Legacy of African Americans in Western Nebraska: Pioneers, Entrepreneurs and Buffalo Soldiers Vol. 1

edited by
Ruby Coleman
Cheri L. Hopkins

Ruby Coleman
rvcole@charter.net
Cheri L. Hopkins
clchopkins@gmail.com

The cover was designed by Cheri L. Hopkins. It depicts the gravestone and military marker of Rufus Slaughter who was buried in the Alliance Cemetery. The lady is Myrtle Chandler Nickens. On the back cover is a photograph of the original house belonging to Robert Ball Anderson, located approximately 14 miles northwest of Hemingford, Box Butte Co., Nebraska.

Dedication

We dedicate these two volumes to LeRoy Hayes Nickens.

LeRoy was born in Alliance, Nebraska where he became an icon in the community. His friends were abundant and from all walks of life. He was loyal and his friends and family knew that LeRoy would always stand up for them should the occasion arise. Community fans followed and cheered LeRoy through his football sports years as a star fullback at Alliance High School. After graduation, LeRoy's work career included 33 years working for the Burlington Northern Santa Fe Railroad before he retired.

Family roots were deep in LeRoy's family, as he had ancestral connections to many people who appear in these volumes. LeRoy Nickens was respected and loved as a father, husband, brother, friend, community leader … and most importantly he was a good man.

LeRoy Hayes Nickens 1948-2012   We will forever miss him.

Table of Contents
Volume 1

Introduction — Walking in Another's Shoes

When my sister-in-law asked me to locate more information about a black Civil War soldier, I became interested in his life. Little did I know that my interest in Thomas Jackson would lead me to walking in another's shoes.

It isn't easy to put yourself into somebody else's shoes. Not only had I never done African American research, but I'm caucasian... white skin, blonde hair (now grey) and blue eyes. While I am a professional genealogist, this was out of my scope of experience. Surely I could walk around in their shoes and learn something, plenty of something. I have no black ancestors, but quite a few ancestors who owned slaves.

Those shoes have at times been painful. I have photos of some people I research, their eyes looking intently at me. They are questioning if I know what their life was like. Children are staring at me with their cute, childish grins, holding a white doll. Did they know the doll was white?

I grew up with a prejudged mother, southern grandparents, relatives and ancestors. I knew the rules and especially learned my lesson when I requested a black doll for Christmas. The signs of segregated restrooms, drinking fountains and lunch counters are still vivid in my mind. What right do I have to pry into their lives, their painful lives?

In 1962 I bid farewell to college friends who were boarding a Nebraska train bound for Hattiesburg, Mississippi. They were going to make a wrong a right. Or were they merely going for the adventure? As if going off to war, they proclaimed that they might not come back alive. I didn't go to experience the Mississippi turmoils and view brutalities first hand. What right do I have now that I'm investigating these black lives?

The shoes are worn through at times, so that I am walking on bare feet. I feel the sting of the rocks on a foreign soil and at times history reminds me of the lashings and beatings as well as the lynchings. Walking in those shoes does not make a wrong a right. My feet are tired at times and I want to stop walking and researching. Later I am compelled to walk again and see what is around the next bend. Who are the masters who owned humans of another color? Wishing to keep going beyond the Emancipation, I pick up only fragments of names, very seldom a surname, or names of parents.

My research comes to a halt quickly as I discover name changes, missing records and I long for written testimonies, other than criminal records or newspaper accounts. As I dig deeper and deeper the frustration mounts as well as the sensitivity to the mental and physical battering of black lives. Was the Peculiar Institution political and economical? Was there no love and compassion in the souls of the masters? I hope that my slave owning ancestors treated their slaves with kindness.

Some of the African Americans of western Nebraska had been slaves and others had parents who were slaves, while even more were third generation blacks who sought land or employment in western Nebraska. There were some who escaped slavery by the Underground Railroad to Canada. A few of them fought in the Civil War and then enlisted as Buffalo Soldiers. When their term of service expired, they were at Fort Robinson in the panhandle of Nebraska. They stayed in the area to continue their life, free from slavery. How free was it? The railroad opened the route of settlement in western Nebraska as well as challenges to the black population.

I cannot walk comfortably in their shoes, but I have a story to tell so they will be remembered.

Ruby Coleman, Co-Editor

Introduction — History is Color Blind

Sixty five years ago as school began, my friends and I were playing together on the Central School playground in Alliance, Nebraska. One of those children has remained as my friend all through our school years and beyond. Over the years we occasionally met up near the city park as she traveled on her long walk to school. We'd laugh together or talk about school and classmates as we walked the rest of the way. Middle and High school years found us again occasionally walking together, she heading towards home as I was going to work in my Mother's downtown dress shop. We made it through High school graduation in 1970 and as time goes, I left for college and marriage while my friend moved to eastern Nebraska to pursue her career. Over the last 50 years we seemed to have lost touch with one another save the occasional short internet posts through our mutual Class of 1970 group. My lifelong friend, Stephanie, is African American.

Looking back, I wish our 'walking conversations' might have been more substantial in their content; that today I might know more of her family and their past. It seems that back then we had more things in common and to me at least, very little that separated us. She is one of the smartest people I have ever known. I will always be grateful that Stephanie is my friend.

Both during my school years and more recently I became acquainted with several other people whom I call my friends: Barb, Florence, LeRoy, and Amber. Nearly thirty years after I graduated, LeRoy's daughter, Amber, would sometimes stop at our home to say hello on the days that she and my sons had walked together after school. Many of my acquaintances as well as good friends were Caucasian like me, but my circle of friends also included Japanese Americans, Mexican Americans, African Americans and American Indians. I treasure each and every relationship to this day. We are all one family; the children of Alliance, Nebraska.

Five years ago, and as a result of a research project undertaken by the Knight Museum and Sandhills Center in Alliance, Nebraska, I embarked on the journey that led to co-authoring these books. Museum volunteers identified and wrote genealogical sketches of all the Civil War soldiers that were buried in Box Butte County and the immediate surrounding area. We pledged to be care-takers of each of their grave sites if no family was already doing so. I adopted as two of my soldiers, Rufus Slaughter and Thomas Jackson, both African American "Buffalo Soldiers". Rufus and Thomas became part of my life and family from then on. I decorate their graves on Memorial Day and speak about them to anyone who has an interest. Both men had been mostly forgotten…but for a lonesome grave and a few simple death records on file to remind us that they had lived. Rufus Slaughter does have a military gravestone of Honor and is known through fairly well documented military records. The other known soldier, Thomas Jackson, is buried near Rufus but has no gravestone and few definitive records.

Thomas Jackson had beckoned to me to retrace his life's trail and that of his friend Rufus. Why did he pick me? Was it because I had chosen him as one of my 'adopted' soldiers to document? I will likely never know. Thomas' was a hard case with few extant records of his existence, plus he had a name in common with several other Black soldiers of his time. I asked my sister-in-law to assist with Thomas' research as she had much more experience working with early military records. Both Thomas and Rufus enlisted, we believe, at Fort Nelson, Ky. Research and study seems to have both men in the same places and at the same time on multiple records. Thomas eventually married Gertrude, daughter of Rufus Slaughter thus their association and friendship became quite evident. Our idea to write something more comprehensive was born and this book began to slowly take shape. It has been a five year labor of love and respect, growing more every year. We have had our bumps along the road, including having to pare down the size of the book to under 1,000 pages… but we have finally prevailed and come to the end of our project.

History should be color blind but it usually is not. Sometimes color and prejudice simply crowd out love and respect. I have learned to respect some of my friends even more as some of their stories have been related to me. It is my hope that neither they nor myself will ever stop learning from or loving one another. Rufus Slaughter and Thomas Jackson should be honored for their military service as 'Buffalo Soldiers" and together they worked as a tag team to push us down this path of discovery! I personally honor Rufus and Thomas, it is for them and in appreciation of my friends that this book has been written.

Undoubtedly there are many more lives to be discovered, those early African Americans who may have settled in the Western Nebraska area but may not have gravestones, or left written records to prove their past history here. Perhaps as time passes more people may be identified and their families documented.

Cheri L. Hopkins,   Co-Editor

Personal note: My Mother-in Law passed away in 2020 and from the day I announced the writing of this book, she was interested and encouraged the endeavor. Every phone call and every visit brought out her question of "When were Ruby and I going to finish our book?" She was a lifelong genealogist, avid reader, and history buff, still interested at age 90 in history and in our book. The last book she requested to read was *Uncle Tom's Cabin* a few weeks before her death. I'm sorry she passed before our book was completed. I know she would have been pleased to have seen it finished and would have read it over and over, cover to cover.

Preface & Acknowledgments

The book in two volumes is divided into four sections. The first section contains information on slavery, laws, and migrations, as well as settlements and military history. It is a prelude for the main part of the book which is Section 3 in both volumes. Section 2 contains Rogues, Rascals and Rooming Houses, The Ku Klux Klan in Alliance and 101 Sweetwater. Photographs and documents are in Section 3 in Volume 1. Readers will discover the histories and genealogies of African American settlers in Section 3 in two volumes.

Photographs were shared by family members and some were retrieved from Internet web sites, such as Ancestry. The support help and legal office of Ancestry advised us about using the photographs on Ancestry public trees. If they are not personally copyrighted on Ancestry, they can be used. If they are over 75 years old, they can be used. The person submitting the photograph does not have control over the photograph because it is in the public domain. Some of the photographs were also used with the permission of museums and research centers.

The co-editors are very grateful for the inspiration and help provided by many people. Our sincere thanks to Florence Nickens of Alliance for providing information and stories that further motivated us to write the book.

We visited many courthouses and museums and found the staff overwhelmingly helpful and also interested in our endeavour to write the book.

Our thanks to Becci Thomas, director of the Knight Museum and Sandhills Center in Alliance. Her knowledge was invaluable. Director Thomas helped us to retrieve relevant documents to aid in our research; many which had not yet been scanned but ultimately proved valuable in the writing of this book. The Knight Museum and Sandhills Center has an extensive collection of books and resources which are extremely valuable for historians and genealogists.

Co-editor Cheri Hopkins wishes to ackowledge her husband, Geoffrey and son, Jason, for the many hours both spent helping to go through the hundreds of documents, papers, and books within several museums and courthouses. They were valued helpers and scanned hundreds of documents for us.

Section 1

Slavery, Laws, Migrations
African American Settlements
Military History

Slavery

"To be given dominion over another is a hard thing; to wrest dominion over another is a wrong thing; to give dominion of yourself to another is a wicked thing."
— *Toni Morrison, A Mercy*

History books relate information about the Transatlantic Slave Trade, normally beginning with the year 1650. However, beginning in 1492, Africans were transported into the regions that were to become the American Spanish colonies. By 1500 they were brought as slaves to Hispaniola.

The second period of migration was between 1650 and 1807 when an estimated seven million Africans were brought to the American continent. There was a high demand for labor on southern plantations that grew crops such as rice, indigo, tobacco, cotton, coffee and cocoa. Slave traders made fortunes during this time period. There were also internal political and religious struggles within Africa which accounted for the excessive deportation of Africans.

Slave trade was high risk. In some instances, local traders would disappear with payment and never produce the captives. Slaves could escape, commit suicide, die from epidemics or be murdered. There was no court or judicial system equipped to handle violations of human rights as they pertained to slaves and the trade.

Most of the slaves were traded from the ports of Luanda (Angola), Whydah (Bight of Benin), Bonny (Blight of Biafra) and the "castles" of Winneba and Koromantin, located on the Gold Coast. Other ports were Old Calabar, Benguela, Cabinda and Lagos. At least half of the Africans deported to America came through those ports. [1]

Slave traders referred to the voyage from Africa to the Americas as the Middle Passage. It is estimated that over 30,000 voyages from Africa to America have been documented. Ships transported only about 350 people, but some handled over 800. Men, women and children were transported. They were branded and stripped naked for the voyage. The voyage usually lasted from one to three months in which time the slaves were forced to lived amidst filfth, stifling heat and endure beatings. They were denied the dignity of even the lowest of animals. During their voyage, they lost any social, personal and cultural identity. It is estimated that at least 20 per cent of the slaves died from epidemics or committed suicide.

Approximately 450,000 Africans were transported to America. Survival rate was low and this number represents only a fraction of those transported. While the south benefited with slave labor, the transportation of slaves also benefited the commerce and economy in New York, Pennsylvania and Massachusetts. In the 1700s there was a higher concentration of African Americans in the lowlands of South Carolinas and Georgia, as well as the Sea Islands. Most of those in the lowlands came from Bantu regions in west-central Africa. Most in Virginia and Maryland came from the Bight of Biafra, with others from Sengambia. In these two regions most of the African Americans came from four zones in Africa.

The third period of migration began with a ban on the importation of captives imposed in 1807 and lasting until the 1860s. Since slave importation was not legal in the United States, they were taken to Cuba, Puerto Rico and Brazil. Even with these restrictions, some were being brought into the United States until the late 1840s, most of them being smuggled.

According to Article I, Section 9, Clause 1 of the United States Constitution "The Migration or

Importation of such Persons as any of the States now existing shall think proper to admit, shall not be prohibited by the Congress prior to the Year one thousand eight hundred and eight, but a Tax or duty may be imposed on such imports, not exceeding ten dollars for each Person." While slave trade from Africa was abolished as of 1 January 1820, it continued until 1860.

The United States Slave Trade Act was enacted in February of 1807 and specified that the Africans illegally brought to slave states would still be sold and enslaved. Penalties consisted of fines and most authorities refused to enforce the law. In 1820 Congress passed another law making international slave trading an act of piracy punishable by death. There was only one American executed for piracy. Slave traders continued transporting slaves to Brazil, Cuba and Puerto Rico where the trade was still legal.

In 1842 the Webster-Ashburton Treaty between Britain and the United States approved an anti-slave trade African Squadron. The harbors of the African coast were patrolled, but slave traders continued to bring slaves to America until the Civil War.

Brutality that began on a slave ship did not end once the Africans were in America. They were subjected to physical punishment, sexual abuse and exploitation. Paternal and maternal rights were dismissed and for the most part kinships were disregarded. Any knowledge of their ancestry in Africa was by memory with no written records. As chattel property, slaves were inherited for perpetuity by descendants of slave owners.

Slaves were often sold several times during their slavehood, families ripped apart, never to find each other again. Slave bills of sale show prices received for slaves, depending upon their age and ability to work. For the most part, house slaves were treated better than those who worked in the fields. Rebellious slaves were sometimes killed by overseers or put back on the slave auction block. The sale of slaves from the family unit was a show of authority and example for the rest of the slaves. Worn out old slaves were quickly replaced by new blood and bodies that could be whipped into submission. As family estates were divided, slaves were often sold at auction unless they were specifically accounted for in the owner's will. There are known cases where those slaves were sold in family units.

When a slave ship was due to arrive, posters went up announcing the sale of slaves on board the ship. The advertisements usually state how many slaves were on board and choice words, such as "cargo" referenced them. Usually slaves were taken off the ship and placed in a pen where they were washed and branded with a hot iron identifying them as slaves. They then stood on a raised platform and could be inspected by prospective buyers. Young slaves retrieved higher bids than the young, very old or sick slaves.

Quite often slave holders leased their slaves. This would sometimes result in the splitting up of families. If they were leased to steamboat captains, the owner risked having his or her slave jump ship or disembark in free states. The profits of leasing slaves outweighed the risk.

Slave holders feared slave rebellions, particularly after the Nat Turner's Rebellion that took place in Southampton Co., Virginia in August of 1831. Led by Turner, the rebel slaves killed between 55 and 65 people. The rebellion was suppressed at Belmont Plantation and Virginia. They executed 56 slaves accused of being part of the rebellion. In the aftermath, more slaves were severely punished or murdered by mobs and militia. Laws were passed in the South that prohibited educating slaves and free persons of color, as well as excluding other privileges. It was the common thought that the more slaves knew by reading and writing the more apt they would turn on their masters. In 1830 the State of North Carolina passed a statue pertaining to teaching slaves to read or write. Any free person attempting to teach any slave in North Carolina to read or write, to learn figures, giving them books or pamphlets will be indicted in any court of record in the State. They were subject to being fined not less than $100 and not more than

$200 or imprisoned. If a free person of color was found guilty of the same, they would be fined, imprisoned or whipped, not exceeding thirty nine lashes, nor less than twenty lashes. 2

To perpetuate slaves and insure a labor force, many slave owners practiced slave breeding. There were forced sexual relationship between male and female slaves as well as sexual relationships between a master and female slaves. Many felt this would encourage stability. 3

It is no wonder that people without names, could not remember their names when families were torn apart by the greed and need of others. When census enumerators began asking questions of blacks for the 1870 federal census, many guessed as to their age and location of birth. From one decennial census to the next, their age sometimes changed drastically, as well as places of birth. Even so, they were survivors and passed the legacy of survival to succeeding generations.

1. The Transatlantic Slave Trade, http://www.inmotionaame.org/migrations/topic.cfm?migration=1&topic=3.
2. History is a Weapon http://www.historyisaweapon.com/defcon1/slaveprohibit.html.
3. Treatment of Slaves in the United States https://en.wikipedia.org/wiki/Treatment_of_slaves_in_the_United_States.

Brief Historical Timeline of Slavery in America

1619

The first African slaves arrived in Virginia.

1787

Slavery was made illegal in the Northwest Territory. The U.S Constitution stated that Congress could not ban the slave trade until 1808.

1793

Eli Whitney's invention of the cotton gin greatly increased the demand for slave labor.

A federal fugitive slave law was enacted which provided for the return to their owners of slaves who had escaped and crossed state lines.

1800

There was a slave revolt which was organized with the intention to march on Richmond, Virginia. The plans were discovered and a number of the rebels were hanged. Virginia's slave laws were tightened as a result.

1808

The U.S. Congress banned the importation of slaves from Africa.

1820

The Missouri Compromise banned slavery north of the southern boundary of Missouri.

1822

An enslaved African American carpenter who had purchased his freedom, planned a slave revolt with the intent to lay siege on Charleston, South Carolina. His plot was discovered, and he and thirty-four others were hanged.

1831

An enslaved African American preacher named Nat Turner, led the most significant slave uprising in American history. He and his band of followers launched a short and bloody rebellion in Southampton County, Virginia. Militia stamped out the rebellion, and Turner was eventually hanged.

The state of Virginia made the state slave laws even stronger after the Turner rebellion.

The first issue of the *Liberator*, a weekly paper that advocated the complete abolition of slavery, was published. The paper's publisher became one of the most famous figures in the abolitionist movement.

1846

The Wilmot Proviso was introduced in Congress and it attempted to ban slavery in the territory gained as a result of the Mexican War. The proviso was blocked by Southerners, but it continued to be a major spark for the debate over slavery.

1849

Harriet Tubman escaped from slavery and became one of the most effective and famous leaders of the Underground Railroad.

1850

The continued debate whether territory gained in the Mexican War should be open to slavery was decided within the Compromise of 1850: California was admitted as a free state, Utah and New Mexico territories were left to be decided by popular sovereignty, and the slave trade in Washington, DC was prohibited. The Compromise of 1850 also established a much stricter fugitive slave law than the original law which had passed in 1793.

1852

Harriet Beecher Stowe's novel, *Uncle Tom's Cabin,* was published. It became one of the most influential literary works and prompted even stronger anti-slavery feelings.

1854

Congress passed the Kansas-Nebraska Act which established the territories of Kansas and Nebraska. The legislation repealed the Missouri Compromise of 1820. This Act enflamed tensions even more among anti- and pro-slavery factions.

1857

The Dred Scott case decision was handed down by the U.S. Supreme Court. Ruling: **1.** No slave or descendant of a slave could be considered a U.S. citizen, (thus could not sue in court or enjoy any other legal rights offered to a citizen) **2.** The Federal government had no power to regulate slavery in the Federal territories. **3.** The Missouri Compromise of 1820 was ruled unconstitutional.

1859

John Brown, a staunch abolitionist, and twenty-one of his followers captured the Federal arsenal at Harpers Ferry, Virginia (now West Virginia). Shortly after the capture of the arsenal, his group attempted to launch a slave revolt which ultimately failed. John Brown and his followers were captured and later hung.

1861

The Confederacy was founded after several states of the South seceded from the Union. The Civil War officially began when Confederate artillery opened fire on Fort Sumter in Charleston Harbor on April 12, 1861.

1863

President Lincoln issued the Emancipation Proclamation. It declared "that all persons held as slaves" within the Confederate States are, and henceforward shall be free."

1865

The Civil War ended on April 9th. President Abraham Lincoln was shot on April 14th and died the next day. The Thirteenth Amendment to the United States Constitution abolished slavery and involuntary servitude, except as punishment for a crime. In Congress, it was passed by the Senate on April 8, 1864, and by the House on January 31, 1865.

1866

President Andrew Johnson **formally** declared the end of the Civil War on August 20, 1866.

A circa 1830 illustration of a slave auction in America. Rischgitz/Hulton Archive—Getty Images

.

Plantation Rules and Ordinances

In 1840 the "Southern Cultivator and Monthly Journal" published the following rules of the plantation:

Rule 1st. The overseer will not be expected to work in the crop, but he must constantly with the hands, when not otherwise engaged in the employer's business, and will be required to attend on occasions to any pecuniary transactions connected with the plantation.

Rule 2nd. The overseer is not expected to be absent from the plantation unless actual necessity compels him, Sundays excepted, and then it is expected that he will, on all occasions, be at home by night.

Rule 3rd. He will attend, morning, noon and night, at the stable, and see that the mules and horses are ordered, curried, and fed.

Rule 4th. He will see that every negro is out by daylight in the morning—a signal being given by a blast of the horn, the first horn will be blown half an hour before day. He will also visit the negro cabins at least once or twice a week, at night, to see that all are in. No negro must be out of his house after ten o'clock in summer and eleven in winter.

Rule 5th. The overseer is not to give passes to the negroes without the employer's consent. The families the negroes are allowed to visit will be specified by the employer; also those allowed to visit the premises. Nor is any negro allowed to visit the place without showing himself to the employer or overseer.

Rule 6th. The overseer is required not to chat with the negroes, except on business, nor to encourage tale bearing, nor is any tale to be told to him or employer, by any negro, unless he has a witness to his statements, nor are they allowed, in any instance, to quarrel and fight. But the employer will question any negro, if confidence can be placed in him, without giving him cause of suspicion, about all matters connected with the plantation, if he has any reason to believe that all things are not going on right.

Rule 7th. As the employer pays the overseer for his time and attention, it is not to be expected he will receive much company.

Rule 8th. As the employer employs an overseer, not to please himself, but the employer, it will be expected that he will attend strictly to all his instructions. His opinion will be frequently asked relative to plantation matters, and respectfully listened to, but it is required they be given in a polite and respectful manner, and not urged, or insisted upon; and if not adopted, he must carry into effect the views of the employer, and with a sincere desire to produce a successful result. He is expected to carry on all experiments faithfully and carefully note the results, and he must, when required by the employer, give a fair trial to all new methods of culture, and new implements of agriculture.

Rule 9th. As the whole stock will be under immediate charge of the overseer, it is expected he will give his personal attention to it, and will accompany the hog feeder once a week and feed them, and count and keep a correct number of the same. The hog feeder is required to attend to feeding them every morning.

Rule 10th. The negroes must be made to obey, and to work, which may be done by an overseer who attends regularly to his business, with very little whipping; for much whipping indicates a bad tempered or an inattentive manager. He must never, on any occasion, unless in self-defense, kick a negro, or strike him with his fist, or butt end of his whip. No unusual punishment must be resorted to without the employer's consent. He is not expected to punish the foreman, except on some extraordinary emergency that will not allow of delay, until the employer is consulted. Of this rule the foreman is to be kept in entire ignorance.

Rule 11th. The sick must be attended to. When sick they are to make known the fact to him; if in the field, he is requested to send them to the employer, if at home; and if not, the overseer is expected to attend to them in person, or send for a physician if necessary. Suckling and pregnant women must be indulged more than others. Sucklers are to be allowed time to visit their children, morning, noon and evening, until they are eight months old, and twice a day from thence until they are twelve months old—they are to be kept working near their children. No lifting, pulling fodder, or hard work is expected of pregnant women.

Rule 12th. The negroes are to appear in the field on Monday mornings cleanly clad. To carry out said rule they are to be allowed time (say one hour by sun) every Saturday evening for the purpose of washing their clothes.

Rule 13th. The overseer is particularly required to keep the negroes as much as possible out of the rain, and from all kind of exposure.

Rule 14th. It will be expected of a good manager, that he will constantly arrange the daily work of the negroes, so that no negro may wait to know what to go to doing. Small jobs that will not reasonably admit of delay must be forthwith attended to.

Rule 15th. It is required of him, to keep the tools, ploughs, hoes &c. out of the weather and have all collected after they are done using them. The wagon and cart must be kept under a shed. He is expected to keep good gates, bars and fences.

Rule 16th. The employer will give him a list of all the tools and farming utensils and place the same in his care, and he is to return them at the years' end to the employer; if any are broke, the pieces are expected to be returned.

Rule 17th. He is not to keep a horse or dog against the employer's approbation—and dogs kept for the purpose of catching negroes will not be allowed under any consideration.

Rule 18th. He is required to come to his meals at the blowing of the horn. It is not expected he will leave the field at night before the hands quit their work.

Rule 19th. It will be expected he will not speak of the employer's pecuniary business, his domestic affairs, or his arrangements to any one. He will be expected to inform the employer of anything going on that may concern his interest.

Rule 20th. He is to have no control whatever over the employer's domestic affairs; nor to take any privileges in the way of using himself, or loaning the employers property to others.

Rule 21st. He is expected to be guilty of no disrespectful language in the employer's presence—such as vulgarity, swearing &c; nor is he expected to be guilty of any indecencies, such as spitting on the floor, wearing his hat in the house, sitting at the table with his coat off, or whistling or singing in the house (Such habits are frequently indulged in, in Bachelor establishments in the South). His room will be appropriated to him, and he will not be expected to obtrude upon the employer's private chamber, except on business.

Rule 22nd. It will be expected of him that he will not get drunk, and if he returns home in that state he will be immediately discharged. He will also be immediately discharged, if it is ascertained he is too intimate with any of the negro women.

Rule 23rd. It is distinctly understood, in the agreement with every overseer, should they separate, from death or other cause—and either is at liberty to separate from the other whenever dissatisfied—without giving his reasons for so doing; in said event the employer, upon settlement, is not expected to pay the cash nor settle for the year, but for the time only he remained in the employer's service, by note, due January next (with interest) pro rata, he was to pay for the year.

American Slavery http://www.american-slave.com/#!plantation-rules/c1j6s

Laws

Bigotry's birthplace is the sinister back room of the mind where plots and schemes are hatched for the persecution and oppression of other human beings.
Bayard Rustin

Researching and studying the history and genealogy of any race involves a study of laws, history and geography. It is doubly important to learn about the laws of various periods as they pertain to or affect African Americans. The laws include federal and state laws. The most significant change in slavery laws took place from 1850 until after the Civil War.

Racial classifications were informal references made by whites and the government upon the appearance of African Americans. Most commonly seen in records is the word mulatto, which was used to identify a mixed race person with white and black ancestry. Usually they were a person with one white and one black parent, or to persons born of a mulatto parent or parents. Quadroon was applied to persons of one-quarter African ancestry and one white parent. Terceroon was synonymous with octoroon. Mustee was used to refer to a person with one-eighth African ancestry. Mustefino referred to a person with one-sixteenth African ancestry. A quintroon was the offspring of an octoroon and a white person.

The **Fugitive Slave Act of 1793** was a federal law with the intent to enforce Article 4, Section 2 of the United States Constitution. This required the return of runaway slaves. If a slave was found in a free state, they were to be returned to their masters. Some of the northern states passed personal liberty laws, that mandated a jury trial before a fugitive slave could be moved. In some cases laws were enforced forbidding the use of local jails or assistance by state officials in the arrest or return of fugitive slaves.

The law of 1793 applied to slaves who escaped to free states without their master's consent. In the case of *Prigg v. Pennsylvania* in 1842, the United States Supreme Court ruled that states did not have to offer aid in locating and capturing slaves.

On 18 September 1850 the United States Congress passed the **Fugitive Slave Law,** also known as the **Fugitive Slave Act**. This was part of the Compromise of 1850 between the slave-holding southerners and the northern free-soilers. Basically the law required that all escaped slaves, upon capture, to be returned to their masters and that officials and citizens of the free state be required to cooperate with the law. It was nicknamed the "Bloodhound Law" by abolitionists. By the mid-1850s several hundred slaves a year were escaping to the North, many being tracked by bloodhounds.

The 1850 law penalized officials who did not arrest runaway slaves, making them liable to a fine of $1,000. If a person was suspected of being a runaway slave because of a claimant's sworn testimony of ownership the law-enforcement officials were required to arrest people. The slave could not seek a jury trial or testify on his or her behalf. If people provided shelter or food to runaway slaves, they were subject to a fine of $1,000 plus six months in jail. As incentive, law enforcement officers who captured runaway slaves were entitled to a bonus or promotion. All the slave owner had to do was provide an affidavit to a Federal marshall for the capture of a slave. Without benefit of a trial, the runaway slave was taken back into slavery.

Not all northern states found favor with the Fugitive Slave Law of 1850. In November of that year, Vermont's legislature passed the "Habeas Corpus Law" requiring Vermont officials to assist captured fugitive slaves, thus rendering the Fugitive Slave Law unenforceable in that state. It caused a good deal of controversy throughout the nation. Five years later the Wisconsin Supreme Court declared the Fugitive Slave Act unconstitutional. The United States Supreme Court overruled the state court.

While there were slaves in the north, the total population was minor in comparison to that in the south where slaves were used for labor. The passage of the Fugitive Slave Law of 1850 placed the responsibility of enforcing slavery on the anti-slavery North and abolitionists. In 1852 Harriet Beecher Stowe wrote *Uncle Tom's Cabin*, detailing the evils of slavery. The plight of the slave was read by many people in the nation.

Even with the enforcement of the 1850 law, people assisted slaves in escaping to Canada, some openly admitting to it. Canada became a major destination and between 1850 and 1860 the black population of Canada increased from 40,000 to 60,000.

In some instances slave owners attempted to manumit their slaves. This was often done in a will after long years of service and normally applied to trusted house slaves instead of field hands. In essence they were no longer useful since they were extremely old. As early as the seventeenth century, slaves were being freed by manumission.

It was also possible that slaves could arrange manumission by agreeing to purchase themselves, by paying the master an agreed amount. The regulation of manumission began in Virginia in 1692. This was changed in 1723 when a law made exception of manumission only for those who had achieved meritorious services or as allowed by the governor and council. In time of war, a master could send a slave as a substitute with the promise of freedom if he survived. In 1782 a law permitted the master to free their slaves on their own accord. In 1778 Virginia passed a law forbidding free negroes from moving into the state. Because of the 1782 law, Virginia's free blacks increased to 7% in 1800, with the free black population increasing to 13.5% of the total black population.

In 1820 the **Missouri Compromise** was passed. It symbolized an effort to preserve the balance of power in Congress between slave and free states. Missouri was admitted as a slave state and Maine as a free state. Slavery, with the exception of Missouri, was prohibited in the Louisiana Territory north of the 36 degree 30' latitude line. The act was repealed in 1854 with the passage of the **Kansas-Nebraska Act** and in 1857 the Missouri Compromise was declared unconstitutional by the United States Supreme Court. The ruling was that Congress did not have the authority to prohibit slavery in the territories. The Kansas-Nebraska Act of 1854 established popular sovereignty or local choice of slavery in Kansas and Nebraska.

Freedom suits were filed by enslaved people against their slaveholders, mainly before 1830. They were known as petitions and the majority were heard in southern or border states. As much as one-third of the suits never went to trial and were settled out of court. Southern states began a series of requirements aimed at the defendants and juries. While most were tried in state courts, there were some that went to the United States Supreme Court.

Dred Scott and Harriet Robinson were owned by military officers. They married in Fort Snelling, Wisconsin Territory. Along with their daughters Eliza and Lizzie, they were still slaves and living in St. Louis, Missouri. Because of their marriage and time spent at Fort Snelling, which was a free territory, Dred and Harriet both filed separate freedom suits in the St. Louis Circuit Court on 6 April 1846. Thus began years of court cases and appeals until 1852 when it was ruled that appeals would be based on the suit filed by Dred Scott. On 6 March 1857 the United States Supreme Court denied Dred and his family their freedom. The case was *Dred Scott v. Sandford*, but became known as the **Dred Scott Decision**. They ruled that Scott nor any other person of African ancestry could claim citizenship in the United States. This decision added fuel to the already heated controversy between southern slave owners and anti-slave supporters and hastened the Civil War. It was nullified by the Emancipation Proclamation in

1863 and the 13th, 14th and 15th Amendments. Dred Scott died one year later in 1858 and Harriet and family received freedom from the family of Dred's former owners. 1

When the Civil War began, the legal status of slaves changed with the masters or owners being in arms. The **Confiscation Act of 1861** was passed in August of 1861. This discharged from service or labor any slave employed in aiding or promoting any insurrection against the government of the United States. On 13 March 1862 Congress passed the **Act Prohibiting the Return of Slaves**. Through this act, any slave belonging to a disloyal master (allegiance to the Confederacy) who was in a territory occupied by Northern troops was declared ipso facto free. The Fugitive Slave Law of 1850 was still enforced in the border states that were loyal to the Union government. On 28 June 1864 the 1850 law was fully repealed.

There was no formal law in the South that controlled the sale of slaves or provided for the marriage of slaves. The law of the planter was the only control. Slave families were torn apart through the sale or removal of members of the family. Unless a sold or inherited slave remained within the white family, their whereabouts usually remained unknown. Slave men and women cohabited with more than one spouse in "slave marriages." The white owners viewed these marriages as not being legal or permanent. Surnames, if taken, were usually that of the master and would change when sold to another owner. Children were considered property of their mother and used a surname of her owner until she was sold. It is not surprising that federal census records beginning in 1870, contain conflicting information. Surnames often changed, people did not know their exact age or date of birth as well as where they were born. With the 1880 federal census where more information was needed, subjects often had no idea where their parents were born, thus simply stated United States or made a guess. That guess often times changed throughout subsequent census enumerations.

On 1 January 1863, President Abraham Lincoln issued the **Emancipation Proclamation**. The document declared that persons held as slaves within the rebellious states were then and forever free. The five page document was limited as it applied only to states that had seceded from the Union. Within the border states, slaves were not free. The wording showed a positive position of a Union victory.

The document was not the end of slavery. With the proclamation came the acceptance of black men into the Union Army and Union Navy. When the Civil War ended almost 200,000 black soldiers and sailors had fought for the Union as well as to secure personal freedom. They were instrumental in battles that led to the end of the Civil War and the rebuilding of the United States. Even so, they were still part of a classification that was not exactly free, living in a society of whites. Freedom was less than total freedom.

Miscegenation was a term first used in 1863 during the Civil War. Journalists in the United States used it to discredit the abolitionist movement. This created concern over black-white intermarriages after the abolishment of slavery. **Anti-miscegenation laws** were established by states. They normally defined miscegenation or interracial marriages as a felony. Because of the nature of some of the marriages they were not charged with miscegenation, but fornication or adultery. Some states criminalized cohabitation between races. Laws against miscegenation were proposed in the United States Congress in 1871, 1912-1913 and 1928, but were never enacted. In the state of Nebraska anti-miscegenation laws were passed in 1855 and repealed in 1963. 2

The **Thirteenth Amendment to the United States Constitution** was adopted on 6 December 1865. It abolished slavery and involuntary servitude, except as punishment for a crime. Article 1, Section 2, Clause 3, known as the Three-Fifths Compromise detailed how a state's total slave population would be factored into its total population count for the apportioning of seats in the House of Representatives and the imposing of direct taxes upon the state. In essence African Americans were considered 3/5ths human. Once slavery was abolished the Three-Fifths Compromise became null and void.

In 1865 all states, with the exception of Iowa, Kentucky, Mississippi, New Jersey, Florida, Texas, Oregon and California ratified the amendment. It was rejected and then ratified by Kentucky Mississippi and New Jersey. Between 1865 and 1870 the states of Iowa, California, Oregon, Texas and Florida did a post-enactment ratification.

The Fourteenth Amendment to the United States Constitution guaranteed equal protection under the law to all Americans. It was adopted on 9 July 1868 as one of the Reconstruction Amendments. **The Fifteenth Amendment to the United States Constitution** prohibits the federal and state governments from denying a citizen the right to vote based on the citizen's race or color or previous condition of servitude. It was ratified on 3 February 1870 as the third and last of the Reconstruction Amendments.

For a brief period of time, with the new amendments in effect, African Americans were able to vote, acquire some land and seek employment. Opponents soon began to make significant changes to this new-found freedom.

Black Codes were laws passed in the Southern states in 1865 and 1866. They placed restrictions on the freedom of African Americans, forcing them to work in a labor economy with low wages. Thus, the discrimination did not end with emancipation or the 13th Amendment. The earlier codes were imposed to reduce any influence of free blacks. Some of the restriction included prohibiting them from voting, bearing arms, learning to read or write and gathering in groups for worship. Within the black codes was the vagrancy law that allowed local authorities to arrest freed blacks for minor infractions, committing them to involuntary labor. This was known as the convict lease system. 3

The first state to pass Black Codes was Mississippi. This served as a model for those passed in other states. In 1865 they were passed by South Carolina, Alabama and Louisiana. The following year they were passed in Florida, Georgia, Virginia, Texas, Arkansas, Tennessee and North Carolina. Even with some modifications, they enacted a racist regime.

In 1828 Thomas "Daddy" Rice (a white man), created a caricature of a minstrel black man called **Jim Crow**. This was for the entertainment of white audiences. Within less than sixty-years later, Jim Crow became synonymous with the system of racial laws and codes in the South. Even though these laws were associated with the South, the first Jim Crow laws were passed in the north prohibiting blacks from voting in all but five New England states along with segregating schools and public accommodations. Blacks were barred from entering the states of Oregon and Illinois. Almost all of the cities in the north restricted blacks to living in ghettos. Eventually Illinois repealed the law barring blacks to move into the state. 4

Black Codes of the 1860s and the Jim Crow laws were not the same. The Black Codes were society's reaction to the abolishment of slavery as well as the South's defeat in the Civil War. The Jim Crow laws were later, closer to the end of the 19th century. The notorious sundown laws were even later. They placed restrictions on where the blacks lived or where they could be found after dark. There were towns that had their own set of sundown laws. 5

With the end of slavery, planters in the South experienced a labor shortage. Many of the blacks did not immediately stop working on plantations, but attempted to work less and have more time for freedoms. Slavery had shielded them, in many instances, from learning to read and write and adapt to society. When some of the blacks became vagrants because of lack of employment, the southern whites viewed them as a dangerous social problem. The whites viewed them as being destined for servitude regardless of the laws. At the same time southern whites blamed the blacks for the Confederacy's defeat in the Civil War. 6

The **Eighteenth Amendment** was approved and ratified as part of the United States Constitution on 16 January 1919. The entire nation went dry on 17 January 1920, prohibiting the sale, production, importation and transportation of alcoholic beverages. This amendment was repealed by the ratification of the **Twenty-first Amendment** to the United States Constitution on 5 December 1933. With the enactment of prohibition, northern newspapers reported that the underlying motive for prohibition in the south was to suppress African Americans. [7]

There were many ways to avoid the law of prohibition as practiced by all races. People began distilling whiskey and bootleg booze was sold in speakeasies or in people's homes. Court records show many instances of blacks arrested for dispensing liquor without a license, illegal manufacture of alcohol and other probation violations.

The **Civil Rights Act** was passed by Congress in 1866. The 39th Congress realized that the Black Codes were promoting a form of quasi-slavery. They also passed the **Second Freedmen's Bureau Bill.** The Reconstruction Acts placed the South under military rule. This was enforced until the military withdrawal by the Compromise of 1877. Immediately after the Civil War, there were attempts in Reconstruction to provide aid to former slaves and integrate them into society. The Reconstruction lasted from 1863 to the **Compromise of 1877**. At the same time, whites who were resentful established local chapters of the **Ku Klux Klan.**

The Compromise of 1877 pulled federal troops out of state politics in the South and ended the Reconstruction Era. It was also based on political struggles and disputes between the Republican and Democratic parties.

A major set back for civil rights was the Supreme Court decision *Plessy v. Ferguson* in 1896. This upheld "separate but equal" racial segregation. The Civil Rights Act was declared unconstitutional by the United States Supreme Court in 1883.

The **Freedmen's Bureau Bill** established the Freedmen's Bureau on 3 March 1865 and was intended to last for one year after the Civil War. [8] It was made part of the United States Department of War and began operations in 1865. The charter was renewed in 1866, but for several years the Bureau lost funding and was weakened due to the Ku Klux Klan violence in the South. It was abandoned by Congress in 1872. There was opposition to the Freedmen's Bureau, with posters and newspaper articles proclaiming "The Freedman's Bureau! An Agency to keep the Negro in Idleness at the Expense of the white man. ..." [9]

While the bureau was hindered by the passage of Black Codes in the South, they were able to help African Americans locate family members from whom they had been separated. They assisted in education, with food and clothing. Agents of the bureau served as advocates in local and national courts and worked with freed blacks in an attempt to gain employment. The bureau also assisted ex-slave couples in formalizing marriages they had entered into during their time as slaves. In some instances, more understanding slave owners allowed slaves to have formal marriages, but for most it was seeking their consent and moving into a cabin together. If the couple were from different plantations, their cohabitation was known as a "broad" marriage. Normally slave men received passes to visit their wives on weekends. Children born of such "broad" marriages were the property of the slave woman's owner. Those children were formally recognized between 1865 and 1867 by most of the southern states as being legitimate.

During the Civil War, free persons found refuge in contraband camps of military officers. In those situations it was possible for chaplains in the Union Army or missionaries to solemnize marriage among the free persons. The word contraband was slang used by the Union referring to escaped slaves who would not be returned to their masters. There were over 100 contraband camps in the South. [10]

The **Ku Klux Klan** (KKK), also known as "the Klan" advocated extremism such as white supremacy, white nationalism and anti-immigration, expressed through terrorism. They flourished in the South in the late 1860s. After being suppressed around 1871, a second group of the Klan was founded in 1915 and flourished nationwide. After 1950 a third group of the Klan emerged focusing on opposition to the Civil Rights Movements. Because of their spirited violence and identification with white robes and burning crosses, many African Americans lived in fear of their oppression.

In the years following the end of the Civil War and after Reconstruction, African Americans began migrating north out of the south to cities and less settled areas, such as in Kansas and Nebraska. They sought out employment in the north, as well as free land. The Black Codes had restricted their right to own property, lease land and move about freely. Their migrations were also an attempt to avoid not only Jim Crow laws, but the Ku Klux Klan and the White League.

In 1922 there were 1,100 members of the Ku Klux Klan in Nebraska and by 1923 there were 45,000 members. In 1924 their demonstrations, cross burning and parades were common throughout Nebraska. That same year a convention was held in Lincoln, Nebraska where over a thousand members paraded openly through the streets. 11

The first **African-American Civil Rights Movement** began in 1896 and ended in 1954. It was usually seen as non-violent, but it exposed the need for social and legal acceptance of civil rights. Overall the movement refers to political struggles to end discrimination against African American, especially in the South. The tone of opposition to blacks was felt and seen primarily in the south with reference to black men as a "boy" and black women as a "girl." Labels were prevalent. Within the movement were other movements, one being the **Lily-white Movement** which was an all-white faction of the Republican Party in the South. They were opposed to the biracial element known as the **Black-and-tan Faction**. Both were factions of the Republican Party in the south from the 1870s into the 1860s. The Black-and-Tan Faction was bi-racial and sought to include most African Americans voters within the party. The faction practically disappeared in 1964.

The **New Negro Movement** was founded in 1916-1917. It was also known as Harlem Renaissance. While the metaphor New Negro had been used since 1895, it became more noticeable during the first part of the twentieth century. Within the movement blacks became more outspoken for dignity and the right to vote. Following World War I blacks gained self-confidence and a voice. Thousands of blacks began moving after the war from the South to the industrial urban areas of the North. There were even greater demands for an end to segregation and political equality. 12

The National Association for the Advancement of Colored People (NAACP) was founded on 12 February 1909. While it is a civil rights organization with members and supporters world-wide, it became voice for African Americans. It was formed partially in response to lynching and race riots. The mission of the NAACP was to secure the rights guaranteed in the 13th, 14th and 15th Amendments to the United States Constitution. 13

An attempt was made by the federal government to pass an anti-lynching bill. It was introduced in April 1918 by Congressman Leonidas C. Dyer of Missouri. The bill was based on a bill drafted by NAACP founder Albert E. Pillsbury in 1901, calling for the prosecution of lynchers in federal courts. The bill also mandated that state officials who did not uphold this would face five years in prison and a $5,000 fine. The heirs of lynching victims could recover up to $10,000 from the county where the lynching occurred. The Dyer Bill was passed on 26 January 1922, but a filibuster by Southern Democrats defeated it in the Senate. 14

In the era of segregation, blacks traveling by car on the open road presented many dangers. Signs were posted at public places warning them they would be banned after nightfall. Victor H. Green, a black postal carrier in Harlem wrote a guide, *The Negro Motorist Green-Book*, in 1937. It applied to the New York metro area and listed places that welcomed blacks. The final publishing of the book was in 1966-1967. Green's books were sold at the Negro Urban League, black churches and Esso gas stations. He died in 1960, four years before the Civil Rights Act was passed by Congress. 15

The second **African-American Civil Rights Movement** began in 1954 and ended in 1968. The primary focus, again, was to end racial segregation and discrimination. This was the era of boycotts, sit-ins, freedom rides and marches. While most were non-violent in nature, there were some that were more criminal in nature. During this second movement the **Civil Rights Act of 1964** was passed. This banned discrimination based on race, color, religion, sex or national origin in employment. It also ended unequal application of voter registration requirements and racial segregation, particularly in schools and work places as well as public accommodations.

While the mid 20th century brought about positive changes, many African Americans today will state that there was always and always will be a faction of Americans who distinguish them unfavorably. It is important to remember that from the beginning of slavehood to the passage of the Civil Rights Act of 1964, albeit a lengthly period of time, there has been progress made toward assimilating the black race into a white culture and without distinction and prejudice.

1. *They Have No Rights: Dred Scott's Struggle for Freedom.* Westport [Ct.]: Greenwood Press, 1979.
2. *The Black Image in the White Mind* by George M. Fredrickson Wesliyan University Press page 7
3. Douglas Blackmon, *Slavery by Another Name: The Re-Enslavement of Black Americans from the Civil War to World War II,* New York: Doubleday, 2008
4. *The Rise and Fall of Jim Crow* by Richard Wormser. New York, NY: St. Martin's Press, 2003.
5. The Keys to Segregation were Black Codes https://thoughtprovokingperspectives.co/2015/12/28/never-forget-black-codes/
6. *Black Codes and Broken Windows* by Stewart 1998 pp 2259-2260
7. Blacks and the Southern Prohibition Movement; Hanes Walton, Jr. and James E. Taylor *Phylon (1960-) Vol. 32, No. 3 (3rd Qtr., 1971), pp. 247-259Published by: Clark Atlanta University*
8. Wormser.
9. "The Post War Years" http://xroads.virginia.edu/~cap/scartoons/caremanc.html
10. https://www.boundless.com/u-s-history/textbooks/boundless-u-s-history-textbook/the-civil-war-1861-1865-18/emancipation-during-the-war-131/the-contraband-camps-707-4621/
11. Jennifer Hildebrand, "The New Negro Movement in Lincoln, Nebraska," Nebraska History 91 (2010) page 169
12. Africana Age http://exhibitions.nypl.org/africanaage/essay-renaissance.html
13. NAACP http://www.naacp.org/pages/naacp-history
14. NAACP History: Anti-Lynching Bill http://www.naacp.org/pages/naacp-history-anti-lynching-bill
15. How the Green Book Helped African-American Tourists Navigate a Segregated Nation http://www.smithsonianmag.com/smithsonian-institution/history-green-book-african-american-travelers-180958506/?no-ist

The Emancipation Proclamation

The original document is at the National Archives in Washington, DC. The following is a transcript of the proclamation.

January 1, 1863
A Transcription

By the President of the United States of America:

A Proclamation.

Whereas, on the twenty-second day of September, in the year of our Lord one thousand eight hundred and sixty-two, a proclamation was issued by the President of the United States, containing, among other things, the following, to wit:

"That on the first day of January, in the year of our Lord one thousand eight hundred and sixty-three, all persons held as slaves within any State or designated part of a State, the people whereof shall then be in rebellion against the United States, shall be then, thenceforward, and forever free; and the Executive Government of the United States, including the military and naval authority thereof, will recognize and maintain the freedom of such persons, and will do no act or acts to repress such persons, or any of them, in any efforts they may make for their actual freedom.

"That the Executive will, on the first day of January aforesaid, by proclamation, designate the States and parts of States, if any, in which the people thereof, respectively, shall then be in rebellion against the United States; and the fact that any State, or the people thereof, shall on that day be, in good faith, represented in the Congress of the United States by members chosen thereto at elections wherein a majority of the qualified voters of such State shall have participated, shall, in the absence of strong countervailing testimony, be deemed conclusive evidence that such State, and the people thereof, are not then in rebellion against the United States."

Now, therefore I, Abraham Lincoln, President of the United States, by virtue of the power in me vested as Commander-in-Chief, of the Army and Navy of the United States in time of actual armed rebellion against the authority and government of the United States, and as a fit and necessary war measure for suppressing said rebellion, do, on this first day of January, in the year of our Lord one thousand eight hundred and sixty-three, and in accordance with my purpose so to do publicly proclaimed for the full period of one hundred days, from the day first above mentioned, order and designate as the States and parts of States wherein the people thereof respectively, are this day in rebellion against the United States, the following, to wit:

Arkansas, Texas, Louisiana, (except the Parishes of St. Bernard, Plaquemines, Jefferson, St. John, St. Charles, St. James Ascension, Assumption, Terrebonne, Lafourche, St. Mary, St. Martin, and Orleans, including the City of New Orleans) Mississippi, Alabama, Florida, Georgia, South Carolina, North Carolina, and Virginia, (except the forty-eight counties designated as West Virginia, and also the counties of Berkley, Accomac, Northampton, Elizabeth City, York, Princess Ann, and Norfolk, including the cities of Norfolk and Portsmouth), and which excepted parts, are for the present, left precisely as if this proclamation were not issued.

And by virtue of the power, and for the purpose aforesaid, I do order and declare that all persons held as slaves within said designated States, and parts of States, are, and henceforward shall be free; and that the Executive government of the United States, including the military and naval authorities thereof, will recognize and maintain the freedom of said persons.

And I hereby enjoin upon the people so declared to be free to abstain from all violence, unless in necessary self-defense; and I recommend to them that, in all cases when allowed, they labor faithfully for reasonable wages.

And I further declare and make known, that such persons of suitable condition, will be received into the armed service of the United States to garrison forts, positions, stations, and other places, and to man vessels of all sorts in said service.

And upon this act, sincerely believed to be an act of justice, warranted by the Constitution, upon military necessity, I invoke the considerate judgment of mankind, and the gracious favor of Almighty God.

In witness whereof, I have hereunto set my hand and caused the seal of the United States to be affixed.

Done at the City of Washington, this first day of January, in the year of our Lord one thousand eight hundred and sixty three, and of the Independence of the United States of America the eighty-seventh.

By the President: ABRAHAM LINCOLN
WILLIAM H. SEWARD, Secretary of State.

Migration

Escape the bondage! Run, never look back. From the onset of slavery on this continent, the slaves were constantly thinking of freeing themselves from the dreadful conditions that oppressed them.

On the mind and in the heart of almost all of the slaves was freedom. It took generations before some were to realize any form of freedom. During the 1800s there was more widespread escapes than ever before. Approximately 50,000 men, women and children ran away, most going to Canada or Mexico and some were returned to their slaveowners. There were four major migration routes from the time of the Revolutionary War to the Civil War. 1

A significant number of slaves escaped to towns and cities in the South where they could assimilate into the population and were given opportunities for autonomy. This is considered the first migration. They were able to create new identities and become free people of color. The black populations entering into cities such as Richmond, Nashville, New Orleans, Baltimore, St. Louis, Mobile and the District of Columbia became more difficult to control by authorities. They also assimilated with regular slaves, hired slaves and other fugitives.

The second migration of fugitives fled to remote, isolated areas such as the backcountry along the Mississippi River Valley, and what later became Texas and Florida. They found shelter in the forests, bayous, swamps and around the southern Indian tribes. People often referred to their colonies as maroons. By 1800 there were thousands of fugitive slaves living in the Great Dismal Swamp that was along the border between Virginia and North Carolina. They also sought refuge within Indian nations in Mississippi and Alabama, as well as with the Seminoles who lived in the Florida Everglades.

Southern slaves, in the third migration, began fleeing to the North. When slavery had ended in Pennsylvania, New Jersey, New York and New England, their refuge was more secure. Slavery was also outlawed in Indiana, Illinois, Michigan and Ohio. Those who made this type of migration were normally from the Upper South in states such as Maryland, Delaware, Kentucky, Virginia and Missouri.

Fugitives fled over the Mason-Dixon line and also across the Ohio River. There were some who went north out of the Philadelphia area to New York City and on further north. In Ohio, specific communities, such as Xenia and Oberlin offered help to fleeing blacks. There were all black communities in Brown and Mercer counties, Ohio. Quaker areas of Indiana offered assistance.

The runaways traveled, often times thousands of miles, primarily at night. Without actual road maps, most followed the North Star. Most of the fugitives slept during the day, in barns, outbuildings, or dense woods. Those in the Deep South became stowaways on steamboats going north on the Mississippi River or vessels that were going north along the eastern seacoast. Those who could pass as white or free persons of color, would ride trains northward, hoping to achieve freedom without being caught.

After the War of 1812 a significant number of slaves used the fourth migration of fleeing to Canada. Because they were on British soil, they were free. In 1833 a Parliamentary Act was passed that abolished slavery in the British colonies. It is estimated that between then and the early 1860s, upwards of two thousand slaves entered Canada each year. Their primary settlements were in Canada West, which is now known as Ontario. There were entire black communities founded by white abolitionists. After the passage of the Fugitive Slave Law in 1850 approximately five thousand blacks entered Canada in one year. There were six black communities in Canada West. They were along the Detroit Frontier, the Chatham area, the central part of Canada West, the Niagara Peninsula, urban center on Lake Ontario and the counties Simcoe and Grey. At the onset of the Civil War approximately thirty thousand former slaves lived in Canada.

Amherstburg in Canada West was the chief Canadian terminal on the Underground Railroad. It was located in the narrowest part of the river, thus easily accessible. Two years before the Civil War there were 800 blacks living there. In 1851 abolitionists from Canada and Michigan formed the Refugee Home Society to assist in locating blacks to Canada West. London, Brantford, Queen's Bush and Wilberforce were black communities in central Canada West. Wilberforce was the first all black settlement in Upper Canada. 2

Once fugitives were in free states, they received help from people known as conductors on the Underground Railroad. They were also assisted by free blacks. The "railroad" was actually a network of safe houses along secret routes that slaves used to escape northward. There was no actual train or railroad tracks and it was not underground. Similar to railroad terms, the harboring points along it were called stations and the routes were called lines. The routes extended through fourteen of the Northern states. There was no one person who knew the entire routes of the Underground Railroad, only about the next station on the route. Nothing was in writing, but passed down by word of mouth. Not only were slaves at risk, but also free blacks who were caught, particularly those involved with escapes. Those persons assisting slaves to escape were also, if caught, arrested. There were more routes and stations in Ohio than anywhere else. It also extended west into Iowa and eastern Nebraska Territory.

The Mississippi River provided an escape route. Leaving the South, they could more easily get to Illinois and the Ohio River by using this river. It is estimated that at least 40,000 people used the Mississippi River and tributaries to gain freedom. The river also had a dual purpose as many slaves sold on the auction block were transported to new locations on the river. This became known as "sold down river."

For the most part, runaways were young males, some married, but usually unmarried. They were able to move faster and defend themselves. Slave women often had children they either took with them or were forced to leave behind. Regardless of sex, they were resourceful and wily. They were forced to survive off the land and always remain on guard. Those who managed to get to southern Ohio, Illinois or Indiana, often discovered the whites had origins in the South and had pro-slavery sentiments. Illinois passed a territorial law in 1813 with penalties against blacks, forcing them to leave. In 1829 a law was passed in the state of Illinois, mandating that blacks post a bond of $1,000 if they wished to stay. In Indiana, the state constitution banned further black settlements beginning in 1841. Whites were fined for employing blacks. Ohio passed laws in 1804 and 1807 that required black residents to possess certificates of freedom. Blacks entering Ohio had to post a $500 bond. With tongue in cheek these states did not want black settlers and at the same time were anti-slavery.

Some of the early black settlements in Ohio included Springfield Township in Clark County. There were 276 blacks there in 1860. The cities, such as Cleveland, Columbus and Cincinnati, were prominent areas for blacks to settle before 1860. In Columbus alone there were 997 blacks enumerated in 1860. Oberlin College in Lorain Co., Ohio began admitting black students in 1835. Large numbers of blacks settled early in Ross County.

During slavehood and attempts to flee from their bondage, slaves often exhibited violence against the owners and overseers. They developed habits, as runaways, of looting and furthering violence. Slaves were continually on the defense and some lived in outlying gang groups. The slaves who had learned to read and write, were more apt to achieve freedom in the North. Overall the number of slaves who escaped their bondage was small compared to the slave population of the South.

After escaping to the North and also after being freed by the Emancipation Proclamation, former slaves were planning and hoping to better their lives. Some remained in the South and others sought out places elsewhere, particularly in the Midwest and Great Plains where they could own land. In an attempt to escape the Black Codes and other problems with Reconstruction, freed slaves began to leave the south. There was a new territory, and perhaps a new future, beyond the Missouri River. Like Moses in the Bible, who led the Israelites out of Egypt, they were also seeking the "Promised Land."

Some Africans came to America in the 17th century as free men, primarily working as sailors on ships. There were some who came as indentured servants, becoming free when they completed their term of indenture. The most common area for these indentured servants was the Chesapeake Bay. The free black population increased when children were born to free black women, mulatto children were born to white indentured women or free women, children born to Native American women and slaves who were freed or escaped.

Once the colonies and eventually slaves were faced with a slavery problem, there was a move to remove them to Africa or other locations. This began in 1714 and the sentiment increased after the Revolutionary War. There was thought given to gradual emancipation and also riding the United States of all but free blacks. In 1815 there was a small number of blacks who emigrated to Sierra Leone where a colony was being established by the British in 1815. In 1816 the American Colonization Society was organized, formally known as the American Society for Colonizing the Free People of Color in the United States. Founders of the organization felt that by removing people of color they would have a better life, less tension in the United States and encourage slave owners to free their slaves.

In 1820 blacks and their families, totaling 86 people, left for Sherbo Island off Africa's west coast. The colony was short lived because of disease and problems with assimilation. Next the society purchased lands on the west coast of Africa near Cape Mersurado. It was to be named Liberia. There were approximately 11,000 black who were located in Liberia, half of whom were newly freed slaves. The transportation to Liberia eventually began to fail because of finances and lack of policy agreement. The society realized failure also when free blacks refused to go back to Africa, many having been born in the United States.

The supporters and activists in the society were diverse in opinion. Some felt their endeavors would lead to gradual emancipation. Others saw the blacks as being dangerous and getting rid of them would get rid of the problem. Yet another group of supporters were opposed to slavery but also the equality of races. Ironically the anti-black feelings were strongest in the states where there were no slaves. The colonization efforts were founded by whites, promoted by whites and benefited by whites. 3

On the eve of the Civil War there were just under four million slaves in the United States. The free black population was almost 500,000. It has been difficult to estimate the number of free blacks because they often kept out of sight when a census enumerator was in the area. In some instances light skinned African Americans passed for white. 4

From 1821 to 1865 slavery had increased over the eastern two-fifths of Texas, with the most rapid growth in the 1840s and 1850s. It was widely accepted that Texas would thrive upon slavery. Settlers could receive 80 acres of land for each slave brought to Texas. The Texas Revolution brought assurance to slaveholders that slavery would exist forever. The Constitution of the Republic of Texas, written in 1836, stated that slaves would remain as property to their owners and settlers could bring their slaves to Texas. By 1845 there were well over 30,000 slaves in Texas. Most of those slaves came with their owners when they migrated into Texas. Others were bought in slave trade. Large concentrations of slave plantations were along Brazos and Colorado rivers in the counties of Matagorda, Wharton, Fort Bend and Brazoria. Sugar was the main crop on the lower Brazos River. When a slave would escape in this area, they went to Mexico. All they had to do to achieve freedom was to get across the Rio Grande River. After the emancipation, some returned to the United States. 5

In 1850 the largest population of free African Americans, 74,723, was in the state of Maryland. The second largest population surprisingly was 54,333 in Virginia. 6 In the northern area of Virginia, particularly in the areas of Fairfax and Loudoun counties, there were large populations of free blacks. Slave population increased from 697,897 in 1790 to 3,953,760 in 1860. The number of free blacks increased from 59,466 in 1790 to 487,970 in 1860. 7 Free blacks who went to Kansas in the 1850s soon realized they were caught in the war between pro and antislavery groups, and a bloody war at that. Even the so-called free states, did not accept free blacks as citizens. People who moved into free states with their slaves, were also caught up in the battle between citizens and politics and the laws.

There were specific early African-American settlements in Ohio. Some were as early as 1807 up until 1860. Freed slaves migrated to the state and then others were attracted to the areas. There were also abolitionists who assisted fugitives in their settlement in Ohio. The counties involved were Adams, Belmont, Brown, Clark, Cuyahoga, Darke, Delaware, Franklin, Gallia, Greene, Lawrence, Guernsey, Hamilton, Highland, Jackson, Logan, Lorain, Mercer, Miami, Monroe, Muskingham, Paulding, Pike, Ross, Scioto, Shelby and Van Wert.

As western territories and states were formed, slave owners and their slaves began migrating from the east. The rich, fertile soil along the Missouri River in Missouri attracted many to obtain land there. The area became known as "Little Dixie." The county of Saline had 341 African-American couples register their marriages between 1865 and 1870.

Because of harsh feelings between former slaves and their masters, some fled from their slavehood environment. Others worked for wages for their former owners. Along with employment there was the need for education. Few knew how to read and write prior to the Emancipation Proclamation. This would change as most had learned to read and write by 1900. During the Reconstruction, missionaries and white teachers from the North traveled into the South hoping to provide an education for the freed slaves. This all made it possible for freed slaves to begin a journey that they thought would fulfill their quest for total freedom.

After the Civil War, African Americans began settling in Iowa along the southern border and also along the Mississippi River. Some settled along the Missouri River. They found work on boats and railroads as well as in the lead and coal mines in Iowa. During World War I, Camp Dodge, located near Des Moines, was the only camp in the United States for training officers, including African Americans. Some brought their families to the area. The camp was also in use for training in World War II.

In 1877 a group of freed slaves from Kentucky established the community of Nicodemus in Graham County, Kansas. The Nicodemus Town Company was incorporated by six black and two white men from Kansas. They became known as the "Exodusters." In March and April of 1879 there were 6,200 Exodusters who arrived in St. Louis on their way to Kansas and Nebraska. Some of the men had fought in Colored Regiments for the Union Army in the Civil War. The settlement in northwest Kansas was significantly different from the Kentucky climate and geography. Along with crop failures and hatred of the white settlers, the black community began to decline.

There were twelve agricultural communities established by 1881 in Kansas. Along with Nicodemus there was Hodgeman, Morton City, the Kansas City area, Dunlap, Wabuansee, Parsons, Summit Township, the Topeka area, Burlington, Votaw Colony and Little Caney. Some of these lasted for only a few years, while Nicodemus lasted well into the 20th century. 8

In 1877, there were approximately 300 blacks who came from Tennessee to a colony near Baxter

Springs, Cherokee Co., Kansas. The settlement encompassed 1,000 acres. The land there was available for purchase by the railroad. The colony struggled. After this colony began to fail, the founder, Benjamin "Pap" Singleton, founded a settlement nearDunlap, Kansas which was a white town. In the 1880s a tuition-free school for all ages was established there. By 1900 settlers began leaving the colony at Dunlap. The school closed in 1890.

The Little Caney Colony was established in Chautauqua Co., Kansas. Black settlers were led there by Alfred Fairfax, an escaped slave. There were approximately 200 families who went there in 1879-1880, settling on a 200 acre farm.

Morton City in Hodgeman County attracted 150 black settlers from Kentucky in September of 1877. It was located about three miles northeast of Jetmore. The Hodgeman Colony was established in 1878 and the David City Colony in 1877.

In Shawnee County there were settlements known as The Bottoms and Tennessee Town. Freed slaves settled within a four-block area south of 10th Street and east of Jackson Street in Topeka. The land was originally owned by John Ritchie, an abolitionist and Underground Railroad supporter. It became known as The Bottoms. Another group of about 500 blacks from Tennessee settled in Topeka in an area bounded by S.W. Clay, S.W. Washburn, Huntoon and 10th. Their settlement became known as Tennessee Town. Other areas settled by blacks were Redmondsville in North Topeka and Mud Town, along the Shunganunga Creek.

The Wabaunsee Colony, southwest of Topeka, was established in 1879 by 30 Exoduster families. They were mostly from Mississippi and many came from a plantation owned by the brother of Jefferson Davis, President of the Confederacy.

In the late 1850s, Quindaro Colony in Wyandotte County was founded by freed slaves and abolitionists. They helped slaves escape to the area. It was located on the Missouri River where steamboats could dock. This colony declined when Leavenworth and Kansas City became more populated. Other black settlements in Wyandotte were Rattlebone Hollow, Mississippi Town, Hoggstown and Juniper Town. 9

In 1881 the Votaw Colony was established on 160 acres north of Coffeyville, Kansas close to the Verdigris River. Daniel Votaw, white and a Quaker, bought the land and sold sections consisting of 16 acres each to former slaves for $100 each section. They attempted to grow cotton on the land which resulted in very little profit. In 1895 the river flooded and did signifiant damage. By about 1900 most of the people had moved out of the area. 10

Large numbers of Texas African-Americans came into Kansas by way of Labette Co., Kansas. Parsons, Kansas was on the Missouri, Kansas and Texas Railroad, which became known as "The Katy." This brought many of the blacks into Indian Territory (now Oklahoma) and into Kansas. It is known that Texas blacks were better off financially than those from Mississippi and Louisiana. Many of them rode "The Katy" as first class passengers. 11

Sully County in Dakota Territory (South Dakota) became a haven for blacks in the late 1800s. It was primarily founded by former-slave Norvel Blair in 1882. In 1906 one his sons, Benjamin, and others formed the Northwestern Homestead Movement in Yankton, South Dakota. This was designed to relocate blacks from the South to farms in South Dakota and the Upper Midwest. Sully County was the only area to survive with approximately 200 members locating there. The Great Depression attributed to the demise of the colony. 12

In western New Mexico, black settlements were created, two being Dora and Blackdom. The settlement of Dearfield, Colorado was established in 1910. While there were former slaves of the Cherokees and other tribes in Oklahoma who remained in Indian Territory, eventually blacks from the South began migrating there, particularly in 1889 during the land run. In this time period, the all black town of Langston was founded. Very early communities in the Indian Territory were North Fork Colored, Arkansas Colored, Marshalltown and Canadian Town. Many of these early towns ceased to exist, but surviving towns included Brooksville, Boley, Clearview, Lima, Langston, Summit, Redbird, Rentiesville, Tullahassee, Taft, Tatums and Vernon.

When Oklahoma passed Jim Crow laws in 1907, many of the blacks began to leave, some going as far away as western Canada to provinces such as Alberta and Saskatchewan. Some went on the ill-fated migrations to Africa and some moved to colonies in Mexico. 13 On the border of Mexico and Texas there were black settlements at Coahulila. Ex-slaves and free persons of color migrated into the area in the 19th century. One specific group was the Mascogos consisting of runaway slaves and free blacks from Texas. In the United States they were known as Black Seminoles and most were descendants of the Seminole Negro Indian Scouts. 14

In 1910 an attempt to establish a black agricultural community on the High Plains was made by Oliver Toussaint Jackson. He and his wife, Minerva, filed a desert claim for 320 acres in Weld Co., Colorado and established the town of Dearfield. Within five years the colonists owned 8,000 acres. Soon jobs in Denver began taking settlers to the big city. 15

The abolitionist, John Brown, assisted slaves in the corner of Missouri, Kansas and Nebraska to escape to freedom. They could not travel along the Missouri River because of the pro-slavery people in Leavenworth, Atchison and other river towns. There was also the Iowa Sac and Fox Indian reservation in the area. Slaves were afraid of the Indians. For the most part, the slaves began their flight to freedom near Topeka, Kansas, traveling until they reached Syracuse in Nebraska and then Falls City. The second station in Nebraska was at Nemaha City from which they would cross the Missouri at Brownsville or Nebraska City. Once they arrived in Tabor, Iowa they were safe and would be outfitted for a journey to Canada. Between 1856 and 1860 John Brown and other anti-slavery men frequented Falls City. Each time Brown visited he brought slaves with him, crossing the Nemaha River and driving through town with his cargo. 16

In the 1870s and 1880s, the white Benton Aldrich family encouraged former slave families to settle in Nemaha County in southeastern Nebraska. Aldrich, who was born in New Hampshire and settled in Nebraska in 1865, was an abolitionist. The area, as well as across the Missouri River in Iowa, was dotted with Underground Railroad stations.

Some of the African Americans who migrated northwest after the Civil War, were Civil War soldiers who re-enlisted in the United States Army. They served in defense of the western frontier areas at forts established to protect freight and settlers against Indians. After their tenure in the army, many remained in the area where they were discharged, oftentimes becoming farmers.

On 20 May 1862 President Abraham Lincoln signed into law the Homestead Act which provided settlers with 160 acres of public domain land. Passed during the Civil War, it was greatly opposed by Southern slave-owners who were still eager to buy up large amounts of land and use slave labor. Millions of acres were available for settlement under the Homestead Act. The land was available to anyone who had never taken up arms against the United States government and was at least 21 years of age or head of the household. They were required to reside on the land for five years and show they had made improvement. Men who had fought or were fighting in the Union Army could deduct some years off their five year requirement with proof of honorable discharge. There was nothing in the act that prohibited

24

blacks from applying for land under the Homestead Act. Even women of any race, if head of a household, could secure land.

This act led to the migration of blacks from various locations in the United States to take up land in states such as Kansas and Nebraska. Being able to secure land meant freedom. At the same time, 1 January 1863, that the Homestead Act went into effect, President Lincoln issued the Emancipation Proclamation.

It is important to realize that in 1863 when the Homestead Act went into effect, African Americans could not secure the land. They were, as yet, not naturalized citizens nor had they filed a declaration to become a citizen. It was not until 1866 that they were granted citizenship under the Civil Rights Act. In 1872 under section 2302 of the Revised Statues of the Homestead Act, it became illegal to make a distinction of an entry person on account or race or color. [17]

Homestead files and patents do not state the applicant's race. In a few cases there are comments about slavery, name changes or race in files. The newspaper notices about the land acquisition also do not specify the race. This is unusual, particularly for the time period, because newspapers normally specified the race or made derogatory comments about blacks.

The Timber Culture Act was passed by Congress in 1873. It allowed homesteaders to acquire another 160 acres of lands provided they plant trees on one-fourth of the land. This amounted to 40 acres and would supposedly solve the problem of the lack of wood. After the trees were planted, the applicant had to reside there for at least five years. Later the act was amended to require they set aside land for trees to 10 acres. When the applicant had claimed 160 acres, at least five acres were to be plowed the first year. This plowed land was to be cultivated in the second year, as well as plowing another five acres. During the third year, the initial five acres was to be planted with trees and the second five acres cultivated. By the fourth year, all of the ten acres had been planted in trees. At the end of eight years, the entry man could make final proof. A total of thirteen years were allowed from the date of entry. At the time of final proof, the settler had to prove that at least 675 trees had survived on each acre.

The land could be claimed under both the Homestead Act and Timber Culture Act. Settlers soon realized that trees would not grow in the sandy soil of the Nebraska sandhills, which was most suited to stock grazing. In Nebraska, there were 8,876,351 acres entered and final proof made on only 2,456,696 acres. Congress repealed the act on 3 March 1891. [18]

Both the Homestead Act and Timber Culture Act applied to other states than just Nebraska. For the purpose of this book, emphasis is placed on land laws primarily of Nebraska. [19]

The Kinkaid Act of 1904 also amended the Homestead Act of 1862. One section of 640 acres of public domain land could be freely acquired, except for a small filing fee. The land had to be located in 37 counties in northwest Nebraska. It was introduced in Congress by Moses Kinkaid who was the 6th congressional district representative from Nebraska. The act was signed on 28 April 1904 and went into effect on 28 June 1904.

The provisions of the Kinkaid Act resembled those of the Homestead Act. Claimants had to prove that improvements equivalent to $1.25 per acre had been made to his or her property. The land was non-irrigable. If a homesteader held land in the area when the act went into force, they could accumulate additional surrounding land that was available in order to acquire 640 acres. Under the Homestead Act, settlers could commute their land by paying cash instead of occupying the land for five years. This did not apply to the Kinkaid Act. Kinkaiders soon realized that non-irrigable land was not suited for raising crops. The Nebraska Sandhills where most of the land was located, was dotted with large ranching operations. The ranch barons were hostile about farmers encroaching on lands that adjoined their ranches. One of the land offices that was kept busy with prospective Kinkaiders was at Alliance in Box Butte County. On the initial day of 28 June 1904 it was reported 400 people were in line. It took three days to process all of the filings. By 1912 almost all of the public lands had been claimed, many through illegal transactions of industrialists, jobbers and cattle ranchers. The Kinkaid Act was repealed on 21 October 1976.

All three acts provided land not only for whites, but other races as long as they qualified. No distinction was made at the land office, except when blacks became involved with fraudulent land claims instigated by ranchers and jobbers.

African American cowboys were introduced to Nebraska when they herded Texas longhorns north to railways in Nebraska. Some stayed on and obtained land or worked for ranching operations in the state.

By the early 1900s railroads had advanced through Nebraska, covering the landscape with iron tracks and blackening the air and sky with plumes of coal dust. The railroad meant employment and black men, married, single, divorced or widowed, found employment in western Nebraska. They were employed as section men, working in the boiler room, coach cleaners or as porters. Shortly after the Civil War, George Pullman hired former slaves to work on his sleeper cars on the railroad. Their work in that capacity continued until the 1960s when sleeping car service declined. Pullman had pioneered sleeping accommodations on trains and easily found former slaves willing to work in the capacity of a porter. This became one of the best jobs available for African American men. Some were still categorized as servants and took verbal abuse, while others were treated well by passengers.

Women, whether married, single or widowed were employed in private families as housekeepers, doing laundry, cooking or working in sporting houses which were also known as brothels. Men who did not find employment on the railroad were employed in saloons or barber shops as porters or doing odd jobs during the day.

In 1929, the Great Depression caused hard times, not only for whites, but also for African Americans. Two-thirds of approximately two million black farmers made no money, many going into debt. Desperate, many left their homes seeking work elsewhere, directly in competition with whites who had lost their jobs. As populations in all-black towns dwindled, it added to the failure experienced by the entire nation. Because of these hard times, researchers realize the instability of the black population by reading census. A sense of the types of jobs available for blacks is also very apparent from the 1920 US Census through the 1940 US Census. Along with other races, blacks were mobile, moving from one location to another where they could obtain work. This also brought about dislocated families as black men sought employment in other towns, cities and states.

2. *The Migration of Fugitive Slaves Within the United States and to Canada* by Loren Schweniger, University of North Carolina
2. "Early Settlements in Canada West for The Fugitives of Slavery" by Buxton Historical Society
3. "Back to Africa?" The Colonization Movement in Early America by Timothy Crumrin, Connor Prairie Historian Also Roll of Emigrants to Liberia, 1820-1843 http://www.disc.wisc.edu/archive/liberia/index.html

4. *Between Slavery and Freedom, Free People of Color in America from Settlement to the Civil War* by Julie Winch, Lanham, Maryland: Rowman & Littlefield, 2014. xiii

5. Slavery, Texas State Historical Association, https://www.tshaonline.org/handbook/online/articles/yps01

6. *Between Slavery and Freedom, Free People of Color in America from Settlement to the Civil War* by Julie Winch, Lanham, Maryland: Rowman & Littlefield, 2014. page 62

7. *Between Slavery and Freedom, Free People of Color in America from Settlement to the Civil War* by Julie Winch, Lanham, Maryland: Rowman & Littlefield, 2014, page 39

8. http://legacy.soulofamerica.com/black-towns-kansas.phtml Black Towns Kansas

9. Blacks Found Hope in post-war Ks. http://cjonline.com/life/2010-04-17/blacks_found_hope_in_post_war_ks

10. http://richmondconfidential.org/2010/01/17/resident-reconnects-slave-colony-descendants/

11. *In Search of Canaan Black Migration to Kansas 1879-1880* by Robert G. Athearn. The Regents Press of Kansas, Lawrence, 1978, page 186

12. http://www.southdakotamagazine.com/sully-county-colored-colony Freedom in Sully County 1 April 2016

13. Crockett, Norman, *The Black Towns.* Lawrence KS Regents Press of Kansas, 1979.

14. Ariane Tulloch. Afro-Mexicans: A short study on Identity (PDF) (MA). University of Kansas. http://www.bjmjr.net/west/mascogos.htm The Mascogos

15. http://www.inmotionaame.org/print.cfm;jsessionid=f83018604414595924654413?migration=6&bhcp=1 The Western Migration

16. Keim, A.R. "John Brown in Richardson County' (1887). *Transactions and Reports, Nebraska State Historical Society.* Paper 12.

17. Revised Statutes of The United States, 43rd Cong., 1st sess. (1873) , Sec. 2302, 424.

18. U.S. Statutes at Large, vol. 17, p. 605. Forty-second Congress Sess. II. Ch. 274-277, 1873.

19. Congress repealed the act on 3 March 1891.

NEBRASKA

HISTORICAL MARKER

DEWITTY
AN AFRICAN AMERICAN SETTLEMENT
IN THE SANDHILLS

Spread out along the North Loup River west of here,
DeWitty, later known as Audacious, was the largest
and longest-lasting African American settlement in
rural Nebraska. The settlers, including former slaves
who had fled to Canada before the Civil War and their
descendants, began to arrive in 1906-07, attracted by
the 1904 Kinkaid Act's offer of 640 acres of free land
in the Sandhills.

The settlement included a church, store, barber,
post office, and baseball team, the North Loup
Sluggers, which competed against teams from nearby
communities. Three rural schools educated the children.
On Independence Day, residents of DeWitty and nearby
Brownlee would come together for a rodeo, baseball
game, and picnic.

The 1910 census recorded 82 black residents. The
number of occupied African American homesteads
peaked in 1914, although some settlers had already
canceled or sold their claims and moved away. The
black homesteaders, like their white counterparts,
found 640 acres in this semi-arid region insufficient
for ranching and marginal for farming. The last African
American resident left the area in 1936. The last
parcel still owned by DeWitty settler descendants
was sold in 1993.

Cherry County Historical Society   Nebraska State Historical Society, 2015
Descendants of DeWitty

28

African American Settlements

Dawson Co., Nebraska

African Americans from Ontario, Canada began settling in Dawson County shortly before 1885. They were primarily in search of land. They lived a couple miles north and east of the village of Overton, which is located north of Lexington, the county seat.

After a few years, they decided to take advantage of more land that was available in Cherry County, just to the north and west. This land was located near the village of Brownlee, south of Valentine.

Some of the family names found in Dawson County include Meehan, Emanuel, Riley, Hatter, Tann and Walker. They raised large families and have many descendants.

DeWitty, Cherry Co., Nebraska

With the passage of the Kinkaid Act, that went into effect in June of 1904, eager settlers began filing for land in Cherry County and elsewhere in the sandhills. Approximately 50,000 acres of unclaimed land were located northwest of the settlement known as Brownlee in Cherry County. The land was primarily located along the North Loup River.

Clem Deaver was employed as an immigrant agent for the Burlington Railroad as it developed through Nebraska and into Wyoming. He located land and promoted settlement in the sandhills of Nebraska. He may have contacted black settlers of Dawson County or else they heard about the available land. It is reported in many accounts that have been published or on Internet that Clem Deaver was a black settler. This is incorrect. He was white and most likely never purchased land in Cherry County.

In about 1905, blacks from the Overton area began claiming the available land in Cherry County. More followed in the spring of 1906. The land was not the best as white settlers had already claimed land near the river and in the valleys. Some of the black settlers began to leave the area and some stayed on hoping for the perfect season and better crops.

There was a village in Cherry County that was named DeWitty, in the area of the black settlements. It was founded in 1907, located about 10 miles north and west of Brownlee, named DeWitty after Miles DeWitty (Dewitty) who patented land under the Homestead Act in the area and was named postmaster of a newly established Cherry County postoffice, DeWitty, on 6 April 1915. 1

The town was renamed Audacious, but is usually referred to as DeWitty. A church was started there in 1910 by Rev. O.J. Burchkardt (Burkhart), a missionary of the African Methodist Episcopal Church in Lincoln, Nebraska. The up and coming village had a post office, barber, general store, school districts and a baseball team. The town was disincorporated in 1936. On 11 April 2016 the Nebraska State Historical Society placed a roadside marker on U.S. Highway 83 to commemorate the DeWitty settlement.

The DeWitty Cemetery was located approximately 10 miles west of Brownlee in Section 27, Township 28 North, Range 30 West. Very little can be seen there as makers have deteriorated. South and east of this old cemetery is the grave of Joshua Emanuel, in Section 32. The following are known people buried in the DeWitty Cemetery or in that general area. 2

Infant Brown (child of Mr. and Mrs. Maurice Brown)
Mrs. George Brown (buried 1/2 mile northwest of the present river bridge)
Hazel Crawford
Grandma Curtis (buried 1/2 mile south of the river, 2 miles each of present river crossing)
Joshua Emanuel
Thomas Henson
Ruthie Masterson (daughter of Clarence and Mary Masterson)
Infant Meehan (child of Mr. and Mrs. Dennis Meehan)
Mrs. Nellie Price
Mrs. Nora Steel
Lewis Thomas
John Williams

Bliss, Nebraska

A black settlement existed near Goose Lake, Ewing, Holt Co., Nebraska and was known as Bliss. Black cowboys began settling there in about 1882. Former slaves who had worked in coal mines in southeastern Iowa were duped into buying land there. They were told by land agents that the Goose Lake area offered fertile land and coal. The agents "salted" some sand blowouts with scoops of coal to entice them. However, some did make homestead entries.

The town of Bliss was never incorporated, but it is estimated that by about 1890 there were 100 to 150 people living there. They had their own church and school. Hector Dixon was well known. He was a former slave and served as a school teacher, justice of peace and a creamery driver. Dixon owned 1,000 acres of ranch land before he died in 1912. A cemetery called "Negro Cemetery" blew open during the Dust Bowl. The remains were reburied at Valley View Cemetery in Holt County.

Buffalo Soldier of the Plains
Fort Robinson, Nebraska landscape

Military History

Black soldiers fought in the Revolutionary War and unofficially in the War of 1812. They had been excluded from state militias. During the second year of the Civil War, it was apparent that the Union Army needed soldiers. The white men who could volunteer were not doing so because the war appeared to be dragging on. Even with a draft law there was a need for soldiers if the Union would win the war.

On July 17, 1862 the Second Confiscation and Militia Act authorized the president "to employ as many persons of African descent as he may deem necessary proper for the suppression of this rebellion … in such manner as he may judge best for the public welfare." While this act did not specifically invite blacks to fight, they began organizing their own infantry units in the south, Kansas and Missouri.

The first actual call for black soldiers came in early February 1863 from Massachusetts' abolitionist governor. Over 1,000 blacks responded and the 54th Massachusetts Infantry Regiment was formed. Soldiers came from slave states, Canada and the Caribbean to serve. The infantry was led by Colonel Robert Gould Shaw, a white offier. They stormed Fort Wagner at the Port of Charleston, South Carolina on July 18, 1863 which was the first time black troops led an infantry attack. Unfortunately they were outgunned and outnumbered and almost half of the troops were killed including Colonel Shaw. 1

There was a risk and danger for blacks serving in battle. If they were captured, they were enslaved or executed immediately. White commanders would also be punished and in some cases executed. Black soldiers were paid significantly less than the white soldiers. In 1864 Congress passed a bill that allowed equal pay.

The war came to an end in 1865 and statistics indicate that about 180,000 blacks served as soldiers in the U.S. Army, approximately 10% of the total fighting force. Approximately 90,000 were former contraband individuals from the Confederate states. There were many from the border states as well as free persons of color from the north. During the war, 40,000 black soldiers died … 10,000 in battle and 30,000 from illness or disease.

"Once let the black man get upon his person the brass letter, U.S., let him get an eagle on his button, and a musket on his shoulder and bullets in his pocket, there is no power on earth that can deny that he has earned the right to citizenship."
Frederick Douglass

At the end of the war, white Union soldiers went home or to a different location, drew their pensions and many took advantage of the Homestead Act to obtain "free" land. The options were limited for the black soldiers. Were they to return to a plantation or try to obtain land in a former slave state? While technically they were free, they were not. They had no pension and only the prospect of owning land, primarily under the Homestead Act, which did not specify the color of the entry man.

As settlers began pushing westward and the government acquired more land from the Indians, there was a need for soldiers to stop Indian uprisings and protect the settlers. In 1866 Congress authorized the formation of the 9th and 10th Cavalry Regiments and the 24th, 25th, 38th, 39th, 40th and 41st Infanty Regiments. They were deployed to the west. Later the infantry regiments were consolidated into the 24th and 25th Infantry Regiments. Because of their experience in battle, many black soldiers, veterans of the Civil War, enlisted in the regular Army. There were approximately 5,000 black soldiers who guarded the frontier from 1866 to 1891. They were called Buffalo Soldiers.

The 9th Cavalry was formed in Louisiana in August of 1866 and seven months later had marched into Texas. The following June four companies of the 9th Cavalry reoccupied the abandoned post at Fort Davis. In September of 1875 the 9th Cavalry was transferred to New Mexico and from the mid to the late 1880s they were in Wyoming, Utah, Nebraska and Kansas. In the spring of 1890 seven 9th Cavalry troops were sent to the Pine Ridge and Rosebud reservations in Dakota during the last uprising of the Sioux Nation. 2

In the summer of 1867, a small regiment of the 10th Cavalry was involved in battles with the Cheyenne as they guarded Kansas Pacific Railroad work crews. They also saw duty in Colorado and Oklahoma. In 1873 there were five companies sent to Texas and two years later Company H was sent to Fort Davis in Texas. In 1882 it was headquarters for the regiment. From 1879 through 1880 the 10th Cavalry became involved in the raid of Victorio, a leader of the Apaches. He and the Indians were raiding in western Texas and northern Mexico. Six companies from the 10th Cavalry and one company from the 24th Infantry guarded and patrolled the area water holes. In 1885 the 10th Cavalry moved to the Department of Arizona where they were involved in the Geronimo Campaign. 3

The 24th Infantry served at Fort Davis from 1869 to 1872 and then again in 1880. They guarded stage stations and constructed roads and telegraph lines throughout western Texas and southeastern New Mexico. Company H was involved in the Battle of Rattlesnake Spring forcing Victorio to retreat to Mexico in 1880. The 24th Infantry was transferred to Fort Sill in Indian Territory (became Oklahoma). In 1888 the regiment moved to New Mexico and Arizona. 4

In July of 1870, companies of the 25th Infantry formed in Louisiana and Mississippi, arrived at Fort Davis. They served ten years at the fort and constructed 91 1/2 miles of telegraph line. In 1880 they were transferred to Dakota Territory, forming garrison tasks until sent to Montana in 1888. The infantry participated in the Pine Ridge Campaign of 1890-1891. They were also involved in the 1890s in the mining district in Idaho to restore peace when labor unions declared war on mine owners. 5

Located in the northern panhandle of Nebraska, Camp Robinson was established in 1874 as a temporary encampment during the Indian Wars. The post was in existence sporadically through World War II. The first four years of the post's existence security was provided for the Red Cloud Agency which was nearby on the White River. The agency was home to approximately 13,000 Indians, having been moved to northwestern Nebraska in August of 1873. The Red Cloud Agency was relocated after 1877 to the Pine Ridge Agency in Dakota Territory.

The soldiers also guarded the Sidney-Deadwood Trail that went into the Black Hills. Chief Crazy Horse surrendered at the camp on May 6, 1877, then was mortally wounded in September of 1877 while resisting imprisonment. The Camp was renamed Fort Robinson in 1878. In the winter of 1879 Northern Cheyenne were being held captive at the fort and escaped. With the discovery of gold in the Black Hills and the migration of settlers, the Fremont, Elkhorn and Missouri Valley was built in the area in the mid-1880s, geographically linking it with north central Nebraska. 6 The 9th Cavalry was deployed to Wyoming during the Johnson County War in 1892.

African American soldiers of the 9th Cavalry arrived in 1885 and served at Fort Robinson as regimental headquarters from 1887 to 1898. There were rumors of agitation among Sioux Indians on the Pine Ridge Indian Reservation to the north of Fort Robinson. Soldiers were sent there during the Ghost Dance movement. After 1900 the fort was headquarters for the 10th, 8th and 12th Cavalry Regiments. In 1916 the units were transferred to the Mexican border.

At one time there were 23 black soldiers stationed there who received the Medal of Honor for bravery during the Indian wars and in Cuba during the Spanish American War. They were Emanuel

33

Stance, George Jordan, William Wilson, Thomas Shaw, Henry Johnson, John Denny, Augustus Walley, Brent Woods, William Tompkins and George Wanton. 7 At a military court in 1894 the African-American Chaplain Henry Vinton Plummer was convicted at the fort of conduct unbecoming an officer and dismissed from his military service.

Serving under white officers often meant unjust treatment. The Adjutant General's Office in Washington, DC, 3 April 1874 reported Geneal Court-Martial Orders No. 23. This involved Captain J. Lee Humfreville of the 9th Cavalry while on detached service at Fort Clark, Texas and in command of an escort consisting of his Company K. They were detailed to protect a surveying party and did, without proper authority, abandon the command near Weatherford, Texas. The company was absent for about ten days visiting in Galveston, Texas. Humfreville while en route from Fort Richardson to Fort Clark, Texas by way of Forts Griffin, Concho and McKett, approximately 450 miles, marched for nineteen days. He illegally punished privates in Company K, being Rufus Slaugher (see Section 4), James Imes, Jerry Williams, Levi Comer, Henry Robinson, Jim Wade and E. Tucker. Humfreville had them handcuffed in pairs and fastened in a gang two abreast by a rope and tied to the back of an army wagon. They had to keep up with the moving wagon for approximately 25 miles a day. Slaughter and the others were forced to carry a log weighing 25 pounds while manacled and walk before a sentinel until midnight. This was accomplished until they reached Fort Clark, Texas. They were fed only bread and meat from 15 December 1872 to 20 January 1873. The men were not allowed any fire for warmth or to dry their clothing. They waded through mud and water in extremely cold weather and had no shelter at night. While Captain Humfreville pled not guilty, he was found guilty and sentenced to be dismissed from service. 8

After their service had been fulfilled, several of the black soldiers from Fort Robinson made Alliance and areas in Dawes and Sioux counties their home.

1. Black Civil War Soldiers https://www.history.com/topics/american-civil-war/black-civil-war-soldiers
2. African Americans in the Frontier Army https://www.nps.gov/foda/learn/historyculture/africanamericansinthefrontierarmy.htm
3. Ibid.
4. Ibid.
5. Ibid.
6. Brief History of Fort Robinson https://history.nebraska.gov/visit/brief-history-fort-robinson
7. Black Past - Fort Robinson, Nebraska (1874-1916) https://www.blackpast.org/african-american-history/fort-robinson-nebraska-1874-1916/
8. *Voices of the Buffalo Soldier* by Frank N. Schubert, pp 55-62.

Discharge, Retirement and Death
Soldiers at Fort Robinson

May their valour be remembered.

Fort Robinson in northwest Nebraska was home to the Buffalo Soldiers. They began arriving there in about 1889. Many of the younger ones reenlisted while there and then served in Cuba. Some died in Cuba. The older soldiers retired and called Dawes or Sioux counties home.

The following retired soldiers lived in Dawes, Sioux and Box Butte counties after their retirement. Those listed below are detailed in Section 4 that contains biographical information.

David Badie
William Bell
Caleb Benson
Allen Briggs
Preston Brooks
Pascal Conley
Benjamin J. Hartwell
William Howard
Thomas Jackson
George Jordan
Henry McClain
Edward McKenzie
Rufus Slaughter
Alexander Stepney
Beverly Thornton
Sandy Tournage/Turnage
Israel Valentine
James W. Williams

Fort Robinson Cemetery

As with all military forts and cantonments, a cemetery was established at Fort Robinson in Sioux Co., Nebraska. 1 In 1947 remains were moved to the Fort McPherson National Cemetery, near Maxwell, Lincoln Co., Nebraska. There are still four visible markers within the original cemetery at Fort Robinson.

No Name

No Name

Lee Pitt, died 4 August 1896, age 17 months, 19 days
    son of W & D Pitt

Ellen Rankin, died 22 January 1901, age 64 years and 1 month

Lee Pitt was the son of Wallace and Della Pitts, who lived in Andrews Prect., Sioux Co., Nebraska. They were white and Wallace was a stock grower. Because the child did not belong to a military family, his remains were left in the Fort Robinson Cemetery. 2

On the 1900 US Census, Sioux Co., Nebraska, White River Prect., Ellen Rankin is shown as white, born June 1842 in Pennsylvania and divorced. She is shown as a stock grower. Because she was non-military related, her remains were left in the Fort Robinson Cemetery. 3

During the years that Fort Robinson was in existence, there were military personnel and civilians buried the cemetery located at the fort. They were removed in 1947 to Fort McPherson National Cemetery, located south of Maxwell in Lincoln Co., Nebraska. 4

The following are known military removals. Information by column is Grave Number, Name, Rank, Regiment, Date of Death. The (c) denotes that they were colored. Some of those shown as white may in fact be black, but not denoted as colored (c) in records.

1037	John Tate	Pvt.	10th Cav.	14 Jan 1905
1038	Benjamin Hartwell (c)	Pvt.	10th Cav.	8 Mch 1934
1039	Richard Carter (c)	Pvt.	9th Cav.	14 Dec 1896
1040	Emanuel Stance (c)	1st Sgt.	9th Cav.	25 Dec 1887
1041	Lewis Tollifer (c)	Sgt.	9th Cav.	25 Sept 1903
1042	Thos. Travillion (c)	Sgt.	10th Cav.	26 April 1904
1043	Preston Brooks (c)	Cpl.	9th Cav.	11 Aug 1905
1044	Howard H. Bond (c)	Pvt.	10th Cav.	5 July 1906
1045	Henry Roberts (c)	Pvt.	9th Cav.	6 Dec 1886
1046	Davis D. Badie (c)	1st Sgt.	9th Cav.	24 Jan 1894
1047	Charles H. Grey (c)	Pvt.	9th Cav.	16 Mch 1890
1048	Carter Smith (c)Sgt.	10th Cav.		3 Oct 1903
1049	Lincoln Passchall (c)	Pvt.	9th Cav.	20 Aug 1894
1050	Sandy Turnage (c)	Pvt.	9th Cav.	
1051	William C. Johnson (c)	Cook	US Army	20 Jan 1914
1052	Willie Carson (c)	Pvt.	10th Cav.	27 June 1902
1069	William Bell	Q.M.Sgt.	10th Cav.	26 July 1904
1070	Rufus Tate (c)	Pvt.	9th Cav.	5 Nov 1890

1071	David D. Scipio (c)	Pvt.	9th Cav.Band	1 March 1892
1072	William Wilson (c)	Pvt.	10th Cav.	8 June 1905
1073	Henry Peck (c)	Pvt.	10th Cav.	15 July 1904
1074	John H. Sanders (c)	Pvt.	9th Cav.	17 May 1894
1075	John W. Harris (c)	Pvt.	10th Cav.	27 June 1904
1076	William Johnson (c)	Pvt.	9th Cav.	24 Oct 1890
1077	William C. Hicks (c)	Pvt.	9th Cav.	6 Oct 1896
1078	Harrison Williams (c)	Pvt.	9th Cav.	2 Oct 1897
1079	George Johnson (c)	Cpl.	10th Cav.Band	16 June 1902
1080	William Matthews (c)	Pvt.	9th Cav.	16 Feb 1888
1081	Henry Trout (c)	Pvt.	9th Cav.	15 Aug 1908
1082	Jordon Taylor (c)	Pvt.	10th Cav.	13 May 1906
1083	Jerome Nellis (c)	Pvt.	9th Cav.	17 June 1896
1100	Neander N. Carter	Pvt.	10th Cav.	24 June 1905
1101	Charles Robinson (c)	Farrier	9th Cav.	4 March 1890
1102	William C. Frye (c)	Pvt.	9th Cav.	14 July 1896
1103	Thomas P. Killean (c)	Pvt.	9th Cav.	13 Oct 1893
1104	Joseph White (c)	Sgt.	10th Cav.	27 Mch 1904
1105	John Prather (c)	Pvt.	10th Cav.	22 May 1905
1106	Thomas Dooms (c)	Cpl.	10th Cav.	17 Mch 1904
1107	Charles Haywood (c)	Pvt.	9th Cav.	30 Dec 1890
1108	Willie P. Talbot (c)	Pvt.	9th Cav.	14 June 1890
1109	Carlton Rand (c)	Pvt.	10th Cav.	8 Sept 1902
1110	Jesse Plowden (c)	Pvt.	9th Cav.	28 Jan 1895
1111	Israel Valentine (c)	Sgt.	9th Cav.	21 June 1892
1112	Dobson Theophilus (c)	Pvt.	9th Cav.	11 July 1890
1113	Harry Walker (c)	Pvt.	10th Cav.	30 May 1904
1114	Theophilus White (c)	Sgt.	9th Cav.	11 Sept 1896
1130	Thomas Morton	Pvt.	9th Cav.	14 Sept 1886
1131	George Jordan	1st Sgt.		24 Oct 1904
1132	John Brown (c)	Pvt.	9th Cav.	27 June 1887
1133	Clayton Woody (c)	Pvt.	9th Cav.	11 Aug 1891
1134	John W. Johnson (c)	Pvt.	9th Cav.Band	14 Dec 1897
1135	Jerry A. Davis (c)	Pvt.	9th Cav.	6 April 1893
1136	William Gibbs (c)	Pvt.	9th Cav.	17 April 1888
1137	John T. Carter (c)	Pvt.	9th Cav.	23 Mch 1888
1138	Charles Johnson (c)	Pvt.	9th Cav.	13 April 1886
1139	Augustus Finley (c)	Pvt.	9th Cav.	5 Dec 1897
1140	William B. Burton (c)	Cpl.	10th Cav.	23 Nov 1906
1141	Benjamin Williams (c)	Pvt.	Infantry	19 Feb 1903
1142	Richard Parker (c)	Pvt.	9th Cav.	2 Mch 1890
1143	George Mason (c)	1st Sgt.	9th Cav.	5 Apr 1916
1144	Louis Steward (c)	Pvt.	9th Cav.	17 Aug.?
1158	Henry Chambers	Pvt.	4th Inf.	23 Sept 1884
1159	Peter McFarland	Sgt.	4th Inf.Artificer	20 Aug 1883
1160	Cornelius Donovan	Pvt.	8th Inf.	15 Oct 1891
1161	John Doyle	Pvt.	8th Inf.	27 Jan 1889
1162	Herbert Coyan	Pvt.	8th Cav.	9 June 1910
1163	Fred R. Friend	Pvt.	8th Inf.	19 Oct 1887
1164	Alex. E. Stepne	Pvt.	9th Cav.	18 May 1918
1165	Henry W. Chaffin	Pvt.	9th Cav.	23 May 1876
1166	John C. Hinley	Cpl.	3rd Cav.	3 Feb 1879

1167	Gorge Sprowl	Pvt.	3rd Cav.	9 Jan 1879
1169	James Brogan	Pvt.	9th Inf.	2 July 1875
1170	Joseph E. Allen	Pvt.	4th Cav.	7 July 1877
1172	George Brown	Farrier	3rd Cav.	22 Jan 1879
1173	Bernard Krome	Pvt.	8th Inf.	14 Nov 1893
1185	William M. Miller	PFC	Signal Corp	31 Aug 1886
1186	William Edwards	Trumpeter	3rd Cav.	16 Feb 1877
1187	Herman Schemerhorn	Pvt.	17th Inf.	25 Jan 1891
1188	David McDaniels	Pvt.	8th Inf.	26 Oct 1890
1189	John Teemer	Pvt.	8th Inf.	28 Nov 1891
1190	Henry A. Deblois	Pvt.	3rd Cav.	24 Jan 1879
1191	James Caraley	Pvt.	3rd Cav.	6 Nov 1877
1192	Con Reardon	Pvt.	9th Inf.	25 Oct 1876
1193	George Nelson	Pvt.	3rd Cav.	22 Jan 1879
1194	Amos J. Barbour	Pvt.	3rd Cav.	17 Jan 1879
1195	Jacob Pehl	Pvt.	3rd Cav.	19 Dec 1878
1196	Bernard Kellog	Pvt.	3rd Cav.	
1197	A.J. Barber	Cpl.	3rd Cav.	
1198	John E. Getts	Pvt.	14th Inf.	26 Sept 1876
1199	William H. Raysner	Pvt.	12th Cav.	15 Sept 1911
1200	Thomas McKenzie	Sgt.	US Army	4 Oct 1892
1210	Eugene Carleton	Pvt.	Co. D, 9th Inf.	29 June 1876
1211	James Taggert	Sgt.	3rd Cav.	22 Jan 1879
1212	William H. Good	Pvt.	3rd Cav.	10 Jan 1879
1213	James Conally	Pvt.	3rd Cav.	
1214	Allen Briggs	Color Sgt	US Army	11 Oct 1901
1215	William W. Everett	Pvt.	3rd Cav.	11 Jan 1879
1216	George Smith	Pvt.	8th Inf.	13 April 1887
1217	Timothy Sullivan	Pvt.	5th Cav.	
1218	John Clayton	Pvt.	2nd Inf.	19 Sept 1889
1219	Charles Canal	Pvt.	4th Cav.	20 Aug 1876
1220	Blanton Hord	Wagoner	8th Cav.	17 Aug 1907
1221	John G. Kaly	Pvt.	9th Inf.	5 Jan 1876
1222	Joseph Mazzee	Pvt.	8th Cav.	10 July 1909
1223	Stanley Speed	Pvt.	12th Cav. Band	20 Oct 1911
1224	Earl Rice	Pvt.	8th Cav.	12 June 1908
1225	John Ollis	Pvt.	5th Cav.	9 July 1884
1231	Peter Hulse	Pvt.	3rd Cav.	24 Jan 1879
1232	Jackson Creed	Pvt.	8th Inf.	8 Sept 1889
1233	Adolphus Hood	Cpl.	1st Cav.	9 Dec 1890
1234	John A. Taylor	Retired Sgt.	US Army	2 Feb 1901
1235	Edson J. Stevens	Pvt.	8th Inf.	4 Oct 1890
1236	Andrew West	Pvt.	8th Inf.	17 Sept 1884
1237	Martin Green	Cpl.	5th Cav.	5 Oct. 1880
1238	Francis Barth	Pvt.	3rd Cav.	19 Feb 1877
1239	Frank Graves	Pvt.	4th Field Artly	2 June 1930
1240	Nels Thurley	S/Sgt.	4th Field Artly	2 July 1931
1241	Clarence Chulk	Pvt.	QMC	14 Aug 1939
1242	Syrenus Singer	S/Sgt.	82 Field Artly	12 Aug 1936
1243	Caleb Benson (c)	1st Sgt. US Army		18 Nov 1937
1244	Fred Lister	1st Sgt.		10 June 1945

1245	William Baird	S/Sgt. QMC		21 Jun 1938
	and infant son, Gottfried Baird			
Lot 68?	James A. Swift	1st Lt.	9th Cav.	9 Jan 1896
Lot 69?	Williamson Markland	2nd Lt.	12th Inf.	24 Feb 1895

The following are civilian removals from the cemetery at Fort Robinson to Fort McPherson National Cemetery. (Grave Number, Name, Additional Information, Date of Death)

5880	Larry Dean Wiltse, son of Tech/Sgt D.W. Wiltse	19 July 1943
5881	Michael Eugene Mallory, son of Pvt. C.H. Mallory	2 Feb 1944
5882	Eugenie Pearl Clark, daughter of Cpl. C.L. Clark	15 Sept 1933
5882	John Edward Clark, son of Cpl. C.L. Clark	15 Nov 1933
5883	Dennis Edward Boettiger, son of Pvt. I.G. Boettiger	12 Aug 1942
5884	D.M. Potts, child of Sgt. M.L. Potts	14 Aug 1931
5884	Gerald M. Potts, son of Sgt. M.L. Potts	27 May 1925
5885	Eliza C. Corliss, wife of Capt. A.W. Corliss	11 Jan 1890
5886	2 unknown children	
5887	2 unknown children	
5888	John and Casey Mooby	24 Aug 1876
5889	Sarah Duncan	12 July 1889
5889	Myrtle Duncan	
5889	Layton C. Duncan	
5889	Silion C. Duncan	
5890	M.W. Duncan	12 July 1889
5891	Charles O'Brien	5 Feb 1877
5892	Snedacher	
5893	Mrs. Snedacher and two children	
5894	Rogers Child	
5895	Ellen Roy	20 April 1896
5896	Mrs. Hand	
5897	Joseph Hand	6 April 1877
5898	Garnier Child	6 Aug 1900
5899	Joseph Garnier	2 Oct 1889
5899	George Crook Garnier	2 Oct 1889
	Child Garnier died 6 August 1900	
5900	Baptiste Garnier "Little Bat" Indian Scout	16 Dec 1900
5901	16 unknowns; same grave	
5902	Edward M. O'Brien	16 Aug 1894
5902	E.J. O'Brien	
5903	Mrs. Daumo	
5904	Edna English	
5905	Edna English	
5905	Jenette Sweetin	
5905	Jewette English	13 May 1923
5906	Guy Bursclough, infant	12 Oct 1920
5907	Early Child	
5908	Joseph Lusk	
5909	Allezandro Martin	24 June 1903
5910	James McCarthy	12 May 1887
5911	Samuel Prisk	14 May 1887
5912	Selma Olson	8 Oct 1876
5913	Wesley Rose	30 Mch 1886

5914	Ferdinand Jones	28 Nov 1911
5915	Mike Hanley	
5916	Willie White Wolf	28 Nov 1897
5918	Benjamin Brooks, child	
5919	James Meeks	23 Sept 1879
5920	John D. Hancock	10 July 1878
5921	Moses Milner, "California Joe" Indian Scout	29 Oct 1876
5922	Scott Child	
5923	Taylor Child	
5924	Hattie Larkins	20 Apr 1905
5925	Alexander F. Buck (c), infant	28 Mch 1893
5926	Herbert A. Walton	20 Feb 1928
5927	Clayton Child	
5928	Rosa McMahon	20 Mch 1892
5929	George Morgan	
5930	Richard Hughes	13 Aug 1883
5931	Henry Oppenheimer, son of Pvt. H.W.	11 Aug 1910
5932	Emma Howard, wife of Sgt. Wm. Howard	20 Aug 1908
5933	George Parry, Infant	4 Sept 1876
5934	Lyman Lester Hoag	12 July 1910
5935	Rodgers Child	
5936	J.D. Wallace, child	24 Feb 1893
5937	Robert Waliski, child	9 July 1876
59938	Eloise Coffin	2 Jun 1890
5939	John H. Donohue, child	9 Feb 1894
5940	Mrs. Berg	13 Apr 1893
5941	Elise Neubauer	
5942	Susie Jonee, child	
5943	Evans Child	
5956	Turnage	
5957	Paris Child	
5958	James O;Brien	10 Feb 1894
5959	Moses Child	
5960	Albert Mitchell	12 Feb 1896
5961	Henry Masters	27 Nov 1881
5962	Margarent Kunz, daughter of 1st Sgt. C.H. Kunz	20 Apr 1908
5963	Kline Child	27 Oct 1901
5964	Henry Russell	13 Mch 1913
5965	C.D.P. Howard	
5966	Bridget Keogh	17 June 1876
5967	Pearl Wheat	
6026	Annie McKenzie (c)	16 Feb 1895
6027	William "Willie" Shidell (c), son of Pvt. J.S. Shidell	3 Apr 1886
6028	Mattie Grayson (c), wife of Cpl. A.L. Grayson	18 Aug 1891
6029	R.C. Richardson (c)	18 Feb 1892
6030	Hector Child (c)	
6031	Helen Carter (c), daughter of Sgt. C.M. Carter	10 Jan 1898
6032	Ella Jackson (c), child	28 Aug 1886
6033	Gertrude Wallace (c), daughter of Sgt. Harry Wallace	
6033	Mattie Wallace (c), daughter of Sgt. Harry Wallace	
6034	Wiley Infant (c)	24 May 1898
6035	Clayton Hunt (c), infant	2 Sept 1895

6036	Celestie F. Hunt (c)	28 Mch 1895
6037	Clarence Ernest Tracey (c), infant	15 Mch 1893
6038	Madden Child (c)	
6039	Sallie Monroe (c)	
6040	Laura Bradden (c)	9 June 1910

1. NebraskaGravestones http://nebraskagravestones.org/cemetery.php?cemID=348
2. Year: 1900; Census Place: Andrews, Sioux, Nebraska; Roll: 941; Page: 5B; Enumeration District: 0191; FHL microfilm: 1240941
3. Year: 1900; Census Place: White River, Sioux, Nebraska; Roll: 941; Page: 9A; Enumeration District: 0191; FHL microfilm: 1240941
4. *Fort McPherson (Nebraska Territory) History, Regiments of the Plains and Grave Removals to Fort McPherson National Cemetery* by Ruby Coleman; pub. by Nebraska State Genealogical Society, Lincoln, NE 2000 pp 51-55

Fort Niobrara

Fort Niobrara was located as a military post in north central Nebraska. It was constructed along the Niobrara River after the Great Sioux War of 1876. There was a need to contain the Lakotas on the reservation lands immediately north in Dakota Territory. The primary intention of the Fort was to oversee Chief Spotted Tail's band of Upper Brule Lakota at the Rosebud Agency. There were approximately 4,000 Indians about 40 miles north of the area selected for Fort Niobrara.

The site for the fort was selected in 1879 by General George Crook and work on the fort began in 1880. It was situated on the south bank of the Niobrara River. In 1882-1883 the Fremont, Elkhorn and Missouri Valley Railroad was built through the area and the fort was used as a distribution point for supplies provided to the Lakota agencies in South Dakota. A few miles west of the post, the village of Valentine was built in 1882. The railroad linked Fort Niobrara with Fort Robinson, further west in the Nebraska panhandle.

Throughout the 1880s Fort Niobrara was garrisoned by units of the 5th Cavalry, 9th Infantry and 9th Cavalry. During the 1880s the soldiers stationed there escorted supply trains to the Indian agencies in South Dakota. They also tried to prevent cattle rustling from the cattle herds on the Indian reservations. The garrison responded to the Ghost Dance affray on the Sioux reservation in December of 1890, by providing security at the Rosebud reservation. Companies A,B, and H of the 8th Infantry and Troops A and G of the 9th Cavalry marched to the Rosebud Agency, establishing a field camp. In the 1890s there were approximately 500 soldiers stationed on the Rosebud Agency.

With the beginning of the Spanish American War in 1898, the post was garrisoned with less than 100 men. In 1902 the black 25th Infantry was stationed there until July 1906 when the fort was abandoned.

People who died at Fort Niobrara were buried in a cemetery on the premises. In June of 1907 the bodies were exhumed and buried in the Fort Leavenworth National Cemetery, Leavenworth, Leavenworth Co., Kansas. 1

The following are the known remains that were removed from Fort Niobrara to Fort Leavenworth National Cemetery in 1907. The date shown is their death. It is unknown if any of those listed below are black as their race was not identified.

George Abbott	10th US Infantry	11 September 1900
Owen Dement Ball	Co H, 5th	30 December 1904
Henry C. Barrett	Co. F, 5th US Cav	25 June 1881
Emma L. Barbour	infant dau Sgt. Barbour	11 May 1906
Infant Beaman	child of Fred Beaman	22 March 1894
George Bivens		12 July 1889
James Bratton	25th US Infantry	16 September 1903
J.Anna Halstensen Cahota	wife of Edward Cahota	15 February 1891
John J. Carroll	Cpl. Co. F 6th Cav	8 June 1888
John M. Carter	Music Co A 9th Cav	1 October 1891
John O. Cathopper	civilian	2 October 1883
James Coleman	civilian	22 January 1896
Lawrence Crane	2nd US Infantry	14 August 1886
Annie Cunningham	wife of Sgt.	27 April 1898
Elijah Custard	Cpl. Co M, 25th Inf.	17 September 1905

William J. Davis	25th US Infantry	20 March 1906
Frank Dillon		6 April 1900
John Dive	civilian	1885
John Donavon	8th US Infantry	21 Sept 1894
Joseph Edward	25th US Infantry	15 May 1906
Joseph Farrell	12th US Infantry	1 April 1898
Elenor Finch	dau Albert & Mary	31 July 1887
Ferdinand Flick	8th US Infantry	4 March 1888
Squaw Frosted Bear	Pvt 6th US Cav	17 August 1883
George Furtsch	Pvt Co G Inf.	29 September 1886
George W. Gardner	Pvt Co G 6th Cav	8 May 1893
Anton Gehringer	Pvt Co. G Cav	9 May 1893
Newman Gibson	Co. G 9th Cav	29 June 1888
Theodore Green	child of Charles	7 February 1894
Fannie Green		2 March 1899
Myrtle Green	infant Charles A.	16 March 1898
John Maston Grimes	son Sgt. E.P. Grimes	2 July 1881
James M. Hale	Pvt Co F 12th Inf	16 March 1898
Cordelia Harmon	wife W.G. Harmon	19 September 1896
(born 19 September 1864)		
David Harris	Co L 25th Inf	25 May 1905
Iron Hawk	Co. L 6th Cav	30 March 1894
Child Humm	child of Pvt Humm	7 May 1900
Samuel Daniel Jenkins	Co A 9th Cav	31 December 1889
Thomas Jones	Co K 25h Inf	6 May 1904
John J. Kane	Co A 8th Inf	10 November 1890
John Kane	Co G 8th Inf	8 December 1894
Kannigiesser	Sgt Band, 12th Inf	26 September 1897
James Kennedy	Co. K, 2nd US Inf	29 December 1886
George King	citizen	23 June 1888
Ida Marion King	dau. Thomas; citizen	15 July 1889
Arnold Krummenacher	Co. A, 12th Inf	5 January 1897
Fannie Kurtzebaum	mother Sgt Dyer	21 May 1896
James Layden	Sgt Co G 6th Cav	31 December 1891
Grace Mangan	wife of James	19 April 1894
Albert E. Maxwell	Co L 25th Inf	24 March 1905
Jesse L. McFerrin	Corp Co C 5th Inf	21 April 1903
Henry McKee	Co D Infantry	17 September 1902
Child Meissner	child of William	19 April 1884
George T. Moles	Co. A 12th Infantry	26 October 1897
Thomas Mosby	Co. G 9th Cav	12 May 1886
Anna Marguerite Muller	child of Pvt Muller	9 August 1894
Infant Noisy Owl		5 July 1891
Howard Noland	Sgt Co G 9th Cav	15 June 1888
John O'Brien	Co B 8th US Inf	24 October 1890
Sioux Perkins	infant dau Sgt Perkins	5 May 1891
Pine, Benjamin P.	Co F 5th Infantry	16 January 1881
Reva Ross	Co B 25th Inf	29 May 1906
John J. Rudman	Co. E 21st Inf	16 January 1891
Mrs. Alice Schall	wife Pvt Schall	17 June 1893
Francis J. Schmidt	Co F 12th Infantry	8 January 1896
Child Schuler/Schooler		27 July 1897

Annie Shaw		30 June 1888
Frank E. Simmons	Co. F 5th MD Cav	5 March 1881
Edith M. Sperling	child Pvt Sperling	20 July 1895
Edwin Joseph Sperling	child Pvt Sperling	17 July 1895
Charles Steele	Corp Co D 5th Cav	22 April 1884
Henry Stokes	Co D 25h Infantry	7 August 1904
Infant Tarpy	child of David Tarpy	no dates
F.F. Tarpy	son of David Tarpy	1 August 1889
Victor Tozoski	Co L 6th Cav	20 May 1893
W.T. Torvend		6 October 1898
William Tully	Co I US Inf	2 July 1904
Indian Woman		no dates
Charles Walser	Co G 6th Cav	24 December 1892
Emily Walters	d/o Wm & Rose	25 June 1881
Joseph R. Weaver	saddler Co F 6th Cav	19 February 1891
William D. Weaver	Co C 12th Inf	27 June 1896
William R. Webb	Sgt Co C 25th Inf	7 February 1903
Jacob Weden	1st Sgt Co D 5th Cav	5 July 1880
Felma D. Wheelan	d/o Corp Wheelan	6 February 1904
Samuel B. Wheeler, Jr	s/o Corpl. Wheeler	10 June 1905
Joseph Whipple	half-breed citizen	no dates
Frank M. Wildt	Co F 12th Inf	30 August 1897
John Williams	Co L 25th Inf	3 July 1903
Henry William	Co B 5th Cav	26 June 1881
White Boy		1 December 1892
Thomas J. Wiggins	Sgt Post QM	22 June 1899
Jacob D. Wilson	Co G 9th Cav	28 February 1891
Eugene Woods	Cpt Co G 9th Cav	30 December 1889
James Yates	Troop G	9 December 1898
Robert Yours	25th Infantry	17 April 1903

1. "The Republican," Valentine, Nebraska, 14 June 1907

World War I Draft Registration

The United States declared war on Germany on 6 April 1917 and officially entered into World War I. On 18 May 1917, the Selective Service Act was passed, authorizing the president to increase the military of the United States. Every male living within the United States between ages eighteen and forty-five was required to register for the draft.

Men were required to register regardless of the citizenship status. Not all men who registered actually served in the military. Some men enlisted and served, but never registered for the draft. There were approximately 24 million men living in the United States in 1917 and 1918 who registered. Since the total population was approximately 100 million, this means close to 25% of the total population is represented in draft records.

There were three separate registration. The first registration was on 5 June 1917 for men aged 21 to 31, thus born between 6 June 1886 and 5 June 1896. The second registration was on 5 June 1918. This included men who had turned 21 years of age since the previous registration; born between 6 June 1896 and 5 June 1897. Men who had not previously registered or not already in the military were registered. There was a supplemental registration taken on 24 August 1918 for men who turned 21 years of age since 5 June 1918. The third registration was on 12 September 1918 for men age 18 to 21 and 31 to 45; men born between 11 September 1872 and 12 September 1900.

The original draft records are kept in the National Archives, Southeast Region in East Point, Georgia. They have been digitized and are available on Ancestry and other large databases.

Draft registrations for World War I show that many African American men were working in the panhandle of Nebraska for the railroad. Depending on the registration, there may be information on relatives, along with addresses. While they may not have lived in Nebraska for any great length of time, their information is included as a reminder of their part in the railroad history of the state.

Information has been taken from the original World War I Draft Registration images found on Ancestry.com. Names are shown as indicated on the registration card.

African Americans — World War I Draft Registration
Cherry Co., Nebraska

Edward Thurman Bonty, Valentine, Nebraska
24, 1 February 1893, Hill City, Kansas
janitor, banks and auditorium, Valentine, Nebraska
married, wife and child; negro
filed 5 June (1917) Valentine, Cherry Co., Nebraska

Joseph Hooker Boyd, Audacious, Cherry Co., Nebraska
25, 21 August, 1892, Kingston, Tennessee
farmining, self, Audacious, Nebraska
mother and sisters to support; negro; single
filed 5 June 1917, Kennedy, Cherry Co., Nebraska

William McKinley Boyd, Audacious, Cherry Co., Nebraska
23, b. 21 March 1894, Harrison, Tennessee
farmer, self, Audacious, Nebraska
single; mother and four children to support; negro
filed 5 June 1917, Kennedy, Cherry Co., Nebraska

Joe Thomas Conrad, Brownlee, Cherry Co., Nebraska
35, b. 14 May 1883
farming, self, Brownlee; negro
wife, Charlotte Conrad, Brownlee
filed 12 September —- Valentine, Cherry Co., Nebraska

Miles Henry DeWitty, Valentine, Cherry Co., Nebraska
45, b. 27 August 1873, negro
farmer, self, Valentine
Myrtle Louise DeWitty, Valentine
filed 12 September 1918, Valentine, Cherry Co., Nebraska

John H. DeWitty, Prentice, Cherry Co., Nebraska
33, b. 2 April 1884
farming, Prentice, Cherry Co., Nebraska; negro
Mrs. Hattie DeWitty, Prentice
filed 12 September 1914, Valentine, Cherry Co., Nebraska

Richard Dewey Emanual, Seneca, Thomas Co., Nebraska
18, b. 11 January 1900
farming for father; Seneca; negro
Joshua Emanual, father, Seneca, Thomas Co., Nebraska
filed 12 September —-, Valentine, Cherry Co., Nebraska

James Alvin Griffith, Wells, Cherry Co., Nebraska
42, b. 6 May 1876
farmer, self; negro
Emma Griffith, wife
filed 10 September 1918, Valentine, Cherry Co., Nebraska

LeRoy Jones, Jr., 1317 S. 20th St. Philadelphia, Pennsylvania
18, b. 26 September 1899
farm hand for Orr and Steadman, Brownlee, Cherry Co., Nebraska; negro
S.G. Saunders, 1317 S. 20th St., Philadelphia, Pennsylvania
filed 12 September 1918, Valentine, Cherry Co., Nebraska

Clem Henry Linear, Wells, Cherry Co., Nebraska
38, b. 17 June 1880
rancher and farmer, Wells Precinct, Cherry Co., Nebraska; negro
Mack Linear, 524 East 3rd St., Alliance, Box Butte Co., Nebraska
right leg paralyzed
filed 12 September 1918, Valentine, Cherry Co., Nebraska
two copies, one certified

Charles Edward Meehan, Wells, Cherry Co., Nebraska
42, b. 22 July 1876
farming for A.P. Curtis and self, Wells, Cherry Co., Nebraska; negro
Hester C. Meehan, mother, Brownlee, Cherry Co., Nebraska
filed 12 September 1918, Valentine, Cherry Co., Nebraska

Arthur Dennis Meehan, Wells, Cherry Co., Nebraska
33, b. 11 May 1885
farming, self, Wells, Cherry Co., Nebraska; negro
Ida Meehan, wife, Wells
filed 12 September —-, Valentine, Cherry Co., Nebraska

Clarence Masterison, Brownlee, Cherry Co., Nebraska
29, b. 28 December 188 at Powhatten, Kansas
farming for self, Brownlee, married; negro
[signed as Masterson]
filed 5 May 1917, Kennedy, Cherry Co., Nebraska

Elmer Lee Plumner, Wells, Cherry Co., Nebraska
18, b. 20 November 1890
farm hand for C.B. Woodson, Wells, Cherry Co., Nebraska; negro
Drucillie Plumner, 2960 West Bell St., St. Louis, Missouri
[signed as Plummer]
filed 12 September —-, Valentine, Cherry Co., Nebraska

Turner Price, Jr., Hood, Nebraska
22, b. 8 August 1894, Atlanta, Georgia
farmer, self, near Hood, supporting father and mother; single; negro
physically disabled, blind one eye
filed 6 June 1917 Cherry County

George Addison Riley, Brownlee, Cherry Co., Nebraska
33, b. 17 Nov. 1884
stock farmer; negro
Truth Riley, wife, Brownlee
filed 12 September —-, Valentine, Cherry Co., Nebraska

Albert Franklin Riley, Brownlee, Cherry Co., Nebraska

32, b. 2 May 1886
farming, self, Brownlee, negro
Leanna V. Riley, wife, Brownlee
12 September —- Valentine, Cherry Co., Nebraska

George William Roberts, Valentine, Cherry Co., Nebraska
35, b. 28 April 1883
day laborer, C&NW RR, Valentine; negro
Annic Roberts, Detroit, Michigan
filed 12 September 1918, Valentine, Cherry Co., Nebraska

Frank Ross, 814 West Eldridge, Coffeyville, Kansas
28, b. 27 June 1880
farm hand, Orr and Steadman, Brownlee, Cherry Co., Nebraska; negro
Frank Ross, East Coffeyville, Kansas
filed 12 September 1918, Valentine, Cherry Co., Nebraska

Charles Speese, Brownlee, Cherry Co., Nebraska
36, b. 8 January 1882
farming & ranch, Loup Precinct; negro
Rosetta Speese, Brownlee
filed 12 September 1918
Valentine, Cherry Co., Nebraska

Harry Tyler, Wells, Cherry Co., Nebraska
37, b. 8 May 1881
farm hand for Turner Price, Loup Precinct, Cherry Co., Nebraska; negro
Edward Walker, Ellwood, Doniphan, Kansas
filed 12 September 1918, Valentine, Cherry Co., Nebraska

Charles Boston Woodson, Wells, Cherry Co., Nebraska
237, b. 19 Januiary 1881
mail carrier, govt., Wells; negro
Lena Woodson, mother, RR1, Horton, Atchison Co., Kansas
filed 12 September —-, Valentine, Cherry Co., Nebraska

African Americans — World War I Draft Registration
Cheyenne Co., Nebraska

Thomas Bates, Sidney, Cheyenne Co., Nebraska
24, born 12 January 1893, Leavenworth, Kansas
section hand, negro
single
filed 5 June 1917, no location shown

William Brown, Potter, Cheyenne Co., Nebraska
43, born 15 December 1874
section hand, UPRR Co., Potter, negro
no relatives
both legs broken 1910
filed 12 September 1918, Sidney, Cheyenne Co., Nebraska

Henry Clay, Potter, Cheyenne Co., Nebraska
34, born 6 August 1884
section hand, UPRR Co., Potter, negro
Dock Clay, Grady, Arkansas
filed 12 September 1918, Sidney, Cheyenne Co., Nebraska

Geddie Dupree, 513 Avenue D, Crowley, Louisiana
37, born 4 July 1881
porter, UPRR Co., Sidney, Cheyenne Co., Nebraska, negro
Caroline Judward, mother, 513 Avenue D, Crowley, Louisiana
filed 12 September 1918, Sidney, Cheyenne Co., Nebraska

William Gary, 1248 Wabash Ave., Chicago, Illinois
26, 28 August 1890, born Mobile, Alabama
mechanic, not employed, negro
support mother, single
filed 5 July 1917, Sidney, Cheyenne Co., Nebraska

Willie H. Harmon, Sunol, Cheyenne Co., Nebraska
24, born 7 February 1893
section laborer, Union Pacific RR Co., Sunol, negro
single
filed 1 June 1917, Colton Prect., Cheyenne Co., Nebraska

Charlie Jackson, Sidney, Cheyenne Co., Nebraska
34, born 9 September 1884
section hand, UPRR Co., negro
Alice Jackson, Oak Ridge, LA
filed 12 September 1918, Sidney, Cheyenne Co., Nebraska

Sam Johnson, Sidney, Cheyenne Co., Nebraska
26, born 11 May 1891, Little Rock, Arkansas
section hand, Union Pacific RR Co., Sidney, negro
single; has a physical defect
home address is 802 East 14th St., Kansas City, Missouri
filed 5 June 1917, Sidney, Cheyenne Co., Nebraska

James Johnson, Sidney, Cheyenne Co., Nebraska
18, born 11 September 1900
porter/dishwasher, Union Pacific Hotel, Sidney, negro
Rosea Johnson, mother, Oklahoma City, Oklahoma
filed 12 September 1918, Sidney, Cheyenne Co., Nebraska

Eddy James Kimbley, Sidney, Cheyenne Co., Nebraska
26, born 12 August 1890, Central City, Kentucky
porter, National Hotel, Sidney, negro
married
filed 5 June 1917, Sidney, Cheyenne Co., Nebraska

George Mother, Potter, Cheyenne Co., Nebraska
19, born 15 September 1899
on section, UPRR Co., Potter, negro

Foras Mother, Columbus, Mississippi
filed 12 September 1918, Sidney, Cheyenne Co., Nebraska

Fred Patterson, Potter, Cheyenne Co., Nebraska
35, born 17 March 1884
laborer, UPRR Co., Potter, negro
Lizzie Patterson, 1319 - 32, Denver, Colorado
filed 12 September 1918, Sidney, Cheyenne Co., Nebraska

Charles Edward Patton, Sidney, Cheyenne Co., California
33, born 4 April 1885
General Cleaning, for self, Sidney, negro
Gertrude Helen Patton, 1814 Divisadero, San Francisco, California, wife
filed 12 September 1918, Sidney, Cheyenne Co., Nebraska

Artie Clarence Richardson, Sidney, Cheyenne Co., Nebraska
34, born 29 December 1884
porter, I.S. Hobbs, Sidney, negro
A.S. Forbush, 2843 Weston, Denver, Denver Co., Colorado
2036 Arapahoe St., Denver, Colorado [written under his signature]
"says he lost an eye"
filed 12 September 1918, Sidney, Cheyenne Co., Nebraska

Mathew Edward Silvers, Sidney, Cheyenne Co., Nebraska
35, born 22 September 1883
section hand, Union Pacific RR Co., negro
Tula Silvers, 1118 Cambell St., Kansas City, Missouri
filed 12 September 1918, Sidney, Cheyenne Co., Nebraska

Isaac Turner, Potter, Cheyenne Co., Nebraska
23, born 20 March 1894, Colliston, Louisiana
section hand, Union Pacific RR, Potter, negro
single
eyes bad
"eyes apparently all right"
filed 5 June 1917, Potter, Cheyenne Co., Nebraska

John Wilson, Jr., Sidney, Cheyenne Co., Nebraska
34, born 24 August 1884
common laborer, UPRR, Sidney
John Wilson, father, Belcher, Louisiana
filed 12 September 1918, Sidney, Cheyenne Co., Nebraska

African Americans — World War I Draft Registration
Dawes Co., Nebraska

William Biggs, Whitney, Dawes Co., Nebraska
41, b. 13 March 1877
farming for E.H. Pilster, Whitney, negro
Cortnay Biggs, mother, Llano, Texas
filed 12 September 1918, Chadron, Dawes Co., Nebraska

John D. Byrd, Arkansas City, Desha Co., Arkansas
34, b. 24 March 1884
section laborer, CB&Q RR Co., Belmont, Dawes Co., Nebraska, negro
Savanah Byrd, Arkansas City, Desha Co., Arkansas
filed 12 September 1918, Chadron, Dawes Co., Nebraska

Lawrence Carrol Bruce, 141 So. 6th St., Canton, Peoria, Illinois
33, b. 11 December 1885
section laborer, CB&Q RR, Belmont, Dawes Co., Nebraska, negro
Minnie Bruce, 141 So. 6th St., Canton, Peoria, Illinois
mail to 158 So. Prairie, Galesburg, Illinois
present address Belmont, Nebraska
filed 12 September 1918, Chadron, Dawes Co., Nebraska

Waller Wesley Craig, St. Louis, Missouri
32, b. 26 February 1886
farmer for George Dorrington, Crawford, Dawes Co., Nebraska, negro
Nicholas Craig, father, 6850 Watson St., St. Louis, Missouri
filed 12 September 1918, Chadron, Dawes Co., Nebraska

Alfred Dandridge, Chadron, Dawes Co., Nebraska
32, b. 29 November 1885
laborer, W.H. Donahue, Chadron, negro
Kinzie Dandridge, Mooresville, Missouri
filed 12 September 1918, Chadron, Dawes Co., Nebraska

Henry Syprus Dodson, Chadron, Dawes Co., Nebraska
42, b. 7 April 1876
janitor for Ray Tierney, Chadron, negro
Mrs. Rose Dodson, Chadron
filed 12 September 1918, Chadron, Dawes Co., Nebraska

Joseph Hill, 124 Ann, Chadron, Dawes Co., Nebraska
40, b. 15 May 1878
teamster, City of Chadron, negro
Mrs. Estella Hill, 124 Ann, Chadron
filed 12 September 1918, Chadron, Dawes Co., Nebraska

Andrew Holley, 2227 S. State St., Chicago, Cook Co., Illinois
36, b. 26 September 1881
section laborer, CB&Q RR. Co, Belmont, Dawes Co., Nebraska
John Holley
present residence Belmont, Dawes Co., Nebraska
filed 12 September 1918, Chadron, Dawes Co., Nebraska

William Huffman, Crawford, Dawes Co., Nebraska
34, b. 29 Jan. 1884
RR laborer, CB&Q RR Co., Crawford, negro
Allen Huffman, father, South ?, Sumner, Tennessee
filed 12 September 1918, Chadron, Dawes Co., Nebraska

Frank Lucas, Marsland, Dawes Co., Nebraska
39, b. 4 October 1878
section man, CB&Q RR, Marsland, Dawes Co., Nebraska
Ida Vincent, 706 E. 1st, Oklahoma City, Oklahoma
mail to 302?, Second St., St. Louis, Missoui
filed 12 September 1918, Chadron, Dawes Co., Nebraska

Samuel William Neighbors, Crawford, Dawes Co., Nebraska
43, b. 14 February 1875
RR Laborer, CB&Q RR Co., Crawford, negro
Rebecca Neighbors, wife, Crawford
filed 12 September 1918, Chadron, Dawes Co., Nebraska

Willie Lewis Small, Crawford, Dawes Co., Nebraska
33, b. 25 December 1885
laborer for R.R. Beatte, Crawford, negro
Willard Small, father, Memphis, Tennessee
filed 12 September 1918, Chadron, Dawes Co., Nebraska

George Isaac Stewart, Crawford, Dawes Co., Nebraska
35, b. 19 September 1882
section hand, CB&Q RR Co., Dawes Co., Nebraska, negro
Mattie May Stewart, daughter, Orville, Alabama
filed 12 September 1918, Chadron, Dawes Co., Nebraska
Bert George Taylor, Chadron, Dawes Co., Nebraska
44, b. 25 July 1874
laborer in Chadron, negro
Maggie Taylor, wife, Chadron
filed 12 September 1918, Chadron, Dawes Co., Nebraska

Ira Webb, Belmont, Dawes Co., Nebraska
34, b. 24 September 1883
Section Laborer, CB&Q RR Co., Belmont, negro
Emiline Webb, Salisbury, Rowan Co., North Carolina
filed 12 September 1918, Chadron, Dawes Co., Nebraska

Ellison Wright, Chadron, Dawes Co., Nebraska
19, b. 25 September 1894
porter, C & NW RR Co., Chadron, negro
Mrs. Belle Wright, Los Angeles, California
filed 10 September 1918, Chadron, Dawes Co., Nebraska

African Americans — World War I Draft Registration
Custer Co., Nebraska

Lacy Conrad
Broken Bow, Custer Co., Nebraska
34, b. 19 April 1888
bus man, transfer line for A.J. Elliott, Broken Bow, Custer Co., Nebrfaska
Hattie Conrad, Broken Bow
filed 12 September 1918

Joseph Daniels
Broken Bow, Custer Co., Nebraska
35, b. 1883
farming for Edward McComas, Broken Bow, Custer Co., Nebraska
Mrs. Amelia Conrad, Broken Bow
filed 12 September 1918

Arthur James Davis
Sumner, Dawson Co., Nebraska
34, b. 15 November 1883
farming for J.M. Downey, Sumner, Dawson Co., Nebraska
wife, Alice Davis, Sumner
filed 12 September 1918

Robert Lee Hunter
Broken Bow, Cusster Co., Nebraska
35, b. 19 December 1883
farmer, self, Broken Bow, Custer Co., Nebraska
Maggie Hunter, Broken Bow
filed 12 September 1918

William Jones
Anselmo, Custer Co., Nebraska
43, does not know date of birth
laborer for C.G. Eupfield, Anselmo, Custer Co., Nebraska
Frony Davis, Galveston, Texas
filed 12 September 1918

African Americans — World War I Draft Registration
Box Butte Co., Nebraska

The following are African Americans who registered for the World War I Draft in Box Butte Co., Nebraska. Their nearest relative was listed, along with identifying information. Some of them were actual residents of Box Butte County, while others were railroad employees whose residence was elsewhere. The last date is when the registration was filed in Alliance, Nebraska.

William Batt, Alliance
born 7 Dec 1874
farmer (self) - Alliance
Victoria Batt, Alliance
12 Sept 1918

Denver C. Burrow, 704 Wyandotte, Kansas City, Missouri
born 27 Nov 1893 Marshall Co., Mississippi
section, CB&Q RR Alliance
single
5 Jan. 1917

Robert Joseph Campbell, 215 1st St., Alliance
born 7 June 1880
cook for L.E. Johnson, 216 Box Butte, Alliance

Helen Campbell, Deadwood, SD
12 Sept 1918

Hayes E. Chandler, Hemingford
born 25 Sept 1880
farming, renter Hemingford
Florence M. Chandler, Hemingford
12 Sept 1918

John Henry Chapman, Alliance
born 7 Feb 1880
bl washer CB&Q RR Alliance
wife Maggie Chapman, Alliance
12 Sept 1918

Dan Cherry
RFD 30, Oceola, Mississippi Co., Ark.
born 20 Feb 1885
boilerwasher CB&Q Burlington Shop, Alliance
Ella Hilbert same address
12 Sept 1918

James M. Clark, Fayetteville, TN
26 April 1896
born Fayetteville TN
section man CB&Q RR Alliance
single
5 Jan 1917

Aaron Engle Collier, 220 126th, New York
4 Dec 1897
Laborer, Alliance steam? 123 E. Third, Alliance, Nebraska
John J. Glover, Kansas City, MO
12 Sept 1918

Henry William Curl
114 Walnut, Emporia, Kansas
14 Aug 1883
laborer for C.L. Hill in Alliance
Ida Curl, 114 Walnut, Emporia, KS
12 Sept 1918

Dock Dale - Durant, Holmes Co., Mississippi
10 May 1898
section worker CB&Q RR Alliance
Ella Dale, mother of Durant, Holmes Co., Mississippi
missing two fingers of left hand
12 Sept 1918

William Edward Darnell, 221 Niobrara, Alliance
5 Nov. 1894
born Lincoln, Nebraska

automobile mechanic Rumer Motor Co., Alliance
single
5 June 1917

Thomas Davis, Cleveland, Ohio
22 Feb 1893 Anderson, South Carolina
sectionman, CB&Q RR Alliance
single
5 June 1917

James Diggs, Alliance
1 Feb 1878
laborer CB&Q Alliance
12 Sept 1918

John Dixon, Alliance
4 Juy 1880
laborer, CB&Q RR Alliance
friend Mary White, 3612 So. State St., Chicago, Cook Co., IL
cannot write
12 Sept 1918

Barshall Dumas, Graceport, Grenada Co., Mississippi
4 Feb 1899
trackworker CB&Q RR Alliance
Oliver Dumas, uncle, Graceport, Grenada Co., Mississippi
12 Sept 1918

Newton Edwards, 4225 Finney, St. Louis, MO
1 Sept 1878
laborer, CB&Q RR Alliance
Sister, Callie Mundy (same address)
12 Sept 1918

John Fanando, 115 Sweetwater, Alliance
born 30 May 1888 in Thurber, Texas
hod carrier for George A. Shane, Alliance
married
5 June 1917

William Fletcher, 523 W. 2nd St., Alliance
born 26 Feb 1891 Marion Co., IL
laborer employed by J.J. Vaner, Alliance
wife and child; married
16 June 1917

Tom Ford, 223 W. 2nd, Alliance
born 6 Feb 1891 Birmingham, Alabama
laborer CB&Q RR Alliance
single
5 June 1917

Cliff Franklin, Alliance
does not know date of birth, born in Bryant, Texas
working for City of Alliance
single; supporting mother
signed with mark
5 June 1917

Ollie Funches, 1417 Lily, Kansas City, MO
born 6 March 1889, St. Louis, MO
dining car waiter CB&Q RR Kansas City, MO
single, supporting mother, sister and brother
filed 5 June 1917 in Alliance

John Gatlin, Hemingford
born 2 March 1901
laborer, CB&Q Alliance
father J.W. Gatlin Carrolville, Missouri
filed 12 Sept 1918

John Gaden, Altherman?, Arkansas
born 15 June 1884
mail handler CB&Q, Burlington Depot, Alliance
Dity Kimp 1614 Forest Ave., Kansas City, Missouri
filed 12 Sept 1918

Hiller Gay, 3206 S. State St., Chicago, Cook Co., Illinois
born 26 Nov 1884
blr washer CB&Q RR Alliance
father, Walter Gay, Oklahoma City, OK
signed as Hilliard Gay
filed 12 Sept 1918

John Glass, 114 Missouri, Alliance, NE
born 17 March 1888 Bryan, Texas
laborer CB&Q RR Alliance
wife; married
5 June 1917

John Henry Green, Elmyra, NY
born 2 Nov 1880
laborer CB&Q RR Alliance
sister Mrs. Alice Bacon, Concord, NH
12 Sept 1918

Eddie William Green, 118 Laramie, Alliance
born 23 Sept 1891, Little Rock, Arkansas
plasterer tender for J. Pryor of Alliance
married
5 June 1917

Charles Willis Griffth, Alliance, NE
permant address Platt City, Missouri

born 25 June 1885
laborer storehouse, CB&Q Alliance
Will Griffeth (no address or relationship shown)
12 Sept 1918

Tom Hand, Indianolo, Mississippi
born August 1900, day unknown
porter for J.M. Miller Alliance
father, Thos. Hand, Indianolo, Mississippi
cannot write, signed with mark
12 Sept 1918

Bert Louis Harris, Hills Addition, Alliance
born 28 May 1879
boilerwasher, CB&Q RR Alliance
Tom Harris, RFD 1 Iuka, Mississippi
12 Sept 1918

Obe Harris, Alliance
born 19 Jan 1895 Carbon Hill, Alabama
boiler washer, CB&Q RR Alliance
single
5 June 1917

Charles C. Harvey, 105 Sweetwater, Alliance
born 25 Dec 1878
laborer storchouse, CB&Q Alliance
John Harvey Althimer, Arkansas
12 Sept 1918

Walter Hayes, Alliance
born 31 May 1885
laborer CB&Q, Alliance
wife Lola Hayes, 3323 Hickory, St. Louis, MO
12 Sept 1918

Thomas Phoenix Hoard, Alliance
born 27 Nov 1874
Evangelist in Alliance
son T.P. Hoard, Jr., 33 West 33 Chicago, Cook Co., IL
12 Sept 1918

Fred Horton, 105 Sweetwater, Alliance
born 3 Oct 1898
common laborer for Jess Miller, Box Butte Ave., Alliance
sister Hattie Horton, Nashville, TN
12 Sept 1918

Lige Wilson Houchins, 319 So. Main, McPherson, Kansas
born 13 June 1881
cook for L.E. Johnson, 216 Box Butte, Alliance
Sam Houchins, Garden City, Kansas

12 Sept 1918

George L. Howell, Alliance
born 13 March 1895, Manhattan Kansas
miner
State of Kansas, Kansas State Penitentiary
single
5 June 1917 at Leavenworth, Kansas; cross filed in Alliance, Nebraska

John Franklin Johnson, 1205 Clara St., New Orleans, LA
12 Aug 1884
laborer CB&Q RR Alliance
father Wm. Johnson, 1205 Clara St., New Orleans, LS
12 Sept 1918

John Johnson, Brownville, TX
born 20 Oct 1898
laborer CB&Q RR Alliance
no nearest relative
16 Sept 1918

Archel Rudolph Johnson, 310 Nicholas, Brookfield, Linn Co., MO
born 26 Jan 1899
cook CB&Q RR Com Dept., Kansas City, Missouri
father J.D. Johnson, 310 Nicholas, Brookfield, MO
12 Sept 1918 in Alliance

Tom Jones Athens, Limsetone Co., Alabama
born in 1876, don't know day and month
sectionman CB&Q RR Alliance
cousin, Mary Walters Athen, AL
12 Sept 1918

Willie Jay Jones, 212 E. 1st, Alliance
born 25 Dec 1892
loco repr CB&Q RR Alliance
G.W. Hill, friend Winston Salem, Tennessee
12 Sept 1918

William Hutchinson Julius, Alliance
born 25 Dec 1878
mail transfer CB&Q RR Alliance
wife, Cora Julius, Alliance NE
12 Sept 1918

Ulysses Kirk, Marshall, Texas
born 14 Oct 1892, Marshall, TX
section, Great Northern RR Great Falls, MT
single
5 June 1917

Leo V. Lennear, Alliance

born 26 May 1887 Beatrice, NE
car cleaner Burlington RR Alliance
married
5 June 1917

Mack Linear 524 East 3rd St, Alliance
born 25 June 1876
farmer Wells Precinct, Cherry Co., Nebraska
Anna Linear, 524 East 3rd St., Alliance
14 Sept 1918

Fonzo Lucas, Alliance
born 15 Feb 1885
laborer section hand CB&Q RR Alliance
Ida Lucas, Galesburg, Illinois
9 Sept 1918

William M. Mack, Alliance
born 2 May 1879
laborer CB&Q RR, Alliance
mother Sallie Smith, Baughn, Maryland
12 Sept 1918

Dan McLandmon, 18th and Ivy, Dayton, OH
born 1 Oct 1884
hotel porter for J.M. Miller 102 Box Butte, Alliance
Jim Thomas, uncle Kansas City, MO
12 Sept 1918

William McKinney, 212 E. 1st, Alliance
born 18 March 1882
laborer/plasterer for self; contractor in Alliance
Sam McKinney, Dallas, Texas
12 Sept 1918

Charley Martin, 725 W. Bond, Denison, Texas
born 26 April 1896 in Denison, Texas
porter in hotel Burlington RR Great Falls, Montana
single
5 June 1917

William Minor, Chicago, IL
born 25 Nov 1880
laborer in shops, CB&Q Alliance
Carry Brown, 429 W. Hunt?, Atlanta, Georgia
12 Sept 1918

John Mitchell, Alice, Kansas
born 22 Aug 1881
blr washer CB&Q Alliance
Rosie Mitchell, daughter, Alice, Kansas
missing end of two fingers

12 Sept 1918

Benjamin H. Moore, Alliance
born 12 Dec 1884
minister A.M.E. Church Alliance
Edna Moore
14 Sept 1918

James Jacob Moore, 1308 St. Louis Ave., Kansas City, MO
born 17 April 1888 Texarkana, Arkansas
laborer on RR CB&Q Great Falls, Montana
wife and mother
5 June 1917

Lenward Marshel Motley, Hemingford
born 12 June 1895 Petersburg, Illinois
farmer and stock raising
single
5 June 1917

Virgil Jerome Motley, Hemingford
born 27 March 1900
farming for father James Motley, Hemingford
James Motley, Hemingford
12 Sept 1918

Barney Napier, 624 Mississippi, Alliance
born 25 May 1892 Cass Co., Missouri
porter/hotel of J.M. Miller, Alliance
single, caring for mother
5 June 1917

Richard Owens, West 2nd St., Alliance
born 10 March 1877
fire ? CB&Q RR Alliance
Bessie Owens, wife, West 2nd, Alliance
12 Sept 1918

L.M. Parker, Kansas City, MO
born 5 Aug 1879
waiter CB&Q RR
Ida B. Boyd, 1518 Park, Kansas City, MO
12 Sept 1918

Ector Penson, Alliance
born 25 March 1881
laborer CB&Q RR Alliance
Sarah Penson, wife 1304 Louisiana, Fort Worth, TX
12 Sept 1918

John Henry Piner, 1012 Oakland, Kansas City, Kansas
born 30 Jan 1898

laborer, round house CB&Q RR Alliance
Mrs. Belle Piner, 1012 Oakland, Kansas City, Kansas
12 Sept 1918

Leslie Porter 1826 Fillmore, Topeka, KS
born 6 Aug 1884
boiler washer CB&Q shops Alliance
Georgia Connely, Buffalo, Wyoming
12 Sept 1918

George Ellis Raglan, 117 2nd Street Alliance
born 5 March 1873
porter for Bruce McDowell, 216 Box Butte, Alliance
Reddick Raglan, 1837 N. 22nd St., Omaha, NE
12 Sept 1918

Dupree R. Raglan 76 6 St., Brookland, Illinois
born 29 Aug 1898
laborer, CB&Q shop, Alliance
Hicksey Raglan, 1811 Pine, St. Louis, Missouri
12 Sept 1918

Will Reed Johns, Jefferson Co., Alabama
born 28 March 1891
porter, CB&Q RR Alliance
John Reed, Logan, West Virginia
12 Sept 1918

Arthur Rice, 212 East 1st, Alliance
born 16 Nov 1891, Little Rock, Arkansas
shoe shining (self employed), Alliance
single
8 June 1917

Frank James Robeertson, 2947 Federal St., Chicago, Cook Co., IL
born 4 July 1898
laborer, CB&Q RR Arvada, Wyoming
F.B. Robertson, father, 2947 Federal St., Chicago, Illinois
12 Sept 1918

Edward Grant Rollins, 544 E. Costella, Colorado Springs, El Paso Co., Colorado
born 22 Oct 1898
laborer, CB&Q freight depot, Alliance
Elwood Grant Rollins, 544 E. Costella, Colorado Springs, Colorado
[shown as College Springs which is most likely Colorado Springs since it is in El Paso Co.]
12 Sept 1918

Joy Ruff, 115 Yellowstone Ave., Alliance
born 18 Feb 1878
fireman, round house, CB&Q RR, Alliance
Shellie Lipscomb, uncle, Fort Gibson, Oklahoma
12 Sept 1918

Jesse Earl Selby, Hills Addition, Alliance
born 29 Dec 1889 Alma, Nebraska
farmer near Alliance
wife and two children
5 June 1917

Samuel Shelton, 109 Box Butte, Alliance
born 2 Oct 1877
restaurant manager (self), 109 Box Butte, Alliance
Julia Shelton, wife, 109 Box Butte, Alliance
12 Sept 1918

James William Shores, 123 Box Butte, Alliance
born 18 Dec 1878
janitor for R.M. Hampton and F.M. Knight Alliance
Nora Bradford, sister, 306 N. Chamber Ave., Georgetown, Kentucky
12 Sept 1918

John Skillen, 105 Sweetwater Ave., Alliance
born 27 Nov 1882
cook for Sam Shelton, Niobrara Ave., Alliance
Hattie Skillen, wife, 1921 W. Fulton, Chicago, Illinois
12 Sept 1918

George Edward Slaughter, 223 W. 2nd Street, Alliance
223 West 2nd St., Alliance
born 13 June 1893 Hot Springs, South Dakota
auto mechanic Lowry & Henry Alliance
single
5 June 1917

Daniel John Smith, West Lawn, Alliance
born 15 Oct 1882
laborer, CB&Q RR Alliance
Leslie Smith, wife, West Lawn, Alliance
12 Sept 1918

Lloyd Alex Smith, 132 Missouri, Alliance
born 22 Sept 1887, Goliad, Texas
Chair Car Porter CB&Q RR Aliance
married
no date shown

Henry Spann, Alliance
born 15 Oct 1875
porter, CB&Q RR Alliance
Mrs. Johanna Spann, Alliance
11 Sept 1918

Oscar Joseph Spriggs, Alliance
born 11 Sept 1884
fire builder CB&Q RR Alliance

Pearl Spriggs, wife, Alliance
12 Sept 1918

Elbert Stark, 211 Laramie, Alliance
born 15 Aug 1878
janitor for F.E. Reddish, 202 Box Butte, Alliance
Ethel Stark, wife, 211 Laramie, Alliance
no date shown

Guy Ansevald Strother, Pine Bluff, Arkansas
born 12 July 1895 Benoit, Mississippi
section man, Great Northern RR, Great Falls, Montana
married
5 June 1917

William Thomas, 1327 W. Walnut, Louisville, Kentucky
born 22 Feb 1899
cook for J.M. Miller, Alliance
Joe Thomas, brother, 2328 Magazine St. Louisville, Kentucky
12 Sept 1918

John Thompson, Hemingford
born 5 May 1885
RR Laborer, CB&Q RR Alliance
Martin Thompson, father, Winona, Carroll Co., Mississippi
12 Sept 1918

James Thornton, 115 Yellowstone, Alliance
born 22 Feb 1875
car cleaner, CB&Q RR Alliance
Fannine Thornton, wife, 115 Yellowstone, Alliance
12 Sept 1918

Walter Walker, 129 Box Butte, Alliance
born 12 Nov 1891, Wagner, Oklahoma
automobile chauffer for Henry Wallace of Alliance
single
5 June 1917

John Ware, 115 Sweetwater, Alliance
born 1 May 1896 Conway, Arkansas
shoe shiner for Bruce McDowel, Alliance
married with wife and child
5 June 1917

Claude McKinley Washington, Bryan, Brazos Co., Texas
born 6 Sept 1900
freight dept Burlington Depot, CB&Q RR Alliance
James Washington, US Army
no date shown

Henry White Alliance

born 15 June 1884
laborer for Chas. Nation, 213 Box Butte, Alliance
Sarah Jane White, Brookhaven, Lincoln Co., Mississippi
12 Sept 1918

Frank George Wilbon, 428 17th St., Jacksonville, Florida
born 4 Sept 1900
store house laborer, CB&Q Alliance
Claude Wilbon, 428 17th St., Jacksonville, Florida
12 Sept 1918

French Whitfield, Waynesboro, Wayne Co., Mississippi
born 23 Jan 1900
trackworker CB&Q RR Alliance
Annie Whitfield, mother, Waynesboro, Wayne Co., Mississippi
12 Sept 1918

Cleveland Williams, Houma, Louisiana
18 years old, does not know when born
RR section man, CB&Q RR Hemingford
Nancy Griffin, Houma, Louisiana
12 Sept 1918

Henry C. Winston Alliance Hotel, Alliance
born 2 Dec 1872
cook, Alliance Hotel, Alliance
Sally Allen, Atler, Virginia
12 Sept 1918

Bolden Wooding, Hurts, Virginia
15 Aug 1897
sectionman, CB&Q RR Alliance
J.H. Wooding, father, Knoxville, Iowa
12 Sept 1918

M.C. Woodlee, 116 Missouri, Alliance
born 5 March 1883
porter, CB&Q RR Alliance
Mrs. M.C. Woodlee, 116 Missouri, Alliance
16 Sept 1918

African Americans — World War I Draft Registration
Dawson Co., Nebraska

Joseph Adams, Lexington, Dawson Co., Nebraska
38, b. 1 January 1880
laborer, Wells & Spies, Lexington; negro
Joseph Adams, Kirksville, Missouri
filed 12 September 1918, Lexington, Dawson Co., Nebraska

John William Riley, Overton, Dawson Co., Nebraska

29, b. 2 Fecember 188?, Overton, Dawson Co., Nebraska
farmer, self, wife and 3 children; negro
filed 5 June 1917 at Overton, Dawson Co., Nebraska

Ivern Williams, #4, Lexington, Dawson Co., Nebraska
35, b. 2 July 1883
section labor, UPRR; negro
John H. Williams, St. Louis, Missouri
filed 12 September 1918, Lexington, Dawson Co., Nebraska

African Americans — World War I Draft Registration
Sioux Co., Nebraska

Adam Debaum, Glen, Sioux Co., Nebraska
35, born 1883
patient Hospital for Insane, Norfolk Madison Co., Nebraska, negro
C. Johnson, Glen, Sioux Co., Nebraska
dementia, prarcox, paranoid
filed 12 September 1918, Harrison, Sioux Co., Nebraska

Charles Edward English, Harrison, Sioux Co., Nebraska
44, born 3 March 1874
farm hand for J.H. Dieckmann, Harrison, negro
friend, J.H. Dieckmann, Harrison
filed 12 September 1918, Harrison, Sioux Co., Nebraska

Burbridge Washington Hughes, Harrison, Sioux Co., Nebraska
34, born 30 June 1884
farming for self, Harrison, negro
Josephine E. Hughes, Harrison
filed 12 September 1918, Harrison, Sioux Co., Nebraska

Floyd Sutton, 2217 State, Richmond, Virginia
24, born 25 March 1893, Richmond, Virginia
section labor, CB&Q RR, Mansfield, Nebraska
negro, single
served as a private in US Regular Army, Cavalry, 3 years
filed 5 June 191, Sugar Loaf Prect., Sioux Co., Nebraska

African Americans — World War I Draft Registrations
Keith Co., Nebraska

Walter Jerome Becton, Paxton, Keith Co., Nebraska
27, born 17 January 1890, Lincoln, Lancaster Co., Nebraska
second hand, UPRR Co., Paxton, negro
married
filed 5 June 1917, Paxton, Keith Co., Nebraska

Artie Campbell, Paxton, Keith Co., Nebraska
23, born 5 December 1894, Wichita, Kansas
railrway laborer, Union Pacific RR Co., Paxton, negro
single

filed 5 June 1917, Paxton, Keith Co., Nebraska

Howard Doss, Paxton, Keith Co., Nebraska
22, born 2 January 1895, Kansas City, Missouri
section hand, UPRR Co., Korty, Nebraska, negro
single
filed 5 June 1917, Paxton, Keith Co., Nebraska

Leroy Gibson, Paxton, Keith Co., Nebraska
25, born 2 June 1892, Lexington, Missouri
section hand, UPRR Co., Korty, Nebraska, negro
single
filed 5 June 1917, Paxton, Keith Co., Nebraska

Louis Harris, Paxton, Keith Co., Nebraska
25, born 18 December 1892, Memphis, Tennessee
section laborer, Union Pacif Railway Co., Korty, Nebraska, negro
single
filed 5 June 1917, Paxton, Keith Co., Nebraska

Robert Johnson, Ogallala, Keith Co., Nebraska,
45, do not know year, possibly 1873
track laborer, UPRR, John Esse, Ogallala, Keith Co., Nebraska
no nearest relative
filed 12 September 1918, Ogallala, Keith Co., Nebraska

Henry Clay Johnsen, Paxton, Keith Co., Nebraska
39, born 25 December 1879
UPRR, Paxton, negro
John Johnsen, Kanas City, MO
filed 12 September 1918, Ogallala, Keith Co., Nebraska

Henry Malone, Ogallala, Keith Co., Nebraska
42, born 1 June 1876
laborer, Union Pacific RR Co., Ogallala, negro
Kate Malone, Route 2, Box 22, Longview, Texas
filed 12 September 1918, Ogallala, Keith Co., Nebraska

Louis Mathers, Paxton, Keith Co., Nebraska
39, born 5 August 1877
secion hand, UPRR, Paxton, negro
address unknown for nearest relative
filed 12 September 1918, Ogallala, Keith Co., Nebraska

Rufus Parks, Paxton, Keith Co., Nebraska
18, born 7 August 1900
Ry. laborer, Union Pacific RR, Paxton, negro
V.G. Parks, Blissville, Drew Co., Arkansas
filed 12 September 1918, Ogallala, Keith Co., Nebraska

Frank Payton, Paxton, Keith Co., Nebraska
20, born 20 January 1898

railroading, UPRR, Paxton, negro
Jerry Payton, Bessiner?, Alabama
filed 12 September 1918, Ogallala, Keith Co., Nebraska

George Phillips, Brule, Keith Co., Nebraska
45, born 2 June 1873
RR Track man, Union Pacific RR Co., Brule, negro
George Ann Phillips, mother, Lebanon, Marion Co., Kentucky
filed 12 September 1918, Ogallala, Keith Co., Nebraska

Charley Venson, Paxton, Keith Co., Nebraska
27, born 20 August 1889, Carterville, Tennessee
seciond hand, UPRR Co., Korty, Nebraska
single
filed 5 June 1917, Paxton, Keith Co., Nebraska

Will Howard Webb, Ogallala, Keith Co., Nebraska
37, born 29 September 1881
laborer, UPRR, John Esse, Ogallala, Keith Co., Nebraska
Dore Webb, Manon, Perry Co., Alabama
filed Ogallala, Keith Co., Nebraska [1918]

Everett Woods, Paxton, Keith Co., Nebraska
28, born 19 December 1891, Shelbina, Missouri
railway laborer, Union Pacific Railway Co., Paxton, negro
supporting mother, single
filed 5 June 1917, Paxton, Keith Co., Nebraska

African Americans — World War I Draft Registration
Lincoln Co., Nebraska

Will Anderson, RR 1, Box 61, North Platte, Lincoln Co., Nebraska
22, born 13 January 1895, Walls, Mississippi
section labor, Union Pacific RR, Birdwood, Nebraska, negro
single, supporting mother
filed 5 June 1917, Hinman Prect., Lincoln Co., Nebraska

William Burnett, General Delivery, North Platte, Lincoln Co., Nebraska
44, born 18 August 1874
porter, Union Station, UPRR, North Platte, Nebraska, negro
Bess Burnett, General Delivery
filed 11 September 1918, North Platte, Lincoln Co., Nebraska

Brooks Chappell, Brady, Lincoln Co., Nebraska
37, does not know day and month
section hand, UPRR, Brady, Lincoln Co., Nebraska, negro
Maud Chappell, wife, Chaliken, Kansas
filed 12 September 1918, North Platte, Lincoln Co., Nebraska

Robert Dewey Cobb, 1012 N. Locust St., North Platte, Lincoln Co., Nebraska
19, born 14 January 1899
laborer, Ford Garage, North Platte, negro

Emma Cobb, Idabell, Oklahoma
filed 11 September 1918, North Platte, Lincoln Co., Nebraska

Henry Culpepper, 116 West 6th, North Platte, Lincoln Co., Nebraska
21, born 25 May 1896, Dallas, Texas
laborer, J.A. Gilbert, North Platte, negro
single
filed 5 June 1917, North Platte, Lincoln Co., Nebraska

Henry Harris, Conway, Faulkner Co., Arkansas
20, born 23 september 1898
track laborer, CB&Q Railroad, Wellfleet, Lincoln Co., Nebraska
Mary Price, sister, Conway, Faulkner Co., Arkansas
filed 12 September 1918, North Platte, Lincoln Co., Nebraska

Willie D. Harris, Giblesn, Louisiana
18, born 25 December 1900
track laborer, CB&Q Railroad, Wellfleet, Lincoln Co., Nebraska, negro
Georgia Warren, cousin, Giblesn, Louisiana
filed 12 September 1918, North Platte, Lincoln Co., Nebraska

Lucian James Mason, Sutherland, Lincoln Co., Nebraska
40, born 12 August 1878
farming, self, Sutherland, negro
Urith Mason, Sutherland
filed 12 September 1918, North Platte, Lincoln Co., Nebraska

William Arthur Mason, 219 No. 9th, Lincoln, Nebraska
29, b. 9 June 1887 Houstonia, Missouri
laborer in sugar beet field of John A. Bender, Sutherland, Lincoln Co., Nebraska, negro
single
filed 5 June 1917, Sutherland, Lincoln Co., Nebraska

Ray Lester Mason, Sutherland, Lincoln Co., Nebraska
20, born 26 September 1897
farmer, self, Sutherland, negro
Pearl Mason, wife, Sutherland
filed 12 September 1918, North Platte, Lincoln Co., Nebraska

Robert Nelson, Brady, Lincoln Co., Nebraska
38, born 15 January 1880
section hand, UPRR Co., Brady, negro
Arthur Nelson, Cincinnati, Ohio
filed 12 September 1918, North Platte, Lincoln Co., Nebraska

Louis Norman, RR 1, Box 61, North Platte, Lincoln Co., Nebraska
21, don't know when born, born Murry City, Tennessee
section labor, Union Pacific Railroad, Birdwood, Lincoln Co., Nebraska, negro
single, supporting mother
filed 5 June 1917, Hinman Prect., Lincoln Co., Nebraska

Charlie Parker, Brady, Lincoln Co., Nebraska

44, born 13 March?
UP Section, UPRR Co., Brady, Lincoln Co., Nebraska, negro
Mary A. Parker, wife, 605 3rd St., Knoxville, Tennessee
filed 12 September 1918, North Platte, Lincoln Co., Nebraska

Harry Robinson, Genl. Delivery, North Platte, Lincoln Co., Nebraska
38, born 29 August 1880
porter for M.S. Rebhausen, North Platte, negro
Addie Robinson, North Platte
filed 11 September 1918, North Platte, Lincoln Co., Nebraska

Novl Simmons, 620 So. Dewey, North Platte, Lincoln Co., Nebraska
33, born 1 January 1885
cook, "myself", North Platte, negro
Mabel Simmons, 620 S. Dewey, North Platte
filed 11 September 1918, North Platte, Lincoln Co., Nebraska

Charles Lorenzo Thomas, RR 1, Box 61, North Platte, Lincoln Co., Nebraska
27, born 8 March 1890 Claiborne, Alabama
section labor, Union Pacific Railroad, Birdwood, Lincoln Co., Nebraska, negro
married, supporting wife
filed 5 June 1917 Hinman Prect., Lincoln Co., Nebraska

Charles Augustus Turner, 620 Maple, North Platte, Lincoln Co., Nbraska
34, born 12 June 1884
no occupation, negro
Bell Turner, 620 Maple, North Platte
filed 12 September 1918, North Platte, Lincoln Co., Nebraska

George Welch, 1012 No. Locust, North Platte, Lincoln Co., Nebraska
34, born 2 August 1884
porter for P.A. Carson, North Platte, negro
Lou Welch, 318 So., Main, Peru, Indiana
filed 11 September 1918, North Platte, Lincoln Co., Nebraska

Walter Wilson, Brady, Lincoln Co., Nebraska
37, born 17 October 1881
section hand, UPRR Co., Brady, negro
Louis Wilson, brother, with the American Army, France
filed 12 September 1918, North Platte, Lincoln Co., Nebraska

Woldridge Oppenheimer Wilson, 115 W. 9th, Bomont, Jefferson Co., Texas
36, born 11 March 1882
porter, I.G. Gilbert, North Platte, Lincoln Co., Nebraska, negro
Della Wilson
filed 12 September 1918, North Platte, Lincoln Co., Nebraska

African Americans — World War I Draft Registration
Kimball Co., Nebraska

Harvey Caldwell, Bushnell, Kimball Co., Nebraska
26, born 15 Feburary 1891, born Paola, Kansas

section hand, UP Railroad, Bushnell, negro
single
filed 5 June 1917, Bushnell, Kimball Co., Nebraska

John Carter, Bushnell, Kimball Co., Nebraska
34, born 22 September 1883
section hand, UPRR, Bushnell, negro
Isick Carter, 2408 F Ave., Kansas City, Missouri
fore finger, right hand
filed 12 September 1918, Kimball, Kimball Co., Nebraska

John Carter, East Plumber, Bedford, Virginia
29, born 8 April 1888, born Bedford, Virginia
labor, Union Pacific RR Co., Dix, Nebraska, negro
married
filed 5 June 1917, Dix, Kimball Co., Nebraska

French Cecil, Kimball, Kimball Co., Nebraska
42, born 5 January 1876
laborer, W.S. Rodman Bldg, Kimball, negro
William Cecil, Pocahontas, Virginia
filed 12 September 1918, Kimball, Kimball Co., Nebraska

Theodore Albert Collins, Kimball, Kimball Co., Nebraska
18, born 24 Dec 1899
laborer, Union Pacific Railroad, Kimball, negro
Selestrin Collins, New Orleans, LA
filed 12 September 1918, Kimball, Kimball Co., Nebraska

Harrison Easley, Bushnell, Kimball Co., Nebraska
30, 16 September 1886, born Topeka, Kansas
section hand on railroad, Bushnell, negro
single
filed 5 June 1917, Bushnell, Kimball Co., Nebraska

Alfred Foreman, 76 South 9, Kansas City, Kansas
25, born 12 April 1892, Vicksburg, Mississippi
laborer, Union Pacific Railroad Co., Dix, Kimball Co., Nebraska, negro
married
filed 5 June 1917, Dix, Kimball Co., Nebraska

Allie Jackson, Bushnell, Kimball Co., Nebraska
33, born 12 July 1885
section hand, UPRR, Bushnell, negro
John Ross, Bushnell, Kimball Co., Nebraska
filed 12 September 1918, Kimball, Kimball Co., Nebraska

Will James, Limmi?, Mississippi
35, born 6 November 1883
farm laborer, Charles Southern?, Dix, Kimball Co., Nebraska, negro
Serveate James, Limmi?, Mississippi
filed 12 September 1918, Kimball, Kimball Co., Nebraska

Frank Johnson, Kimball, Kimball Co., Nebraska
32, born 12 February 1886
farmhand, self, Kimball, negro
Amanda Johnson, Central City, Nebraska
filed 12 September 1918, Kimball, Kimball Co., Nebraska

Harrison Mack, Bushnell, Kimball Co., Nebraska
27, born 12 February 1890, born Nelson, Missouri
plasterer or mason, self, Bushnell, negro
married, wife, two children
filed 5 June 1917 Bushnell, Kimball Co., Nebraska

Thomas A.C. Robison, Kimball, Kimball Co., Nebraska
34, born 24 December 1883
section, UPRR, Kimball, negro
Flossie Timmon, address not known
filed 12 September 1918, Kimball, Kimball Co., Nebraska

William Robinson, Bushnell, Kimball Co., Nebraska
29, born 22 March 1888, Olathe, Kansas
section hand, Union Pacific RR, Bushnell, negro
single
filed 5 June 1917, Bushnell, Kimball Co., Nebraska

John Ross, Bushnell, Kimball Co., Nebraska
34, born 25 August 1884
section hand, UPRR, Bushnell
Marry E. Ross, 2836 S. 31, Kansas City, Kansas
filed 12 September 1918, Kimball, Kimball Co., Nebraska

Cedrick Stewart, 1031 College Ave., Rosdale, Kansas
25, born 10 June 1891, Kansas City, Missouri
laborer, Union Pacific Railroad Co., Dix, Kimball Co., Nebraska, negro
single
filed 5 June 1917, Dix, Kimball Co., Nebraska

Emmett White, Kimball, Kimball Co., Nebraska
37, born 25 December 1881
section, UPRR, Kimball, negro
Lucy White, 11721 Devonshire St., Boston, Massachusetts
filed 12 September 1918, Kimball, Kimball Co., Nebraska

Eddie Young, Bushnell, Kimball Co., Nebraska
28, born 25 September 1889, born West Point, Mississippi
labor, UP Railroad, Bushnell, negro
married
filed 5 June 1917, Bushnell, Kimball Co., Nebraska

African Americans — World War I Draft Registration
Scotts Bluff Co., Nebraska

Clarence Banks, Gering, Scotts Bluff Co., Nebraska

34, born 28 May 1884
factory hand, Great Western Sugar Co., Gering, negro
Daws Davis, Chicao, Illinois
filed 12 September 1918, Gering, Scotts Bluff Co., Nebraska

Wallace Conley, Scottsbluff, Scotts Bluff Co., Nebraska
32, born 1 November 1885
porter, Ray Roash, Main Street, Scottsbluff, negro
Ethel Conley, Scottsbluff
filed 12 September 1918, Gering, Scotts Bluff Co., Nebraska

George Milton Curtis, Scottsbluff, Scotts Bluff Co., Nebraska
23, born 28 February 1894, born Yucatan, Missouri
mechanic, Scottsbluff Motor Co., Scottsbluff, negro
wife and 1 child
filed 5 June 1917, Gering, Scotts Bluff Co., Nebraska

George Washington Dale, Gering, Scotts Bluff Co., Nebraska
38, born 22 June 1880
factory porter, Great Western Sugar Co., Gering, negro
Mrs. Anna Dale, Gering
filed 12 September 1918, Gering, Scotts Bluff Co., Nebraska

George Leonard Dean, Scottsbluff, Scotts Bluff Co., Nebraska
32, born 12 April 1886
laborer for A.T. Crawford, Scottsbluff, negro
Maggie Deal, Scottsbluff
filed 12 September 1918, Gering, Scotts Bluff Co., Nebraska

Fred Ellis, Scottsbluff, Scotts Bluff Co., Nebraska
37, born 28 July 1881
fireman for E.J. Peterson, Scottsbluff, negro
Josephine Holford, mother, Alma, Kansas
mail registration certificate
filed 12 September 1918, Gering, Scotts Bluff Co., Nebraska

Steve Fletcher, Gering, Scotts Bluff Co., Nebraska
39, born 10 February 1879
factory hand, Great Western Sugar Co., Gering, negro
Mrs. Lulu F. Jones, 2325 Pine St., St. Louis, Missouri
has no permanent address
filed 12 September 1918, Gering, Scotts Bluff Co., Nebraska

Hubert French Hall, Scottsbluff, Scotts Bluff Co., Nebraska
31, born 3 October 1887
fireman, Great Western Sugar Co., Scottsbluff
Theoia Hall, wife, Scottsbluff
filed 12 September 1918, Gering Scotts Bluff Co., Nebraska

Cash Henderson, Scottsbluff, Scotts Bluff Co., Nebraska
37, born 17 July 1881
laborer, Scottsbluff

Lavania Henderson, wife, Scottsbluff
filed 12 September 1918, Gering Scotts Bluff Co., Nebraska

Raymond Scott Henderson, Scottsbluff, Scotts Bluff Co., Nebraska
34, born 26 April 1884
citizen of Mexico
laborer, Int. R. Light & Power Co., Scottsbluff, negro
no nearest relative listed
filed 12 September 1918, Gering, Scotts Bluff Co., Nebraska

Charles Ross Henderson, Scottsbluff, Scotts Bluff Co., Nebraska
33, born 2 November 1894
laborer, Great Western Sugar Co., Scottsbluff, negro
Ella Henderson, wife, Scottsbluff
filed 12 September 1918, Gering, Scotts Bluff Co., Nebraska

Al Lester Hester, Scottsbluff, Scotts Bluff Co., Nebraska
33, born 1 January 1885
laborer for cement contract, John Rochelt, Potash Pit, Scottsbluff, negro
Ida Hester, Scottsbluff
filed 12 September 1918, Gering, Scotts Bluff Co., Nebraska

Charles Higgenbothen, Gering, Scotts Bluff Co., Nebraska
36, born 8 February 1882
factory hand, Great Western Sugar Co., Gering, negro
Mrs. Cora Higgenbothen, Hill City, Graham Co., Kansas
filed12 September 1918, Gering, Scotts Bluff Co., Nebraska
Ed Hollands, Gering, Scotts Bluff Co., Nebraska
35, born 25 June 1883
factory hand, Great Western Sugar Co., Gering, negro
Mrs. Maggie Williams, Yoakum, DeWitt Co., Texas
filed 12 September 1918, Gering, Scotts Bluff Co., Nebraska

Will Johnson, Gering, Scotts Bluff Co., Nebraska [Scotts Bluff crossed through the
Chicago below it]
35, born 15 April 1883
factory hand, Great Western Sugar Co., Gering, negro
no relative
filed 12 September 1918, Gering, Scotts Bluff Co., Nebraska

John Jones, General Delivery, Scottsbluff, Scotts Bluff Co., Nebraska
37, born 7 April 1881
cement laborer, John Rochett, c/o The Great Western Sugar Co., Scottsbluff, negro
Mrs. Lillie Jones, General Delivery, Bredett, Arkansas
filed 12 September 1918, Gering, Scotts Bluff Co., Nebraska

Lewis Jordon, Chocta, Folk Co., Oklahoma
41, born 24 December 1879
miner, Scottsbluff, negro
Maria Jordon, Chocta, Folk Co., Oklahoma
filed 12 September 1918, Gering, Scotts Bluff Co., Nebraska

Ernest Kissine, Ave. C, Scotttsbluff, Scotts Bluff Co., Nebraska
32, born 15 May 1886
porter, Bickford & Davis Barber Shop, 16th St., Scottsbluff
Mary Jane Simms, 1207 Ross St., Waco, McClellen Co., Texas
filed 12 September 1918, Gering, Scotts Bluff Co., Nebraska

William Hamilton Mitchell, Scottsbluff, Scotts Bluff Co., Nebraska
23, born 24 November 1893, White Springs, Florida
mechanic helper, Platte Valley Motor Co., Scottsbluff, negro
single, supporting sister
filed 5 June 1917, Gering, Scotts Bluff Co., Nebraska

Clem Robinson, Scottsbluff, Scotts Bluff Co., Nebraska
36, born 17 February 1882
laborer for Concrete Contractor, John Rochett, Potash Pit, Scottsbluff, negro
Mamie Robinson, Scottsbluff, Scotts Bluff Co., Nebraska
filed 12 September 1918, Gering, Scotts Bluff Co., Nebraska

Albert Sinton, General Delivery, Mitchell, Scotts Bluff Co., Nebraska
39, born 21 December 1879
hostler, George Mollring, Alliance, Box Butte Co., Nebraska, negro
Ida Sinton, wife, General Delivery, Indianapolis, Indiana
Dead At Alliance
filed 12 September 1918, Gering, Scotts Bluff Co., Nebraska

George Thomas, Gering, Scotts Bluff Co., Nebraska
39, born 15 July 1879
factory hand, Great Western Sugar Co., Gering, negro
no relatives
filed 12 September 1918, Gering, Scotts Bluff Co., Nebraska

Harry Hockles Thomas, Scottsbluff, Scotts Bluff Co., Nebraska
38, born 16 March 1880
shining ?, negro
Blanch Ruth Thomas, Scottsbluff
filed 12 September 1918, Gering, Scotts Bluff Co., Nebraska

Solomon Woods, Scottsbluff, Scotts Bluff Co., Nebraska
37, born 22 September 1880
porter at barber shop, Ed Vandenburg, 1512 Broadway, Scottsbluff
Edna Woods, wife, Scottsbluff
filed 12 September 1918, Gering, Scotts Bluff Co., Nebraska

African Americans — World War I Draft Registration
Thomas Co., Nebraska

Thomas Booker Bythwood, Seneca, Thomas Co., Nebraska
21, b. 5 September 1897
Section Hand, CB&Q RR, Seneca, negro
Henry Bythwood, brother, 1840 State, Chicago, Cook Co., Illinois
filed 12 September 1918, Thedford, Thomas Co., Nebraska

Dennis Evans, Halsey, Thomas Co., Nebraska
37, 6 August 1883
laborer, CB&Q, Halsey, negro
Elizabeth Evans, Love Joy, Illinois
filed 12 September 1918, Thedford, Thomas Co., Nebraska

George Walter Ware, Halsey, Thomas Co., Nebraska
42, b. 10 October 1875
laborer, CB&Q, Halsey, negro
Bill Wilburn, 3426 Hickory St., St. Louis, Missouri
filed 12 September 1918, Thedford, Thomas Co., Nebraska

Buck Ware, Seneca, Thomas Co., Nebraska [Brownsen, Nebraska also shown]
33, b. 26 February 1885
no occupation, negro
Osker Ware, brother, 1016 Wyandotte, Kansas City, Missouri
filed 12 September 1918, Thomas Co., Nebraska

Charles Williams, Seneca, Thomas Co., Nebraska
34, b. 25 October 1883
RR laborer, CB&Q RR Co., Seneca, negro
Nellie Williams, mother, Minden Webster, Louisiana
filed 12 September 1918, Thedford Co., Nebraska

Section 2

Rogues, Rascals, and Rooming Houses
The Ku Klux Klan in Alliance
101 Sweetwater

Information is shown as written in court documents and newspapers and is not attributable to the editors.

Rogues, Rascals, and Rooming Houses

Alliance, Nebraska was on the route of the railroad. There were black workers on the railroad, some who did not remain there long and others who settled and called Alliance home. During the time of prohibition, plenty of bootlegging went on. The African Americans appear to have been on the radar by the Alliance police department. Along with the bootlegging there were murders, assaults and attempted murders. The following information is arranged chronologically as to the time period and most information appeared in the Alliance newspapers. Court records of Box Butte County have also been included. Undoubtedly there is more information that has not been included. The popular rooming house, aka brothel, aka the chicken house, was located at 101 Sweetwater in Alliance.

The Alliance Times, Alliance, Box Butte Co., Nebraska
1 June 1900
"Murdered Without Cause
Edgar G. Wait Loses His Life as the Result of an Unexpected Blow at the Hands of Henry W. Mathews
Concussion of the Brain Causes Death

Alliance was horrified last Saturday by one of the most unprovoked crimes in the annals of the state. At eleven o'clock in the forenoon E.G. Wait was struck by Henry Mathews, and ten hours later life had passed from the body of the victim. It is a most deplorable affair, but the citizens of Alliance are incensed and resolved that the perpetrator shall not go unpunished. The story may be learned by the following summary of evidence adduced at the Coroner's Inquest:

At nine o'clock Sunday morning Coroner Dr. W.K. Miller impaneled a jury, composed of six of Alliance's most substantial citizens, the inquest being held in the undertaking rooms of Thos. Beck & Co.

H.C. Armstrong was the first witness, Harry Thomason, Jay Newcomb, bartender, E.G. Wait and the witness were present in the saloon of Corneal & Co. Wait and the witness had been having a friendly bout 'boxing hats'. Henry Mathews and R.T. Boone came in. All 'lined up' at the bar for a drink 'on the house.' Mathews then said, 'Have one on me.' In paying for this he exhibited a handful of silver. Wait joyously remarked that he had 'better pay him for fixing that watch.' Mathews responded that 'it had taken six weeks to get the watch fixed, now he could wait six weeks for the money.' Mr. Wait told Mathews that he needed the money, and reached out his hand as if to take the money. Mathew was carrying a gunny sack containing irons. Witnesses judged they would weigh from eight to fifteen pounds. Heard the irons crash together and looked just in time to see Wait falling to the floor. Mathews was standing within about two feet of the falling man, and there had been no quarrel or other words of particular importance except as related, and neither party was drunk. Wait rolled over on his side and slowly sat …. (missing newspaper)
——- the Red Light saloon, passed through, out the back door and fell to the walk unconscious. Witnesses ran to his side, dragged him into the shade and then ran for a doctor. Saw no signs of vitality and thought Wait was dead.

J. Newcomb, the bartender at the Corneal saloon, was the next witness. He corroborated Mr. Armstrong's testimony, but had not seen the blow struck, his back being turned for an instant.

Albert Renswold said he was a blacksmith by trade and acquainted with all the parties. Mathews and Boone had come to his shop between eleven and twelve o'clock on May 26th. The former still had the irons in the gunny sack and wanted some implements for working stone made from them. There were two pieces of iron, the smaller being about six inches long, one inch in diameter, with a jagged end. The other was twenty inches in length, with one inch square sides. The combined weight was four or five pounds, he thought. He was shown both pieces and identified them. Had no conversation with Mathews relating to the affair.

Dr. W.S. Bellwood was called to attend Wait shortly after eleven o'clock. Found him unconscious, a wound about an inch in length near the left temple and bruise on nose. The skull was not fractured. In his opinion the blow and wound were sufficient to cause death, and had caused Wait's death.

Dr. J.W. Moore was called in consultation about four o'clock in the afternoon when he first saw Wait. His testimony coincided in every particular with that of the previous witness. Death was caused by bursting of blood vessels and pressure of blood on the brain.

R.T. Boone saw all the trouble in the saloon, but was not looking just as the blow was struck. His testimony was similar to that of Mr. Armstrong. He accompanied Mathews when he left the saloon and was with him all the time until the blacksmith shop was reached. He had thrown a large iron in the scrap-pile at the blacksmith shop because he thought it might get Mathews into trouble, but produced it later at the command of Sheriff Sweeney.

An autopsy was performed by Dr. W.S. Bellwood and Dr. Moore, assisted by Coroner Miller, a photograph of the wound having previously been taken by W.T. Caldwell. The brain was removed and the skull carefully examined at the point where the blow had been struck. The bone was found uninjured. Small clots of blood were found on the left side of the brain and the opposite side, or the right lobe, was badly clotted. This also was photographed. The combined testimony of the doctors who performed the autopsy was about as before. They found death had been caused by concussion from the blow, bursting the blood vessels and causing congestion of the opposite side of the brain. Their description of the wound was that it was one inch in length, one-fourth inch deep, six-sixteenths of an inch at the base, and triangular shape. It was two inches from the arch of the left eye to the center of the wound, above and to the right of the eye, about two inches from the edge of the scalp.

Verdict of the Jury

At an inquisition holden at Alliance, in Box Butte county on the 27th day of May, A.D. 1900, before me, W.K. Miller, coroner of said county, upon the body of Edgar G. Wait, lying dead, by the jurors whose names are hereunto subscribed, the said jurors upon their oath do say that Edgar G. Wait came to his death from a deadly and mortal wound inflicted on the left side of his head from a blow struck by Henry W. Mathews with two pieces of steel or iron enclosed in a gunny sack. In testimony whereof the said jurors have hereunto set their hands the day and year aforesaid.

> W.D. Rumer
> J. Shafer
> E.A. Hall
> L.W. Emery
> N. Hart
> C.A. Newberry

County Attorney Tuttle interrogated the witnesses at this hearing and forty or fifty of the most influential citizens were in attendance. The sentiment was then, and has since been frequently heard, that the blot on the fair name of our city must be removed by drastic punishment of the author of the crimes. Mathews had been arrested on the charge of assault and battery shortly after the occurrence. He was admitted to bail in the sum of $500 by Justice of the Peace Berry. When the serious condition of his victim was learned the amount of bail was increased and he was re-arrested.

The Preliminary Hearing occurred Monday at 1:30 o'clock before Judge Berry. It was held in the court house …. district court for Box Butte county, when the case will come up for trial. The complaint was read by Mr. Tuttle, charging Mathews with murder in the first degree. The defendant stood up and plead, 'not guilty.' R.C. Noleman then stated that the defense would waive preliminary hearing, but urged that the court admit the prisoner to bail. Attorneys for the state objected to this and after some discussion Judge Barry bound the prisoner over without bail.

Mathews was taken to Lincoln on the afternoon train Monday, being in charge of Sheriff Sweeney and Marshal D.W. Lee. He was placed in the county jail for safe keeping until district court convenes next fall. Sheriff Sweeney said to the *Times* man that he would give strict orders that no possible chance be allowed the prisoner for escape. The case is a desperate one for the defendant, and it is believed he would avail himself of the slightest opportunity to evade the grasp of the law.

The sentiment is decidedly strong against Mathews here, and lynching was even hinted by many Saturday night. *Times* believes this crime was committed by the prisoner on the impulse of the moment, believing that he would knock Wait and nothing more serious would come from it perhaps than a minor fine. It is a deplorable fact that there is a considerable element in most every locality who consider it evidence of prowess to 'smash' a human fellow being. To such the terrible end of E.G. Wait and inevitable long term of imprisonment that await Henry Mathews should prove a warning.

Mr. Armstrong has rendered every possible aid, financially and otherwise to the bereaved. Further than this, he is determined to aid the law in the punishment of the perpetrator of such a wanton and cruel act.

It has developed since the hearing that Edgar Chapman, an employee at the round house, entered the back door of the saloon and saw the blow struck. His testimony will be forthcoming with the others at the proper time in the forging of a chain of evidence that it will be impossible to break. Wm. Mitchell has been engaged by the Waits as an attorney to assist with the prosecution.

Mr. Armstrong says that he considered both men friends, and had he noticed the slightest probability of a quarrel in the saloon at the time it happened, he would promptly have suppressed this and ordered them outside. But it came without warning, and a widow and sons mourn the loss of a husband and father, while in the other family a devoted and most estimable woman must grieve with her little ones the absence and disgrace of the father."

Obituary
Edgar G. Wait was born at Ottawa, Ill., July 12, 1864. His parents moved to Marshalltown, Iowa, in his infancy, where he remained until he reached the age of nineteen, learning his trade. Deceased first engaged in business at Macon City, Mo. He was married in 1884 at the age of twenty years, his wife being seventeen. They moved to McCook, spending one year there, seven at Broken Bow and five at Alliance where his demise occurred Saturday evening, May 26, at fourteen minutes to nine o'clock, aged thirty-five years, ten months and fourteen days. At Broken Bow he was honored with many high offices, being a member of the Knights of Pythias. He was possessed of a generous, kindly nature and made many friends here.

He leaves a wife and two sons, Earl, aged eleven, and Edgar, aged six. A father and mother and one sister sadly lament his untimely end. Funeral services were conducted at the M.E. church in this city Monday evening. Rev. E.C. Horn discoursed to a congregation taking the capacity of the edifice. The remains were bourne to the depot that evening by six of the business men of Alliance, and placed on board the 11:18 train for transportation to Marshalltown, Iowa, where the relatives of the deceased reside. Mrs. Wait and two sons left at the same time to attend the obsequies after which they will return to this city."

In the 12 October 1900 newspaper, there is notice that Henry Mathews who was charged with killing of E.G. Wait was found not guilty and was discharged. He was thought to have left the area immediately.

Editor's note: Edgar Wait and family were whites. The saloon where the incident occurred was managed by W.N. Corneal, black.

****

Box Butte County, Nebraska
District Court
Case 1236, Docket F, Page 1236
filed 20 May 1901

Injunction
Charles Tierman
vs
Miller and Leith and Co.

Plaintiff for cause of action says that he is a resident of Box Butte County, Nebraska engaged in the ranch business, that he ranches about 500 head of cattle and some few horses, that his range has been on sections 15, 17, 18, 19, 20, 30, 29, 28, 31, 32, 33 and 34 of Township 24 Range 51 Box Butte County Nebraska and to the south along the north part of township 23 range 51 Cheyenne County, Nebraska; that theretofore and prior to dates herein after fixed said land was practically all government land save and except that plaintiff is the owner of the following land to wit: S 1/2, SW 1/4, Sec 15 and N 1/2 NW 1/4 Sec 22 and NE 1/4 Sec 21 and a lien of mortgage and tax title on SE 1/5 Sec 15 and N 1/2, S 1/4 Sec 14 and have a lease hold interest in S 1/2, NW 1/4 and N 1/2, SW 1/4 Sec 15. Upon the last named tract your petitioner maintains his home ranch. That in addition to the above holdings by fee simple and similar titles your petitioner has permission to use and does use the following land which are held by bonafide Homesteaders to wit N 1/2, NE 1/4, Sec 20, NW 1/4 and N 1/2, SW 1/4 Sec 21 the N 1/2 Sec 22 and W 1/2 NW 1/4 Sec 26, all in Township 24, Range 51, Box Butte County, Nebraska.

Your petitioner says that on or about the 18 day of June 1888 one John H. Finnegan made a homestead entry upon the following land to wit: S 1/2, SE 1/4, Sec 20 and the S 1/2, SW 1/4, Sec. 21. That the claimant never resided on said tract but on the contrary was never known to have been in the country and was not known to the oldest inhabitants. That said land was supposed to be government land, that on or about February 1899 one Patrick J. Tiernan squatted upon said land and caused valuable improvements to be erected thereon, that in March following he offered his filing at the U.S. Local Land Office at Alliance when it became known that said land was an abandoned Homestead entry. That same having been reported for cancellation said Patrick J. Tiernan, made application to enter said land deposited the necessary money in the Land Office and at once established and maintained his residence on said tract, that there is valuable improvements thereon to wit: a well of abundant and good water, that there has been placed thereon a windmill and tanks, and made as a watering place and that this plaintiff has procured the right to water his cattle at said well and from said tanks; that the plaintiff occupies said land for his range and for the water privilege, and that there is no other place near where water can be had, that the wells are very deep and water is hard to get; that there is no running water near to this land and none controlled by plaintiff and plaintiff has no other place to water his cattle, except this place above being procured from Patrick J. Tiernan. Further that plaintiff has occupied said lands as heretofore mentioned for ten years last past. That during said time plaintiffs stock had run upon said range undisputed and unmolested, that the water place is the only place where plaintiff can water his cattle. Plaintiff says that the ranges of western Nebraska are crowded with cattle and that the water supply is all taken and that it is impossible for the plaintiff to find other range or place to water his cattle; that he has no remedy

80

according to the strict rules of law for the injuries and threatened injuries hereinafter complained of; that unless this court afford plaintiff a remedy he will suffer irreparable injury, that the defendants have been guilty of the following.

II
The defendants are a company composed of H.H. Miller and John Leith they sign themselves Miller and Leith, the said company as a firm and as individuals, by the firm and by themselves by their agents and attorneys have been and are now guilty of divers frauds practiced upon and against this plaintiff and against the United States government in this to wit: said defendants Miller and Leith have conspired to destroy the range and drive the plaintiff away and to fence plaintiff out from said watering place and to deprive plaintiffs cattle of water and of grass, by the following false fraudulent transactions in the manner hereinafter set out;

III
On or about the first week in April 1901 defendants by themselves and through their agents and attorneys; did procure one Lizzie Duncan a colored woman, and 26 other colored persons and 2 white persons to make entries upon the following described land as is set out on the exhibit hereto attached marked Exhibit "A".

IV
That the defendants procured said Lizzie Duncan and the 28 others to make Homestead application similar to Exhibit "B" and did procure the said Lizzie Duncan and 28 others to make sign and swear to homestead affidavit similar to Exhibit "C" hereto attached and made a part of this petition.

V
That said Lizzie Duncan and 28 others falsely testified that said entry was made for their own benefit; when in fact said entries and entry was made for the benefit of the defendants; that the defendants were guilty of fraud as against the government of the United States and were conspiring to destroy the property and rights of plaintiff by thus procuring said parties to commit the fraud upon the government and to thus cover up the government domain; that said defendants, for each application and affidavit so falsely made and for each corrupt entry so procured and for each filing obtained by fraud to defeat the aim of the Homestead law the said defendant paid to the said Entry so fraudulently procured the sum of $5.00 and some few of them defendants paid $10.00 that immediately after said entry was made the defendants procured a relinquishment to said entry and a lease upon the said land and immediately took charge of the filing receipt of the entry man and retained the same; that the defendants paid the filing fee of $14.00 on each claim to the United States Land office and did pay for all clerical work in preparing the necessary papers and did pay the additional sum of $5.00 and $10.00 to the said Lizzie Duncan and others named in exhibit "A".

VI
That each of said entries are founded in fraud and are not entitled to recognition, and that said land is and has been at all time U.S. Government land, that the fraudulent acts of the defendants has not divested the government of the United States of its rights and the said Lizzie Duncan and others named in exhibit "A" have no rights in and to said lands and the said defendants have acquired no rights by reason of said lease for reason same is founded in fraud, perjury and a conspiracy on the part of the defendants to defraud the government of the United States and to defraud this plaintiff. That said entries so made are in direct violation of the laws of the United States.

VII
Plaintiff says that on the ___ (blank) day of April 1901 the said defendants served the following notice upon him, naming Tiernan and Burke, meaning this Plaintiff and one G.G. Burke who is having cattle

81

kept by the plaintiff. A copy of said notice is hereto attached and made a part of this petition marked exhibit "D".

VIII

Plaintiff says that the defendants have driven plaintiffs stock from said lands, now claims said lands, by reason of corrupt and fraudulent entries, and is commencing to build a fence enclosing the land claimed and mentioned in the said notice; that about one half of a mile of said fence has already been built, and the remainder is going to be built by defendants at once; and defendants are going to prevent the cattle of plaintiff from getting to said well and of having water and feed. That defendants by their agents and themselves are armed and threaten violence to the person of the plaintiff and are thus armed and with force are carrying out the false, fraudulent, perjured and corrupt design - relying wholly upon the rights acquired by reason of said false, fraudulent, corrupt, conspiring and perjured Homestead entries as made by the parties named in exhibit "A" and upon no other right or rights; that said defendants are trespassers upon the government domain.

IX

Further that at this time there is pending before the U.S. Land department an investigation and the rights of said parties named in said exhibits "A" have been ordered for investigation that the said plaintiff says that said action can not be heard until after the irreparable injury has been done to this plaintiff and that unless said injunction be at once allowed and granted the plaintiff will be driven from his range and he has no place to water or range his cattle and that the said defendants are not capable to respond in damages and the damages cannot be measured in money; And that all the rights claimed by defendants are based upon fraud and founded in fraud and a conspiracy against the United States Government and that said fraud while against the government works directly against this plaintiff.

Plaintiff therefore prays that the defendants and their agents, attorneys and representatives be enjoined from asserting any control of the land described in exhibit "A" and of fencing or from exerting, maintaining any fencing thereon as shown on said exhibit to the lands described in within Box Butte County, Nebraska, in exhibit "A" or from driving the stock of plaintiff from off said lands or in any way interfering with the range of the plaintiff and that a temporary restraining order be issued and that on a final hearing of said cause that this injunction be made perpetual and for such other and further relief as the premises may require.

Exhibit A
(all land unless denoted is in Box Butte County, Nebraska)
Lizzie Duncan SW, Sec 29
Henry Payne S 1/2, SW 1/4, Sec 28; W 1/2, NW 1/4, Sec 33
Ben Johnson NE 1/4, Sec 32
Ben Williams SW 1/4, Sec 29
Thomas Jackson SE 1/4, Sec 32
William Shore NW 1/4 Sec 29
Fred Stewart W 1/2, SE1/4, Sec 28; NW 1/4, NE 1/4, NE 1/4, NW 1/4, Sec 33
Stephen Jackson NW 1/4, Sec 32
Annie Graves E 1/2, NE 1/4, NE 1/4, SE 1/4, Sec 33; SW 1/4, NW 1/4, Sec 34
Peter Martin S 1/2, NE 1/4, NW 1/4, SE 1/4 Sec 27; NE 1/4, SW 1/4, Sec 34
Hattie Houseley S 1/2 NW, SW 1/4, SE 1/4, Sec 27; NE 1/4, NW 1/4, Sec 34
Lucretia Green W 1/2, NW 1/4, NW 1/4, SW1/4 Sec 28
John Corneal SW 1/4, SW 1/4, Sec33 and Lots 2, 3, and 4 in Sec 4, Twp 23, Range 51 in
        Cheyenne County, Nebraska
Farmie Trefre (white former colored) SW 1/4, Sec 17
Abraham Trefren (white) NW 1/4 Sec 17

The following land in Cheyenne County, Nebraska in Township 23, Range 51
Edward Baker SE 14, Sec 4
James Woodward W 1/2, NE 1/4, SW 1/4, NW 1/4, Sec 10
Jessie Cobb S 1/2, NE 1/4, W 1/4 NW 1/4 Sec 33
Ida Taylor Lots 1, 2, 3, 4 in Sec 4
Addie Taylor SW 1/4, NW 1/4, Sec 3; S 1/2, NE 1/4, SE 1/4, NW 1/4, Sec 4

Charles Peper N1/2, NE 1/4 Sec 9, N 1/2, NW 1/4 Sec 16
Mattie Parkes S 1/2, SW 1/4, NW 1/4, SW 1/4, SW 1/4, NW 1/4, Sec 5
Ben Carter S 1/2, NE 1/4, SE 14, NW 1/4, NE 1/4, SW 1/4 Sec 5
Louise Carter NW 1/4, SE 1/4, SE 1/4, SE 1/4 Sec 3; NE 1/4, NE 1/4, Sec 10

Exhibit D
Alliance, Nebr.
To Charles Tiernan and George Burke Respectfully,
You are hereby notified that we the undersigned have either leased or deeded the following tract of land:
Beginning on the NW 1/4 of the NW 1/4 of Sec. 165, Town 24, Range 51 West to the NW corner of Sec.
17 of the same town and range thence south five miles thence east to the fence between the Vaughn ranch
and the Miller & Leith ranch thence east to the Sollenberg ranch including the Wells ranch thence west to
the starting point, except such lands as held by you yourselves by deed or lease of homestead.

You are hereby further notified that after April the 22nd 1901 you are expected to keep your stock off the
above described tract of land. Our deeds are on record our leases can be seen at the house of H.H. Miller,
in Alliance.

Signed this 15 days of April 1901
John Leith
H.H. Miller

Demurer
The defendants demur to the petition of the plaintiff for the following causes, which appear on the face of
the petition:

1st The court has no jurisdiction of the subject matter of the action.
2nd The petition does not state facts sufficient to constitute a cause of action.

Miller and Leith et al, Dfts.
by W. Mitchell their atty.
came up for hearing on 28 May 1901
Having heard the demur, the Court overruled the same. The Defendants excepts.

Motion to Vacate 31 May 1901
The defendants move the court to vacate the injunction heretofore granted in the case for the following
reasons:
1.   The petition does not state facts sufficient to authorize the issuing of the same.
2.   The facts and allegations set forth in said petition upon which said injunction was granted are untrue.
Signed by Miller & Leith et al, Defendants
by Wm. Mitchell and B.F. Gilman, their attorneys
This was overruled by the court.

Chares Tiernan, plaintiff
vs

Miller and Leith a firm composed of H.H. Miller and John Leith
H.H. Miller, John Leith the agents and attorneys of Miller and Leith
and the agents and attorneys of H.H. Miller and John Leith individually

Statement that the defendants have disobeyed the order of injunction so granted in this to wit: That on the 16th day of July 1901 the defendants began the construction of a barb wire fence at the northwest corner of section 28 Town 24 Range 51 in said county and have since built the said fence from the said corner to the southeast corner of the northeast quarter of said section 29, and that the defendants have stated to this affiant that they intend to build the said fence from the said latter point one mile west. Affiant further says that the defendants have the material on the ground to construct the fence which they stated they intended to build all of which is in open violation of courts restraining order. By the summons issued in the above suit the defendants were directed to answer on or before the 21st day of June 1901 and to this day they have failed and neglected to answer and are now in default. That said order of injunction is being openly violated by Miller and Leith, John Leith, H.H. Miller as principals and by their agents seven colored men whose names so far known are as follows Nathan Taylor, Thomas Jackson, ___ Johnson, first name unknown, ____ Mitchell, first name unknown, John Doe, real name unknown, Richard Roe, real name unknown, Smith, real name unknown. But as persons and individuals are known by sight to Affiant. Wherefore Affiant asks of the court that the defendants and each of them and the agents of the defendants and each of them be cited to appear at such a time and such a place as the Court may direct to show cause why they should not be punished for the violation of the Injunction heretofore issued and now in full force in the above cause and that they be required to answer for said violation and contempt of the Court. 17 day of July 1901

Statement from W.Mitchell stating that as acting county attorney he cannot act on behalf of Miller & Leith, et all for the violation of said injunction and asks the court to relieve him and appoint some qualified attorney. 31 July 1901

Document dated 2 August 1901 asking the Sheriff of Box Butte County to remove within three days any and all fence he may find on the lands mentioned in the injunction to which orders defendants W.N. Corneal and Ben Johnson, except

States Exhibit G
Answer
In answer to paragraph #1 of the plaintiff's petition, defendants deny each and every allegation there contained except that which is admitted herein. Defendants deny that plaintiff had any right to range on said sections 15, 17, 18, 19, 20, 30, 29, 28, 31, 32, 33 and 34 of Township 24 Range 51, Box Butte Co., Nebr. to the South along the north part of Town 28 Range 51 Cheyenne County Nebraska, any more than any other person or that his live stock ranged on said land any more than livestock of other persons, or that plaintiff has any claim or interest in said sections that exceeded interest of any other person or persons.

Plaintiff admits that plaintiff uses and says that that plaintiff has fenced N 2, NE 4 Sec. 20; NW1/4 and N1/2, SW 1/4 Sec 21; N 1/2 Sec 22 and W 1/2, NW 1/4 Sec 26 all in Township 24, Range 51, Box Butte County, Nebraska. Plaintiff says that said land last described herein were entered at the U.S. Land Office at Alliance, Nebraska by persons at the instigation of this plaintiff and that he has — said land to exclusion of every other person and is using same for his own benefit. That said lands were entered exclusively for the benefit of this plaintiff and that persons entering same have not lived on or resided on said lands in — with the U.S. Land Laws. Defendants say that the said lands were entered in the same manner plaintiff alleges the lands described in his petition were entered by said Lizzie Duncan and — other entry men. That fencing said lands plaintiff has prevented the cattle and horses of defendants from grazing and — on said or using on same; That by fencing said lands plaintiff has kept cattle of defendant from waters on Snake Creek immediately north of said fenced entries, and thus damaging the defendants by his acts. Defendants deny that Patrick H. Tierman has ever made or maintained his residence on S 1/2, SE 1/4, Sec 20 and S 1/2, SW 1/4, Sec 21 — the John H. Finnegan, H.E., or that he has ever placed a wind mill and tanks on said place or made a watering place on said land. Defendants say that said wind mill, tank and watering place were placed on paid land by this plaintiff who now owns said and that said Patrick H. Tierman has no interest in said improvements and owns no cattle of his own that range or occupy said fenced lands. Defendants deny that water is hard to get near said land, but on contrary defendants say that the Snake Creek a stream of running water is over 1/2 mile from where plaintiff lives and not over 1 miles from where the Finnegan land is and that water is easy to procure any place near the Finnegan land, wells not being over 34 feet deep and in places not over 15 feet. Defendants deny that plaintiff has occupied lands heretofore mentioned for 10 years except possible lands he may have — or where his buildings are located. Defendants deny that plaintiff has occupied said lands unmolested or that he has any rights to same also deny that water is hard to get and that plaintiff can get any place by digging wells. Defendants deny that plaintiff has been injured or that they or anyone of them has injured or threatened to injure plaintiff. Defendants say that if plaintiff has more cattle than he can pasture, — or feed and — it is no fault of theirs and that if they have injured plaintiff he has his remedy at law as the defendants John Leith and H.H. Miller are well over and above all their debts and exemptions the sum of.

Defendants say that theirs or their agents have never at any time interfered with the cattle or horses of the plaintiff on the Finnegan land nor have they driven them from the watering place on said or interfered with their grazing thereon, nor have they ever fenced or attempted to fence said Finnegan land or in any way interfere with same or exercise control of same. In answer to paragraph 2 of said petition of plaintiff defendants say each and every allegation therein contained. Defendants say that H.H. Miller and John Leith are not — and never have been that they simply run their stock together on range.

In answer to paragraph #3 deny each and every allegation there contained, except that Lizzie Duncan and 28 other persons made the homestead therein claimed as seen out in Exhibit A of plaintiff's petition. The defendants deny each and every allegation in paragraph #4 of plaintiff's petition. In answer to paragraph #5 of plaintiff's petition defendants deny each and every allegation there contained. In answer to paragraph #6 of plaintiff's petition defendants deny each and every allegation contained. The defendants admit for paragraph 7 of plaintiff's petition. Defendants deny each and every allegation as contained in paragraph 8 of plaintiff's petition, except that defendants claim said lands by lease, which will be further described hereafter, but that said leases, are [word "not" crossed through] based on consent and fraudulent entires and admit that defendants have commenced to fence lands described in Exhibit D attached to plaintiff's petition.

The defendants deny each and every allegation contained in paragraph 9 of plaintiff's petition. The defendants — answering plaintiff's petition say that on or about the first week in April 1901 Lizzie Duncan and 28 other persons entered the lands described in Exhibit attached to plaintiff's petition as homesteads, under the U.S. Land Laws, at the U.S. Land Office at Alliance, Nebraska. That said entries were made in good faith and for the promises of actual settlement and residence by said Lizzie Duncan and said 28 entry men, so far as is known to defendants. That these defendants did not procure either in person or by their agents, said Lizzie and said 28 other entry men or any of them to make said — entries, nor did said defendants — theirsevles or by their —— from said entry men relinquishments for said nor have the defendants ever attempted to so. Defendants say that they did not pay the sum of $5.00 or $10.00 nor any sum whatsover for relinquishments to said entries nor have they relinquishments for said entries. Defendants say they were not parties to said entries in any way nor did they procure them to be made, nor have they — for any entries being made either to Lizzie Duncan or said other 28 entry men nor have they paid for the work of preparing the papers for said entry men, nor have defendants been guilty of fraud toward plaintiff of the U.S. in modius said entries nor have said defendants had said entries made to injure or hurt the plaintiff in person or by preventing his livestock from pasturing or watering on said lands described in said entries. Defendants say they did not say or cause to be said the filing fee of $14.00 to make any of said entries, nor have they caused same to be done. Defendants say that they have had nothing to do with making said entries nor have the[y] solicited same to be made and that they are not interested in same in any way except that they being in the stock business have arranged with the entry men to use the grass on said land for pasture, but they have no control over nor have they anything to do with said land in any other — to get the benefit of said grass. Defendants obtained permission to fence said land which they were doing when enjoined[?] by this plaintiff. Defendants say that all they did was to try to get the benefit of the grass they had leased on —. Defendants say that at no time have they — the plaintiff with force or arms nor have they armed themselves and — violence to the person of the plaintiff. Defendants say that said Lizzie Duncan, said other 28 entry men have made actual settlement and residence on lands described in plaintiff's exhibit "A" and now residing upon same having houses and furniture on said lands and having complied with the land laws of the U.S. in every —. Defendants say they have done nothing contrary to law nor have they injured or conspired to injure the plaintiff nor have they conspired with said entry men to defend the U.S. Defendants say they are not bankrupt but that they are worth over and above all debts and exemptions the sum of [left blank].

Wherefore plaintiff prays that said injustices may be dissolved and that the — heretofore granted may be dissolved and set aside and that said — investigation — for may be demurred and that defendants recover their costs herein and for such others and — relief as may be just and equitable.
Signed by Miller and Leith by attorneys B.F. Gilman and Em. Mitchell
1 May 1902 - recorded

Motion

Comes now the plaintiff and moves the Court to strike the defendant's answer from the files, for reason same was filed out of time and without leave of court and without any authority for the filing of the same, in this; that the defendants had been in default for more than eleven months at the time of filing said

answer without authority therefor. Signed by Charles Tiernan.
Supplemental Petition of the Plaintiff
Comes now the plaintiff and shows to the Court that since the filing of the petition in said cause the following material changes have taken place in this to wit: The Government of the United States through its Department of the Interior has suspended the entry of John Corneal and 24 others, the said John Corneal and the said 24 others being parties with whom the said Miller & Leith are charged with conspiring, and that notices were issued directly to the said John Corneal and 24 others from the United States local Land Office at Alliance, Nebraska on or about May 28, 1902. That a copy of the notice issued against John Corneal is hereto attached to this Supplemental Petition marked exhibit "A"; that similar notices and similar actions were had by the United States against each and all of the said 24 others and the names of the parties referred to in this Supplemental Petition together with their entry and the description of their land is attached to and made a part of this Supplemental Petition marked exhibit "B". Wherefore the plaintiff prays for an injunction as heretofore requested, adopting and making the prayer of the petition heretofore filed the request of this Supplemental Petition and praying that this Supplemental Petition be filed and considered along and together with the original petition filed in this case.
Signed by his attorneys
26 June 1902

Letter from Department of the Interior, United States Land Office
Alliance, Nebr., May 28, 1902
Marked Exhibit "A"
John Corneal, Alliance, Nebr.

Sir:
You are hereby notified that the Commissioner of the General Land Office by letter dated April 21, 1902 has suspended your Homestead No. 4148 for the Lots 2-3 & 4 Sec 4, Twp. 23, N Range 51W, Alliance Nebraska Land District on charges contained in a report by a special agent.

The charges on which said Homestead is suspended are summarized as follows: On personal examination of the tract it is found to be grazing land. Improvements, board shack built on dividing line between H E 4148 and adjoining entry to cover both entries. Barbed wire fence around house at two feet distance there from. Door nailed up, two windows, no floor or chimney; claimant never resided on claim or attempted to break or cultivate any land. Leased on date of filing to H.H. Miller and John Leith who paid all fees and expenses of making entry and in whose interest filing was made.

You will be allowed thirty days within which to file application in this office for a hearing and your failure to apply for a hearing within the time specified will be taken as an admission of the truth of the charges against said Homestead 4148, and the same will be cancelled.

Very respectfully,
W.R. Akers, Receiver

The Defendants demur to the petition of the plaintiff for the following reason which appears on the face of the petition: 1. Because the petition does not state facts sufficient to constitute a cause of action.
26 June 1902

Supersedeas Bond
We, Charles Tiernan as principal and G.G. Burke and Tom G. Burke as sureties are held and firmly bound until Miller & Leith, the agents and attorneys of Miller & Leith and H.H. Miller and John Leith as individuals, and their agents and attorneys in the sum of $1,000 for the payment of which we jointly bind ourselves, our heirs, assigns administrators and executors. The condition of this obligation is such that whereas the said Charles Tiernan has appealed to the Supreme Court of Nebraska from the decree

vacating a temporary injunction and dismissing the petition above entitled suit and entered on the 26th day of June, 1902, dissolving the said injunction theretofore granted to the said Charles Tiernan in the said entitled suit, and said Court has fixed the amount of bond to be given for the purpose of continuing the said temporary injunction in force during the pendency of such appeal at the sum of $1,000. Now if the said Charles Tiernan will prosecute such appeal without delay, and will pay all costs which may be found against him on the final determination of the said cause in the said Supreme Court, then this obligation is to be void, otherwise to remain in full force.
27 June 1902

Mandate #13058
Supreme Court of the State of Nebraska
Sitting at Lincoln, September Term 1903
To the District Court of the 15th Judicial District sitting in and for the County of Box Butte
Charles Tiernan, Plaintiff
Miller and Leith, a firm etal, Defendants
Box Butte County District Court prosecuted an appeal to the Supreme Court of the State of Nebraska. Judgment rendered in favor of Defendant against said Plaintiff; Plaintiff taxed $15.65.

The State of Nebraska
vs
H. H. Miller, et all
Contempt
Case 1250, Docket F, Page 120
Filed 1 August 1901

In the District Court of Box Butte County
In the matter of The State of Nebraska
vs
H.H. Miller and John Leith
individuals and Miller and Leith
W.N. Corneal, agent of Miller and Leith
Ben Johnson, agent of Miller and Leith
Ben Carter, agent of Miller and Leith

Comes now R.C. Noleman duly appointed County Attorney of Box Butte County, Nebraska having on the 31st day of July 1901 been especially appointed in open court by J.J. Harrington the then presiding Judge. And on behalf of the County Attorney and the State, Complaint makes and gives the Court to be informed, That heretofore to-wit on the 20th day of May 1901 that one Charles Tiernan brought suit in the District Court of Box Butte County, Nebraska against H.H. Miller and John Leith as a firm under the style of Miller and Leith and as individuals under the names of H.H. Miller and John Leith. Their agents and attorneys of which was to obtain an injunction restraining the said defendants from exercising any control over the homestead entries of Lizzie Duncan and 28 others, and from fencing the lands homesteaded by the said Lizzie Duncan and 28 others and from preventing the stock of the plaintiff from watering at their accustomed watering place. That in keeping with the prayer of said petition, the District Judges and each of them being absent from the County of Box Butte, Bruce Wilcox issue(d) a temporary injunction in keeping with the prayer of the plaintiffs petition as above set fourth [sic]. Whereby Miller and Leith as a firm and H.H. Miller and John Leith as individuals and the attorneys and agents of Miller and Leith and the attorneys and agents of John Leith and H.H. Miller were enjoined from exercising any control over and from fencing the following lands to wit SW 1/4 Sec 29, S 1/2 NW 1/4 Sec 28, W 1/2 NW 1/4, Sec 33, NE 1/4 Sec 32, SE1/4 Sec 29, SE 1/4 Sec 32, NW 1/4 Sec 29, W 1/2 S/E 14/ Sec 28, NW 1/4, NE 1/4 & NE 1/4 NW 1/4 Sec 33, NW 1/4 Sec 32, E 1/2 NE 1/4 NE 1/4 SE 1/4 Sec 33 Sw 14 NW 1/4 Sec 34, S 1/2

NE 1/4 NW 1/4, NW 1/4, SE 1/4 and NE 1/4 SW 1/4 Sec 34, NW 1/4 and NW 1/4 SW 1/4 Sec 28, SW1/4 SW 1/4 Sec 33 and Lots 2, 3, 4, Sec 4 of Town 23 Range 51 SW 1/4 Sec 17, NW 1/4 Sec 17. All of the above lands excepting the tract described in Town 23 being in Box Butte County Nebraska. That afterwards to wit on the 27th day of May 1901 the same being one of the days of the regular Term of the District Court [sic] of Box Butte County Nebraska, the said cause came on for hearing on the demurrer of the defendants, on consideration of which the court overruled the demurrer. That at a subsequent day of said term to wit on June 4th 1901 the said cause came on to be heard on motion of the defendant in said case in said injunction to vacate the injunction, after consideration of which the court on said day overruled the said motion. That no further proceedings has been had in said cause and the answer day as fixed in the original summons is long past and the defendants and each of them are now in default and the said injunction as granted on May 20th 1901 is now in full force and effect and has been in full force and effect at all times since said date. Your Complainant further states that the defendants Miller and Leith as a firm and the defendants John Leith and H.H. Miller as individuals have violated the injunction as heretofore issued. And also one W.N. Corneal an Agent of Miller and Leith and one Ben Johnson An Agent of Miller and Leith and also one Ben Carter an Agent of Miller and Leith have violated the injunction heretofore issued and set out in this complaint. Complainant says that the said Agents W.N. Corneal, Ben Johnson and Ben Carter well knew said injunction was in full force and effect and the said H.H. Miller and John Leith well knowing that said injunction was in full force and effect they and each of the aforesaid and aforenamed H.H. Miller, John Leith, W.N. Corneal, Ben Johnson and Ben Carter, purposely intentionally and with full knowledge of the injunction and with an intention to disobey the order of the court did willfully and intentionally violate said injunction in this to wit H.H. Miller and John Leith and W.N. Corneal, Ben Johnson and Ben Carter, purposely intentionally and with a full knowledge of the injunction and with an intention to disobey the order of the court did willfully and intentionally violate said injunction in this to-wit H.H. Miller and John Leith and W.N. Corneal, Ben Carter and Ben Johnson did on or about the 16 day of July 1901 exercise control over the following land the W 1/2 NW 1/4 and NW 1/4 SW 1/4 of Sec 28 and S 1/2 of Sec 29 all of Town 24 Range 51 Box Butte County Nebraska by fencing on the north and west side of said land and did on or about the said day erect a two wire, barbed wire fence, commencing at the northeast corner of the northwest quarter of section 28 then running due west on the north line of said section to the northwest corner of said section then south on the west line of said section one half mile then west three fourths of a mile through the center of section 29 then southwest to the southwest corner of the southwest corner of the south west quarter of section 29 Township 24, Range 51 Box Butte County, Nebraska and the said parties and each of them did aid, assist, council and advise in the construction of the said fence and they and each of them full well knew that said injunction was in full force and effect.

Wherefore your Complainant makes information and says that the said H.H. Miller and John Leith as individuals and the said Miller and Leith as partners and the said W.N. Corneal the said Ben Carter and the said Ben Johnson are guilty of contempt of court, committed in manner and form as heretofore set out. And that said defendants and each of them are guilty of contempt of court, of the District Court in and for Box Butte County Nebraska and that said contempt was committed within Box Butte County Nebraska in manner and form as heretofore set out in this information

R.C. Noleman, Specialy[sic] appointed County Attorney
14 August 1901
States Witnesses
Charles Tiernan, John Tiernan, George Burke, Dock Wirts, E. Dukker, John Henderson, R.C. Noleman, R.M. Hampton, Thos. Beck, Frank Darling, H.C. Armstrong, Everrett Logan, George Clark, George L. Turner, F.Wm. Hargarten, Nathan Taylor, E.P. Sweeney, D.K. Spacht
Journal Entry
State of Nebraska
vs
H.H. Miller, John Leith, W.N. Corneal, Benjamin Johnson - Defendants

On this 2nd day of August 1901 this cause came on to be heard on the application of each of these defendants who were present in court and on consideration of said application the court grants the same and continues said cause to the next regular term of said court and it is ordered that each defendant give bond for their appearance to the next term of court in the sum of $200.00.

The State of Nebraska to the Sheriff of Box Butte County Nebraska
Greeting:
We command you to take H.H. Miller, John Leith, W.H. Corneal, Ben Johnson and Ben Carter, and them and each of them safely keep so that you have the bodies of each of them before the Judge of the District Court for the County of Box Butte, forthwith, to answer unto the State of Nebraska to the information exhibited against them and each of them for Contempt of Court, and have you then and there his writ. Witness my hand and seal of said Court at Alliance, this 1st day August 1901
S.M. Smyser?, Clerk District Court

The State of Nebraska vs H.H. Miller, John Leith, W.N. Corneal, Ben Johnson and Ben Carter
Be it remembered that on the 2nd day of August, A.D. 1901 John Leith of Box Butte County, State of Nebraska, and H.H. Miller of the County and State aforesaid, appeared personally before the District Court in and for said County, and jointly and severally acknowledged themselves to owe and be indebted to the State of Nebraska in the penal sum of $200.00, to be made and levied upon their respective goods, chattels, lands and tenements; to be void, however, if the said John Leith shall personally be and appear before the District Court of said County on the first day of the next term of thereof, to-wit: on the 18th day of November, A.D., 1901 to be and remain from day to day of said term and from term to term, to answer a charge preferred against him for Contempt of Court, and to do and receive what shall be enjoined by said Court upon him, and shall not depart said court without leave.

[The exact same document was issued for H.H. Miller, Ben Johnson and W.N. Corneal to appear in court.]

State of Nebraska to the Sheriff of Box Butte County, Nebraska
Greeting:
You are hereby commanded to summon Charles Tiernan, John Tiernan, George Burke, Dock Wirtz, E. Dukker, John Henderson, R.M. Hampton, Nathan Taylor, Everett Logan, George Clark, George L. Turner, F. Wm. Hargarten, H.C. Armstrong, Ed Burke, John Brubaker and C.A. Newberry to appear before the District Court of Box Butte County on 18 November 1901 at 11 a.m. to give evidence in a suit between The State of Nebraska and John Leith, H.H. Miller, W.N. Corneal and Ben Johnson, defendants on the part of said Plaintiff. Dated 7 November 1901

Officer's Return of Service
served on 11 November 1901 but after diligent search John Henderson, Ed Burk and John Brubaker cannot be found in this county

State of Nebraska to the Sheriff or Any Constable of Box Butte County, Nebraska
Greeting
You are commanded to summon Ed Dickker, John Henderson, John Tiernan, George Burke, S.H. Wirtz, C.A. Newberry, R.M. Hampton, Charles Tiernan, M.V. Tiernan, G.C. Turner to appear in the District Court of Box Butte County Nebraska on 26 June 1902 at 9 a.m. and then and there to give testimony about a pending case wherein the State of Nebraska prosecutes John Leith and H.H. Miller on behalf of the plaintiff. Dated 14 June 1902
[There are two summons on file for the State of Nebraska asking to summon Geo. Clark to appear in District Court of Box Butte County on 18 November 1901 at 11 a.m. and one for Tom Burke to appear in District Court of Box Butte County on 26 June 1902 at 9 a.m.]

In the District Court for Box Butte County, Nebraska

State of Nebraska, Plaintiff
vs
H.H. Miller, John Leith, W.M. [sic] Corneal, Agent, Ben Johnson, Agent and Ben Carter, Defendants
Motion to Strike

Now comes the above named defendants, H.H. Miller, John Leith, W.M. [sic] Corneal and Ben Johnson in their own proper persons and move the court to strike from the files herein the information filed on the first day of August 1901, by R.C. Noleman Esq., special county attorney, for the following reasons:

1. Because said R.C. Noleman, Esq., special county attorney, is not dis-interested in the prosecution of this cause.
2. Because said R. Noleman was and still is the attorney of record for the plaintiff in the injunction suit mentioned and set forth in the information herein, and was by reason of such fact disqualified from appointment as such special county attorney, and disqualified from prosecuting these defendants herein; and disqualified from making and filing the information filed herein.
3. Because said information does not state facts sufficient to constitute an offense.
4. Because said information does not state facts sufficient to constitute a criminal contempt.
5. Because said information information does not state facts sufficient to constitute a civil contempt.
6. Because said information does not state facts sufficient to constitute the contempt of the injunction order mentioned in said information.
7. Because said information is not verified upon the oath of any person.
8. Because said information is not sworn by any person.

Signed by John Leith 26 June 1902

Following this document was a corrected document changing the word information contained herein to affidavit. Two more additions were made.
9. Because the court has no jurisdiction over this cause.
10. Because the information filed herein confers no jurisdiction.
Signed by John Leith on 26 June 1902

District Court of Box Butte County, Nebraska
State of Nebraska, Plaintiff
vs
H.H. Miller, John Leith, W.M. [sic] Corneal, Agent, Ben Johnson, Angent and Ben Carter, Defendants
Plea in Abatement

And now comes the above named defendants, H.H. Miller, John Leith, W.M. [sic] Corneal and Ben Johnson in their own proper persons and for plea in abatement to the information filed herein, and respectively show to the court that they ought no further to be held to answer said information or to be put upon trial thereon for the following reasons:

Said information is filed in said district court and not before a judge thereof as an examining magistrate. Because these pleading defendants have not been examined on said charge before any justice of peace, county judge, or other magistrate having authority to examine the offense therein alleged, and to recognize these defendants to answer said charge in said District Court.
Because these pleading defendants have never had any examination before any examining magistrate upon said charge and have never been recognized to answer the same in court.
Because the order of injunction it is claimed was violated, has been dissolved and case dismissed and the contempt if any peurged [sic].
Said information is filed in said district court and not before a judge thereof as an examining magistrate. Because of these pleading defendants have not been examined on said charge before any justice of peace,

county judge, or other magistrate having authority to examine the offense therein alleged, and to recognize these defendants to answer said charge in said District Court.

Because these pleading defendants have never had any examination before any examining magistrate upon said charge and have never been recognized to answer the same in court.

Because the order of injunction it is claimed was violated, has been dissolved and case dismissed and the contempt if any peurged [sic].

Signed by John Leith on 26 June 1902

District Court of Box Butte County Nebraska
The State of Nebraska
vs
John Leith et al
Comes now R.C. Noleman specially appointed County Attorney to prosecute the above cause and demurs to defendants plea in abatement.
1. Because said plea does not state any facts which is a cause of abating said action.
2. Because said plea does not state any reason good in law.
3. Because said plea is insufficient.

Signed by R.C. Noleman on 26 June 1902

District Court of Box Butte County Nebraska
State of Nebraska, Plaintiff
vs
H.H. Miller, John Leith, W.M.[sic] Corneal, Agent, Ben Johnson, Agent and Ben Carter, Defendants
Demand for Jury
And now comes the above named defendants, H.H. Miller, John Leith, W.M.[sic] Corneal and Ben Johnson in their own proper persons and demand that a jury come to try the issues joined herein upon the information, and the plea of not guilty, which has heretofore been entered in this cause. Signed by John Leith and H.H. Miller 26 June 1902

District Court of Box Butte County Nebraska
The State of Nebraska, Plaintiff
vs
John Leith, H.H. Miller, W.N. Corneal, Ben Johnson and Ben Carter
Motion to Retax Costs
And now comes the defendant in H.H. Miller in this case and moves to retax the costs as assessed against him.
1. That fees of witnesses E.E. Decker, John Henderson, John Tiernan, George Burke, S.H. Wirtz, C.A. Newberry, R.M. Hampton, Charles Tiernan, M.V. Tiernan, G.L. Turner, Tom Burke, E.P. Sweeney in the sum of $101 be stricken out and be not charged to him for reason that said witnesses and their testimonies were not material to any issue raised in said cause and were in attendance on court at that time by virtue of a subpoena issued in and [sic] injunction suit pending in this court and their mileage and daily compensation was properly chargeable in said injunction suit, to wit case of Charles Tierman vs John Leith and H.H. Miller.
2. That said costs only $8 be taxed to this defendant for the reason that all of the costs in this case was incurred in a prosecution against four of the defendants and this defendant should only be charged with the costs necessarily incurred in due action against him.

Signed by H.H. Miller by his attorney B.F. Gilman
filed 14 August 1902

The Alliance Herald, 16 February 1905
"Two Robbers Caught
A Pair of Colored Burglars Caught Red Handed

The 13th is certainly unlucky for a couple of wandering colored men. On Monday Feb. 13th Mr. Sanford Smith in his desire for booze, broke into the back door of Eph Corneal's saloon and stole a quantity of whiskey. How much was not found out but Mr. Smith filled up on the stuff Monday night and Tuesday morning he was lying on the soft side of a snow drift in West Lawn and brought in by sheriff Reed in a partially congealed condition. On going to his house or room, six bottles of the stolen firewater were found. When arraigned before Judge Spacht he plead guilty to the charge of house breaking which means a term at the Lincoln broom factory.

The same night, William Johnson a chocolate colored traveling minstrel performer, thinking to increase his wardrobe, broke into Beckwith & Bresee's clothing store and appropriated three pairs of late style trousers, some shoes, half dozen pairs sox and a complete outfit of modern stylish wearing apparel. Beckwith took the scent — you know Beckwith is a hunter — and finally located the stolen property in a grip or suit case that belonged to Mr. Johnson. When confronted with the evidence of his guilt, he too made a clean breast of it and plead guilty in Judge Spacht's court and was bound over to await the arrival of District Judge Westover, who has been sent for and he too may take up his residence in Lincoln. The law provides from one to ten years in the pen as the penalty for house breaking."

****

The Alliance Herald, 9 March 1905
"Robber Breaks Jail
Sanford Smith, the colored inmate of the county jail who had plead guilty to the charge of house breaking a couple weeks ago, escaped Monday night.

The sheriff had secured the jail for the night, and locked everything up in good order when for some reason the janitor who has or had a key went into the jail. The colored man took advantage of the man and the night to get away. An alarm was given but the thief was gone.

The sheriff and marshals scoured the country all day but no trace of him could be found. Tuesday night about 10 o'clock the coon came back and asked the jailer to admit him, which was done and the sheriff notified. When Reed arrived Smith was toasting his shins at a comfortable fire and seemed pleased to be allowed to get back in his cell and go to bed. When asked to tell why he left he said he guessed he was crazy. Judge Westover is expected here daily to pass sentence on the trio.

It now appears that the object of the return of the prisoner was to release the other two, hoping to find the jailer there to admit him to his cell. Instead the wily jailer put him in the corridor, locked the door and called the sheriff."

Sanford Smith
born about 1881
sentenced for burglary for three years; Box Butte Co., Nebraska
Prisoner Number 4409 ₁

****

"The Alliance Herald", 2 March 1905
"Another Coon Caught
Nigger Payne was captured by Policeman Cardwell Friday night and landed in the 'jig' to keep company

with Sanford Smith for the Beckwith store robbery last week. Payne was wearing more new clothes than Cardwell thought he owned and pinched him. Payne confessed to having helped to the job at The Right store and told where the balance of the plunder was which Cardwell found. This makes a clean case and Payne will probably change his residence as soon as Judge Westover arrives. This makes five candidates for the pen that have fallen into the meshes of Detective Ardwell's drag net and four of them are 'coons.'"

****

Alliance Semi-Weekly Times
Alliance, Box Butte Co., Nebraska
17 May 1907, page 1
"Killed A Negress

Clinton Hollman, Colored, Sends Mistress to the Other World Without An Instant Warning
Appears Case of Self Defense
A shooting among some of the colored population last night at about 11 o'clock developed into a serious matter. It occurred at the small frame dwelling back of the opera house block, and which has been allotted to the use of the janitors of that building the past several years. Clifton (sometimes called George) Hollman, janitor of the block, is the party who did the shooting, firing one shot at a woman variously known as Sadie Bolch, Sadie Halbram or Sarah Bowles, and said to hail originally from Kansas City. The weapon used was a 38-calibre, and Hollman, who immediately hunted up Night Marshal Cox and surrendered, that the deed was committed in self-defense. The woman has been living with Hollman as his wife the past four or more months. She came here from Crawford, and is said to have been concerned in a murder there. Hollman was formerly in the U.S. army, served in the Philippines, and when discharged at Crawford, came here and accepted employment. He was a quiet, apparently inoffensive fellow, honest and industrious, and those who know him best are loth to believe the shooting was without some provocation. He claims that the woman had made threats, he had been told of them, that the doors were locked and she attacked him with a large dirk. The room was small and powder from the weapon scorched the sleeve of her dress. The ball entered at the collarbone, deflected downward and passed through the top of the heart, death being instantaneous. Four other colored men were in an adjoining room and heard the shot, but said they were afraid to open the door for some minutes. The woman was then about dead lying on the floor and with the knife near her own hand. It is believed these witnesses, who have been required to furnish bonds in the sum of $100 each for their appearance in district court, know much more than they tell and that a melee, with jealousy as the motive occurred.

Dr. J.E. Moore, coroner, impanelled a jury this forenoon and an inquest was held in the Lockwood undertaking rooms. The verdict was to the effect that Sadie Bolch came to her death from the effects of a gunshot wound inflicted by George Hollman, fired with felonious intent. The prisoner, who was immediately given into the custody of Sheriff Wiker and placed in the county jail, was not present at the hearing. Those composing the coroner's jury were: A.S. Reed, foreman; W.O. Barnes, H. Renneau, W.C. Mounts, Horace Bogue and L.A. Suprise. Hollman was bound over to the district court, and Judge Harrington expresses the intention of hearing the case as soon as the Maynard-Barnes case is disposed. For the purpose of making it easier to obtain a jury and saving the county expense, we have been requested not to give more minute details, so the fuller facts in detail will be published later."

****

The Alliance Herald, 31 December 1908
"Dies Christmas Morning In Down Town Stairway

While the world was singing its praises to the new born King of Bethlehem and strains of Christmas anthems burst forth in praise of the Messiah, there was another side to life in this city which was sad and

94

touching. Fred Pride, a colored man in the employ of Contractor Sang Reck, for a year or more, was discovered in the early morning in the stairway leading to the Elks lodge room cold to death. The last seen of Pride was during the night when he and several associates were enjoying the event of Christmas by imbibing of liquor. It is thought that Pride got more than his share and with the cold that prevailed brought on his death. He and his companions were roving about town and it was in front of the Elks hall that he was last seen alive. Here the party of colored men were singing and laughing most heartily. Then Pride went to the Elks stairway to lie down on his couch of death. A colored companion named Jackson was horrified when he discovered the body and running across the street almost white with terror announced to the passers that 'Dat coon am surely dead.'

The remains were taken to the undertaking rooms of the Gadsby store and an inquest held. A thorough dissection of the body gave no evidence of foul play and a jury composed of Ira Reed, W.O. Barnes, Jos. Smith, Sang Reck, C.W. Brennan and Wm. James, returned a verdict of death by exposure.

Deceased own two horses and possessed some money. He was about thirty-five years of age and a jolly, good-hearted soul. It is said that his mother lives in Brownsville, Texas. The funeral took place last Sunday afternoon from Holy Rosary church and the remains are buried in the Catholic cemetery."

****

The Alliance Herald, 16 December 1909
"Death of a Stranger

On Sunday, Dec. 12, occurred the death of John Lewis, the funeral being held next day at the Gadsby undertaking rooms, Rev. J.N. Huston conducting the same. Mr. Lewis' death was sudden, heart failure being the cause. He was a stranger in Alliance, a colored man, whose home and relatives, if had them, were in Georgia. Interment was made in Greenwood cemetery."

****

Box Butte County, Nebraska Criminal Court Record
District Court
Case 2124 Docket J page 64

State of Nebraska
vs
Samuel Shelton
selling intoxicating liquor without a license
11 April 1912
(complete Record "N" 595)
complaint of Bert G. Plummer

Samuel Shelton, late of the county, on 16 Aug 1911 in Box Butte County did unlawfully sell and give away malt liquors and intoxicating drinks to wit: beer to one Babe Moran without having first complied with the provisions of Chapter 32 of Cobbey annotated Statutes of the State of Nebraska for the year 1911 entitled "liquors" without having first obtaining a license to sell intoxicating liquors, as in such chapter provided and against the peace and dignity of the State of Nebraska.

Second Count:
Samuel Shelton, late of the county, on 16 August 1911 in Box Butte County did sell and give away malt liquors and intoxicating drinks to wit: beer, to one Harry Czarnososki, without having first complied with [above wording exactly]

Third Count:
Samuel Shelton, late of the county, on 17 August 1911 in Box Butte County did sell and give away malt
liquors and intoxicating drinks to wit: beer, to one Bert G. Plummer [above wording exactly]
Fourth Count:
Samuel Shelton, late of the county, on 17 August 1911 in Box Butte County … same as above to wit:
beer and whiskey to George Kiser [above wordiing exactly]
Fifth Count:
Samuel Shelton, late of the county, on 17 August 1911 in Box Butte County … same as above to wit:
beer to one John Wallace [above wording exactly]
Sixth Count:
Samuel Shelton, late of the county on 17 August 1911 in Box Butte County … same as above to wit:
beer to Jerry Steel [exact wording exactly]
Seventh Count:
Samuel Shelton late on the county did on 18 August 1911 in Box Butte County … same as above to wit:
whiskey to Bert G. Plummer

24 August 1911 — warrant was issued for the arrest of Samuel Shelton; arrested on 5 April 1912. Shelton
asked for continuance to 8 April 1912 and posted $500 bond, signed by Samuel Shelton and William
King.

8 April 1912 — Samuel Shelton and attorney B.F. Gillman and Joe Westover appeared in court.

11 April 1912, special April term of court Samuel Shelton fined $100 and committed to county jail until
said fine and costs are paid.

****

Alliance Semi-Weekly Times, Alliance, Nebraska 22 November 1912, page 1
"Drunken Negress Shoots Another Woman In Frenzy of Rage This Morning
Single Barrel Shotgun Used in Murderous Attack. Feet are Almost Shot Off Blood Poison May be Result

Mrs. Georgia Coleman this morning shot Mrs. Janie Street, using a shotgun. Mrs. Street's feet received
the charge of No. 5 shot from a single barrel gun and it is probable that amputation will be necessary. The
shooting occurred almost midnight, at the home of Mr. Guy, a colored man. All the folks are colored. One
version of the shooting is that Mrs. Coleman was very drunk and attempted to follow the Street woman's
husband into a closet, outside the home. He locked her out and this enraged her. She then went into the
house and secured the shotgun, which she deliberately loaded. In the meantime Mrs. Street came out to
learn what the trouble was about. The Coleman woman didn't waste any words with the Street woman,
but raised the gun and fired. For a wonder, her aim was good, although lower than intended. The other
inmates of the house were alarmed and at once notified the police, who came and took the Coleman
woman to jail. None of the parties have very much to say about the trouble. Mrs. Coleman has been in
trouble considerably of late and has a bad reputation. A state case will be made against her, and if she
escapes the penitentiary it will be because of some technicality of the law."

Alliance Semi-Weekly Times, Alliance, Nebraska 26 November 1912
"Coleman Woman Is Bound Over

Georgia Coleman was arraigned in Justice Zurn's court Monday morning and pleaded not guilty to the
charge of shooting Mrs. Janie Street. She waived preliminary examination and was bound over to the
action of the district court. Georgia is the Negress who has been giving considerable trouble to the local
police authorities and her latest scrape is very likely to be her last, at least for some time, as a penitentiary

sentence is about the least she can hope for. The story of the shooting of the Street woman is one which clearly fixes Georgia's guilt. That she was drunk at the time should not mitigate the offense in the least.

She had been out carousing, in fact, she had been drunk all day, growing drunker as the hours lengthened toward midnight. She and Mr. Street were out around the premises a few minutes before the shooting occurred. He went into a closet and while there his wife came outside the house and started to talk to Georgia. The latter either had or quickly secured a single barrel shotgun and raised the barrel and aimed it at Mrs. Street. The shot was fired from the rear of the unfortunate woman and the charge pierced her feet and a few scattering shot struck her above the ankles. A large hole was torn out of one foot, the other not being injured so badly. The physician in charge states that the woman will never be able to use her feet as formerly. He fears that the one most severely injured may have to be amputated. Tetanus may also set in, although all precautionary measures are being taken to prevent this.

The wounded woman is determined to prosecute. She hardly knew Georgia and had had no words at all with her, according to the story told by her husband. They are homesteaders near Harrison and had been here but a short time. Mr. Street says that Georgia spoke during the day of having a shotgun which she would use before the day was over, and it is probable that to shoot someone had become a manta with her."

District Court, Box Butte Co., Nebraska
Criminal Court
#2194 Docket J page 134
State of Nebraska vs Georgia Coleman
shooting with intent to do great bodily injury
filed 9 Dec 1912

21 Nov 1912 Georgia Coleman unlawfully, feloniously and maliciously did make an assault upon Jennie Streets with a shot gun, loaded with gun powder and leaden bullets with intent to wound.
Filed by C.A. Laing

Georgia Coleman was arrested on 25 Nov 1912 and brought before the Justice of the Peace, Gregory Zurn. Arrested by Sheriff, C.M. Cox.

Witnesses, 16 Dec 1912
Steve Jackson
Janie Streets
C.A. Laing
C.M. Cox

Georgia Coleman appeared in court on 16 Dec 1912 was informed of the charges and allegations and entered a plea of guilty. When asked if she had anything to say as to why judgment should not be pronounced, she replied "I have nothing to say." Decision to imprison her in the penitentiary of the State of Nebraska at Lincoln, Nebraska, kept at hard labor, Sundays excepted, for a minimum of one year and maximum of five years, none of which would be in solitary confinement. No costs for the prosecution were listed.

****

Alliance newspaper
3 October 1913 - Friday
"Coroners Jury Refuses to Hold Jordan As an Accessory to Killing of Edwards Woman
Blame Place Upon Paramour, Who Is Still At Liberty

Body of Woman Slain in Wednesday Night's Shooting Affair may be Turned Over to Medical College. Detail of Crime as Told by Witnesses

Coroner's Jury composed of T.H. Barnes, foreman; A.D. Rodgers, Ellis Ray, W.R. Harper, Geo. Duncan and L.F. Smith found that Bertie Edwards came to her death at the hands of Archie Edwards, while she was resisting arrest.

Bertie Edwards was a negress who was killed on Niobrara Ave. about 10 p.m. Wednesday night, when her paramour, Archie Edwards, attempted to rescue her from the hands of Officer Ben Jordan, also colored, who had arrested her. Jordan was shot through the left knee and the left thumb. At the coroner's jury was in session at Darling's morgue, nearly twenty witnesses were examined. The jury was divided if the bullets fired by Jordan or those fired by Edwards killed her. They were in deadlock for nearly two hours. Some felt she had come to her death because of the duel between Jordan and Edwards. Her body was recommended either to be buried in the cemetery at the county's expense or be sent to the medical institution if the institution will pay the transportation expenses. At the time of the newspaper article, Edwards was still at large and it was thought that he had been captured at Bingham. However, the description of the colored man at Bingham did not match that of Edwards.

Testimony of the Night Marshall: he was near Rodgers Grocery when he heard the shooting. He found Ben Jordan lying and hollering in the road. He was in the middle of Niobrara Ave. 100 feet south of Second Street. The night marshall discovered a woman, gasping and he could not detect any heart beats. There was no other man around. He was told by the crowd that the woman was named Edwards. The police had been watching her for about two wccks.

Testimony of Ben Jordan: he had seen the woman two weeks prior and told her she would have to keep off the streets. Wednesday night he saw her talking to a white man near the corner of First and Niobrara. The man came toward the Burlington Hotel and the woman going East. He did not know the white man. Jordan followed her to Niobrara Ave. and told her that she was under arrest. She began to scream for 'Arthur' as they approached the house on the east side of Niobrara. Jordan was on the inside of the walk as they passed the house. The man came out and asked what Jordan was going to do with her and was informed that he intended on locking her up. The man walked from behind Jordan and Edwards around in front of them and began firing. The first shot hit Jordan in the left hand and the second in the left knee. Jordan began firing back and didn't know positively what he had shot at. He didn't see the woman after he fell. He fired shells blindly in the direction of the man who shot him. He thought the man shot four times.

Testimony of F.H. Highland, cook at Alliance cafe: he was talking to Jordan on Wednesday night when they saw the colored woman and white man talking at the east end of the depot. He heard the man make a date with the woman. Jordan left to follow them. The white man wore a black hat and blue suit. When Highland heard three shots, he ran around to the Dismer house and the shooting re-commenced. He dodged behind the building. He saw a man in shirt sleeves running south just before the shooting stopped. Jordan fired two more shots after he started running. He didn't know if the woman was alive or dead because her eyes were open. Jordan and the woman lay about 30 feet apart.

Testimony regarding the guns: Sheriff Cox produced the gun that was used by Ben Jordan. Dick Waters, an expect on guns and bullet wounds examined the body. After examining the bullet wound in the right breast of the woman where the bullet went in and the hole in the left side, where it came out, and comparing the lead bullets from the .38 carried by Jordan the witness didn't think that the wound was caused by a lead bullet, but by a bullet from a smaller gun, like an automatic shooting a steel bullet. A lead bullet would have produced a hole twice as large. Waters was shown a bullet picked up in the nearby house and pronounced it similar to a Jordan bullet, also the flattened loose bullet found in the woman's clothes.

Testimony of L.W. Jackson, undertaker: testified as to the removal of the bullet and the bullet pierced clothes of the woman.

Testimony of Samuel Shelton, porter at the Elks club: having served 5 years in the regular army and 3 years in the Philippines, he noticed that steel jacketed bullets went through bodies, leaving a clean hole, but hole where the lead bullets came out was almost always larger that the place it went in.

Testimony of Gertrude Jackson, colored woman: she was not acquainted with the parties until recently. She had only met Bertie Edwards the morning of her death. She described the missing negro as being light brown colored, rather tall and slender, with two upper teeth missing. She said they had heard loud talking Wednesday night which sounded like somebody calling Oscar with the answer being, 'All right in a minute.' Then there were four shots that sounded light, then eight that sounded heavier, almost like a cannon. After the shooting they heard a man walk into the house, slam the door after him, stay a minute or two and come out. They were scared and did not see where he went.

Testimony of Sheriff Cox: he and Officer Hill entered the shack occupied by Edwards and the woman and found a complete opium smoking outfit. The pipe was still warm as though it had been recently used. The door was locked and had to be kicked open.

Testimony of Chief of Police Jeffers: Jordan had been a duly appointed officer of the law for the past two weeks and that his instructions were to attend to the colored quarter alone and have nothing to do with the white people. Jordan had talked about the dead woman and Jeffers told Jordan if she did not stay off the streets at night to arrest her and lock her up. Jordan was acting on instructions. Jeffers was asked why there was need of having a colored man on the police form. He stated that the past summer the Burlington had shipped ten or twelve loads of negroes to the Wyoming railroad work and the treatment and wages accorded has not been sufficient to pay their way back to the starting point after a summer's work. Lots of them drop off in Alliance as this is the first place of importance after quitting their job. They have no money and can't find work. Others take up with some women and the least work they can do the better they like it. Conditions in the colored quarter were getting worse each day. After some consideration, and a talk with the mayor it was decided to put Jordan on the the force as a special deputy whose duty it was to look after the colored section and attempt to clear it up. It was felt that he would understand their habits and traits. He was not to receive any pay unless he made arrests. Conditions have greatly improved since Jordan started working for the police and undesirables have been forced to leave town.

The woman had been in Alliance about three weeks and part of this time was spent in walking the streets after night. Jordan told her several times prior to the murder to keep out of sight and she paid little attention to him. The woman called, "Arthur, Arthur" as she and Jordan approached her home near the corner of Niobrara and Second.

Account of Shooting: Jordan saw the body on the ground and thought he had killed the assailant. Crawling closer he discovered it was the body of the woman. She had died within four minutes. Blood poured from her mouth and trickled onto the ground around her head. Upon examination it was determined that one of the bullets had entered her body near her waist, coming out at the arm pit on the left side. The other entered the right side. A description of the assailant was wired to all ranches and towns in the area. All outgoing trains were stopped at the city limits and searched. The railroad yards and colored quarters were searched. The morning after the shooting, automobiles searched the hills and ranches. He was identified as Archie Edwards, five feet eight inches tall, weighing 135 to 140 pounds, white shirt and no cap, no coat, two teeth out in front. Blue pants hole in seat, very thick lips.

Police carefully searched the house occupied by the couple. It is possible that Edwards was an opium fiend and the lack of funds had made it impossible for him to receive another supply. When the woman called out his name, it is thought he was crazed and grabbed the gun, commencing to shoot."

10 October 1913
"Edwards Waives The Preliminary
Alleged Slayer Returned to Jail Without Bail. His Story of the Trouble

Archie Edwards, accused of murder appeared before Judge Zurn the morning of 10 October 1913.
Through his attorney, H.M. Bullock, Edwards entered a plea of not guilty and waived examination. He
was held for the next term of District Court without bail.

Sheriff Cox brought Edwards, handcuffed, back to Alliance, earlier in the week, from Lincoln. He was
taken from the Lincoln jail to the train and put in leg irons. Once the train arrived in Alliance he was
taken to sheriff's office. At that time he made the following statement, 'I was figuring on starting a
shining parlor in the room formerly owned by George Curtis. In order to get enough money to swing the
deal I tried to pawn a gun at several of the saloons, and finally at the second hand store. The proprietor of
the store told me to get the gun and he would see what it was worth. I had just entered the house to get
the gun .... I rushed out of the house in time to see a colored man wrestling with her and seemed as
though they were on the ground. Just as I got near them, the man, whom I afterwards found out was
Jordan, told me to put my hands up. I did so and while they were in the air he commenced shooting at
me. I backed up and stumbled over a fence, falling to the ground. It was then that I pulled my gun and
commenced shooting in self defense. One of Jordan's bullets hit me on the finger before I commenced to
shoot. I was a little rattled as the report of Jordan's gun sounded like a cannon and kept ringing in my
ears all the next day. I only had three shells in my gun and as soon as they were fired I retreated to the
house, grabbed my hat and coat from the table in the kitchen, slammed the door shut and made off to the
East. I walked to Antioch and caught a freight train and finally landed in Lincoln Sunday. It was then
that I heard for the first time that my wife was dead. Had I known that she had been killed I never would
have left Alliance as she was the only friend I had and it was to protect her that I first commence to shoot.

Edwards was asked about the opium pipe found in his room and he said he knew nothing of it and never
used drugs of any kind. If there was any opium done in the house, he knew nothing about it. Apparently
there was a shooting in Lincoln involving Edwards. He stated that the people with whom he was staying
were bootleggers and they opened fire on the officers, thinking that the law was descending on them. The
officers had reported that Edward was the one shooting and his gun was still warm when handed over to
them. Officers reported that the opium pipe was still warm when they raided his house after the shooting
in Alliance. The bed showed marks of being recently occupied. If his story was true that he was going to
show the gun to the second hand dealer, that is untrue as the store was closed at that time of night.

Edwards stated that he was twenty-nine years of age, born in Durham, North Carolina, where his mother
was still living. His deceased wife's folks live in St. Louis. Archie Edwards had lived in Nebraska for
eighteen years, with this being his first arrest. He was a chef and worked in many of the larger hotels."

Omaha-World Herald, Omaha, Nebraska, 6 October 1913, page 1
"Arrested in Lincoln After Gun Battle
Archie Edward, Wanted at Alliance for Murder of Wife, is Captured
Patrolman Shot in Leg and Companion of Colored Man Is Wounded
(Special Dispatch to the World-Herald from a Staff Correspondent)
Lincoln, Neb., Oct 5. — Archie Edwards, colored, who killed his wife at Alliance last Tuesday and who
shot and wounded Special Officer Jordan in a pistol duel afterwards, was captured here today following a
gun fight between the local police, the murderer, and two negro women. In the melee Patrolman H.A.
Burns was severely wounded in the groin, and Herman McCurly, at whose house Edwards was captured,
was shot through the leg. Edwards was finally overpowered by Captain Barrett and Patrolman Erickson.
The two negro women made their escape.

Edwards reached Lincoln shortly after noon today. According to his story told to the Chief of Police Malone after he was arrested, he walked from Alliance to Antioch Tuesday night. Since then he has been stealing night rides on freight trains. During the day time he hid in outbuildings and hay stacks. As soon as he reached this city he took a street car to McCurly's home. The two, together with the pair of negro women, were just sitting down to a late dinner when the police broke in on them.

Edward retreated at once to the kitchen, followed by Officers Erickson and Burns. He opened fire at once with a .28 caliber revolver. Officer Burns had fired only twice when he went down, struck by a bullet from Edwards' gun. Erickson covered Edwards the next instant, and the negro at once gave up the fight, without offering further resistance.

The negro women who had opened fire on the officers stationed outside the house, made their getaway, while the policemen were shackling Edwards, and attending to their wounded fellow patrolman.

Chief Malone was the first man to discover Edwards' presence in the city. As he was riding down the street in his automobile he saw a negro turn in at a tobacco store. The chief began reviewing the burly black man's physical and facial characteristics in his mind, and had not gone far when he was convinced that it was the Alliance colored man. He stopped at the Burlington depot and called the police station at once. There he was informed that a call had just come in from a local negro who said that Edwards was in the city and on the way to McCurly's home.

Alliance officials were notified during the afternoon and word was received that Sheriff Cox would come here at once to take the negro back to the scene of the first crime."

Box Butte County, Nebraska Criminal Case
District Court
Case 2277 Docket J page 217
The State of Nebraska vs Archie Edwards
Murder
filed 15 Oct 1913

Complaint - 5 Oct 1913 Archie Edwards, late of Box Butte County on 1 Oct 1913 in Box Butte County killed Bertie Edwards with a pistol or revolver, charged with gunpowder and leaden or steel bullets. Declared deliberate and premeditated malice that he killed her. She was shot in the right side of her breast receiving a mortal wound and died instantly. A warrant was issued for his arrest on 5 Oct 1913 and he was pursued to Lincoln, Nebraska and arrested, brought back to Alliance. He pled not guilty as charged and waived preliminary hearing. He was held without bail. His attorney was H.M. Bullock. 28 Oct 1913 in court he pled guilty to murder in the second degree.
Witnesses: Ben Jordan, L.W. Corlss (Corliss?)

Verdict: imprisonment in the state penitentiary of Lincoln, Nebraska and kept at hard labor, Sundays excepted, for 22 years, none in solitary confinement.

Archie Edwards, born about 1882
sentenced from Box Butte Co., Nebraska
murder
22 years
Prisoner Number 6180 2

1920 US Census, Lancaster Co., Nebraska, State Penitentiary, ED 103, Page 4B 3
    A. Edward, black, 37, single, b. MT, father b. NC, mother b. NM, cook

Within the file detailed above, Case 2277 Docket J page 217, several letters are found. They are as follows.

Letter - 6 October 1920
" Mr. Eugene Barton, Alliance, Neb.
Dear Mr. Burton: We have a young colored boy here, by the name of Archie Edwards who came in from your town and was prosecuted by you. Archie is one of our best prisoners and I am anxious that he get consideration before the board of pardons. He can get no recommendations of all the officials here and a word from you would be of great help to him. He has had no work of a —- here for several years and I have a close personal acquaintance with him, and am interested in his welfare. Sincerely yours, Thos. A. Maxwell, Chaplain"

Letter - 12 November 1920, Alliance, Nebr.
"Thos. A. Maxwell, Lincoln, Nebr.
Dear Brother Maxwell: Your letter at hand this morning. Will be glad to give you needed information. Eugene Burton's law partner is Robert O. Reddish. Attorney H.M. Bullock died about two months ago and I conducted his funeral services. Since writing you before I had a consultition [sic] with a colored man of Alliance, Sam Shelton by name. Sam was a special officer at the time of Archie Edwards' trouble here. He tells me that he was one of the first if not the first on the scene of the shooting and that he is sure that the killing of the girl was unintentional. He also says that Attorney Burton was mistaken about confusing Archie with a coke fiend at that time. Hoping that this information will be helpful to you and extending best wishes, I am, Yours fraternally, Stephen J. Epler"

Letter - 17 November 1920
"Mr. Robt. O. Reddish, Alliance, Nebr. Dear Mr. Reddish: We have a young man here, sentenced from Alliance 7 years ago. Your law partner was the prosecuting attorney at that time, and will remember the case … Archie Edwards. His prison record here is fine and the circumstances of the case are such that if the proper effort is made he may get consideration from the pardon board. What would be the probable expense of having you get a satisfactory and helpful letter as possible from Judge Westover, Mr. Burton and Sam Shelton, the party mentioned in the enclosed letter? Let me hear from you as soon as possible, giving your terms for handling the case for Archie. Your truly, Thos. G. Maxwell, Chaplain, Neb. State Pen., Lincoln, Nebr. P.S. We are desirous of having you handle this, as it would be difficult for Mr. Burton to push it as instantly as it ought to be worked. TGM"

The following letter in the file folder is not signed.
Letter - 19 November 1920
"Rev. Thomas A. Maxwell, Chaplain, State Penitentiary, Lincoln, Nebraska. Dear Sir: Your letter of October 6, directed to me and your letter of November 17, addressed to Robert O. Reddish, was handed me and in response to same beg to state: On the 6th day of October 1913, I, as County Attorney, filed a complaint against Archie Edwards, charging him with the murder of Beatrice Edwards, his wife, on the first day of October 1913. As I recall the facts in this matter, Edwards for a short time prior to October 1, had been running a cleaning and pressing establishment here in Alliance, and on the night of September 30 or the morning of October 1, there had been some disturbance about his place and a colored man by the name of Ben Jordan, who was at that time a special officer, went to investigate the trouble at the Edwards house and shortly afterwards the shooting started. Ben Jordan using a .38 calibre revolver, shooting lead bullets, Edwards using an automatic revolver, shooting steel bullets, and during the affray Edward's wife was killed and Edwards escaped, and Ben Jordan was also wounded during the shooting. At the Coroner's inquest it was gone into as thoroughly as could be done at that time and from the witnesses who were called and the statement of the Doctor who made the examination of the body, there was no question but that Edwards had fired the shot that killed his wife. The next we learned of Edwards was when he has been captured and arrested in Lincoln, after having shot a police man there, and my recollection is that it was Officer Burns, (However I might be mistaken as to the name). Upon learning of

his arrest, C.M. Cox, Sheriff of this county at that time, went to Lincoln and brought Edwards back and on the 28th day of October, he entered a plea of guilty to murder in the second degree and was sentenced on said day to a term of twenty-two (22) years in the penitentiary, and I have had no knowledge of him from that time up until the receipt of your letters. I had no personal acquaintance with Edwards prior to this trouble and know nothing as to his character prior to this trouble, but I was informed at that time that he was either a morphine or cocaine addict, and when under the influence of the drug was a very dangerous man. As stated above, as to this I have no personal knowledge and I presume you could get some first hand information from the Police force at Lincoln, relative to this man and also relative to the wounding of one of the officers. I have no knowledge as to whether Sam Shelton was a special officer at that time or not, but know that he was one of the parties who gave some information relative to the shooting. I am of the opinion that the killing of Edward's wife was unintentional on his part and that his intentions were and he was attempting to kill Ben Jordan, and that his attempt was malicious and for this reason filed complaint for murder in the first degree, as the accidental killing of one to maliciously kill another would be murder in the first degree. You can see from the above statements that I have no personal knowledge relative to Edwards prior to this crime and of course I have no knowledge of him since; and for these reasons I am not in a position to make any recommendations as to a pardon or parol; and for the same reasons I am not in a position and have no reasons or inclination to file any protest to his application to either, and if the Pardon Board sees fit to either pardon or parol, if his conduct has been such as to deservance, there is no objection whatever on my part, but before so doing or taking any action in this matter I would suggest that you interview the Police force of Lincoln relative to making his arrest. In response to your letter to Mr. Reddish as to getting letters from Judge Westover, myself and Sam Shelton, and the terms for fees and same, beg to advise you that neither Mr. Reddish or myself ask fees for given information to the Pardon board and I presume that Judge Westover is in the same position as myself, and knows nothing relative to Edwards other than is shown by the court records in the Information and Sentence. Sam Shelton is a colored man here who is thought well of as a colored man, and if you will write direct to him I feel safe in saying that Sam will give you the information he has as to Edwards."

The following letter was not signed.
Letter - 16 December 1921
"Board of Pardons, Lincoln, Nebraska. Gentleman: In Re: Archie Edwards, No. 6180
Relative to the application of Archie Edwards for a pardon from the sentence for a period of twenty-two years in the penitentiary of the state of Nebraska imposed upon him on the 28th day of October 1913 by the district court of Box Butte County, Nebraska beg to advise; That I, the undersigned, was at that time the county attorney of Box Butte County and filed a complaint against Archie Edwards for murder in the first degree, and as I recall the facts, and after having talked the matter over with some of the witnesses who appeared before the Coroner I believe the following statements to be correct; that either on the night of September 30th or the morning of October 1st, 1913, during a difficulty or controversy between a colored man by the name of Ben Jordon and Archie Edwards, some trouble arose, on which I have no knowledge, and that during the controversy there was shooting by both Edwards and Jordon, and in which Edwards' wife was killed. We made an investigation of the matter at that time and from the best evidence we could secure we came to the conclusion that Edwards had fired the shot that killed his wife. One further investigation convinced us that the killing of this woman was accidental and that there was no intent on the part of Edwards to kill or injure this woman. I believed at the time that Edwards deserved some punishment in as much as his wife had been killed in a shooting affray between himself and another colored man, although the killing of this woman was not intentional, and for that reason filed the complaint. I also believe that Edwards has been sufficiently punished for the crime he committed and would respectfully recommend that he be pardoned, paroled, or his sentence commutated, depending upon his conduct during the time already served in the penitentiary. I will gladly furnish any further information in my possession that may be desired in this matter. Yours very truly,"

Omaha World-Herald, Omaha, Nebraska, 1 October 1911, page 12

"Archie Edwards, negro who has served nearly ten years of a twenty-two year term for the accidental shooting of his wife during a gun fight with a negro policeman, Ben Jordan, at Alliance, is asking a commutation. A.D. Rogers, mayor of Alliance, at that time, writes the board that Mrs. Edwards was killed by a steel-jacket bullet similar to that used in the policeman's gun. Edward was defending his wife from arrest at that time. He fled to Lincoln after the shooting and was captured after he had barricaded himself in a house and shot Police Officer H.P. Burns, a member of the posse which captured him."

Alliance newspaper - 27 October 1922
"Box Butte Slayer is Given Commutation
Archie Edwards, negro, who was sent to the penitentiary from Box Butte county in 1913, on a charge of second degree murder in connection with the shooting of his wife, has been granted a commutation of sentence, according to an Omaha newspaper. Edwards' sentence was ten years to life imprisonment and he has now served about nine years…"

According to the *Omaha World-Herald*, Omaha, Nebraska, 29 October 1922, page 12, Archie Edwards' sentence was commuted to fifteen years. It appears that Archie Edwards, upon release from prison, made his way east to New Jersey, where he is shown on the 1930 US Census.

> 1930 US Census, Essex Co., New Jersey, Newark, ED 11, Page 10B   4
> 48-195 Mary Legon, rents, $18 month, negro, 45, widow, b. VA, both parents b.
>   VA, days work, private family
> Cutter Harris, brother, negro, 32, married, married at age 22, b. NJ, both
>   parents b. VA, chauffeur, private family
> Alla Harris, sister-in-law, negro, 32, married at age 22, b. VA, both parents b. VA,
>   days work, private families
> A. Adams, roomer, male, negro, 45, single, b. NC, both parents b. NC, laborer,
>   buildings
> Archie Edwards, roomer, negro, 47, single, b. MT, both parents b. MT, street
>   paving, city
>
> 1940 US Census, Essex Co., New Jersey, Newark, ED 25-474, Page 3A 5
> 160 James St.
> rents $10 month Archie Edwards, negro, 57, 5th grade, b. NC, same place
>   1 April 1935, chef, hotel
> Lulu, wife, negro, 47, 3rd grade, b. GA, same place 1 April 1935

****

The Alliance Weekly Times, Alliance, Box Butte Co., Nebraska, 20 January 1914
"Victims of Sunday Morning's Shooting Affray Reported Considerably Better Tuesday
Tom and Neely Smith Shot by Sollie Woods, who is Captured and Lodged in County Jail, Outgrowth of Game of Craps.

Tommy Smith, The Young Colored Boy Who Was Seriously Wounded While Gambling In The Colored Quarter Last Saturday Night, Is Reported as Considerably Better Today And The Attending Physician States That He will Recover, Barring Unforeseen Complications

A little bad whiskey, a game of craps with high stakes and a reckless negro with a big .38 caliber Colt revolver were responsible for a shooting affair among the colored population of Alliance shortly after one o'clock Sunday morning. As the result of the affray, which occurred at the home of "Sonny" Smith, 210 East First Street, "Sollie" Woods is locked up at the county jail awaiting the outcome of the injuries of his two victims, half a dozen other negroes are under arrest and Tom Smith, aged 22 and Neely Smith, aged

19, are lying at their home badly wounded, with chances against the recovery of the first named. Tom Smith is shot through the left breast, the bullet making a clean hole about an inch above the lung and not far from the heart. Neely Smith is shot through the left knee, although the bullet did not hit the knee cap. If he escapes infection from the wound, he will probably be lame for life.

The negroes state that they began shooting craps at Smith's house shortly after midnight Saturday night laying a blanket on the floor and shaking the dice to the accompaniment of the mystic 'Come eleben, come eleben.' That the stakes were large enough to make the game interesting is shown by the fact that it was of the $2.55 to $4.05 variety and that Ed May had a twenty dollar bill in the game. Some time after one o'clock, the game came to a sudden halt, when Tom Smith, who had loaned Ed May $1.05 because the latter had no small change, demanded his money back. May refused and ran to Woods, who was taking no part in this stage of the game and asked him for his revolver. In the meantime Tom Smith had gone downstairs and was besought by his father to remain down there and leave the game. Tom, however, ran upstairs again and his brother Neeley went to the stair door to persuade him to go back. As Tom entered the room, Woods fired. The first shot hit Neely in the leg and the second struck Tom in the breast. After the shooting, Woods blew out the light in the room and the Smith boys, getting down stairs as fast as they could, were followed by the rest of the frightened bunch of players.

Neely Smith's report of the shooting is this: 'Ed May owed Tommy a dollar and five cents and said he wouldn't pay. Tom said he would get it. Tom went downstairs with father and then came back again to get his money. In the meantime, Ed May ran to Sollie to get his gun. 'No' said Sollie 'I'll keep it and jes' let him darken the door and I'll knock his d—-heart out.' I went over to Sollie and asked him to have nothing to do with this, that it was just an affair between Tommy and Ed May. Then Tommy came upstairs and I ran to the door to shove him back. Just then Tommy opened the door Sollie fired, the first shot hitting me and the second, striking Tommy, just as he turned around to go back. Tommy fell against the wall and then we went down stairs and the rest followed us. We weren't more than ten feet from Sollie when he fired.

We went on the porch and Solllie came down and said he would kill the whole d—- bunch. He cocked the gun and was going to shoot Tommy, but Jes Thomas stepped in front of Tommy and saved him. We didn't do anything to Sollie to have him shoot us.'

The father of the two injured boys said: 'I was downstairs when Tommy started back upstairs. I followed and was up two or three steps when I heard the shots and Tom yelled 'Papa, I'm shot.' Both of the boys came down stairs and the bunch went out on the porch and scattered to their homes. I called up night officer J.A. Witowac and found him at the police station. We called Dr. Slagle to come and look after the boys.'

The *Times* interviewed Sollie Woods at the county jail Monday night. He claimed that he thought Tommy threatened the whole crowd with (missing area of newspaper). 'I was afraid he was going to kill me, so I shot first. He had a Winchester.' said Sollie. There is no evidence further than this, that Tom Smith either drew a razor or had a gun and that Sollie did anything else than to interfere in the quarrel of the other men.

After the shooting, Woods had the nerve to wake up Judge Zurn and was starting to swear out a warrant for the Smiths, when Sheriff Cox entered and said: 'You're the man I want' and took him to the county jail. Woods had thrown away the gun that did the shooting, but the sheriff found out where it was cached and retrieved it. It is a big Colt …. The power of the gun is so great that the bullet passed through Tom Smith's body, through the side of the house and into the air.

After Woods' arrest, the sheriff spent the rest of the night rounding up the rest of the crap shooters and at daylight had Ed May and his wife, Lilly May, three Smiths, Jesse Thomas, Dusty Norwood and H. Peat.

105

All except Woods were placed in the city prison to await their trial for gambling Tuesday morning. Part were able to get bail Sunday. When the sheriff went to arrest Ed May, the negro was in bed. He went to the door and told the sheriff that Ed was not there. He then went to the back door and attempted to flee and, although several shots were fired after him, he continued until darkness swallowed him up. He ran in his bare feet for some distance, but when he was finally caught at the round house … he was wearing a dilapidated pair of shoes."

Box Butte County, Nebraska Criminal - District Court
District Court
Criminal
Case No. 2317 Docket J page 257
The State of Nebraska vs. Sollie Woods
Shooting with intent to do great bodily injury
24 April 1914

Sollie Woods on 17 Jan 1914 in Box Butte Co., Nebraska did unlawfully, feloniousy and laiciously make and assault upon one Tommy Smith with a pistol loaded with gun powder and one leaden bullet, with intent to wound.

17 April 1914 — Sollie Wood brought into court and pled not guilty. Called Tommy Smith and Neeley Smith as witnesses.
Summoned into court: Ed Mays, Sony Smith, Tommie Smith, Mealy Smith and Dan Norwood on 5 May 1914.
27 May 1914 came into court Sollie Woods and his attorney E.H. Boyd and entered a plea of guilty and indicated … "I have nothing to say."

Verdict: imprisonment in the penitentiary of the state of Nebraska located in Lincoln; kept at hard labor, Sundays excepted, for the minimum period of one year and a maximum of one year, none to be in solitary confinement.

Sollie Woods was seeking the material testimony of Jesse Thomas, witness and was unable to procure it. Jesse Thomas was a resident of Alliance on 17 Jan 1914 and at the time of the hearing was living in Kansas City, Missouri, which was recently discovered. Thomas was present at the time of the shooting. Tommy Smith stated at the incident that he was going after a gun when he went down stairs after the quarrel and before the shooting in question. Smith said he was going to use the gun if necessary to get his money and drew a knife on Sollie Woods before going down stairs. He had been drinking just enough that he probably would have used the gun if he had succeeded. Sollie Woods asked for a continuance of the trial.

Another list of witnesses:
Sonny Smith, Tommie Smith, Neeley Smith, Ed Mays, Dr. C.E. Slage, Chuck Watkins, Dave Norwood, Jess Thomas, C. M. Cox, C.W. Jeffers
Sallie [sic] Woods was sentenced from Box Butte Co., Nebraska to the penitentiary in Lincoln, Lancaster Co., Nebraska. The cause was shooting and he was sentenced for one year. He was born about 1881. 6

****

The Alliance Times 12 April 1916
"Gunplay Flares During Battle At Spann Home
Colored Woman Says Man Johnson Attacked Her When She Remonstrated Against Profanity Heard by Children

Man Johnson, 41, colored, sometimes resident of Alliance and believed to have been a former convict in both Idaho and Wyoming penitentiaries, was shot and killed in a fight last night with Mrs. Louise Perkins, 34, also colored, at the home of Nathaniel and Willie Spann, 101 Sweetwater Avenue. Mrs. Perkins, being held in the county jail today awaiting an inquest into the killing, told officers last night that she shot Johnson in self-defense.

County Attorney William Hein said an inquest will probably be held sometime this afternoon at the Lan(?) Funeral Home, where the body of Johnson was taken.

The first report of trouble at the Spann home came to officers at ? clock last night when Mrs. William [Willie] Spann called the police station and reported a fight was in progress at her home. The call was taken by County Attorney Hein, who happened to be at the police station at the time. Chief of Police Barnum, Office ? and Hein left the station at once and drove to the Spann home. The shooting took place just before their arrival. As the officers entered the back door of the Spann home, Mrs. Perkins fled out the front door, clad only in a house dress and in her stocking feet. She was not located until about 11:30 p.m. when Frank Wright, colored resident of south Alliance, reported that she was at his home and desired to surrender to police.

Woman Tells Her Story
Questioned at the police station last night, Mrs. Perkins said she was eating supper at the Spann home with the Spann children when Johnson entered the house and started using profanity. She remonstrated against his use of such language before the youngster she said and Johnson became enraged at her. Johnson, formerly married to Mrs. Spann's sister, said he thought Mrs. Perkins, who has made her home at the Spann residence since coming here a month ago from North Platte, was 'trying to run the place,' the woman said.

Johnson dragged her from her room, to which she had fled, according to the story of Mrs. Perkins and that of Mr. and Mrs. Spann. With the help of the Spanns she got away from him the first time and returned to her room and procured a gun which had been the property of her ...."
[article could not be located for continuation]

"Negro Killed Here Witness in Recent Killing at Bluffs
James 'Man' Johnson, negro, who was slain here Monday evening in a battle with Mrs. Louise Perkins, also colored, was to have been a witness for the state in the murder trial of Bert Williams, alleged slayer of Happy Joe Camper, at Scottsbluff yesterday. In the Scottsbluff case it is alleged that Williams went to a house in Scottsbluff where Johnson was staying soon after the slaying of Camper. Johnson is reported to have said that Williams told him then that he had 'just shot a man.' John had appeared at Scottsbluff about a week before and left for Alliance when he learned the date for which Williams' trial was set."

****

The Alliance Herald, 7 May 1918
"Arrested on Rape Charge, Now in Jail
George Shields was arrested in Broken Bow on information supplied by Sheriff Cox, charging him with intent to commit rape against Edna Saunders, a thirteen year old colored girl. The crime is alleged to have been committed in a box car in the Burlington yards.

Soon after he committed his crime Shields, also colored, took a train for Broken Bow and he was arrested that Sunday afternoon. Sheriff Cox left Monday and returned today with his prisoner. The preliminary hearing was held before Judge Tash today."

****

107

Alliance newspaper   19 September 1916
"Colored Folks Get Sex Mixed and Show off

Man or woman? That is the questions that has been puzzling folks on the west side of town for the past several weeks. Robert Smith, colored, was arrested by Marshal Wheeler Monday afternoon and he will be prosecuted on a vagrancy charge. According to the complaints he has been running a boarding house and masquerading as a woman.

Jesse Wilson, a corpulent colored woman, is also under arrest for making indecent exposures of her person. She has formed the rather queer habit of making public exhibitions along the railroad track when passenger trains were in sight. The woman has been boarding with Smith, but she swears, and rather vehemently, too, that she supposed him to be a woman and never had any reason for believing otherwise. The officers have plenty of evidence against the pair by people who have witnessed their actions. Smith made several trips about town dressed in woman's attire and on rare occasions he put on male habiliments."

****

The Alliance Herald, Alliance, Nebraska, 6 February 1919, Page 1
"Young Forger Lands In The Pen Quick
Colored Laborer Wrote Check on Wrong Bank and Causes Suspicion of Merchant

Wilbur Wright, young colored laborer, who had been employed by Contractor Charles Fuller, signed the name of the latter to a check for $14.25 and tried to pass the same on an Alliance merchant Monday afternoon. The merchant had cashed smaller checks for Wright but his suspicions were aroused because the check was written on a different bank than formerly.

Wright was captured the same evening. He was taken before Judge Tash Tuesday morning and bound over to district court. He was then taken before Judge Westover and pled guilty to the charge of passing a forged check. He was immediately sentenced to from one to twenty years at hard labor and the sum of $100 and costs and started with acting Deputy Sheriff Jeffers for Lincoln that night. Wright was raised at Chadron and had gone as far as the tenth grade in high school."

****

The Alliance Herald, Alliance, Box Butte Co., Nebraska, October 1918

"One Colored Man is Sentenced in Murder
Simon Pitts, colored, was sentenced to a life term in the penitentiary at a special session, Monday, of the district court, Judge Westover presiding. Pitts was arraigned before the court and pleaded guilty as a party to the killing of Ray Wilson of Lisco, who was murdered in Alliance on the evening of September 20th, shortly after he had displayed a roll of bills. At first Pitts denied taking an active part, but when cross examined, admitted that he knew a great deal about it, but implicated another colored man, whom the officials have been after since the killing.

During the trial the officials secured some additional information regarding the leading man wanted in the case and the wires have been kept busy and they expect soon to land the other party behind the bars, to receive the same sentence as Pitts. Pitts was picked up on the main street of Alliance the next morning by Sheriff Cox and at that time told the officers they had the wrong nigger, but no chances were taken and as a result Pitts will land where he will be at home."

Alliance Newspaper - 1918
"Murderer of Ray Wilson Caught at East Moline
Albert O. Lewis, the colored barber who shot and killed Ray Wilson, of Lisco, on the streets of Alliance Sept 21, has been captured by the chief of police in East Moline, Ill. He will be brought to Alliance the last of this week for trial. Lewis left here the night of the tragedy for Denver and he finally made his way to Terre Haute, Ind., and East Moline, where he was captured. He went under various names at different places, but his right name is Albert O. Lewis. His mother lives in Chicago. He is 23 years old and stands 5 ft 6 in. A description of Lewis was sent to all of the larger cities in the country and he was recognized as the man who was convicted in Terre Haute in 1915 on a charge of shooting with intent to kill. He is also wanted by the government for desertion from the army. The gold teeth in Lewis' mouth were the chief identification mark which resulted in is arrest by the Moline officers."

The Alliance Herald, Alliance, Box Butte Co., Nebraska, 6 February 1919
"Negro Plead Guilty to Murder - Sentenced to Pen For Life Simon Pitts, Colored Accomplice, Brought from Penitentiary to Testify Against Barber Who Shot Ray Wilson

Alfred Sheffield, colored barber who was arraigned before the district court on Monday morning on the charge of murder and who pled guilty at the time, changed his plea when brought before the court this morning. On his plea of guilty he was sentenced for life in the penitentiary at Lincoln, thereby saving his neck. It is believed that a jury would have found him guilty of murder in the first degree and that the death sentence would have been the penalty.

Sheffield was charged with being the one who fired the shots that killed a white man, Ray Wilson of Garden county, on a side street in Alliance on the night of September 20, 1918. Wilson had been drinking and had flashed a roll of money at the auto races. Early that evening shots were heard on West Second street and Wilson staggered under a street light and fell dead. Suspicion was directed toward Sheffield and Pitts at once. Sheffield escaped but Pitts was captured, pled guilty and was sentenced to the pen for life, being taken to Lancaster in October.

Sheffield was captured in Illinois and brought back to Alliance some weeks ago. County Attorney — had lined up an array of evidence against him that would have undoubtedly caused his conviction on the charge of murder in the first degree. On finding Monday that Sheffield intended to stand trial, acting Deputy Sheriff Charles Jeffers went to Lincoln and brought back Pitts, who had confessed in October that Sheffield had used the gun that caused Wilson's death. Sheffield, on learning that Pitts had been brought back to testify against him, changed his plea. Pitts proved rather a hard one for deputy Jeffers to handle. He told the deputy that he had all 'they could give him' and that unless he was treated tip-top he would refuse to testify against Sheffield. Two officers will accompany the murderer back to Lincoln."

Box Butte County, Nebraska
District Court
Criminal Record
Docket L page 123 Case
State of Nebraska vs
Alfred Sheffield alias Henry McCray alias Henry Lewis
Murder
filed 18 Dec 1918

Summoned: C.M. Cox, George Darling, George Stafford, Alta Phillips, George J. Hand and Ruth McKinney 4 Feb 1919
Receipt from Nebraska State Penitentiary stating that J.W. Miller, Sheriff of Box Butte County had

delivered Alfred Sheffield on 19 Feb 1919.

On 20 Sept 1918 Alfred Sheffield (aliases) willfully, unlawfully, violently and feloniously made an assault with intent by force and violence against Ray Wilson to take a roll of currency valued at $200 from him. At the same time using a pistol loaded with gun powder and five leaden bullets, holding it in his right hand in an attempt to rob Ray Wilson shot him with the intent to kill him. Wilson sustained a mortal wound in and through the back. He died instantly.

Wittnesses: Clifford Sward, C.M. Cox, George Darling, George Stafford, Lena Lape, Simon Pitts, Ruth McKinney, Lyle Burrows, Mrs. Allany Burrow, Wm. Wilson, Dr. George J. Hand, Alta Phillips and Lee Basye. William Mitchell and Harry E. Gantz were appointed counsel for Alfred Sheffield. Sheffield pled not guilty on 4 Feb 1919.

He was charged with the crime of murder in the first degree. Simon Pitts who was then in the State Penitentiary was brought for testimony. Pitts and Sheffield both planned to rob Ray Wilson of a large sum of money. The plan was originated by Alfred Sheffield, who agreed to divide the money that they should get from Wilson, if Pitts would assist in the robbery. In the attempt Sheffield shot and killed Ray Wilson.

After counsel, Sheffield agreed to enter a plea of guilty in the second degree, which was accepted by the State of Nebraska. He was sentenced to the Penitentiary of the State of Nebraska in Lincoln for his natural life and kept at hard labor, Sundays and holidays excepted, not to be kept in solitary confinement. Sheffield was to pay $154.10 in costs.

Simon Pitts
born about 1847
murder, sentenced from Knox County
life sentence #7396 7

Alfred Sheffield, aka Henry Lewis, aka Al McCray
born about 1898
murder, sentenced from Box Butte County
life sentence #7448 8

1920 US Census, Lancaster Co., Nebraska, State Penitentiary, ED 103, Page 1A 9
Al Sheffield, black, 21, single, b. OH, both parents b. PA, barber

****

The Alliance Times 9 February 1919
"Brown, Woodley and Sheffield Are Defendants in Criminal Cases Which Opened Before Jury This Afternoon

The principal session of the February 1919 term of the district court convened at 1:30 this afternoon when the case of the State vs Brown opened for jury trial. The case is the aftermath of a gambling game which ended in a row. The colored men got into a fight, and one of them received a gash in the face which nearly severed his head. The prosecution will attempt to prove that Brown wielded the knife.

The case of the State vs Woodley is on appeal from the county court where Woodley was convicted of selling whiskey. Woodley is a porter in a chair car.

The third and most important case on the docket is that of the State vs. Sheffield, the colored man brought back from Chicago to stand trial for the murder of Arthur Wilson last September. Sam Pitts, the colored man who plead guilty to a share in the crime, will be brought back from Lancaster, where he is serving a twenty-year term to give testimony to this case. Sheffield intimated when he was first brought back that he would plead guilty, but he has changed his mind and now enters a plea of not guilty to first degree murder."

NEBRASKA STATE PENITENTIARY

TO THE CLERK OF COURT,   , LANCASTER, NEB.,   FEB 13 1919   191

This Doth Certify, That _____ D. W. Miller _____ Sheriff of _____ Box Butte _____ County,

Nebraka, did, on the day of the date hereof, deliver to me at the Penitentiary, at Lancaster, the body of

_____ Clarence Pitts, _____

who was, tried, convicted, and sentenced, at the _____ taken out as a Witness _____ Term 191__, of the District Court of said County,

in the case of Alfred Sheffield, at Alliance Nebr.

held at _____ Neb., 191__   Jas. O'Connell

                                                                  Chief Clerk

The Alliance Herald, Alliance, Nebraska 11 May 1920
"Charles Brown is Found Guilty
Convicted by Jury of Felonious Assault on Willie Brown … To Be Sentenced Today

Charles Brown, colored, was found guilty by a jury in district court Saturday of felonious assault on Willie Brown, colored with intent to do great bodily injury. The jury was out only a s short time. Judge Paine has not yet passed sentence, but this is expected to be done today, in order that Brown may be taken to the penitentiary with John Gill, convict, who was here to testify in the Lackey case.

The evidence offered by the state was to the effect that Brown had been keeping company with Miss Foster. On March 1, she was down town and passed by the Sam Shelton cafe, where Brown was eating breakfast. The time was about 11:30 a.m. He left the restaurant, followed her up the street a distance of half a block behind, and continued to stick around until she started for home, when he struck in ahead of her. At a point near her home Brown crossed the street, stopped her and her companion, Mrs. English, and after telling her that he had 'told her not to go out of the house' struck her with his open hand. In his other hand was an open knife. Willie ducked and ran into the house while Mrs. Essie English, Willie's companion, picked up a couple of convenient quart bottles and calmed him down. Brown stayed outside for some time, trying to pick up a quarrel and was finally arrested by Chief Nova Taylor.

The testimony was highly interesting, and furnished fully as good entertainment as it did in the county court when the preliminary was held. The witnesses were, on motion by Attorney Harry Gantz, excluded from the court room until they had testified.

Willie Foster, the first witness called, said that she had lived in Alliance three years. She is now staying at the home of Mrs. English. She had known Charles Brown for two years, and had been his sweetheart for six months. She told of the events leading up to the attack, and positively declared that the knife held in Brown's hand was open.

Brown's defense was that he had not followed Miss Foster; that he had remained on the street because a band with a minstrel show in town March 1 was giving a concert, and that he had done nothing more than strike Miss Foster was his open hand. The knife he declared, was not drawn until Mrs. English 'butted in' and that he had no intention of using it, though he had threatened to do so ... on Mrs. English. He denied that the knife introduced in evidence by the state was his property, although he admitted he had a knife. He did not explain by what right he had ordered the plaintiff to stay off the street, or why he had 'promised her a beating.'

Mrs. Essie English was the second witness called by the state and she corroborated Miss Foster's testimony in every detail, and told a lot more beside. It was she who advised Willie to run after Charles had struck her. She said that she reached for the quart bottles as soon as she saw him draw back his hand. When she had them in her hand, she addressed Charles thusly: 'If you touch that girl again, I'll bust your head wide open.' To which Charles gallantly made reply: 'If you butt in here, I'll slit your throat from ear to ear.'

Whereupon, seeing that Willie was safe, she retreated to the house, Brown remaining outside, daring them to come out. Mrs. English quoted him as saying: 'If you don't believe I'll kill her, just throw her out. Just you throw her out, that's all.' Mrs. English said she threatened to 'call the law.' 'Damn the law," was the way Charles expressed his sentiments.

On cross-examination, she denied that she told Charles that she'd take a 'pistol and blow his ___ brains out if it wasn't for the fact that he wasn't worth going to Lincoln for.' 'No, sah," she told the court, 'I don't use that kind of language.'

Willie G. James, 115 Sweetwater, was the state's next witness. She said she lived next door, and on hearing the noise of the racket came to the door. She said she saw the open knife in Brown's hand. On cross-examination she denied that she had quarreled with the defendant over a gambling debt of $5. Brown testified that she had lost that sum to him, but that she had paid only half of it, and that he had to threaten to tell her husband before she would kick in with the balance. When asked what Brown did for a living, she said: 'I never did know Charles to work anywhere.'

Nova Taylor told of making the arrest and searching Brown, taking a knife off him. She said that Brown told him, on the way to the station that he would have 'cut her ____ guts out if it hadn't been for Mrs. English.' Taylor also testified that Brown didn't work.

Sheriff Miller identified the knife as having been given to him by the Alliance police as Brown's. Brown then testified in his own behalf. He had finished a late breakfast, and that he had no intention to following the ladies when they passed by. He was listening to the band. He denied the conversation with Chief Taylor. When asked what he did for a living, he said, 'I work some ... and play some ... just like the rest of them.' According to his evidence, he had held a job just two months out of the three years he had been in the city."

****

The Alliance Herald, 30 December 1904
"Special Term of Court
Charles H. Brown, colored, who broke into the section house at Girard Christmas day securing a considerable amount of money and jewelry, also plead guilty and was given three years at hard labor."

The Alliance Herald, 6 February 1919, page 1

"Charles Brown, colored, charged with wielding a knife which caused serious injury to another colored man, plead guilty to assault and battery. A fine of $100 and costs was imposed and Brown promised to leave the country."

****

The Alliance Herald, Alliance, Nebraska, 11 May 1920
"Colored Gamblers In Police Court

Eight gentlemen of color, and one lady of the same complexion, received fines in police court after a legal struggle of four hours in which there was both testimony and oratory. Attorney Earl Meyer substituted for City Attorney Metz during the trial, which was one of the most interesting in weeks. The charge was gambling. The eight men received fines of $10 and costs, a piece, a total of $15, while Willie James, the woman, was assessed $25 and costs, largely because it was in the rooming house conducted by her that the gambling was going on.

Arrest was made at a raid at 115 Sweetwater Friday evening by Chief of Police Taylor and Night Watch Trabert. They told of surrounding the premises, and lying in wait till the game started. The chief then took a look through one of the windows, and saw a large number of men gathered about a table. He heard the rattle of dice, and words sounding like 'Big Dick' and 'Little Joe' and others which furnished sufficient evidence to convince him that money was changing hands pretty rapidly. He then entered the house, gained entrance to the room by shoving his foot where it was needed when the door was opened. There was a general scattering, the chief managed to hold eight men and capture one deck of cards, one pair of bones and a trifle over $8 in money.

Every one of the captured men failed to be impressed by a night in jail and in firm, strong voices they pleaded not guilty to the charge of gambling. It was only an innocent card game, and every one of them averred that they were just playing whist to pass away the weary hours, and they proved that they knew how to play whist, too. They hinted that Chief Taylor was trying to 'get' them. It was a peaceful story that they told, every one of them, with little variation in the details.

It seems that the evenings are sometimes long and dull on Sweetwater. There is no place down town where a colored man may spend his leisure hours and Willie James, in her rooming house, has set apart a sort of back parlor as a club room. There is a piano, a card table and a refrigerator, from which the land-lady sells Bevo and pop and other harmless liquors at a reasonable price. The evening in question, then people testified, they were playing whist. One man was at the piano, furnishing music. Every now then someone would buy Bevo for the house. Into this peaceful scene the police thrust themselves, noisily, rudely and with profanity.

The men were backed up against the wall, ordered to hold up their hands and be searched. The land-lady was relieved of a second pair of dice, but she came by them in a right and proper way, having taken them off 'her aunt's little boy' only that noon. Willie also explained the presence of the money on the table. It seems that some brother had just given her a ten-dollar bill to buy the drinks (soft drinks) for the crowd, and she had gone into her room, adjoining, to get the correct change for this money. It seems that she had brought the wrong amount — or that he had decided to pay his room rent, too, while he had the money, and she had to go back for more change. Instead of taking the money she had brought back to her room with her, she had laid it down on the table. Unfortunately, that was the moment that the police came in.

It was plain to be seen that everything was open and above-board, and that everyone of them denied there was so much as a hint of gambling. The court wasn't convinced. Judge Roberts listened to the evidence and the pleas, and proceeded to assess fines right and left. Only two escaped, one of whom was the piano player."

113

[Bevo was a non-alcoholic malt beverage, also referred to as near beer. It was popular during prohibition when beer, wine and distilled liquors were illegal.] 10

Willie James, the landlady was the same Willie James who married Nathaniel Spann. She was the madam of a house on Sweetwater Avenue in Alliance. Refer to the Spann in Section 4 for more information.

****

Alliance, Box Butte Co., Nebraska newspaper June, 1920s
"Colored Woman Fined for Sale of Intoxicants

'Jedge, ah knew there was a law agin' sellin' moonshine, but ah didn't know there was one again peddlin' beah.' declared Emma Mandez, 28, colored, when arraigned before County Judge Ira E. Tash Tuesday afternoon on a charge of selling beer. The court holding that ignorance of the law is no excuse for violations, netted out a fine of $100 and costs and the dusky maiden immediately began making arrangements to pay it. After about an hour she obtained funds to meet the fine.

State, county and city officers paid a visit to the Mandez place in South Alliance last Monday evening. The raid resulted in the arrest of the woman and the seizure of several bottles of beer.

Two other liquor cases were disposed of Tuesday by Judge Tash. Alvin Riley of three miles northwest of the city pleaded guilty to charges of illegal possession and was fined $100 and costs. James H. Dougherty pleaded guilty to a similar charge and received a fine of the same amount."

****

The Alliance Herald, 20 July 1920, Page 1
"Railroad Sends out Colored Men
City Authorities Should Call Their Attention to Effect of Their Policy

For the past several weeks, Alliance has been flooded with negroes. Every freight train brings in a new gang, and it keeps the city police officers busy filling out their walking papers and urging them to be on their way. No sooner has one batch been disposed of than another one comes in. They fill the passenger station and accumulate in cool, shady spots outside.

And the railroad is to blame for it, according to information which reaches this office. These men are all sent out here from points east to work on various railroad projects in Wyoming, Montana and Nebraska. But a large portion of them do not go to work or remain at work. If their ticket reads Alliance, they are quite apt to get off at Seneca. If their ticket reads to some point further west, they are quite likely to decide that Alliance is as far as they care to go. If they do go on to their destination, they seldom work longer than it takes them to get one or two pay checks, and then they rest.

It wouldn't be so bad if they'd go back to Chicago or some of the places where they were recruited. When winter comes along, it is quite probably that they will do that very thing. But it is several months before winter, and in the meantime Alliance and every other place where a number of trains come and go will be flooded with them. By this time, the railroad ought to realize that the floaters they have been hiring won't stick on the job. But the trainloads that come to and through Alliance don't show any let-up. There is an inexhaustible supply in the cities, and so long as the colored men are willing to accept a free ride without any intention to work, it is probable that the railroads will dig up transportation, unless some of the cities that have … real grief call attention to the imposition in no uncertain terms.

Now, there are hundreds of colored people in Alliance who work hard and who stay on the job. This sort

114

of employee is indispensable no matter what his color. But there are a lot of others who hang around, living as best they can and working as little as they can. When the court records are consulted, and it is discovered that of those sent to the penitentiary, less than one out of ten comes from this county, it's time that someone let out a howl. It costs money to arrest and convict these floaters. Some of them will come here anyway, but the railroads shouldn't shoot them out here in carloads.

Here's a fair sample. Dee Winters, colored, arrested by Special Agent Smith, arrived in Alliance on freight train No. 46 Sunday morning. He admitted to the court that he had beat his way. On search, it was discovered that he had $100 in Burlington pay checks in his pockets. He had worked just a month, and grown tired of labor. Instead of using the money to get back to Chicago, he decided to beat his way. He took the first train out, and landed in Alliance. Ten minutes later he landed in jail. Monday morning in justice court he was fined $5 and costs, a total of $10, paid the fine, and probably beat his way to the next town.

And another story: Mitchell Field, likewise colored, was sent out to Mitchell, Neb., on a railway labor gang. He probably came for the ride for his arrival at Mitchell he told the court, things didn't suit him. He couldn't get a place to sleep. Trouble with him was that he didn't want to work. The Burlington furnishes its workmen a place to bunk. So Mitchell Field walked (at least he says so, and far be it from us to disbelieve him, no matter how often the freight trains run or how good his shoes look) to Bridgeport. Here, it seems, he was unable to find work, and he drifted to Alliance. He was just on his way to ask for a job at the roundhouse when the police nabbed him as a vagrant. Judge Roberts fined him $5 and costs, and suspended the fine for twenty-four hours, during which time Mitchell was given to understand that he was to get his job or get out of town.

These are just a couple of cases. If you want to get an idea of the number of idle men in the city, take a walk to the passenger station or the railroad yards and use your eyes. Then ask yourself why the railroad companies can't, in the interest of the cities they serve, use a little more care in sorting out laborers. You'll probably have to answer your own riddle, but it will do no harm to ask it."

****

The Alliance Herald, 20 July 1920
"Four Fined For Playing Poker
Two More Produce Plausible Alibis, But Finley's Tale Fails to Get By

Jim Johnson drew a fine of $25 and costs, and Joe Collier, Henry Washington and Albert Finley $15 and costs each in police court Monday morning when tried before Judge Roberts on a gambling charge Monday morning. Charles Smith and Dave Brown were discharged, due to lack of sufficient evidence to convict. All of the defendants are colored and all of them told substantially the same story.

The arrest was made by Chief of Police Reed, Burlington Special Agent T.J. Smith and Night Watchman Al Roland at Johnson's home on Sweetwater about 11 o'clock Saturday evening. The officers testified that before they entered the room they heard sounds which could be used only in a poker game, and on their entrance they discovered five of the men seated at a table with five cards dealt out to each one. There was some $28 on the table. This number of cards, so we are informed, is the regulation poker hand. One man, Smith, was lying on a bed in an adjoining room apparently sleeping soundly. It required some labor to awaken him to place him under arrest. The men were escorted to the station and some of them gave cash bail for appearance Monday morning. The others were guests of the city until the trial.

Albert Finley, colored, has a vivid imagination. Moreover, he has a poker face. With impassive countenance and every evidence of sincerity he told the court a wild tale of the way in which the money happened to be on the table when the officers entered. This is the tale:

It seems that for three years, Albert has carried a 'lucky piece,' a $20 gold coin. Of late he has been doubtful whether this was really lucky. He had begun to think it might be 'jonah.' Only last week he was arrested at his place of employment, the Harvey cafe, on the charge of manufacturing intoxicants and he finally admitted to City Attorney Metz that the court had found him guilty of the charge and he paid a fine. It was this unfortunate experience that led him to believe that his lucky coin was a jinx, and so he decided to part with it.

On Saturday evening, Finley said, he had got through work about quarter after ten, and there being no place of recreation or amusement in Alliance where a colored man was welcome, he wandered up to his friend's home. There he found a number of other colored men, all in the same fix. These men sitting about the table visiting. Dave Brown was awaiting a phone call from Casper, Wyo. Charley Smith was taking a nap. The others were passing the time away in conversation. Suddenly Finley thought about the jinx. He told the others and one of them offered to buy it. Thereupon Finley, in order to make it worth while and to avoid trading money, which everybody knows is unlucky offered the $20 coin and a ring for $25. His offer was accepted. The purchaser was counting out the cash when the police came. Finley denied there were any cards on the table or in the house, so far as he knew. His testimony was substantiated by the others.

The police officers didn't bring the cards into court, but their testimony convinced the judge that there had been gambling, and the fines were imposed. The session was enlivened by the pleas of Attorney H.E. Gantz who pointed out the sad plight of the colored man in Alliance. Another interesting feature was the refunding of the money taken at the time of the raid. Every colored witness insisted that the money in sight belonged to Finley, but when they commenced paying it back every one crowded around and looked interested. One of them claimed a portion of it, but when reminded of his testimony that the money was Finley's, explained that 'the cops didn't get any of his money, but if any of it did belong to him, he wanted it.' Finley got it all, and paid his fine with it. After all, it was his story and he should have stuck with it."

****

District Court
Box Butte Co., Nebraska
Criminal Court
Case No. 2039 — Docket "H" 106
Burglary
State of Nebraska vs Willie Sneed
16 July 1920

On 12 July 1920 Willie Sneed willfully, unlawfully and feloniously and burgulary about the house of eleven o'cock in the night season of the same day in said county, break and enter the dwelling house of Heubert Adams in Box Butte County, Nebraska, with the intent then and there to steal and take and carry away the property of Adams situated in said dwelling house. Willie Sneed was late of the county of Box Butte.

He took from the dwelling house of Heubert Adams, one gold watch chain, one coin purse of the value of $40, the personal property of said Adams. Sneed was arrested and brought into court, arraigned and pled to both counts. The court found that there was enough evidence to charge the defendant as guilty. Willie Sneed was to appear for trial the next term of District Court, with bond fixed at $500 and confinement in the Box Butte County Jail.

Journal Entry-District Court 3 August 1920
Willie Sneed pled guilty. Adjudged by the court that Sneed be taken to the State Penitentiary located in

Lancaster Co., Nebraska and to remain for not less than one year and no more than ten years.

The Alliance Herald, 20 July 1920, Page 1
"Willie Sneed, colored, who was arrested by Chief of Police Reed at the colored church last Wednesday evening and who was charged with breaking and entering, as well as larceny, pleaded guilty in county court Saturday afternoon, and was bound over to district court for trial. Bond was placed at $500, which was not furnished."

Nebraska Prison Records Database
William Sneed, born about 1902
sentenced from Box Butte County
Prisoner number #7889
sentence for 1-10 years
Reel Number RG034#4 11

****

The Alliance Herald, 27 July 1920
"Alliance A Poor Place to Loaf

Some of these days the word will be passed, as they say in the navy, that Alliance is an unhealthy place for hoboes, either white or colored. Since the last issue of *The Herald*, no less than four vagrants have been tried and fined in police court, and at present four tired men are at work on the city's streets and will continue to labor until their fines are worked out.

The roster includes Charles Rogers, colored, who will work out a fine of $20 and costs; Sam Keith, likewise colored, whose fine and costs amount to $30; and John Williams, colored too, who was nicked $25 and costs. One white man, Lloyd Samson, was picked up Monday and is out with the colored brethren in an effort to satisfy a fine of $10 and costs. These arrests were made Saturday and Monday. One of these men, Sam Keith, was charged with carrying concealed weapons as well as vagrancy.

There is no letup as yet in the number of the Sons of Rest who come into Alliance riding on freight trains. They still infest the depot and yards, and the police are busy shooing them out of town or picking them up when they get nasty. Some of these fellows get pretty hard boiled when told to move on, but a little persuasion generally convinces them that they have no kick coming.

'Sergeant' Reed, the black dog belonging to Chief Reed, is an invaluable aid in rounding up the loafers. He is a mild mannered dog, who likes to scratch for fleas as well as any hound, but he resents it when anyone uses rough language to the chief. If you have any doubts, try it."

****

The Alliance Herald, 27 July 1920
"Still On Lookout for Colored Men

The police are still doing their best to locate 'Red Mike' and Charles Smith, two colored men who are said to have broken into the home of Gertrude Jackson, colored, at 105 Sweetwater, last week, as well as having robbed two colored employees of Sam Shelton of $257 and $46 respectively. A report came in from Gering that two men answering the descriptions had been captured but they proved to be only two of the regulation loafers that have been infesting this part of the country for the last month or two.

'Red Mike' and his friend made their last evening in Alliance a busy one. The first place they visited was the Jackson home where they made away with a gun. They next visited the place about a mile and half out of town where Sam Shelton keeps horses and wagons for his scavenger business. They knocked at the door and it was opened by an old colored man. They shoved the gun in his face and relieved him of his roll, which was quite sizable, figuring some $257. Another employee was asleep on a bed, and without waking him they removed $46 from one of his pockets. The alarm was not given to the police until some time after midnight and the stickups had time to make good their escape. Neighboring towns were notified."

****

The Alliance Herald, Alliance, Nebraska
19 November 1920
"Box Butte County Convicts Released

Two colored men sentenced from Box Butte county were among the thirty-eight paroled by Governor McKelvie last Saturday. Alonzo Isaiah was sentenced a couple of months ago along with another colored man yelpt [?] Price on charge of stealing a pocketbook from P.S. Lohr in the local yards. Isaiah and Price concealed the pocketbook by throwing a coat over it, and later attempted to dispose of liberty bond coupons and to cash railway pay checks contained in it.

The other Box Butte convict released was Will E. Foster, who was sentenced a little over a year ago on a charge of shooting with intent to kill. Charles Brown, likewise colored, was the victim, and the fray occurred as a result of a gambling game. About seven months ago, Brown followed Foster to the penitentiary. Sheriff Miller says that within the past two years he has escorted seventeen colored men to the penitentiary from this county, and the most of them have been released, some without serving more than a slight portion of their sentence."

Joe Price, born about 1906 was sentenced to the penitentiary from Box Butte County on charges of grand larceny. He was sentenced to serve 1-7 years; prisoner number 7719. 12

Lozie Isaiah, aka Isaiah Lozie, born about 1854, was sentenced to the penitentiary from Box Butte County on charges of grand larceny. He was sentenced to serve 1-7 years; prisoner number 7718. 13

Charles Brown, born about 1873, was sentenced to the penitentiary from Box Butte County on charges of assault. He was sentenced to serve 1-5 years; prisoner number 7794. 14

William Foster, born about 1883, was sentenced to the penitentiary from Box Butte County on charges of shooting. He was sentenced to serve 1-20 years; prisoner number 7588. 15

****

The Alliance Herald, 6 May 1921
"Colored Man Stages a Marathon With the Cops Tuesday Evening

A burly colored man, whose name is unknown, but who hails from Brownlee, Neb., left Alliance Tuesday evening with a greatly increased respect for the law and the cops. On the same evening, three police officers learned that all is not moonshine which gurgles. It all happened this way:

Chief Jeffers, Night Watch Stillwell and Burlington Special Agent T.J. Smith were talking over the hobo situation in the passenger station about 9 o'clock Tuesday evening. Alongside one of the benches, near the south wall of the main waiting room, they saw two gunnysacks, each pretty well filled. Their very appearance was suspicious. One of them contained a quantity of clothing. The other was tied, roped, wired and strapped as tight as could be and to the practiced eyes of the officers looked like equipment for a bootlegger. They held it up and shook it. Their ears heard the rattle of glass and the kicking of white mules imprisoned therein.

Two bystanders, noticing the police at the work of investigation, stepped up and told a story which greatly strengthened the belief of the cops. They said that the sacks had been left there by a colored man, who didn't stay in the waiting room with them, but who had been coming back every five minutes or less to see if they were still there. While the bystanders were telling their story the form of the colored man appeared at the window. Although the lights were on in the station, he produced a flashlight, threw its rays on the sacks and walked away. T.J. Smith slipped out the south door, and the colored man fled. He waited not on the order of his going, but went at once.

The special agent drew his automatic and shot a bullet in the air above the man of color. He didn't halt, even when asked to do so in the most pleading tones. Chief Jeffers ran to the northwest corner of the station, and saw a whirl of arms and legs treking for the livery barn. The chief fired a couple of shots above the figure, but the only effect was to increase the speed. The colored man took off his hat, got about three feet nearer the ground and fairly dug his toenails into the earth. He simply clawed up the ground. The three officers took up the chase, and once Officer Stillwell had an opportunity to fire a shot like the rest of the officers.

The colored man sought refuge at the home of a friend in West Lawn. The friend persuaded him that the thing to do was to show up at the police station, for 'if you don't, the law'll shoot you on sight," he said. The colored man, accompanied by the friend, appeared at the station an hour or so later and everything was explained satisfactorily. The muchly wrapped gunnysack was finally undone. It contained, first of all, a suitcase. Inside the suitcase were no bottles of home brew, but a quantity of canned fruit. These, the colored fugitive explained, had been given him by his mother. There was, however, a B&M switchman's lantern, which was retained by Special Agent Smith, the colored man's explanation of how he came into possession of it being rather thin.

The officers asked him why he didn't come in to look at the sacks instead of using the flashlight. 'When I seen all you fellows standing around,' he answered, 'I just thought I'd better move along.' They asked him why he had run, he explained that when he saw Smith come out of the depot, he looked to him just like a drunk man, and he didn't care to have no truck with drunk men."

****

The Alliance Herald, 19 July 1921, Page 4
"Colored Man Languish in City Bastile Due to Fines of $50 Each

Sam Brown and Tom Young, both colored are spending a few hot days in the city bastile, due to their inability to raise fines of $50 each, together with the costs. The fines were assessed by Police Judge L.A. Berry late Saturday afternoon, following a fracas in the Alliance Billiard Parlors. The story, as developed by examination of the witnesses, was about as follows:

Brown and a white floater, — Clarence De Ford, were playing pool in the place. Apparently they had a small bet on the outcome of the game, and when the stranger won, the colored man was slow to pay and an argument followed. Oscar Haverson, white, a partner of De Ford's testified that Brown came at De Ford with an open knife, and the latter retaliated by grabbing a billiard cue from a rack and breaking it twice over the colored man's head. Brown went to the floor for the count, just as Young, colored porter in a barber shop, entered the building. The two white men decided to get while the getting was good, and they ambled to the depot to see about outgoing freights. Halverson testified that Young followed them and when next they saw him, he toted a big club and made for them.

De Ford escaped in the mixup, and Young chased Halverson, down the street, brandishing the club. They ran smack into Chief Jeffers who took Halverson into custody, and a few months [moments] later, when Brown had recovered, took him also. Judge Berry assessed $50 fines against the two colored men on a charge of disturbing the peace by fighting. There was no evidence to show that Halverson was mixed up in the scrap and he was allowed to go. The two colored men were still in jail this morning."

****

The Alliance Herald, 1 November 1921 Page 1
"Alabama Man Starts Feud With Porter
Stages Private War on Sunday Evening
Borrow Jacknife to Slay Colored Man and Police Surgeon Takes Four Stitches in His Scalp

Fred Grizzell, Burlington brakeman, who comes from Alabama, put in a busy hour or two Saturday evening. He began with an overabundance of white mule and before the evening had ended had managed to start a race war all of his own, had attempted to slay a colored man who had offended his sense of the proprieties, had been knocked down a couple of times, getting a badly bruised head and a scalp wound that required four stitches to close, and had inflicted a wound in the neck with a pocket-knife upon Frank Weaver, colored porter in the W.G. Ezell barber shop. Shortly afterward he was knocked out and when he came to was in the city bastile, where he had an opportunity to get his wounds sewed up and dressed, and where he was given an opportunity to sober up.

The trouble started Sunday evening shortly after 6:30 o'clock. According to Grizzell's story, he had been walking past an alley to the rear of the Rodgers grocery, and had come upon a group of colored men. Weaver was arguing with another colored man, he said, and he had made some mild inquires concerning the argument. His interest was rewarded by a question as to how the dispute concerned him. 'I was the only white man there,' he said sadly, but that didn't deter him from telling the colored man what would happen to a negro if he acted that way in Alabama. Weaver then called him a vile name, he said, and he walked away.

Shortly afterward his hot southern blood got the better of him, and he realized that the colored man was in a way the victor. He followed the porter over to the Shelton restaurant, 'called him out' and began angling for an apology. He didn't get it and then he started hostilities by hitting Weaver. The answer came quickly. Weaver returned the blow. And once more hostilities ceased.

Grizzell then started out for revenge. Nothing would satisfy his Alabama tradition and avenge the blow he had received, or the insult, but the blood of the man who had wronged him. He started out to borrow a knife or a gun. Ten or fifteen people he approached, asking for some instrument with which to do damage to the colored man who had offended his idea of race proprieties. At the Army and Navy store he tried to buy a knife, and finding none on sale, inquired as to the chance of getting an army rifle. At the Alliance Billiard Parlor he bought a bottle of near beer and told the proprietor that he wanted to borrow a knife to kill a colored man who had insulted him. He spoke to several men. 'Don't think I won't kill him,' he told one man whom he asked for the loan of a knife.

Finally a brakeman let him have a pocket knife. He selected the sharp blade, again called out his enemy and attacked him with it, inflicting a wound in the neck. That was the finish of his aggressive tactics, for the knife was knocked out of the hand and he hit the pavement. Friends of the colored man urged him not to do any carving on his own account, and the Alabama crusader walked up the street. Weaver's anger then got the better of him, and he followed his assailant and in front of the Keep-U-Neat the blow was struck which put an end to this private race war. Officer Stilwill, Burlington Agents Short and Martin approached, and they found him in front of the Keep-U-Neat, lying in a small pool of blood. He was taken to the station and surgical assistance was called. Weaver gave himself up to the police within an hour.

Grizzell, in police court Monday morning, pleaded guilty to a complaint charging him with drunkenness and fighting, and was assessed a fine of $25 and costs. Weaver, arraigned at the same time, pleaded not guilty and Monday afternoon appeared in police court with a bunch of witnesses to testify in his defense. At the morning session, he had declared that he struck in self-defense.

Grizzell gave the story of his wrongs, omitting some of the details concerning acts of aggression on his part and the search for a knife or gun. He admitted he never saw the colored man with a knife and that he didn't know whether he was hit in the eye or fell on it. He had come to Box Butte county only a short time ago, had worked on the Clay ranch a short time and since October 18 had been laboring on the rip track. Special Agent Short told of finding Grizzell on the sidewalk and of recovering the knife with which the colored man was carved. The brakeman who had lent it, he said, had picked it up from the street, wiped the blood off the blade and stuck it back in his pocket. He said he could not say that the colored man had been drinking, but he saw nothing that would indicate it. Officer Stilwill and George W. Powell also testified.

Weaver had charge of his own defense, but the fact that he brought his witnesses into court and had them tell their story in a way worked against him. He was not fully acquainted with his right to go on the stand, but thought the court and prosecuting attorney would question him. Ray Tompkins, Bud Charlton, Frank L. Thomas of the Army and Navy store and John Velous gave testimony showing that Grizzell had tried to borrow of [sic] knife, but the charge on which Weaver was being tried was that of disturbing the peace by fighting. He was fined $25 and costs.

'They didn't ask me any questions.' said Weaver, when it was all over. 'I could have told them how it happened and that he said things to me that gave me the right to hit him. He hunted me up and made an insulting remark concerning a colored woman. I told him I ought to hit him in the face. He said that in Alabama, where he came from, colored men got off the street when white men came along. I said I didn't know what they did in Alabama, but they didn't do it here. He said some other things and I got mad. He deserved to be hit.'"

****

Box Butte County, Nebraska
Criminal Case
District Court
Case 3949 Docket O page 313

State of Nebraska vs. John Lewis
Burglary
filed 2 April 1927

1 April 1927 complaint of P.E. Romig, County Attorney, charging John Lewis with the crime of burglary in Box Butte County. Warrant issued for arrest of John Lewis, the same day. He waived arraignment and his right to a preliminary hearing, entering a plea of not guilty. Bond set at $500 and court costs at $7.80.

Lewis willfully, unlawfully, maliciously and forcibly broke and entered into the granary of A.H. Hann with intent to steal, take and carry away property of value within the building carrying away 20 skunk hides and one weasel hide valued at $45, property of A.E. Hann.

8 April 1927 brought to court

John Lewis was late of the county and on 22 Dec 1926, in Box Butte County broke into granary of A.E. Hann, stealing goods valued at $45. Defendant then pled guilty.

Verdict - taken to state penitentiary in Lincoln and confined at hard labor, Sundays and Holidays excepted for one full year. He was to pay prosecution costs of $19.95.
Receipt from Nebraska State Penitentiary is dated 15 April 1927

****

Alliance, Nebraska newspaper
10 July 1928
"Darktown Loses Some Citizens
Two Families Do Fadeway to Evade Change of Residence to City Jail

Alliance's colored section lost two families from its ranks on Monday, presumably a very short time after a certain joint hearing in city police court before Police Judge Highland at 2 p.m. yesterday. When the sun arose this morning as usual it very likely disclosed a Studebaker and an Oakland sedan headed elsewhere and traveling at a fairly good speed.

Henry Washington and Gertrude his wife, came to Alliance from Sidney shortly before the rodeo. They came to visit friends, and hadn't intended to remain here very long but Henry became ill — much too ill to travel. Henry Lilly, and Janey, his wife arrived in town about the same time as the Washingtons, only they came from Rapid City, S.D. Henry is a barber and even worked at the trade. Janey is a hair-dresser — a marceller — but she hadn't bothered to hunt up a job.

Both of these couples live over in the Sweetwater district, and neighbors have written indignant letters to the police, to the effect that the home(s) were public nuisances. The police staged a little raid late Saturday night and captured both couples, together with some corn liquor, in the possession of Henry Lilly. The police also arrived before Harry Arthur, a young white ranch hand, had been able to secure delivery of a certain package for which he had given Janey his last $2.35.

And so they were all taken to jail and all appeared before Judge Highland, who assessed the usual fines. Janey and Gertrude were assessed $50 and costs each on the charge of conducting disorderly resorts, when Officers Minnick and Police Chief Horton testified to conditions. Henry Lilly drew $100 and costs on a charge of possessing intoxicating liquor, and they were a blue-looking bunch until Police Judge Highland told them to report at 8 a.m. this morning to begin serving out their time. Henry Lilly was pretty dumb, but he finally got it through his head that he wasn't going to be closely guarded during the night. When 8 a.m. came the quartet were elsewhere by a large majority."

****

Alliance newspaper — 16 September 1931
"Grave Charges Made Against 'Barbecue' in Statement of Woman

'Barbecue Charley' Moore, pudgy colored proprietor of a soft drink parlor south of the tracks in Hills Addition is seriously under fire authorities state, being implicated by a signed statement of Miss Dorothy Lucas, 18, colored, who made a hasty departure from Moore's place last Thursday night. Her statement declares that Moore brought her and two other colored girls, Lolita Ashford and Lavito Penney, from Denver on August 3, 1931 for immoral purposes. Miss Lucas said that she was cruelly mistreated and beaten. She displayed bruises to officers and blamed the colored man for inflicting them. Miss Lucas stated that she had failed in previous attempts to leave the Moore institution and would be shut up in a room for three or four days at a time. She is being held in the woman's ward of the county jail pending

122

contemplated action in her case by the county authorities. Officers say that Miss Lucas ran out of the Moore house while they were on patrol duty in front of the place. She was apparently ill and was given treatment before placed in the women's quarters of the jail. Action is being taken by Ellis Kincaid, owner of the property rented by Moore, to eject him as a tenant. Sometime would be required to eject Moore through the courts."

****

Alliance newspaper
20 April 1937
"Alliance Colored Folks in Trouble

Jackson Linear, Alliance colored man, was fined $50 and costs in police court at Scottsbluff Monday on a petit larceny charge. Linear was accused of stealing $30 from Myrtle Collins, also formerly of Alliance.

The Collins woman left Alliance recently after being accused of having 'rolled' an Alliance white man for $60 when he visited the residence at 101 1/2 Sweetwater. Before she left town she sustained injuries which she said resulted from a fall, but which officers believed resulted from an altercation with someone else over 'business dealings.'"

****

Alliance newspaper - date unknown
"Alleged White Slaver Arrested
Colored Woman — Arrested Here and Placed Under $3,000 Bonds

A colored woman named Lizzie Lane was taken off Burlington passenger No. 43 in Alliance Friday afternoon by the local officials. The woman is charged with being a violator of the "White Slave" act, and was arrested upon telegraphic authority from the U.S. District Attorney Howell at Omaha. A man who was supposed to have been traveling out of Omaha with her was also wanted, but he was not found at Alliance. Sheriff Cox went as far as Crawford, hoping to find him, but was unsuccessful.

The woman was large, powerfully built, and rather good looking, and was about fifty years old. She claimed she was a married woman, living in Sheridan. The Omaha officials allege she was known in Omaha as 'Miss Lizzie.' She made no objection to being taken from the train and denied that she was traveling with or had left Omaha with a man. 'Miss Lizzie' was pretty well dressed, with a handsome brown fur coat and diamond earrings.'"

The White-Slave Traffic Act, better known as the Mann Act, was passed on 25 June 1910. The law made it a felony to engage in interstate or foreign commerce transport of any woman for the purpose of prostitution or debauchery or any other immoral purpose.

****

Alliance Times Herald, Friday 1 January 1943
"Bill Lyons Is Victim of Bullets
Killing Took Place at 101 Sweetwater at 1 A.M. Today

The second "killing" in the last six months to occur at 101 Sweetwater, notorious local negro boarding house, took place early this morning while New Year's revelry was still at its height in the downtown district, Joe Johnson, 39-year-old negro, shooting two bullets from close range into the body of Bill Lyons, 22, another negro. One bullet struck Lyons above the right eyebrow and emerged on the opposite side of his head behind the ear, while the other penetrated his left forearm.

The assault, witnessed by Police Officer Foster Green who attempted to stop it, occurred at 1 a.m. Dr. G.L. Johnston was immediately called to the scene, and the Landa ambulance removed the victim to the hospital a few minutes later.

Lived Five Hours
Lyons died at 6:35 this morning at St. Joseph's hospital. He never regained consciousness.

Witnesses, who were questioned early this morning by County Attorney Leo M. Bayer, declared that the two men had been together earlier in the evening and had quarreled over a dice game. Mrs. Naomi Jones, who resides at 101 Sweetwater said that Lyons has been living there since last September, and he and Johnson were both employed by Ben Nelson, Alliance city scavenger. Early in the evening, she said, the two men appeared to be on good terms. Then Johnson and Lyons went into a room, and a short time later a quarrel began. Abe Scott and Nelson were also in the room. Both were questioned by Bayer this morning. After the quarrel Johnson left, only to return with a gun. Nelson said that the gun, a .38 automatic, was his, and had been taken from his home a mile east of town. Nelson said that when he returned after midnight he found the house broken into, and the gun "and some cash" missing.

Fired Inside House
Mrs. Jones disclosed that Johnson fired four shots in the inside hallway of the building, but said she didn't know whether he was shooting at Lyons then. She sent her daughter, Barbara Jones, after the police, and Patrolman Foster Green arrived in the police car just as the men were in the yard on the south side of 101 Sweetwater. Green declared that he shouted at Johnson to put down the gun, and drew his own revolver just as the shots were fired. Johnson was taken to the city jail. Charges have not been filed.

The shooting occurred almost on the same spot where John Fountain, 17-year-old Omaha negro was fatally stabbed last August by Jim Boone, another negro now serving a six-year sentence in the state penitentiary for manslaughter. Other parallels to the previous killing noted in last night's affair were facts that police arrived at that time just as the stabbing took place, and Russell Finnell, a witness of the shooting last night, also witnessed the stabbing of Fountain."

"First Degree Murder filed in Negro Case
Joe Johnson, 33-year-old negro will be arranged before County Judge P.E. Romig tomorrow morning on a charge of first degree murder in connection with the slaying of Bill Lyons, 22, at 101 Sweetwater early last Friday morning. Johnson was transferred to the county jail from the city jail yesterday. He will be defended by Attorney S.L. O'Brien. The information charging Johnson with first degree murder for the shooting of Lyons, was filed in the county judge's office yesterday morning by County Attorney Leo M. Bayer. The preliminary hearing has been set for tomorrow at 10 a.m., when Bayer is expected to call at least six witnesses of the alleged quarrel between the two men, and of the shooting, including Police Officer Foster Green, Russell Finnell, Mrs. Ralph Jones, Ben Nelson, Abe Scott and others.

Lived in Illinois
Relatives of Lyons have been located at East St. Louis, Ill, and they have directed the Landa funeral home, where arrangements are being made, to ship the body there for burial.

Since the shooting Friday, local authorities have found that neither of the two had resided here long. Lyons arrived here in September from East St. Louis to work on the project. Johnson's home before coming here early in the fall was at Sioux City, Ia. After working on the Air Base project, both men were employed by Ben Nelson, city scavenger, and the investigation made just after the shooting by County Attorney Bayer revealed that they had quarreled on previous occasions. Details of these quarrels are expected to come out at the preliminary hearing.

I have also learned since the shooting that a local taxi driver transported Johnson to Nelson's house, a mile east of the city, where it has been reported he broke in and took the automatic pistol used in the killing."

Prison Records
Joseph Johnson
born 1 August 1909
sentenced from Box Butte County
Prisoner number 15008
17 years for murder 16

****

Alliance newspaper - no date
John Graham, negro, convicted in District court Tuesday on charge of breaking and entering a garage April 10 on the farm of Fred Marsh, three miles south of Alliance. Graham was accused of having attempted to steal gasoline from a pickup truck in Marsh's garage and having fled when a fire broke out which destroyed the garage, truck and a chicken house and about 100 chickens. Marsh testified at the trial to finding a can under the gas tank of the truck after the fire. He had never seen the can before, he said. His hired man, Mernlee Barker, told of awakening early in the morning and seeing the fire from a window and a man leaving the yard. Ward Hall testified that on his way to the fire he observed Graham on the highway about a mile from the Marsh farm. Deputy Sheriffs Shelmadine and Dowart testified to having seen a man's footprints in the vicinity of the fire and to having taken a plaster paris cast of them. Shoes allegedly belonging to Graham and the casts were submitted by County Attorney Leo Bayer as evidence. Sentence has not been made as yet.
Note: John Graham was sentenced to the Nebraska Prison in Lincoln, Nebraska from Box Butte Co., Nebraska for breaking and entering. He was born 20 July 1901 and sentenced for four years, prison number 13446   17

1. Nebraska State Historical Society RG34#4
2. Nebraska State Historical Society Reel RG934#2
3. Year: 1920; Census Place: State Penitentiary, Lancaster, Nebraska; Roll: T625_997; Page: 4B; Enumeration District: 103; Image: 104
4. Year: 1930; Census Place: Newark, Essex, New Jersey; Roll: 1333; Page: 10B; Enumeration District: 0011; Image: 356.0; FHL microfilm: 2341068
5. Year: 1940; Census Place: Newark, Essex, New Jersey; Roll: T627_2426; Page: 3A; Enumeration District: 25-474
6. Nebraska State Historical Society, RG034#5
7. Nebraska State Historical Society, RG034#3
8. Nebraska State Historical Society, RG034#4
9. Year: 1920; Census Place: State Penitentiary, Lancaster, Nebraska; Roll: T625_997; Page: 1A; Enumeration District: 103; Image: 97
10. Bevo, https://en.wikipedia.org/wiki/Bevo 4 June 2013
11. Nebraska State Historical Society, http://nshs.hallcountyne.gov/cgi-bin/prisoner_records_search.cgi
12. Nebraska State Historical Society, RG 034#3
13. Nebraska State Historical Society, RG 034#2
14. Nebraska State Historical Society, RG 034#1
15. Nebraska State Historical Society RG034#2
16. Nebraska State Historical Society, RG034#2
17. Nebraska State Historical Society, RG034#2

Willie Spann Pays Fine and Goes Free

Willie Spann, Alliance colored woman who was convicted in district court on charges of selling liquor without a license and ordered to pay a fine of $100 and costs on one of two counts or go to jail made her choice. She paid yesterday. The total

SIMON PITTS, COLORED ACCOMPLICE, BROUGHT FROM PENITENTIARY TO TESTIFY AGAINST BARBER WHO SHOT RAY WILSON

TWO ROBBERS CAUGHT

A Pair of Colored Burglars Caught Red Handed.

The 13th is certainly unlucky for a couple of wandering colored men. On Monday Feb. 13th Mr. Sanford Smith in his desire for booze, broke into the back door of Eph Corneal's saloon and stole a quantity of whisky. How much, was not found out but Mr. Smith filled up on the stuff Monday night and Tuesday morning he was lying on the soft side of a snow drift in West Lawn and brought in by sheriff Reed in a partially congealed condition. On going to his house or room, six bottles of

The Ku Klux Klan in Alliance

There appear to be no written reports of violence associated with the Ku Klux Klan in Alliance. It is known that they met and wore white robes and perhaps burned a wooden cross. Older African Americans recall knowing they were present and at least seeing them. They were also known to be in other communities and counties in western Nebraska where blacks were living.

The Alliance Herald, 18 October 1921, Page 2
"The Ku Klux Klan
There is no need blinding our eyes to the fact that the organization of a Ku Klux Klan in Alliance is one of the most widely discussed subjects in the city today. We're tolerably well used to new organizations. Our citizens have been fair game for any organizer for any society, business, social, fraternal or otherwise, who has visited us in the past two years.

… But this mysterious secret Klan is arousing a storm of resentment, and has a host of supporters. Some there are who consider that the Klan is everything that its organizers claim —- the salvation of the country in the dark carpetbagging days following the civil war, and its chief protection now against plots and conspiracies of one kind and another.

… The officers and organizers of the Klan now in Alliance have not furnished this newspaper with any statement of the aims of the organization, and its editor has received no invitation to attend any meeting.

… The various elements and classes in Alliance have always lived and worked in harmony. … It seems inconceivable that any organization of men in this city should deliberately set out to destroy this harmony, and if this is not the intention someone should take steps to see that any misunderstanding is cleared."

The Alliance Herald, 9 August 1921, Page 6
"Ku Klux Klan in Nebraska
Klans have been organized in Omaha, Lincoln, Hastings, Sutton, Neligh, McCook, North Platte, Council Bluffs, Fremont, Grand Island, Minden, Holdrege, Sioux City and Nebraska City."

The Alliance Herald, 14 October 1921, page 1
"Ku Klux Klan Chief Topic of Conversation
Mysterious Organiation Holds Meetings in City
Local Klan Said to Have Elected officers Wednesday Evening —- Some Resentment is Apparent
The newly organized Ku Klux Klan has been the chief topic of conversation in Alliance since last Tuesday evening, when the principal sessions of members, present and prospective, was held at Reddish hall. There have been local and outside workers in the city for the past ten days or more, and strenuous efforts had been made to get certain men to attend the meeting. One Alliance business man was solicited six times in one day and received a couple of telephone calls before his 'No' was accepted as final. Others did not need so much persuasion.

The meeting was not open to the public generally, although it was generally understood that those interested could gain admittance, provided they passed the rigid tests that the clan organizers prescribed. The men who had been asked to attend were in most cases told they might bring others for whom they could vouch. Over fifty men were on hand at the hall at 8 p.m.

The mystery and secrecy, commonly believed to be connected with the klan, were preserved. There were sentinels inside and outside the door, and before any man was admitted he was questioned. It is said that all adherents of a certain religion were denied admittance.

The organizer, the Rev. Basil Newton, at present or at one time pastor of a Christian church in St. Louis, Mo., was the principal speaker at the meeting, according to reports from some of those who attended. Mr. Newton is said to be possessed of considerable oratorical powers, and to know how and when to use them. According to the reports, the speaker explained the aims of the klan, denied that it is responsible for outrages in the south and elsewhere with which it has been charged by its enemies; defended it against attacks of various newspapers over the country, some of which are publishing so-called exposures and then launched into some exposures of his own, in which a number of things were attacked.

At the close of the address, an appeal was made for members. Preliminary application blanks, which called for information concerning the candidate for membership, were passed around, and the opportunity to sign them given. Those who did not sign were requested to leave and placed upon their honor by the speaker not to reveal the names of any person present at the meeting.

It is estimated by one of thsoe present that over half of the men present remained in the room for the secret session which followed.

Another meeting was held the following evening, at which it is reported that the formal organization was completed. The head of the local organization, or king kleagle, is reported to be in the employ of the Burlington. The attendance at the second meeting was even larger than at the first.

It is not known how many members have been secured for the klan to date, but strenuous effort is being made to get at least 150, which is said to be the minimum requirement for a separate klan. Where the membership falls below that figure, it is stated that the organization is ranked as a branch.

Considerable ill feeling and resentment has been engendered on the part of many who are opposed to the formation of a Klan, and who feel they have been descriminated against. On Tuesday evening, a closed automobile was packed near the entrance to the hall, and the names of all men who attended the meeting were taken down. The names of those who left early were carefully noted, it is said.

On Wednesday evening, when word of the name recording had been passed about, it is said that several men entered and left the hall by a rear entrance to the building. The names of these men were secured and carefully filed for future reference.

A number of Alliance citizens were already members of the Klan, before the organizers appeared on the scene, it is declared. These men affiliated with the Klan in Denver and several Nebraska points. It is estimated that there have been fifteen or twenty Klan members in the city for several months.

Those who profess to be acquainted with the Klan's activities say there is absolutely no need for alarm; that the organization does not sponsor violence of any kind and is in effect simply a secret lodge. On the other hand, there are a number who have been receiving reports from various places, via the newspapers and other routes, and these say the Klan is a trouble-breeder. The mere fact that its membership is secret and that it does not make public what it intends to do, they say, leaves the way open for imagining all sorts of terrors and outrages, and this, it is charged, is exactly what the Klan desires. There is no question that a number of people are agitated over the matter in Alliance today, and it may be that an anti-Klan organization will result."

101 Sweetwater

The address of 101 Sweetwater in Alliance went by a variety of names. The property originally belonged to the Spann family. A large number of black individuals and families lived on Sweetwater in that vicinity. For many years the house was associated with gambling, illegal alcohol distribution, prostitution and a place where blacks could room, albiet for a day or two. There were also a number of shoot-outs and murders that occurred there.

Years later it was an old run-down shack about 34 feet by 34 feet near the depot and railroad tracks. The Burlington Railroad black porters and waiters were not allowed to stay in the Alliance Hotel or the Barry House. George Edward Slaughter was approached by the railroad superintendent about possibly buying 101 Sweetwater. Slaughter went by a variety of names, such as Eddie, Ed or Sparky. He was also black and knew of the need for a place where the black employees of the railroad could board.

Eddie was given $1,500 by the railroad to fix it up, but that was not for public knowledge. The money was put in the bank and everything was kept a secret. His plans were to enclose the porch and have six bedrooms, three on each side of the hall, a small kitchen and a large room where they would play poker or get drunk. It would cost $3 a night to stay at 101 Sweetwater. Eddie's bedroom was on the southeast part of the building. As construction began they added two more bedrooms on the front porch and two in the garage behind.

After six weeks it became the railroad house for porters, car waiters, transients and a few tramps. It was also a place where the men could bring the "girls." The house was in an ideal location, close to the tracks and in a dark neighborhood. Gert Slaughter cooked the evening meal and people brought their own bottle. While Eddie commented he wasn't going to run a "cat house," the girls were brought in through the east door where they would not be seen.

In 1941 the air base was built outside of Alliance and blacks needed a permanent room. Eddie rented them a room for $3.50 a night or $50 a month. Gert's food prices got higher also. Fewer porters and waiters came because it became a rough place. The same year Eddie applied for a liquor license from the City of Alliance, but was turned down. He was paying about $30 a month to the Guardian State Bank and it was all kept a secret. Soon Eddie had the bank paid off and added more to the house, including better beds.

By 1941 his sister, Neoma Jones, was running the food portion of 101 Sweetwater. Some of the blacks renting by the month could not afford the $50 unless it was right after a nightly crap game. Eddie became involved in loaning money to the black population. With his cleaning business for the Guardian State Bank and Robert Reddish's office, along with the income from 101 Sweetwater and interest on loans, Eddie was financially well off. He also did some bootlegging.

On June 21, 1943, Eddie was arrested and charged with selling liquor without a license. He pled guilty to a charge filed by County Attorney Leo M. Bayer and was fined $200 and costs. After that he leased 101 Sweetwater to his sister, Neoma Jones. Once again Eddie was arrested. In January of 1946 he was charged with selling liquor without a license and having liquor in his possession. Judge Meyers went easy on Eddie and once again he was fined $200 and costs. The whites that Eddie knew had also provided him a way out with the law. LeRoy Abbott, President of the Guardian State Bank, posted his bond of $800 cash and testified as to his character.

Things got worse for Eddie and 101 Sweetwater. In the early part of 1950 two smooth, city-slickers came to Alliance. They were Alfred Mickens and James Hubbard. Eddie gave them a written lease for one year at $150 per month and they would pay for the heat and hot water. On November 1, 1950 Eddie was charged with receiving stolen property of one James C. Fraudsen of Dalton, Nebraska, who was a tavern and liquor store owner. The police also arrested Alfred Mickens, James E. Hubbard, Harley Toney and Tillie Trimble. Hubbard was wanted for escaping jail in Nebraska and a murder in Montana. Toney and Trimble had their charges dropped provided they left Alliance. Eddie maintained he knew nothing about the robbery of the Fraudsen Liquor Store. Mickens was keeping most of the booze in the walls of 101 Sweetwater.

The case went to a jury trial on April 17, 1951. Hubbard was brought back from the penitentiary in Lincoln to testify. He testified Eddie knew nothing about the booze or where it had been. Testifying were a number of Alliance businessmen who knew that Eddie had leased to Mickens and Hubbard. Mickens testified that Eddie didn't know about the liquor store robbery. The jury returned a verdict of not guilty. Eddie once again took possession of 101 Sweetwater.

Eddie's troubles were just beginning. On February 3, 1956 County Attorney Robert A. Moran filed a complaint against Eddie for selling liquor without a license. The stool pidgeons were Jon McWilliams of Sidney and Wilson Fitzpatrick. McWilliams was a football player at the University of Nebraska. On the night of April 14, 1957 they showed up at 101 Sweetwater. Fitzpatrick kept asking for booze and Eddie handed over a pint for $5. The men took the $5 back and said "you are under arrest." Officers were stationed outside. Eddie was found guilty, fined $50 and costs of $124.80.

On February 24, 1960 Eddie took ill and died. That did not signal the end of 101 Sweetwater. When his will was probated his estate was $2,500 with Howard Litchey acting as executor. It was divided among his two sisters, Goldie Bartley of Detroit and Neoma Jones of California. On July 28, 1960 Goldie sold 101 Sweetwater to William W. Sessions and his wife, Barbara for $2,000. Sessions who had a barbeque in Rapid City, South Dakota, paid $500 down. His wife, Barbara, was in the women's reformatory in York, Nebraska where she was serving seven years for a murder. Sessions named the property "Pick A Rib." He was on a scouting mission in Amarillo, Texas when he died suddenly on January 5, 1962. Shortly after that his widow was released from prison and she sold 101 Sweetwater to Saul Hardin.

Saul Hardin was a gambler and pimp and also a very handsome black man with fancy clothes. He had connections with the brothels in Kansas City, Missouri and North Platte, Nebraska. Saul began making improvements to the property with fancy red carpet, paneling and new mattresses. Every two weeks he brought in girls from Kansas City and North Platte. He also drove a white Cadillac.

On the morning of March 11, 1965 Saul was supposedly visiting a brother and sister in California. His wife had left him earlier. The U.S. Alcoholic Tax officers from Omaha came to the east door of 101 Sweetwater. One of the officers was David Finney, a former Alliance resident, who appeared to be drunk and wanted a drink. Saul was arrested and taken to Gering. He was later arraigned in Omaha and entered a plea of not guilty. His bond was set at $1,000 which was posted. As the case drug on Saul changed his plea to nolo contendere on September 20, 1967 in front of U.S. Judge Richard E. Robinson in North Platte. He was fined $50 and released.

Less than a month later on October 16, 1967 a force of seventeen county and city police made a raid on Saul's "Pick-A-Rib." Saul was arrested with about fifty others … Indians, colored people, Mexicans and also ranchers, businessmen, a prominent insurance man, a banker and white and black prostitutes. Under the direction of County Attorney Laurice Margheim, those arrested were brought to court in a large bus. The bus made two trips with prisoners. Some of Alliance's prominent men left before the bus came back.

The headlines of *The Alliance Daily Times-Herald* of Monday, October 16, 1967 read "Over 50 Arrested Here After Raid at 101." Saul Hardin was charged with pandering [keeping a prostitute] and selling liquor without a license. He was released on a bond of $250. From the door of 101 Sweetwater was hung a sign "Closed." Approximately half of those arrested were taken to the County Building and the other half to the Municipal Building. Court was held by Police Magistrate Nell Johnstone and County Judge S.L. O'Brien. Saul's trial was moved to District Court at Rushville in Sheridan County. He was found guilty and it was ordered that the furniture and 101 Sweetwater be sold. Saul was released from jail on May 3, 1968 and left town for parts unknown.

After various sales, foreclosures and legal actions, the City of Alliance bought 101 Sweetwater for $13,000 with HUD money. The house still stands as a reminder of Alliance's sordid past.

101 Sweetwater before the 1967 raid

The Alliance Times Herald, Alliance, Nebraska
26 June 1980, page 11

Section 3
Part 1

Photographs and Documents
Genealogies and Histories

Introduction to Photographs and Documents

Photographs were shared by family members and some were retrieved from Internet web sites, such as Ancestry. The support help and legal office of Ancestry advised us about using the photographs on Ancestry public trees. If they are not personally copyrighted on Ancestry, they can be used. If they are over 75 years old, they can be used. The person submitting the photograph does not have control over the photograph because it is in the public domain. Some of the photographs were also used with the permission of museums and research centers or from personal collections.

Documents that were scanned are part of the public record available freely to researchers. Many were made from actual documents and other were located on genealogical Internet web sites, such as FamilySearch and Ancestry. Photographs are numbered as the family or individuals are located in either Volume 1 or Volume 2

Introduction to Section 3, Part 1 and Part 2

The family genealogies and biographical information pertain to many of the blacks who settled in western Nebraska. We have tried to select those who remained within the area or had connections already established to the area. If we have not included someone, it was not our intention. We welcome any additions or corrections.

Our research is not exhaustive. What is contained herein will give the readers an idea of the lives we have researched. By using original documents we have been able to piece together their lives. We have also received information regarding ancestors from their descendants. The federal census enumerations were taken every ten years, except in certain states, such as Iowa, Kansas and Nebraska, where there were state censuses between the ten year intervals. These enumerations allow us to follow people as they migrated, married, had children and died.

Within the genealogies, the census enumerations are shown, if possible, beginning with the 1870 US Census, which was the first enumeration after the emancipation of slaves. In many circumstances, people changed their names or drifted apart from their families. When reporting information, many did not know their exact age or where they were born. Beginning with the 1880 US Census, the place of birth for parents is shown. Unfortunately, the 1890 US Census was destroyed, with only some fragments remaining and none for Nebraska, except the US Veterans Schedule. The 1900 US Census was the only one to list the month and year of birth. Sometimes these are not correct. The 1940 US Census contains only the subject's place of birth. Enumerators asked where the subject was living on 1 April 1935, as well as the number of years educated. The 1930 and 1940 US Census specifically reported blacks as "negro." Prior to that they were usually shown as black or mulatto. People who were freed persons of color prior to the emancipation are usually reported as black or mulatto and sometimes just as free persons of color. The enumerator reported their race according to how he or she viewed them.

Many of the subjects researched had connections with other blacks who settled not only in Box Butte County, but primarily in Dawson, Dawes, Cherry and Custer counties. It is interesting to see how their lives intertwined. While the railroad provided employment for many who chose to settle in western Nebraska, others were attracted to free or inexpensive land, particularly after the passing of the Homestead Act and the Kinkaid Act. Still others served their country as Buffalo Soldiers at Fort Robinson, either retired from service there or remained in the area. Significantly they all left their mark and legacy upon western Nebraska.

134

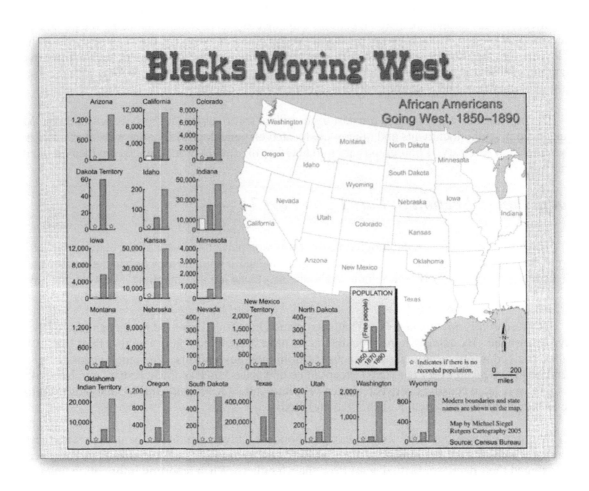

Designed by Cheri L. Hopkins

135

The old A.M.E.
Church building
Alliance, Nebraska
(W. 2nd St.-taken 2016)

136

African Methodist Episcopal Church (AME)
North Platte, Lincoln Co., Nebraska

Robert Ball Anderson - 1927

Daisy Graham Anderson

Record for Robt Ball 650

Date, and No. of Application, Mch 26 66
Name of Master, Robt Ball
Name of Mistress, Mary Ball
Plantation,
Height and Complexion, 5 7 Blk
Father or Mother? Married? Billy Anderson
Name of Children,
Regiment and Company, Co I 125 USCI
Place of Birth, Green Co Ky
Residence, " "
Occupation,
REMARKS, Scar left side lower jaw

Signature, Robert Ball

Volume 1

Hayes Chandler
Volume 1

Florence Motley Chandler
wife of Hayes Chandler Volume 1

Hayes Chandler giving rides on his wagon to
children in Alliance, Nebraska.
Volume 1

Joshua Emanuel   Alfred Emanuel

Volume 1

Mary Robinson Emanuel

Joshua Emanuel and Family
Volume 1

Ephraim Corneal
Volume 1

James "Nigger Jim" Kelly
Volume 2

Beatrice Woodlee holding her niece
Betty Buckley (Riley)

Volume 2

Harry L. Buckley

Jesse Ford - age 1

Volume 2

Fay and Jesse Ford - 1923

Florence Nickens
high school photo

Volume 2

LeRoy Nickens
high school photo

148

Shore Family in Custer Co., Nebraska
used with permission from Custer County
Historical Society/Museum and Research Center,
Broken Bow, Nebraska

Volume 2

Speese Family in Custer Co., Nebraska
used with permission from Custer County
Historical Society/Museum and Research Center,
Broken Bow, Nebraska
Volume 2

Truth Hannahs

Truth Hannahs

Volume 2

George Riley, Truth Hannahs Riley,
Glen Riley

Turner Price
Volume 2

Price sod house in the sandhills.

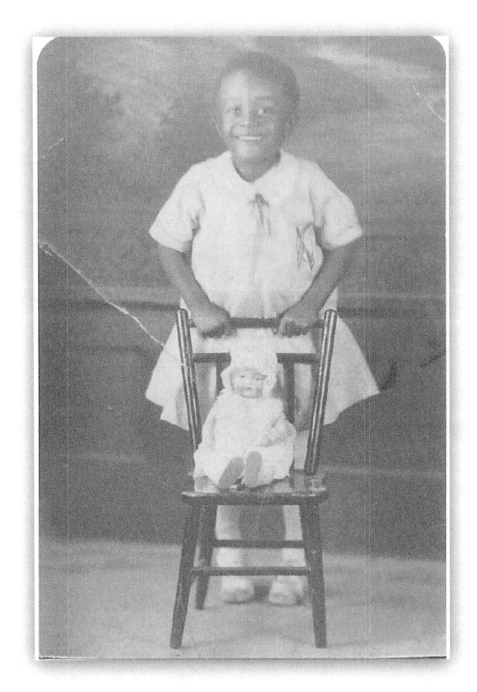

Harriet Spann Volume 2

Henry and William Spann
Volume 2

Nathaniel Spann

Leslie and Lula Spann
Volume 2

Volume 2

Mary Jane Sayers

Sophia Napier Watkins

156

Photographs of William Ford
Volume 2

Charles Henry Meehan and wife
Hester Catherine Freeman
Volume 2

Charles Henry Meehan
and sons

Volume 2

Charles Edward Meehan

159

Grandchildren of Charles and Hester Meehan
taken Christmas 1913 in DeWitty, Cherry Co.,
Nebraska   Volume 2

Volume 2

Charles Speese and wife Rosetta Meehan

William Meehan

Children of Gertie Meehan and Maurice Brown
Volume 2

Joseph (Livas) Anderson Volume 2

Darnell Children Volume 1

Rev. Russell Taylor at Bellevue College, Omaha, NE
about 1896   Volume 2

Robert Greggs   Volume 2

St. James A.M.E. Church, DeWitty, Nebraska
(Great Plains Black History Museum)

Lucy Young Woods - age 100
Volume 2

Harriet - Alliance, Nebraska
last name unknown

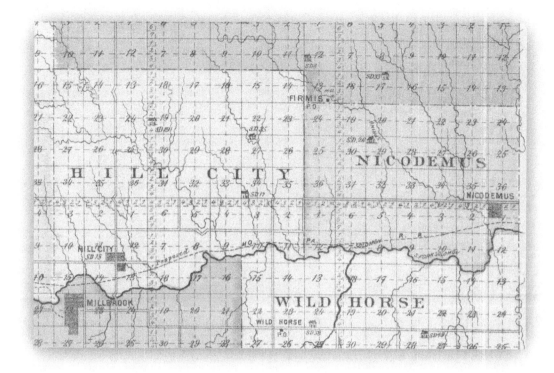

Nicodemus, Graham Co., Kansas

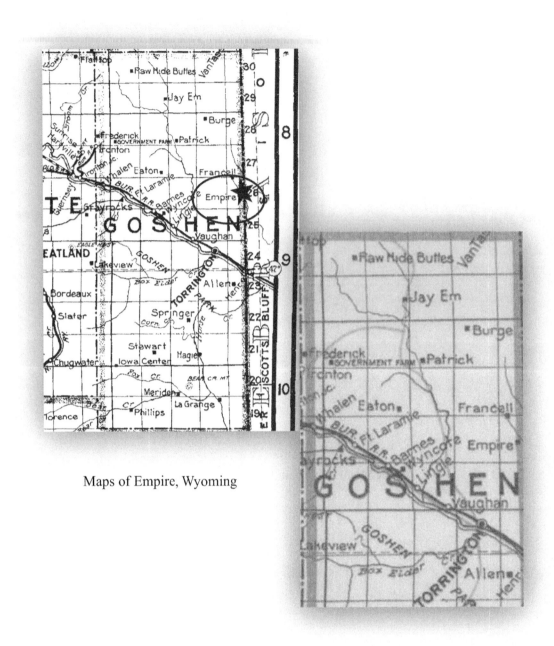

Maps of Empire, Wyoming

171

171

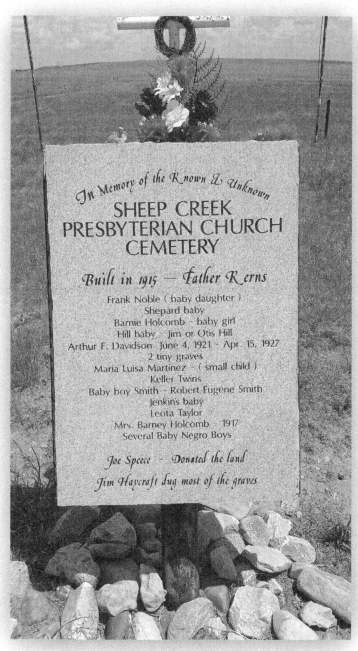

In Memory of the Known & Unknown

SHEEP CREEK
PRESBYTERIAN CHURCH
CEMETERY

Built in 1915 — Father Kerns

Frank Noble (baby daughter)
Shepard baby
Barnie Holcomb – baby girl
Hill baby – Jim or Otis Hill
Arthur F. Davidson June 4, 1921 – Apr. 15, 1927
2 tiny graves
Maria Luisa Martinez – (small child)
Keller Twins
Baby boy Smith – Robert Eugene Smith
Jenkins baby
Leota Taylor
Mrs. Barney Holcomb – 1917
Several Baby Negro Boys

Joe Speece – Donated the land

Jim Haycraft dug most of the graves

Sheep Creek Cemetery
near Empire, Wyoming

Alliance Cemetery, Alliance, Nebraska
Rufus Slaughter and his son Samuel

Volume 2

Hayes Jerome Chandler
Volume 1

174

Neuswanger Award For '75 Goes To Chandler

Hayes Chandler

Hayes Chandler, who began his employment as a part time helper while still attending high school in Hemingford in 1928, was named the Outstanding Employe in 1975 of Neuswangers, Inc. by a committee of his fellow employes.

Chandler became a full time employe in 1929, and except for a period of 5 years spent in the military service, has been continuously employed since that time. His first jobs were involved with livestock and local delivery, and the majority of his years have been driving trucks in all phases of the business. He drove long distance trips for many years hauling petroleum products, grain, and feed products. During this time he made many friends throughout the state and has received a number of commendations for his acts of courtesy and help along the highways.

In 1974, Chandler began devoting his full time to his current responsibility of Tank Wagon Driver serving Neuswangers customers with petroleum products throughout their trade area.

During the period of 1941 to 1946, Chandler was in the military service in various parts of the country and served 28 months in the European Theater as a driver and assistant motor pool sergeant. He married Mildred Jackson of Alliance on Dec. 31, 1941, and they had two children.

Criteria for selection for this annual award included customer service attitudes, cooperation with fellow employes, willingness, interest in the organization, and care in the operation of equipment.

Gene Neuswanger, president of the firm commented that "I've worked with Hayes these many years, and I've never known him not to have a smile and a good word for everyone. His father worked for us too for something like 17 years, and I'm proud to have known and worked with both of them."

Hayes Jerome Chandler
Volume 1

Robert Ball Anderson and wife Daisy Graham on their
honeymoon, Colorado Springs, CO, 1922.
From Daisy Graham Anderson memoirs, "Have You No
Shame" in Knight Museum & Research Center

Volume 1

Robert Ball Anderson's original house
located about 14 miles northwest of Hemingford,
Box Butte Co., Nebraska   Volume 1

Grand Army of the Republic members, Hemingford,
NE; Robert Ball Anderson, colorbearer
1920s   Volume 1

From "Slavery to Affluence, Memoirs of Robert
Anderson, Ex-Slave' - Knight Museum & Research
Center, Alliance, Nebraska

Robert Ball Anderson's houses located about 14 miles
northwest of Hemingford, Nebraska   Volume 1

From "Slavery to Affluence, Memoirs of Robert
Anderson, Ex-Slave' - Knight Museum & Research
Center, Alliance, Nebraska

Charles "Charlie" Horn(e)
Volume 1

List of Genealogies and Histories
Volume 1

Alexander Brown

Alexander "Alex" Brown and his wife, Harriet, came to Sheridan Co., Nebraska with J. Buford "Buff" Tinnin. According to information in the Tinnin family, the Browns were slaves of Buff's parents, but more likely they were slaves of Buff's grandparents. Alexander Brown married Harriet Miller on 28 April 1879 in Bastrop Co., Texas. An exact match for Alexander Brown and wife has not been found on the 1880 US Census.

The Tinnin family were from Bastrop Co., Texas. J. Buford "Buff" Tinnin was born 9 July 1876 in McDade, Bastrop Co., Texas to John Tinnin and Elizabeth Eleanor Herron. Buff married Bess Helen Antenen on 16 January 1911 in Gordon, Sheridan Co., Nebraska. He died on 11 September 1946 in Denver, Colorado and was buried in the Fairmount Cemetery Mausoleum in Denver, Colorado. Buff retired to Denver in about 1940. John Tinnin was born March 20, 1840 in Hinds Co., Mississippi and died on 20 August 1917 in Georgetown, Williamson Co., Texas. He married Elizbaeth Eleanor Herron in about 1874. She was born in Texas on 15 November 1854 and died on 11 November 1925 in Torrington, Goshen Co., Wyoming. Because of the dates of birth, it is probably John Tinnin's father who owned Alexander "Alex" Brown, because Alexander was born in Mississippi and the Tinnins were from Hinds Co., Mississippi.

According to his tombstone, Alex was born in 1850 and died in 1932. However, he was deceased by the 1930 when the US Census was taken. He and his wife were buried in the Merriman Cemetery, Merriman, Cherry Co., Nebraska. According to her tombstone, Harriet was born in 1854 and died in 1949. She was found dead in her small house in east Gordon, Nebraska in the blizzard of 1949. The federal census enumerations indicate more about where they were living.

> 1900 US Census, Sheridan Co., Nebraska, Village of Gordon, ED 178, Page 7A 1
> 121-121 Alex Brown, black, b. September 1851, 48, married 22 years, b. MS,
>   father b. MS, mother b. VA, day laborer
> Harriett, wife, black, b. Jan 1865, 35, married 22 years, 1 child, 0 living, b. TX,
>   both parents b. TX
>
> 1910 US Census, Cherry Co., Nebraska, Merriman Prect, ED 55, Page 5B 2
> 66-66 Alex Brown, black, 59, married 30 years, b. MS, both parents b. MS,
>   rancher
> Harriet, wife, black, 45, married 30 years, 1 child, 0 living, b. TX, father b. TX,
>   mother b. AL, laundress
>
> 1920 US Census, Cherry Co., Nebraska, Merriman Prect, ED 58, Page 15B 3
> 46-46 Alex Brown, owns, free, negro, 54, b. TX, both parents b. TX
> Harriet, wife, negro, 53, b. TX, both parents b. TX
>
> 1930 US Census, Cherry Co., Nebraska, Merriman Village, ED 27, Page 2B 4
> 44-44 Philip Menisinger HH - proprietor of hotel
> Harret Brown, servant, negro, 54, widow, b. TX, both parents b. TX, hotel laborer
>
> 1940 US Census, Cherry Co., Nebraska, Merriman Village, ED 16-28, Page 1A 5
> owns #300
> Harriet Brown, informant, negro, 75, widow, b. TX, same house 1 April 1935

Alexander Brown obtained land in Cherry Co., Nebraska under the Homestead Act. It is described as follows. 6

Alexander Brown
Homestead Act - patent issued 11 July 1907
160 acres
Valentine Land Office, Cherry Co., Nebraska
6th PM, T 31N, R 40W, Section 15
South 1/2 of Northeast 1/4
North 1/2 of Southeast 1/4
Located in northwest Cherry County near the Sheridan County border and southeast of Gordon, Nebraska.

Alexander Brown
Homestead Act - patent issued 10 October 1912
480 acres
Valentine Land Office, Cherry Co., Nebraska
6th PM, T 34N, R 38W
Section 27 Southwest 1/4 of Northwest 1/4 and North 1/2 of Southwest 1/4
Section 28 North 1/2 of Southeast 1/4, Southwest 1/4 of Southeast 1/4 and
East 1/2 of Southwest 1/4
Section 33 East 1/2 of Northwest 1/4 and West 1/2 of Northeast 1/4
Located along Leander Creek, east of Merriman in Cherry County, about five miles west
and two miles south.

The complete Homestead file for Alexander Brown indicates that he made homestead proof on land in Section 15, Township 31 North, Range 40 on 5 January 1907. It was approved on 8 June 1907 and the patent was issued on 11 July 1907. His initial application for the land was 27 March 1900. At the time the patent was issued he was shown as "of Gordon, Nebraska." His affidavit indicated that he was a native born citizen of the United States. It was filed at Cooper, Cherry Co., Nebraska. The newspaper advertisement of November 21, 1906 shows he was living at Lavacca, Nebraska. On that date he notified the US Land Office at Valentine that he had lost his filing papers and did not know his homestead number. He built a sod house 16x24 feet, frame stable 12x24 feet, granary, hen house, good well with pump and windmill. One-half acre was put to garden, fenced with woven wire. His claim was fenced and cross fenced, valued at $700. The sod house was built in August 1900. His wife and family resided continuously on the land. 7 According to 1900 and 1910 US Census, Harriet had given birth to one child who was no longer living. The affidavit that Alexander filed for patent of the land in 1907 indicated that his wife and "family" had resided continuously on the land. The child most likely died in Cherry County.

1. Year: 1900; Census Place: Gordon, Sheridan, Nebraska; Roll: 940; Page: 7A; Enumeration District: 0178; FHL microfilm: 1240940
2. Year: 1910; Census Place: Merriman, Cherry, Nebraska; Roll: T624_840; Page: 5B; Enumeration District: 0055; FHL microfilm: 1374853
3. Year: 1920; Census Place: Merriman, Cherry, Nebraska; Roll: T625_981; Page: 15B; Enumeration District: 58; Image: 956
4. Year: 1930; Census Place: Merriman, Cherry, Nebraska; Roll: 1268; Page: 2B; Enumeration District: 0027; Image: 919.0; FHL microfilm: 2341003
5. Year: 1940; Census Place: Merriman, Cherry, Nebraska; Roll: T627_2240; Page: 1A; Enumeration District: 16-28
6. U.S. Department of Interior, Bureau of Land Management, General Land Office http://www.glorecords.blm.gov/results/default.aspx?searchCriteria=type=patent|st=NE|cty=031|ln=Brown|sp=true|sw=true|sadv=false
7. Fold3 http://www.fold3.com

Alexander Stepney

Alexander Stepney was a private in the 9th Cavalry. According to military records he was born in Anne Arundel Co., Maryland. He was a former slave and during the Civil War, was a servant to a Confederate officer. Alexander was born in about 1847. There were many free persons of colored living in Anne Arundel Co., Maryland before the Civil War. After the Civil War he is shown on the 1870 US Census at Fort Clark, Texas.

> 1870 US Census Kinney Co., Texas, Fort Clark, US Military Reservation, Page 7   1
> PO Fort Clark
> Company D 25th Regimental H.S. Infantry Enlisted Soldiers
> Alexander Stepney, 23, black, b. Maryland

The Returns from Regular Army Cavalry Regiments indicate the following entries for Stepney. 2

A. Stepney
Co. I, 9th US Cavalry
private
31 July 1876
Fort Defiance, New Mexico

A. Stepney
Co. I, 9th US Cavalry
private
11 August 1876
Fort Defiance, New Mexico

A. Stepney
Co I, 9th US Cavalry
Colonel Edward Hatch
private
24 December 1877
Ute Country - detached driver

Alex T. Stepney
Co. I, 9th US Cavalry
Colonel Edward Hatch
private

24 December 1877
Fort Bayard, New Mexico

Alex Stepney
Co I, 9th US Cavalry
Colonel Edward Hatch
private
30 April 1881
Fort Wingate

A. Stepney
9th US Cavalry
private
5 August 1881
Fort Wingate

Alex Stepney
Co I, 9th US Cavalry
Colonel Edward Hatch
private
9 May 1882
Fort Reno

While these records do not indicate he was at Fort Robinson, it is known that he actually was there and was discharged there. Stepney retired from the military in 1891 at Fort Robinson. He was employed at the 0-4 Ranch in Sioux County, then was a cook as is shown on the 1900 US Census, which also indicates he was widowed. If he had married during his military career, there is no record found of the marriage.

The 1890 Veterans Schedules for Nebraska exist even though the population schedules for the most part have been destroyed. The 1890 Veterans Schedule for Dawes Co., Nebraska, Dry Creek show Eelander [sic] Stepney, Private Co. G, 4th Md? Infantry, enlisted June 1863; discharged March 1865. His post office address is shown as Chardon, Nebraska and he had rheumatism. 3

> 1910 US Census, Sioux Co., Nebraska, Fort Robinson, ED 226, Page 10A 4
> 4-4 James R. Church household, white, surgeon US Army

Alexander Stepney, servant, black, 60, widowed, b. MD, both parents b. MD,
        cook, private family

Alexander Stepney married Mrs. Fannie Jones in Crawford, Dawes Co., Nebraska on 10 March
1915. He was 56 years old, born Maryland, a resident of Nebraska, son of William Stepney, born in
Maryland and Jane Watkins, born in Maryland. Alexander was a mail carrier. Fannie was 21, colored,
born Hot Springs, Fall River Co., South Dakota daughter of William Taylor, birth place unknown and
Birdie Anderson, born in Kansas. It was her second marriage and she was divorced. They were married
on 10 March 1915. The witness to their wedding was Mrs. Mae Sprague of Crawford. 5

On 3 September 1912 in Crawford, Dawes Co., Nebraska, Fannie Taylor married Seth Jones of
Co. A 9th Calvary. On their marriage license, Jones is shown as age 65, resident of Crawford, Nebraska,
born in Wilmington, North Carolina, a soldier. His parents were shown as Homer Johnson Jones and
Rhodia Johnson. Fannie is shown as Fannie Butler, age 21, resident of Crawford, Nebraska, born at
Crawford, works in laundry. Her parents are shown as Sam Butler and Birdie Taylor. Their marriage
ended soon in divorce. 6

Jones was stationed at Fort Wingate, New Mexico on 15 December 1876. On the 1910 US
Census, he was living in Sioux Co., Nebraska, Andrews Prect. and is shown as black, age 63, divorced,
born NC, birth place of parents is unknown. He was a blacksmith. 7

Alexander Stepney and Fannie lived in Crawford, Dawes Co., Nebraska after their marriage
where he worked as a mail carrrier between the railroad and Fort Robinson. 8

On the 1900 US Census Fannie's mother, Birdie Taylor, was living in Crawford, Dawes Co.,
Nebraska. She is shown as single, but may have been divorced, or never married. However, on the 1900
US Census, Sheridan Co., Nebraska, Fannie is shown in the household of Samuel Butler. On the 1910 US
Census, Sam and Fannie Butler were living in Crawford, Dawes Co., Nebraska. The daughter Fannie was
not in their household, but in the household of Wm. Birdie Boone next door.

1900 US Census, Sheridan Co., Nebraska, Village of Gordon, ED 178, Page 6B 9
 119-119 Samuel M. Butler, black, b. Oct 1867, 32, married 8 years, b. NE, both
        parents b. VA, day laborer
Fannie, wife, black, b. Feb. 1870, 30, married 8 years, 1 child, 1 living, b. MO,
        both parents b. KY
Fannie, daughter, black, b. May 1893, 7, b. SD, father b. NE, mother b. MO

1900 US Census, Dawes Co., Nebraska, Crawford, ED 81, Page 6B   10
Ash Street
135-136 George Jordan, colored, b. Nov 1848, 51, single, b. KY, parents birth
        place unknown, retired soldier USA
Birdie Taylor, servant, colored, b. Dec 1877, 22, single, b. KS, father b. KS,
        mother b. unknown, housekeeper
William Boone, boarder, colored, b. Dec 1871, 28, single, b. KY, both parents
        b. KY, day laborer

1910 US Census Dawes Co., Nebraska, Crawford, Ward 2, ED 93, Page 10A 11
Block 21
245-251 Wm. Boone, black, 37, married 18 years, b. KY, both parents b. US,
        butcher
Birdie, wife, black, 31, married 18 years, 1 child, 1 living, b. KS, both parents
        b. KY

Fannie, daughter, black, 17, single, b. SD, father b. KY, mother b. KS

246-252 Sam Butler, black, 43, b. NE, both parents b. US, bar tender
Fannie, wife, black, 40, b. KS, both parents b. KY

The following describes land that Alexander Stepney purchased at the Chadron Land Office in Dawes Co., Nebraska. It totaled 160 arcres, and was dated 12 October 1891, located in Dawes County. The land was east of Chadron and approximately one to two miles west of the Dawes and Sheridan counties line. 12

      6th PM, Twp 33N, Range 47W, Section 14
            West 1/2, Southwest 1/4
            Northeast 1/4, Southwest 1/4
            Northwest 1/4, Southeast 1/4

Alexander Stepney died 18 May 1918 and was buried in the Fort Robinson Cemetery in Dawes Co., Nebraska. In 1947, his remains were transferred to the Fort McPherson National Cemetery at Maxwell, Lincoln Co., Nebraska, Plot F, 1164.

1.   Year: 1870; Census Place: Fort Clark US Mil Res, Kinney, Texas
2. U.S., Buffalo Soldiers, Returns From Regular Army Cavalry Regiments, 1866-1916 [database on-line]. Provo, UT, USA: Ancestry.com Operations, Inc., 2012
3. Year: 1890; Census Place: Dry Creek, Dawes, Nebraska; Roll: 37; Page: 1; Enumeration District: 172
4. Year: 1910; Census Place: Fort Robinson, Sioux, Nebraska; Roll: T624_855; Page: 10A; Enumeration District: 0226; FHL microfilm: 1374868
5. Dawes Co., Nebraska Marriage Book 5 page 324
6.   Dawes Co., Nebraska Marriage Book 5, page 63.
7. Year: 1910; Census Place: Andrews, Sioux, Nebraska; Roll: T624_855; Page: 2B; Enumeration District: 0224; FHL microfilm: 1374868
8. Frank N. Schubert, *Buffalo Soldiers, Braves and the Brass*, Shippensburg, PA: This White Mane Publishing Company, Inc., page 153
9. Year: 1900; Census Place: Gordon, Sheridan, Nebraska; Roll: 940; Page: 6B; Enumeration District: 0178; FHL microfilm: 1240940
10. Year: 1900; Census Place: Crawford, Dawes, Nebraska; Roll: 921; Page: 6B; Enumeration District: 0081; FHL microfilm: 1240921
11. Year: 1910; Census Place: Crawford Ward 2, Dawes, Nebraska; Roll: T624_841; Page: 10A; Enumeration District: 0093; FHL microfilm: 1374854
12. US Department of the Interior, Bureau of Land Mangement, General Land Office Records http://www.glorecords.blm.gov/details/patent/default.aspx?accession=NE0660___.396&docClass=STA&sid=ngrtgquf.qzo

Alfred Bradden

Alfred Bradden was a Civil War soldier and a Buffalo Soldier who remained in Dawes Co., Nebraska for some time after his discharge. He was born in Alabama in April of 1849 and began his military career, enlisting on 8 February 1864 in Nashville, Tennessee as a private in Co. C, 17th Regiment United States Colored Troops. He was discharged there on 25 April 1866, General Orders #15. He had chronic articular rheumatism. Alfred enlisted again at Nashville on 23 November 1866 as a Sgt. in Co. C, 38th US Infantry and was discharged on 17 November 1869 at Fort Clark, Texas, due to expiration of service. 1

According to the Descriptive Book, 24th Infantry NCS and Band, he served in the 17th US Colored Troops until 25 April 1866; served in Co. C 28th Infantry and discharged as a sergeant on 17 November 1869; in Co. H 24th Infantry, discharged as a sergeant on 16 August 1875; in Co. B 24th Infantry, discharged as a sergeant 18 February 1881; enlisted in the Band, 24th Infantry, Fort Supply, Indian Territory on 19 February 1881. He was the principal musician on 1 October 1881 and resigned on 24 June 1884. According to his discharge information he was "a good E flat cornet player." He was married and had five children as dated 18 February 1886. Alfred was listed on the Roster of the 9th Cavalry in 1893 as being in the 9th Cavalry Band since 11 August 1892. He was residing with his wife at Fort Robinson, Nebraska and retired from there in November 1893. He worked as an attendant in the post exchange billiard room. 2

Returns from the Regular Army Cavalry Regiments (US Buffalo Soldiers) indicates that in May of 1892, Alfred Bradden, Band, 9th Cavalry, was at Hot Springs, South Dakota on 16 April 1892, regiment commanding officer Colonel James Biddle. 3

On the 1900 US Census, Bradden and his wife, Laura, were living at Fort Robinson where he is shown as being an employer at the post exchange. In 1910 they were living in Crawford. There is no pension file for Alfred Bradden.

1900 US Census, Dawes Co., Nebraska, Fort Robinson, ED 208, Page 1A 4
7-7 Alfred Bradden, black, b. April 1849, 51, married 18 years, b. AL, both
    parents b. AL, post exchange employer
Laura, wife, black, b. June 1853, 46, married 18 years, 4 children, 0 living, b. GA,
    both parents b. SC, nurse
Robert Jackson, boarder, black, b. Nov 1866, 33, single, b. Canada, father b. KY,
    mother b. Canada, came to US in 1881, naturalized, teamster (post
    exchange)

1910 US Census, Dawes Co., Nebraska, Crawford, Ward 2, ED 93, Page 8A 5
Block E
190-196 Alfred Bradden, black, 64, widowed, b. TN, both parents b. TN, retired

Laura Bradden died at Fort Robinson on 9 June 1910. She was buried in the cemetery at Fort Robinson. In 1947 her remains were removed to Fort McPherson National Cemetery, near Maxwell, Lincoln Co., Nebraska. On 12 May 1915 Alfred was admitted to the US National Home for Disabled Volunteer Soldiers in Leavenworth, Kansas. He is shown as born in Alabama, age 66, 5 feet 8 1/2 inches in height, brown complexion, black eyes and grey hair. He could read and write and was a retired soldier. The records indicate that he was a widower. His nearest relative was his son, William Bradden, who was living in Chicago, Illinois. He died in the hospital at the home in Leavenworth on 27 April 1916 and was buried in the National Cemetery there on 29 April 1916 in Section 31, Row 8, Grave #0342. His personals were disposed to his daughter, Mary Ferris, 4th and Marion Street, Leavenworth, KS. 6

1. Historical Register of National Homes for Disabled Volunteer Soldiers, 1866-1938; (National Archives Microfilm Publication M1749, 282 rolls); Records of the Department of Veterans Affairs, Record Group 15; National Archives, Washington, D.C.
2. *On The Trail of the Buffalo Soldier*, Schubert, pp 49, 50
3. *Returns From Regular Army Cavalry Regiments, 1833-1916.* NARA microfilm publication M744, 16 rolls. Records of U.S. Regular Army Mobile Units, 1821-1942, Record Group Number 391. National Archives, Washington D.C.
4. Year: 1900; Census Place: Fort Robinson, Dawes, Nebraska; Roll: 921; Page: 1A; Enumeration District: 0208; FHL microfilm: 1240921
5. Year: 1910; Census Place: Crawford Ward 2, Dawes, Nebraska; Roll: T624_841; Page: 8A; Enumeration District: 0093; FHL microfilm: 1374854
6. Historical Register of National Homes for Disabled Volunteer Soldiers, 1866-1938; (National Archives Microfilm Publication M1749, 282 rolls); Records of the Department of Veterans Affairs, Record Group 15; National Archives, Washington, D.C.

Robert I. Allen

Sometime before 1880, Robert I. Allen and his family of Kentucky, moved to Dawson Co., Nebraska. They cannot be located after the Nebraska State Census of 1885. The following census enumerations show their household. On the state census of 1885 everybody in the household is shown as white.

1880 US Census, Dawson Co., Nebraska, Covington Prect., ED 1, Page 338A 1
5-5 Robert I. Allen, mulatto, 50, farmer, b. KY, father b. KY, mother b. VA
Mary J., black, 40, wife, keeping house, b. KY, both parents b. KY
Thomas, black, 17, son, herding, b. KY, both parents b. KY
Edward, black, 15, son, attending school, b. KY, both parents b. KY
Lizzie, black, 14, daughter, attending school, b. KY, both parents b. KY
Lucy, black, 12, daughter, attending school, b. KY, both parents b. KY
George T., black, 10, son, attending school, b. KY, both parents b. KY
Julia, black, 7, daughter, b. KY, both parents b. KY
Robert D., black, 2, son, b. KY, both parents b. KY
Elijah Tann, black, 37, single, farmer, b. NY, nothing shown for birth place
        of parents

1885 Nebraska State Census, Dawson Co., Nebraska, Overton Precinct, ED 191, Page 7 2
59-59 R.I. Allen, 48, farmer, b. KY, father b. MO, mother b. VA
Mary, 44, wife, keeping house, b. KY, both parents b. KY
Lizzie, 18, daughter, at school, b. KY, both parents b. KY
Lucy, 17, daughter, at school, b. KY, both parents b. KY
George, 15, son, b. KY, both parents b. KY
Julia, 13, daughter, b. KY, both parents b. KY
Robt., 7, son, b. Canada, both parents b. KY

The son, Thomas Allen, died on 25 May 1883 and was buried in the Evergreen Cemetery in Lexington, Dawson Co., Nebraska. Also buried there is his father, R.I. Allen, with no identifying dates on his stone.

There are infant children of a Milo E. Allen buried in the Evergreen Cemetery. The plaque on their graves is identical to that of Thomas Allen. One of them is identified as having died on 10

November 1911 and another died 20 October 1922. There is a Milo Everett Allen buried in the Evergreen Cemetery, died 24 September 1997 in Rooks Co., Kansas. No date of birth is shown.

1. Year: 1880; Census Place: Covington, Dawson, Nebraska; Roll: 746; Family History Film: 1254746; Page: 338A; Enumeration District: 001; Image: 0118
2. "Nebraska State Census, 1885," database with images, *FamilySearch* (https://familysearch.org/ark:/61903/1:1:X3X2-426 : 2 April 2016), R L Allen, 1885; citing NARA microfilm publication M352 (Washington, D.C.: National Archives and Records Administration, n.d.); FHL microfilm 499,540.

Allen Briggs

Allen Briggs was a Sergeant in Co. H, 9th Cavalry. He was at Fort Robinson, Nebraska in 1895 and had been a sergeant since 1881. In March of 1896 he was detailed as a regimental standard-bearer.

Special Order 170, Adjutant General's Office, 27 July 1897, provides information about his retirement at Fort Robinson. He retired with $8.30 retained and had $60.70 in clothing and $100 in deposits due him. 1

On the 1870 US Census, Allen Briggs was at Fort McKavett, Menard Co., Texas. He is shown as age 24, black, soldier, born NC, cannot read or write. 2

Returns for US Army Cavalry Regiments, Buffalo Soldiers, reveal the following information pertaining to Allen Briggs. 3

Allen Briggs
Sgt. - Co. H, 9th Cavalry
Colonel Edward Hatch
20 Jan 1878
Fort Union, New Mexico

Allen Briggs
Sgt - Co. H, 9th Cavalry
Colonel Edward Hatch
20 Jan 1879
Tularosa, New Mexico

Allen Briggs
Sgt - Co. H, 9th Cavalry
Colonel Edward Hatch
9 Feb 1879
Fort Stanton, New Mexico

Allen Briggs
Sgt - Co. H, 9th Cavalry
Colonel Edward Hatch
25 June 1880
Fort Bayard, New Mexico

Allen Briggs
Sgt - Co. H, 9th Cavalry
Colonel Edward Hatch
7 July 1880
Fort Bayard, New Mexico

Allen Briggs
Sgt - Co. H, 9th Cavalry
Colonel David Perry
Colonel David Perry
Fort Robinson, Nebraska

4 Aug 1897
Colonel Edward Hatch
7 July 1885
North Platte, Nebraska - Brady Island

Allen Briggs
Sgt - Co. H, 9th Cavalry
Colonel James Biddle
27 August 1894
Bellevue, Nebraska

Allen Briggs
Sgt - Co. H, 9th Cavalry
Colonel James Biddle
6 July 1895
Fort Robinson, Nebraska

Allen Briggs
Sgt - Co. H, 9th Cavalry
Colonel James Biddle
22 August 1896
Fort Robinson, Nebraska

Allen Briggs
Sgt - Co. H, 9th Cavalry
Colonel James Biddle
6 September 1896
Fort Robinson, Nebraska

Allen Briggs
Sgt - Co. H, 9th Cavalry

Briggs remained in Dawes County after his retirement and is found on the 1900 US Census on Second Street in Crawford. He is shown as born June 1849 and a single person, born in North Carolina and his parents were born in Virginia. 4

He died of consumption at Crawford, Nebraska on 11 October 1901 and was buried in the Fort Robinson Cemetery. In 1947 he remains were entered at Fort McPherson National Cemetery, Maxwell, Lincoln Co., Nebraska.

1. *On the Trail of the Buffalo Soldier*, Frank Shubert, Wilmington, DL, Scholarly Resources Inc. 1995, page 53
2. 1870 U.S. census, population schedules. NARA microfilm publication M593, 1,761 rolls. Washington, D.C.: National Archives and Records Administration
3. *Returns From Regular Army Cavalry Regiments, 1833-1916*. NARA microfilm publication M744, 16 rolls. Records of U.S. Regular Army Mobile Units, 1821-1942, Record Group Number 391. National Archives, Washington D.C.
4. Year: 1900; Census Place: Crawford, Dawes, Nebraska; Roll: 921; Page: 6B; Enumeration District: 0081; FHL microfilm: 1240921

Members
AME Church - North Platte, Lincoln Co., Nebraska

The St. Mary's African Methodist Episcopal Church in North Platte finally had a building for worship in 1953. They began working to fulfill their dream of a church building in about 1951. The church building was built at Eighth and Curtis in North Platte. Before the building was erected, members met every other Sunday in the Salvation Army Outpost. Miss Belva Spicer of Lincoln came every other Sunday for two years to preach.

There were two houses already on the lot when the members purchased it. They were sold which provided funds for the church building. Members of the congregation had dinners and other acitivies to raise money.

Plans for the building included the main sanctuary about 22 by 50 feet, the entry room measuring 8 feet by 10 feet, rest rooms and a study for the minister. Plans also included a playground for children in the area.

The *North Platte Telegraph Bulletin* of 4 June 1953 published a photograph of the church cornerstone with members Mrs. Easter Hicks, Mrs. Dolly Ross, Mrs. Helen Hawkins, Mrs. Ada Ryan and Prime Hicks, Jr.

A special service was held in September 1953 to dedicate the new church, located at 1021 West 8th Street. The congregation consisted of about eighteen people. The first meeting of the congregation was held on 12 December 1949. Trustees of the church were Roy Hawkins, Mrs. Rebecca Hopkins, Mrs. Helen Hawkins, Prime Hicks, Mrs. Dolly Ross and Mrs. Easter Hicks. Stewards were Mrs. Rebecca Hopkins, Mrs. Helen Hawkins and Mrs. Dolly Ross. Stewardesses were Mrs. Rebecca Hopkins, Mrs. Helen Hawkins and Mrs. James Johnson. Ushers were Clint Mathis and Booker Nelson. *North Platte Telegraph Bulletin* 16 September 1953

Dolly (Dollie) Ross was in North Platte by 1929, when she witnessed the warning out of the blacks after the shootings at the Hummingbird Inn. She was born 11 October 1901 and died 2 March

1982. She married William F. Ross before 1929. He was born 12 January 1894 and died 9 June 1972. William served as a private in the 805th Pioneer Infantry during World War I. Both were buried in Fort McPherson National Cemetery near Maxwell, Lincoln Co., Nebraska.

Another member of the black community in North Platte was Pearl K. Duncan, born 12 October 1900 in Denver, Colorado to George Ogden Duncan and Maggie Lancaster. Pearl married George Kennedy who was born 6 September 1891 in Minneapolis, Minnesota and died 14 January 1950 in Red Oak, Montgomery Co., Iowa. Pearl died 17 May 1953 in Hastings, Adams Co., Nebraska. They were both buried in the North Platte Cemetery, North Platte, Lincoln Co., Nebraska.

George Kennedy died intestate. The Lincoln County court petitioned for the probate of his estate naming his wife Pearl and sister Helen Hawkins. The following are named with no relationship shown: Evelyn F. Dryden, James Dale Dryden, Jr., Karen J. Dryden, John K. Dryden, Dan R. Dryden and Cecil Goodwin. [1]

Evelyn Theodora From married James Dale Dryden. She was born 1907 and died 1982. James Dale Dryden was born 1907 and died 1948. They were both buried in the North Platte Cemetery, North Platte, Lincoln Co., Nebraska. The Drydens were caucasian.

Pearl's parents were living in Denver, Colorado on the 1900 and 1910 US Census. By 1910 her parents were divorced.

1900 US Census, Arapahoe Co., Colorado, Denver, ED 0007, Page 6B [2]
1122 California Street
95-96 George O. Duncan, black, b. Oct, 1871, married 6 years, b. CO, father b. KY, mother b. MO, porter drug store
Maggie, wife, black, b. March 1875, 25, married 6 years, 6 children, 3 living, b. KY, both parents b. KY
Helen, daughter, black, b. June 1895, 4, b. CO, father b. CO, mother b. KY
Lizzie P., daughter, black, b. Oct 1893, 1, b. CO, father b. CO, mother b. KY
Bert E., brother, black, b. Sept 1874, 25, married 1 year, b. CO, father b. KY, mother b. MO, common laborer
Rebecca, sister in law, black, b. April 1875, 25, married 1 year, 1 child, 1 living, b. GA, both parents b. GA

1910 US Census - Denver Co., Colorado, Denver Ward 9 ED 120 [3]
2537 Washington
97-114 Maggie Duncan, mulatto, 33, divorced, 5 children, 2 living, b. KY, both parents b. US, cook private family
Pearl, daughter, mulatto, 11, b. CO, father b. CO, mother b. KY
Helen Stewart, daughter, mulatto, 16, married 0 years, b. CO, father b. CO, mother b. KY servant, private family
John E. Stent, nephew-in-law, mulatto, 28, married 2 years, b. KS, father b. US, mother b. DC, porter, hotel
Eva B. Stent, niece, 18, married 2 years, 0 children, b. CO, father b. US, mother b. KY, maid, hotel

Helen Georgia Duncan, shown above, also came to North Platte. She married David Stewart in Colorado on 2 March 1910. She was age 16 and he was 17 years of age. [4] When she lived in North Platte her last name was Hawkins. She was born 24 June 1895 in Denver, Colorado and died 26 May 1974 in North Platte. She was buried in the North Platte Cemetery.

George Ogden Duncan, father of Helen and Pearl, was born 27 October 1871 in Denver, Colorado. He was the son of Merritt Duncan and Lilly A. Bosher. 5 However, his mother is shown as Mary on the 1880 US Census.

1880 US Census, Arapahoe Co., Colorado, Denver, ED 13, Page 285B   6
403   Merritt Duncan, 30, mulatto, janitor, b. MO, both parents b. MO
Mary, 23, wife, mulatto, keeping house, b. MO, both parents b. MO
George, 9, son, mulatto, at school, b. CO, both parents b. MO
Bertie, 4, son, mulatto, b. CO, both parents b. MO
Merritt, 3, son, mulatto, b. CO, both parents b. MO
Florence, 6/12, December, daughter, mulatto, b. CO, both parents b. MO

Merritt Duncan was born in 1836 and died March 1909; buried 14 March 1909; buried in the Fairmount Cemetery, Denver, Denver Co., Colorado.

Prime and Easter Hicks were instrumental members of the AME Church in North Platte. Prime Hicks (Jr) was born 24 May 1896 in Lampton, Marion Co., Mississippi to Prime Hicks, Sr. and Lizzie Jones. He married Easter Fox. Because she was much younger than Prime, she may have been a second wife.

1930 US Census, Yazoo Co., Mississippi, Beat 3, ED 13, Page 14A   7
Little Italy
417-417 Joseph Fox, rents, negro, 56, divorced, b. MS, both parents b. MS
Gussie H., daughter, negro, 12, b. MS, both parents b. MS
Joe By, son, negro, 10, b. Mississippi, both parents b. MS
Easter, daughter, negro 4 9/12, b. MS, both parents b. MS
Ealbert, son, negro, 3 1/12, b. MS, both parents b. MS

Easter (Ester) Fox Hicks was born 29 May 1925 in Mississippi and died 25 July 1993. According to the Social Security Death Index, her last residence was Lincoln, Lancaster Co., Nebraska. 8 She was buried in the Wyuka Cemetery, Lincoln, Lancaster Co., Nebraska. According to the Social Security Claims Index she was born in Asia City, Yazoo Co., Mississippi to Joe Fox and Harriet Hoges [Houge?]. 9

Prime Hicks, Jr. died in North Platte, Lincoln Co., Nebraska on 13 September 1963 and was buried in Floral Lawn Memorial Gardens in North Platte. He and Easter had two known children, Leroy and Glen H. Hicks. Prime and Easter moved to North Platte in 1945.

Leroy Hicks was born 9 November 1944 in Eden, Yazoo Co., Mississippi. He grew up in North Platte, Nebraska, attending Roosevelt Elementary School and Adams Junior High School. He worked for Hirschfelds in North Platte and was active in the Jaycees and the Community Play House. In 1979 he moved to Visalia, California and in 1995 to Las Vegas, Nevada. In 1999 he met Gracy Lynette Thomas and they lived together for eleven years. They married in North Platte on 10 February 2004. He died on 28 November 2009 in North Platte and was buried in Floral Lawn Memorial Gardens in North Platte, Lincoln Co., Nebraska. 10 Glen H. Hicks was born 4 December 1947 and died 1 January 2004. He was also buried in Floral Lawn Memorial Gardens, North Platte.

Another member of the AME Church in North Platte was Jessie Mae Nelson Brown. She was born on 15 November 1932 in Yazoo City, Yazoo Co., Mississippi to Murray Nelson and Chadie Hicks. She came to North Platte in 1952. Her mother, Chadie Hicks Nelson, was born 10 October 1914 in Mississippi to Prime and Elizabeth Hicks. She was a niece to Prime Hicks who also settled in North Platte.

Jessie married Booker T. Brown, Sr. who was born 29 September 1930 in Morgan City, Leflore Co., Mississippi, son of Henry Brown. Booker died 8 March 1960 in Omaha, Douglas Co., Nebraska and was buried in the North Platte Cemetery, North Platte, Lincoln Co., Nebraska. Jessie died 2 March 2005 in North Platte and was buried in the North Platte Cemetery.

She was a volunteer of several organizations, including chairwoman and director of the Commission on Christian Concern, president of the first Family Planning Clinic Board and a board member of Western Nebraska Legal Services from 1982 to 1989.

Jessie's obituary indicates that she was survived by daughters Chadie Holmes and Bettie J. Brown of Lincoln, Nebraska and Jennifer Brown of Colorado Springs, Colorado. She was survived by sons Honor Brown of Colorado, Tea Brown, Leander Brown and Isaiah Brown all of Lincoln, Nebraska and Jonathan "Tom" Brown of North Platte. A son, Booker T. Brown, Jr. was born in Nebraska on 23 May 1955 and died on 26 November 1977 in Cozad. He was buried in the North Platte Cemetery, North Platte, Lincoln Co., Nebraska. Jessie was also survived by sisters Flora Mae Holmes and Betty Hines of Mississippi and a brother Booker T. Nelson of Lincoln, Nebraska.

1 Scott Abstract Index, North Platte Public Library, Genealogy Room, North Platte, Lincoln Co., Nebraska.
2. Year: 1900; Census Place: Denver, Arapahoe, Colorado; Roll: 117; Page: 6B; Enumeration District: 0007; FHL microfilm: 1240117
3. Year: 1910; Census Place: Denver Ward 9, Denver, Colorado; Roll: T624_116; Page: 5A; Enumeration District: 0120; FHL microfilm: 1374129
4. "Colorado Statewide Marriage Index, 1853-2006," database with images, *FamilySearch* (https://familysearch.org/ark:/61903/1:1:KNQP-D4V : 3 December 2014), David Stewart and Helen Duncan, 02 Mar 1910, Colorado, United States; citing no. 48227, State Archives, Denver; FHL microfilm 1,690,138.
5. Ancestry.com. *U.S., Social Security Applications and Claims Index, 1936-2007* [database on-line]. Provo, UT, USA: Ancestry.com Operations, Inc., 2015.
6. Year: 1880; Census Place: Denver, Arapahoe, Colorado; Roll: 88; Family History Film: 1254088; Page: 285B; Enumeration District: 013; Image: 0392
7. Year: 1930; Census Place: Beat 3, Yazoo, Mississippi; Roll: 1173; Page: 14A; Enumeration District: 0013; Image: 347.0; FHL microfilm: 2340908
8. Ancestry.com. *U.S., Social Security Death Index, 1935-2014* [database on-line]. Provo, UT, USA: Ancestry.com Operations Inc, 2011.
9. Ancestry.com. *U.S., Social Security Applications and Claims Index, 1936-2007* [database on-line]. Provo, UT, USA: Ancestry.com Operations, Inc., 2015.
10. *North Platte Telegraph* 2 December 2009.

Robert Ball Anderson

An early homesteader in Box Butte County was Robert Ball Anderson. He was born in Green Co., Kentucky on 1 March 1843 to a female slave owned by Colonel Robert Ball. Her name has never been ascertained. She had six children. When the Civil War began, Colonel Ball, lived in Green Co., Kentucky and owned slaves. They were as follows. 1

    1 black, male, age 60
    1 black, male, age 35
    1 black, female, age 26
    1 black, male, age 20
    1 black, male, age 19
    1 black, female, age 15
    1 black, female, age 14
    1 black, male, age 14
    1 black, male, age 13
    1 black, male, age 10
    1 mulatto, female, age 4
    2 mulatto, females, age 2

Approximately six miles away from the Ball plantation was the plantation of Alfred Anderson, who owned 67 slaves. He was among the largest slave owners in Kentucky. Robert's father was one of his slaves. Twice a week he was allowed to visit his family on the Ball plantation. Robert's father was known as Anderson's Bill or Bill Anderson, and often referred to as "Uncle Billy." Robert's master, Robert Ball, considered him a favorite slave, so he was named Robert Ball. 2

In about 1849 Robert's mother was sold to a tracker who took her to Louisiana. After this, the children never saw their mother again and infrequently saw their father. The oldest sibling, Sylvia, took over her mother's job in the kitchen of the Ball plantation along with caring for the younger children. According to Robert's memoirs, Colonel Robert Ball's wife, his mistress, was overbearing and drunk much of the time. She mistreated Robert a good deal of the time, in one instance beating him with a raw-hide whip until he could not stand. To add injury to insult, she rubbed red pepper into his wounds and then bathed them with salt water.

Robert's father, Alfred Anderson, eventually married another woman from a different plantation. They did not have children, but she conceived a child by her master. When his mother left, Robert had a brother, William (two years older than Robert) and three sisters, Silva, Agga and Emma, but according to his memoirs, his mother had six children. When the mother left, Emma was only about three years old.

The Ball plantation, and most likely also the Anderson plantation raised flax and hemp. They mixed it with cotton or wool and spun it into thread. Even the children had to help with day to day functions on the plantation. Slave mothers made sure their children learned how to take care of themselves. Robert described the kitchen where his sister (and previously his mother) worked as being about eight feet from the plantation house. It was a log building about fifteen feet square. There was a large fireplace across one end, about eight feet long and five feet deep.

Robert described his clothing as somewhat like a gunny sack with a hole cut in the bottom for his head to go through and the corners cut out for arm holes. Only male children who had achieved the age of ten to twelve were given pants and a shirt to wear. They did not wear undergarments.

On rare occasions the slaves were permitted to hunt and bring in possum, rabbit and woodchuck. They would cook possum and yams together and dip their corn bread in the grease. Robert's master would sometimes leave scraps of food for him on his plate. Because he was a houseboy, he had to pass cake and wine when there were visitors. The cake was counted ahead of time to make sure a slave did not take any. When young, Robert was assigned the duty of pulling weeds in the garden.

The arranged marriage of slaves residing on different plantations was referred to as a broad marriage. This type of marriage was often of concern to the owners as the married couple would take time off to see each other, which sometimes caused ideas of independence. The male slave would usually be given a pass to visit his wife on a different plantation. Any children born of the marriage became the property of the mother's slave owner. 3

The Anderson and Ball plantations are shown next to each other on the 1850 US Census, Green Co., Kentucky, District 1. Alfred Anderson is shown as age 54, estate valued at $22,822, born in Virginia. Robert Ball is shown as 75, estate valued at $8,000, born in Virginia. Robert's wife, Mary was age 46, born in Virginia. 4 Colonel Robert Ball was born 29 February 1776 in Middlesex Co., Virginia and died 5 November 1866 in Green Co., Kentucky. His first wife, Anna Webb was born in 1779 and died in Green Co., Kentucky on 4 March 1818. Mary was his second wife.

When Robert turned 21, he left the plantation and went to Lebanon in Marion Co., Kentucky where he enlisted in the Union Army. He was not the only slave who was born in Green Co., Kentucky who enlisted in the US Colored Troops. There were about ninety-five who enlisted showing that as their place of birth. There were 2,052 black slaves and 317 mulatto slaves in the county in 1860. 5

Robert Ball enlisted as a private in Co. K, 125th US Colored Infantry. 6 He was in the Army only six months when Colonel Robert E. Lee surrendered at Appomatox Courthouse, Virginia. At that time his unit was sent to Kansas. In his memoirs he recalled helping to corral the Indians and put them on reservations. He claimed to have hiked on foot over 3,200 miles. Two years and eight months later he was discharged at Louisville, Jefferson Co., Kentucky.

After his discharge, Ball visited his family who were still living on the Ball plantation in Green County. They decided to take their father's last name and thus he became known as Robert Ball Anderson. He left Kentucky for Iowa where he worked from 1867 to about 1870. With his army pay he purchased some land from a dishonest real estate agent in Davenport, Scott Co., Iowa.

In 1870, Robert Ball Anderson, came to Butler Co., Nebraska where he secured land under the Homestead Act, through the Lincoln Land Office. His name is shown as Robert Anderson alias Robert Ball. The 80 acres was located in Township 14 N, Range 3 E, Section 18, West 1/2 of the South East 1/4. Within his land file there is a certificate of discharge signed by James E. Brown, 1st Lt., US Army and dated at Jefferson Barracks, Missouri, 31 October 1867. Anderson was discharged at Jefferson Barracks on that day. Statements of Final Proof within the land file indicate that he was not married and made settlement on the land on 28 May 1870. He built a sod house 12x14 feet, with one door and two glass windows. He also built a sod stable 15x30 feet and dug a well. Anderson entered the army under the name of his master, Robert Ball, discharged under that name, but his true name was Robert Anderson. He received final certificate # 2411 on 22 August 1874. 7

After loosing everything because of drought and grasshoppers, Anderson left Butler County in 1881 and moved to northeast Kansas. He worked and saved his money there for three years then decided to move to the far northwest part of Nebraska where there was an abundance of land. The government was issuing land under the Timber-Culture Act. If the settler could get trees to grow on the arid land, they could eventually own it.

On 19 July 1884 Robert Anderson, Fort Robinson, Nebraska, applied for 160 acres under the Timber-Culture Act of June 14, 1878. It was located in T28, R51, Section 35, SW 1/4. He applied at the Valentine, Nebraska Land Office. He paid $14 to file for the land. His testimony for proof was filed on 23 May 1893. He stated that he was 51 years of age, resident of Lawn, Nebraska, born in Kentucky. He broke six acres in 1885 and five and half acres in 1886. In 1886 he cultivated six acres and eleven and half acres in 1887. Six acres were planted to seeds in 1887. He planted it to ash and box elder trees, measuring the tract planted. In 1888 he planted the entire eleven and half acres to ash and box elder trees, almost measuring the tract planted. In 1889 he applied for an extension by making an affidavit ... the trees are in good, healthy condition, having made a personal examination on 22 May 1893.

In order to plant trees on land, settlers had to find them somewhere. Robert was able to get trees from the Pine Ridge, about 15 miles from where he lived. After planting his trees, he built a sod house, all this about fourteen miles northwest of Hemingford, Box Butte Co., Nebraska. He borrowed money from a bank in Hemingford at 3 % interest and bought oxen and a plow. He eventually was able to purchase more land as some settlers gave up and left. By 1895 he had 480 acres and by 1900 he had 1,120 acres and eventually around 2,000 acres. He would take his wagon into Hemingford and sell produce grown on his land.

By 1920 Robert gave up on farming and sold his ranch. He was then living in a two story, eight room house. In 1922 he went on a trip to Forrest City, St. Francis Co., Arkansas. His brother was living there. It was there he met Daisy Graham at church. Thirty days later they were married on 19 March 1922. 8 He was 79 years old and Daisy was 21 years old. Because his land was valued at $61,000, she was more than eager to return with him to Nebraska. They first went to Colorado Springs, Colorado on a honeymoon. About five years later, Robert told her his story and she wrote it down for publication.

Robert was old and tired in 1928. Some of her relatives came to help out, but were not good managers. In March of 1930 he deeded his land to his wife. In 1930 he had traveled by automobile to Forrest City, Arkansas to visit his brother. On 30 November 1930 he was in an accident near Lincoln, Nebraska and killed. Daisy was with him and bruised. Her brother, Ernest Graham, was also traveling with them and driving the vehicle. Robert was buried on 4 December 1930 in the Hemingford Cemetery, Hemingford, Box Butte Co., Nebraska. Throngs of people showed up to pay their respects. The graveside services were conducted by the Grand Chaplain of the G.A.R. from Omaha along with the Chaplain of the Alliance Chapter.

Through the years Robert had become very well known and respected in Box Butte County. He was active in the Grand Army of the Republic (GAR), a member of the Masonic Lodge and Methodist Church. When the Civil War veterans marched in a parade, Robert always carried the flag.

In addition to the sisters Emma, Sylvia and Agga, Robert had a sister, Harriet Anderson, who was the mother of Bettie Anderson. Refer to Chandler-Motley, Volume 1.

1880 US Census, Butler Co., Nebraska, Center Prect., ED 154, Page 33A 9
10-11 George W. Matingly, black, 33, widowed, farmer, b. KY, both parents
    b. KY, farmer
Robert Anderson, black, 35, boarder, single, farm laborer, b. KY, both parents
    b. KY
James Upson, white, 20, servant, single, b. IL, both parents b. IL

1900 US Census, Box Butte Co., Nebraska, Lawn Prect., ED 9, Page 1B 10
22-22 Robert Anderson, black, b. March 1842, 58, single, b. KY, father b.
    VA, mother b. unknown, farmer

1910 US Census, Box Butte Co., Nebraska, Lawn Prect. ED 11, Page 3B [11]
64-66 Robert Anderson, black, 68, single, b. KY, both parents b. KY, farmer
Harrison Tanner, hired man, black, 20, married 2 years, b. AR, both parents
      b. AR, farm laborer

1920 US Census, Box Butte Co., Nebraska, Lawn Prect., ED 15, Page 3A [12]
60-61 James Motley, rents, black, 58, b. KY, both parents b. KY, farmer
Sara E., wife, black, 56, b. KY, both parents b. KY
Virgil J., son, black, 19, single, b. KY, both parents b. KY
Joseph W. Crittenden, son-in-law, mulatto, 49, b. TX, father b. TN, mother
      b. VA, farm laborer
Cora B. Crittenden, daughter, black, 37, b. KY, both parents b. KY
Robert Anderson, uncle, black, 80, single, b. KY, both parents b. KY

There is no evidence that this could also be the same Robert Anderson in St. Francis Co.,
Arkansas. It is known he had a brother William who lived in St. Francis Co., Arkansas. If it is him, he
may have just been visiting or assisting his brother on their farm.

1920 US Census, St. Francis Co., Arkansas, Madison Township, ED 223, [13]
Page 7B
138-138 William Williams, owns, free, black, 79, b. KY, both parents b. US,
      no occupation
Katie, wife, black, 63, b. TN, father b. VA, mother b. TN
Robert Anderson, brother, black, 76, single, b. KY, both parents b. VA, farmer

1930 US Census, Box Butte Co., Nebraska, Lawn Prect., ED 10, Page 2A [14]
32-32 Robert Anderson, negro, 87, married at age 79, b. KY, both parents b.
      VA, farmer
Daisy, wife, negro, 29, married at age 21, b. TN, both parents b. TN
William Graham, brother-in-law, negro, 24, single, b. TN, both parents b. TN
Earnest Graham, brother-in-law, negro, 22, single, b. TN, both parents b. TN

"After all is said and done, I find that there is no greater rule for making and holding friends, for
happiness and contentment, and real enjoyment of life, than in doing unto others as I would like them to
do unto me and try to do it just a little better."
— Robert Ball Anderson

Daisy Graham

Daisy Graham who married Robert Anderson, was born in Tennessee in about 1901. She was
living in St. Francis Co., Arkansas when they married there on 19 March 1922. Her parents were John
Wesley Graham and Alice Davy. Daisy died 19 September 1998 in a nursing home in Denver, Denver
Co., Colorado. She had no children, but raised nieces, Rosemarie, Mary Loretta and Rita Ann. She was
the last surviving widow of a Civil War Union veteran. A memorial service was held at the Most Precious
Blood Catholic Church. On 17 October 1998 she was inducted posthumously into the Arkansas Black
Hall of Fame.

She wrote her own memoirs under the title of *Have You No Shame?*. The booklet was re-written
several times and supposedly changed a bit through the years. Daisy's personality is seen in the memoirs
as being strong-willed and very opinionated. In her book she does not mention the brother, Charles. Two
years older than Daisy, he possibly died between 1910 and 1920. She does mention brothers Ruben and

Otis who are not found on census enumerations. Her father, John Wesley Graham, worked on steamboats until he was injured and then began farming. Daisy recalled living in a one-room building and sleeping four children at one end of the bed and four at the other end of the bed.

At the age of eleven Daisy went to work for other people. Her first pay was a gallon of milk to take home for the family. It is unknown how she got to St. Francis Co., Arkansas where she married Robert Ball Anderson, but they were introduced at church by the preacher.

Daisy was not a good manager of the land or finances that Robert had acquired. They were deeded to her in March of 1930. Her husband had been generous and she was a spendthrift during the depression when she should have been thrifty. She moved to South Dakota and then in 1937 to Steamboat Springs, Colorado where her sister was living. The following is a court case in Box Butte Co., Nebraska pertaining to Daisy.

Box Butte County, Nebraska
Civil Case
District Court
Case 5141   Docket S   page 231

Daisy Anderson
vs
Clyde Ray, et al
filed 28 Feb 1935
Suit for Damages
Plaintiff is resident of Box Butte County for many years; defendants are residents of Box Butte County.

On 28 July 1934 and for about 12 years prior Daisy resided on Section 35-28-51 in Box Butte County; she was a widow; for several years owner of about 2,000 acres of land and lost ownership by reason of foreclosure and subsequent sale in July 1934.

She vacated the premises on 28 July 1934 by command and order of the sheriff and moved onto the premises known as the NE 1/4 of Section 4, Township 27, Range 51 in Box Butte County.

On 30 July 1934 at 10 pm in the night, the defendants, Jones, Sheriff; Shelmadine, Deputy Sheriff; Clyde Ray, William Clark and Harry Pierce came to her home and maliciously, unlawfully and illegally and without cause with no complaint being filed and without a search warrant and without her consent or any authority, entered and searched her home for several hours. They searched and ransacked her home, disturbed and disquieted the plaintiff. They searched the wagons upon which her furniture and other possession were stored, the stack of fodder there stored, by tearing same apart and overturning same, and said defendants searched the yard and premises immediately surrounding said home. They searched the cave near said home, tore off parts of the roof and boards of said cave. They claimed to have a search warrant for 19 window screens and one door belonging to and being a part of the building located on Section 3, Township 27, Range 51, East of the 6th P.M. claimed by the defendant Clyde Ray. She told them she had no window frames or door from that location. She demanded a search warrant and they said they had no copy for her. Jones took out a pocket flash light and read to her from a piece of paper which he claimed to be a search warrant. He refused to give her the copy. They continued the search until about one in the morning and found no door or window screens.

Finding none she was arrested and they forcibly took her without consent and warrant to Alliance and put her in jail. She was there until about 2 p.m. on 31 July 1934. She was taken by the Deputy Sheriff to the office of William Hein, County Attorney where she was questioned about removing the window screens and door. She informed him she had not taken them and did not know where they were located. Hein sent her back unlawfully and illegally to jail and imprisoned her for several hours. She was then released and given her freedom.

The defendants, Jones and Hein, again came to her home on 1 August 1934 and again searched for the window screens and door. She informed them she did not have them. They did not have a search warrant.

On 28 July 1934 she moved her personal proptery away from the premises of Section 35, 28, 51 and the deputy sheriff was present and assisted her in moving the personal property by furnishing one truck and two men who moved it into trucks and vehicles. Deputy Sheriff Shermadine told Hein that she did not remove said window screens or door while he was assisting her with the move.

Plaintiff alleges damages in the amount of $25,000. Being compelled to move out of Box Butte County she suffered great financial loss, and had to sell and dispose of all her personal property worth $1,000.

Order of Dismissal 17 Nov. 1934 oral motion of William H. Hein that the action be dismissed for reason that there is insufficient evidence upon which to base a conviction of said Daisy Anderson. Case dismissed.

28 March 1935 Special Appearance of Defendant William Hein
Objected to the purported jurisdiction of the district court over his person and moved the court to quash the summons which does not contain on the back side the seal of the Clerk of the District Court.

Motion for Security for Costs 1 April 1935
Defendants George P. Jones and Fred M. Shelmadine move the court to require Daisy Anderson to give security for costs, for reason that plaintiff is now and was at the time of her filing the petition a non-resident of Box Butte County, Nebraksa.

Court 15 May 1936 defendants require plaintiff to give security for costs; court found the motion for costs should be sustained and action dismissed at plaintiff's cost for want of prosecution. Dismissed at plaintiff's costs.

After moving to Colorado, Daisy and her parents and relatives discovered that because of the color of their skin, they were not welcome. They lived in an area called Strawberry Park where she grew strawberries that had been plucked and put into a weed pile. Eventually those few strawberries grew into an eight acre crop. She was industrious and also raised hundreds of chickens, rented out cabins in the summer and worked as a hunting guide. After a while she became somewhat of a celebrity. In 1993 she met Pope John Paul when he visited in Denver. She met President Clinton in 1997 and gave him flowers along with her husband's autobiography.

Her father, John Wesley Graham was born in July of 1874 in Savannah, Hardin Co., Tennessee. He married 20 December 1896 in Hardin Co., Tennessee to Alice Davy, born in November of 1875 in Tennessee to Daniel T. Davy and Mary E. Graves. John Wesley was the son of Joseph Ned and Maria Graham (Grayham). Alice Davy Graham died 4 February 1958. According to family information, Alice's grandmother was a full-blooded Indian and her father was white.

> 1900 US Census, Hardin Co., Tennessee, Civil Dist. 8, ED 41, Page 12B 15
> 234-234 John W. Graham, black, b. July 1874, 25, married 4 years, b. TN, both
>   parents b. VA, farmer
> Allice, wife, black, age unknown, married 4 years, 2 children, 2 living, b. TN,
>   both parents b. unknown
> Chesley L., son, black, b. Oct 1897, 2, b. TN, both parents b. TN

Daisy, daughter, black, b. Nov. 1899, b. TN, both parents b. TN

1910 US Census, Hardin Co., Tennessee, Civil Dist. 8, ED 83, Page 11A 16
203-203 Wesley Graham, black, 33, married 14 yars, b. TN, parents place
        b. unknown, farmer
Alice, wife, black, 28, married 14 years, 7 children, 5 living, b. TN, both
        parents b. TN
Charlie, son, black, 12, b. TN, both parents b. TN
Dasie, daughter, black, 10, b. TN, both parents b. TN
Gracie, daughter, black, 9, b. TN, both parents b. TN
William, son, black, 8, b. TN, both parents b. TN
Earnest, son, black, 7, b. TN, both parents b. TN

1920 US Census, Hardin Co., Tennessee, ED 83, Page 6B 17
121-121 Weslie Graham, owns, free, black, 47, b. TN, both parents b. US,
        farmer
Alice, wife, black, 45, b. TN, both parents b. TN
Daisy, daughter, black, 19, single, b. TN, both parents b. TN
Gracy, daughter, black, 16, b. TN, both parents b. TN
William, son, black, 14, b. TN, both parents b. TN
Earnest, son, black, 12, b. TN, both parents b. TN
May Ella, daughter, black, 8, b. TN, both parents b. TN

1930 US Census, Box Butte Co., Nebraska, Lawn Prect., ED 10, Page 2A 18
living next door to Robert and Daisy Anderson
33-33 John Graham, rents $10 month, negro, 55, married at age 22, b. TN, both
        parents b. TN, laborer, farm
Alice, wife, negro, 50, married at age 18, b. TN, both parents b. TN
May, daughter, negro, 18, single, b. TN, both parents b. TN

1940 US Census, Box Butte Co., Nebraska, Liberty Prect., ED 7-15, Page 2A 19
rents $2 month
John W. Graham, informant, negro, 70, 2 years education, b. TN, rural Box Butte
        Co. 1 April 1935
Alice, wife, negro, 64, 6th grade, b. TN, rural Box Butte Co. 1 April 1935

The following are the known children born to John Wesley Graham and Alice Davy.

1. Charlie L. Graham, born October 1897 in Hardin Co., Tennessee
2. Chesley L. Graham, born 17 October 1898 in Hardin Co., Tennessee
3. Daisy Graham, born about 1901 in Hardin Co., Tennessee (see above)
4. Gracy Graham, born about 1904 in Tennessee md. a Carpenter
5. William Graham, born about 1906 in Tennessee
6. Earnest Graham, born about 1908 in Hardin Co., Tennessee
7. Mae Ella Graham, born about 1912 in Tennessee

Chesley L. Graham, son of John Wesley Graham and Alice Davy, was born 17 October 1898 in
Hardin Co., Tennessee. He filed his papers for the World War I Draft Registration on 12 September 1918
in Hardin Co., Tennessee. His address is shown as Right, Hardin Co., Tennessee. He was a laborer for
L.A. Blankenship at Right in Hardin County. The nearest relative shown was his father, Wesley Graham
also of Right. On the 1920 US Census, Chesley was living with his employer Lloyd A. Blankenship, who
was a white farmer. Chesley was 21 and single, b. TN, both parents b. TN, a farm laborer. 20

Earnest Graham, son of John Wesley Graham and Alice Davy, was born about 1908 in Hardin Co., Tennessee. He was a Master Sgt. in the US Army.

Mae Ella Graham, daughter of John Wesley Graham and Alice Davy, was born about 1912 in Tennessee. She graduated from Hemingford High School, Hemingford, Box Butte Co., Nebraska. Her husband was Lee Williams who was born about 1915 in Kansas. They had three daughters, Rosie M., Mary Loretta and Rita Anne. After Mae Ella's tragic death, the girls lived with their Aunt Daisy Anderson. On the 1940 US Census, their previous location in 1935 should have been Box Butte, Nebraska instead of Kansas.

> 1940 US Census, Routt Co., Colorado, Steamboat Springs, ED 54-2, Page 61B 21
> owns $200
> Lee Williams, informant, mulatto, 25, 8th grade, b. KS, rural Box Butte, Kansas
>   1 April 1935, farmer, truck farm
> May, wife, mulatto, 26, 1 year college, b. NE, rural Box Butte, Kansas 1 April
>   1935
> Rosie M., daughter, mulatto, 4, 1st grade, b. NE, rural Box Butte, Kansas, 1 April
>   1935
> Mary L., daughter, mulatto, 2, b. NE

Joseph Ned Graham, the father of John Wesley Graham, was born about 1855 in Tennessee, the son of York Graham and Rosetta "Rose" Roberts. According to family records he married Maria —- in about 1875 in Savannah, Hardin Co., Tennessee and she was the mother of John Wesley Graham and others. There are also other wives listed. Maria —- was born about 1857 in Tennessee and died between 1900 and 1910.

> 1880 US Census, Hardin Co., Tennessee, District 6, ED 46, Page 70D 22
> 194-221 Ned Grayham, black, 25, laborer, born TN, father b. NC, mother b.
>   VA
> Maria, black, 23, wife, keeping house, b. TN, nothing shown for parents
> Wesley, black, 6, son, b. TN, both parents b. TN
> Manerva, black, 2, daughter, b. TN, both parents b. TN

> 1900 US Census, Hardin Co., Tennessee, Savannah, ED 32, Page 5B 23
> 109-109 Ned Graham, black, b. 1831, 48, married 25 years, b. TN, both
>   parents b. TN, farmer
> Delmar, son, black, b. June 1890, 10, b. TN, both parents b. TN
> Ella E., daughter, black, b. Oct 1891, 9, b. TN, both parents b. TN
> Lewis, son, black, b. Nov. 1892, 7, b. TN, both parents b. TN
> Clyde, son, black, b. Feb 1895, 5, b. TN, both parents b. TN
> W. H., son, black, b. May 1898, 2, b. TN, both parents b. TN

> 1910 US Census, Hardin Co., Tennessee, Civil District 8, ED 83, Page 15A 24
> 287-287 Ned G. Graham, black, 59, widowed, b. TN, both parents b. TN,
>   farmer
> Eller, daughter, mulatto, 17, b. TN, both parents b. TN
> Louis, son, mulatto, 16, b. TN, both parents b. TN
> Henry, son, mulatto, 13, b. TN, both parents b. TN

The following are the children born to John Ned and Maria Graham. Because of the gap of age between Manerva and Delmar, it is possible that the first two children were Maria's children and the others possibly had a different mother.

1. John Wesley Graham, born July 1874 in Savannah, Hardin Co., Tennessee
    (see above)
2. Manerva Graham, born about 1878 in Tennessee
3. Delmar Graham, born June 1890 in Savannah, Hardin Co., Tennessee
4. Ella E. Graham, born October 1891 in Savannah, Hardin Co., Tennessee
5. Lewis Graham, born 1894 in Savannah, Hardin Co., Tennessee;
    died 3 July 1918 in Massac Co., Illinois; buried in Shady Grove
    Community Cemetery, Shady Grove, Massac Co., Illinois
6. Clyde Graham, born February 1895 in Savannah, Hardin Co., Tennessee
7. W. Henry Graham, born May 1898 in Savannah, Hardin Co., Tennessee

York Graham, father of Ned G. Graham, was born about 1826 in North Carolina. He married Rosetta "Rose" Roberts who was born May 1825 in Virginia. On the 1870 US Census they are shown as Grimes which is also used as a form of Graham. There are two sons shown, one as Ned and one as Joseph. The two names are usually combined.

1870 US Census, Hardin Co., Tennessee, District 6, PO Savannah, Page 18   25
130-130 York Grimes, 44, black, farmer $25-500, b. NC
Rosetta, 45, black, keeping house, b. VA
George, 20, black, works on farm, b. TN
Robert, 16, black, works on farm, b. TN
Ned, 14, black, works on farm, b. TN
Joseph, 12, black, works on farm, b. TN
Mary, 10, black, b. TN
Martha, 8, black, b. TN
Ann, 6, black, b. TN
Belle, 3, black, b. TN
Thomas, 1, black, b. TN

1880 US Census, Hardin Co., Tennessee, District 6, ED 46, Page 70C 26
191-222 York Grayham, black, 52, farmer, b. NC, father b. NC, nothing shown
    for mother
Rosetta, black, 52, wife, keeps house, b. VA, both parents b. VA
Mary, black, 20, daughter, single, b. TN, father b. NC, mother b. VA
Martha, black, 18, daughter, single, b. TN, father b. NC, mother b. VA
Ann, black, 17, daughter, single, b. TN, father b. NC, mother b. VA
Belle, black, 14, daughter, b. TN, father b. NC, mother b. VA
John, black, 8, son, b. TN, father b. NC, mother b. VA

The following children were born to York Graham and Rosetta "Rose" Roberts.

1. George Washington Graham, born 1846 in Savannah, Hardin Co., Tennessee
2. Robert Graham, born about 1854 in Hardin Co., Tennessee
3. Joseph Ned Graham, born about 1855 in Tennessee (see above)
4. Mary Graham, born 4 October 1858 in Savannah, Hardin Co., Tennessee; died
    31 August 1945 Savannah, Hardin Co., Tennessee
5. Martha Graham, born about 1862 in Hardin Co., Tennessee
6. Ann Graham, born 15 October 1865 in Savannah, Hardin Co., Tennessee; died
    1 November 1923 in Savannah, Hardin Co., Tennessee
7. Belle Graham, born about 1867 in Hardin Co., Tennessee
8. Thomas Graham, born about 1869 in Hardin Co., Tennessee; died 1870-1880
9. John Graham, born about 1872 in Tennessee

George Washington Graham, son of York Graham and Rosetta "Rose" Roberts, was born in 1846 in Savannah, Hardin Co., Tennessee. He married Jennie Dillahaunty on 7 October 1880 in Savannah, Hardin Co., Tennessee. She was born about October 1862 in Tennessee. George died 17 April 1936 in Savannah, Hardin Co., Tennessee.

The Will of Alfred Anderson

Greeen County, Kentucky
Will Book 3
page 350
14 December 1870

Alfred Anderson, the owner of Robert Ball Anderson's father, William, and others, left his will, dated 14 December 1870 in Green Co., Kentucky. He allocated money to be given by his executors to former "servants."

> Walker Anderson, Sr. $100
> Jacob Anderson, Sr. $110
> Abram Anderson, $50
> Louisa Anderson $100
> John Caldwell $100
> Nathan his son $100
> Martha $100
> Mary $60
> Eliza $60
> Mara $60
> Susan $60
> America $60
> Nelly $60
> Total $1,020

In addition to those allocations, he left Evelina $100; Frank and Alfred, Martha's sons $25 each, bringing the final total to $1,170. His will was probated 20 January 1874 in Green Co., Kentucky.

1. Ancestry.com. *1860 U.S. Federal Census - Slave Schedules* [database on-line]. Provo, UT, USA: Ancestry.com Operations Inc, 2010.
2. *From Slavery to Affluence Memoirs of Robert Anderson, Ex-Slave*, published by The Hemingford Ledger, Hemingford, Nebraska 1927
3. Prologue Magazine http://www.archives.gov/publications/prologue/2005/spring/freedman-marriage-recs.html
4. Year: 1850; Census Place: District 1, Green, Kentucky; Roll: M432_202; Page: 109B; Image: 224
5. Notable Kentucky African Americans Database http://nkaa.uky.edu/record.php?note_id=2356
6. NARA Film Number M589, roll 4
7. Homestead Application No. 5282 http://www.fold3.com
8. Ancestry.com. Arkansas, County Marriages Index, 1837-1957 [database on-line]. Provo, UT, USA: Ancestry.com Operations, Inc., 2011.
9. Year: 1880; Census Place: Center, Butler, Nebraska; Roll: 744; Family History Film: 1254744; Page: 33A; Enumeration District: 154; Image: 0070
10. Year: 1900; Census Place: Lawn, Box Butte, Nebraska; Roll: 917; Page: 1B; Enumeration District: 0009; FHL microfilm: 1240917

11. Year: 1910; Census Place: Lawn, Box Butte, Nebraska; Roll: T624_838; Page: 3B; Enumeration District: 0011; FHL microfilm: 1374851

12. Year: 1920; Census Place: Lawn, Box Butte, Nebraska; Roll: T625_979; Page: 3A; Enumeration District: 15; Image: 1120

13. Year: 1920; Census Place: Madison, St Francis, Arkansas; Roll: T625_80; Page: 7B; Enumeration District: 223; Image: 1029

14. Year: 1930; Census Place: Lawn, Box Butte, Nebraska; Roll: 1266; Page: 2A; Enumeration District: 0010; Image: 1000.0; FHL microfilm: 2341001

15. Year: 1900; Census Place: Civil District 8, Hardin, Tennessee; Roll: 1576; Page: 12B; Enumeration District: 0041; FHL microfilm: 1241576

16. Year: 1910; Census Place: Civil District 8, Hardin, Tennessee; Roll: T624_1504; Page: 11A; Enumeration District: 0083; FHL microfilm: 1375517

17. Year: 1920; Census Place: Civil District 8, Hardin, Tennessee; Roll: T625_1744; Page: 6B; Enumeration District: 83; Image: 1118

18. Year: 1930; Census Place: Lawn, Box Butte, Nebraska; Roll: 1266; Page: 2A; Enumeration District: 0010; Image: 1000.0; FHL microfilm: 2341001

19. Year: 1940; Census Place: Liberty, Box Butte, Nebraska; Roll: T627_2237; Page: 2A; Enumeration District: 7-15

20. Year: 1920; Census Place: Civil District 8, Hardin, Tennessee; Roll: T625_1744; Page: 2B; Enumeration District: 83; Image: 1110

21. Year: 1940; Census Place: Steamboat Springs, Routt, Colorado; Roll: T627_479; Page: 61B; Enumeration District: 54-2

22. Year: 1880; Census Place: District 6, Hardin, Tennessee; Roll: 1260; Family History Film: 1255260; Page: 70D; Enumeration District: 046

23. Year: 1900; Census Place: Savannah, Hardin, Tennessee; Roll: 1576; Page: 5B; Enumeration District: 0032; FHL microfilm: 1241576

24. Year: 1910; Census Place: Civil District 8, Hardin, Tennessee; Roll: T624_1504; Page: 15A; Enumeration District: 0083; FHL microfilm: 1375517

25. 1870 U.S. census, population schedules. NARA microfilm publication M593, 1,761 rolls. Washington, D.C.: National Archives and Records Administration

26. Year: 1880; Census Place: District 6, Hardin, Tennessee; Roll: 1260; Family History Film: 1255260; Page: 70C; Enumeration District: 046

David Badie

David Badie was born in about 1847-1849 in Bourbon Co., Kentucky. He had enlisted by 1870 when he is shown on the US Census at Fort Clark in Texas.

1870 US Census, Fort Clark US Military Reservation, Kinney Co., Texas 1
Co. G, 9th Regiment
David Badie, 24, mulatto, born Kentucky, cannot read or write

He served as a 1st Sergeant in Co. B, 9th Cavalry. In October of 1879 David was praised for bravery against Victorio, by Major Albert P. Morrow. On 16 August 1881 he led a detachment of fourteen soldiers against Indians in Nogal Canyon, New Mexico. Victorio was a warrior and chief of the Warm Springs band of the Tchihendeh division of the central Apaches. In 1879 and 1880 the 9th Cavalry pursued Victorio, engaging in numerous fights against the Apaches. This came to an end in October of 1880 when Mexican soldiers, backed by the US Army troops, killed Victorio in the mountains of Chihuahua.

On 15 October 1887 he was authorized for a four-month furlough at Fort Duchesne, Utah. By

1888 he was serving as a 1st Sergeant at Fort Robinson, Nebraska. He died at Fort Robinson on 24 January 1924 of interstitial nephritis. His funeral was held at the Fort Robinson post hall on 26 January 1924 and burial was in the cemetery at Fort Robinson. In 1947 his remains were removed to Fort McPherson National Cemetery, Maxwell, Lincoln Co., Nebraska. David's wife, Katie was living in California in 1910 and 1920, as shown on census enumerations. [2]

There is a marriage record in Dawes Co., Nebraska for Solomon Hollomon and Ida Badie. She was 17, born Trinidad, Colorado, residing in Dawes County; daughter of David Badie and Catherine J. Holland. The marriage was on 16 February 1893 at Fort Robinson. [3] The following census enumerations show more about these families.

1880 US Census, Grant Co., New Mexico, Fort Bayard, ED 15, Page 352B [4]
6-6 Kate Badie, black, married, 22, laundress, b. MD, both parents b. MD
Ida L., black, 3, daughter, b. CO, father b. KY, mother b. MD
Wm. A., black, 1, son, b. NM, father b. KY, mother b. MD

1900 US Census, Pinal Co., Arizona Territory, Fort Grant, ED 88, Page 2A [5]
31-31 Soloman Holloman, black, b. Aug 1848, 51, married 7 years, b. NC, both parents
      b.VA, 1st Sgt. US Cav.
Ada L., wife, black, b. Dec 1876, 23, married 7 years, 3 children, 2 living, b. CO,
      father b. KY, mother b. MD, cook
Solloman J., son, black, b. Nov 1893, 6, b. NE, father b. NC, mother b. CO,
      at school
William M., son, b. Nov 1899, 6/12, b. AZ Territory, father b. NC, mother b.
      CO
John Adams, boarder, black, b. Feb 1850, 50, single, b. MD, both parents b.
      MD, laundry man

By 1910 Ida Halloman (Holloman) was living with her mother in California and is shown on the census enumeration as a widow with three young children.

1910 US Census, Monterey Co., California, Monterey, ED 13, Page 19B [6]
176-178 Katie Badie, black, 56, widow, 1 child, 1 living, b. MD, both parents
      b. MD, laundress, at home
Ida Halloman, daughter, black, 32, widow, 4 children, 4 living, b. CO, father
      b. KY, mother b. MD, laundress, at home
William Halloman, grandson, black, 10, b. AZ, father b. NC, mother b. CO
Arthur Halloman, grandson, black, 7, b. NE, father b. NC, mother b. CO
Mattie, granddaughter, black, 9/12, b. NE, father b. NC, mother b. CO

1920 US Census, Monterey Co., California, New Monterey, ED 20, Page 13A [7]
815 McClellan
323-349 Katie Badie, rents, black, 56, widow, b. MD, both parents b. MD, father
      b. US, mother b. MD, laundress, at home
Mattie Holloman, granddaughter, black, 10, b. NE, father b. NC, mother b. CO

1. Ancestry.com. *1870 United States Federal Census* [database on-line]. Provo, UT, USA:Ancestry.com Operations, Inc., 2009.
2. *On the Trail of the Buffalo Soldier* by Frank N. Schubert Wilmington, DL: Scholarly Resources, Inc. 1955 page 21
3. Dawes Co., Nebraska Marriage Book B page 234 Dawes Co., Nebraska Marriage Book B page 234

4. Year: 1880; Census Place: Fort Bayard, Grant, New Mexico; Roll: 802; Family History Film: 1254802; Page: 352B; Enumeration District: 015; Image: 0711
5. Year: 1900; Census Place: Fort Grant, Pinal, Arizona Territory; Roll: 47; Page: 2A; Enumeration District: 0088; FHL microfilm: 1240047
6. Year: 1910; Census Place: Monterey, Monterey, California; Roll: T624_89; Page: 19B; Enumeration District: 0013; FHL microfilm: 1374102
7. Year: 1920; Census Place: Monterey, Monterey, California; Roll: T625_122; Page: 13A; Enumeration District: 20; Image: 1011

Daniel Baxter

Daniel Baxter was born in July of 1839 in North Carolina. He enlisted on 29 April 1865 in the Union Army, serving as a Corporal in Co. K, 40th United States Colored Infantry. The 40th was organized on 29 February 1864 in Nashville, Tennessee. Men in the 40th spent their entire service guarding railroad lines and depots in Tennessee. Their guard duty was primarily along the Nashville and Louisville Railroad, the Northwestern Railroad and railroad depots in the District of East Tennessee. Daniel Baxter probably served about one year as the 40th United States Colored Infantry was mustered out of service on 25 April 1866. [1]

According to the US Colored Troops Military Service Records, Daniel was born in Lincoln Co., North Carolina. The Company Descriptive Book indicates that he was 24 years of age, 5 feet 4 inches in height and a farmer. Daniel enlisted at Greenville, Tennessee under Capt. Thornton for three years, as a private. He was promoted to corporal on 1 July 1865. When the 1890 Veteran enumeration was taken, Daniel indicated that his discharge date was lost. The muster rolls indicate he was mustered out on 23 April 1866 at Chattanooga, Tennessee. [2]

He and his wife, Manerva, were from Forsyth Co., North Carolina where she died probably in about 1880-1881. He came to Nebraska in about 1888, settling in Seward Co., Nebraska and then moved to Ansley, Nebraska before 1890, then to Broken Bow, Nebraska. Daniel died 27 August 1901 and was buried in the Westerville Cemetery, Westerville, Custer Co., Nebraska. The following enumeration shows their household in North Carolina before coming to Nebraska.

> 1870 US Census, Forsyth Co., North Carolina, Vienna Twp. [3]
> 106-106 Daniel Backster, 34, black, farming, b. NC
> Manerva, 23, black, keeping house, b. NC
> Mary, 3, black, b. NC
> Robert, 1, black, b. NC
> Mary Transon, 9, black, b. NC

The following is the enumeration of 1880 for the Baxter family in Forsyth Co., North Carolina. His wife is shown as Manerva on the 1870 US Census, but on the 1880 she is shown as D. Baxter. Records in the Custer County Historical Society Museum in Broken Bow, Custer Co., Nebraska, indicate he was married to Dorcus Prier instead of a Manerva.

> 1880 US Census, Forsyth Co., North Carolina, Vienna Twp., ED 77, Page 344C [4]
> 78-78 D. Baxter, black, 35, father, b. NC, both parents b. NC
> D. Baxter, black, female, 33, mother, b. NC, both parents b. NC
> M.A. black, female, 11, daughter, b. NC, both parents b. NC
> William Baxter, black, 2, son, b. NC, both parents b. NC

The 1890 Veterans Schedules (Union Army) have survived for Nebraska. Daniel Baxter is shown in Ansley, Custer Co., Nebraska. He served as a Corporal in Co. K, 40th US Colored Infantry, enlisted 29 April 1865. There is a notation that the discharge date was lost and unknown. 5 Daniel applied, from Nebraska, for a military pension on 15 June 1891 and received it; application 1032187, certificate 764896. 6

>1900 US Census, Custer Co., Nebraska, Ansley, ED 58, Page 9B 7
>191-192 Daniel Baxter, black, b. July 1839, 60, widowed, b. NC, parents b.
>>unknown, pension
>Clara M., daughter, black, b. April 1878, 22, single, b. NC, both parents b. NC

Mary Ann E. Baxter, daughter of Daniel and Manerva or Dorcus Baxter, was born about 1867 in North Carolina. On 6 February 1887 she married William S. Shores in Custer Co., Nebraska. He was the son of Jeremiah and Rachel Shores. 8 Refer to Shores and Speese , Volume 2.

Clara Magdalene Baxter, daughter of Daniel and Manerva or Dorcus Baxter, was born 27 April 1878 in Forsyth Co., North Carolina, perhaps at or near Winston-Salem. She married Radford L. Speese on 7 April 1901 on Westerville, Custer Co., Nebraska. He was the son of Moses Speese and Susan Kirk, and born in March of 1872 in North Carolina. Radford died in 1924 and was buried in the Fairview Cemetery in Scottsbluff, Scotts Bluff Co., Nebraska. Clara died 3 April 1976 in Omaha, Douglas Co., Nebraska, and was buried in the Forest Lawn Cemetery in Omaha, Douglas Co., Nebraska. Clara was selected as Mother of the Year to St. John A.M.E. Church in Omaha, Nebraska for the year 1959. She joined the Methodist Church at the age of fourteen and joined the St. John African Methodist Episcopal Church in 1924 when she moved to Omaha. For more information on the children of Clara and Radford, refer to Shores and Speese in Volume 2.

The following desribes the land in Nebraska that was purchased by Daniel Baxter. He purchased the land, comprised of 160 acres, at the Grand Island Land Office, Grand Island, Nebraska, issue date 28 October 1890. It was located in Custer County approximately four to five miles southwest of Westerville. 9

>6th PM Twp 16N Range 19W Section 12
>East 1/2 Northeast 1/4
>Southwest 1/14 Northeast 1/4
>Southeast 1/4 Northeast 1/4

Baxter Slave Owners in North Carolina

If Daniel Baxter assumed the surname of Baxter from his master, then he possibly was a slave of Peter Zimmerman Baxter who lived, before the Civil War, in Lincoln Co., North Carolina. Peter Z. Baxter served in the Confederate Army as a Captain. He was born in 1821 and died in 1884. His wife was Sarah Bess, daughter of Bastian "Boston" Bess and Mary "Polly" Carpenter. Peter's parents were William Baxter and Sarah Carpenter. On the 1850 US Census Slave Schedule, Lincoln Co., North Carolina, Peter Z. Baxter is shown with seven slaves; one male was age 12 and one male was age 8. On the 1860 US Census Slave Schedule, Lincoln Co., North Carolina, Peter Z. Baxter owned fifteen slaves; two males were age 20 and one male was age 25. 10

On the 1860 US Census, Lincoln Co., North Carolina, Peter Zimmerman Baxter's real estate was valued at $10,000 and his personal property at $22,500. The personal property included his fifteen slaves. On the 1870 US Census, Lincoln Co., North Carolina his real estate had increased to $15,000 and his personal property had decreased to $500, due to the emancipation of slaves.

1. NARA Publications https://www.archives.gov/research/microfilm/m1993.pdf used 26 July 2016
2. The National Archives at Washington, D.C.; Washington, D.C.; Compiled Military Service Records of Volunteer Union Soldiers Who Served with the United States Colored Troops: Infantry Organizations, 36th through 40th; Microfilm Serial: M1993; Microfilm Roll: 101
3. 1870 U.S. census, population schedules. NARA microfilm publication M593, 1,761 rolls. Washington, D.C.: National Archives and Records Administration, n.d.Minnesota census schedules for 1870. NARA microfilm publication T132, 13 rolls. Washington, D.C.: National Archives and Records Administration
4. Year: 1880; Census Place: Vienna, Forsyth, North Carolina; Roll: 963; Family History Film: 1254963; Page: 334C; Enumeration District: 077; Image: 0169
5. Year: 1890; Census Place: Ansley, Custer, Nebraska; Roll: 37; Page: 1; Enumeration District: 136
6. National Archives and Records Administration. U.S., Civil War Pension Index: General Index to Pension Files, 1861-1934 [database on-line]. Provo, UT, USA: Ancestry.com Operations Inc, 2000. Original data: *General Index to Pension Files, 1861-1934*. Washington, D.C.: National Archives and Records Administration. T288, 546 rolls.
7. Year: 1900; Census Place: Ansley, Custer, Nebraska; Roll: 921; Page: 9B; Enumeration District: 0058; FHL microfilm: 1240921
8. Custer Co., Nebraska Marriage Book 1 page 366
9. U.S. Department of the Interior, Bureau of Land Management, General Land Office Records http://www.glorecords.blm.gov/details/patent/default.aspx?accession=NE0840__.330&docClass=STA&sid=uapz4hnv.h5i
10. Ancestry.com. *1850 and 1860 U.S. Federal Census - Slave Schedules* [database on-line]. Provo, UT, USA: Ancestry.com Operations Inc, 2010.

William C. Beckett

Sergeant William C. Beckett served in Co. E, 10th Cavalry. He was born in Virginia and served first as a private from 21 December 1887 to 20 December 1892. He was in Co. G, 10th Cavalry on 10 April 1893 and again in Co. E, 10th Cavalry on 5 June 1893. Beckett was promoted to corporal on 16 January 1896. The following year he was stationed at Fort Custer, Montana.

After his initial enlistment he was at Fort Apache, Arizona. In 1898 he served in Cuba. After his discharge, Beckett lived in Crawford, Dawes Co., Nebraska. He had been stationed at Fort Robinson from 1902 to 1907. Beckett was a good friend of Henry McClain, a fellow comrade. It appears that Beckett never applied for a pension. [1]

Along with Sgt. Caleb Benson, he was present at the dedication of twin mouments at Fort Robinson on 5 September 1934. The monuments were in memory of Lieutenant Levi H. Robinson, the fort's namesake and Crazy Horse, Oglala Sioux. [2] Even though his surname is spelled incorrectly, William and wife Anne are shown on the 1930 US Census in Dawes Co., Nebraska.

1930 US Census, Dawes Co., Nebraska, Crawford, ED 9, Page 4B [3]
86-103 William C. Beckes, owns, $1,400, negro, 58, age 22 at first marriage,
     b. MD, both parents b. MD, no occupation
Anne C., wife, negro, 64, age 44 at first marriage, b. MD, both parents b. MD

1. *On the Trail of the Buffalo Soldier*, Shubert, page 32
2. Buffalo Soldiers, etc. by Shubert, page 183
3. Year: 1930; Census Place: Crawford, Dawes, Nebraska; Roll: 1271; Page: 4B; Enumeration District: 0009; Image: 148.0; FHL microfilm: 2341006

William Bell

William Bell was a Quarter Master Sergeant in Co. B, 10th Cavalry. He was recommended for the Medal of Honor for heroism in the assault on San Juan Hill on 1 July 1898.

Bell's wife, Lulu, worked at Fort Robinson, Nebraska as a servant for one of the officers. She was expelled from this position during Colonel Biddle's hostility over dependents living on the post. After this William and Lulu lived in Crawford.

On 25 July 1904 he and his wife, Lulu, were at a dance at Fort Robinson, which was in honor of Sergeant Perry of Co. L, 10th Cavalry. After quarreling with her husband, she shot him twice with a pistol. He died 26 July 1904 at Fort Robinson, having been a twenty-three year veteran. At the time he and his wife were residing in the southwest part of Crawford. He was buried on 27 July 1904 at the Fort Robinson Cemetery. In 1947 his remains were removed to Fort McPherson National Cemetery at Maxwell, Lincoln Co., Nebraska. 1

The following are Returns from Regular Army Cavalry Regiments that detail information regarding William Bell. 2

William Bell
recruit
Co. B, 10th Cavalry
Colonel John K. Mizner
19 November 1893
Fort Custer, Montana

William Bell
Sergeant
Co. B, 10th Cavalry
18 July 1898

William Bell
Sergeant
Co. B, 10th Cavalry
1 November 1899
St. Lucia, Cuba

William Bell
Quartermaster Sergeant
Co. B, 10th Cavalry
16 April 1901
Holguin, Cuba
Colonel Samuel M. Whitside

William Bell
Quartermaster Sergeant
Co. B, 10th Cavalry
Colonel Samuel M. Whitside
16 April 1901
Holguin, Cuba

William Bell
Quartermaster Sergeant
Co. B, 10th Cavalry
Colonel Jacob A. Agur
28 August 1902
Fort Robinson, Nebraska

William Bell
Quartermaster Sergeant
Colonel Jacob A. Agur
Co. B, 10th Cavalry
27 April 1904
Fort Robinson, Nebraska

1. *Buffalo Soldiers, Braves and the Brass The Story of Fort Robinson* by Frank N. Schubert, The White Mane Publishing Company, Inc., Shippensburg, PA, 1993, pp 67, 68
2. *Returns From Regular Army Cavalry Regiments, 1833-1916*. NARA microfilm publication M744, 16 rolls. Records of U.S. Regular Army Mobile Units, 1821-1942, Record Group Number 391. National Archives, Washington D.C.

Ben Nelson

On the 1930 US Census, Ben Nelson appears in the household of Julia Shelton, widow of Samuel "Sam" Shelton who had died the previous year in Alliance, Box Butte Co., Nebraska. Ben is shown as a cousin, age 19, born in Nebraska. His father was born in Kentucky and his mother was born in Kansas. He was a truck driver for the city scavingers. He was still in Box Butte County in 1940. [1]

1940 US Census, Box Butte Co., Nebraska, Boyd Prect., ED 7-8, Page 5A [2]
rents
Ben Nelson, informant, negro, 30, single, 3 years high school, b. NE,
     same house Alliance 1 April 1935, scavenger, city scavenger
Ernest Nickens, boarder, negro, 39, married, wife elsewhere, 6th grade,
     b. MO, residing Alliance, Box Butte Co., NE on 1 April 1935,
     laborer, city scavenger

On 2 September 1940 in Alliance, Box Butte Co., Nebraska, Ben married Martha Crawford of Omaha. He is shown on the marriage record and license as Benjamin F. Nelson, resident of Alliance, colored, 30, first marriage, born in Lincoln, Lancaster Co., Nebraska. His parents are shown as Margaret Cloyd, born Kansas and William Nelson, born Kentucky. His wife, Martha Crawford was of Omaha, negro, age 30, divorced, second marriage. She was also born in Lincoln, Lancaster Co., Nebraska. Her parents are shown as Toby James, born in Texas and Leigh Reeves, born in Kansas. They were married by Rev. G.W. Brown. The witnesses were Birdie E. Murphy and Wilma Darnell. [3]

Before coming to Box Butte County, he was living with Charles and Birdie Murphy in Cherry County. The Murphys also moved to Box Butte County. They are shown on the 1920 US Census in Cherry County.

1920 US Census, Cherry Co., Nebraska, Kennedy Prect, ED 54, Page 2B [4]
36-36 Charles H. Murphy, owns, mortgaged, mulatto, 56, b. KY, both
     parents b. MO, farmer, stock farmer
Birdie E., wife, black, 48, b. IA, father b. TN, mother b. MO
Benjamin F. Nelson, mulatto, 9, b. NE, father b. KY, mother b. KS

Prior to 1920, Benjamin "Ben" Nelson was living with his parents in Lincoln, Nebraska. Both of his parents died when he was very young and he was apparently taken in by Charles and Birdie Murphy who also lived in Lincoln.

His mother, Margaret L. Cloyd Nelson, was born 2 April 1868 in Kentucky and died 7 July 1914. She was buried in Wyuka Cemetery, Lincoln, Lancaster Co., Nebraska. His father, William H. Nelson was born 28 August 1861 in Kentucky and died 28 March 1919. He was also buried in the Wyuka Cemetery.

The Evening State Journal and Lincoln Daily News 26 March 1919 page 14
"William H. Nelson, fifty-five years of age, died at 5 p.m. Tuesday in Lincoln. The body is being held at Brown's parlors pending funeral arrangements. Mr. Nelson lived in Lincoln more than twenty years."

In 1908 Wm. H. Nelson is shown as living at 1941 N. 30th St. in Lincoln, Nebraska. He was a janitor at the post office. In 1913 they had moved to 3533 N. 9th St. in Lincoln, Nebraska. They are shown as colored, his wife was Margaret L. and he was still a janitor at the post office. [5]

1900 US Census, Lancaster Co., Nebraska, Lincoln Ward 1, ED 44, Page 4B [6]

824 P Street

55-68 Wm. H. Nelson, black, b. Aug 1861, 39, married 6 years, b. KY, both
parents b. KY, barber

Margaret, wife, black, b. April 1866, 24, married 6 years, 4 children, 3 living,
b. KY, both parents b. KY

Wm. M., son, black, b. April 1894, 6, b. NE, both parents b. KY, at school

Margarette, daughter, black, b. Dec 1896, 3, b. NE, both parents b. KY

Jenette, daughter, black, b. Feb 1899, 1, b. NE, both parents b. KY

Henry Taylor, lodger, black, b. Jan 1860, 40, married, married 1 year, b. PA, both
parents b. KY, day laborer

Isaac Maxwell, lodger, black, b. May 1857, 43, single, b. KY, both parents
b. KY, hotel waiter

Julius Sapington, lodger, black, b. Nov 1854, 45, single, b. KY, both parents
b. KY, hotel waiter

Dan'l. Daughterty, lodger, black, b. Jan 1862, 38, single, b. KY, both parents
b. MS, porter

Wm. Lewis, lodger, black, b. Oct 1864, 35, married 1 year, b. KY, both
parents b. KY, hotel waiter

Emmary Cloyd, mother-in-law, black, b. Dec 1841, 58, married, married
40 years, 9 children, 2 living, b. KY, both parents b. KY

1910 US Census, Lancaster Co., Nebraska, Lincoln, Ward 5, ED 78, Page 11A 7

2127 South 10th Street

277-286 William H. Nelson, black, 47, married 18 years, b. KY, both parents b.
KY, janitor, post office

Margaret L., wife, black, 42, married 18 years, 9 children, 8 living, b. KY,
both parents b. KY

Margaret O., daughter, black, 13, b. NE, both parents b. KY

Irma G., daughter, black, 11, b. NE, both parents b. NE

Mary, daughter, black, 7, b. NE, both parents b. KY

Mack, son, black, 6, b. NE, both parents b. KY

David, son, black, 4, b. NE, both parents b. KY

Vernon, son, black, 2, b. NE, both parents b. KY

Benjamin, son, black, 10/12, b. NE, both parents b. KY

There is a Vernon J. Nelson born 29 June 1909 and died on 4 May 1913. He was buried in Wyuka Cemetery, Lincoln, Lancaster Co., Nebraska and may be the son of William H. Nelson and Margaret L. Cloyd.

Margaret Cloyd, the mother of Benjamin F. "Ben" Nelson, was born 2 April 1868 in Kentucky. She was the daughter of Alfred and Emma Cloyd as shown on the 1870 US Census. The Cloyds cannot be located on the 1880 US Census, but Emma was living in Lincoln, Lancaster Co., Nebraska, with her daughter and son-in-law when the 1900 US Census was taken. Emma was born 17 February 1842 in Kentucky and died 16 April 1912. She was buried in Wyuka Cemetery in Lincoln, Lancaster Co., Nebraska.

1870 US Census, Cumberland Co., Kentucky, Marrowbone, Page 37, PO 8

Burksville

6275 Alfred Cloyd, 32, black, farmer $2,000 b. KY

Emma, 30, black, keeping house, b. KY

Anderson, 12, black, on farm, b. KY

Mary, 9, black, b. KY

Susan, 6, black, b. KY
Margaret, 2, black, b. KY

1910 US Census, Lancaster Co., Nebraska, Lincoln, Ward 3, ED 64, Page 2A 9
1959 Vine Street
37-37 Emma Cloyd, black, 67, widow, 9 children, 2 living, b. KY, father b. VA,
     mother b. KY, domestic, general house work

Benjamin Nelson, was born 13 April 1910 and died 8 April 1986 in Santa Clara Co., California. His wife, Myrtha Leigh James Nelson, was born 9 September 1909 and died 28 June 1982 in San Mateo Co., California. According to her death record she was born in Tennessee which is incorrect. 10

James and Reeves

Martha (Myrtha) Crawford who married Benjamin F. Nelson was married first to Lovejoy Crawford. They divorced by 1940 when she married Benjamin F. Nelson in Alliance, Box Butte Co., Nebraska. The correct spelling of her given name was Myrtha. According to her marriage record and license to Benjamin F. Nelson, she was age 30, born in Lincoln, Lancaster Co., Nebraska to Toby James and Leigh Reeves.

On the 1940 US Census, Lovejoy Crawford was living at 2505 Maple Street in Omaha, Douglas Co., Nebraska. He owned his property, valued at $2,000. He is shown as negro, 37, divorced, 1 year college, b. Oklahoma, occupation lineman, county surveyor's office. Also in his household are his daughter and father. The daughter was Florentine, negro, age 9, 3rd grade, born in Nebraska. His father, John, was the informant. He was 70, widowed, born in Missouri. John was a janitor at a retail bakery. All three had been living in the same house on 1 April 1935. Lovejoy and Myrtha were living with his parents in Omaha in 1930. 11

1930 US Census, Douglas Co., Nebraska, Omaha, ED 16, Page 11A 12
2507 Maple Street
184-187 John Crawford, owns, $2,500, negro, 60, married at age 29, b. MO,
     both parents b. MO, janitor, apartments
Henrietta, wife, negro, 65, married at age 20, b. Canada, both parents b. Canada
Lovejoy, son, negro, 28, married at age 27, b. NE, father b. MO, mother b.
     Canada, news advertising manager, news paper office
Mertha, daughter-in-law, negro, 20, married at age 21, b. IA, both parents b. US

According to the Omaha City Directory, Lovejoy and Myrtha Crawford were living at 2505 Maple in 1936. 13 On the Social Security Death Index, Lovejoy M. Crawford is shown as born 16 August 1902, died 8 June 1992; number issued in Nebraska. His last residence was Downingtown, Chester Co., Pennsylvania. 14

Lovejoy Crawford and Myrtha James had a daughter, Florentine Lee. She was born about 1931 in Omaha, Douglas Co., Nebraska. Apparently her father had custody of her after the divorce of her parents. She graduated from Central High School in Omaha, Nebraska and attended the University of Nebraska in Lincoln. She married Nelson P. Williams who was born 8 March 1923 in Florida to Nelson P. Williams, Sr. and Frances Miller. He died 7 September 2008 at Coatesville, Chester Co., Pennsylvania. Florentine died 11 July 2002 in Downingtown, Chester Co., Pennsylvania. Both Florentine and her husband Nelson P. Williams, Jr. were buried in Indiantown Gap National Cemetery in Annville, Lebanon Co., Pennsylvania. Nelson Williams served in the United States Marine Corps.

213

Myrtha James Crawford Nelson was the daughter of Manitoba Chester "Toby" James and Leigh Reeves. They were married on 22 May 1906 in Fort Scott, Bourbon Co., Kansas, both are shown as colored. He was 24 years of age and she was 21 years of age. They were married by Rev. M. Whooten of the A.M.E. Church. 15. The family are first shown on the 1910 US Census in Grand Island, Nebraska.

1910 US Census, Hall Co., Nebraska, Grand Island, Ward 1, ED 101, Page 9A 16
1206 Fourth
187-190 Tobe James, white, 24, married 4 years, b. TX, both parents b. TX,
          signwriter, at home
Lee, wife, black, 25, married 4 years, 2 children, 2 living, b. TN, both parents
     b. TN
Maunne, son, black, 3, b. NE, father b. TX, mother b. TN
Martha, daughter, black, 1, b. NE, father b. TX, mother b. TN
Nannie (Carthen, crossed through for surname), mother, black, 40, widow,
     b. TX, father b. MO, mother b. VA, cook

On 12 September 1918 in Lancaster Co., Nebraska, Manitoba Chester James filed his World War I Draft Registration. He was living at 830 No. 17th in Lincoln, Lancaster Co., Nebraska. He was a cleaner and dryer at Evans Laundry, 333 No. 12th Street in Lincoln. His nearest relative was Leigh James of the home address. 17

1920 US Census, Lancaster Co., Nebraska, Lincoln, Ward 3, ED 63, 2B 18
42 N. 17th Street
850-42 Manitoba James, rents, black, 34, b. NE, parents birth place unknown,
          cleaners
Lee, wife, black, 35, b. KS, both parents b. TN
Maraunce, son, black, 12, b. NE, father b. NE, mother b. KS
Myrtha, daughter, black, 11, b. NE, father b. NE, mother b. KS
Edna, daughter, black, 9, b. NE, father b. NE, mother b. KS

1930 US Census, Douglas Co., Nebraska, Omaha, ED 17, Page 1A 19
2427 Maple Street
6-8 Manitoba James, owns $2,724, negro, 44, married at age 19, b. TX, father
          b. US, mother b. TX, spotter, dry cleaners
Leigh, wife, negro, 45, married at age 20, b. TN, both parents b. TN
Edna Mae, daughter, negro, 19, single, b. NE, father b. TX, mother b. TN,
          lynotype operator, newspaper
Clinton, son, negro, 17, b. NE, father b. TX, mother b. TN
Betty Jean, daughter, negro, 8, b. NE, father b. TX, mother b. TN

The World War II Draft Registration for Manitoba Chester James, indicates he was living at 935 Campbell, Oakland, Alameda Co., California. He was age 56, born in Fort Worth, Texas on 1 November 1885. His relative was Leigh James of the same address. He was employed at Campbell Cleaners, 4476 Emery, Emeryville, Alameda Co., California. Under physical characteristics, he stated his hand was burned. It was filed on 11 September 1943 in Alameda Co., California. 20

Manitoba Chester "Toby" James and his wife, Leigh, were both buried in the Evergreen Cemetery, Garden of Prayer, Oakland, Alameda Co., California. According to the California Death Index, Manitoba was born 1 November 1885 in Texas, died 12 January 1951 in Alameda Co., California. His mother's maiden name was Arnet. According to the California Death Index, Leigh was born 9 December 1885 in Tennessee and died 9 November 1954 in Alameda Co., California. Nothing is shown for the surnames of her parents. 21

The following are the children born to Manitoba Chester "Toby" James and Leigh Reeves.
1. Maurance M. James, born 10 April 1907 in Nebraska
2. Myrtha Leigh James, born 9 September 1909 in Nebraska
3. Edna Mae James, born 18 June 1911 in Nebraska
4. Clinton James, born about 1913 in Nebraska
5. Betty Jean James, born 5 July 1921 in Nebraska

Maurance M. James, son of Manitoba Chester "Toby" James and Leigh Reeves, died on 17 April 1963 in Alameda Co., California. He was buried in the Evergreen Cemetery, Garden of Prayer, Oakland, Alameda Co., California. His wife Winifred D., 1909-1973 was also buried there. Both Maurance and his sister, Myrtha are shown in the 1925 Grand Island High School Yearbook, Grand Island, Hall Co., Nebraska. They had apparently transferred there from Lincoln High School, Lincoln, Lancaster Co., Nebraska. 22

Edna Mae James, daughter of Manitoba Chester "Toby" James and Leigh Reeves, was married to —- Dotson. She died 15 December 1992 in Contra Costa Co., California. Betty Jean James, daughter of Manitoba Chester "Toby" James and Leigh Reeves, married —- Jacobs. She died 19 October 1943 in Alameda Co., California.

Leigh Reeves, wife of Manitoba Chester "Tobe" James, was the daughter of Pleasonton or Pleasant and Lula Reeves. She was born in 8 December 1885 in Tennessee according to the 1900 US Census and her death information. The 1895 Kansas State Census and subsequent US Censuses provide significant information about them.

1895 Kansas State Census, Bourbon Co., Kansas, Marmaton, Page 33   23
2128-233 Pleze Reeves, 50, black, b. TN, laborer
Lula, 39, black, b. TN
James, 18, black, b. TN
Jennie, 16, black, b. TN
Edward, 15, black, b. TN
Lee, female, 11, black, b. TN
Unice, 9, black, b. KS
Oscar, 5, black, b. KS
Sarah, 1, black, b. KS

1900 US Census, Bourbon Co., Kansas, Fort Scott, Ward 2, ED 34, Page 2A   24
309 Towman St.
34-35 Plesenton Reeves, black, b. April 1846, 54, married 24 years, b. TN, both
          parents b. TN, farmer
Lula, wife, black, b. Sept 1856, 43, married 24 years, 9 children, 8 living, b. TN,
          both parents b. TN
Edward, son, black, b. September 1880, 19, single, b. TN, both parents b. TN,
          farmer
Leigh, daughter, black, b. Dec 1884, 15, b. TN, both parents b. TN, at school
Eunice, daughter, black, b. Dec 1886, 13, b. KS, both parents b. TN, at school
Oscar, son, black, b. Oct 1892, 7, b. KS, both parents b. TN, at school
Sadie, daughter, black, b. Feb 1894, 6, b. KS, both parents b. TN, at school
Beatrice, daughter, black, b. Oct 1897, 2, b. KS, both parents b. TN
Jaunetta, daughter, black, b. March 1899, 1, b. KS, both parents b. TN

1910 US Census, Bourbon Co., Kansas, Scott, ED 56, Page 9B   25

189 Pleasant Reeves, black, 64, married 30 years, b. TN, both parents b. TN,
        farmer
Lula, wife, black, 54, married 30 years, 9 children, 7 living, b. TN, both parents
        b. TN
Oscar, son, black, 18, single, b. KS, both parents b. TN, laborer, home farm
Sarah, daughter, black, 16, b. KS, both parents b. TN
Beatrice, daughter, black, 14, b. KS, both parents b. TN
Waneta, daughter, black, 11, b. KS, both parents b. TN
George, grandson, black, 8, b. KS, father b. TN, mother b. MO
James, grandson, black, 6, b. KS, father b. TN, mother b. MO
Loyd Richie, nephew, black, 17, single, b. KS, father b. KS, mother b. TN

1915 Kansas State Census, Bourbon Co., Kansas, Fort Scott, Page 48   26
owns, free
#248 Ples Reeves, 70, black, b. TN, came to KS from TN, retired
Lula, 65, black, b. TN, came to KS from TN, house wife
Sadie, 21, black, b. KS, dress maker
Beatrice, 18, black, b. KS
Juanita, 16, black, b. KS
James, 13, black, b. KS
Geo., 11, black, b. KS

1920 US Census, Bourbon Co., Kansas, Fort Scott, Ward 2, ED 40, Page 11B   27
523 Couch Street
275-297 Lula Reeves, owns, freen, mulatto, 65, married, b. TN, both parents
        b. TN, retired invalid
Beatrice, daughter, mulatto, 22, single, b. KS, both parents b. TN, teaching,
        city school
Jaunita [sic], daughter, mulatto, 19, single, b. KS, both parents b. TN
James, grandson, mulatto, 15, b. KS, both parents b. KS
Pleasant, husband, mulatto, 75, married, b. TN, both parents b. KS,
        washing, private family

On the above 1920 enumeration, Pleasant was undoubtedy confused with the information about
Lula and placed at the end of the family. He is most likely the retired invalid and Lula is washing for a
private family.

1925 Kansas State Census, Bourbon Co., Kansas, Fort Scott   28
Lula Reaves, owns, colored, 70, b. TN, came to KS from TN, housewife

1930 US Census, Bourbon Co., Kansas, Fort Scott, Ward 2, ED 4, Page 18B   29
523 Burk Street
433-506 Lula Reeves, owns, $800, negro, 70, widow, married at age 20, b. TN,
        both parents b. TN, no occupation

Pleasant Reeves, born in 1843, died in 1922. He was buried in the Evergreen Cemetery at Fort
Scott, Bourbon Co., Kansas. His wife, Lula, was born 1858 and died in 1938. She was also buried in the
Evergreen Cemetery. The following children were born to Pleasant and Lula Reeves.

1. James C. Reeves, born 16 May 1878 in Shelbyville, Bedford Co., Tennessee
2. Jennie Reeves, born about 1879 in Tennessee
3. Edward Reeves, born September 1880 in Tennessee

4. Leigh Reeves, born 9 December 1885 in Tennessee (see above)
5. Eunice Reeves, born December 1886 in Kansas
6. Oscar Reeves, born October 1892 in Kansas, died October 1926; buried
    Evergreen Cemetery, Fort Scott, Bourbon Co., Kansas
7. Sarah/Sadie Reeves, born February 1894 in Kansas
8. Beatrice Reeves, born 16 October 1896 in Kansas, died 6 April 1924;
    buried Evergreen Cemetery, Fort Scott, Bourbon Co., Kansas
9. Juanita Reeves, born 1899 in Kansas, died 1921; buried Evergreen
    Cemetery, Fort Scott, Bourbon Co., Kansas

James C. Reeves, son of Pleasant and Lula Reeves, was born in about 1877 in Tennessee. He married Nellie Garrelt on 11 March 1900 in Fort Scott, Bourbon Co., Kansas. The marriage license indicates he was age 22 of St. Louis, Missouri and she was age 23 of Fort Scott, Kansas. 30

James C. Reeves died in the General Hospital No. 2 in Kansas City, Jackson Co., Missouri on 9 August 1946 of brochogenic carcinoma. He had been in the hospital for 144 days. According to his death certificate he was widowed, wife's name was Mable (penciled in). He was born 16 May 1878 at Shelbyville, Tennessee to Pleasant Reeves, born Tennessee and Lula McLean, born Tennessee. His normal resident address was 2425 Olive Street in Kansas City, Missouri. While he was unemployed at the time of his death, his normal occupation was porter, maintenance. The informant was his nephew James W. Reeves of the same address in Kansas City. He was buried in Fort Scott, Bourbon Co., Kansas on 12 August 1946. 31

It appears that James' first wife, Nellie Garrelt, either died or they divorced before 1942. There is a death certificate for Mabel Reeves, colored, married to James C. Reeves. She died at Kansas City, Jackson Co., Missouri on 30 August 1942 of carcinoma of the cervix and secondary anemia. Mabel was born 6 September 1890 at Jefferson City, Missouri to Roy Abraham and Frankie Webb, both born in Missouri. The informant was her husband James C. Reeves of 2427 Prospect, Kansas City, Missouri. She was buried in Jefferson City, Missouri. 32

In 1900 James C. Reeves, son of Pleasant and Lula Reeves, and his wife, Nellie was living with his cousin, John Reeves and wife Myra J. at 2502 Leffingwell Avenue in St. Louis, Missouri. John Reeves was the son of Monroe Reeves and his wife America. Monroe was probably a brother to Pleasant Reeves, thus making both of them sons of Albert Reeves, who was born about 1816.

1880 US Census, Bedford Co., Tennessee, District 22, ED 16, Page 358A   33
153-156 Albert Reeves, mulatto, 64, widowed, farmer, b. VA, both parents b.
    VA
James, black, 23, son, single, sick with consumption, b. TN, father b. VA,
    mother b. TN
Columbus, black, 18, son, single, works on farm, b. TN, father b. VA, mother
    b. TN
Mary, black, 12, daughter, b. TN, father b. VA, mother b. TN
Monroe Reeves, mulatto, 34, son, farmer, b. TN, father b. VA, mother b.
    TN
America, 25, wife, black, housekeeping, b. TN, both parents b. TN
John, 5, son, black, b. TN, both parents b. TN
Georgiana, 2, daughter, black, b. TN, both parents b. TN
Allen Campbell, 55, brother-in-law, black, works on farm, b. TN, both
    parents b. TN

1900 US Census, St. Louis, Missouri, Ward 20, ED 300, Page 3B   34

2502 Leffingwell Avenue

72 John Reeves, black, b. Sept 1874, 25, married 2 years, b. TN, both
      parents b. TN, porter

Myra J., wife, black, b. Dec 1876, 23, married 2 years, 0 children, 0 living,
      b. MO, both parents b. IL

James C., cousin, black, b. May 1877, 23, married 0 years, b. TN, both parents
      b. TN, porter

Nellie M., cousin, black, b. April 1876, 24, married, 0 years, 0 children, 0 living,
      b. KS, both parents b. KY

1910 US Census, Cook Co., Illinois, Chicago, Ward 3, ED 227, Page 5B [35]

734 East 38th Street

22-77 John A. Reeves, mulatto, 31, married 11 years, b. TN, father b. PA,
      mother b. TN, groom, livery stable

Myra J., wife, mulatto, 29, married 11 years, 2 children, 1 living, b. MO,
      both parents b. IL, hair dresser, parlors

Jesse M., son, mulatto, 9, b. MO, father b. TN, mother b. MO

1920 US Census, Cook Co., Illinois, Chicago, Ward 2, ED 102, Page 3A [36]

3803 Rhodes Ave.

#61 John Reeves, rents, black, 45, b. KY, both parents b. KY, teamster, stables

Myra, wife, black, 43, b. MO, both parents b. MO

Jessie M., son, black, 19, single, b. MO, father b. KY, mother b. MO, chauffeur

1930 US Census, Cook Co., Illinois, Chicago, Ward 4, ED 146, Page 24B [37]

Wabash Avenue

#261 John A. Reeves, rents $66 month, negro 50, married at age 20, b. TN, father
      b. PA, mother b. TN, agent, insurance

Myra H., wife, negro, 45, married at age 15, b. MO, both parents b. IL

James C. Patton, lodger, negro, 48, married, married at age 36, b. KY, both
      parents b. KY, photographer, photographic studio

Edward Reeves, son of Pleasant and Lula Reeves, was born in September of 1880 in Tennessee. He married Georgia Etta Julian on 28 May 1910 at Fort Scott, Bourbon Co., Kansas. She is shown as age 18 on their marriage record and he is shown as age 19. [38] Edward and Georgia/Georgetta were parents of James and George, the grandchildren living in the household of Edward's parents as children.

James William Reeves, son of Edward Reeves and Georgetta Julian, was born 6 September 1903 in Fort Scott, Bourbon Co., Kansas. He lived at 2425 Olive Street in Kansas City, Missouri. According to his death certificate, he died on 16 November 1954 at the Veterans Administration Hospital in Kansas City, Jackson Co., Missouri, where he had been for 28 years. He was married to Charline —- and had served in World War II. His normal occuaption was an elevator operator. He died of uremia, due to renal tuberculosis and pulmonary tuberculosis. He was buried on 19 November 1954 in the Fort Leavenworth National Cemetery at Fort Leavenworth, Leavenworth Co., Kansas. [39]

Eunice Reeves, daughter of Pleasant and Lula Reeves, was born in December of 1886. She married G.W. Allison on 27 December 1909 in Fort Scott, Bourbon Co., Kansas. They are both shown as colored on their marriage license. He was of Hutchinson, Kansas, age 25 and she was of Fort Scott, Kansas. They were married by Rev. J.F. Sage, Pastor of the AME Church. [40]

1. Year: 1930; Census Place: Boyd, Box Butte, Nebraska; Roll: 1266; Page: 3A; Enumeration District: 0006; Image: 942.0; FHL microfilm: 2341001

2. Year. 1940, Census Place. Boyd, Box Butte, Nebraska, Roll. T627_2237, Page. 5A, Enumeration District: 7-8

3. Box Butte Co., Nebraska Marriage Book J, page 225 #5305

4. Year: 1920; Census Place: Kennedy, Cherry, Nebraska; Roll: T625_981; Page: 2B; Enumeration District: 54; Image: 866

5. Ancestry.com. *U.S. City Directories, 1822-1995* [database on-line]. Provo, UT, USA: Ancestry.com Operations, Inc., 2011.

6. Year: 1900; Census Place: Lincoln Ward 1, Lancaster, Nebraska; Roll: 933; Page: 4B; Enumeration District: 0044; FHL microfilm: 1240933

7. Year: 1910; Census Place: Lincoln Ward 5, Lancaster, Nebraska; Roll: T624_850; Page: 11A; Enumeration District: 0078; FHL microfilm: 1374863

8. 1870 U.S. census, population schedules. NARA microfilm publication M593, 1,761 rolls. Washington, D.C.: National Archives and Records Administration, n.d.Minnesota census schedules for 1870. NARA microfilm publication T132, 13 rolls.

9. Year: 1910; Census Place: Lincoln Ward 3, Lancaster, Nebraska; Roll: T624_850; Page: 2A; Enumeration District: 0064; FHL microfilm: 1374863

10. Ancestry.com. *California, Death Index, 1940-1997* [database on-line]. Provo, UT, USA: Ancestry.com Operations Inc, 2000.

11. Year: 1940; Census Place: Omaha, Douglas, Nebraska; Roll: T627_2269; Page: 6A; Enumeration District: 94-24

12. Year: 1930; Census Place: Omaha, Douglas, Nebraska; Roll: 1273; Page: 11A; Enumeration District: 0016; Image: 652.0; FHL microfilm: 2341008

13. Ancestry.com. *U.S. City Directories, 1822-1995* [database on-line]. Provo, UT, USA: Ancestry.com Operations, Inc., 2011

14. Ancestry.com. *U.S., Social Security Death Index, 1935-2014* [database on-line]. Provo, UT, USA: Ancestry.com Operations Inc, 2011.

15. Kansas County Marriages, 1855-1911," database with images, FamilySearch (https://familysearch.org/pal:/MM9.3.1/TH-1951-21618-37261-68?cc=1851040, Bourbon > Marriage licenses, Index, 1905-1910, v. J > image 61 of 349; citing district clerk, court clerk, county clerk and register offices from various counties.

16. Year: 1910; Census Place: Grand Island Ward 1, Hall, Nebraska; Roll: T624_847; Page: 9A; Enumeration District: 0101; FHL microfilm: 1374860

17. Registration State: *Nebraska;* Registration County: *Knox;* Roll: *1711702;* Draft Board: *1*

18. Year: 1920; Census Place: Lincoln Ward 3, Lancaster, Nebraska; Roll: T625_996; Page: 2B; Enumeration District: 63; Image: 377

19. Year: 1930; Census Place: Omaha, Douglas, Nebraska; Roll: 1273; Page: 1A; Enumeration District: 0017; Image: 674.0; FHL microfilm: 2341008

20. United States, Selective Service System. *Selective Service Registration Cards, World War II: Fourth Registration*. Records of the Selective Service System, Record Group Number 147. National Archives and Records Administration.

21. State of California. *California Death Index, 1940-1997*. Sacramento, CA, USA: State of California Department of Health Services, Center for Health Statistics.

22. Ancestry.com. *U.S., School Yearbooks, 1880-2012* [database on-line]. Provo, UT, USA: Ancestry.com Operations, Inc., 2010

23. Kansas State Historical Society; Topeka, Kansas; *1895 Kansas Territory Census;* Roll: *v115_9;* Line: *1*

24. Year: 1900; Census Place: Fort Scott Ward 2, Bourbon, Kansas; Roll: 471; Page: 2A; Enumeration District: 0034; FHL microfilm: 1240471

25. Year: 1910; Census Place: Scott, Bourbon, Kansas; Roll: T624_432; Page: 9B; Enumeration District: 0056; FHL microfilm: 1374445

26. Kansas State Historical Society; Topeka, Kansas; Roll: *ks1915_17;* Line: *1*

27. Year: 1920; Census Place: Fort Scott Ward 2, Bourbon, Kansas; Roll: T625_525; Page: 11B; Enumeration District: 40; Image: 106

28. Kansas State Historical Society; Topeka, Kansas; *1925 Kansas Territory Census;* Roll: *KS1925_10;* Line: *1*

29. Year: 1930; Census Place: Fort Scott, Bourbon, Kansas; Roll: 694; Page: 18B; Enumeration District: 0004; Image: 92.0; FHL microfilm: 2340429

30. Kansas County Marriages, 1855-1911," database with images, FamilySearch (https://familysearch.org/pal:/MM9.3.1/TH-1951-21618-13989-69?cc=1851040, Bourbon > Marriage licenses, Index, 1897-1902, v. H > image 212 of 362; citing district clerk, court clerk, county clerk and register offices from various counties.

31. Missouri Death Certificate # 27322.

32. Missouri Death Certificate #26473.

33. Year: 1880; Census Place: District 22, Bedford, Tennessee; Roll: 1244; Family History Film: 1255244; Page: 358A; Enumeration District: 016

34. Year: 1900; Census Place: St Louis Ward 20, St Louis (Independent City), Missouri; Roll: 897; Page: 3B; Enumeration District: 0300; FHL microfilm: 1240897

35. Year: 1910; Census Place: Chicago Ward 3, Cook, Illinois; Roll: T624_243; Page: 5B; Enumeration District: 0227; FHL microfilm: 1374256

36. Year: 1920; Census Place: Chicago Ward 2, Cook (Chicago), Illinois; Roll: T625_307; Page: 3A; Enumeration District: 102; Image: 451

37. Year: 1930; Census Place: Chicago, Cook, Illinois; Roll: 421; Page: 24B; Enumeration District: 0146; Image: 148.0; FHL microfilm: 2340156

38. Kansas County Marriages, 1855-1911," database with images, FamilySearch (https://familysearch.org/pal:/MM9.3.1/TH-1942-21618-14562-85?cc=1851040 :Bourbon > Marriage licenses, Index, 1897-1902, v. H > image 223 of 362; citing district clerk, court clerk, county clerk and register offices from various counties.

39. Missouri Death Certificate #37557.

40. Kansas County Marriages, 1855-1911," database with images, FamilySearch (https://familysearch.org/pal:/MM9.3.1/TH-1942-21618-37376-79?cc=1851040 : Bourbon > Marriage licenses, Index, 1905-1910, v. J > image 322 of 349; citing district clerk, court clerk, county clerk and register offices from various counties

Bert Harris

On 30 March 1919 Bert Louis Harris married Grace Louisa Emanuel in Alliance. His marriage license indicates he was born in Alabama to Tom Harris and Maria Hampton. Bert was born 8 May 1882 in Tuscumbia, Colbert Co., Alabama. Grace was the daughter of Joshua Dawson Emanuel and Mary Ann Robinson, born 8 January 1894 in Nebraska. [1] The following census enumerations show more about the Bert and Grace Harris family. Refeer to information pertaining to the Emanuel family in Volume 2.

1920 US Census, Box Butte Co., Nebraska, Alliance, ED 11, Page 22B [2]
Wyoming Addition - First Street
Bert L. Harris, rents, Indian, 33, b. AL, both parents b. AL, cuprod, railroad
Grace L., wife, black, 26, b. NE, father b. NY, mother b. Canada

1930 US Census, Box Butte Co., Nebraska, Alliance ED 2, Page 8A [3]
134 Missouri Avenue
158-171 Bert L. Harris, owns $1,800, negro, 45, married at age 32, b. AL,
        both parents b. AL, janitor, office building
Grace E., wife, negro, 36, married at age 25, b. NE, father b. NY, mother b.
        Canada

Joseph, son, negro, 7, b. NE, father b. AL, mother b. NE
Dora Lee, daughter, negro, 4 4/12, b. NE, father b. AL, mother b. NE
Junior, son, negro, 3 4/12, b. NE, father b. AL, mother b. NE

1940 US Census, Box Butte Co., Nebraska, Alliance, ED 7-2A, Page 1B 4
134 Missouri   owns $1,800
Bert Harris, 55, white, 4 years high school, b. AL, same place 1 April 1935,
      janitor, Masonic Temple
Grace, 44, wife, white, 4 years high school, b. NE, same place 1 April 1935
Joe, 17, son, white, 3 years high school, b. NE, same place 1 April 1935
Dorla, 14, daughter, white, 8th grade, b. NE, same place 1 April 1935
Bert J., 13, son, white, 6th grade, b. NE, same place 1 April 1935

On 12 September 1918, Bert registered for the World War I Draft in Alliance, Box Butte Co., Nebraska. He is shown as living in the Hills Addition in Alliance. He was 39, born 28 May 1879 and working as a boiler washer for the CB&Q Railroad in Alliance. His nearest relative was Tom Harris of RFD 1, Iuka, Mississippi. 5

There was an Obe Harris who filed his World War I Draft Registration in Alliance, Box Butte Co., Nebraska on 5 June 1917. He is shown as living in Alliance and working as a boiler washer for the CB&Q Railroad. He was born 14 January 1895 in Carvin Hill, Alabama and single. It is not known if he relates to Bert Harris. 6 He registered for the World War II draft indicating that he was living on the Carpame Farm near Clear Clake, Mississippi Co., Arkansas, PO Box 447 Blytheville, Arkansas. He was born 19 January 1895 at Carvin Hill, Alabama. The person who would know where he was located is shown as C.W. Graham, PO Box 447, Blytheville, Arkansas. Obe was farming in the Clear Lake community. There are notes that he had a one inch scar on the 3rd joint of the index finger, left hand and a scar through the center finger nail on the middle finger of his left hand. His registration was filed 27 April 1942 in Mississippi Co., Arkansas. 7 According to the applications for military headstones, Obe Harris enlisted in World War I, 1 August 1918 and was discharged honorably on 7 July 1919. He served as a private in Co. C 805th Pioneer Infantry. The application shows that he was born 19 January 1895 and died 18 December 1953, buried in Oak Hill Cemetery, Gary, Lake Co., Indiana. 8

Bert registered for the World War II Draft from Alliance, Nebraska. He is shown as Bert Louis Harris, 57, born 18 May 1885 in Tuscumbia, Alabama; relative Mrs. Grace L. Harris of Alliance. He was working for the WPA at Mirage Flats in Dawes Co., Nebraska. He is shown as a negro. It was filed 27 April 1942 in Box Butte Co., Nebraska. 9

Bert Louis Harris died on 11 April 1961 in Alliance and was buried in the Alliance Cemetery, Alliance, Box Butte Co., Nebraska. Prior to his death he had been employed for 46 years in the freight house of the Burlington Railroad in Alliance. His wife, Grace Emanuel Harris died 30 September 1970 in her home at 134 Missouri, Alliance, Nebraska. She was a member of the Salvation Army, the Amaranth Chapter of the Order of Eastern Star and the Daughter of Isis. Grace was buried in the Alliance Cemetery, Alliance, Box Butte Co., Nebraska. 10 They were parents of the following children.

1. Joseph Harris, born about 1923 in Nebraska.
2. Dora Lee Harris, born about 1927 in Nebraska.
3. Bert Louis Harris, Jr. "Junior", born 10 November 1926 in Nebraska.

Joseph Harris may be the Joseph P. Harris who is shown on the Social Security Death Index as born 1 February 1923, died 20 May 1998, last residence Seattle, Washington. His Social Security number was issued in Nebraska. According to the obituary of Bert Louis Harris, Jr., Joseph died before 2004.

Dora Lee Harris, daughter of Bert Louis Harris and Grace Emanuel, married Virgil Lee Snoddy on 14 November 1943 in Alliance, Nebraska by Rev. H.L. Powel. Dora was a resident of Alliance, her first marriage, born in Alliance to Bert L. Harris, born in Tuscumbia, Alabama and Grace Emanuel, born in Overton, Nebraska. Virgil was a resident of Troy, Doniphan Co., Kansas, age 21, first marriage and a typist for the US Army. He was born in Troy, Kansas, single and the son of John Wallace (step father, own father's name unknown) and Joyce V. Snoddy, born in St. Joseph, Missouri. 11 At the time of the death of Dora's mother in 1970, Dora was married to Henry Jones and living in Denver, Colorado. Dora passed away on 11 September 2016 in Rehobeth, Houston Co., Alabama. She worked in the Air Force Accounting and Finance Center at Lowery Air Force Base, as a Secretary Stenographer, retiring in June of 1989 after 32 years. In 1994 she became an ordained minister for the State of Colorado. According to her obituary she was survived by her son, Lee and his wife, Joanne, grandchildren and great grandchildren. 12

Bert Louis Harris, Jr. "Junior", son of Bert Louis Harris and Grace Emanuel, married Charlotte Brooks on 4 September 1946 in Alliance, Box Butte Co., Nebraska, officiant being Rev. Walter A. Ashby. The witnesses were Mrs. Mildred Chandler and Mrs. Mabel Ashby. According to their marriage license, Bert was born in Alliance to Bert Harris, born in Alabama and Grace Emanuel, born in Overton, Nebraska. He was age 19, a railroad worker in Alliance. Charlotte Brooks was a resident of Alliance, age 21, born in Tacoma, Washington to James Brooks and Mary Pollard, both born in Virginia. The mother of Junior gave her consent for her underage son to marry. 13 Bert attended elementary and high school in Alliance, Nebraska. In 1943 he entered the Cavalry as a Buffalo Soldier at Fort Riley, Kansas, 10th Cavalry Division. He took his basic training on horseback using a McClellan saddle, then transferred to Camp Lockett, California.

After their marriage, Bert and Charlotte lived in Washington state. Bert married second in 1965 to Lorraine Beatrice Curvey of Seattle, Wshington. Bert was employed for sixteen years in Tacoma, Washington at Madigan General Hospital and for twenty-eight years with the US Postal Service in Seattle. He died in Seattle, King Co., Washington on 13 September 2004. He was survived by his widow, children, grand children and great and great, great grandchildren, as well as his sister Dora Lee Jones of Denver, Colorado and a cousin Jimmy Smith of Denver, Colorado. 14

The obituary for Bert Harris, Sr. indicates he was survived by a sister, Mrs. Katie House of Cleveland, Ohio and a brother, Thomas Harris, Jr., of St. Louis, Missouri. Nothing conclusive can be located with regard to them or pertaining to their parents.

2. Box Butte Co., Nebraska Marriage Book F, page 83 #2609
2. Year: 1920; Census Place: Alliance, Box Butte, Nebraska; Roll: T625_979; Page: 22B; Enumeration District: 11; Image: 1045
3. Year: 1930; Census Place: Alliance, Box Butte, Nebraska; Roll: 1266; Page: 8A; Enumeration District: 0002; Image: 820.0; FHL microfilm: 2341001
4. Year: 1940; Census Place: Alliance, Box Butte, Nebraska; Roll: T627_2237; Page: 1B; Enumeration District: 7-2A
5. Registration State: *Nebraska;* Registration County: *Box Butte;* Roll: *1711448*
6. Registration State: *Nebraska;* Registration County: *Box Butte;* Roll: *1711448*
7. United States, Selective Service System. *Selective Service Registration Cards, World War II: Fourth Registration.* Records of the Selective Service System, Record Group Number 147. National Archives and Records Administration
8. *Applications for Headstones for U.S. Military Veterans, 1925-1941.* Microfilm publication M1916, 134 rolls. ARC ID: 596118. Records of the Office of the Quartermaster General, Record Group 92. National Archives at Washington, D.C.*Applications for Headstones, compiled 01/01/1925 - 06/30/1970, documenting the period ca. 1776 - 1970* ARC: 596118. Records of the Office of the Quartermaster General, 1774–1985, Record Group 92. National Archives and Records Administration, Washington, D.C.

9. The National Archives at St. Louis; St. Louis, Missouri; Draft Registration Cards for Fourth Registration for Nebraska, 04/27/1942 - 04/27/1942; NAI Number: 598911; Record Group Title: Records of the Selective Service System; Record Group Number: 147
10. Obituary Collection, Knight Museum, Alliance, Nebraska
11. Box Butte Co., Nebraska Marriage #230
12. "Denver Post," Denver, Colorado 2 October 2016
13. Box Butte Co., Nebraska Marriage License #6425
14. Obituary Bert Louis Harris, Jr. "The Seattle Times" http://www.legacy.com/obituaries/seattletimes/obituary.aspx?page=lifestory&pid=2616114

Beverly Thornton

Sgt. Beverly F. Thornton was a cook in Co. K, 10th Cavalry at Fort Robinson. He married Sallie Conley, sister of Paschall Conley, a sergeant in the 10th Cavalry. She was of Huntsville, Alabama, age 43 and Beverly was age 42. They married at Fort Robinson on 21 April 1904, officiated by William L. Anderson, Chaplain of the 10th Cavalry. 1

Thornton was born 5 September 1863 at Ware Neck, Gloucester Co., Virginia to Paul Thornton and Mary A. Foxwell. He attended Hampton Institute at Hampton, Virginia. This was a school for "Negroes and Indians." Before enlisting in the US Army, he taught six sessions in Lunenburg and Gloucester counties in Virginia. During his service he wrote to the Hampton Institute, stating that he was "away out on the western frontier, where civilization is practised by a little." In his letter he stated, "Of course we have a great deal of scouting to do, but as I am rough and hard, I am just suit for the business. I do not know whether I am doing so much for my people or not, but I am going to stand by my country, no matter how great the danger." 2

1880 US Census, Elizabeth City Co., Virginia, Chesapeake Magisterial Dist., ED 3
13, Page 23A
B.F. Thornton, mulatto, 18, student, good health, b. VA, both parents b. VA

As reflected in the 1900 US Census, he married prior to his marriage at Fort Robinson to Sallie Conley. On 29 September 1898 he married Nora Ransom in Gloucester Co., Virginia. She was born in 1863 in Gloucester Co., Virginia to Robert and Betty Ransom and died 24 January 1901 in Philadelphia, Philadelphia Co., Pennsylvania.

The Register of Enlistments, US Army shows information for Beverly F. Thornton. On 22 June 1888 in Baltimore, Maryland, he enlisted in the 10th Cavalry, United States Army. He is shown as being a school teacher, enlisting in the 11th Cavalry, Co. L. He was discharged on 20 October 1888 at Fort Dowell, Arizona Territory because of disability, rank private. On 8 July 1893 he re-enlisted at Washington, DC and his occupation is shown as a soldier. He enlisted in Co. K, 10th Cavalry and was discharged on 2 July 1898 at Lakeland, Florida because of expiration of service. He is shown as an "excellent" private. On 3 July 1898 he re-enlisted at Lakeland, Florida in Co. K, 10th Cavalry. He was discharged on 2 July 1901 at Holquin, Cuba; cook. On 3 July 1901 he re-enlisted at Holquin, Cuba, Co. K, 10th Cavalry. He was discharged 2 July 1904 at Fort Robinson, Nebraska, expiration of service, cook. The next day he re-enlisted at Fort Robinson in Co. K, 10th Cavalry, and was discharged at Fort Robinson on 27 January 1907. He re-enlisted on 28 January 1907 at Fort Robinson, Nebraska, in Co. K, 10th Cavalry. He was discharged at Fort Ethan Allen, Vermont on 27 January 1910. On 28 January 1910 he enlisted at Fort Ethan Allen, Vermont in Co. K, 10th Cavalry. He was discharged on on 27 January 1913 at Fort Ethan Allen where he had served as a cook. 4

During the Spanish American War he remained in the United States. However, he did service in Cuba.

1900 US Census, Military and Naval Forces, Holguin, Cuba, , Co., K, 10th 5
Cavalry, ED 110
Beverly F. Thornton, cook, residence Gloucester Co., VA, black, b. Sept.
　　　1860, 39, married 1 year, b. Gloucester Co., VA, both parents b.
　　　Gloucester Co., VA

1910 US Census, Chittenden Co., Vermont, Colchester, Fort Ethan Allen, 6
Military Post, ED 78, Page 4B
Barrack Road
Beverly F. Thornton, private, black, 50, married 6 years, b. VA, both parents
　　　b. VA, soldier, US Army

1920 US Census, Chittenden Co., Vermont, Colchester, ED 56, Page 6B 7
Franklin Street
115-120 Beverly Thornton, owns, free, mullato, , 74, b. VA, both parents b.
　　　VA, janitor, church
Salie, wife, mulatto, 58, b. AL, both parents b. AL
Zan Scruggs, son-in-law, mulatto, 45, b. AL, both parents b. AL
Jennie, daughter, mullato, 40, b. AL, both parents b. AL
Levi, grandson, mullato, 18, single, b. AL, both parents b. AL
Margaret, granddaughter, mullato, 16, b. AL, both parents b. AL
Thornton, grandson, mullato, 14, b. AL, both parents b. AL
Edgar, grandson, mullato, 12, b. AL, both parents b. AL
Louise, grandson, mullato, 10, b. AL, both parents b. AL
Ellen, granddaughter, mulatto, 9, b. VT, both parents b. AL
James, grandson, mullato, 1 1/12, b. VT, both parents b. AL

According to his death certificate, Beverly Thornton died at the Fanny Allen Hospital in Colchester, Vermont, where he had been hospitalized for 23 days. He is shown as negro, age 75 years, 4 months, 3 days, retired soldier; born 5 September 1846 in Virginia. His parents are shown as Paul Thornton and Mary Foxwell, both born in Virginia. He died 8 January 1922 of chronic endocarditis and arterio scelerosis. He was married. 8

Sallie Ann Conley, wife of Beverly F. Thornton, was the daughter of Jesse and Maria Conley, according to census. She was born 12 December 1864 at Huntsville, Madison Co., Alabama and died 8 February 1931 at Winooski, Chittenden Co., Vermont. According to her death record, shown as Sallie A. Thornton, she died at her home at 40 Franklin Street. She was born 12 December 1865 and the widow of Beverly F. Thornton. Her parents are shown as Paschal Conley and Mary Steiger, both born in Huntsville, Madison Co., Alabama. The informant for her death was Jessie Scruggs of Winooski, Vermont. She died of hemiplegia and high blood pressure. 9   On Sallie's marriage license to marry Beverly F. Thornton in Dawes Co., Nebraska, her parents are shown as Paschal Conley and Mary Stegger. The Jesse Connally [sic] shown on the 1870 US Census is undoubtedly in error and meant to be Pascal or Paschal.

1870 US Census, Madison Co., Alabama, Township 3, Range 1, Subdivision 53 10
83-86 Jesse Connally, 50, black, farm laborer, b. AL
Maria, 35, black, b. AL
Mahala, 17, black, b. AL

Fanny, 12, black, b. AL
Paschal, 8, black, b. AL
Sally Ann, 6, black, b. AL
Jesse, 4, male, black, b. AL
Babe, 2, female, black, b. AL

It appears that Sally/Sallie Conley was married prior to her marriage to Beverly F. Thornton. In their household in 1920 Chittenden Co., Vermont are members of the Scruggs family, with an indication that Jennie Scruggs was a daughter. In 1900 Sallie is shown in Kansas City, Missouri and married.

1920 US Census, Jackson Co., Missouri, Kansas City, Ward 7, ED 67, Page 8B [11]
2842 East Seventh Street
151-168 George N. Petty HH, white
Sallie Conley, servant, black, b. June 1864, 35, married 16 years, 1 child, 0 living,
      b. AL, father b. AL, mother b. VA

On the 1929 City Directory, Burlington, Vermont, Sally A. Thornton is shown as the widow of Beverly, living at 40 Franklin. [12] She applied for a widow's pension on 12 July 1922, indicating her husband Beverly F. Thornton had served in Co. K, 10th US Cavalry as a 1st Sgt., retired USA. She applied from Vermont, application no. 1191853, certificate 934,734. [13]

Beverly F. Thornton and his wife, Sallie A. Conley, were both buried in the Lakeview Cemetery, Burlington, Chittenden Co., Vermont. His tombstone indicates he was a Sergeant in Troop K, 10th Cavalry. [14]

Also buried in the Lakeview Cemetery is Jessie I. Conley Scruggs, born 1879 and died 1947. This indicates that she was born a Conley, thus probably a daughter born out of wedlock to Sallie Conley Thornton. Jessie's husband Zan M. Scruggs is also buried in the Lakeview Cemetery, born 1875 in Alabama and died 1954. Their son, James Thomas Scruggs, was born in 1918 in Winooski, Chittenden Co., Vermont. He married Beverly Eastman on 12 December 1943 in Burlington, Chittenden Co., Vermont and died there on 30 July 2005. James worked at St. Michael's College in Colchester, Vermont. [15]

1. Dawes Co., Nebraska Marriage Book 3 page 333 *On the Trail of the Buffalo Soldier* by Frank N. Schubert, Wilmington, DL: Scholarly Resources, Inc., 1995, page 427
2. https://archive.org/stream/twentytwoyearswo00hamp#page/n7/mode/2up
3. Year: 1880; Census Place: Chesapeake, Elizabeth City, Virginia; Roll: 1363; Family History Film: 1255363; Page: 23A; Enumeration District: 013
4. Register of Enlistments in the U.S. Army, 1798-1914; (National Archives Microfilm Publication M233, 81 rolls); Records of the Adjutant General's Office, 1780's-1917, Record Group 94; National Archives, Washington, D.C.
5. Year: 1900; Census Place: Holguin, Cuba, Military and Naval Forces; Roll: 1838; Enumeration District: 0110; FHL microfilm: 1241838
6. Year: 1910; Census Place: Colchester, Chittenden, Vermont; Roll: T624_1614; Page: 4B; Enumeration District: 0078; FHL microfilm: 1375627
7. Year: 1920; Census Place: Colchester, Chittenden, Vermont; Roll: T625_1872; Page: 6B; Enumeration District: 56; Image: 41
8. Vermont State Archives and Records Administration; Montpelier, Vermont; Vermont Death Records, 1909-2008; User Box Number: PR-01923; Roll Number: S-30890; Archive Number: M-2051939
9. Vermont State Archives and Records Administration; Montpelier, Vermont; Vermont Death Records, 1909-2008; User Box Number: PR-01923; Roll Number: S-30890; Archive Number: M-2051939

10. Year 1870 U.S. census, population schedules. NARA microfilm publication M593, 1,761 rolls. Washington, D.C.: National Archives and Records Administration
11. Year: 1900; Census Place: Kansas City Ward 7, Jackson, Missouri; Roll: 862; Page: 8B; Enumeration District: 0067; FHL microfilm: 1240862
12. Ancestry.com. *U.S. City Directories, 1822-1995* [database on-line]. Provo, UT, USA: Ancestry.com Operations, Inc., 2011
13. National Archives and Records Administration. U.S., Civil War Pension Index: General Index to Pension Files, 1861-1934 [database on-line]. Provo, UT, USA: Ancestry.com Operations Inc, 2000. Original data: *General Index to Pension Files, 1861-1934*. Washington, D.C.: National Archives and Records Administration. T288, 546 rolls.
14. FindAGrave http://www.findagrave.com
15. ibid.

William Biggs

William Biggs came from Texas to Nebraska. He and his wife are shown on pre-1930 US Census enumerations in Texas. He married Rushie Moore on 20 May 1896 in Llano Co., Texas. He is shown as W.E. Biggs. [1] The following census enumerations show more about the Biggs.

1900 US Census, Brown Co., Texas, Brownwood, ED 4, Page 21B [2]
396-405 David S. Camp HH, white
William Biggs, servant, black, b. March 1877, age 23, married 4 years,
     b. TX, both parents b. TX
Ruisha Biggs, servant, female, black, b. August 1873, 26, married 4 years,
     0 children, 0 living, b. TX, father b. TX, mother b. TN

1910 US Census, Jones Co., Texas, Stanford, ED 137, Page 6B [3]
312 Campbell Street
113-119 Will Biggs, black, 35, married 14 years, b. TX, father b. US,
     mother b. TX, cook sanitariam
Russie Biggs, wife, black, 33, married 14 years, 0 children, 0 living, b. TX,
     both parents b. TN, servant, private family
Rufus D. Taylor, boarder, black, 45, married, second marriage, married 8
     years, b. TX, both parents b. US, clergyman, Baptist Church

William Biggs filed his World War I Draft Registration in Dawes Co., Nebraska on 12 September 1918. He is shown as living at Whitney, Dawes County and farming for E.H. Pilster of Whitney. His nearest relative is shown as Cortnay Biggs, his mother, of Llano, Texas. [4]

It is unknown if William E. Biggs and Rushie Moore had any children. They are not shown on the 1920 US Census. He is in Box Butte Co., Nebraska without her in 1930, rooming with Lucille James. Lucille and Biggs were still in the same house on the 1940 US Census.

1930 US Census, Box Butte Co., Nebraska, Alliance, 3rd Ward, ED 3, Page 2A [5]
Railroad Yards
    South Platte Street
    35-35 Lucille James, rents, $10 month, negro, 54, divorced, married at age 27,
        b. MO, both parents b. TX, general household labor, in homes
    William Biggs, roomer, negro, 53, single, b. TX, both parens b. TX, laborer,
        scavenger wagon

1940 US Census, Box Butte Co., Nebraska, Alliance, ED 7-2B, Page 8A 6
111 Sweetwater
Bill Biggs, owns, $1,200, informant, 68?, b. TX, 3rd grade, same place 1 April
     1935, janitor, local newspaper
Lucille James, housekeeper, 64, widow, 7th grade, b. MO, same place 1 April
     1935, house keeper, private home
Jimmie Shores, housekeeper's, grandson, 9, 2nd grade, b. NE, same place
     1 April 1935
Tommy Shores, housekeeper's grandson, 5, b. NE, same place 1 April 1935

William Biggs was born 13 March 1877 in Llano Co., Texas. He had resided in Alliance for
twenty-one years before his death on 27 July 1946 in Alliance. He was survived by a sister, Mrs. M.E.
Carter and a brother, both of Llano, Texas. His spouse was listed as Raisha on funeral records and they
were not divorced. The lot where he was buried was owned by Priscilla James.

His sister may have been the following Elizabeth Carter who was living in Llano, Llano Co.,
Texas in 1940, a widow. Courtney Biggs may have been his brother.

1900 US Census, Llano Co., Texas, Llano, ED 150-1, Page 27B 7
614 South Llano owns, $300
Elizabeth Carter, negro, 65, widow, 3rd grade, b. TX, living at Benson, Kanabec
     Co., TX 1 April 1935
Jennie Carter, daughter, negro, 24, single, 3 years high school, b. TX, living at
     San Antonio, Bexar Co., TX 1 April 1935, servant, private home
Ethlyn Brudy, granddaughter, negro, 20, single, 1 year high school, b. TX,
     living at Benson, Kanabec Co., TX 1 April 1935, servant, private home

1900 US Census, Llano Co., Texas, Justice Prect. 1, ED 125, Page 8A 8
141-143 Courtney Biggs, black, b. May 1858, 42, divorced, 9 children, 7
     living, b. TX, both parents b. MO, laundress
Ed Biggs, son, black, b. August 1879, 20, single, b. TX, both parents b. TX,
     day laborer
John Biggs, son, black, b. July 1881, 18, b. TX, both parents b. TX, day laborer
Nathan Taylor, son, black, b. Feb 1882, 12, b. TX, both parents b. TX
Tommie Taylor, son, black, b. Aug 1891, 8, b. TX, both parents b. TX
Ruby Taylor, daughter, black, b. Feb 1893, 7, b. TX, both parents b. TX
Minnie Lemons, niece, black, b. Sept 1886, 13, b. TX, both parents b. TX
Mary Mabry, mother, black, b. Aug 1831, 68, single, b. MO, both parents
     b. TX

1. Texas Marriages, 1837-1973," database, FamilySearch (https://familysearch.org/ark:/
61903/1:1:FXQF-3MS, W. E. Biggs and Rushie Moore, 20 May 1896; citing , Llano, Texas, , reference
2:W8R49X; FHL microfilm 982,995.
2. Year: 1900; Census Place: Brownwood, Brown, Texas; Roll: 1650; Page: 21B; Enumeration District:
0004; FHL microfilm: 1241615
3. Year: 1910; Census Place: Stanford, Jones, Texas; Roll: T624_1569; Page: 6B; Enumeration District:
0137; FHL microfilm: 1375582
4. Registration State: *Nebraska;* Registration County: *Dawes;* Roll: *1711524*
5. Year: 1930; Census Place: Alliance, Box Butte, Nebraska; Roll: 1266; Page: 2A; Enumeration District:
0003; Image: 856.0; FHL microfilm: 2341001
6. Year: 1940; Census Place: Alliance, Box Butte, Nebraska; Roll: T627_2237; Page: 8A; Enumeration
District: 7-2B

7. Year: 1940; Census Place: Llano, Llano, Texas; Roll: T627_4096; Page: 27B; Enumeration District: 150-1
8. Year: 1900; Census Place: Justice Precinct 1, Llano, Texas; Roll: 1655; Page: 8A; Enumeration District: 0125; FHL microfilm: 1241655

Billy Smith

In 1894, Billy Smith, a black man of the south, came to Nebraska. He worked for about four years around Alliance and Crawford in the Nebraska panhandle. In about 1898 he went to Broken Bow, Custer Co., Nebraska.

According to his obituary he was born 11 September 1869 in Lexington, Fayette Co., Kentucky. After arriving in Broken Bow, he went to Comstock in Custer County where he lived for over fifty years with the Gibbons family on the Walter Gibbons ranch at Wescott near Comstock. Billy had a love of horses. Probably before hiring on at the Gibbons ranch he had served as a cook on the Olive Ranch. Billy apparently never married. He died on 20 September 1951. His funeral was held at the Walter Gibbons ranch home and he was buried in the Douglas Grove Cemetery near Comstock in Custer Co., Nebraska. The following census enumerations reveal more about Billy.

1900 US Census, Custer Co., Nebraska, Broken Bow, ED 62, Page 1B   1
11-11 William Smith, colored, b. June 1876, 24, single, b. KY, father b. OH,
  mother b. KY, farm laborer

1910 US Census, Custer Co., Nebraska, Douglas Grove Twp., ED 77, Page 1B   2
#18 Frank F. Hale HH, white, farmer
William Smith, black, 33, single, b. KY, both parents b. KY, farm laborer

1920 US Census, Custer Co., Nebraska, Douglas Grove Twp., ED 83, Page 6A   3
118-118 Edward C. Gibbons, owns, mortgaged, 64, widowed, b. NY, both
  parents b. NY, farmer
Walter E. Gibbons, son, 21, single, b. NE, father b. NY, mother b. WI, farm helper
William Smith, hired man, black, 50, single, b. KY, both parents b. US, farm
  laborer

1930 US Census, Custer Co., Nebraska, Douglas Grove Twp., ED 17, Page 7B   4
138-142 Walter C. Gibbons, owns, 32, married at age 25, b. NE, father b. NY,
  mother b. WI, farmer
Silvia M., wife, 28, married at age 21, b. NE, father b. NE, mother b. KY
Walter E., son, 5/12, b. NE, both parents b. NE
William Smith, servant, negro, 60, single, b. KY, both parents b. KY, farm laborer

1940 US Census, Custer Co., Nebraska, Douglas Grove Twp., ED 21-18, Page 7A 5
#134 Walter Gibbons HH, farmer
Billie Smith, laborer, shown as black and then crossed over to white, 66, 0
  education, b. KY, same house 1 April 1935, laborer, farm

1. Year: 1900; Census Place: Broken Bow, Custer, Nebraska; Roll: 921; Page: 1B; Enumeration District: 0062; FHL microfilm: 1240921
2. Year: 1910; Census Place: Douglas Grove, Custer, Nebraska; Roll: T624_841; Page: 1B; Enumeration District: 0077; FHL microfilm: 1374854

3. Year: 1920; Census Place: Douglas Grove, Custer, Nebraska; Roll: T625_985; Page: 6A; Enumeration District: 83; Image: 292
4. Year: 1930; Census Place: Douglas Grove, Custer, Nebraska; Roll: 1270; Page: 7B; Enumeration District: 0017; Image: 285.0; FHL microfilm: 2341005
5. Year: 1940; Census Place: Douglas Grove, Custer, Nebraska; Roll: T627_2242; Page: 7A; Enumeration District: 21-18

Arthur Blackwell

Arthur Blackwell who resided in Alliance, was finally lured into marriage by his common-law wife, Josephine Johnson. The following is reported in an Alliance, Box Butte Co., Nebraska newspaper in 1919.

"Two weeks ago Arthur Blackwell was fined $50 for beating his then common-law wife, Josephine Johnson. Being unable to pay the fine he was sentenced to thirty days hard work. He took up his duties shoveling snow in front of the court house, washing windows and singing bass in the colored quartette.

While he was thus engaged, Josephine came along and on the hypothesis that sympathy is akin to love, she proposed marriage to Arthur. He secured a job as porter at a salary of $60 a month and when arrangements were made to pay the balance of his fine the couple secured a license and proceeded to get married.

When the judge questioned Josephine if she fully realized what she was doing, she said: 'I love that man, judge; and if we can keep liquor away from him he will be all right.' Thereupon she paid the judge the fee and took Arthur away to head her household."

The Alliance Herald, 21 February 1918 indicates that Arthur Blackwell was taken to Chadron by US Marshall A.N. White, charged with treasonable utterances.

Arthur and Josephine were married in Alliance, Box Butte Co., Nebraska on 13 February 1919. Their marriage record indicates that he was 34, black, first marriage, born in Kansas, laborer. His parents are shown as Chas. Blackwell, born in Missouri and Mattie March, born in Tennessee. Josephine was age 33, first marriage, black, daughter of Joe Johnson, born Missouri and Anna Show, born Missouri. The witness at their marriage was Cyrus A. Lang. 1

Shortly after their marriage in 1919, Arthur and Josephine Blackwell moved to Kansas City, Missouri where they are shown in 1920 living with his mother.

1920 US Census, Jackson Co., Missouri, Kansas City, Ward 10, ED 155, Page 5B 2
2635 Michigan Avenue
108-137 Mattie Blackwell, owns, mortgaged, black, 59, widow, b. TN, both
      parents b. TN, no occupation
Charles E., son, black, 23, single, b. KS, father b. MO, mother b. TN, laborer,
      general
Chester A., son, black, 35, married, b. KS, father b. MO, mother b. TN,
      laborer, any kind
Josephine, daughter-in-law, black, 33, married, b. MO, both parents b. MO,
      laundry, private families

1930 US Census, Jackson Co., Missouri, Kansas City, Ward 9, ED 121, Page 2B 3
1400 Pacific St.

—57 Florence Terrell, rents $8 month, negro, 46, widow, married at age 30, b.
IL, both parents b. VA, servant, private family
Arthur Blackwell, roomer, negro, 46, married at age 32, b. KS, father b. MO,
mother b. TN, laborer, street bldg.
Josephine Blackwell, roomer, negro, 46, married at age 32, b. MO, father b.
unknown, mother b. MO, laundress, laundry
Josephine Blackwell, roomer's daughter, negro, 9, b. MO, father b. KS, mother
b. MO
Lualie Blackwell, roomer's daughter, negro, 6, b. MO, father b. KS, mother
b. MO

1940 US Census, Jackson Co., Missouri, Kansas City, Ward 2, ED 116-38,   4
Page 62B
1008 Vine - rents $9 month
Arthur A. Blackwell, informant, negro, 56, widowed, 4th grade, b. KS, residing
Kansas City 1 April 1935, laborer, WPA Project
Josephine, daughter, negro, 18, single, 4 years high school, b. MO, residing
Kansas City 1 April 1935, maid, private home

Josephine Blackwell died on 20 July 1934 in Kansas City, Jackson Co., Missouri in her home at
1838 E. 9th St. According to her death certificate she died of acute alcoholism. She was married to C.A.
Blackwell and born 23 January 1884 in St. Louis, Missouri to Joe Johnson, mother unknown. The
informant was her husband C.A. Blackwell, of the home address. 5

Chester Arthur Blackwell died on 29 May 1947 in General Hospital No. 2 in Kansas City,
Jackson Co., Missouri. According to his death certificate he had been in the hospital for 29 days. He
apparently remarried after the death of Josephine as his wife is shown as 50 year old Sadie Blackwell.
His home address was 1227 E. 11th Street in Kansas City, Jackson Co., Missouri. He was born 22
September 1883 in Ottowa, Kansas to Charlie Blackwell and Mattie Morris, born Tennessee. His wife,
Sadie was the informant, and she may not have known too much about him. His occupation was a
minister. Arthur died of pulmonary infarction, central nervous system and syphilis. His body was
removed on 2 June 1947 to Westlawn Cemetery in Kansas City, Wyandotte Co., Kansas. 6

Blackwell and March

According to the Social Security Claim Index, Arthur Blackwell was born 22 September 1883 in
Ottowa, Franklin Co., Kansas, son of Charley Blackwell and Mattie March. He is shown in his parents'
household on the 1900 US Census.

1900 US Census, Miami Co., Kansas, Paola, 2nd Ward, ED 130, Page 15A 7
West Shawnee Street
337-345 Charles Blackwell, black, b. April 1853, 47, married 19 years, b. MO,
both parents b. VA, day laborer
Mattie, wife, black, b. Jan 1860, 40, married 19 years, 10 children, 7 living, b.
TN, father b. NC, mother b. MD
Hattie, daughter, black, b. Feb 1878, 22, single, b. KS, father b. MO, mother
b. TN
Maggie, daughter, black, b. May 1881, 19, b. KS, father b. MO, mother b. TN
Pearl, daughter, black, b. Mar 1883, 17, b. KS, father b. MO, mother b. TN
Arthur, son, black, b. Sept 1884, 15, b. KS, father b. MO, mother b. TN
Alberta, daughter, black, b. Nov. 1886, 13, b. KS, father b. MO, mother b. TN

Lizzie, daughter, black, b. Aug 1888, 11, b. KS, father b. MO, mother b. TN
Ollie, son, black, b. July 1890, 10, b. KS, father b. MO, mother b. TN
Earl, son, black, b. May 1896 4, b. KS, father b. MO, mother b. TN
Emma D, daughter, black, b. Feb 1900, 3/12, b. KS, father b. MO, mother b. TN

According to the 1900 US Census (above), Charles and Mattie Blackwell had been married about 19 years. There are two daughters born prior to that, Hattie in 1878 and Maggie in 1881. The 1880 US Census indicates that Charles was widowed. Also living in Franklin Co., Kansas was Martha "Mattie" March, as yet umarried. They were married on 23 October 1880 in Franklin Co., Kansas. He is shown on their marriage record as 27 and she is 19. 8

1880 US Census, Franklin Co., Kansas, Lincoln Twp., ED 84, Page 72A 9
59-62 HH of W.H.H. McGee, white
Charles Blackwell, black, 27, servant, farm laborer, b. MO, both parents b. TN

1880 US Census, Franklin Co., Kansas, Centropolis Twp., ED 78, Page 17A 10
86-87 Jacob March, black, 35, widowed, b. NY, nothing shown for parents, no
       occupation
Martha March, black, 30, sister, single, keeping house, b. TN, father b. TN
William March, black, 11, son, works on farm, b. TN, father b. NY, mother b. TN
Susie March, black, 10, daughter, b. TN, father b. NY, mother b. TN
Mec. March, black, female, 8, daughter, b. TN, father b. NY, mother b. TN
John March, black, 6, son, b. TN, father b. NY, mother b. TN
Lula March, black, 3, daughter, b. TN, father b. NY, mother b. TN

1910 US Census, Wyandotte Co., Kansas, Kansas City, Ward 3, ED 167, 11
Page 18B
726 Oakland
30-31 Charles T. Blackwell, black, 50, second marriage, married 32 years, b.
       MO, father b. VA, mother b. MO, wagon driver, coal company
Mattie, wife, black, 48, first marriage, married 32 years, 6 children, 7 living,
       b. TN, father b. SC, mother b. MD
Ollie, son, black, 18, single, b. KS, father b. MO, mother b. TN, wagon driver,
       transfer company
Earl, son, black, 12, b. KS, father b. MO, mother b. TN
—32 William W. Jones, black, 23, married 6 years, b. OK, both parents b. OK,
       janitor, club house
Elberta, wife, black, 21, married 6 years, 1 child, 1 living, b. KS, father b.
       MO, mother b. TN
Alfred, son, black, 4, b. KS, father b. OK, mother b. KS

1920 US Census, Jackson Co., Missouri, Kansas City, Ward 8, ED 133, Page 2B 12
1818 Sixteenth Street
Charlie Blackwell, lodger, black, 49, divorced, b. MO, father b. MO, mother b.
       KY, janitor, flat

Even though Mattie March Blackwell indicates in 1920 that she was widowed, it appears that she and Charles were divorced. They were both living in Kansas City, Missouri and in 1920 her son Chester Arthur Blackwell and his wife Josephine were living with her (see above). As Charles and Martha "Mattie" cannot be located on the 1930 US Census, they may have died between 1920 and 1930. The following are the known children born to them. The daughters, Hattie and Maggie, were undoubtedly born to Charles by his first wife.

1. Pearl Blackwell, born March 1883 in Kansas
2. Chester Arthur Blackwell, born 22 September 1883 in Ottowa, Franklin Co., Kansas (see above)
3. Alberta Blackwell, born November 1886 in Kansas
4. Lizzie Blackwell, born August 1888 in Kansas
5. Oliver "Ollie" Blackwell, born 24 July 1889 in Ottowa, Franklin Co., Kansas
6. Charles Earl Blackwell, born 9 May 1896 in Ottowa, Franklin Co., Kansas
7. Emma D. Blackwell, born February 1900 in Kansas

Alberta (Elberta) Blackwell, daughter of Charles Blackwell and Martha "Mattie" March, was born in November 1886 in Kansas. She married William W. Jones. He was born about 1883 in Oklahoma. They were living with her parents in Kansas City, Kansas in 1910. They had a son, Alfred Jones, born about 1906 in Kansas.

Ollie Blackwell, son of Charles Blackwell and Martha "Mattie" March, was born 24 July 1889 in Ottawa, Franklin Co., Kansas. He filed his World War I Draft Registration on 5 June 1917 in Kansas City, Wyandotte Co., Kansas. Ollie was an ice setter for Crystal Springs Ice Co., 7th & NW Tracts, Kansas City, Kansas. He was married, supporting a wife, two children and his mother. Under comments he stated that he had some rheumatism. 13

1915 Kansas State City, Wyandotte Co., Kansas, Kansas City, Ward 3, Page 38 14
3-3 rents Lizzie Blackwell, 22, black, house wife, b. KS
Ollie Blackwell, 25, black, laborer, b. KS
Marie Blackwell, 2, black, b. KS
Helen Blackwell, 1, black, b. KS

1920 US Census, Wyandotte Co., Kansas, Kansas City, Ward 3, ED 158, Page 4A 15
2816 North 6th Street
79-85 Ollie Blackwell, rents, black, 30, b. KS, both parents b. US, teamster, coal yard
Lottie, wife, black, 26, b. KS, both parents b. KS
Marie, daughter, black, 7, b. KS, both parents b. KS
Helen, daughter, black, 5, b. KS, both parents b. KS
Ollie, son, black, 2 6/12, b. KS, both parents b. KS
Marcell, daughter, black, 9/12, b. KS, both parents b. KS

1930 US Census, Wyandotte Co., Kansas, Kansas City, Ward 3, ED 8, Page 20B 16
2505 North Hallock Street
259-271 Oliver Blackwell, rents $10 month, negro, 39, married at age 19, b. KS, both parents b. US, laborer, freight house
Lottie, wife, negro, 33, married at age 17, b. KS, father b. LA, mother b. KY
Oliver, Jr., son, negro, 12, b. KS, both parents b. KS
Marcell, daughter, negro, 11, b. KS, both parents b. KS
Marie Alexander, daughter, negro, 17, married at age 17, b. KS, both parents b. KS
Louie Blackwell, son, 8, b. KS, both parents b. KS

Ollie Blackwell, son of Charles Blackwell and Martha "Mattie" March, died on 30 March 1935 at 6th and Bluff in Kansas City, Jackson Co., Missouri. According to his death certificate he died from his chest being crushed in an automobile accident. He was a passenger. Ollie was married to Lottie Blackwell. He was born 24 July 1889 in Ottawa, Franklin Co., Kansas, son of Chas. Blackwell, born

Kansas; mother unknown. He was a laborer for Western Storage Co. The informant was Ollie C. Blackwell, Jr. of 801 Pacific, Kansas City, Jackson Co., Missouri. Ollie was buried on 3 April 1935 in the Westlawn Cemetery in Kansas City, Wyandotte Co., Kansas. 17

Charles Earl Blackwell, son of Charles Blackwell and Martha "Mattie" March, was born 9 May 1896 in Ottowa, Franklin Co., Kansas. According to his World War I Draft Registration he was living at 732 Locust Street, Kansas City, Missouri. He was a porter, but not employed, single and supporting his mother. It was filed 12 February 1918, in Kansas City, Wyandotte Co., Kansas. 18

1.Box Butte Co., Nebraska, Marriage Book F, page 73 #2599
2. Year: 1920; Census Place: Kansas City Ward 10, Jackson, Missouri; Roll: T625_926; Page: 5B; Enumeration District: 155; Image: 860
3. Year: 1930; Census Place: Kansas City, Jackson, Missouri; Roll: 1198; Page: 2B; Enumeration District: 0121; Image: 6.0; FHL microfilm: 2340933
4. Year: 1940; Census Place: Kansas City, Jackson, Missouri; Roll: T627_2166; Page: 62B; Enumeration District: 116-38
5. Missouri Death Certificate #24769
6. Missouri Death Certificate # 20833
7. Year: 1900; Census Place: Paola, Miami, Kansas; Roll: 490; Page: 15A; Enumeration District: 0130; FHL microfilm: 1240490
8. Kansas County Marriages, 1855-1911," database with images, FamilySearch (https://familysearch.org/pal:/MM9.3.1/TH-1-16089-68169-5?cc=1851040 : 16 February 2016), Franklin > Marriage records, 1879-1883, v. D > image 63 of 199; citing district clerk, court clerk, county clerk and register offices from various counties.
9. Year: 1880; Census Place: Lincoln, Franklin, Kansas; Roll: 381; Family History Film: 1254381; Page: 72A; Enumeration District: 084; Image: 0592
10. Year: 1880; Census Place: Centropolis, Franklin, Kansas; Roll: 381; Family History Film: 1254381; Page: 17A; Enumeration District: 078; Image: 0482
11. Year: 1910; Census Place: Kansas City Ward 3, Wyandotte, Kansas; Roll: T624_460; Page: 18B; Enumeration District: 0167; FHL microfilm: 1374473
12. Year: 1920; Census Place: Kansas City Ward 8, Jackson, Missouri; Roll: T625_926; Page: 2B; Enumeration District: 133; Image: 655
13. Registration State: *Kansas;* Registration County: *Wyandotte;* Roll: *1643581;* Draft Board: *2*
14. Kansas State Historical Society; Topeka, Kansas; Roll: *ks1915_261;* Line: *1*
15. Year: 1920; Census Place: Kansas City Ward 3, Wyandotte, Kansas; Roll: T625_555; Page: 4A; Enumeration District: 158; Image: 595
16. Year: 1930; Census Place: Kansas City, Wyandotte, Kansas; Roll: 727; Page: 20B; Enumeration District: 0008; Image: 254.0; FHL microfilm: 2340462
17. Missouri Death Certificate #9451
18. Registration State: *Kansas;* Registration County: *Wyandotte;* Roll: *1643581;* Draft Board: *2*

Bonty Family

The widow Ella Bonty and her children were living on Ray Street in Valentine, Cherry Co., Nebraska when the 1920 US Census was taken. They had come from Hill City Twp. in Graham Co., Kansas between 1916 and 1920. Ella was the widow of Thomas Elias Bonty.

Luella "Ella" Glenn was born 12 October 1869 in Kentucky, the daughter of John F. Glenn and Mary Knuckles. She married Thomas Elias Bonty. Ella died 11 May 1964 in Los Angeles, Los Angeles Co., California. Thomas was born on 16 July 1855 in Newcastle, Henry Co., Kentucky. He died on 7 August 1916 in Hill City, Graham Co., Kansas and was buried in the Hill City Cemetery. Thomas Bonty lived in Denver, Colorado in 1891 and 1892 and on city directories is shown as "colored labor." The Bonty family members are shown on the following enumerations.

1900 US Census, Graham Co., Kansas, Hill City Twp., ED 39, Page 7A [1]

154-154 Thomas S. Bonty, black, b. July 1855, 44, married 11 years, b. KY, both parents b. KY

Ella, wife, black, b. Oct 1869, 30, married 11 years, 3 children, 3 living, b. KY, both parents b. KY

Kenneth W., son, black, b. Jan 1891, 9, b. CO, both parents b. KY

Thurman E., son, black, b. Feb 1893, 7, b. KS, both parents b. KY

Emery E., son, black, b. Feb 1896, 4, b. KS, both parents b. KY

1910 US Census, Graham Co., Kansas, Hill City Twp., ED 48, Page 8A [2]

164-168 Thomas S. Bonty, black, 53, married 19 years, b. KY, both parents b. KY, farmer

Ella, wife, black, 42, married 19 years, 6 children 2 living, b. KY, both parents b. KY

Thurman, son, black, 18, b. CO, both parents b. KY

Emery, son, black, 13, b. KS, both parents b. KY

Ervin, son, black, 7, b. KS, both parents b. KY

Geneva, daughter, black, 3, b. KS, both parents b. KY

1920 US Census, Cherry Co., Nebraska, Valentine, ED 68, Page 10A [3]

Ray Street

202-213 Thurman Bonty, owns, mortgaged, black, 26, b. KS, both parents b. KY, laborer, general work

Jennie, wife, mulatto, 25, b. KS, both parents b. MO

Bolivia, daughter, mulatto 1 6/12, b. NE, both parents b. KS

Louis(e) Rosebud, sister-in-law, mulatto, 12, b. KS, both parents b. MO

Page 10B 210-222 Ella Bonty, rents, black, 52, widow, b. KY, both parents b. KY, laundress, private family

Ervin, son, black, 17, single, b. KS, both parents b KY, laborer, common

Geneva, daughter, black, 13, b. KS, both parents b. KY

The following are the known children of Thomas Elias Bonty and Luella "Ella" Glenn.

1. Kenneth E. Bonty, born January 1891 in Colorado
2. Thurman Edward Bonty, born 1 February 1892 in Kansas
3. Emery Thomas Bonty, born 4 February 1897 in Kansas
4. Ervin Bonty, born 23 March 1903 in Nebraska
5. Genettia Bonty, born 12 December 1906 in Hill City, Graham Co., Kansas; died 15 July 1909 in Hill City, Graham Co., Kansas
6. Genevieve A. Bonty, born 2 December 1907 in Kansas

Thurman Edward Bonty, son of Thomas Elias Bonty and Luella "Ella" Glenn, was born 1 February 1892 probably in Kansas. He married Amanda (Amenda) Jane Lewis, daughter of Philander Lewis and Bolivia Jane Hare. She was born 5 February 1896 in Cloud Co., Kansas and died 15 April 1958 in Pasadena, Los Angeles Co., California. Thurman and his family were living in Beatrice, Gage Co., Nebraska when the 1930 US Census was taken. His wife is shown as Jane. Between 1935 and 1940 they moved to Pasadena, Los Angeles Co., California. Thurman married second on 17 November 1959 in Los Angeles Co., California to Carrie Bell Bluitt. She was born 1 August 1903 in Somerville, Burleson Co., Texas to Jerry Myers Bluitt and Fannie Patterson. Carrie died 17 April 1996 in Los Angeles Co., California. Thurman died 28 December 1977 at Compton, Los Angeles Co., California.

Emery Thomas Bonty, son of Thomas Elias Bonty and Luella "Ella" Glenn, was born 4 February 1897 in Kansas. He married Ida Frances Miller. She was born 4 November 1900 in Kansas, daughter of Edward and Cora Miller. Ida died on 25 September 1994 in Rialto, San Bernardino Co., California. Emery died on 18 September 1976 in Kern Co., California.

Ervin Bonty, son of Thomas Elias Bounty and Luella "Ella" Glenn, was born 23 March 1903 in Nebraska. He married Arlee Helen Jones McLemore, who was born 2 December 1909 in Tennessee and died 1 January 1996 in Tulare, Tulare Co., California. Ervin was employed as a cowboy on ranches and in shows. He then became an auto maker and race car driver. He died 20 January 1966 in Tulare, Tulare Co., California.

Genevieve A. Bonty, daughter of Thomas Elias Bonty and Luella "Ella" Glenn, was born 2 December 1907 in Kansas. She married James Roberts. He was born about 1896 in Kansas. She graduated on 2 June 1927 from Lincoln High School, Lincoln, Lancaster Co., Nebraska. Genevieve died on 1 January 1999 in Los Angeles Co., California. She was buried in Inglewood Park Cemetery, Inglewood, Los Angeles Co., California.

John F. Glenn was born March 1846 in Newcastle, Henry Co., Kentucky. Only his mother's name, Jennie, is known. On 13 September 1864 in Louisville, Jefferson Co., Kentucky, John enlisted in Co. A, 5th U.S. Colored Cavalry. He was mustered out as a private on 16 March 1866 in Helena, Arkansas. Also in 1864 he married Mary Knuckles. She was born 12 March 1847 in New Castle, Henry Co., Kentucky. Mary died 23 May 1926 in Hill City, Graham Co., Kansas. John F. Glenn died 12 July 1920 in Hill City, Graham Co., Kansas. They were both buried in the Hill City Cemetery, Hill City, Graham Co., Kansas. They were parents of the following children.

1. Luella "Ella" Glenn, born 12 October 1869 in Kentucky (see above)
2. Frank G. Glenn, born 7 June 1871 in Kentucky
3. Lenora M. Glenn, born 19 Sept 1873 in Kentucky
4. Joseph William Glenn, born 28 February 1879 in Newcastle, Henry Co., Kentucky
5. Almeada Glenn, born 13 October 1879 in Hill City, Graham Co., Kansas
6. Katherine A. Glenn, born 21 May 1880 in Kansas
7. Myrtle Gertrude Glenn, born 21 May 1885 in Kansas
8. Thomas M. Glenn, born 11 September 1885 in Hill City, Graham Co., Kansas

Frank G. Glenn, son of John F. Glenn and Mary Knuckles, was born 7 June 1871 in Kentucky. He married Bettie M. ____ in 1894. She was born 14 January 1868 in Arkansas and died 7 November 1955 in Hill City, Graham Co., Kansas. Frank died on 14 May 1942 in Hill City, Graham Co., Kansas.

Lenora M. Glenn, daughter of John F. Glenn and Mary Knuckles, was born 19 September 1873 in Kentucky. On 27 December 1895 in Valentine, Cherry Co., Nebraska she married George Washington Caulton. He was born 16 August 1871 in Georgia to Wiley L. Caulton and Polly A. Williams and died 31 January 1950 in Colorado. Lenora died on 31 December 1948 in Los Angeles Co., California.

Joseph William Glenn, son of John F. Glenn and Mary Knuckles, was born 28 February 1879 in New Castle, Henry Co., Kentucky. On 8 July 1917 in Logansport, Logan Co., Kansas, he married Vergie E. Clark. She was attending Kansas State University. Vergie was born 5 January 1887 in Kansas to John

Clark and Julia Jones. She died on 18 September 1984 in Hill City, Graham Co., Kansas. Joseph died 28 February 1953 in Hill City, Graham Co., Kansas.

Almeada Glenn, daughter of John G. Glenn and Mary Knuckles, was born 13 October 1879 in Hill City, Graham Co., Kansas. She married Lewis Neal Grimes in 1904 in Hill City. He was born 2 November 1874 in Frankfort, Franklin Co., Kentucky to E.I. and Muranda Grimes. Lewis died on 2 December 1946 in Junction City, Geary Co., Kansas. Almeada died there on 8 January 1948.

Kathcrinc A. Glenn, daughter of John G. Glenn and Mary Knuckles, was born 21 May 1880 in Kansas. She married Alexander "Alex" Alexander. He was born 26 June 1873 in Cumberland Co., Kentucky, the son of Andrew James and Polina Alexander. Alex died in November of 1971 at Nicodemus, Graham Co., Kansas. Katherine died on 3 December 1967 in Colorado.

Myrtle Gertrude Glenn, daughter of John G. Glenn and Mary Knuckles, was born 21 May 1885 in Kansas. She married Oscar Ernest Ramsey. He was born 24 July 1897 at Jamestown, Cloud Co., Kansas to Deloss Ramsey and Lillian Graham and died 3 March 1934 in Garden City, Finney Co., Kansas. Myrtle died 19 August 1958 in Los Angeles Co., California.

Thomas M. Glenn, son of John F. Glenn and Mary Knuckles, was born 11 September 1885 in Hill City, Graham Co., Kansas. He married Peggy —. On 18 November 1943, Thomas was seriously burned in an accident while working on a county road. He was burning weeds and the feed spout on the gas tank burst, throwing gasoline over his clothing which immediately caught on fire. Between 1952 and 1957 he moved to Wichita, Sedgwick Co., Kansas.

1. Year: 1900; Census Place: Hill City, Graham, Kansas; Roll: 481; Page: 7A; Enumeration District: 0039; FHL microfilm: 1240481
2. Year: 1910; Census Place: Hill, Graham, Kansas; Roll: T624_440; Page: 8A; Enumeration District: 0048; FHL microfilm: 1374453
3. Year: 1920; Census Place: Valentine, Cherry, Nebraska; Roll: T625_981; Page: 10A and 10B; Enumeration District: 68; Image: 1138

Arthur Edward Bray

Arthur Edward Bray, wife and children, lived in Whitman Prect., Grant Co., Nebraska. They came there in about 1909 or early 1910. Arthur married Virginia Thompson. The following enumeration shows them living in Grant Co., Nebraska in 1910.

1910 US Census, Grant Co., Nebraska, Whitman Prect., Township 24, Range 36, 1
ED 119, Page 1A
3-3 James W.T. Thompson, black, 34, second marriage, married 9 years, b. TX, father b. US, mother b. TX, farmer
Mollie, wife, mulatto, 29, first marriage, married 9 years, 8 children, 2 living, b. TX, both parents b. TX
Lizzie, daughter, mulatto, 6, b. TX, both parents b. TX
Anna, daughter, mulatto, 5, b. TX, both parents b. TX
Arthur B. Bray, brother-in-law, mulatto, 30, married 4 years, b. OK, father b. TN, mother b. OK, plumber
Virginia Bray, sister, black, 31, married 4 years, 2 children, 2 living, b. TX, both parents b. US, seamstress
Dorothy E. Bray, niece, mulatto, 3, b. TX, father b. OK, mother b. TX
Margaret Bray, niece, mulatto 1 3/12, b. OK, father b. OK, mother b. TX

Arthur Bray filed his World War I Draft Registration in Hyannis, Grant Co., Nebraska on 12 September 1918. His address was Whitman, Grant County where he was employed by F. Conothers as a ranchman. He was 38, born 18 February 1880, wife Virginia Bray of Whitman. 2

Arthur and Virginia Bray continued to live in Whitman Prect., Grant Co., Nebraska as evidenced from the federal census enumerations. The son Roscoe was not shown on the 1910 US Census, so perhaps remained behind in Texas or Oklahoma.

1920 US Census, Grant Co., Nebraska, Whitman, ED 131, Page 1A   3
2-2 Arthur B. Bray, rents, black, 38, b. TX, both parents b. TX, laborer, stock
    ranch
Virginia, wife, black, 41?, b. TX, father b. TX, mother b. US
Roscoe, son, black, 16, b. TX, both parents b. TX, laborer, stock ranch
Dorothy, daughter, black, 13, b. TX, both parents b. TX
Margaret, daughter, black, 10, b. TX, both parents b. TX

1930 US Census, Grant Co., Nebraska, Whitman, ED 4, Page 2B   4
43-49 Arthur B. Bray, rents, negro, 50, married at age 24, b. TX, both parents b.
    TX, feed store, own
Virginia, wife, negro, 54, married at age 28, b. TX, both parents b. TX

Even though he is shown as Arthur B. Bray in some records, his full name was Arthur Edward Bray, born 18 February 1880 in Texas to Maynard Bray and Katie Johnson. Athur married Virginia "Gammie" Thompson on 19 December 1904 in Lamar Co., Texas. She was born 8 January 1877 at Medill, near Paris in Lamar Co., Texas to Monroe Thompson and Susan Fleming. Arthur died on 4 October 1932 at the Hastings State Hospital near Hastings, Adams Co., Nebraska. It was also called Ingelside. He was buried on 7 October 1932 in the Forest Lawn Cemetery in Omaha. Virginia died 16 July 1961 in Omaha, Douglas Co., Nebraska and was also buried in the Forest Lawn Cemetery. They were parents of the following children.

1. Roscoe Bray, born 13 March 1903 in Texas
2. Dorothy Bray, born about 1907 in Texas, died August 1922 in Omaha,
    Douglas Co., Nebraska, buried Forest Lawn Cemetery, Omaha, Douglas
    Co., Nebraska
3. Margaret Bray, born 6 January 1909 in Texas, died 3 January 1983 in
    Inglewood, Los Angeles Co., California

Roscoe Bray, son of Arthur Edward Bray and Virginia "Gammie" Thompson, was born 13 March 1903 in Texas. He was living with his wife, Katherine in Grant Co., Nebraska and between 1930 and 1935, they had moved to Oklahoma. He died 3 November 1967 and was buried in the Odd Fellows Cemetery, Ponca City, Kay Co., Oklahoma.

1930 US Census, Grant Co., Nebraska, Whitman prect., ED 4, Page 3A   5
59-66 Roscoe Bray, rents, negro, 27, married at age 17, b. TX, both parents
    b. TX, farmer, cattle ranching
Katherine, wife, negro, 17, married at age 15, b. OK, both parents b. Louisiana

1940 US Census, Kay Co., Oklahoma, Ponca City, Ward 3, ED 36-36, Page 9B   6
1529 South Street; owns, $1,000
Roscoe Bray, negro, 37, 7th grade, b. TX, same place 1 April 1935, porter, auto
    garage

Kathrine, informant, wife, negro, 28, 1 year high school, b. OK, same place
1 April 1935, servant, private family

Margaret Bray, daughter of Arthur Edward Bray and Virginia "Gammie" Thompson, was born 6 January 1909 in Texas. She married Malcolm G. Allen. He was born 17 April 1907 in Texas to Malcolm G. Allen and Luella Wiley. He died on 13 December 1990 in Los Angeles, California. Margaret died 3 January 1983 in Inglewood, Los Angeles Co., California.

Arthur Bray's father, Maynard Bray was born in March of 1846 in Mississippi. He was the son of Orange and Lucy Bray. Maynard married Katie Johnson in 1866. She was born in May of 1851 in Texas. They were parents of the following known children.

1. Mary Bray, born about 1867 in Lamar Co., Texas
2. Orange Bray, born about 1872 in Lamar Co., Texas
3. Arthur Edward Bray, born 18 February 1880 in Texas (see above)
4. Raz Bray, born 30 July 1884 in Lamar Co., Texas, died 21 September 1931
   in Lamar Co., Texas
5. Dan Bray, born 12 September 1885 in Lamar Co., Texas
6. Fannie Bray, born 5 December 1892 in Lamar Co., Texas; died 4 April 1975
   in Paris, Lamar Co., Texas

Raz Bray, son of Maynard Bray and Katie Johnson, was born 18 February 1880 in Texas. Raz never married. He died on 21 September 1931 in Precinct 1 of Lamar Co., Texas from an "accidental burning." He was buried on 23 September 1931 in the Family Cemetery, Paris, Lamar Co., Texas. 7

Fannie Bray, daughter of Maynard Bray and Katie Johnson, was born 5 December 1892 in Lamar Co., Texas. She married Gaither Burrell and at the time of her death she was a widow. She died at home, 631 7th St., S.W., Paris, Lamar Co., Texas, on 4 April 1975. The informant was her daughter, Wilma Burrell. Fannie died of natural causes and was buried on 7 April 1975 in the Restlawn Garden Cemetery, Paris, Lamar Co., Texas. 8

Orange Bray, father of Maynard Bray and others, was born in about 1792 in Tennessee. He married a lady named Lucy. She was born 5 September 1800 in Tennessee and died 18 June 1884 in Lamar Co., Texas. Orange died 5 February 1895 in Lamar Co., Texas. They were both buried in the Bray-Bryam Cemetery in Lamar Co., Texas. Their known children were as follows.

1. Maynard Bray, born March 1846 in Mississippi (see above)
2. Jesse Bray, born about 1848 in Tennessee
3. Luke Bray, born about 1848 in Tennessee
4. Orange Bray, born about 1849 in Tennessee

Orange Bray, Jr., son of Orange and Lucy Bray, was born about 1849 in Tennessee. In 1870 he was in the Texas State Penitentiary at Huntsville, Walker Co., Texas. He was imprisoned for defending himself with an axe, for 3 years, and had his "eye shot out by owner." 9

Virginia "Gammie" Thompson who married Arthur Edward Bray on 19 December 1904 in Lamar Co., Texas (see above), was the daughter of Monroe Thompson and Susan Fleming. She was born 8 January 1877 at Medill, near Paris, Lamar Co., Texas. She died 16 July 1961 in Omaha, Douglas Co., Nebraska. Virginia, and along with her husband Arthur and daughter Dorothy was buried in the Forest Lawn Cemetery in Omaha, Douglas Co., Nebraska.

Monroe Thompson was born about 1842 in Alabama. He married Susan Fleming after emancipation, on 18 December 1870 in Lamar Co., Texas. Susan was born about 1843 in Alabama. They were parents of the following children, some born before their legal marriage in 1870.

1. Dean Thompson, born about 1865 in Texas
2. Lizzie Thompson, born about 1868 in Texas
3. Jimmy Thompson, born about 1869 in Texas
4. Rhody Thompson, born about 1872 in Texas
5. Bee Thompson, male, born about 1873 in Texas
6. Virginia "Gammie" Thompson, born 8 January 1877, Medhill, near Paris, Lamar Co., Texas (see above)
7. Oscar Thompson, born about 1879 in Texas
8. Cora Thompson, born about 1889 in Texas

Cora Thompson, daughter of Monroe Thompson and Susan Fleming, was born in about 1889 in Texas. She married Zethro Brooks. He was born about 1890 in Texas and died in April of 1983 in Omaha, buried in Forest Lawn Cemetery, Omaha, Douglas Co., Nebraska. Cora died 29 December 1968 in Omaha and was also buried in the Forest Lawn Cemetery.

1. Year: 1910; Census Place: Whitman, Grant, Nebraska; Roll: T624_847; Page: 1A; Enumeration District: 0119; FHL microfilm: 1374860
2. Registration State: *Nebraska;* Registration County: *Grant;* Roll: *1711695*
3. Year: 1920; Census Place: Whitman, Grant, Nebraska; Roll: T625_992; Page: 1A; Enumeration District: 131; Image: 16
4. Year: 1930; Census Place: Whitman, Grant, Nebraska; Roll: 1281; Page: 2B; Enumeration District: 0004; Image: 982.0; FHL microfilm: 2341016
5. Year: 1930; Census Place: Whitman, Grant, Nebraska; Roll: 1281; Page: 3A; Enumeration District: 0004; Image: 983.0; FHL microfilm: 2341016
6. Year: 1940; Census Place: Ponca City, Kay, Oklahoma; Roll: T627_3301; Page: 9B; Enumeration District: 36-36
7. Ancestry.com. *Texas, Death Certificates, 1903-1982* [database on-line]. Provo, UT, USA: Ancestry.com Operations, Inc., 2013. Original data: Texas Department of State Health Services. Texas Death Certificates, 1903–1982. iArchives, Orem, Utah.
8. Ancestry.com. *Texas, Death Certificates, 1903-1982* [database on-line]. Provo, UT, USA: Ancestry.com Operations, Inc., 2013.Original data: Texas Department of State Health Services. Texas Death Certificates, 1903–1982. iArchives, Orem, Utah.
9. The Freedmen's Bureau Online; Texas State Penitentiary at Huntsville, Walker Co., Texas http://freedmensbureau.com/texas/texasstateprison2.htm

Preston Brooks

Corporal Preston Brooks of Co. D, 9th Cavalry, is probably one of the best known Buffalo Soldiers who served as a commander at Fort Robinson, Nebraska. The following details his service.

Fort Riley, KS 1 Jan-19 Jul 1884
Chicaskia River, Indian Territory 21 Jul-19 Oct 1884
Fort Riley, KS Oct 1884-27 Feb 1885
Chilicco Creek, Indian Territory Mar-May 1885
Fort Riley, 14 June 1885
Fort McKinney, WY 19 Aug 1885-Aug 1887
Fort Robinson, NE, post engineer

Brooks enlisted on 22 August 1882 at Cincinnati, Ohio. He was born in Columbia, South Carolina, a carpenter. His physical characteristics are shown as 5 feet 8 inches in height, yellow complexion. He enlisted in Co. D, 9th Cavalry and was discharged on 21 August 1887 at Fort McKinney, Wyoming, due to expiration of service.

While stationed at Fort McKinney, Wyoming he sustained an injury to his right hip, ankle and back on 16 December 1885. He fell 28 feet off scaffolding while weatherboarding a building at the post. In the line of duty at the post on 10 May 1887 he sprained his right ankle while mounting a horse. [1]

Brooks managed the waterworks and sawmill at Fort Robinson after being discharged on 21 August 1887, and served in this capacity until 1904. He lost his job after severely thrashing a white employee, clerk J.A. Habeggar. Brooks claimed that his son had been framed by Habeggar and wife. The son was accused of theft of Fort Robinson mail. His son was never convicted. [2]

Preston S. Brooks was born about November 1851 in South Carolina, the son of John Hamden Brooks and Janie Gist Adams. Preston Brooks married Anna Griffin Ford at Fort Riley, Kansas in about 1883. He died 10 August 1905 and was buried at the Fort Robinson Cemetery on 11 August 1905 with Masonic Rites. The 10th Cavalry band played at the funeral. His remains were removed on 22 July 1947 to the Fort McPherson National Cemetery near Maxwell, Lincoln Co., Nebraska. [3]

There is a Preston S. Brooks, age 10 shown on the 1870 US Census, in a very confusing household. The entire family is shown as white, and their financial status is very well-to-do. However, there is a J. Hamden Brooks, age 36 in the household with $5,000 in real estate and $3,000 in personal property. Preston is shown as born in South Carolina. They were living at Saluda in Edgefield Co., South Carolina. [4]

1900 US Census, Dawes Co., Nebraska, Fort Robinson, ED 208, Page 2A [5]
29-29 Preston S. Brooks, black, b. Nov 1851, b. SC, both parents b. SC,
        engineer
Annie, wife, black, b. Sept 1853, 56, 9 children, 7 living, b. KY, both parents
        b. KY
Ada, step-daughter, black, b. Feb 1882, 18, single, b. TX, father b. AL,
        mother b. KY
Preston C., son, black, b. June 1884, 15, b. KS, father b. SC, mother b. KY
Hattie, daughter, black, b. Nov 1886, 13, b. WY, father b. SC, mother b. KY
Mamie, daughter, black, b. Nov 1886, 13, b. WY, father b. SC, mother b. KY
Marguerite, daughter, black, b. Aug 1894, 5, b. NE, father b. SC, mother b. KY

1920 US Census, Dawes Co., Nebraska, Crawford, Ward 2, ED 93, Page 8A [6]
Block E
194-200 Annie Brooks, black, 51, widow, b. KY, both parents b. KY
Hattie, daughter, black, 22, single, b. WY, both parents b. KY
Margaret, daughter, black, 16, single, b. NE, both parents b. KY

1930 US Census, Dawes Co., Nebraska, Crawford, ED 9, Page 5A [7]
10 Paddock St.
98-114 Margaret E. Brooks, owns $1,200, negro, 26, married, married at
        age 17, b. NE, father b. SC, mother b. KY, servant, general practice
Andrew J. Brooks, son, nego, 8, b. WY, father b. SD, mother b. NE
Hattie Brooks, sister, negro, 40, married, married at age 18, b. WY, father
        b. SC, mother b. KY
Henry Brooks, nephew, negro, 14, b. NE, father b. NE, mother b. WY

Anna Brooks, mother, negro, 73, widow, married at age 18, b. KY, both
parents b. WY

The wife of Preston Brooks is shown in military records as Annie Griffin and in family genealogical records as Annie Ford. The 1900 US Census indicates that she had a daughter Ada (going by the surname of Brooks), who was born in February 1882 in Texas. This was about a year before she married Preston Brooks at Fort Riley, Kansas. Annie was born 15 September 1853 at Bowling Green, Warren Co., Kentucky. She died on 7 June 1930 at Crawford, Dawes Co., Nebraska. The following children were born to Preston Brooks and Annie Ford Griffin.

1. Preston Clyde Brooks, born 4 June 1884 at Fort Riley, Kansas
2. Hattie Brooks, born November 1886 in Wyoming, died in Chicago, Cook Co., Illinois
3. Mamie Brooks, born April 1891 in Wyoming
4. Margaret/Marguerite Brooks, born August 1894 in Nebraska

Preston Clyde Brooks, son of Preston S. Brooks and Annie Ford Griffin, was born on 4 June 1884 at Fort Riley, Kansas. He married Lydia Rae Terrell on 6 November 1918 in Pennsylvania. She was born 7 August 1891 in Pennsylvania to William Henry Terrell and Mary Charlotte Bell Truman. Lydia died 10 October 1964 at Chicago, Cook Co., Illinois. Preston died on 13 August 1954 in Pittsburgh, Allegheny Co., Pennsylvania. Preston Clyde Brooks and Lydia Rae Terrell had the following children.

1. Margaret Ann Brooks, born 6 November 1919 at Pittsburgh, Allegheny Co., Pennsylvania; married Robert Kenten Cole on 26 January 1946 in Pittsburgh; died 14 August 1976 in Chicago, Cook Co., Illinois
2. Preston Simmons Brooks, born 19 March 1925 in Pittsburgh, Allegheny Co., Pennsylvania; died 12 May 1976 in Chicago, Cook Co., Illinois
3. Mary Ellen Gertrude Brooks, born 21 June 1926 in Pittsburgh, Allegheny Co., PA; married Elmer Burroughs, Sr. on 8 June 1947 in Chicago, Cook Co., Illinois; died 28 December 1987 in Chicago, Cook Co., Illinois
4. Brooks child (still living, private)

Mamie Brooks, daughter of Preston S. Brooks and Annie Ford Griffin, was born in April of 1889 in Wyoming. She married Vincent Lopez on 16 January 1909 in Crawford, Dawes Co., Nebraska. He was age 21, born in the Philippine Islands, the son of Ambrose Lopez and Esodora Duiling. Mamie was age 19 and residing at Crawford, Nebraska. The marriage license indicates she was born at Fort Robinson. 8 She and her husband lived at Fort Robinson where they were in the employ of 1st. Lt. Lawrence Carson (white) of the 8th US Cavalry.

1910 US Census, Sioux Co., Nebraska, Fort Robinson, ED 226, Page 10A 9
9-9 Lawrence Carson household (white)
Vicente Lopez, 20, married 1 year, b. Philippines, both parents b. Philippines, cook, private family
Mamie, wife, mulatto, 19, married 1 year, 0 children, 0 living, b. NE, father b. SC, mother b. KY, chamber maid, private family

Between 1910 and 1920, the Lopez family moved to Valentine, Cherry Co., Nebraska where they are found on census enumerations.

1920 US Census, Cherry Co., Nebraska, Valentine, ED 68 Page 3B 10
Katrona Street

70-72 Lazartt M. Lopez, rents, Fil., 32, b. Philippine Islands, both parents b.
        Philippine Islands, cook, restaurant
Mamie, wife, mulatto, 28, b. WY, father b. SC, mother b. KY
Anita, daughter, Fil., 8, b. NE, father b. Philippine Islands, mother b. WY
Alberto, son, Fil, 6, b. NE, father b. Philippine Islands, mother b. WY
Christina, daughter, Fil., 3 4/12, b. NE, father b. Philippine Islands, mother b. WY

1930 US Census, Cherry Co., Nebraska, Valentine, ED 43, Page 1A 11
Block 20
7-7 Vincent M. Lopez, rents $20 month, Fil., 42, married at age 22, b. Philippine
        Islands, both parents b. Philippine Islands, came to US in 1907, cook,
        restaurant
Mamie L., wife, negro, 38, married at age 18, b. WY, both parents b. US
Anita B., daughter, negro, 18, b. NE, father b. Philippine Islands, mother b. WY,
        waiter, restaurant
Christina, daughter, negro, 13, b. NE, father b. Philippine Islands, mother b. WY
Vincent M., son, negro, 10, b. NE, father b. Philippine Islands, mother b. WY
Margaret, daughter, negro, 7, b. NE, father b. Philippine Islands, mother b. WY
Leon, son, negro, 5, b. NE, father b. Philippine Islands, mother b. WY
Rita, daughter, negro, 3 5/12, b. NE, father b. Philippine Islands, mother b. WY
Josephine, daughter, negro, 1 5/12, b. NE, father b. Philippine Islands, mother b.
        WY

1940 US Census, Cherry Co., Nebraska, Valentine, ED 16-43, Page 21B 12
213 Edna Street   owns $1,000
Vincent Lopez, informant, Fil., 53, 8th grade, b. Manilla, same house on 1 April
        1935, cook, hotel
Mamie, wife, Fil., 49, 2 years high school, b. WY, same house on 1 April 1935
Christina, daughter, Fil, 22, 2 years of school, single, b. NE, same house on 1
        April 1935
Vincent, son, Fil, 19, 4 years high school, single, b. NE same house on 1 April
        1935, attendant, service station
Margaret, daughter, Fil., 17, 8th grade, b. NE, same house on 1 April 1935
Leon, son, Fil., 15, 1 year high school, b. NE, same house on 1 April 1935
Rita, daughter, Fil. 13, 7th grade, b. NE, same house on 1 April 1935
Josephine, daughter, Fil., 11, 5th grade, b. NE, same house on 1 April 1935
Doretha, daughter, Fil., 7, 1st grade, b. NE

Vincent(e) M. "Louie" Lopez was born 7 September 1887 in Manila, Philippines. He and his
wife, Mamie Brooks Lopez, were buried in Mount Hope Cemetery in Valentine, Nebraska. Vincent died
on 27 April 1964. Mamie was born on 20 April 1891 in Wyoming and died on 20 June 1961. 13 They
were parents of the following children.
    1. Anita B. Lopez, born about 1912 in Nebraska
    2. Preston Alberto Lopez, born 1913 in Nebraska; died 17 July 1924; buried in
            Mt. Hope Cemetery, Valentine, Cherry Co., Nebraska
    3. Christina Lopez, born 10 December 1917 in Valentine, Cherry Co., Nebraska
    4. Vincent M. Lopez, Jr., born May 1920 in Nebraska
    5. Margaret Lopez
    6. Leon "Louie" Lopez, born 26 August 1924 in Valentine, Cherry Co., Nebraska;
            died 15 December 2003 in Valentine, Cherry Co., Nebraska; buried in Mt.
            Hope Cemetery, Valentine, Cherry Co., Nebraska
    7. Rita Lopez

8. Josephine "Jo" Lopez born 13 Nov 1928 in Valentine, Cherry Co., Nebraska; died 24 January
   1921 in Valentine, Cherry Co., Nebraska
9. Dorthea Lopez

Christina "Teeny" Lopez, daughter of Vincent M. Lopez and Mamie Brooks, was born 10 December 1917 in Valentine, Cherry Co., Nebraska. She died on 19 July 1985 in Valentine and was buried in the Mt. Hope Cemetery, Valentine, Cherry Co., Nebraska. Her funeral was held at St. Nicholas Catholic Church in Valentine. She never married.

Vincent M. Lopez, Jr., son of Vincent M. Lopez and Mamie Brooks, was born in May of 1920 in Nebraska. He was a 2nd Lt. in 82 AAF Trp. Carrier 50 in World War II. Vincent was killed in action on 14 April 1945 and was buried in the Mount Hope Cemetery, Valentine, Cherry Co., Nebraska.

Dorthea "Dort" Lopez, daughter of Vincent M. Lopez and Mamie Brooks, was born 15 August 1932 in Valentine, Cherry Co., Nebraska. She married James "Jim" Cook in Pierre, South Dakota on 21 November 1966. They had one daughter, Jodi. Dort died on 16 October 2020 at Parkside Manor, Stuart, Holt Co., Nebraska. Burial was on 20 October 2020 in the Mt. Hope Cemetery, Valentine, Cherry Co., Nebraska. 15

Josephine "Jo Lopez was born 13 November 1928 in Valentine, Cherry Co., Nebraska and died there on 24 January 2021. She apparently never married, but had a son Kent born in 1958. She was buried on 30 January 2021 in the Mt. Hope Cemetery, Valentine, Cherry Co., Nebraska. 16

There is a marriage record in Dawes Co., Nebraska for Bertie J. Brooks, age 19, to Drayton H. Moffett, age 29, married on 18 January 1893 at Crawford, Dawes Co., Nebraska. Drayton was born in Newberry, South Carolina to Orange Moffett and Addaline Golleman. Bertie was born in Brown Co., Texas to Preston Brooks and Anna Morson. It is known that Preston's wife had a daughter Ada born previous to her marriage to Preston. Ada went by the name of Brooks. It is possible that Bertie was also Annie's daughter. 14

1. *On the Trail of Buffalo Soldiers*, page 55
2. *The Story of Fort Robinson* by Schubert, page 154
3. Interment Control Forms, A1 2110-B. Records of the Office of the Quartermaster General, 1774–1985, Record Group 92. The National Archives at College Park, College Park, Maryland.
4. 1870 U.S. census, population schedules. NARA microfilm publication M593, 1,761 rolls. Washington, D.C.: National Archives and Records Administration
5. Year: 1900; Census Place: Fort Robinson, Dawes, Nebraska; Roll: 921; Page: 2A; Enumeration District: 0208; FHL microfilm: 1240921
6. Year: 1910; Census Place: Crawford Ward 2, Dawes, Nebraska; Roll: T624_841; Page: 8A; Enumeration District: 0093; FHL microfilm: 1374854
7. Year: 1930; Census Place: Crawford, Dawes, Nebraska; Roll: 1271; Page: 5A; Enumeration District: 0009; Image: 149.0; FHL microfilm: 2341006
8. Dawes Co., Nebraska Marriage Book 4 page 112
9. Year: 1910; Census Place: Fort Robinson, Sioux, Nebraska; Roll: T624_855; Page: 10A; Enumeration District: 0226; FHL microfilm: 1374868
10. Year: 1920; Census Place: Valentine, Cherry, Nebraska; Roll: T625_981; Page: 3B; Enumeration District: 68; Image: 1125
11. Year: 1930; Census Place: Valentine, Cherry, Nebraska; Roll: 1268; Page: 1A; Enumeration District: 0043; Image: 1005.0; FHL microfilm: 2341003
12. Year: 1940; Census Place: Valentine, Cherry, Nebraska; Roll: T627_2240; Page: 21B; Enumeration District: 16-43
13. FindAGrave   http://www.findagrave.com

14. Dawes Co., Nebraska Marriage Book B page 199
15. Sandoz' Chapel of the Pines https://www.sandozfuneralhome.com/obituary/dorthea-cook
16. Sandoz' Chapel of the Pines https://www.sandozfuneralhome.com/obituary/josephine-lopez

Rev. Oliver Johnson Burckhardt (Burkhart)

In 1910 Rev. Burkhart organized the St. James A.M.E. Church in Cherry Co., Nebraska near DeWitty. Church meetings were held in the home of William P. Walker and others. Rev. H.W. Mance eventually built a parsonage on land that he homesteaded. The church was built across the river from the post office in DeWitty.

Prior to establishing the church in Cherry County, the Burckhardts were living in Lancaster Co., Nebraska. Apparently he and his wife did not stay too long in Cherry County as they were back in Lincoln, Lancaster Co., Nebraska when the 1910 and the 1920 US Censuses were taken.

1900 US Census, Lancaster Co., Nebraska, Lincoln Ward 3, ED 48, Page 6B [1]
810 N. 17th Street
124-129 O.J. Burkhart, black, b. April 1868, 32, married 2 years, b. MO, parents
        place of birth unknown, R.R. porter
A., wife, black, b. 1869, 30, married 2 years, b. IA, father b. unknown, mother b.
    MO
T. Rogers, inmate, black, b. 1884, 16, single, b. unknown, parents born unknown

1910 US Census, Lancaster Co., Nebraska, Lincoln, Ward 5, ED 77, Page 11B [2]
1236 Washington
256-266 O.J. Burkhardt, black, 43, second marriage, married 12 years, b. MO,
        both parents b. MO, evangelist for M.E. Church
Anna, wife, black, 40, second marriage, married 12 years, b. IA, father b. MO,
        mother b. AL, artist

Oliver Johnson Burckhardt, age 31, married Anna Jones on 25 May 1898 in Burlington, Des Moines Co., Iowa. He was the son of James Burckhardt and Hattie Monroe. Anna Jones was age 29, daughter of John Jones and Tillie Preverl. [3]

Rev. Oliver J. Burckhardt was born in April of 1868 and died 23 December 1949. He was buried in Wyuka Cemetery, Lincoln, Lancaster Co., Nebraska. His wife, Anna, was born 11 November 1868 and died 20 June 1945. She was also buried in the Wyuka Cemetery. [4]

Oliver Johnson Burckhardt (Burkhart) was the son of James Burckhardt and Harriett "Hattie" Monroe. In 1880 this family was living in Howard Co., Missouri. Prior to that, the 1870 US Census shows the Burkhart blended family in Howard Co., Missouri. Apparently both Jim Burhardt (Burkhart) and Harriett had been previously married. Oliver appears to have gone by the name of John which stood for his middle name of Johnson. According to the marriage records of Howard Co., Missouri, James Burckhartt married Harriet Edwards on 24 March 1867. [5]

1870 US Census, Howard Co., Missouri, Franklin Twp., PO Fayette, Missouri, page 37   [6]
217-217 Jas. Burkhart, 50, black, farmer, b. NC
Harriet, 37, black, keeping house, b. MO
William Burkhart, 21, black, farm hand, b. MO
Chas. Lee, 19, black, farm hand, b. MO
Rose Burkhart, 16, black, b. MO

Henry Burkhart, 14, black, b. MO
Lucy Burkhart, 12, black, b. MO
Jennie Burkhart, 10, black, b. MO
Jefferson Burkhart, 8, black, b. MO
Beckie Burkhart, 6, black, b. MO
John Burkhart, 2, black, b. MO

1880 US Census, Howard Co., Missouri, Franklin, ED 93, Page 226C 7
63-64 Jim Burkhardt, black, 37, laborer, b. NC, both parents b. NC
Harriett, mulatto, ?age, wife, wash woman, b. MO, father b. MO, mother b. KY
John, mulatto, 11, son, b. MO, father b. NC, mother b. MO
Beckie Lee, mulatto, 16, step daughter, b. MO, both parents b. MO
Jeff Lee, black, 17, step son, laborer, b. MO, both parents b. MO

Anna Jones was the daughter of John Jones and his wife, Tillie Preverl. They were living in Burlington, Iowa when the 1870 and 1880 US Censuses was taken, shown as follows.

1870 US Census, Des Moines Co., Iowa, Burlington, Ward 7, page 27, PO 8
Burlington
John Jones, 26, black, cistern maker $700-100, b. AL
Matilda, 22, mulatto, keeping house, b. VA
William A., 3, mulatto, b. IA
Anna, 1, mulatto, b. IA

1880 US Census, Des Moines Co., Iowa, Burlington, ED 118, Page 320B 9
1200 14th Street
57-58 John Jones, black, 36, plasterer, b. AL, father b. AL
Matilda, black, 35, wife, keeping house, b. MO
William, black, 14, son, at school, b. IA, father b. AL, mother b. MO
Anna, black, 11, daughter, at school, b. IA, father b. AL, mother b. MO
Harrison, black, 9, son, at school, b. IA, father b. AL, mother b. MO
Donald, black, 6, son, at school, b. IA, father b. AL, mother b. MO

1. Year: 1900; Census Place: Lincoln Ward 3, Lancaster, Nebraska; Roll: 933; Page: 6B; Enumeration District: 0048; FHL microfilm: 1240933
2. Year: 1910; Census Place: Lincoln Ward 5, Lancaster, Nebraska; Roll: T624_850; Page: 11B; Enumeration District: 0077; FHL microfilm: 1374863
3. Ancestry.com. *Iowa, Marriage Records, 1880-1937* [database on-line]. Provo, UT, USA: Ancestry.com Operations, Inc., 2014. FHL Film #1675730
4. FindAGrave http://www.findagrave.com
5. "Missouri Marriages, 1750-1920," database, *FamilySearch* (https://familysearch.org/ark:/61903/1:1:V28J-99R : 6 December 2014), James Burckhartt and Harriet Edwards, 24 Mar 1867; citing Howard,Missouri; FHL microfilm 963,473.
6. Ancestry.com. *1870 United States Federal Census* [database on-line]. Provo, UT, USA: Ancestry.com Operations, Inc., 2009. Images reproduced by FamilySearch.
7. Ancestry.com. *1870 United States Federal Census* [database on-line]. Provo, UT, USA: Ancestry.com Operations, Inc., 2009. Images reproduced by FamilySearch.
8. Ancestry.com. *1870 United States Federal Census* [database on-line]. Provo, UT, USA: Ancestry.com Operations, Inc., 2009. Images reproduced by FamilySearch.
9. Year: 1880; Census Place: Burlington, Des Moines, Iowa; Roll: 337; Family History Film: 1254337; Page: 320B; Enumeration District: 118; Image: 0642

Caleb Benson

Between the Civil War and World War I, there were many black soldiers who were stationed at Fort Robinson in northwest Nebraska. They are referred to as Buffalo Soldiers. Some retired at the post and remained in western Nebraska. One such soldier was Caleb Benson.

Benson was born 25 June 1861, but sometimes the date is shown as 1860. Records list his place of birth as Aiken, South Carolina, but on some of his military forms it is shown as Jacksonville, Florida.

He was the son of Jacob Benson. When Caleb was six years old, his family moved to Charleston, South Carolina. As a teenager and with deceased parents, he enlisted on 2 February 1875 in the US Army, filling out his forms at Columbia, South Carolina. He was underage, but declared that he was 21 years and 7 months of age, whereas he was only about fourteen or fifteen years of age. He was unable to write, so signed his name with an "X." Caleb is shown as five feet, four inches tall, slight of build, weighing about 135 pounds. His previous occupation was listed as a waiter.

Benson's military career began with the signing of the papers for a five year enlistment. On 6 May 1875 he joined Company D under the command of Francis S. Dodge, at Fort Clark in Texas. The Ninth Cavalry in Texas was to protect the mail and stage lines from the Indians. During the winter of 1875-1876 the 9th Cavalry was ordered to the District of New Mexico. Men from Company D were sent to Santa Fe, where they arrived on 30 April 1876 and were stationed at Fort Union. Within a few months, Company D was sent north into Colorado, but Benson remained behind in confinement. Like so many others who eventually were stationed at Fort Robinson in Nebraska, Benson eventually rejoined his company at Ojo Caliente where they scouted and guarded the Apache reservation.

His military career involved reenlistments and many assignments to various posts throughout the west. In May of 1902, he was with troops who were assigned to Fort Robinson in Nebraska. He was in Troop K, 9th Cavalry. He had been reported as a poor marksman in previous military records, but his aim apparently improved at Fort Robinson as he received a sharpshooter's badge. By 1903 he had over twenty years of service in the United States Army and was able to qualify for a pension. Because he had served in Cuba, that was counted double toward his retirement.

In August of 1903 a detachment from Fort Robinson went into a wood reserve five miles to the west to cut lumber. Benson was sent with them as a cook. A wind came up which caused the fire and flare up from his field stove to blow flames and ashes into his face. Once at the post hospital, it was discovered that he had lost most of his eyesight and had also suffered a head injury from the fall, causing a loss of memory. Even so, in June of 1904 he applied for a reenlistment. The application was refused by the post surgeon. Thus ended his military career.

Many of the older, retired soldiers remained around Fort Robinson after being discharged. Benson worked for an officer, assisting in the kitchen. In 1904 he applied for a pension. Benson wrote to the government, "After having put in the best years of my life [27] ... I therefore beg of you to hasten assistance which of right I should have from my government." 1 Benson wanted to not only have a pension, but also reenlist so he could complete thirty years of service. Officers of the 10th Cavalry along with troops conveyed their consent to having him enlist. On 29 January 1907 Caleb Benson reenlisted in his old troop.

He was on board one of the twelve passenger trains that left Fort Robinson on 1 March 1907 bound for San Francisco. There the troops boarded the ship *Thomas* for the Philippine Islands. The war there had ended five years prior, but there was still a United States military presence on the island.

Benson and his troops of Co. K were stationed at Fort McKinley. In 1908 Benson was ordered to The Presidio in San Francisco and promoted to first sergeant. At The Presidio on 15 September 1908, the War Department issued Special Order Number 215, placing 1st Sgt. Caleb Benson on the retired list created by an act of Congress on 2 March 1907. 2

After years of serving in various locations of the west and southwest, as well as Cuba, Benson felt that northwest Nebraska was home. He returned to Crawford in Dawes County. On 27 March 1909 in Crawford, Dawes Co., Nebraska, Caleb Benson married Miss Percilla Smith of Crawford, Nebraska. She was of Virginia and a graduate of Hampton Institute. She had moved to Crawford from Philadelphia. Their marriage application indicates that she was born in Gloucester Co., Virginia and was a resident of Philadelphia, daughter of Joseph Smith and Agnes Thornton. The birthplace for Caleb is shown as Jacksonville, Florida. Witnesses at their wedding were John H. and Kittie Farr. 3

On the 1880 US Census, Priscilla/Percilla is shown as Scilla in the home of her parents Joseph and Agnes Smith in Gloucester Co., Virginia. According to the marriage application information Priscilla's mother was Agnes Thornton. Beverly Thornton who was also a Buffalo Soldier at Fort Robinson was from Gloucester Co., Virginia.

> 1880 US Census, Gloucester Co., Virginia, Ware District, ED 26 Page 213A 4
> 655-666 Joseph Smith, black, 35, farm laborer, b. VA, both parents b. VA
> Agnes, black, 28, wife, farm laborer, b. VA, both parents b. VA
> Mahaley, black, 10, daughter, b. VA, both parents b. VA
> Annie, black, 8, daughter, b. VA, both parents b. VA
> Benjamin, black, 6, son, b. VA, both parents b. VA
> Scilla, black, 3, daughter, b. VA, both parents b. VA

On the 1900 US Census, Precilla Smith was living in Manhattan. On that census, Caleb was in Cuba with the military. This may have been why she and Caleb went to Manhattan to live between 1920 and 1930.

> 1900 US Census, New York Co., New York, Manhattan, ED 828, Page 17B   5
> 1383 Lefington Avenue
> 64-44 HH of Homer B. and Mathilda Sprague, whites
> Precilla Smith, servant, black, b. March 1876, 24, single, b. VA, both
> parents b. VA

> 1900 US Census, Holguin, Cuba, Military and Naval Forces, ED 110   6
> Caleb Benson, private, resident of Akin, SC, black, b. August 1861
> 38, single, b. Jacksonville, FL, parents place of birth unknown

Under the Homestead Act, Caleb Benson, secured 640 acres of land located in Sioux Co., Nebraska, through the Alliance Land Office. The following is the land descriptions. The land was located west of Fort Robinson south of Soldier Creek and north of the White River. 7

> 6th PM, T 31 N, R 54 W, Section 25, W 1/2
> 6th PM, T 31 N, R 54 W, Section 24, SW 1/4
> 6th PM, T31 N, R 54 W, Section 23, E 1/2 SE1/4
> 6th PM, T 31N, R 54 W, Section 26, E 1/2 NE 1/4

On the 1910 and 1920 US censuses, the Bensons were living in Sioux Co., Nebraska. The 1910 US Census indicates that his wife was Marcella which should have been Persilla or Pricilla.

247

1910 US Census, Sioux Co., Nebraska, Andrews Prect., ED 224, Page 2A 8
40-42 Caleb Benson, black, 51, married 1 year, b. FL, father b. SC, mother
        b. VA, farmer
Marcella S., wife, black, 30, married 1 year, b. VA, both parents b. VA

1920 US Census, Sioux Co., Nebraska, Andrews Prect., ED 247, Page 12A 9
75-79 Caleb Benton, owns, mortgaged, black, 73, b. SC, both parents b.
        SC, farmer
Pricilla, wife, black, 32, b. VA, both parents b. VA

After living on their own land near Fort Robinson for four years, the Bensons moved to Fort
Robinson. They were both employed by Capt. Henry Whitehead of the 12th Cavalry. Shortly after World
War I, Caleb and Percilla continued to work at Fort Robinson for Lt. Col. Edward Calvert. Their travels
continued as they accompanied Calvert to Wisconsin. In about 1925 they moved to New York City, living
in Harlem on West 137th Street. There they took in a foster child, young Jimmie Amos and he assumed
their last name. In July of 1934 they once again returned to Crawford in Dawes Co., Nebraska. They still
owned their original property. The foster son, Jimmie, came to Nebraska with them.

1930 US Census, New York Co., New York, Manhattan, ED 982, Page 1B 10
178 West 137th Street
#14 Caleb Benson, rents $60 month, negro, 73, married at age 53, b. FL, both
        parents b. US
Percilla, wife, negro, 44, married at age 24, b. VA, both parents b. VA, cook,
        restaurant
James Amos, lodger, negro, 25, single, b. FL, both parents b. FL, porter,
        dress factory

1940 US Census, Dawes Co., Nebraska, Crawford, ED 23-7, Page 3A 11
12 Paddock Street   owns, $2,000
Percilla Benson, negro, 54, widow, 4 years high school, b. VA, same house
        1 April 1935, maid, private homes
James A. Benson, nephew, negro, 34, single, 8th grade, b. FL, same house
        1 April 1935, laborer, painter

On 19 November 1937, Caleb Benson died of coronary thrombosis. His funeral was held in the
old African Methodist Episcopal Church in Crawford. He was buried in the cemetery at Fort Robinson.
A year later Percilla applied for a widow's military pension. She moved to Virginia, but later both she and
her sister returned to Crawford. Percilla died at the Grand Island Veteran's Hospital in Grand Island, Hall
Co., Nebraska on 25 August 1966. In 1947 the remains of soldiers and civilians buried in the Fort
Robinson Cemetery were removed to Fort McPherson National Cemetery, near Maxwell, Lincoln Co.,
Nebraska. Percilla is buried with Caleb at Fort McPherson National Cemetery. According to her
tombstone she was born 19 March 1875.

The foster son or nephew, as stated by Percilla on the 1940 US Census, James A.
"Jimmie" (Amos) Benson, was born 4 August 1904 and died 24 November 1988. He is buried in the
Crawford Cemetery, Crawford, Dawes Co., Nebraska.

1. Letter to Commissioner of Pensions, Washington, DC, 22 August 1905, VA File XC 249912
2. Original in Caleb Benson Collection, Nebraska State Historical Society.
3.   Dawes Co., Nebraska Marriage Book 4, page 146
4. Year: 1880; Census Place: Ware, Gloucester, Virginia; Roll: 1367; Family History Film: 1255367;
Page: 213A; Enumeration District: 026

5. Year: 1900; Census Place: Manhattan, New York, New York; Roll: 1154; Page: 17B; Enumeration District: 0828; FHL microfilm: 1241118

6. Year: 1900; Census Place: Holguin, Cuba, Military and Naval Forces; Roll: 1838; Enumeration District: 0110; FHL microfilm: 1241838

7. Bureau of Land Management http://www.glorecords.blm.gov/details/patent/default.aspx? accession=214516&docClass=SER&sid=no2aqyql.3po

8. Year: 1910; Census Place: Andrews, Sioux, Nebraska; Roll: T624_855; Page: 2A; Enumeration District: 0224; FHL microfilm: 1374868

9. Year: 1920; Census Place: Andrews, Sioux, Nebraska; Roll: T625_999; Page: 12A; Enumeration District: 247; Image: 1054

10. Year: 1930; Census Place: Manhattan, New York, New York; Roll: 1575; Page: 1B; Enumeration District: 0982; Image: 1074.0; FHL microfilm: 2341310

11. Year: 1940; Census Place: Crawford, Dawes, Nebraska; Roll: T627_2243; Page: 3A; Enumeration District: 23-7

Chandler and Motley Families

Hayes Ezekiel Chandler was a beloved citizen of Alliance, Nebraska, well known for his horse drawn wagon that he drove through the streets, picking up trash and gardenings. He drove his wagon for years after most people owned automobiles. As he drove the wagon on the streets of Alliance, children rushed to get a ride on the back of it. While the clop of the horse hooves and the clank of the wagon wheels can no longer be heard, they live on in the memory of the people of Alliance.

He was born 25 September 1879 in Clay Co., Mississippi to parents who had been slaves. Hayes married Florence M. Motley who was born on 9 April 1886 in Kentucky. Hayes and Florence were married in Checotah, McIntosh Co., Oklahoma on 5 January 1913. They came to Box Butte County in about 1915 from Oklahoma and farmed in the county until just before 1930 when they moved into Alliance. The story is told that Hayes and Florence came to Box Butte County to farm near Hemingford for her uncle, Robert Ball Anderson. The Chandler story begins much earlier in Mississippi into Texas and Oklahoma. The following enumerations shed more light on their lives.

1920 US Census, Box Butte Co., Nebraska, Lawn Prect., ED 15, Page 3A 1
59-60 Hayes E. Chandler, rents, black, 39, b. MS, both parents b. MS, farmer
Florence M., wife, black, 33, b. KY, both parents b. KY
Hayes J., son, black, 6, b. OK, father b. MS, mother b. KY
Oggereta, daughter, black, 4 11/12, b. OK, father b. MS, mother b. KY
Maude, daughter, black, 2 6/12, b. NE, father b. MS, mother b. KY
Myrtle, daughter, black, 2 6/12, b. NE, father b. MS, mother b. KY

1930 US Census, Box Butte Co., Nebraska, Alliance, ED 3, Page 4B 2
Platte Ave.
76-95 Hayes Chandler, rents, $15 month, negro, 50, married at age 33, b. MS, both parents b. MS, farmer
Florence, wife, negro, 43, married at age 26, b. KY, both parents b. KY, laundress, at home
Hayes, Jr., son, negro, 16, b. OK, father b. MS, mother b. KY, farm laborer
Oggereta, daughter, negro, 15, b. OK, father b. MS, mother b. KY
Maude, daughter, negro, 12, b. NE, father b. MS, mother b. KY
Myrtle, daughter, negro, 12 b. NE, father h. MS, mother b. KY

1940 US Census, Box Butte Co., Nebraska, Alliance, ED 73-B, Page 10B 3

84 Platte Avenue, owns, $350

Hayes Chandler, negro, 58, 7th grade, b. MS, same house 1 April 1935, laborer,
    grain elevator

Florence, informant, wife, negro, 53, b. KY, same house 1 April 1935

Maude, daughter, negro, 22, single, 4 years high school, b. NE, same house
    1 April 1935

Myrtle, daughter, negro, 22, single, 4 years high school, b. NE, same house
    1 April 1935

Hayes Chandler, Jr., informant, rents $4 month, negro, 26, single, 7th grade,
    b. OK, same place 1 April 1935

Hayes Chandler died in St. Joseph's Hospital in Alliance, Box Butte Co., Nebraska on 14 December 1966. He had fallen downtown and fractured his leg. Hayes had faithfully served the citizens of Alliance plowing gardens, mowing weeds and hauling trash. Up until about two years prior to his death, he continued to use a wagon and team of horses. In 1963 the Chamber of Commerce presented him with an outstanding Citizenship award. In 1965 the Dale Carnegie Alumni Chapter of Alliance held a testimonal and award program in his honor. Since moving from the farm near Hemingford, the Chandler family had lived at 220 S. Platte in Alliance. Hayes was buried in the Alliance Cemetery.

Florence Motley, wife of Hayes E. Chandler, Sr., was born 9 April 1886, the daughter of James Motley and Elizabeth "Bettie" Anderson. She was born in Kentucky. Stories are told within the Chandler family that Florence was light skinned and often mistaken for a white woman. In 1986 when she turned age 100, Florence was asked her secret for living a long, healthy life and she replied, "Simple. Just good hard work, a lot of prayer and good clean living." At the age of 100 she was living with her daughter Maude and family at 212 Grand in Alliance, Nebraska. On 9 April 1990 the Alliance City Council proclaimed the day as Grandma Chandler Day in Alliance. Florence died at the age of 105 on 8 July 1991 at her home, 212 Grand, in Alliance. She was buried in the Alliance Cemetery beside her husband, Hayes Chandler. Her mother, Bettie Motley, 20 December 1861 - 20 January 1925 is buried in the Seward Memorial Cemetery in Logan Co., Oklahoma. 4

When interviewed by *The Alliance Times Herald* in 1986, Florence stated that she got up every morning at 4 a.m. and began by reading the Bible. Asked about her husband, Hayes, she replied, "He worked for the newspaper for a while. Then he did landscaping. He did the Baptist church lawn. Hayes did hauling, with his horses and wagons, down alleys and the kids would run and get on his wagon. Oh, he'd have the wagon full. They'd get out of a Cadillac to ride in Hayes' wagon. Hayes helped build the first pool and the big city park." Family members state that Florence told her children and grandchildren that they should not be prejudiced, but to treat everybody with respect. 5

Florence was born in Kentucky, but grew up for a while in Illinois. That was where she first encountered Indians, who were part of a medicine show. She found the Oklahoma Indians to be nothing like those in Illinois. When she was about age twenty, she moved to Oklahoma along with her parents and siblings. "I remember tornadoes and an Indian uprising led by Chief Crazy Snake." The uprising happened in 1909 and was viewed as a war between the Creek people and American settlers, also involving African Americans who were Creek Freedmen. 6

Her oldest children, a boy and girl, were born in Oklahoma and the twins were born in Hemingford. The Chandlers lived in a sod house near Hemingford on her great uncle, Robert Ball Anderson's ranch near Hemingford. Refer to Anderson, Volume 1. The children of Hayes Ezekiel Chandler and Florence Motley are as follows.
1. Hayes Jerome Chandler (called Hayes, Jr.), born 5 October 1913 at Guthrie,
    Logan Co., Oklahoma
2. Oggereta Chandler, born 8 February 1915 at Checotah, McIntosh Co., Oklahoma

3. Myrtle Chandler, born 6 June 1917 in Hemingford, Box Butte Co., Nebraska
4. Maude Chandler, born 6 June 1917 in Hemingford, Box Butte Co., Nebraska

Hayes Jerome Chandler, son of Hayes Ezekiel Chandler and Florence Motley was born in Guthrie, Logan Co., Oklahoma on 5 October 1913. His obituary states that he was born in Checotah, McIntosh Co., Oklahoma. He married Anna Mildred Jackson, daughter of Viney Jackson and Florence Copen, on 31 December 1941 in Alliance. They were married by Rev. V.J. Barnes. Witnesses to their marriage were Mrs. Ophelia Barnes and Helen Jackson. Refer to Viney Jackson Volume 2. Anna was born 2 October 1913 in Montgomery, Montgomery Co., Missouri, and went by her middle name of Mildred.   Hayes, Jr. served in the US Army from 1941 to 1945. He was employed by Neuswangers, Inc. and then Heitz East Side Texaco in Alliance. He died on 21 April 1991 at the Box Butte General Hospital in Alliance, Nebraska and was buried in the Alliance Cemetery. Anna Mildred Jackson Chandler died on 16 September 1995 in Alliance, Box Butte Co., Nebraska and was buried in the Alliance Cemetery. Hayes Jr. and Mildred had two daughters, Beverly Joan and Barbara Jean.

Beverly Joan Chandler, daughter of Hayes Jerome Chandler and Anna Mildred Jackson, was born 5 February 1949 in Alliance, Nebraska. She died on 1 March 1955 in St. Joseph's Hospital in Alliance, following surgery. Barbara Jean Chandler, daughter of Hayes Jerome Chandler and Anna Mildred Jackson, never married. She was born 11 November 1950 in Alliance and died 22 July 2016 in Scottsbluff, Scotts Bluff Co., Nebraska, buried in the Alliance Cemetery. Barbara has two daughters, Charity Jones and Fawn Sullivan. 7, 8

Oggereta Chandler, daughter of Hayes E. Chandler and Florence Motley, was born 8 February 1915 at Checotah, McIntosh Co., Oklahoma. She married John Forrest Shores on 9 August 1939 in Scottsbluff, Scotts Bluff Co., Nebraska. He was born 23 August 1908 at Halsey, Thomas Co., Nebraska to John W. Shores and Mildred "Millie" Keyser. Forrest died on 2 January 1984 at Greeley, Weld Co., Colorado. He and Oggereta had moved there in 1948. Prior to his retirement he was a maintenance man at the University of Northern Colorado in Greeley. Ogeretta died 2 August 1998 in Greeley, Weld Co., Colorado. They were both buried in the Alliance Cemetery. Forrest and Ogeretta had two children, John C. and Kerry.   Refer to Shores and Speece Volume 2.

Myrtle Chandler, daughter of Hayes E. Chandler and Florence Motley, was born 6 June 1917 in Hemingford, Box Butte Co., Nebraska. She had a twin sister, Maude. Myrtle married Ernest Nickens who was born 15 September 1900 in Missouri and died 19 October 1951. Myrtle died 3 December 1957 in Nebraska and was buried in the Alliance Cemetery. Refer to Nickens Volume 2.

Maude Chandler, daughter of Hayes E. Chandler and Florence Motley, was born 6 June 1917 in Hemingford, Box Butte Co., Nebraska. She married Freeman L. McGuire who was born 3 March 1922 in Indianapolis, Marion Co., Indiana and died there on 16 October 1989. Maude died in Indianapolis on 24 May 2000. Maude had a daughter, Myrtle McGuire, who was raised by Maude's parents and took the name of Chandler. Myrtle was born 1 August 1943 in Kansas City, Missouri and died 26 September 2018 at the University of Colorado Hospital in Denver, Colorado. Maude had Marsha, Fredric "Freddy", Freeman "Buddy" and Marlene by Freeman McGuire.

Smith Chandler & Mary Cousins

The parents of Hayes Ezekiel Chandler were Smith Chandler and Mary Cousins. They were both born in Mississippi as slaves. Smith was born about 1847 in Chickasaw Co., Mississippi to Edward "Ned" and Martha Chandler. Edward "Ned" was born in 1814 in Halifax Co., Virginia and brought to Chickasaw with the Chandler family. Martha was born in 1820 in Virginia and died in 1870 at Sparta, Chickasaw Co., Mississippi.

Smith Chandler and Mary Cousins were married on 25 December 1867 in Chickasaw Co., Mississippi. Mary was born in October of 1852 in Mississippi, most likely in Chickasaw County. There was a John Cousins living in Chickasaw Co., Mississippi in 1860 and is shown on the slave schedule that year as having an 11 year old black female and two 4 year old black females. Smith and Mary died between 1920 and 1930 in Seward, Logan Co., Oklahoma. They are shown on the following enumerations.

1870 US Census, Chickasaw Co., Mississippi, Township 15, Page 19, PO Sparta [9]
143-140 Smith Chandler, 24, black, farm laborer, $300, b. MS
Mary, 19, black, farm laborer, b. MS
James, 1, black, farm laborer, b. MS
Nancy Hoagsone, 12, mulatto, domestic servant, b. MS

1880 US Census, Clay Co., Mississippi, Beat 5, ED 46, Page 302A [10]
133-143 Smith Chandler, black, 33, farmer, b. MS, both parents b. VA
Mary, black, 26, wife, keeping house, b. MS, both parents b. VA
James, black, 10, son, b. MS, both parents b. MS
Lexter, black, 8, son, b. MS, both parents b. MS
Lynch, black, 6, son, b. MS, both parents b. MS
Walter, black, 4, son, b. MS, both parents b. MS
Maritea, black, 2, daughter, b. MS, both parents b. MS
Hays, black, 10/12, b. Aug, son, b. MS, both parents b. MS
Rebecca Yeates, black, 28, sister, widow, laborer, b. MS, both parents b. VA
Savannah Yeates, black, 10, niece, b. MS, both parents b. MS
Winny Yeates, black, 8, niece, b. MS, both parents b. MS
Bud Yeates, black, 4, nephew, b. MS, both parents b. MS

1900 US Census, Navarro Co., Texas, Justice Prect. 2, ED 10, Page 5B [11]
86-85 Smith Chandler, black, b. Aug 1847, 52, married 32 years, b. MS,
        both parents b. VA, farmer
Mary, wife, black, b. Oct 1852, 47, married 32 years, 9 children, b. MS,
        both parents b. VA
Walter, son, black, b. June 1878, 21, single, b. MS, both parents b. MS,
        farmer
Martha, daughter, black, b. Aug 1880, 19, b. MS, both parents b. MS
Hays, son, black, b. July 1881, 18, b. MS, both parents b. MS
Mamie, daughter, black, b. Dec 1883, 16, b. MS, both parents b. MS
Florence, daughter, black, b. Dec 1885, 14, b. MS, both parents b. MS
Florence, daughter, black, b. Dec 1888, 11, b. MS, both parents b. MS
[The second Florence is shown on another page, so may not be correct. The second Florence may be the 20 year old daughter shown in their 1920 household.]
87-86 Lex Chandler, black, b. Oct 1875, 24, single, b. MS, both parents b.
        MS, farmer

1910 US Census, McIntosh Co., Oklahoma, Checotah Twp., ED 70, Page 9B [12]
18-18 Smith Chandler, black, 65, married 43 years, b. MS, both parents b. MS,
        farmer
Mary, wife, black, 56, married 43 years, b. MS, both parents b. MS, farm
        laborer
Kansas, daughter, black, 20, single, b. MS, both parents b. MS, farm laborer
19-19 Hase Chandler, black, 20, single, b. MS, both parents b. MS, farm
        laborer

1920 US Census, Logan Co., Oklahoma, Seward Twp., ED 69, Page 1A   13
6-6 Lee Allen, owns, free, black, 34, b. TX, both parents b. TX, farmer
Mamie Allen, wife, black, 34, b. MS, both parents b. MS
Leon Allen, son, black, 13, b. OK, father b. TX, mother b. MS
Smith Chandler, father-in-law, black, 72, b. MS, both parents b. VA
Mary Chandler, mother-in-law, black, 65, b. MS, both parents b. VA
Tim Mottley, brother-in-law, black, 24, b. KY, both parents b. VA, laborer, farm
Cansas Mottley, sister, black, 28, b. MS, both parents b. MS
Hugh Mottley, nephew, black, 5, b. OK, father b. KY, mother b. MS
Mary Mottley, niece, black, 3, b. OK, father b. KY, mother b. MS
Thedford Mottley, nephew, black, 9/12, b. NE, father b. KY, mother b. MS

The following are the known children born to Smith Chandler and Mary Cousins.

1. James "Jim" Chandler, born 12 March 1867 in Mississippi
2. Lexter "Lex" Chandler, born about 1872 in Mississippi
3. Lynch Chandler, born in December1874 in Mississippi
4. Walter C. Chandler, born June 1878 in Mississippi
5. Maritea Chandler, born about 1878 in Mississippi
6. Hayes Ezekiel Chandler, born 25 September 1879 in Clay Co.,
   Mississippi (see above)
7. Mamie Chandler, born December 1883 in Mississippi
8. Florence Chandler, born 9 April 1886 in Mississippi
9. Kansas Chandler, born about 1890 in Mississippi

James "Jim" Chandler, son of Smith Chandler and Mary Cousins, was born 12 March 1867 in Mississippi. He married Eula Tankersley. She was the daughter of James Samuel Tankersley and Mollie Cobb, born 21 June 1879 in Alabama. Eula died at John Petersmith Hospital in Fort Worth, Tarrant Co., Texas on 30 January 1959. 14 James died 15 Jan 1951 at Rice, Navarro Co., Texas. He was buried in the Rice Negro Cemetery, Rice, Navarro Co., Texas. 15. Jim and Eula were parents of two children, Willie Lee and Hayes.

Willie Lee Chandler, daughter of James "Jim" Chandler and Eula Tankersley, was born 13 August 1903 at Rice, Navarro Co., Texas. She married Eddie Surell and they divorced. She married second to Washington McBride. Her third marriage was to a Mr. Penn. She died on 3 March 1935 in Corsicana, Navarro Co., Texas, 20 Warring Quarters. Her death was from eclampsia, relevant to pregnancy. She was buried in the Rice Negro Cemetery, Rice, Navarro Co., Texas. 16

Hayes Chandler, son of James "Jim" Chandler and Eula Tankersley, was born 9 August 1905 in Navarro Co., Texas. He married Alice —- in about 1927 and married second to Catherine —-. Hayes died 20 February 1955 at Fort Worth, Tarrant Co., Texas. His death certificate indicates that he was a laborer in motor truck equipment. He was buried in the Rice Colored Cemetery, Rice, Navarro Co., Texas. 17

Lexter "Lex" Chandler, son of Smith Chandler and Mary Cousins, was born about 1872 in Mississippi. In 1900 he was single and living in Navarro Co., Texas. In about 1901 he married Annie Joiner. She was born 16 July 1881 in Texas to Frank L. Joiner and Elizabeth Lanier. Annie died 5 January 1932 in Dallas, Dallas Co., Texas. She is buried in the Woodlawn Cemetery, Dallas, Dallas Co., Texas. Texas Death Certificate #1072 Lexter died on 15 September 1957 at Ferris, Ellis Co., Texas. He is shown on the Convict Record Ledgers, Texas State Penitentiary at Huntsville, Texas, as being admitted on 24 April 1923 for manufacturing liquor in violation of the law, for one year. He had entered a plea of not guilty. He was discharged on 2 February 1924. Earlier in 1912 he was on the Convict Record Ledgers, Texas State Penitentiary for robbery, convicted to 5 years on 4 November 1912 from Dallas Co., Texas. He was pardoned on 5 Aug 1915 by the Texas governor, Jas. E. Ferguson, Prc.#13119. [18] Lexter and Annie had two daughters, Myrtle and Meathel.

Myrtle Chandler, daughter of Lexter "Lex" Chandler and Annie Joiner, was born in about 1902 in Texas. She married —- Jones.

Meathel Chandler, daughter of Lexter "Lex" Chandler and Annie Joiner, was born about 1903 in Rice, Navarro Co., Texas. She married Tom Fields.

Lynch Chandler, son of Smith Chandler and Mary Cousins, was born in December of 1874 in Mississippi. On the 1900 US Census he is shown with his wife, Margaret, and daughter in Clay Co., Mississippi. They were probably married on 27 September 1898 in Clay Co., Mississippi.

> 1900 US Census, Clay Co., Mississippi, Lacross Prect., Beat 5, ED 34, Page 14B [19]
> Lynch Chandler, black, b. Dec 1874, 25, married 2 years, b. MS, both parents b.
>   MS, farmer
> Margaret, wife, black, b. May 1880, 20, marrmed 2 years, 1 child, 1 living, b. MS,
>   both parents b. MS
> Russel, daughter, black, b. Dec 1899, 5/12, b. MS, both parents b. MS

Lynch remarried in about 1909 and is shown on the 1910 US Census with wife Roberta and the daughter Roxie who is Russel as shown on the 1900 US Census.

> 1910 US Census, Okibbeha Co., Mississippi, Beat 3, ED 99, Page 8A [20]
> 131-133 Link Chandler, black, 30 second marriage, married 1 year, b. MS,
>   both parents b. MS
> Roberta, wife, black, 25, first marriage, married 1 year, b. MS, both parents
>   b. US
> Roxie, daughter, black, 11, b. MS, both parents b. MS

Lynch filed his World War I Draft Registration in Navarro Co., Texas on 12 September 1918. He was age 41, born 12 August 1877, working as a farm hand for W.N. Marshall at Rice, Navarro Co., Texas. His nearest relative is shown as Roburter Chandler. [21]

On the 1930 US Census Census, Lynch had married for the third time, to Julia Jackson Bonner. Her children are shown in the household as step children.

> 1930 US Census, Ellis Co., Texas, Ennis, Ward 3, ED 23, Page 2B [22]
> 1102 Glasscock
> 43-48 Lynch Chandler, rents $16 month, negro, 63, both MS, both parents
>   b. MS, laborer, odd jobs
> Julia, wife, negro, 63, b. TX, father b. GA, mother b. AL, laundress, home
> Ellis Thomas, step son-in-law, negro 29, b. TX, both parents b. TX, laborer,
>   oil mill
> Roberta Thomas, step daughter-in-law, negro, 27, b. TX, father b. LA, mother
>   b. TX, general housekeeping, private homes
> Herman Thomas, step grandson, negro, 8, b. TX, both parents b. TX
> Lucille Bonner, step grand daughter, negro, 15, b. TX, father b. LA, mother b. TX,
>   maid, private home
> Louise Bonner, step grand daughter, negro, 5, b. TX, father b. LA, mother b. TX

Eddie M. Bonner, step grand daughter, negro 3 2/12, b TX, father b. LA,
        mother b. TX

According to the Social Security Applications and Claims Index, Lynch Chandler, was born 12 August 1887 at West Point, Mississippi to Smith Chandler and Mary Couzzens. The date is not correct. [23]

The death certificate for Lynch Chandler indicates that he was born at West Point, Clay Co., Mississippi on 1 January 1900 to Mary Chandler. The informant was Elnora Bonner. He was divorced and died after a ten day stay at Riverside General Hospital in Houston, Harris Co., Texas. [24]

Even with the confusion of the date of birth, the death certificate and Social Security information pertains to the same person. Lynch and his first wife Margaret "Maggie" had one child, Roxie Elnora. She was born 25 December 1899 in Clay Co., Mississippi and died on 25 June 1969 Houston, Harris Co., Texas, buried in the Paradise South Cemetery in Pearland, Brazoria Co., Texas. Roxie married Eddie Bonner son of Dave Bonner and Julia Jackson. Eddie's mother, Julia Jackson Bonner, became the third wife of Roxie's father, Lynch Chandler. Eddie was born 11 January 1896 in Texas and died 30 December 1928 in Houston, Harris Co., Texas.

Walter C. Chandler, son of Smith Chandler and Mary Cousins, was born in about 1876 in Mississippi. He married Matilda Cooksey who was born in March of 1885 in Texas to Rufus Cooksey and Maria Taylor. He filed his World War I Draft Registration on 12 September 1918 in McIntosh Co., Oklahoma, listing his address as RT 1, Box 116, Checotah, McIntosh Co., Oklahoma. [25] Walter died in 1963 in Checotah, McIntosh Co., Oklahoma. He and Matilda had the following known children.

1. Jessie C. Chandler, born 21 March 1903 in Fayette Co., Texas; married
        Leona —-.
2. Robert E. Chandler, born 13 January 1905 in Oklahoma
3. Obelia Chandler, born about 1907 in Oklahoma
4. Sherman J. Chandler, born 4 December 1908 in Oklahoma; died May 1987
        in Tulsa, Tulsa Co., Oklahoma; buried Crown Hill Cemetery, Tulsa, Tulsa
        Co., Oklahoma
5. Nathella Lois Chandler, born 28 April 1913 in Oklahoma
6. Francis E. Chandler, born 12 March 1919 in Oklahoma
7. Opal Chandler, born about 1922 in Oklahoma

Robert E. Chandler, son of Walter C. Chandler and Matilda Cooksey, was born 13 January 1905 in Oklahoma. He married Viola Barnes in 1939 in Oklahoma. She was born 7 August 1912 in Okmulgee, Okmulgee Co., Oklahoma to William Barnes and Willa Mae Brown. Viola died 12 April 1991 in Tulsa, Tulsa Co., Oklahoma. Robert died 17 March 1989 in Tulsa, Tulsa Co., Oklahoma.

Nathella Lois Chandler, daughter of Walter C. Chandler and Matilda Cooksey, was born 28 April 1913 in Oklahoma. She married —- Jones and died 31 August 1992 in Los Angeles, Los Angeles Co., California. Nathella was buried in the Riverside National Cemetery, Riverside, Riverside Co., California.

Francis E. Chandler, son of Walter C. Chandler and Matilda Cooksey, was born 12 March 1919 in Oklahoma. He enlisted in the US Army on 1 February 1941 in Tulsa, Tulsa Co., Oklahoma as a private. Francis was single. He achieved the rank of corporal. He died on 7 December 1987 in Oklahoma and was buried in Fort Gibson National Cemetery, Fort Gibson, Muskogee Co., Oklahoma.

Mamie Chandler, daughter of Smith Chandler and Mary Cousins, was born December 1883 according to census enumerations. However, the Social Security Application and Claim Index shows her birth as 25 November 1894 in Clay Co., Mississippi. She married Henry Lee Allen who was born on 8 October 1885 in Ennis, Ellis Co., Texas to Prince and Bettie Allen. 26 Mamie and Henry divorced on 7 February 1936 in Oklahoma Co., Oklahoma. 27 Mamie married second to —- Minner. She died in 1965 in Logan Co., Oklahoma and was buried in Seward Memorial Cemetery, Logan Co., Oklahoma. Mamie and Henry had the following children.

1. Leoma Allen, born 1902, died 1929 in Logan Co., Oklahoma
2. Leon Allen, born 22 November 1906 in Oklahoma; died 11 Feb 1927 in
       Logan Co., Oklahoma
3. Myrtle Lee Allen, born 1921; died 1934 in Logan Co., Oklahoma

Kansas Chandler, daughter of Smith Chandler and Mary Cousins, was born about 1890 in Mississippi. She married Timothy Hudell Motley. Refer to Motley information. Kansas died in 1923 in Logan Co., Oklahoma. She was buried in the Seward Memorial Cemetery, Logan Co., Oklahoma.

There were Cousins living in 1870 in Chickasaw Co., Mississippi who are undoubtedly related to Mary Cousins Chandler. Robert and Mary Cousins may be her parents. They were living very close to some of the Chandlers in 1870. Two houses from them is William D. Cousens, age 24, white, b. Alabama. 28

1870 US Census, Chickasaw Co., Mississippi, Township 15, Page 18,
PO Sparta
137-134 Robert Cousins, 47, black, farm laborer, b. AL
Mary, 39, black, farm laborer, b. AL

1870 US Census, Chickasaw Co., Mississippi, Township 15, Page 17, PO
Sparta
Henry Cousins, 30, black, farm laborer, b. AL
Charlott, 24, black, farm laborer, b. VA
Leroy D., 1, black, b. MS

1870 US Census, Chickasaw Co., Mississippi, Sparta, page 3
14-14 John Cousins, 28, black, farm laborer, b. AL
Silva, 21, black, keeping house, b. VA
Kelea, 4, black, b. MI

There were Cousins living in Chickasaw Co., Mississippi after 1870, but Robert and Mary are not shown on censuses after 1870.

Edward "Ned" Chandler

Smith Chandler, father of Hayes E. Chandler, was the son of Edward "Ned" and Martha Chandler. Edward was born in about 1814 in Halifax Co., Virginia. Martha was born in about 1820 in Virginia and died in 1870 in Sparta, Chickasaw Co., Mississippi. After the death of Martha, Smith married Araminta "Minnie" Jennings on 17 September 1871 in Chickasaw Co., Mississippi. She was born about June 1849 in South Carolina. Ned Chandler married third to Alice Westbrook on 5 July 1877 in Clay Co., Mississippi. There were children born in all three marriages. The daughter, Emma Chandler, age 19 on the 1880 US Census (see below) was probably a daughter of Araminta and took the name of Chandler. Edward "Ned" Chandler paid taxes in 1892 in LaCross, Clay Co., Mississippi as tax payer #2593; $1.35 for one mule valued at $75 and one horse valued at $60. 29 In 1870 Edward "Ned" Chandler was enumerated twice in Chickasaw Co., Mississippi

1870 US Census, Chickasaw Co., Mississippi, Township 15, Page 21, PO Sparta   30
159-156 Ned Chandler, 56, black, farm laborer, $800 b. Va
Martha, 50, black, keeping house, b. VA
Dilworth, 14, black, farm laborer, b. MS
Susan, 12, black, farm laborer, b. MS

1870 US Census, Chickasaw Co., Mississippi, Township 15, page 27
173-170 Ned Chandler, 56, farm laborer $150, b. VA
Martha, 50, black, keeping house, b. NC
Dilworth, 14, black, farm laborer, b. MS
Susan, 9, black, b. MS
Jane McGee, 18, black, farm laborer, b. VA
Barney [Barry?] Chandler, 28, black, farm laborer, b. MS

1880 US Census, Clay Co., Mississippi, Beat 5, ED 46, Page 298B   31
75-82 Edward Chandler, black, 65, farmer, b. VA, both parents b. VA
Araminta, black, 34, wife, keeping house, b. GA, both parents b. SC
Emma, black, 19, daughter, laborer, b. MS, father b. VA, mother b. SC
Grant, black, 7, son, b. MS, father b. VA, mother b. SC
Lousianna [sic], black, 6, daughter, b. MS, father b. VA, mother b. SC
Prudence, black, 4, daughter, b. MS, father b. VA, mother b. SC

1900 US Census, Clay Co., Mississippi, Lacross Prect., ED 34, Page 13A   32
246-238 Ped [sic] Chandler, black, b. May 1818, 92, married, married 28 years,
          b. VA, both parents b. VA, farmer
Minnie, wife, black, b. June 1849, 50, married 28 years, 4 children, 3 living,
          b. SC, father b. SC, mother b. VA, farmer
Louisiana, daughter, black, b. January 1876, 24, single, b. MS, father b. VA,
          mother b. SC, farm laborer

Edward "Ned" Chandler and his first wife, Martha had the following children. She was still living when the census enumeration was taken in 1870, but was deceased by September 1871 when Ned remarried.

1. Barry Chandler, born about 1842 in Chickasaw Co., Mississippi
2. Smith Chandler, born about 1847 in Chickasaw Co., Mississippi (see above)
3. Rebecca Chandler, born 4 July 1851 in Mississippi
4. Dilworth Chandler, born October 1855 in Starksville, Chickasaw Co., Mississippi
5. Susan Chandler, born in 1858 in Mississippi

Edward "Ned" Chandler and his second wife, Araminta "Minnie" Jennings, had the following children. She probably had Emma, who went by the name of Chandler, by another marriage or out of wedlock. It is unknown if Ned and Minnie divorced, separated or if she died before his marriage to Alice Westbrook. Descendants indicate that Minnie had a daughter Eugenia Chandler by Ned, born in 1885.

1. Grandville "Grant" Chandler, born about 1873 in Mississippi
2. Prudence Chandler, born about 1876 in Mississippi
3. Louisiana Chandler, born January 1876 in Mississippi

Edward "Ned" Chandler and his third wife, Alice Westbrook, had one child.
1. Edward Chandler, born 28 October 1882, probably in Mississippi

257

Barry Chandler, son of Edward "Ned" Chandler and his first wife, Martha, was born about 1842 in Chickasaw Co., Mississippi. He married Caroline Metcalf on 16 January 1884 in Clay Co., Mississippi. She was born about 1864 in Mississippi to Armstead and Nellie Metcalf.

Rebecca Chandler, daughter of Edward "Ned" Chandler and his first wife, Martha, was born 4 July 1851 in Mississippi. She married Wiley Yeates on 22 December 1866 in Oktibbeha Co., Mississippi. Wiley was born in about 1846 in Oktibbeha Co., Mississippi. His father was Juniper Yeates. In Oktibbeha Co., Mississippi in 1876, Wiley Yeates received a bond for the title of a tract of land, being 250 acres, bought from Francis and John Stevens. The land was paid for with 35 bales of lint cotton. Wiley died in about 1876 in Oktibbeha Co., Mississippi. After his death, Rebecca was living in 1880 with her brother, Smith Chandler, in Clay Co., Mississippi. She married Clifford Brownlee on 22 April 1894 in Chickasaw Co., Mississippi. He was born in 1832 in Mississippi to Edmond "Ned" Brownlee and his wife Priscilla "Cella." Clifford died before 1910 in Clay Co., Mississippi. Rebecca had no children by Brownlee. She died 7 March 1938 in Pulaski Co., Illinois and was buried in the Thistlewood Cemetery, Mounds, Pulaski Co., Illinois. 33

1870 US Census, Oktibbeha Co., Mississippi, Police Beat 2, PO Starkville,
Page 39
310-310 Wiley Yeates, 24, black, farm laborer, $230, b. MS
Rebecca, 19, black, farm laborer, b. MS
Martha, 1, black, b. MS

Rebecca Chandler and Wiley Yeates had the following children. Some researchers indicate she had John Yeates, born 1879 and Sam Yeates, born 1880. They were born after the death of Wiley Yeates and before her marriage to Clifford Brownlee. The only children listed with her in 1880 in her brother Smith Chandler's household were Martha, Savannah, Nancy and Bud.

1. Martha Yeates, born about 1869 at Starkville, Oktibbeha Co., Mississippi
2. Savannah "Tennessee" Yeates, born about 1870 in Mississippi
3. Nancy "Winny" Yeates, born about 1872 at Starkville, Oktibbeha Co., Mississippi
4. Wiley "Bud" Yeates, born May 1876 in Mississippi

Savannah "Tennessee" Yeates, daughter of Rebecca Chandler and Wiley Yeates, was born in about 1870 in Mississippi. She supposedly had a child by Jackson Ford, who was born about 1868 in Mississippi to Franklin and Faithie (Hall) Ford. He died in Michigan and married in 1888 in Clay Co., Mississippi to Martha A./Margaret ——. The child born to them was Frank Ford, born about 1891 in Montpelier, Clay Co., Mississippi. He married Lula Richardson on 29 March 1923 in the Zion Congregational Church of God in Christ in Detroit, Wayne Co., Michigan. Lula was born about 1897 in Mississippi to Lee and Catherine with no surname shown on the marriage record. She is shown as being divorced and a maid. He was a bricklayer. Frank worked for Ford Motor Co. and died on 3 September 1926 of pulmonary tuberculosis. 34.

On 12 April 1891 in Clay Co., Mississippi, Savannah married Major Ford, who was born in September 1869 in Oktibbeha Co., Mississippi, a brother to Jackson Ford. She died in 1908. They had the following children.

1. Mary A. Ford, born about 1892 in Clay Co., Mississippi
2. Wiley Ford, born 15 March 1895 in Woodland, Chickasaw Co., Mississippi
3. Major Ford, Jr., born about 1896 in Montpelier, Clay Co., Mississippi
4. Rosa "Rosie" Ford, born about 1898 in Mississippi
5. Cora Ford, born about 1900 in Mississippi

6. Martha J. Ford, born 10 July 1903 in Mississippi
7. Cannie Bell Ford, born 13 January 1905 in Montpelier, Clay Co., Mississippi
8. Amorie Ford, born June 1906 in Mississippi
9. Savannah Ford, born 15 September 1906 in Clay Co., Mississippi

Mary A. Ford, daughter of Savannah "Tennessee" Yeates and Major Ford, was born about 1892 in Clay Co., Mississippi. She married Thomas James Ligon on 4 Jauary 1912 in Clay Co., Mississippi. He was born about 1875 in Mississippi, the son of Larkin and Leah Ligon and died 20 November 1946 in Woodruff Co., Arkansas. In about 1924 Mary and her children moved to Illinois. She and Thomas were separated and then divorced. In about 1925 in Pulaski Co., Illinois she married Henry McClary. He was born 6 August 1866 in Tennessee and died 2 October 1931 in Pulaski Co., Illinois. On 22 November 1938 she married George Washington Figgures, Jr. in Charleston, Mississippi Co., Missouri. He was born 6 February 1881 in West Point, Clay Co., Mississippi and died 5 December 1980 in Grand Rapids, Kent Co., Michigan.

Wiley Ford, son of Savannah "Tennessee" Yeates and Major Ford, was born 15 March 1895 in Woodland, Chickasaw Co., Mississippi. He married Sofronia Tate who was born about 1897 in Mississippi and died 23 Jan 1961 in Toledo, Lucas Co., Ohio. Wiley registered for the World War I Draft at Portland, Chicot Co., Arkansas on 5 June 1917. He was farming in Chicot County for W.H. Wells, single, negro. 35 Wiley's obituary indicates that he died 2 April 1973 in Toledo, a retired janitor from Mercy Hospital. He was buried in Forest Cemetery, Toledo, Lucas Co., Ohio. 36

Rosa "Rosie" Ford, daughter of Savannah "Tennessee" Yeates and Major Ford, was born about 1898 in Mississippi. She lived with her sister Savannah and suffered with rheumatoid arthritis. She died in Vardaman, Calhoun Co., Mississippi.

Cora Ford, daughter of Savannah "Tennessee" Yeates and Major Ford, was born about 1900 in Mississippi. She lived with her sister Savannah and never married. According to family stories she my have had a mental disability and suffered with rheumatoid arthritis. She died in about 1969 in Vardaman, Calhoun Co., Mississippi.

Martha J. Ford, daughter of Savannah "Tennessee" Yeates and Major Ford, was born 10 July 1903 in Mississippi. She married Garfield Shotwell in 1918 in Clay Co., Mississippi. He was born 18 March 1897 in Clay Co., Mississippi to William Shotwell and Nancy Brownlee. Garfield died on 22 August 1977 in East St. Louis, St. Clair Co., Illinois. He served in World War I, at Camp Funston, Geary Co., Kansas. 37 Martha died in February of 1980 in Jackson, Madison Co., Tennessee.

Cannie Bell Ford, daughter of Savannah "Tennessee" Yeates and Major Ford, was born 13 January 1905 in Montpelier, Clay Co., Mississippi. She married John Shotwell on 22 February 1920 in Chickasaw Co., Mississippi. 38 He was born 16 March 1900 in Montpelier, Clay Co., Mississippi to Nancy Springer and William Shotwell. John died on 30 November 1972 at Pheba, Clay Co., Mississippi and was buried in the Pleasant Ridge Missionary Baptist Church Cemetery, Sparta, Chickasaw Co., Mississippi, with no marker on his sunken grave. Cannie Bell died 26 August 1974 in Montpelier, Clay Co., Mississippi and was buried in the Lower Prairie Creek Cemetery, also known as Dixie Cemetery, in Montpelier, Clay Co., Mississippi. Nancy Springer Shotwell married second to Mose Chandler. They are shown on the 1940 US Census, Chickasaw Co., Mississippi. Mose was 63, married 0 years, b. Mississippi, farmer. Nancy, who was the informant was 57, married 0 years, b. Mississippi. 39

Savannah Ford, daughter of Savannah "Tennessee" Yeates and Major Ford, was born 15 September 1906 in Clay Co., Mississippi. She married first to Dan Roberson who was born about 1871 in Eupora, Webster Co., Mississippi and died about 1949 in Mississippi. She married second to Sam Henry

Clark who was born 6 March 1895 in Woodland, Chickasaw Co., Mississippi and died there 15 September 1967. Savannah died on 8 February 1993 in Vardaman, Calhoun Co., Mississippi.

Wiley "Bud" Yeates, son of Rebecca Chandler and Wiley Yeates, was born in May of 1876 in Mississippi. He married Zipporah Chandler on 17 January 1899 in Clay Co., Mississippi. 40. She was born in about 1877 in Montpelier, Clay Co., Mississippi to a Mr. Chandler and Eliza Clark Calvert. Bud supposedly married also to Sue Kilpartrick who was born about 1875 in Mississippi.

Dilworth Chandler, son of Edward "Ned" Chandler and Martha was born 27 October 1855 at Starksville, Chickasaw Co., Mississippi. He married Harriet Clark in Clay Co., Mississippi on 22 December 1877. She was born in 1859 in Mississippi to George and Agnes Clark. Dilworth died 18 November 1936 in Chicago, Cook Co., Illinois. They were parents of the following children.

1. Georgia Chandler, born October 1885 in Pheba, Clay Co., Mississippi
2. John J. Chandler, born December 1887 in Pheba, Clay Co., Mississippi
3. Agnes Chandler, born 18 April 1895 in Pheba, Clay Co., Mississippi
4. Silla Chandler, born March 1899 in Pheba, Clay Co., Mississippi

John J. Chandler, son of Dilworth Chandler and Harriet Clark, was born December 1887 in Pheba, Clay Co., Mississippi. He married Martha Poker who was born 24 December 1894 in Arkansas and died in June of 1979 in Chicago, Cook Co., Illinois. John died 8 March 1961 in Chicago, Cook Co., Illinois and was buried in the Restvale Cemetery in Chicago.

Agnes Chandler, daughter of Dilworth Chandler and Harriet Clark was born 18 April 1895 in Pheba, Clay Co., Mississippi. She married first to Joseph Jones who was born about 1895 in Alabama. She married second to Alfred Brothers. In 1920 she is shown on the census enumeration as being divorced. She died 2 December 1956 in Chicago, Cook Co., Illinois, buried in the Restvale Cemetery in Chicago.

Grandville "Grant" Chandler, son of Edward "Ned" Chandler and Araminta "Minnie" Jennings, was born in 1873 in Mississippi. In 1896 he married Judith "Dudie" Chandler, daughter of Solomon and Celia Chandler. She was born in about 1873 in Mississippi. They were parents of the following children.

1. Lucretia Chandler, born 1897 in Mississippi
2. Jesse Chandler (male), born about 1897 in Mississippi
3. Solomon Chandler, born December 1899 in Mississippi
4. Luereby Chandler, born about 1901 in Mississippi
5. Frank Chandler, born about 1903 in Mississippi
6. Oleans Chandler (male), about 1904 in Mississippi
7. Andreas Chandler (male), born about 1906 in Mississippi
8. Ulysses Grant "US" Chandler, born about 1911 in Mississippi

Lucretia Chandler, daughter of Grandville "Grant" Chandler and Judith "Dudie" Chandler, was born in 1897 in Mississippi. She had two children, Lee H. Johnson, born in 1934 and Daisy E. Johnson, born in 1936.

Ulysses Grant "US" Chandler, son of Grandville "Grant" Chandler and Judith "Dudie" Chandler, was born about 1911 in Mississippi. He married Thora Mae Kilgore. She was born 30 May 1920 in Clay Co., Mississippi to Joe and Tennessee Kilgore and died 10 February 2011 in Clay Co., Mississippi.

Eugenia Chandler, the daughter shown as born 14 March 1885 in Mississippi to Araminta

"Minnie" Jennings Chandler, married Dan D. Coleman. He was born about 1879 in Mississippi. On the 1930 US Census, Eugenia was living in Pemiscot Co., Missouri, divorced.

Chandler Slave Owners

The Chandlers and their slaves came to Chickasaw Co., Mississippi in about 1847 from Halifax Co., Virginia. Willis Chandler was born in about 1778 in Halifax Co., Virginia to Robert C. Chandler and Mary Hamblin. He married Rebecca "Polly" Hill on 19 June 1802 in Halifax Co., Virginia. She was born 2 July 1780 in Halifax Co., Virginia. Willis died in Halifax Co., Virginia on 27 December 1847. When some of the Chandlers migrated from Halifax Co., Virginia to Mississippi, they brought with them their slaves. Willis and Rebecca had the following children.

1. Hartwell Chandler, born 1802 in Halifax Co., Virginia; died there 7 November 1854
2. John James Chandler, born 1806 in Halifax Co., Virginia; married 10 December 1840 in Halifax Co., Virginia to Susan Anne Moore; probably remained in Halifax Co., Virginia
3. Rowena Chandler, born 17 June 1808 in Halifax Co., Virginia; married John A. Williams, 2 December 1823 in Halifax Co., Virginia; married Phillip Edgington in 1843, Halifax Co., Virginia; died 1 January 1855 in Clay Co., Mississippi
4. Stanfield Chandler, born 17 June 1808 in Halifax Co., Virginia; married Eliza Edwards Dunlap in 1851; died 29 May 1883 in Texas
5. Malachi "Kyle" Chandler, born 17 Marh 1810 in Halifax Co., Virginia; married Paulina Petty in 1837 in Halifax Co., Virginia; married Sarah Elizbeth Robinson in 1841; died 22 November 1878 in Clay Co., Mississippi
6. Erastus Chandler, born about 1812 in Halifax Co., Virginia; married Jane Coats in about 1840; killed in 1862 at the Battle of Malvern Hill
7. Diana Robert Chandler, born about 1813 in Halifax Co., Virginia; married Thomas Johnson on 5 June 1833 in Halifax Co., Virginia
8. Gilderoy "Roy" Chandler, born 8 March 1814 in Halifax Co., Virginia; married Louisa Garner (1813-1867) in 1842 in Lowndes Co., Mississippi; died 16 May 1854 in Chickasaw Co., Mississippi
9. Willis Chandler, born about 1818 in Halifax Co., Virginia
10. Robin Chandler, born about 1820 in Halifax Co., Virginia
11. Rebecca Jane Chandler, born 16 March 1825 in Halifax Co., Virginia; married 12 February 1844 in Halifax Co., Virginia to William E.A. Moseley; died 16 December 1875 in Sparta, Chickasaw Co., Mississippi

Edward "Ned" Chandler came to Chickasaw Co., Mississippi with one of these Chandler slave owners, originally from Halifax Co., Virginia. On the 1850 US Slave Schedule, Stanfield Chandler is shown owning a black male age 35. The age would fit to be that of Edward "Ned" Chandler. On the 1860 US Slave Schedule, Louisa Chandler (widow of Gideroy "Roy" Chandler) is shown as owning a black male age 45. Erastus Chandler (relationship to the others unknown) owned a black male age 50.

Most likely Edward "Ned" Chandler was owned by Stanfield Chandler. On the 1860 US Census, the widow Louisa Chandler, age 44, was living in Chickasaw Co., Mississippi on a large plantation. Her son, Andrew, age 16, born Mississippi was in her household, along with two other sons, Benjamin, age 12, born Mississippi and Kyle, age 11, born Mississippi. The son, Andrew Martin Chandler served in the Civil War and took with him his black body servant, Silas Chandler. Andrew served in the Confederate

Army as a private in Co. F, 44th Regiment, Mississippi Infantry. The slaves owned by Louisa Chandler and Stanfield Chandler were freed by the end of the Civil War, so there is no probate record which would indicate which slaves were owned by either of them.

Stanfield Chandler was a larger slave owner than his sister-in-law, Louisa Chandler. On the 1860 US Census he was living in Chickasaw Co., Mississippi owning $4,000 in real estate and $50,000 in personal property which would have included slaves. His wealth had decreased significantly after the Civil War, when he is shown as age 62 living in Chickasaw Co., Mississippi. He was living in Clay Co., Mississippi in 1880 with his wife and by 1883 he was living in Texas where he died. He was buried in the Dobie McShorter Cemetery at Lagarto, Live Oak Co., Texas.

An inventory of the estate of E.C. Chandler of Chickasaw Co., Mississippi was taken in 1865. It is unknown how he relates to the white planters of that name in the same county. However, the inventory listing his "negroes" supplies some names. They had been hired out and are Washington, a man; Ellick, a man; Thos., a man; Soloman, a man; Patrick, a boy; Bettie Ussey Casterah and Josephine; Larkin, a boy; James, a boy; Warren, a man; Booker, a boy, Wm. a man; Hannah and 2 children; Mariah and child; Salusa, a girl; Savannah, a woman; Martha and five children. 40

It is impossible to know the exact relationship of all the slaves that were owned by the Chandlers in Chickasaw and Clay counties, Mississippi. Some may be related and some may not be related. The following are the African American Chandlers who were living in Chickasaw Co., Mississippi in 1870 as shown on the US Census. 41

135-132 Martha Chandler, 37, black, farm laborer, b. VA
Lisa, 16, black, farm laborer, b. VA
Ellick, 15, black, farm laborer, b. VA
Ted, 14, black, farm laborer, b. VA
Molly, 12, mulatto, domestic servant, b. VA
Richard, 6, mulatto, b. MS
Dock, 5, black, b. MS

322-320 Mary Chandler, 35, black, farm laborer, b. VA
Randle, 5, black, b. MS
William, 4, black, b. MS
Mary L., 1, black, b. MS

167-164 Sam Chandler, 64, black, farm laborer, $100 b. VA
Agnes, 41, mulatto, farm laborer, b. TN
Sam, 15, black, farm laborer, b. MX
Thomas, 12, black, farm laborer, b. MS
Moses, 4, black, b. MS

165-162 Homer? Chandler, 45, black, farm laborer, $1,000, b. VA, married
        September 1869
Minnie, 38, mulatto, keeping house, b. AL
Booker, 18, mulatto, farm laborer, b. MS
Bark, 14, mulatto, male, farm laborer, b. MS
Terael, 13, mulatto, male, farm laborer, b. MS
Silas, 11, mulatto, b. MS
Milas, 11, mulatto, b. MS
Hugh, 9, mulatto, b. MS
Mary, 65, black, blind, b. VA

In 1885 a School Census was taken in Clay Co., Mississippi, Pine Bluff Election District. The following Chandler children (black) are shown, along with their age and their parent. [42]

> Benjamin Chandler, age 7, son of Allen Chandler
> Lenon Chandler, 7, son of Patrick Chandler
> Hale Chandler, 7, son of Smith Chandler [Hayes]
> Walter Chandler, 9, son of Smith Chandler
> Linch Chandler, 11, son of Smith Chandler
> Lister Chandler, 15, son of Smith Chandler
> James Chandler, 16, son of Smith Chandler
> Sina Chandler, 11, daughter of William Chandler
> Arrena Chandler, 6, daughter of William Chandler
> Tom Chandler, 20, son of Gordon Chandler
> Amus Chandler, 18, son of Gordon Chandler
> Calvin Chandler, 14, son of Gordon Chandler
> Liza Chandler, 12, daughter of Gordon Chandler
> Millie Chandler, 8, daughter of Gordon Chandler
> Laura Chandler, 6, daughter of Gordon Chandler
> John Chandler, 5, son of Gordon Chandler

Rebecca Chandler, daughter of Edward "Ned" Chandler and his first wife, Martha married second to Clifford Brownlee (1832-1910), son of Edmond "Ned" Brownlee and Priscilla "Cella" Brownlee. Clifford married first to Nancy Chandler, parents unknown. She was born about 1840 in Virginia. They had the following children.

1. Georgianna Brownlee, born Feb 1862 in Mississippi; married Dick E. Keaton
   in 1887 in Chickasaw Co., Mississippi; married second to Mr. Nichols
2. Mary Brownlee, born about 1864 in Mississippi
3. James K. "Polk" Brownlee, born about 1864 in Mississippi; married Mattie
   Johnson
4. Margaret Brownlee, born 17 July 1868 in Mississippi; married Redwood
   Danzy in 1890; died 2 March 1944 in Memphis, Shelby Co., Tennessee
5. Emma R. Brownlee, born 1869 in Mississippi
6. Amos Brownlee, born about 1873 in Mississippi; married Lula Glenn
7. John Brownlee, born June 1875 in Mississippi
8. Emmett Brownlee, born 14 September 1878 in Mississippi; married Susie A.

Nancy Springer, daughter of Mac Springer and Nancy Brownlee Shotwell, was born in 1886 in Clay Co., Mississippi. She married second to Mose Chandler, born in 1875 in Mississippi, died in East St. Louis, St. Clair Co., Illinois. She also married Sim "Nigger" Chandler, born 14 November 1889 in Montpelier, Clay Co., Mississippi, son of Thomas Chandler and Mahalia Foster. They had a son named Tensy Chandler. Sim died in October of 1970 in Pheba, Clay Co., Mississippi.

Thomas Chandler was born about 1859 in Mississippi. He was supposedly the son of Sam and Agatha Chandler. Thomas married Mahalia Foster on 31 March 1885 in Clay Co., Mississippi. She was born in about 1869 in Mississippi. Thomas died before 1930 in Mississippi.

Sam Chandler was born about 1806 in Virginia, most likely owned by the Chandlers of Halifax Co., Virginia who went to Chickasaw and Clay counties, Mississippi. He married Agatha Chandler who was born about 1830 in Virginia. Sam died in December of 1879 in Clay Co., Mississippi of colic.

Motley

Florence M. Motley who married Hayes Ezekiel Chandler, was born about 9 April 1886 in Kentucky, the daughter of James Motley and Bettie Anderson. James was fondly referred to as "Grandpa Bear." He was born about 25 Decmber 1855 in Kentucky, the son of Ruben/Reuben and Amanda "Mandy" Motley. James married Bettie Anderson who was born 20 December 1861 in Kentucky, the daughter of Harriet Anderson. The Motleys lived in Taylor Co., Kentucky and then moved to McIntosh Co., Oklahoma. James died in 11 July 1948 in Alliance, Box Butte Co., Nebraska and was buried in the Alliance Cemetery. Bettie died 20 January 1925 in Logan Co., Oklahoma.

> 1880 US Census, Green Co., Kentucky, Grove Twp., ED 55, Page 624C 43
> 4-4- James Motley, black, 25, farming, b. KY, both parents b. KY
> Bettie, 19, keeping house, black, b. KY, both parents b. KY

In 1900 Ruben and Mandy Motley were living with James and Bettie Motley in Taylor Co., Kentucky. Mandy indicates she had had only one child, being James. On the 1870 and 1880 enumerations, Rubin/Ruebin/Reubin and Mandy Motley were living in Green Co., Kentucky. Clearly on the 1870 US Census, there is a female in their household who is two years older than James and may have been a daughter. It is also possible she was a niece, as no relationships were shown by the enumerator.

> 1870 US Census, Green Co., Kentucky, Prect. No. 2 44
> 163-167 Reubin Motley, 40, black, works on farm, b. KY
> Amanda, 40, mulatto, keeping house, b. KY
> Palina?, female, 17, mulatto, b. KY
> James, 15, mulatto, b. KY
> Nancy, 30, black, b. KY
> Mary Ball, 13, mulatto, b. KY

> 1880 US Census, Green Co., Kentucky, Groves, ED 55, Page 625A 45
> 5-6 Reubin Motley, black, 51, farm hand, b. KY, both parents b. VA
> Amanda, mulatto, 51, wife, keeping house, b. KY, both parents b. KY
> Easter Cobble, black, 26, single, b. KY, both parents b. KY
> George Cobble, black, 4, son, b. KY, both parents b. KY

> 1900 US Census, Taylor Co., Kentucky, Magistorial District, Campbellsville, ED 46
> 117, Page 6A
> 108-111 James Motley, black, b. 1852, 48, married 21 years, b. KY, both parents
>   b. KY, farmer
> Bettie, wife, black, b. Dec 1868, 31, 6 children, 6 living, b. KY, both parents b.
>   KY
> Florance, b. April 1886, black, 14, b. KY, both parents b. KY
> Tim, b. July 1891, black, 8, b. KY, both parents b. KY
> Lenard, b. June 1895, black, 4, b. IL, both parents b. KY
> James, b. March 1900, black, 3/12, b. KY
> Ruben, father, black, b. 1830, 70, married 44 years, b. KY, father b. VA,
>   mother b. KY
> Mandy, mother, black, b. 1830, 70, 1 child, 1 living, b. KY, father b. VA,
>   mother b. KY

> 1910 US Census, McIntosh Co., Oklahoma, Checotah Twp., Checotah, ED 69, 47
> Page 1A

Okmulgee Street

4-5 James Motley, black, 55, married 30 years, b. IL, both parents b. IL, farmer
Bettie, wife, black, 47, 6 children, 6 living, b. KY, both parents b. KY, laborer,
      odd jobs
Flourance, 24, black, single, b. KY, laundress
Tim, 19, black, single, b. KY, farm laborer, home farm
Lenwood, 14, black, b. KY, farm laborer, home farm
Virgil, 10, black, b. KY, farm laborer, home farm

While Bettie Anderson Motley, wife of James Motley, did not die until 1925 in Logan Co., Oklahoma, James Motleyy is shown with another wife, Sara E., on the 1920 US Census in Box Butte Co., Nebraska.

1920 US Census, Box Butte Co., Nebraska, Lawn Prect., ED 15, Page 3A 48
60-61 James Motley, rents, black, 58, b. KY, both parents b. KY, farmer
Sara E., wife, black, 56, b. KY, both parents b. KY
Virgil J., son, black, 19, b. KY, both parents b. KY
Joseph W. Crittenden, son-in-law, mulatto, 49, b. TX, father b. TN,
      mother b. VA, farm laborer
Cora B. Crittenden, daughter, black, 37, b. KY, both parents b. KY
Robert Anderson, uncle, 80, single, b. KY, both parents b. KY

According to James Motley's obituary from the Alliance, Nebraska newspaper he was survived by his six children, being Mrs. Hayes Chandler and Mrs. Cora Crittenden of Alliance, Nebraska, Dr. Robert Motley of Tulsa, Oklahoma, T.H. Motley of Fresno, California, L.M. Motley of Lincoln, Nebraska and Virgil G. Motley of New York City. He was also survived by Jim Motley, champion, amateur prize fighter, one of eleven grandchildren.

1. Cora Motley, born 25 September 1882 in Taylor Co., Kentucky (see Crittenden Volume 1
2. Florence M. Motley, born 9 April 1886 in Kentucky (see above)
3. Timothy Hudell "Tim" Motley, born 29 July 1890 in Kentucky
4. Lenard/Leonard Marshel Motley, born 12 June 1899 in Illinois
5. James Motley, b. March 1900 in Kentucky (Robert)
6. Virgil Gerome Motley, b. 27 March 1900 in Kentucky

Timothy Hudell "Tim" Motley, son of James Motley and Bettie Anderson, was born 29 July 1890 in Kentucky. He married Kansas Chandler, the daughter of Smith Chandler and Mary Cousins. She was born in 1890 in Mississippi and died in 1923 in Logan Co., Oklahoma. Tim died 26 June 1975 in Fresno, Fresno Co., California. He registered for the World War I Draft on 5 June 1917 in McIntosh Co., Oklahoma. He was shown as living at 415 6th Street in Checotah, McIntosh Co., Oklahoma, age 30, born 29 July 1896 in Campbellville, Taylor Co., Kentucky. He was a smelter worker for US Smelting Co. at Checotah. His race is shown as African. He had a wife and two children. 49

1940 US Census, Fresno Co., California, ED 10-148, Page 8A 50
rents $10 month
Tim H. Motley, negro, 49, 2 years college, b. IL, residing Topeka, KS 1 April
      1935, laborer, farm
Hudell, son, negro, 25, 4 years high school, b. KS, residing Topeka, KS 1 April
      1935, laborer, farm

Hudell Orville Motley, son of Timothy Hudell Motley and Kansas Chandler, was born 17

November 1914 in Oklahoma. He married Mamie Harris on 26 February 1957 in Kings Co., California. Hudell died 7 December 2009 in Lemoore, Kings Co., California and was buried in the Lemoore Cemetery. Mamie was born 3 March 1916 in Okmulgee, Okmulgee Co., Oklahoma to John Robert Harris and Rosella Willis Harris. She married first to Milton Burton. She died 14 September 1996 in Lemoore, Kings Co., California and was buried in the Lemoore Cemetery. 51

Hugh Motley, son of Timothy Hudell Motley and Kansas Chandler, was born about 1915 in Logan Co., Oklahoma and died in 1982 in Tulsa Co., Oklahoma

Mary Elizabeth Motley, son of Timothy Hudell Motley and Kansas Chandler, was born 9 April 1916 in Checotah, McIntosh Co., Oklahoma. She married William McKinley Reese. He was born 4 December 1899 in Texas and died 19 July 1967 in Oklahoma City, Oklahoma Co., Oklahoma. Mary died 10 June 1990 in Oklahoma City, Oklahoma Co., Oklahoma.

Thedford W. Motley, son of Timothy Hudell Motley and Kansas Chandler, was born 25 March 1919 in Logan Co., Oklahoma. He married Elene High, born 29 November 1919 and died 28 April 2013. Thedford died in 1995 in Oklahoma City, Oklahoma Co., Oklahoma.

Lenard/Leonard Marshel Motley, son of James Motley and Bettie Anderson, was born 12 June 1899 in Illinois. He was sentenced in Dawes Co., Nebraska for robbery, serving 3 to 15 years in the Nebraska State Penitentiary in Lincoln, Nebraska. He also was sentenced from Box Butte Co., Nebraska for burglary, in which case his name is shown as Leon M. Motley. 52

He is also shown as Lenward M. Motley, when his wife, Nora F. Motley filed for a divorce in Box Butte Co., Nebraska.

Box Butte Co., Nebraska
District Court - Civil Records
Case #4147 Docket P Page 190
filed 6 November 1928

Nora F. Motley
vs
Lenward M. Motley

The plaintiff and defendant were married at Hot Springs, Fall River Co., South Dakota on 18 July 1924. The plaintiff has resided in Box Butte Co., Nebraska since 18 July 1924. On 19 April 1926 in Box Butte Co., Nebraska, the defendant was convicted of a felony; crime of burglary and larceny and was sentenced to the State of Nebraska Penitentiary for not less than ten years. The sentence is still in effect. The plaintiff seeks a divorce. The defendant was served a summons on 10 December 1928.

Journal Entry Case #4147
31 October 1932, plaintiff asked to dismiss the case without prejudice to a new action and that plaintiff pay the costs.

In September of 1950 at Fremont, Dodge Co., Nebraska, Leonard Motley was standing trial for the death of Clayton Annon, Sr., which took place on 23 July 1950. As the second degree murder trial was progressing, Motley changed his plea to guilty to a charge that he shot Annon when he found him with Motley's wife. He was given the minimum sentence of fifteen years in the Nebraska State Penitentiary in Lincoln. 53 Leonard died 9 September 1957 while in prison and was buried in the Yankee Hill Cemetery, Lincoln, Lancaster Co., Nebraska. 54

James Motley, son of James Motley and Bettie Anderson, is most likely the Dr. Robert Motley shown in his father's obituary. He was born in March of 1900 in Kentucky. Motley was in the Navy and after discharge came back to Alliance where he was a truck driver. James became a heavyweight boxer, having engaged in boxing matches in the Navy. In April of 1947, Motley was in the National AAU Boxing Tournament in Boston. During a bout with Joe Brown of Abington, Massachusetts, Motley's left arm was broken, forcing him to forfeit the match. [55]

Virgil G. Motley, son of James Motley and Bettie Anderson, was born 27 March 1900 in Kentucky. He married Minnie Pearl Motley on 31 March 1921 in Greensburg, Green Co., Kentucky. She was the daughter of Jessie and Nellie Motley and was born about 1904. Their first child, Sarah Bell Motley, was born and died on 12 May 1922 in Box Butte Co., Nebraska. She was buried in the Alliance Cemetery, Alliance, Box Butte Co., Nebraska. Her tombstone is inscribed with "Baby Motley." The marriage of Virgil and Minnie ended in divorce. [56]

Box Butte Co., Nebraska
District Court
Divorce
filed 3 September 1938
Case #5558, Docket T, Page 303

Minnie Motley
vs
Virgil Motley

They were married on 31 March 1921 in Greensburg, Green Co., Kentucky and came to Alliance, Box Butte County about 15 March 1922. She was treated cruelly and inhumanely. Virgil Motley had a violent, unruly temper and displayed fits of rage, calling her vile, obsene names. He struck her and had daily quarrels with her until 1 November 1937 when he neglected her for two years. She has no money or property. A restraining order was issued 3 September 1938 and a hearing was held on 19 September 1938.

The defendant demurred and denied all the charges. The children born to the couple were James Motley, 15, Ella Motley, 14, Bernice Motley, 7 and Teresa, age 4. The court found in favor of the plaintiff on 29 July 1940, awarding her $20 a month for the support of the children.

> 1930 US Census, Box Butte Co., Nebraska, Alliance, ED 3, Page 4B [57]
> Platte Ave.
> 75-94 Virgil Motley, rents $10 month, negro, 29, married at age 21, b. KY,
>   both parents b. KY, laborer, odd jobs
> Minnie, wife, negro, 27, married at age 19, b. KY, both parents b. KY
> James, son, negro, 6, b. NE, both parents b. KY
> Marjory, daughter, negro, 5, b. KY, both parents b. KY
>
> 1940 US Census, Box Butte Co., Nebraska, Alliance, ED 7-3B, Page 9B [58]
> 1024 W 1st Street, rents $7 month
> Minnie Motley, informant, negro, divorced, 8, b. KY, same place 1 April
>   1935, housework, odd jobs
> James, son, negro, 16, 2 years high school, b. NE, same place 1 April 1935
> Montori, daughter, negro, 15, 7th grade, b. KY, same place 1 April 1935
> Bernice, daughter, negro, 8, 2nd grade, b. NE, same place 1 April 1935
> Terese, daughter, negro, 7, 1st grade, b. NE, same place 1 April 1935

On 12 September 1918, Virgil Jerome (Gerome) Motley of Hemingford, Box Butte Co., Nebraska registered for the World War I draft. He was born 27 March 1900, age 18, negro. He was farming for his father, James Motley at Hemingford. 59

Virgil Gerome Motley served as a private in the US Army during World War II. He died on 7 June 1977 and was buried in the Fort Logan National Cemetery, Denver, Denver Co., Colorado, Plot 0, 1290. 60

Minnie Pearl Motley who married Virgil Gerome Motley, was the daughter of Jessie and Nellie Motley. On the 1920 US Census, she was living with her grandparents John M. and Minnie Johnston in Gresham Twp., Green Co., Kentucky. 61 She was also living with them in Green Co., Kentucky on the 1910 US Census, age 6, b. Kentucky. They are shown as Marsh and Minnie Johnson. 62 Virgil Gerome Motley and Minnie Pearl Motley were married on 31 March 1921 in Green Co., Kentucky. Her parents are shown as Jessie Motley and his wife, Nellie. 63 Therefore, it appears that Virgil went from Nebraska to Kentucky to marry her. Minnie's father does not appear to have been born a Motley. According to the 1900 US Census, he was the stepson of a Buffy Motley. Buffy may not have been his actual given name.

1900 US Census, Green Co., Kentucky, Gresham, ED 36, Page 1A 64
7-7 Buffy Motley, black, b. Sept 1875, 54, married 12 years, b. KY,
        both parents b. KY, farmer
Harret, wife, black, b. July 1861, 39, married 12 years, 4 children, 4 living,
        b. KY, both parents b. KY
Perley, daughter, black, b. Nov. 1887, 12, b. KY, both parents b. KY
Jessey, stepson, black, b. May 1879, 20, single, b. KY, both parents b. KY, farm
        laborer

James Motley's parents, Ruben/Reuben and Amanda "Mandy" Motley, were both born in Kentucky and lived in Green Co., Kentucky. They were both born in about 1830 in Kentucky. Mandy died on 2 November 1911 in Green Co., Kentucky. She is buried in the Cabell Cemetery at Gresham, Green Co., Kentucky. There were Motleys in Green Co., Kentucky who owned slaves. They originated in Amelia Co., Virginia.

Bettie Anderson who married James Motley, was the daughter of Harriet Anderson, and a sister to Robert Ball Anderson who also came to Box Butte Co., Nebraska. More information on the Andersons can be found in Volume 1. They were from Green Co., Kentucky.

Harriet Anderson, the mother of Bettie, was born in 1835 in Henderson Co., Kentucky. According to her death certificate, she died 14 April 1912 in Henderson Co., Kentucky. She was a widow and her parents are shown as unknown. The informant was Bettie Anderson of Henderson Co., Kentucky. Bettie Anderson was married to James Motley by then, but apparently gave her maiden name on the form. Harriet died of penumonia and old age and was buried on 15 April 1912 in the Mt. Zion Colored Cemetery in Henderson Co., Kentucky. 65

In 1870 Bettie and her sister were living with their mother in Henderson Co., Kentucky. Some researchers indicate that Harriet Anderson was married to Zackary Motley by whom she had the daughter Bettie who went by the surname of Anderson. He was born about 1822 in Virginia.

1870 US Census, Henderson Co., Kentucky, Henderson, Ward 3, PO Henderson 66
146-179 James Brown, 39, black, day laborer, $75, b. KY
Sallie, 32, black, keeping house, b. KY
America, 13, black, b. KY
Carrie, 11, black, b. KY

268

Alice, 3, black, b. KY
Mary E., 1/12, black, b. KY in May
Harriet Anderson, 44, black, cook, b. KY cannot read or write
Carrie Anderson, 10, mulatto, b. KY
Bettie Anderson, 6, mulatto, b. KY

Bettie is shown as being married to James Motley when the 1870 US Census was taken, Green Co., Kentucky. She is also shown, probably enumerated just before her marriage, living in Warren Co., Kentucky.

1880 US Census, Warren Co., Kentucky, Bowling Green, ED 226, Page 10C 67
156-149 B.F. Proctor, 34, white, lawyer, b. KY, both parents b. KY
Lilah, 29, white, wife, keeps [house], b. KY, father b. VA, mother b. KY
Bettie Anderson, 19, black, servant, single, cook, b. KY, both parents b. KY

Green Co., Kentucky Census - Motley

Unless a slave had been emancipated, they are not shown on any federal enumeration until the 1870 US Census. It is difficult to determine blood relationships from census. In the case of emancipated slaves, many took the surname of their master. In the course of time, there were some who changed their surname. With regard to race, it was in the enumerator's instructions to show the degree of color as it appeared to him or as he was told. Thus, from one census to another a person might be shown as black on one and mulatto on another. Names were also an obstacle. The enumerator spelled them as he heard them. Nicknames were not to be used, but often they were used on the census schedule. In some cases, a person would be shown as William J. on one census and as J. William on another. The middle name was sometimes used as the given name or "known name."

The following African American people showing the surname of Motley are shown on the 1870 and 1880 US Censuses in Green Co., Kentucky. They may or may not have been related in some degree. It is known from census that they all lived within close proximity of each other, so undoubtedly knew each other.

1870 US Census, Green Co., Kentucky, Prect. 2, PO Haskinsville

41-45 Diner [Dinah] Motley, 58, female, black, keeping house, b. VA
Louciller, 24, female, black, b. KY

42-46 Harrod Motley, 63, black, farmer, b. VA
Mira, 40, black, keeping house, b. KY
Taylor, 20, black, b. KY
Mary E., 18, black, b. KY
Edward, 10, black, b. KY
Lettie, 7, black, b. KY
Palmer, 5, black, b. KY
Luler, 2, female, b. KY
Leller, 2, female, b. KY
Henry A., 2/12, b. KY

47-51 Quincy Motley, 27, black, farmer $100, b. KY
America, 24, black, keeping house, b. KY
Doctor, 17, black, male, works on farm, b. KY

Thomas, 14, black, attending school, b. KY
Catharine, 10, black, b. KY

112-116 John Motley, 30, black, works on farm, b. KY
Agnis, 23, black, keeping house, b. KY

121-125 Lieullen Motley, 21, black, male, works on farm, b. KY
Susan, 21, black, keeping house, b. KY

163-167 Reubin Motley, 40, black, works on farm, b. KY
Amanda, 40, mulatto, keeping house, b. KY
Palina?, female, 17, mulatto, b. KY
James, 15, mulatto, b. KY
Nancy, 30, black, b. KY
Mary Ball, 13, mulatto, b. KY

1880 US Census, Green Co., Kentucky, Grove
5-6 Reubin Motley, black, 51, farm hand, b. KY, both parents b. VA
Amanda, mulatto, 51, wife, keeping house, b. KY, both parents b. KY
Easter Cobble, black, 26, single, b. KY, both parents b. KY
George Cobble, black, 4, son, b. KY, both parents b. KY

8-9 Harrod Motley, black, 70, widowed, farm hand, b. VA, both parents b. VA
Letha, black, 18, daughter, b. KY, both parents b. KY
Farmer, black, male, 16, son, farm hand, b. KY, both parents b. KY
Leler, black, female, 9, daughter, b. KY, both parents b. KY
Lulu, black, female, 9, daughter, b. KY, both parents b. KY
James, black, 7, son, b. KY, both parents b. KY

1-1 Emma or Emmer Motley, black, female, 50, single, keeping house, b. KY,
         both parents b. KY
Laura, black, 25, single, daughter, b. KY, both parents b. KY
Joseph, black, 19, single, son, b. KY, both parents b. KY
William, black, 17, son, b. KY, both parents b. KY
Frank, black, 10, son, b. KY, both parents b. KY

4-4 Filman Motley, mulatto, 25, married, b. KY, both parents b. KY
Salley, mulatto, 17, married, b. KY, both parents b. KY

7-7 Ella Motley, black, 65, widow, farming, b. VA, both parents b. VA
Silvey, black, 29, daughter, single, b. KY, father b. KY, mother b. VA
Berry or Beny, black, 18, grandchild, farm hand, b. KY, both parents b. KY
Henry, black, 9, grandchild, farm hand, b. KY, both parents b. KY
Allen, black, 8, grandchild, b. KY, both parents b. KY
Newman, black, 6, grandchild, b. KY, both parents b. KY
Nannie, black, 4, grandchild, b. KY, both parents b. KY

9-9 Watkins Motley, black, 45, farming, b. KY, father b. KY, mother b. VA
Frances, mulatto, 45, wife, keeping house, b. KY, father b. KY, mother b. VA
Sarah, black, 8, daughter, b. KY, both parents b. KY

3-3 William Motley, black, 30, farming, b. KY, both parents b. KY

Emily, mulatto, 27, wife, keeping house, b. KY, both parents b. KY
Henry, black, 10, son, b. KY, both parents b. KY
Savanah, mulatto, 1/12, daughter, b. KY, both parents b. KY

4-4 James Motley, black, 25, farming, b. KY, both parents b. KY
Bettie, black, 19, keeping house, both parents b. KY

5-5 Quincy Motley, black, 37, widowed, farming, b. KY, both parents b. KY
Peter C., black, 9, son, b. KY, both parents b. KY
Magline, black, 6, daughter, b. KY, both parents b. KY
Hite Motley, black, 23, farm hand, b. KY, both parents b. KY
Martha, mulatto, 24, wife, keeping house, b. KY, both parents b. KY
Amelia, mulatto, 70, mother, b. KY, both parents b. KY
America Motley, black, 25, single, servant, b. KY, both parents b. KY
Andy, black, 9, b. KY, both parents b. KY
Charles, black, 5, b. KY, both parents b. KY
Amelia, black, 3, b. KY, both parents b. KY

7-7 John Motley, black, 35, farm hand, b. KY, father b. KY, mother b. VA
Aggie, black, 30, wife, keeping house, b. KY, both parents b. KY
Hite, black, 4, son, b. KY, both parents b. KY
John, black, 2, son, b. KY, both parents b. KY
Amelia Ingram, black, 70, mother, widow, b. VA, both parents b. VA

10-10 Frank Motley, black, 27, farm hand, b. KY, both parents b. KY
Ellen, black, 23, wife, keeping house, b. KY, both parents b. KY
Lue, black, female, 4, b. KY, both parents b. KY
Addom, black, male, 1, b. KY, both parents b. KY

2-2 Household of Martha Lane, white
Edward Motley, black, 22, single, farm hand, b. KY, both parents b. KY

9-9 Household of George W. Walker, white
Lincon Motley, black, 19, farm hand, b. KY, both parents b. KY
Jessey Motley, black, male, 16, farm hand, b. KY, both parents b. KY

7-9 Allen Motley, black, 60, farmer, b. KY, both parents b. VA
Agnis, black, 56, wife, b. KY, both parents b. VA
Elizabeth, black, granddaughter, 16, b. KY, both parents b. KY

From these enumerations it appears that the oldest Motleys were Diner [Dinah] Motley, age 58, born in Virginia, shown on the 1870 US Census of Green Co., Kentucky. This would make her birth at approximately 1812. On the 1880 enumeration, Amelia Ingram, 70, born in Virginia, was living in the household of John Motley, age 35. She is shown as his mother. Also on the 1880 enumeration, Amelia (assumed to be Motley), age 70, born Kentucky was living in the household of Quincy Motley and shown as his mother. Obviously, Amelia was living back and forth between the two sons and caught up in both households on the enumeration. However, was she a Motley or an Ingram?

The Bishop Family Tree by Ruby Motley on Ancestry contains information regarding a Harry Ingram and wife Amelia. All of their children were shown as Motleys. 68 The information on this public site indicates that Harry Ingram was born in Adair Co., Kentucky and died before 1870. His wife,

Amelia, was born about 1810 in Green Co., Kentucky and died in May of 1870 in Green Co., Kentucky. There is no record shown if they married or why the children went by the surname of Motley.

According to this information, Amelia is shown on the 1870 US Mortality Schedule for Precinct No. 2, Green Co., Kentucky. There are two Motleys shown on that, one being a Nellie Motley who Ruby Motley apparently thought was Amelia. It is possible that Nellie was a nickname. She is shown as 80 years of age, black, a widow, born in Virginia and died in May of 1870 of debility. The other person on the mortality schedule is Silvy Motley, one month old, black, b. Kentucky, died October 1869 of an unknown cause.69 From the 1880 US Census, it is apparent that Amelia Motley aka Ingram did not die in 1870. Therefore, the Nellie Motley on the 1870 US Mortality Schedule is not her.

Harry Ingram served in Co. G, 123rd United States Colored Troops. His widow, Amelia Ingram applied for a widow's pension from the federal government on 1 March 1869. She apparently died in about 1894 when Dock Ingram applied for a minor's pension on 10 August 1894, from Kentucky. 43 According to the military record of Harry Ingram he served as a private in Co. A, 13th Regiment US Colored Heavy Artillery and appears on the M and D Roll of men transferred from Co. C, 120th at Camp Nelson, Kentucky on 23 June 1865. He enlisted on 24 November 1864 for three years.70

According to the public tree, Bishop Family Tree by Ruby Motley, on Ancestry, the following children are shown as being born to Harry Ingram and his wife, Amelia. They are all shown with the surname of Motley.

1. Ruben Motley, born about 1823 (see above)
2. Watkins Motley, born about 1831 in Kentucky; died 7 January 1923 at
    Roswell, Chaves Co., New Mexico
3. John Motley, born about 1834 in Green Co., Kentucky; died 2 September 1915
    in Green Co., Kentucky
4. Quincy A. Motley, born May 1844 in Kentucky; died 15 August 1915
5. William Motley, born about 1845 in Kentucky; died 1 April 1913
6. Frank Motley, born December 1854 in Kentucky
7. Hite Motley, born about 1857 in Kentucky

One of the most noticeable things about the listing of children is that there is a gap of eight years between the birth of Ruben and that of Watkins. There is a gap of ten years between the birth of John and Quincy. There is a gap of nine years between the birth of William and Frank. These gaps could allow for the birth of children who did not live to adulthood or are simply not known. At this time, we cannot assume that all seven children were brothers.

In an attempt to understand the Motleys who lived in Green Co., Kentucky pre and post emancipation, the Kentucky birth records, colored for that county have been consulted. The earliest registration of colored births was done by Sylva W. Motley and Elizabeth Ingraham [as spelled] who both owned slaves. In October of 1852 these women registered slave births as follows. Notice that the mother is shown, but not the father. Unfortunately not every slave birth was consistently registered within the county as the next registration of black births began in 1874. 71

Sylva W. Motley's slave birth registrations
Cornilia of color, daughter of Harrit of color
Milley of color, daughter of Amelia of color
Catharine of color, daughter of Nancy of color

Elizabeth Ingraham slave birth registration
Jesse of color, no mother shown

It is possible, but lacking proof, that Amelia "Milley," slave of Sylva W. Motley, was the same person who is shown by Ruby Motley to be the wife of Harry Ingram.

On the 1850 US Census, Elizabeth Ingram [as spelled] was living in District 1, Green Co., Kentucky. She was 52 years of age, farmer, $8,000 and born in Jassamine Co., Kentucky, white. While it is not denoted on that enumeration, she appears to have been a widow or divorced. Two males in her household are Isaac W. Ingram, age 22, born in Adair Co., Kentucky and Benjamin T. Ingram, age 14, born in Green Co., Kentucky. 72

The 1850 US Federal Census, Slave Schedules for Green Co., Kentucky show both Sylva W. Motley and Elizabeth Ingraham [as spelled] as being slave owners. Elizabeth owned seventeen slaves, ranging in age from 80 to two months. 73

Neither the census enumerations or the birth records provide proof as to the father of any of the Motleys in Green Co., Kentucky. Even if a slave woman had children during slavehood and then married, it is no proof that the man she married was their father. The Motleys may have been related in some degree, but no records contain that information.

1. Year: 1920; Census Place: Lawn, Box Butte, Nebraska; Roll: T625_979; Page: 3A; Enumeration District: 15; Image: 1120
2. Year: 1930; Census Place: Alliance, Box Butte, Nebraska; Roll: 1266; Page: 4B; Enumeration District: 0003; Image: 861.0; FHL microfilm: 2341001
3. Year: 1940; Census Place: Alliance, Box Butte, Nebraska; Roll: T627_2237; Page: 10B; Enumeration District: 7-3B
4. FindAGrave http:www.findagrave.com.
5. Interview with Florence Nickens on 3 March 2016, Alliance, Nebraska.
6. Crazy Snake Rebellion https://en.wikipedia.org/wiki/Crazy_Snake_Rebellion.
7. Interview with Florence Nickens.
8. Obituary for Barbara J. Chandler, *Alliance Times Herald,* Alliance, Nebraska, 26 July 2016.
9. 1870 U.S. census, population schedules. NARA microfilm publication M593, 1,761 rolls. Washington, D.C.: National Archives and Records Administration, n.d.Minnesota census schedules for 1870. NARA microfilm publication T132, 13 rolls. Washington, D.C.: National Archives and Records Administration, n.d.
10. Year: 1880; Census Place: Beat 5, Clay, Mississippi; Roll: 645; Family History Film: 1254645; Page: 302A; Enumeration District: 046; Image: 0025
11. Year: 1900; Census Place: Justice Precinct 2, Navarro, Texas; Roll: 1661; Page: 5B; Enumeration District: 0100; FHL microfilm: 1241661
12. Year: 1910; Census Place: Checotah, McIntosh, Oklahoma; Roll: T624_1260; Page: 9B; Enumeration District: 0070; FHL microfilm: 1375273.
13. Year: 1920; Census Place: Seward, Logan, Oklahoma; Roll: T625_1470; Page: 1A; Enumeration District: 69; Image: 1116
14. Texas Death Certificate #5308.
15. Texas Death Certificate #3780.
16. Texas Death Certificate #15055.
17. Texas Death Certificate #9680.
18. Conduct Registers, vols. 1998/038-177–1998/038-236. Texas Department of Criminal Justice. Archives and Information Services Division, Texas State Library and Archives Commission, Austin, Texas. Convict Registers, vols. 1998/038-138–1998/038-176. Texas Department of Criminal Justice. Archives and Information Services Division, Texas State Library and Archives Commission, Austin, Texas.
19. Year: 1900; Census Place: LaCross, Clay, Mississippi; Roll: 805; Page: 14B; Enumeration District: 0034; FHL microfilm: 1240805

20. Year: 1910; Census Place: Beat 3, Oktibbeha, Mississippi; Roll: T624_754; Page: 8A; Enumeration District: 0099; FHL microfilm: 1374767

21. Registration State: *Texas;* Registration County: *Navarro;* Roll: *1983495;* Draft Board: *2.*

22. Year: 1930; Census Place: Ennis, Ellis, Texas; Roll: 2327; Page: 2B; Enumeration District: 0023; Image: 92.0; FHL microfilm: 2342061.

23. Ancestry.com. *U.S., Social Security Applications and Claims Index, 1936-2007* [database on-line]. Provo, UT, USA: Ancestry.com Operations, Inc., 2015.

24. Texas Death Certificate #50116.

25. Registration State: *Oklahoma;* Registration County: *McIntosh;* Roll: *1851809.*

26. Oklahoma County Marriage Record Book 89 page 113.

27. Oklahoma County Divorces Book 34, page 113.

28. 1870 U.S. census, population schedules. NARA microfilm publication M593, 1,761 rolls. Washington, D.C.: National Archives and Records Administration, n.d.Minnesota census schedules for 1870. NARA microfilm publication T132, 13 rolls. Washington, D.C.: National Archives and Records Administration, n.d.

29. Clay Co., Mississippi Tax Roll page 79.

30. 1870 U.S. census, population schedules. NARA microfilm publication M593, 1,761 rolls. Washington, D.C.: National Archives and Records Administration, n.d.Minnesota census schedules for 1870. NARA microfilm publication T132, 13 rolls. Washington, D.C.: National Archives and Records Administration, n.d.

31. Year: 1880; Census Place: Beat 5, Clay, Mississippi; Roll: 645; Family History Film: 1254645; Page: 298B; Enumeration District: 046; Image: 0018.

32. Year: 1900; Census Place: LaCross, Clay, Mississippi; Roll: 805; Page: 13A; Enumeration District: 0034; FHL microfilm: 1240805.

33. FHL Film #1818556 Digital Folder Number: 4008477 Image Number: 313 Film Number: 1818556 Volume/Page/Certificate Number: 11947 Collection: Illinois, Deaths and Stillbirths, 1916-1947 // buried in Mounds, Pulaski, IL at Thistlewood Cemetery.

34. Ancestry.com. *Michigan, Marriage Records, 1867-1952* [database on-line]. Provo, UT, USA: Ancestry.com Operations, Inc., 2015. Original data: Michigan, Marriage Records, 1867–1952. Michigan Department of Community Health, Division for Vital Records and Health Statistics.

35. United States, Selective Service System. *World War I Selective Service System Draft Registration Cards, 1917-1918.* Washington, D.C.: National Archives and Records Administration. M1509, 4,582 rolls.

36. Lucas Co., Ohio Blade obituary Index, 1970-2010; ancestry.com.

37. The National Archives at Washington, D.C.; Washington, D.C.; Series Title: Lists of Men Ordered to Report to Local Board for Military Duty in the District of Columbia; NAI Number: 1159403; Record Group Title: Records of the Selective Service System (World War I), 1917-1939; Record Group Number: 163.

38. Chickasaw Co., Mississippi Marriage Book 13, page 374, file #0011642.

39. Year: 1940; Census Place: Chickasaw, Mississippi; Roll: T627_2013; Page: 12A; Enumeration District: 9-17.

40. Ancestry.com. Mississippi, Wills and Probate Records, 1780-1982 [database on-line]. Provo, UT, USA: Ancestry.com Operations, Inc., 2015.

41. 1870 U.S. census, population schedules. NARA microfilm publication M593, 1,761 rolls. Washington, D.C.: National Archives and Records Administration, n.d.Minnesota census schedules for 1870. NARA microfilm publication T132, 13 rolls. Washington, D.C.: National Archives and Records Administration, n.d.

42. Mississippi Enumeration of Educable Children, 1850-1892; 1908-1957," database with images, FamilySearch (https://familysearch.org/ark:/61903/1:1:QK6W-2S78), Smith Chandler in entry for Hale Chandler, 1885; citing School enrollment, , Clay, Mississippi, United States, Mississippi Department of Archives & History, Jackson.

43. Year: 1880; Census Place: Grove, Green, Kentucky; Roll: 416; Family History Film: 1254416; Page: 624C; Enumeration District: 055; Image: 0654.

44. Year: 1870; Census Place: Precinct 2, Green, Kentucky; Roll: M593_465; Page: 449A; Image: 439001; Family History Library Film: 545964.

45. Year: 1880; Census Place: Grove, Green, Kentucky; Roll: 416; Family History Film: 1254416; Page: 625A; Enumeration District: 055; Image: 0656.

46. Year: 1900; Census Place: Campbellsville, Taylor, Kentucky; Roll: 552; Page: 6A; Enumeration District: 0117; FHL microfilm: 1240552.

47. Year: 1910; Census Place: Checotah Ward 1, McIntosh, Oklahoma; Roll: T624_1260; Page: 1A; Enumeration District: 0069; FHL microfilm: 1375273.

48. Year: 1920; Census Place: Lawn, Box Butte, Nebraska; Roll: T625_979; Page: 3A; Enumeration District: 15; Image: 1120.

49. United States, Selective Service System. *World War I Selective Service System Draft Registration Cards, 1917-1918*. Washington, D.C.: National Archives and Records Administration. M1509, 4,582 rolls.

50. Year: 1940; Census Place: Fresno, California; Roll: T627_206; Page: 8A; Enumeration District: 10-148.

51. FindAGrave.

52. Nebraska State Historical Society, Reel RG034 #3.

53. *Omaha World-Herald*, Omaha, Nebraska, 18 September 1950, page 6.

54. FindAGrave.

55. *Omaha World-Herald*, Omaha, Nebraska, 10 April 1947, page 17 "Omaha World Herald," Omaha, Nebraska, 22 February 1948, page 32 BoxRec http://boxrec.com/boxer/47141.

56. FHL Microfilm 1877080.

57. Year: 1930; Census Place: Alliance, Box Butte, Nebraska; Roll: 1266; Page: 4B; Enumeration District: 0003; Image: 861.0; FHL microfilm: 2341001.

58. Year: 1940; Census Place: Alliance, Box Butte, Nebraska; Roll: T627_2237; Page: 9B; Enumeration District: 7-3B

59. United States, Selective Service System. *World War I Selective Service System Draft Registration Cards, 1917-1918*. Washington, D.C.: National Archives and Records Administration. M1509, 4,582 rolls.

60. FindAGrave.

61. Year: 1920; Census Place: Gresham, Green, Kentucky; Roll: T625_572; Page: 16A; Enumeration District: 46; Image: 723.

62. Year: 1910; Census Place: Gresham, Green, Kentucky; Roll: T624_478; Page: 8B; Enumeration District: 0043; FHL microfilm: 1374491.

63. "Kentucky Marriages, 1785-1979," database, FamilySearch (https://familysearch.org/ark:/61903/1:1:F49L-NDQ : 4 December 2014), Jessie Motley in entry for Virgil Motley and Minnie Pearl Motley, 31 Mar 1921; citing , reference 17; FHL microfilm 1,877,080.

64. Year: 1900; Census Place: Gresham, Green, Kentucky; Roll: 523; Page: 1A; Enumeration District: 0036; FHL microfilm: 1240523

65. Kentucky Death Certificate #9902.

66. 1870 U.S. census, population schedules. NARA microfilm publication M593, 1,761 rolls. Washington, D.C.: National Archives and Records Administration, n.d.Minnesota census schedules for 1870. NARA microfilm publication T132, 13 rolls. Washington, D.C.: National Archives and Records Administration, n.d.

67. Year: 1880; Census Place: Bowling Green, Warren, Kentucky; Roll: 444; Family History Film: 1254444; Page: 10C; Enumeration District: 226; Image: 0409

68. Ancestry Public Tree, Bishop Family Tree by Ruby Motley http://person.ancestry.com/tree/74559787/person/44313066560/facts.

69. National Archives and Records Administration (NARA); Washington, D.C.; Federal Mortality Census Schedules, 1850-1880, and Related Indexes, 1850-1880; Archive Collection: T655; Archive Roll Number: 15; Census Year: 1869; Census Place: Precinct 2, Green, Kentucky; Page: 519

70. National Archives and Records Administration. U.S., Civil War Pension Index: General Index to Pension Files, 1861-1934 [database on-line]. Provo, UT, USA: Ancestry.com Operations Inc, 2000.

Original data: *General Index to Pension Files, 1861-1934*. Washington, D.C.: National Archives and Records Administration. T288, 546 rolls.

71. Ancestry.com. *U.S., Colored Troops Military Service Records, 1863-1865* [database on-line]. Provo, UT, USA: Ancestry.com Operations Inc, 2007. Original data: Compiled Military Service Records of Volunteer Union Soldiers. The National Archives at Washington, D.C.

72. Kentucky Birth Records, 1847-1911, http://interactive.ancestry.com/1213/
KYVR_994036-0264/307366?backurl=http%3a%2f%2fsearch.ancestry.com%2fcgi-
bin%2fsse.dll%3fdb%3dKYbirths%26gss%3dsfs28_ms_db%26new%3d1%26rank%3d1%26msT%3d1%
26MS_AdvCB%3d1%26gsln%3dMotley%26gsln_x%3dNP%26msbpn__ftp%3dGreen%2520County%2
52C%2520Kentucky%252C%2520USA%26msbpn%3d1206%26msbpn_PInfo%3d7-
%257C0%257C1652393%257C0%257C2%257C0%257C20%257C0%257C1206%257C0%257C0%257
C0%257C%26msbpn_x%3d1%26msbpn__ftp_x%3d1%26_83004002%3dblack%26_83004002_x%3d1
%26MSAV%3d2%26uidh%3dpa1&backlabel=ReturnSearchResults.

73. Year: 1850; Census Place: District 1, Green, Kentucky; Roll: M432_202; Page: 106B; Image: 218.

Charles Alfred Brown

Charles Alfred Brown came to Dawson Co., Nebraska from Canada, settling with other blacks who had journeyed from Canada. He was born 5 October 1864 in North Buxton, Ontario, Canada to Thomas Brown and Margaret Walker.

His wife was Mary Eliza Pierce who was born 24 May 1864 in Tilbury, Ontario, Canada. They were married on 22 April 1888 in Kent, Ontario, Canada. Mary Eliza was the daughter of Job and Cynthia Pierce. 1 Charles died 15 January 1946 in Hill City, Graham Co., Kansas. Mary Eliza died 28 March 1969 in Hill City, Graham Co., Kansas. They are both buried in the Hill City Cemetery, Hill City, Graham Co., Kansas. 2

Charles and Mary migrated from Canada to Nebraska shortly after their marriage. Their daughter Evedelle is shown on the 1900 US Census as born November 1889 in Nebraska.

1900 US Census, Dawson Co., Nebraska, Logan Prect., ED 93, Page 4B 3
72-72 Charles A. Brown, black, b. Oct 1867, 32, married 11 years, b. Canada,
        father b. KY, mother b. OH, farmer
Mary E., wife, black, born May 1869, 5 children 5 living, b. Canada, both parents
        b. OH
Evedelle C., daughter, black, b. Nov. 1889, 10, b. NE, at school
Loyola A., son, black, b. Oct. 1891, 8, b. NE at school
Bertha L., daughter, black, b. July 1894, 5, b. NE at school
Neil D., son, black, b. Feb 1898, 2, b. NE
Vergil E., son, black, b. May 1900 1/12, b. NE

Between 1906 and 1910, Charles A. Brown and his family moved to Graham Co., Kansas.

1910 US Census, Graham Co., Kansas, Hill City Township, ED 48, Page 8B 4
176-180 Charles A. Brown, mulatto, 42, married 22 years, b. Canada, father b.
        KY, mother b. OH, operator, farm
Mary E., wife, mulatto, 40, married 22 years, b. NE, both parents b. Canada
Evedella, daughter, mulatto, 20, single, b. NE, father b. Canada, mother b. NE
Loyola, daughter, mulatto, 18, b. NE, father b. Canada, mother b. NE
Bertha, daughter, mulatto, 15, b. NE, father b. Canada, mother b. NE
Neil, son, mulatto, 12, b. NE, father b. Canada, mother b. NE

Virg S., son, mulatto, 10, b. NE, father b. Canada, mother b. NE
Mabel, daughter, mulatto, 6, b. NE, father b. Canada, mother b. NE
Thomas, son, mulatto, 4, b. NE, father b. Canada, mother b. NE

[Note: on the 1900 US Census, Mary E. Brown is shown as born in Canada. The child Loyola is shown as a male on the 1900 US Census and as a female on the 1910 US Census.]

The following are the known children of Charles Afred Brown and Mary Eliza Pierce.

1. Evedelle/Evadella C. Brown, born November 1889 in Nebraska
2. Loyola A. Brown, born October 1891 in Nebraska (female)
3. Bertha L. Brown, born July 1894 in Nebraska
4. Neil Dowl Brown, born 13 February 1899 in Dawson Co., Nebraska
5. Virgil Touceant Brown, born 4 May 1900 in Nebraska
6. Mabel Brown, born about 1904 in Nebraska
7. Thomas Brown, born about 1906 in Nebraska

Evedelle/Evadella C. Brown, daughter of Charles Alfred Brown and Mary Eliza Pierce, was born in November of 1889 in Nebraska. She married Edd B. Williams who was born in March of 1886 in Kansas.

Bertha L. Brown, daughter of Charles Alfred Brown and Mary Eliza Pierce, was born in July of 1894 in Nebraska. She married William Alfred Schnebley. He was born 11 June 1892 in Kansas.

Neil Dowl Brown, son of Charles Alfred Brown and Mary Eliza Pierce, was born 13 February 1899 in Dawson Co., Nebraska and died on 13 March 1986 in Denver, Colorado. He was buried in the Hill City Cemetery, Hill City, Graham Co., Kansas. Neil married Anna Belle Jennings who was born about 1898 in Kansas. He filed his World War I Draft Registration in Hill City, Graham Co., Kansas on 12 September 1918. He was living there and shown as a school teacher. His nearest relative was his father, Charlie A. Brown of Hill City. Neil enlisted in the US Army on 1 October 1918 and was discharged on 21 December 1918. 5

Virgil Toceant Brown, son of Charles Alfred Brown and Mary Eliza Pierce, was born 4 May 1900 in Nebraska. He died in 1945 in Olathe, Johnson Co., Kansas and was buried in the Hill City Cemetery, Hill City, Graham Co., Kansas. Virgil filed his World War I Draft Registration in Graham Co., Kansas on 12 September 1918. He was a resident of Hill City, farming for his father and also a student. He listed his mother as his nearest relative. 6

Thomas Brown was born about 1810 in North Buxton, Ontario, Canada. He was the son of Hezekiah and Daphne Brown. Thomas married Margaret Walker, daughter of Stewart and Ann Walker. She was born about 1840 in Ohio and died 15 May 1921 in North Buxton, Ontario, Canada. Thomas died 13 October 1889 in North Buxton, Ontario, Canada. They were parents of the following known children.

1. Charles Alfred Brown, born 5 October 1864 in North Buxton, Ontario, Canada
   (see above)
2. Charlotte Ann Brown, born February 1874 in Canada

Charlotte Ann Brown, daughter of Thomas Brown and Margaret Walker, was born in February of 1874 in Canada. She married Alpheus Gregory Prince. They lived for a while in Illinois and then returned to Canada. They were living in Ontario, Canada by 1911 and appear to have had no children.

1900 US Census, Cook Co., Illinois, Chicago, Ward 34, ED 1088, Page 6B   7

126 — Alpheus G. Prince, black, born April 1867, 33, married 4 years, b. Canada,
      both parents b. Canada, came to US in 1874; naturalized, janitor
Lottie A., wife, black, b. February 1874, 26, married 4 years, 0 children, 0 living,
      b. Canada, father b. VA mother b. OH, came to US in 1887

Hezekiah Brown, father of Thomas Brown, was born about 1790 in Kentucky. His wife Daphne was born about 1790, probably in Kentucky.

1. Archives of Ontario; Toronto, Ontario, Canada; *Registrations of Marriages, 1869-1928*; Series: *MS932*; Reel: *60*
2. FindAGrave http://www.findagrave.com
3. Year: 1900; Census Place: Logan, Dawson, Nebraska; Roll: 922; Page: 4B; Enumeration District: 0093; FHL microfilm: 1240922
4. Year: 1910; Census Place: Hill, Graham, Kansas; Roll: T624_440; Page: 8B; Enumeration District: 0048; FHL microfilm: 1374453
5. Registration State: *Kansas;* Registration County: *Graham;* Roll: *1643518* Ancestry.com. *U.S., Department of Veterans Affairs BIRLS Death File, 1850-2010* [database on-line]. Provo, UT, USA: Ancestry.com Operations, Inc., 2011
6. Registration State: *Kansas;* Registration County: *Graham;* Roll: *1643518*
7. Year: 1900; Census Place: Chicago Ward 34, Cook, Illinois; Roll: 289; Page: 6B; Enumeration District: 1088; FHL microfilm: 1240289

Clem Deaver

Many accounts, published, not published and on Internet indicate that a railroader named Clem Deaver, is credited with being the first black person to file for land under the Kinkaid Act in Cherry Co., Nebraska. The Kinkaid Act went into effect in June 1904. According to the stories, Clem journeyed from Seneca in Thomas Co., Nebraska to the land office in Valentine, Cherry Co., Nebraska to file for land.

Once there he learned that approximately 50,000 acres of unclaimed land was available ten miles northwest of a settlement known as Brownlee. The land was along the North Loup River. He returned to Seneca and relayed this information to "his people" living in Nebraska. Initial settlements began in 1907. After his efforts, Clem Deaver, dropped out of sight.

Who was Clem Deaver? Was he black? What was his interest in the land? Finding him in the 1900 and 1920 enumerations in Omaha, Nebraska, along with his occupations, raises questions about his race and interest in the land.

1900 US Census, Douglas Co., Nebraska, Omaha, Ward 8, ED 87, Page 6A 1
2114 Chicago Street
94-99 David Deaver, white, b. August 1864, 35, married 11 years, b. OH, both
      parents b. LA, newspaper editor
Theresa, wife, white, b. August 1869, 30, married 11 years, 2 children, 2 living, b.
      NE, both parents b. Ireland
Quinton, son, b. Dec 1889, 10, b. NE, father b. OH, mother b. MO, at school
Blanche, daughter, b. Sept 1892, 7, b. NE father b. OH, mother b. MO, at school

1910 US Census, Douglas Co., Nebraska, Omaha, Ward 4, ED 27, page 3B 2
520 So. 21st Avenue
62-68 D. Clem Deaver, white, 45, married 21 years, b. OH, both parents b. OH,
      agent, railroad

Theresa, wife, white, 40, married 21 years, 2 children, 2 living, b. MO, both
    parents b. Ireland
Quintin, son, white, 20, single, b. NE, father b. OH, mother b. MO, claim clerk,
    railroad
Blanche, daughter, white, 17, single, b. NE, father b. OH, mother b. MO, student
Edward Devorak, lodger, white, 32, single, b. IA, parents b. unknown, accountant

David Clement "Clem" Deaver was born 28 August 1864 in Perry Co., Ohio. He came to
Omaha, Douglas Co., Nebraska in about 1887. By 1900 he was employed as a newspaper editor. His
next position was an immigrant agent for the Burlington Railroad that was developing westward through
Nebraska and into Wyoming. Therefore, he was instrumental in locating land and promoting settlement
through the sandhills of Nebraska. He was not black, but at some point either contacted black people in
Dawson Co., Nebraska about the availability of land, or else they had heard about his promotion of land.
There are no federal government records that indicate he purchased land for himself in Cherry Co.,
Nebraska.

Deaver was one of the founders of the populist party and prominent up to the time they affiliated
in 1900 with the democratic party. In 1892 he was a candidate for Congress and in 1900 he supported
President McKinley who appointed him as receiver of the land office in O'Neill, Holt Co., Nebraska.
Congressman Kinkaid who promoted the Kinkaid Act of 1904, was from O'Neill. In 1907 President
Theodore Roosevelt reappointed Deaver to the same position, but he resigned. At that time he accepted
the office of land and colonization agent for the Burlington and Missouri Railroad. 3

On 22 February 1914 he died of a heart attack in Omaha, Douglas Co., Nebraska and was buried
in the Holy Sepulchre Cemetery in Omaha. Posthumously in 1917, a town in the Big Horn Basin in
Wyoming was named in his honor as Deaver, Wyoming.

1. Year: 1900; Census Place: Omaha Ward 8, Douglas, Nebraska; Roll: 925; Page: 6A; Enumeration
District: 0087; FHL microfilm: 1240925
2. Year: 1910; Census Place: Omaha Ward 4, Douglas, Nebraska; Roll: T624_843; Page: 3B;
Enumeration District: 0027; FHL microfilm: 1374856
3. *Omaha Memories* by Edward Francis Morearty

Cole and Johnson

Lloyd M. Cole was a long-time employee of Bernie's Hardware Store and Newberry's Hardware
in Alliance, Nebraska, working in the hardware and paint departments. He was well known throughout
the community. Lloyd was born on 16 March 1919 at Smithton, Pettis Co., Missouri. His parents were
Eddie "Ed" Cole and Betty Duvall. Lloyd married Ophelia Beckett who was born 28 November 1915 in
Petty, Lamar Co., Texas to Joe Beckett and Rosie Johnson. They were married on 8 August 1952 in
Lincoln, Lancaster Co., Nebraska. Lloyd died on 5 March 1982 at the Box Butte General Hospital in
Alliance, Nebraska and was buried in the Alliance Cemetery. Ophelia died on 24 March 2013 in the Box
Butte General Hospital and was also buried in the Alliance Cemetery.

Pettis Co., Missouri is located in the middle of the State. In the years after the Civil War the state
of Missouri was split in two with regard to the slavery issue. The Battle of Sedalia was fought 14-15
October 1864 when blacks assisted in building the earthen barricade stretching in an arc north of the
railroad tracks close to Main Street in Sedalia. Under the mandate of General Jeff Thompson of the
Confederate Army, they were executed and their shanties were buried. 1

Eddie "Ed" Cole, father of Lloyd M. Cole was born 3 August 1883 at Beaman, Pettis Co.,

Missouri to George C. Cole and Matilda Williams. Ed married Betty Duvall who was born 20 November 1895 in Smithton, Pettis Co., Missouri, daughter of Joseph Benjamin "Joe" Duvall and Ellen Anderson. Ed Cole died 13 February 1938 in Sedalia, Pettis Co., Missouri. Betty died 16 May 1961 in Sedalia, Pettis Co., Missouri. According to her death certificate, she died at home at 204 E. Jefferson in Sedalia, Missouri. She was a house maid in a private family. She died of coronary occlusion. Both Edward and Betty Cole were buried in the Glenwood Cemetery in Sedalia, Pettis Co., Missouri. 2 On the 1920 US Census of Pettis Co., Missouri Ed and Betty were living close to Ellen Duvall, Betty's mother who was a widow.

1920 US Census, Pettis Co., Missouri, Bowling Green Twp., ED 126   3
18-18 Ed Cole, rents, black, 42, b. MO, both parents b. MO, farmer
Bettie, wife, black, 24, b. MO, both parents b. MO
Dorothy M., daughter, black, 7, b. MO, both parents b. MO
Alvin E., son, black, 3, b. MO, both parents b. MO
Loyd M., son, black, 1, b. MO, both parents b. MO

—-20 Ellen Duvall, rents, black, 50, widow, b. MO, both parents b. MO, washer
        woman, private families
Harrison, son, black, 21, single, b. MO, both parents b. MO, farm laborer
Mary, daughter, black, 19, single, b. MO, both parents b. MO
Mable, daughter, black, 17, b. MO, both parents b. MO
Gertrude, daughter, black, 14, b. MO, both parents b. MO
Eunice, daughter, black, 10, b. MO, both parents b. MO

Ed and Bettie Cole are shown on the 1930 US Census, still living in Pettis Co., Missouri, but had moved into the community of Sedalia.

1930 US Census, Pettis Co., Missouri, Second Ward, Sedalia, ED 20, Page 1A   4
401 Pettis
6-6 Eddie D. Cole, rents $15 month, negro, 40, married, married at age 23, b.
        MO, father b. VA, mother b. MO, janitor, private home
Bettie E., wife, negro, 32, married at age 18, b. MO, father b. VA, mother b. MO
Dorthy M., daughter, negro, 14, b. MO, both parents b. MO
Alvin E., son, negro, 11, b. MO, both parents b. MO
Loyd M., son, negro, 9, b. MO, both parents b. MO
William M., son, negro, 7, b. MO, both parents b. MO
George B., son, negro 3 5/12, b. MO, both parents b. MO
Anna J., daughter, negro, 1 7/12, b. MO, both parents b. MO
Matilda Wheeler, grandmother, negro, 96, widow, married at age 18, b. VA, both
        parents b. VA

Ed died in 1938 and Betty is shown on the 1940 US Census as a widow, living in Sedalia, Pettis Co., Missouri.

1940 US Census, Pettis Co., Missouri, Sedalia, ED 80-21, Page 4B   5
400 No. Washington
Betty D. Cole, informant, negro, 43, widow, 2 years high school, b. MO, same
        house on 1 April 1935, seamstress, works at sewing room
Alvin E., son, negro, 22, single, 3 years high school, b. MO, same house on 1
        April 1935
Wm. M., son, negro, 17, 1 year high school, b. MO, same house on 1 April 1935

George B., son, negro, 13, 8th grade, b. MO, same house on 1 April 1935
Anna J., daughter, negro, 10, 5th grade, b. MO, same house on 1 April 1935
Ellen Duvall, mother, negro, 65, widow, 0 schooling, b. MO, same house on 1
      April 1935

George C. Cole and Matilda Williams were married on 30 October 1873 in Pettis Co., Missouri. The marriage was solemnized by Rev. J.M. Hawkins and returned to the Pettis County courthouse for recording on 10 November 1873. This is evidence that they married, however, census emunerations confuse the name issue. Edward Cole's grandmother was Matilda Wheeler. 6

1880 US Census, Pettis Co., Missouri, Bowling Green Twp., ED 119, page 118A   7
175-189 Tilda Wheeler, black, 45, widow, farming, b. VA, father b. VA, mother b.
    KY
 Joe, son, black, 30, single, tends farm, b. MO, father b. VA, mother b. KY
Jessie, son, black, 5, son, b. MO, father b. VA, mother b. KY
Mattilda, daughter, 26, single, b. MO, father b. VA, mother b. KY
Authur, son, black, 6, b. MO, father b. VA, mother b. KY
Eddie, son, black, 2, b. MO, father b. VA, mother b. KY
Bob, son, black, 12, b. MO, father b. VA, mother b. KY

On the 1900 US Census, Edward Cole is shown living with an uncle, Jesse Wheeler in Pettis Co., Missouri. His grandmother Matilda Wheeler is in the household, but his mother is not there. On the 1910 US Census, he is living with his grandmother, Matilda Wheeler. On the 1920 US Census, Matilda Wheeler was living alone. As shown above, Matilda was living with her grandson, Eddie D. Cole and his wife Betty Duvall on the 1930 US Census.

1900 US Census, Pettis Co., Missouri, Bowling Green Twp., ED 94, Page 4B   8
76-76 Jesse Wheeler, black, b. Jan 1876, 24, married, married 3 years, b. MO,
      father b. TN, mother b. VA, farmer
Emma, wife, black, b. Oct 1876, 23, married 3 years, 3 children, 1 living, b. MO,
      father b. MO, mother b. VA, school teacher
Jesse C., son, black, b. July 1899, 11/12, b. MO, both parents b. MO
William, nephew, black, b. July 1891, 8, b. MO, father b. VA, mother b. MO
Edward Cole, nephew, b. Aug 1876, 23, single, b. MO, both parents b. MO
Matilda Wheeler, mother, b. Jan 1833, 67, widow, 8 children, 6 living, b. VA,
      both parents b. VA

1910 US Census, Pettis Co., Missouri, Bowling Green Twp., ED 110, Page 7A   9
137-146 Matilda Wheeler, black, 77, widow, 8 children, 6 living, b. VA, both
      parents b. VA, laborer, wash woman
Eddie Cole, grandson, black, 33, b. MO, father b. AR, mother b. unknown, no
      occupation

1920 US Census, Pettis Co., Missouri, Bowling Green Twp., ED 126, Page 7A   10
Matilda Wheeler, owns, free, black, b. Jan 1833, 75, widow, b. VA, both parents b.
    VA

The death certificate for Matilda Wheeler indicates that she died at Sedalia, Pettis Co., Missouri on 5 April 1934 of angina pectoris, myocraditis. She was the widow of Thomas Wheeler, born 3 January 1833, making her 101 years, 3 months and 2 days of age. She was born at Lynchburg, Virginia, parents unknown. The informant was Jessie Wheeler. She was buried in the Providence Baptist Church Cemetery at Smithton, Pettis Co., Missouri on 8 April 1934. 11

It is from the death certificate of Thomas and Matilda Wheeler's son Jesse, that we learn more about Matilda. Jesse died at the Sedalia Nursing Home on 4 February 1958. He was born at Beaman, Pettis Co., Missouri on 1 January 1876 to Thomas Wheeler and Matilda Majors. 12

On the 1870 US Census there is a Melinda Majors living in the household of Eliza Majors, male, white, in Pettis Co., Missouri. The names Melinda and Matilda are often confused.

1870 US Census, Pettis Co., Missouri, Blackwater Twp., Page 23, PO Ionia City   13
151-151 Eliza Majors, white, 44, male, farmer $600, b. MO
Sarah, white, 35, keeping house, b. MO
Mary E., white, 21, b. MO
Susan, white 19, b. MO
Benjamin, white, 15, b. MO
Rebecca, white, 13, b. MO
William, white, 9, b. MO
Melinda Majors, 32, black, housekeeping, b. NC

As for Eddie Cole's father, George Cole, he most likely was George Cole living in the household of Thomas Wheeler on the 1870 US Census, Pettis Co., Missouri. He is shown as age 28, so would have been of an appropriate age to have married Matilda Wheeler three years later. According to family records, George C. Cole was born in Forsyth, Taney Co., Missouri. If correct, this enumeration would make his year of birth at approximately 1842. He either died or separated from Matilda, his wife, shortly after 1878. They had a son, Arthur Cole, born in about 1874 and Edward or Eddie born in 1878. What cannot be explained is that Matilda Wheeler Cole appears to have taken back her maiden name of Wheeler. Nothing further is known about Arthur Cole.

The obituary for George C. Cole can be found in the newspaper, *Sedalia Capital,* Sedalia, Missouri, Saturday, 2 June 1928. The confusing part of this is that his mother is shown as Mrs. Matilda Wheeler, who was actually his mother-in-law.

"George C. Cole, aged 75 years, well known negro and a former Sedalia resident, died at 9 o'clock Thursday night at the General Hospital in Kansas City. Fred Ferguson, local undertaker, will make a trip to Kansas City for the body which will be brought here for burial. No arrangements for the funeral have been made. Cole is survived besides his mother, Mrs. Matilda Wheeler, almost a hundred years old, of this city, by two brothers and two sisters."

George Cole's death certificate indicates that he died on 31 May 1928 in the Old City Hospital in Kansas City, Jackson Co., Missouri. His birth is indicated as 15 April 1855 in Missouri. Only his father, Henry Cole, born in Missouri, is listed. George's statistics indicate that he was married, colored and a carpenter. The Old City Hospital, located at 2444 Highland, supplied the information. George died of hypostatic lobar pneumonia and was buried on 2 June 1928 in Beaman, Pettis Co., Missouri. 14

Old City Hospital in Kansas City was originally the Kansas City Municipal Hospital, located on Holmes Street, overlooking the Belt railroad tracks. It was built in 1873 and cared for whites and non-whites. 15

Duvall

Betty Duvall who married Eddie "Ed" Cole on 18 Nov 1912, was the daughter of Joseph Benjamin "Joe" Duvall and Ellen Anderson. Betty and Ed were parents of Lloyd Cole who lived in Alliance, Nebraska. Betty was born 20 November 1895 in Smithton, Pettis Co., Missouri and died 16 May 1961 in Sedalia, Pettis Co., Missouri, buried in Glenwood Cemetery, Sedalia, Pettis Co., Missouri.

More information on the Duvalls can be found on census enumerations. On the 1900 US Census, the enumerator mis-calculated many of the dates.

1900 US Census, Pettis Co., Missouri, Bowling Green Twp., ED 94, Page 1B   16
13-13 Joseph Duval, black, b. Jan 1845, 55, married 11 years, b. VA, both parents
       b. VA, farmer
Ella, wife, black, b. Jan 1875, 25, married 11 years, 4 children, 4 living, b. MO,
       both parents b. KY
William, son, black, b. July 1890, 9, b. MO, father b. VA, mother b. MO
George, son, black, b. Jan 1895, 5, b. MO, father b. VA, mother b. MO
Bettie, daughter, black, b. Feb 1897, 3, b. MO, father b. VA, mother b. MO
Harrison, son, black, b. Feb 1898, 2, b. MO, father b. VA, mother b. MO

1910 US Census, Pettis Co., Missouri, Bowling Green Twp., ED 110, Page 3B   17
60-60 Joe B. Duvall, black, 56, married 20 years, b. VA, both parents b. VA
       farmer
Ellen, wife, black, 36, married 20 years, 9 children, 9 living, b. MO, nothing
       shown for parents
William, son, black, 18, b. MO, father b. VA, mother b. MO, farmer
Harrison, son, black, 11, b. MO, father b. VA, mother b. MO
Bettie, daughter, black, 14, b. MO, father b. VA, mother b. MO
Mary, daughter, black, 9, b. MO, father b. VA, mother b. MO
Mabel, daughter, black, 7, b. MO, father b. VA, mother b. MO
Gertrude, daughter, black, 5, b. MO, father b. VA, mother b. MO
Baby, daughter, black, 8/12, b. MO, father b. VA, mother b. MO

Joseph Duvall died sometime between 1910 and 1920. His wife, Ellen, is shown as a widow on the 1920 US Census, living next door to her daughter Bettie and husband, Ed Cole. On the 1930 US Census, Ellen was living in Sedalia with two daughters in her household. The census enumerator has several household on various streets attached to an Alvin W. Gamber who is white and not living near them.

1920 US Census, Pettis Co., Missouri, Bowling Green Twp., ED 126, page 1B   18
20 Ellen Duvall, rents, black, 50 widow, b. MO, both parents b. MO, washer
       woman, private family
Harrison, son, black, 21, single, b. MO, both parents b. MO, farm laborer
Mary, daughter, black, 19, b. MO, both parents b. MO
Mable, daughter, black, 17, b. MO, both parents b. MO
Gertrude, daughter, black, 14, b. MO, both parents b. MO
Eunice, daughter, black, 10, b. MO, both parents b. MO

1930 US Census, Pettis Co., Missouri, Sedalia, ED 20, Page 9B   19
401 Pettis
19-19 Ellen Duvall, negro, 58, widow, married at age 21, b. MO, both parents b.
       MO
Eunice L., negro, 19, single, b. MO, both parents b. MO, maid, private family
Gertrude J., negro, 22, single, b. MO, both parents b. MO, maid, private family

According to the World War I Draft Registration of Harrison Jessie Duvall, he was living at RR No. 1, Smithton, Pettis Co., Missouri. He was 19 years old, born 15 September 1898 and a laborer. His nearest relative was Ellen Duvall of Smithton, Missouri. The registration was filed on 12 September 1918. [20]

The parents of Ellen Anderson Duvall were William "Will" Anderson and Nellie Hickman. Nellie was born 24 December 1853 in Louisville, Jefferson Co., Kentucky and died 1 June 1943 in Sedalia, Pettis Co., Missouri. According to Ellen's death certificate she is shown as born in 1873 and her tombstone indicates she was born in 1872. She was buried in Crown Hill Cemetery, Pettis Co., Missouri. The death certificate for Nellie Hickman Anderson lists no parents. She was also buried in the Crown Hill Cemetery. Proof of Nellie's maiden name can be found on the death certificate of her daughter, Josie Anderson Blackstone, died 8 July 1910 and shown as parents, William "Will" Anderson and Nellie Hickman.

Johnson

Ophelia, wife of Lloyd Cole was the daughter of Rosie Johnson who also lived in Alliance, Nebraska. According to Ophelia's obituary she was the daughter of Joe Beckett and Rosie Johnson, but raised by her grandmother Lizzy Williams. Her family lived in Clarksville, Red River Co., Texas then moved to Omaha where she attended school and married Lloyd Cole. Ophelia was born 28 November 1915 in Petty, Lamar Co., Texas. She was possibly married before her marriage to Lloyd Cole.

Rosie Johnson was in Alliance, Nebraska by 1930. Rose L. "Rosie" Johnson was buried in the Alliance Cemetery. She lived in Alliance for thirty-four years before her death in the Hemingford Nursing Home on 30 September 1963, at age 83. She is shown on census enumerations as follows.

1930 US Census, Box Butte County, Nebraska, Alliance, ED 2, Page 13A [21]
115 Sweetwater Ave.
257-277 James J. Wimes, rents $10 month, negro, 54, married, married at age 39,
      b. TN, both parents b. TN, porter, barber shop
Jessie, wife, negro, 48, married at age 23, b. CO, both parents b. KS
Rose Johnson, boarder, negro, 47, widow, married at age 19, b. AR, father b. AR,
      mother b. TN, servant, private family

1940 US Census, Box Butte Co., Nebraska, Alliance, ED 7-2B, Page 63B [22]
115 Sweetwater Ave.
Rosie Johnson, rents $4 month, informant, 64, widow, b. AR, same house 1 April
      1935, no occupation shown

1. Rose M. Nolen Black History Library, http://rosemnolenblackhistorylibrary.org.
2. Missouri Death Certificate #61-018491/.
3. Year: 1920; Census Place: Bowling Green, Pettis, Missouri; Roll: T625_939; Page: 1B; Enumeration District: 126; Image: 939
4. Year: 1930; Census Place: Sedalia, Pettis, Missouri; Roll: 1218; Page: 1A; Enumeration District: 0020; Image: 111.0; FHL microfilm: 2340953
5. Year: 1940; Census Place: Sedalia, Pettis, Missouri; Roll: T627_2139; Page: 4B; Enumeration District: 80-21
6. Black Marriage Registry 1865-1874, Pettis Co., Missouri, http://projects.cousin-collector.com/index.php/pettis-county/families/1071-black-marriage-registry-1865-1874.
7. Year: 1880; Census Place: Bowling Green, Pettis, Missouri; Roll: 708; Family History Film: 1254708; Page: 118A; Enumeration District: 119; Image: 0492
8. Year: 1900; Census Place: Bowling Green, Pettis, Missouri; Roll: 881; Page: 4B; Enumeration District: 0094; FHL microfilm: 1240881

9. Year: 1910; Census Place: Bowling Green, Pettis, Missouri; Roll: 1624_800; Page: 7A; Enumeration District: 0110; FHL microfilm: 1374813
10. Year: 1920; Census Place: Bowling Green, Pettis, Missouri; Roll: T625_939; Page: 7A; Enumeration District: 126; Image: 950
11. Missouri Death Certificate #13778.
12. Missouri Death Certificate # 2274.
13. Year: 1870; Census Place: Blackwater, Pettis, Missouri
14. Missouri Death Certificate #17429
15. Missouri Valley Special Collections http://localhistory.kclibrary.org/cdm4/item_viewer.php?
CISOROOT=/Local&CISOPTR=19783&CISOBOX=1&REC=4
16. Year: 1900; Census Place: Bowling Green, Pettis, Missouri; Roll: 881; Page: 1B; Enumeration District: 0094; FHL microfilm: 1240881
17. Year: 1910; Census Place: Bowling Green, Pettis, Missouri; Roll: T624_800; Page: 3B; Enumeration District: 0110; FHL microfilm: 1374813
18. Year: 1920; Census Place: Bowling Green, Pettis, Missouri; Roll: T625_939; Page: 1B; Enumeration District: 126; Image: 939
19. Year: 1930; Census Place: Sedalia, Pettis, Missouri; Roll: 1218; Page: 9B; Enumeration District: 0020; Image: 128.0; FHL microfilm: 2340953
20. Registration State: *Missouri;* Registration County: *Pettis;* Roll: *1683497*
21. Year: 1930; Census Place: Alliance, Box Butte, Nebraska; Roll: 1266; Page: 13A; Enumeration District: 0002; Image: 830.0; FHL microfilm: 2341001
22. Year: 1940; Census Place: Alliance, Box Butte, Nebraska; Roll: T627_2237; Page: 63B; Enumeration District: 7-2B

Conrad, Hunter and Roan Families

The Conrad and Hunter families came to Custer Co., Nebraska from North Carolina and their families, as slaves, undoubtedly connect to the Shores and Speese families as they came from the same general area.

Robert Conrad was born about 26 November 1849 in North Carolina. He married Sarah Levinia Conrad in about 1872. She was born on 25 Sept 1841 in Lewisville, Forsyth Co., North Carolina. Robert died on 17 April 1909 in Broken Bow, Custer Co., Nebraska and was buried in the Broken Bow Cemetery. Sarah died on 18 July 1925 in Hollywood, California and was buried in the Broken Bow Cemetery. She died at the home of her son in Hollywood, where she had gone in December of 1924 for a visit. 1

Robert and Sarah moved to Broken Bow, Custer Co., Nebraska in 1900. The follow census enumerations pertain to them.

> 1880 US Census, Forsyth Co., North Carolina, Vienna, ED 77, Page 338C   2
> 160-165 Robert Conrad, black, 28, farmer, b. NC, both parents b. NC
> Sarah L., wife, mulatto, 29, b. NC, both parents b. NC
> L.J., daughter, mulatto, 6, b. NC, both parents b. NC
> H.W., son, mulatto, 4, b. NC, both parents b. NC
> M.L. daughter, mulatto, 3, b. NC, both parents b. NC
> L.M., daughter, mulatto, 1, b. NC, both parents b. NC
> —-166 Jane Conrad, mulatto, 55, widow, keeping house, b. NC, both parents
>   b. NC
> M.C., mulatto, daughter, 11, b. NC, both parents b. NC
> M.A., mulatto, daughter, 19, housework, b. NC, both parents b. NC
> J.A., mulatto, grandson, 1, b. NC, both parents b. NC

1900 US Census, Custer Co., Nebraska, Broken Bow, ED 62, Page 1B   3

18-18   Robert Conrad, colored, b. Nov 1849, 50, married 26 years, b. NC, both
          parents b. NC
Sarah, wife, colored, b. Sept 1848, 51, married 26 years, 10 children, 8 living,
          b. NC, both parents b. NC
Eliza Jane, daughter, colored, b. Aug 1874, 25, single, b. NC, both parents b.
          NC
Amanda A., daughter, colored, b. July 1878, 21, single, b. NC, both parents b.
          NC
John A., son, colored, b. Nov 1881, 18, single, b. NC, both parents b. NC
Joseph T., son, colored, b. May 1886, 14, b. NC, both parents b. NC
Robert L., son, colored, b. April 1888, 12, b. NC, both parents b. NC
David C., son, colored, b. Jan 1892, 8, b. NC, both parents b. NC
Stella L., daughter, colored, b. Oct 1893, 6, b. NC, both parents b. NC

1910 US Census, Custer Co., Nebraska, Broken Bow, ED 71, Page 1A   4

9-9   Sarah L. Conrad, black, 50, widow, 10 children, 10 living, b. NC,
          father b. NC, mother b. VA
Eliza J., daughter, black, 28, single, b. NC, both parents b. NC, servant,
          private family
Stella L., daughter, black, 14, b. NC, both parents b. NC

1920 US Census, Custer Co., Nebraska, Broken Bow, Nebraska, ED 77, Page 3B   5

66-66 Sarah L. Conrad, owns, free, black, 60, widow, b. NC, father b. NC, mother
          b. VA, farmer
Ruth L. Shores, granddaughter, black, 16, b. NE, father b. US, mother b. NC
Felix F. Shores, grandson, black, 11, b. NE, father b. US, mother b. NC
Margaret M. Shores, granddaughter, 10, b. NE, father b. US, mother b. NC

Their children were born in North Carolina. They are as follows.

1. Henry Conrad, born about 1873 in North Carolina
2. Eliza Jane Conrad, born August 1874 in North Carolina
3. Amanda A. Conrad, born July 1878 in North Carolina
4. Minnie Conrad, born 13 September 1880 in North Carolina
5. John A. "Jack" Conrad, born November 1881 in North Carolina
6. Joseph Thomas "Joe" Conrad, born 14 May 1886 in North Carolina
7. Robert Lacy Conrad, born 16 March 1888 in North Carolina
8. Frank S. Conrad, born 15 July 1889 in North Carolina
9. David Clinton Conrad, born 11 January 1890 in North Carolina
10. Stella L. Conrad, born October 1893 in North Carolina

    Henry Conrad, son of Robert and Sarah Levinia Conrad, was born about 1873 in North Carolina.
He died in November of 1947 in Scottsbluff, Scotts Bluff Co., Nebraska. The city firemen were called to
a blaze at his home and found Henry on the bedroom floor. The bed and his clothing were on fire and the
kitchen floor splashed with kerosene. Two blacks were suspected of arson and the killing of Conrad.
They were arrested in Casper, Wyoming and returned to Scottsbluff, Nebraska. An empty kerosene can
was found at the death site and traced to a house where the two men, Harold Yancy of Louisville,
Kentucky and Otis Jenkins of Omaha, were staying. 6

    Eliza Jane Conrad, daughter of Robert Conrad and Sarah Levinia Conrad, was born in August of
1874 in North Carolina. Some researchers indicate she was the same person as her sister, Minnie Conrad,

who was born 13 September 1880 in North Carolina. By the time the 1910 US Census was taken she was not married, age 28 and living with her mother in Broken Bow, Custer Co., Nebraska (see census above). There is a Liza Conrad, colored, buried in the Broken Bow Cemetery. She was born about 1875 and died 21 December 1917 of kidney disease. She is known to be a sister to Lasey [sic] Conrad, so undoubtedly this is Eliza Jane Conrad, daughter of Robert Conrad and Sarah Levinia Conrad. 7

Amanda A. Conrad, daughter of Robert Conrad and Sarah Levinia Conrad, was born in July of 1878 in North Carolina. She married James A. Shores, son of Jeremiah and Rachel Shores. He was born about 1857 in North Carolina. Amanda died on 10 December 1910 in Denver, Colorado. She was pregnant with twins, who died at birth. Amanda died at the same time. She was buried in the Broken Bow Cemetery, Broken Bow, Custer Co., Nebraska. James A. Shores died on 29 January 1932 and was buried in the Riverside Cemetery, Denver, Denver Co., Colorado. 8 Refer to Shores and Speese in Volume 2.

Minnie Conrad, daughter of Robert Conrad and Sarah Levinia Conrad, was born 13 September 1880 in North Carolina. She married Henry Moss. They lived in Philadelphia, Pennsylvania and in 1964 she was living in New Jersey. In 1944 she was living in Pleasantville, Atlantic Co., New Jersey. The following enumeration strongly indicates that this is Minnie Conrad who married Henry Moss, however, she should have known that she was born in Nebraska and not in Illinois. Even more confusing is the fact that Minnie is shown as born in Virginia on the 1930 US Census.

> 1940 US Census, Atlantic Co., New Jersey, Egg Harbor Twp., ED 1-91, Page 11B   9
> owns $1,000
> Henry Moss, negro, 59, 6th grade, b. VA, same house 1 April 1935, laborer, road
>   construction
> Minnie, informant, wife, negro, 58, 6th grade, b. IL, same house 1 April 1935
> Bernice Henderson, daughter, negro, 28, married, spouse elsewhere, 4 years
>   high school, b. NE, same house 1 April 1935
> James Henderson, grandson, negro, 6, b. PA, same house 1 April 1935
> Dorothy Henderson, granddaughter, negro, 3, b. PA

> 1930 US Census, Atlantic Co., New Jersey, Egg Harbor City, ED 44, Page 2B   10
> 21-21 Henry Moss, rents $5 month, negro, 49, married at age 20, b. VA, both
>   parents b. VA, both parents b. VA, laborer, house wrecking
> Minnie, wife, negro, 48, married at age 19, b. VA, both parents b. VA

John A. "Jack" Conrad, son of Robert Conrad and Sarah Levinia Conrad, was born in November 1881 in North Carolina. He died in June of 1964 in a rest home in Broken Bow, Custer Co., Nebraska, buried in the Broken Bow Cemetery, Broken Bow. 11 John and his brothers, Lacy, Frank and Clinton were all working at the hotel in Broken Bow when the 1910 US Census was taken.

> 1910 US Census, Custer Co., Nebraska, Broken Bow, ED 72, Page 4A   12
> 85-86 Hotel - Main Street
> John Conrad, servant, black, 27, single, b. NC, both parents b. NC, cook,
>   hotel
> Lacey Conrad, servant, black, 25, single, b. NC, both parents b. NC, bus
>   driver
> Frank Conrad, servant, black, 24, single, b. NC, both parents b. NC, dining
>   room, hotel
> Clinton Conrad, servant, black, 19, single, b. NC, both parents b. NC, waiter,
>   hotel

Joseph Thomas "Joe" Conrad, son of Robert Conrad and Sarah Levinia Conrad, was born in May of 1886 in North Carolina. The following newspaper information indicates that he was supposed to have married Charlotte Ann Crawford.

Custer County Republican, Custer Co., Nebraska, 18 February 1909, page 3
"Joe Conrad 'colored' was arrested Friday by the Sheriff on the charge of bastardy, filed by Miss Charlotte Crawford 'colored.' The trial is set for March 15th and Conrad was allowed to go out on bail. His father put up his bond for his appearance on the 15th. Miss Crawford claims that she and Conrad were to be married about Christmas and she got ready to marry him, but he put off the marriage from time to time and finally left the country."

Joe Conrad ended up marrying Charlotte Crawford and on the 1920 US Census, they were living in Cherry Co., Nebraska. Between 1920 and 1930, the Conrads had moved to Lincoln, Lancaster Co., Nebraska.

1920 US Census, Cherry Co., Nebraska, Kennedy Prect., ED 54, Page 2B 13
47-47 Joseph Conrad, black, 36, b. NC, both parents b. NC, farmer
Charlotte A., wife, black, 36, b. Canada (American Citizen), father b. TN,
        mother b. NY
Joy L.A., daughter, black, 10, b. NE, father b. NC, mother b. Canada
Claud W.J., son, black, 9, b. NE, father b. NC, mother b. Canada

1930 US Census, Lancaster Co., Nebraska, Lincoln, Ward 3, ED 19, Page 18B 14
1970 U Street
383-446 Joseph Conrad, rents $30 month, negro, 45, married at age 23, b. NC,
        both parents b. NC, janitor, department store
Charlott, wife, negro, 47, married at age 23, b. Canada (American Citizen),
        father b. TN, mother b. NY, cook, restaurant
Claud, son, negro, 19, single, b. NC, father b. NC, mother b. Canada
Blossom Williams, roomer, female, negro, 69, single, b. KY, both parents b. KY
Joy Conrad, daughter, negro, 21, single, b. NC, father b. NC, mother b. Canada,
        artist

1940 US Census, Lancaster Co., Nebraska, Lincoln, Ward 4, ED55-28B, Page 15
        64B
#203 rents $10 month
Joseph Conrad, informant, negro, 45, widowed, 4th grade, b. NC, same place
        1 April 1935, janitor, department store

Charlotte Conrad, possibly the wife of Joseph Conrad, obtained land in Cherry Co., Nebraska under the Homestead Act. It consisted of 640 acres. The patent was issued on 13 June 1916 at the Valentine Land Office, Valentine, Nebraska. The land was located in the vicinity of DeWitty, Nebraska. It was located in 6th PM, Twp 28N, Range 31W, all of Section 14. 16

According to census enumerations, Joseph Conrad was born May 1886. Burial records indicate that he was born 14 May 1888. He died 20 August 1949 and was buried in the Yankee Hill Cemetery, Lincoln, Lancaster Co., Nebraska. There is no stone on his grave. His wife, Charlotte Ann Walker Conrad, was born 13 March 1883 and died 14 May 1934. She was buried in Wyuka Cemetery, Lincoln, Lancaster Co., Nebraska. 17

Robert Lacy Conrad, son of Robert Conrad and Sarah Levenia Conrad, was born in North

Carolina on 16 March 1886. This may be in error and probably should be 1888. He went by the name of Lacy. He filed his World War I Draft Registration in Broken Bow, Custer Co., Nebraska on 12 September 1918. He is shown as age 34, born 19 April 1888, working as a bus man, transfer line for A.J Elliott of Broken Bow. His nearest relative is shown as Hattie Conrad of Broken Bow. 18

Lacy married Naline Locke on 14 June 1927 in Grand Island, Hall Co., Nebraska. On 3 February 1936 he petitioned the District Court of Custer Co., Nebraska for a divorce from her. They had only one child, Zenobia Conrad, born 7 July 1928. He asked for custody of the child, due to his wife's infidelity. The original divorce petition was modified on 22 June 1936 when the court found that Naline was fit and proper to have custody of the child. The court stipulated $5 a month for child support, beginning on 15 September 1939. The child started to live with the mother on 10 July 1937.

He died on 11 August 1944, intestate, in Custer Co., Nebraska and was buried in the Broken Bow, Custer Co., Nebraska Cemetery. The appointed administrator stated that at the death of Lacy Conrad, he owned the south half of the northeast quarter of the northwest quarter of Section 29, Township 17, North, Range 20 West of the 6th PM, containing 20 acres of land. The child, Zenobia Conrad, was reported as married and Naline Locke Conrad had remarried to a Mr. Hunter. 19

Lacy filed his World War I Draft Registration in Custer Co., Nebraska on 27 April 1942, showing his name as Lacy R. Conrad of Broken Bow, Custer Co., Nebraska, born 19 April 1889 in Louisville [Lewisville], North Carolina. His nearest relative was his brother, Clinton Conrad of Broken Bow. Lacy was self-employed at the Lunch Room in Broken Bow. 20

Naline Locke Conrad married second to Harold Hunter. Depositions taken in Grand Island, Hall Co., Nebraska indicated she was born on 2 October 1910 at Atchison, Kansas to Caroll and Zenobia Locke. Harold B. Hunter was born 9 November 1905 in Pennsylvania to Robert and Maggie Hunter. He married earlier to Rosa Jackson and they were divorced. There is a marriage record in Omaha, Douglas Co., Nebraska for Harold B. Hunter age 53 and Naline F. Hunter, age 48, both of York, January 1960. 21 Naline Fannie Locke Conrad Hunter died on 16 January 2004 in Omaha, Douglas Co., Nebraska. Her husband, Harold Hunter had preceded her in death. Funeral services were held from St. John's African Methodist Episcopal (AME) Church in Omaha. 22

Robert Lacy Conrad was well known as the operator of a lunch wagon for many years in Broken Bow. He loved fine horses and was a trainer of good pacers and race horses. In addition Lacy operated a "hack" service from the railroad depot to hotels in Broken Bow. He began this with a team of spirited horses and a four wheel passenger hack. He met every train coming into town. Eventually he purchased a motor car. 23

Lacy and Naline were parents of only one child who lived. Zenobia was born in Custer Co., Nebraska on 7 July 1928. There is a Zenobia E. Jackson who divorced Junior S. Jackson in Omaha, Douglas Co., Nebraska in January of 1962. 24 Lacy and Naline also had a child who died in infancy in June of 1930 and another child who died in infancy in April of 1931, both of whom were buried in the Broken Bow Cemetery, Broken Bow, Custer Co., Nebraska. 25

Frank S. Conrad, son of Robert Conrad and Sarah Levinia Conrad, was born in North Carolina on 15 July 1889. He married Clara Chiles of Omaha, Nebraska, on 27 November 1919 in Broken Bow, Custer Co., Nebraska. She was age 23, black, born in Nebraska daughter of Samuel Sullivan and Lina Boine or Brown. The ceremony was witnessed by Clinton Conrad and E.S. Hammond, both of Broken Bow. 26

Frank and family are shown on the 1930 US Census. His sister Stella Talbert is also shown in

1930 in a tuberculosis sanatarium in Los Angeles. In 1940 Stella's daughters, Clara and Louise, were living with Frank and Clara.

> 1930 US Census, Los Angeles Co., California, Los Angeles, ED 292, Page 23B   27
> 1046 East 24th Street
> 302-457 Frank F. Conrad, negro, 37, married at age 26, b. SC, both parents b. SC
> Clara, wife, negro, 44, married at age 33, b. GA, both parents b. GA
> Louise Talbert, niece, negro, 9, b. NE, father b. SC, mother b. GA
> Naoma Talbert, niece, negro, 7, b. NE, father b. SC, mother b. GA
> Charles Phillips, uncle, negro, 60, married at age 25 b. GA, both parents b. GA
> Mary Phillips, wife, negro, 48, married at age 18, b. GA, both parents b. GA
> Stella Talbert, sister, negro, 33, married at age 21, b. SC, both parents b. SC

> 1940 US Census, Los Angeles Co., California, Los Angeles, ED 60-821, Page 3A   28
> 1046 East 24th Street   owns $5,000
> Frank S. Conrad, negro, 55, 4 years high school, b. NC, same place 1 April 1935,
>   boot black, shine stand
> Clara, informant, wife, negro, 50, 7th grade, b. GA, same place 1 April 1935
> Louise Talbert, niece, negro, 19, single, 5th grade, b. NE, same place 1 April 1935
> Naomi Talbert niece, negro, 17, single, 2 years high school, b. NE, same place
>   1 April 1935

Frank Conrad died on on 2 July 1986 in Los Angeles Co., California. His wife, Clara, died 29 August 1971 in Los Angeles Co., California. 29

David Clinton Conrad, son of Robert Conrad and Sarah Levinia Conrad, was born in North Carolina on 11 January 1890. He went by the name of Clinton. He filed is World War II Draft Registration in Broken Bow, Custer Co., Nebraska on 27 April 1942. The registration indicates he was Clinton David Conrad, 45, born 11 January 1897, a resident of Broken Bow. According to cemetery information, he was born 11 January 1890 and died 20 October 1985. He was buried in the Fairview Cemetery, Lincoln, Lancaster Co., Nebraska.   Clinton married Esther L. Shores, daughter of John Wesley Shores and Mildred Keyser. A 1923 newspaper article indicates that he was a chef at the Grand Central Hotel in Broken Bow. After spending a few days in Halsey, Nebraska, he returned home with a bride, Miss Esther Shores. She was a graduate of Broken Bow High School. Esther was born on 1 November 1899 in Nebraska. She and Clinton married on 27 January 1923 in Thedford, Thomas Co., Nebraska. Esther died 10 September 1971 and was buried in the Fairview Cemetery in Lincoln. Refer to Shores and Speese in Volume 2.

Clinton Conrad worked for many years as a chef at the Arrow Hotel in Broken Bow, beginning when it opened in 1928 until his retirement in 1966. After his retirement he moved to Lincoln, Nebraska. He was well known for his chez pie, a southern dish, which he served for almost forty years at the Arrow Hotel. He also made orange-creame fancy pies. His recipes were kept secret.

Stella Conrad, daughter of Robert Conrad and Sarah Levinia Conrad, was born in North Carolina in October of 1893. She married Dakota S. Talbert and according to obituaries of family members prior to 1930 she was living in Lincoln, Nebraska. Stella and Dakota are shown on the 1924 Lincoln, Nebraska City Directory as colored, living at 2235 S Street in Lincoln. He was a cook.

On the 1930 US Census she is shown twice. She is shown in the household of her brother, Frank Conrad in Los Angeles (see above) and also as Stella Talbert who was in the Olive View Sanatorium on Fort Hill Boulevard in Los Angeles, Los Angeles Co., California. She is shown as divorced, age 35, born North Carolina, both parents born North Carolina. 30 The Sanatorium is now Olive View - UCLA

Medical Center. It is located in the Sylmar neighborhood of Los Angeles. Originally it was a tuberculosis sanatorium founded on 27 October 1920. Stella died before August of 1944.

Stella and Dakota Talbert had Louise, born about 1911 in Nebraska and Naoma, born about 1913 in Nebraska.

Another Conrad family in Custer Co., Nebraska was William Conrad and his wife, Amelia Williams. They also came from Forsyth Co., North Carolina. While it is possible that William Conrad and Robert Conrad were related, it is also possible that they were born of different parents but on the same master's plantation.

William Conrad was born about 1857 in North Carolina, probably in Forsyth County. He married Amelia Lavina Williams on 28 December 1880 in North Carolina. She was born 12 October 1866 in Forsyth Co., North Carolina. Shortly after coming to Custer Co., Nebraska, William died on 13 January 1910 at Broken Bow, Custer Co., Nebraska, and was buried in the Broken Bow Cemetery. There is a marriage record for a Mrs. Melia Conrad to Bob Thomas on 22 December 1933 in Broken Bow, Custer Co., Nebraska. Bob Thomas was living in Broken Bow, age 33, born in Indiana, the son of Albert Thomas and Martha Williams. However, Amelia Lavina Williams Conrad died before 1933, so this is apparently a marriage for somebody else. 31 Amelia died on 28 May 1926 at Hastings, Adams Co., Nebraska and was buried in the Broken Bow Cemetery. The Conrads came to Nebraska in 1901, settling near Westerville in Custer County. In 1905 they moved to Broken Bow.

> 1910 US Census, Custer Co., Nebraska, Broken Bow, ED 72, Page 12B   32
> Campbell Street
> 272-283 Amelia Conrad, mulatto, 35, widow, 10 children, 7 living, b. NC,
>   b. NC, washer woman, working out
> Henry, son, mulatto, 24, single, b. NC, both parents b. NC, laborer, odd jobs
> Will W., son, 19, single, b. NC, both parents b. NC, laborer, odd jobs
> Arthur R., son, 14, b. NC, both parents b. NC, boot black, on streets
> Alma C., daughter, mulatto, 11, b. NC both parents b. NC
> Frank L., son, mulatto, 9, b. NC, both parents b. NC
> Sabra R., daughter, mulatto, 6, b. NE, both parents b. NC

> 1920 US Census, Custer Co., Nebraska, Broken Bow, ED 78, Page 22A   33
> 14th Avenue
> 97-99 Melia Conrad, owns, free, black, 47, widow, b. NC, both parents b. NC,
>   washer woman, private family
> Henry C., son, black, 34, single, b. NC, both parents b. NC, butcher, packing
>   house
> Winifred T., daughter, black, 9, b. NE, both parents b. NC
> —-100 William Jones, rents, black, 28, b. AR, both parents b. AR, laborer, garage
> Alma C. Jones, wife, black, 19, b. NC, both parents b. NC

There were reportedly eleven children born to William Conrad and Amelia Lavina Williams. The following are their known children.
1. Henry C. Conrad, born 31 August 1888 in North Carolina
2. William W. Conrad, born about 1891 in North Carolina
3. Arthur Robert Conrad, born 1 February 1896 in North Carolina
4. Alma C. Conrad, born about 1899 in North Carolina
5. Frank L. Conrad, born about 1901 in North Carolina
6. Sabra R. Conrad, born about 1904 in Nebraska

7. Winifred T. Conrad, born 4 December 1910 in Nebraska

Henry C. Conrad, son of William Conrad and Amelia Lavina Williams, was born 31 August 1888 in North Carolina. He registered for the World War I Draft in Douglas Co., Nebraska, filed on 12 September 1918. His residence is shown as 2306 No. 26th Street in Omaha and his birth date is shown as 31 August 1884. Henry was working as a butcher for the Armour Co. Pack House in South Omaha. His nearest relative was Amelia Conrad of Broken Bow, Nebraska. 34 When Henry filed his World War II Draft Registration he was living at 2831 Decatur St. in Omaha and still working for Armour Packing Co. at 28th & Q Streets in Omaha. His relative is shown as Mrs. Cora Conrad. Henry is shown as age 54, born 31 August 1888 in North Carolina. It was filed in Douglas County on 27 April 1942. 35

He is shown on the following enumerations, having moved from Custer County to Omaha, Nebraska by 1918.

1930 US Census, Douglas Co., Nebraska, Omaha, ED 16, Page 10B   36
2634 Corby Street
171-174 Henry Conrad, rents $15 month, negro, 40, married at age 37, b. NC,
         parents b. US, butcher, meat house
Cora, wife, negro, 40, b. MO, father b. MO, mother b. KY
Maxine Fields, granddaughter, negro, 7, b. MO, father b. NE, mother b. MO

1940 US Census, Douglas Co., Nebraska, Omaha, ED 94-31, Page 16B   37
2831 Decatur rents $15 month
Henry Conrad, negro, 50, 4th grade, b. NC, same place 1 April 1935, beef kill
         packing
Cora, informant, wife, negro, 52, 2 years high school, b. MO, same place 1 April
         1935

The Social Security Application and Claims Index shows that Henry Conrad was born 31 August 1888 and a life claim was filed on 8 November 1954. 38

Alma C. Conrad, daughter of William Conrad and Amelia Lavina Williams, was born in North Carolina in about 1899. She married William Eugene Jones in Broken Bow, Nebraska on 18 September 1919. According to their marriage record William was born in Kansas, the son of A. Jones and Emma Green. 39 William Jones was born 1 October 1892 in Joplin, Jasper Co., Missouri and died on 27 April 1933 in Broken Bow, Custer Co., Nebraska, buried in the Broken Bow Cemetery. Jones served in World War I for twenty-two months. From 1922 to 1925 Alma and William Jones lived in Kearney, Buffalo Co., Nebraska. Alma died in January of 1970 in Omaha, Douglas Co., Nebraska. 40 The Jones family are shown on the following census enumerations.

1930 US Census, Custer Co., Nebraska, Broken Bow, ED 9, Page 10A   41
219-263 William M. Jones, owns $500, negro, 37, married at age 27, b. MO,
         both parents b. MO, coml. ? of vegetables
Alma C., wife, negro, 29, married at age 19, b. NC, both parents b. NC
Clarence E., son, negro, 9, b. NE, father b. MO, mother b. NC
Maxine S., daughter, negro, 5, b. NE, father b. MO, mother b. NC
Donald M., son, negro, 2 3/12, b. NE, father b. MO, mother b. NC

1940 US Census, Custer Co., Nebraska, Broken Bow, ED 21-9, Page 61B   42
rents $2 month
Alma Jones, negro, 40, widow, 8th grade, b. NC, same house 1 April 1935,
         laundress, home

Bob, son, negro, 18, single, 3 years high school, b. NE, same house 1 April 1935
Maxine, daughter, negro, 15, 8th grade, b. NE, same house 1 April 1935
Donald, son, negro, 12, 5th grade, b. NE, same house 1 April 1935
Winifred, daughter, negro, 9, 4th grade, b. NE, same house 1 April 1935
Billy Jean, daughter, negro, 6, 0 grade, b. NE, same house 1 April 1935

The following children were born to Alma C. Conrad and William Eugene Jones.

1. Clarence E. Jones, born about 1921 in Nebraska; died after 1933
2. Robert Lawrence "Bobby" Jones, born 17 February 1922 in Broken Bow,
        Custer Co., Nebraska
3. Selina Maxine Jones, born about 1925 in Nebraska, married —- Scott
4. Donald M. "Don" Jones, born 7 November 1927 in Broken Bow, Custer Co.,
        Nebraska
5. Winifred Mamie "Winnie" Jones, born 30 May 1930 in Broken Bow, Custer
        Co., Nebraska
6. Billie Jean Jones, born about 1933 in Nebraska, married —- Young

Robert Lawrence "Bobby" Jones, son of Alma C. Conrad and William Eugene Jones, was born in Broken Bow, Custer Co., Nebraska on 17 February 1922. He graduated from Broken Bow High School in 1940 and was an outstanding athlete in basketball and football. After his graduation he attended Tuskegee Institute in Alabama and then joined the United States Navy, serving twenty years. Robert served aboard the *USS Spearfish* which took nurses and army doctors off the besieged Cooregidor in the Philippines. After retiring he worked for the *Omaha World Herald* in Omaha, Nebraska. He died on 2 January 2002 in Suffolk, Virginia. Robert married Gladys Giles and then had Phyllis, Zelma, Carlethia, Robert A. and Willie. 43

Donald M. "Don" Jones, son of Alma C. Conrad and William Eugene Jones, was born 7 November 1927 in Broken Bow, Custer Co., Nebraska. He graduated from Broken Bow High School. Don enlisted in the US Army in 1950. He was injured during the Korean War and honorably discharged on 17 July 1952. After his discharge Don worked for Swift Packing Company in Omaha, Nebraska for forty years. He died on 29 April 2008 in Omaha, Douglas Co., Nebraska and was buried in Forest Lawn Memorial Park, Omaha, Douglas Co., Nebraska. Don and his wife, Aline Black, had Joseph, Donald M., Jr, and Valerie. 44

Winifred Mamie "Winnie" Jones, daughter of Alma C. Conrad and William Eugene Jones, was born in Broken Bow, Custer Co., Nebraska on 30 May 1930. She graduated from Broken Bow High School. On 3 November 1962 she married Edward S. Johnson in Omaha, Douglas Co., Nebraska. They had one child, Edward O. Johnson, born 19 April 1966. Winifred worked for twenty-three years in the Omaha public school system. Edward S. Johnson died on 4 March 1993. Winifred died on 20 October 1996 and was buried in the Forest Lawn Memorial Park, Omaha, Douglas Co., Nebraska. 45

Arthur Conrad, son of William Conrad and Amelia Lavina Williams, was born 1 February 1896 in North Carolina. He died on 7 December 1974 in Omaha, Douglas Co., Nebraska. He was buried in the Veterans Section of Mt. Hope Cemetery in Omaha. Residents of Broken Bow called him "Rabbit Conrad." 46

Winifred T. Conrad, daughter of William Conrad and Amelia Williams, was born 4 December 1910 in Broken Bow, Custer Co., Nebraska. She married Rev. Trago O. McWilliams, son of Trago Travis McWilliams and Idabelle Elder. Refer to Corneal, Volume 1. They were married on 29 March 1928 in Council Bluffs, Pottawattamie Co., Iowa. Winifred and Trago had one child, Richard McWilliams. She died on 20 June 1929 and was buried in Wyuka Cemetery in Lincoln, Lancaster Co., Nebraska. Trago married second to Margaret Emily Stephens. He died on 30 December 1986 and was buried in the Fairview Cemetery in Lincoln, Lancaster Co., Nebraska. 47

Sabra Conrad was born in about 1849 in Lewisville, Forsyth Co., North Carolina. She married Pleasant "Pleas" Hunter. Most likely Sabra was a sister to Robert Conrad, also of Forsyth Co., North Carolina, who came to Custer Co., Nebraska. She married Pleas Hunter in Forsyth Co., North Carolina. He died there before April 1901 when Sabra arrived in Broken Bow, Custer Co., Nebraska. She died in Broken Bow on 24 April 1930 and was buried in the Broken Bow Cemertery. On the 1900 US Census, Sabre [sic] was living in the household of Charles Hayden in Forsyth Co., North Carolina. Her children are not in the household.

> 1900 US Census, Forsyth Co., North Carolina, Winston, Ward 1, ED 37, Page   48
>   12B
> 310-B Cherry St.
> 194-222 Charles Hayden, black, age unknown, b. NC, both parents b. NC,
>   laborer
> Mary, wife, black, age unknown, b. NC, both parents b. NC, cook
> Mattie, niece, black, age unknown, single, b. NC, both parents b. NC
> Sabre Hunter, boarder, black, age unknown, single, b. NC, both parents b. NC,
>   laborer
> Warren Dudley, boarder, black, b. 1846, 54, widowed, b. NC, both parents b.
>   NC, laborer

The following children were born to Sabra Conrad and Pleas Hunter. There may have been others who died young.

> 1. Mary Ella Hunter, born 25 July 1877 in North Carolina
> 2. Robert Hunter
> 3. Laura Hunter, died as a small child

Mary Ella Hunter, daughter of Sabra Conrad and Pleas Hunter, was born 25 July 1877 in Lewisville, Forsyth Co., North Carolina. 49 She married William Roan on 26 May 1898 in Winston, Forsyth Co., North Carolina. 50 Following an operation at a hospital in Hastings, Adams Co., Nebraska, Mary Ella Hunter Roan died there on 23 August 1920. 51 She was buried in the Broken Bow Cemetery, Custer Co., Nebraska.

Ella and William Roan are first shown on the 1910 US Census in Custer Co., Nebraska. On the 1920 US Census, Sabra is shown in the household of her daughter Ella Hunter Roan in Custer Co., Nebraska.

> 1910 US Census, Custer Co., Nebraska, Broken Bow, ED 72, Page 12B   52
> Miller Street
> 269-280 William Roan, mulatto, 33, married 11 years, b. NC, both parents b. NC,
>   laborer, odd jobs
> Ella, wife, mulatto, 34, married 11 years, 1 child, 1 living, b. NC, both parents b.
>   NC
> J. Paul, son, mulatto, 9, b. NC, both parents b. NC

> 1920 US Census, Custer Co., Nebraska, Broken Bow, ED 78, Page 22B   53
> 15th Avenue
> 103-106 William Roan, owns, free, mulatto, 44, b. NC, father b. NC, mother b.
>   VA, farmer

Ella, wife, black, 44, b. NC, both parents b. NC
John P., son, mulatto, 19, single, b. NC, both parents b. NC, cleaner, clothing
Sabra L. Hunter, mother, black, 69, widow, b. NC, both parents b. NC

North Carolina Conrads and Hunters

The following are possibilities for Robert Conrad and Sarah Lavenia Conrad in the 1870 US Census for Forsyth Co., North Carolina. Most likely Robert Conrad who settled in Custer Co., Nebraska, was the son of Wilson and Eliza Conrad. They had a daughter Sabra who is probably Sabra Conrad who married William Hunter and also went to Custer County. All of the Conrads may be related in some way.
54

1870 US Census, Forsyth Co., North Carolina, Vienna Twp., Page 5, PO Vienna
39-39 John Conrad, 51, black, farmer, b. NC
Lucy, 45, black, keeping house, b. NC
Tyon, 25, female, black, day laborer working, b. NC
Adda, 23, black, day laborer working, b. NC
Robert, 19, black, laborer on farm, b. NC
Rena, 14, female, black, b. NC
Rhoda, 6, b. NC

1870 US Census, Forsyth Co., North Carolina, Vienna Twp., Page 13, PO Vienna
104-104 Wilson Conrad, 48, black, farmer, b. NC
Eliza, 49, black, keeping house, b. NC
Sabra, 20, black, b. NC
Robert, 18, black, laborer on farm, b. NC
Amanda, 17, black, b. NC

1870 US Census, Forsyth Co., North Carolina, Vienna Twp., Page PO Vienna
126-126 Sandy Conrad, 50, black, farmer, b. NC
Jane, 45, black, keeping house, b. NC
Sarah, 18, black, b. NC
Fanny, 17, black, b. NC
Alexandra, 16, male, black, labor on farm, b. NC
Clinton, 13, black, b. NC
Ida, 12, black, b. NC
Eliza, 11, female, b. NC
Laura, 8, black, b. NC
Flora, 5, black, b. NC
Martha, 2, black, b. NC

While the age is different than what is usually shown for William Conrad who came to Custer Co., Nebraska, the William Conrad shown below on the 1870 US Census, is the only one in Forsyth Co., North Carolina. The same family is shown on the 1880 US Census and William would logically be in their household as he did not marry until October of that year. His wife, Amelia Lavina Williams cannot be found on any of these enumerations.

1870 US Census, Forsyth Co., North Carolina, Vienna Twp., PO Vienna 55
91-91 Adam Conrad, 35, black, miller, $35, b. NC
Martha, 35, black, keeping house, b. NC
Elijah, 14, black, labor on farm, b. NC
David, 12, black, labor on farm, b. NC

Louisa, 11, black, b. NC
John, 9, black, b. NC
William, 8, black, b. NC
George, 3, black, b. NC

1880 US Census, Forsyth Co., North Carolina, Vienna Twp., ED 77, Page 338D   56
167-178 A.A. Conrad, black, 45, farmer, b. NC, both parents b. NC
Martha, black, 45, wife, keeping house, b. NC, both parents b. NC
L.A., black, 21, daughter, b. NC, both parents b. NC
J.W., black, 19, son, farmer, b. NC, both parents b. NC
Wm. B., black, 17, son, b. NC, both parents b. NC
James, black, 2, son, b. NC, both parents b. NC

1. *Custer County Chief,* Broken Bow, Nebraska, 23 July 1925.
2. Year: 1880; Census Place: Vienna, Forsyth, North Carolina; Roll: 963; Family History Film: 1254963; Page: 338C; Enumeration District: 077; Image: 0177.
3. Year: 1900; Census Place: Broken Bow, Custer, Nebraska; Roll: 921; Page: 1B; Enumeration District: 0062; FHL microfilm: 1240921
4. Year: 1910; Census Place: Broken Bow, Custer, Nebraska; Roll: T624_841; Page: 1A; Enumeration District: 0071; FHL microfilm: 1374854
5. Year: 1920; Census Place: Broken Bow, Custer, Nebraska; Roll: T625_985; Page: 3B; Enumeration District: 77; Image: 127
6. *Custer County Chief,* Broken Bow, Nebraska, 6 November 1947.
7. Broken Bow Burials, Vital Statistics, Custer County Historical Society, Broken Bow, Nebraska
8. Records of burial, Denver Riverside Cemetery, FHL Film #2712.
9. Year: 1940; Census Place: Egg Harbor, Atlantic, New Jersey; Roll: T627_2302; Page: 11B; Enumeration District: 1-91
10. Year: 1930; Census Place: Egg Harbor City, Atlantic, New Jersey; Roll: 1309; Page: 2B; Enumeration District: 0044; Image: 529.0; FHL microfilm: 2341044
11. *Custer County Chief,* Broken Bow, Nebraska, 15 June 1964.
12. Year: 1910; Census Place: Broken Bow, Custer, Nebraska; Roll: T624_841; Page: 4A; Enumeration District: 0072; FHL microfilm: 1374854
13. Year: 1920; Census Place: Kennedy, Cherry, Nebraska; Roll: T625_981; Page: 2B; Enumeration District: 54; Image: 866
14. Year: 1930; Census Place: Lincoln, Lancaster, Nebraska; Roll: 1285; Page: 18B; Enumeration District: 0019; Image: 506.0; FHL microfilm: 2341020
15. Year: 1940; Census Place: Lincoln, Lancaster, Nebraska; Roll: T627_2253; Page: 64B; Enumeration District: 55-28B
16. U.S. Department of the Interior, Bureau of Land Records, General Land Office Records http://www.glorecords.blm.gov/details/patent/default.aspx?accession=533393&docClass=SER&sid=ktoeavar.4ed
17. FindAGrave http://www.findagrave.com.
18. Registration State: Nebraska; Registration County: Custer; Roll: 1711523; Draft Board: 9.
19. District Court, Custer County, Nebraska, Case No. 11,753, Appearance Docket 41, page 110.
20. United States, Selective Service System. *Selective Service Registration Cards, World War II: Fourth Registration.* Records of the Selective Service.
21. *Omaha World-Herald,* Omaha, Nebraska, 13 January 1960, page 34
22. *The Grand Island Independent*, Grand Island, Nebraska, January 2004
23. *The Custer County Chief,* Broken Bow, Nebraska 17 August 1944.
24. *Omaha World-Herald,* Omaha, Nebraska, 17 January 1962, page 48.

25. Broken Bow, Custer Co., Nebraska Cemetery Records, http://www.rootsweb.ancestry.com/~necuster/cmterys/bbcemc.html.

26. Custer County, Nebraska Marriage Book 10, page 562

27. Year: 1930; Census Place: Los Angeles, Los Angeles, California; Roll: 144; Page: 23B; Enumeration District: 0292; Image: 179.0; FHL microfilm: 2339879

28. Year: 1940; Census Place: Los Angeles, Los Angeles, California; Roll: T627_415; Page: 3A; Enumeration District: 60-821

29. California Death Certificates, http://vitals.rootsweb.ancestry.com/ca/death/search.cgi.

30. Year: 1930; Census Place: Los Angeles, Los Angeles, California; Roll: 156; Page: 9A; Enumeration District: 0605; Image: 391.0; FHL microfilm: 2339891.

31. Custer Co., Nebraska Marriage Book 11 page 457.

32. Year: 1910; Census Place: Broken Bow, Custer, Nebraska; Roll: T624_841; Page: 12B; Enumeration District: 0072; FHL microfilm: 1374854

33. Year: 1920; Census Place: Broken Bow, Custer, Nebraska; Roll: T625_985; Page: 22A; Enumeration District: 78; Image: 188

34. Registration State: *Nebraska;* Registration County: *Douglas;* Roll: *1711763;* Draft Board: *5.*

35. The National Archives at St. Louis; St. Louis, Missouri; Draft Registration Cards for Fourth Registration for Nebraska, 04/27/1942 - 04/27/1942; NAI Number: 598911; Record Group Title: Records of the Selective Service System; Record Group Number: 147.

36. Year: 1930; Census Place: Omaha, Douglas, Nebraska; Roll: 1273; Page: 10B; Enumeration District: 0016; Image: 651.0; FHL microfilm: 2341008

37. Year: 1940; Census Place: Omaha, Douglas, Nebraska; Roll: T627_2269; Page: 16B; Enumeration District: 94-31

38. Ancestry.com. *U.S., Social Security Applications and Claims Index, 1936-2007* [database on-line]. Provo, UT, USA: Ancestry.com Operations, Inc., 2015.

39. Custer Co., Nebraska Marriage Book 10, page 521.

40. obituary, William Eugene Jones, *The Custer County Chief,* Broken Bow, Nebraska, 4 May 1933

41. Year: 1930; Census Place: Broken Bow, Custer, Nebraska; Roll: 1270; Page: 10A; Enumeration District: 0009; Image: 136.0; FHL microfilm: 2341005

42. Year: 1940; Census Place: Broken Bow, Custer, Nebraska; Roll: T627_2242; Page: 61B; Enumeration District: 21-9

43. *Custer County Chief,* Broken Bow, Nebraska, 21 February 2002.

44. *Custer County Chief,* Broken Bow, Nebraska, 5 June 2008.

45. *Custer County Chief,* Broken Bow, Nebraska, 19 December 1996, page 2A.

46. obituary *The Omaha World-Herald*, Omaha, Nebraska, 9 December 1974.

47. FindAGrave.

48. Year: 1900; Census Place: Winston Ward 1, Forsyth, North Carolina; Roll: 1195; Page: 12B; Enumeration District: 0037; FHL microfilm: 1241195.

49. Burial Records, Broken Bow Cemetery, Broken Bow, Custer Co., Nebraska.

50. FHL Film #899604.

51. Death notice Mary Ella Hunter Roan, *Custer County Chief,* Broken Bow, Nebraska, 26 August 1920.

52. Year: 1910; Census Place: Broken Bow, Custer, Nebraska; Roll: T624_841; Page: 12B; Enumeration District: 0072; FHL microfilm: 1374854

53. Year: 1920; Census Place: Broken Bow, Custer, Nebraska; Roll: T625_985; Page: 22B; Enumeration District: 78; Image: 189.

54. NARA microfilm publication M593, 1,761 rolls. Washington, D.C.: National Archives and Records Administration, n.d.Minnesota census schedules for 1870. NARA microfilm publication T132, 13 rolls. Washington, D.C.: National Archives and Records Administration.

55. 1870 U.S. census, population schedules. NARA microfilm publication M593, 1,761 rolls. Washington, D.C.: National Archives and Records Administration, n.d.Minnesota census schedules for

1870. NARA microfilm publication T132, 13 rolls. Washington, D.C.: National Archives and Records Administration.
56. Year: 1880; Census Place: Vienna, Forsyth, North Carolina; Roll: 963; Family History Film: 1254963; Page: 338D; Enumeration District: 077; Image: 0178.

Ephraim Corneal

Ephraim Corneal who lived in Ward 2 of Alliance, was very popular and well-known. He was called "Eph" and at least one newspaper article referred to him as "Toad." His actual name was William Nelson Corneal.

He was born in Missouri on 26 June 1864 and early in life went with his parents to Kansas. They were farmers. In about 1884 he roamed about, going to Falls City, Nebraska; Wichita, Kansas; Kansas City; Lincoln and finally ended up at Cripple Creek where he spent three years as a special policeman.

In 1887, he married Mrs. Phannie Bolts (also shown as Botts) in Lincoln, Lancaster Co., Nebraska. She was born Phannie Stepney and had been married to Henry Bolts. Various articles in the *Omaha World Herald*, Omaha, Nebraska indicate that in the late 1890s the Corneals lived in Lincoln where he had a saloon. By 1900 they were living in Alliance, Nebraska.

> 1900 US Census, Box Butte Co., Nebraska, Alliance, Ward 2 ED 6, Sheet 21A 1
> 113-126 Ephraim Corneal, black, b. June 1863, 36, married 13 years, b. MO,
> both parents b. MO; saloon keeper
> Phannie, wife, black, b. December 1864, 35, 5 children, living, b. MO, both
>   parents b. MO
> Harry, black, b. October 1883, 17, single, b. KS, porter, barbershop
> Beulah, black, b. Nov. 1887, 12, b. NE, at school
> Grazie, black, b. March 1891, 9, b. NE, at school
> Sy H., black, brother, b. Oct. 1871, 28, single, b. MO, both parents b. Mo
>   porter, saloon

William (Ephraim) Corneal did porter work and tended a bar belonging to Henry C. Armstrong. Eventually Armstrong sold the bar to Corneal. 2 For three years prior to his death he had saloons in Sheridan and Crawford. *The Alliance Herald*, 19 March 1908, reported, " In March of 1908, W.N. Corneal, Jack Riordan and Everett Cook were arrested in Box Butte County for selling unbranded liquor."

Corneal and his family appear to have lived at various times in Alliance and also in Lincoln, perhaps going back and forth. Apparently Phannie and the children were not always with him when he shows up on city directories of Lincoln, Nebraska, Council Bluffs, Iowa, and St. Paul, Minnesota.

> 1893 Lincoln, Nebraska City Directory
> Benjamin Corneal, col'd. barber, A. Ivison
> Cyrus H. Corneal, col'd laborer, r. 931 N. 17th
> Fannie Corneal, col'd domestic, 1216 H
> Wm. H. Corneal, col'd barber, A. Ivison, rents 2232 O

> 1909 Council Bluffs, Iowa City Directory
> Benjamin F. Corneal (c), saloon, 1029 W. Broadway, lives at same
> Beulah L.S. Corneal, boards, 204 Frank
> Grazia W.S. Corneal, boards, 204 Frank
> Harvey A. Corneal, bartender, boards, 204 Frank

Wm. N. Corneal, res. 204 Frank

1910 Council Bluffs, Iowa City Directory
Billard and Pool Halls
Wm. N. Corneal (c) 1015 W. Broadway

1913 St. Paul, Minnesota City Directory
Wm. Corneal, porter, 204 Granite
Wm. N. Corneal (Crayton & Corneal), res. 204 Granite

When the 1910 US Census was taken, Corneal was living in Minneapolis, Minnesota. He is not shown on the 1907 City Directory for that city.

1910 US Census, Hennepin Co., MN, Ward 5 Minneapolis, ED 89, page 212   3
Phannie Corneal, mulatto, 46, second marriage, married 23 years, five children,
    3 living, b. MO, nothing for parents' places of birth
Beulah Corneal, daughter, mulatto, 22, single, b. NE, father b. KY, mother b. MO
    dressmaker
Grazia Corneal, 19, b. NE, father b. KY, mother b. MO, musician
Josie Galbreath, mulatto, 25, married, married 5 years, b. NE, father b. KY,
    mother b. MO
William N. Corneal, mulatto, 46, b. KY, married 23 years, both parents b. KY
    porter railroad
Howard Crews, son in law, mulatto, 29, married 10 years, b. KS, father b. KY,
    mother b. MO, porter railroad
Oleary Crews, daughter, mulatto, 31, married 10 years, b. KY

Using the 1900 US Census for Box Butte Co., Nebraska and the 1910 US Census for Hennepin Co., Minnesota, it appears that Phannie had daughters, Josie and Oleary and a son Harry before her marriage to William N. Corneal in about 1887. Harry appears only on the 1900 US Census and is shown as a Corneal, even though his birth is shown as 1883. By Corneal, Phannie had daughters Beulah and Grazia.

Beulah Corneal died in Denver, Colorado from consumption on 30 March 1911. She was 23 years, 4 months and 2 days old. The newspaper article in *The Alliance Herald,* 15 June 1911, indicates that her mother was residing in Minneapolis. Beulah was buried in the Minneapolis Pioneers and Soldiers Memorial Cemetery in Minneapolis. Also buried there is William Nelson Corneal who died 19 January 1917 at St. Paul, Ramsey Co., Minnesota.

Grazia Corneal married Melvin Barnes between 1930 and 1940, probably in St. Louis Co., Missouri. According to the Social Security Death Index, she and her husband were residents of Nelson, Saline Co., Missouri. Grazia was born 13 March 1891 and died in July of 1973. Melvin Barnes was born 12 March 1885 and died May 1977.

1920 US Census, Tulsa Co., Oklahoma, Sand Springs, ED 189 page 93   4
111 Elm Street
459-545 Grevia Corneal, rents, black, 28, single, b. NE , father b. KS, mother b.
    MO, teacher in high school
Phannie Corneal, mother, black, 54, widow, b. MO, both parents b. MO, no
    occpuation
Henry Carter, roomer, black, 37, divorced, b. AR, both parents b. MO, laborer
    glass factory

1930 US Census - St. Louis Co., Missouri, Richmond Heights, ED 53, page 225 5
1704 Aberdeen
153-188 Phannie Corneal, rents, $40 month, negro, 65, widow, married at age
          16, b. MO, father b. US, mother b. KY, no occupation
Grazie Corneal, daughter, negro, 35, single, b. NE, father b. KS, mother b. MO,
          music teacher, music studio
Donald Smith lodger, negro, 7, b. MO, both parents b. US
Alphonse Woods, lodger, negro, 13, b. MO, both parents b. US
William Woods, lodger, negro, 10, b. MO, both parents b. US
Dave Clark, lodger, negro, 20, single, b. MS, both parents b. MS, mill hand, saw
          mill
Dave Shudley, lodger, negro, 34, married, b. TN, both parents b. TN, teamster,
          excavating co.

1940 US Census, St. Louis Co., Missouri, Richmond Heights, ED 95-170,   6
Sheet 9-B
1704 Lincoln Street
owns $3000
Melvin R. Barnes, negro, 51, 4 years high school, b. MO, residence 1 April 1935
          Richmond Heights, St. Louis Co., MO, chauffeur private family
Grazia Barnes, informant, wife, negro, 49, 3 years college, b. NE, residence 1
          April 1935 same place
Phannie L. Corneal, mother-in-law, negro, 74 (husband living else), 4 years high
          school; residence 1 April 1935, Lincoln, Lancaster Co., NE
Hattie Lee Harper, lodger, negro, 16, 3 years high school, b. MO, residence 1
          April 1935 White Grove, St. Louis Co., MO
Louise Harper, lodger, negro, 15, 1 year high school, b. MO

Josephine Bolts Galbreath died on 11 July 1914 at 91 So. 13th Street, Minneapolis, Hennepin Co., Minnesota. She was age 30, colored, widow and a domestic. According to her death record she was born in Nebraska on 11 October 1883. Her parents were Henry Bolts, born Kansas and Phannie, born Missouri. Josephine "Josie" was buried in Layman's Cemetery, 2945 Cedar Avenue South, Minneapolis, Minnesota. 7

Evan Corneal and Hardenia Hutchinson

William Nelson Corneal was the son of Evan Corneal and Hardenia Hutchinson. Evan Corneal was born about 1837 in Kentucky and died on 24 April 1923 in Lincoln, Lancaster Co., Nebraska. Hardenia was born 16 August 1840 in Howard Co., Missouri and died on 23 November 1910 in Brown Co., Kansas. According to the obituary for Evan Corneal, he was an old resident of Hiawatha, Kansas, having reared his family there. After the death of his wife, Hardenia, in 1910 he went to live with his children in Lincoln, Nebraska. He died at the home of his daughter, Mrs. Olive L. Howard, 2153 U Street in Lincoln. There is no marker on his grave, but according to cemetery records, he was buried in the Mount Hope Cemetery in Hiawatha, Brown Co., Kansas. 8

Hardenia Hutchinson Corneal was also buried in the Mount Hope Cemetery and there is a marker on her grave. According to her obituary, she was living at 105 Kickapoo Street in Hiawatha. She died of pneumonia. She moved to Brown County, Kansas in 1864, having previously married and joined a church. 9 Evan and Hardenia Corneal had eleven known children. They are as follows.
1. Sally, born about 1862 in Missouri
2. William Nelson "Ephraim", born 26 June 1864 in Missouri (see above)

3. Abraham L., born about 1867 in Kansas
4. Benjamin F., born about 1869 in Kansas
5. Cyrus H., born about 1871 in Kansas
6. Fannie, born 5 December 1872 in Kansas
7. Lydia, born 1874 in Kansas
8. Commora, born in 1877 in Kansas
10. Ellen B.. born in March of 1880 in Kansas
11. Martha F., born in March of 1880 in Kansas
12. Olive M., born October 1881 in Kansas

Ida Corneal,, daughter of Evan Corneal and Hardenia Hutchinson, was born about 1857-1859 in Missouri. She married first to John Miller on 23 March 1889 in Brown Co., Kansas. On her mother's obituary she is shown as Mrs. Ida Coffer of Kansas City. From the 1910 US Census, she states it was her second marriage and she had been married 15 years. She had nine children, only two living. 10

1885 Kansas State Census, Linn Co., Kansas, La Cygne 11
62-70 John Coffer, 51, laborer, b. MO, black
Ida May Coffer, 17, b. KS, black
Fred Coffer, 15, b. KS, black
Frank Coffer, 8, b. KS, black
Gus Coffer, 6, b. KS, black
Gus Tutt, 18, laborer, b. KS, black

1910 US Census, Wyandotte Co., Kansas, 16th Precinct, Kansas City, ED 167 12
page 171
834 State Street
31-32 Fred Coffer, black, 44, first marriage, married 15 years, b. KS, nothing
shown for birth place of parents, brick hod carrier
Ida Coffer, wife, black, 51, second marriage, married 15 years, 9 children, 2
living, born MO, both parents b. MO, washerwoman in private families
John Miller, step son, black, 21, single, b. KS, father b. KY, mother b. MO,
driver, furniture wagon

1920 US Census, Wyandotte Co., Kansas, 49th Precinct, Kansas City, ED 173 13
page 193
1134 Ann Ave.
167-185 Fred Coffer, rents, black, 50, b. KS, both parents b. MO, laborer for
house builder
Ida Coffer, wife, mulatto, 60, b. MO, both parents b. MO, laundress at home

1930 US Census - Linn Co., Kansas, Pleasanton, ED 11 Sheet 10B 14
407 Broad
— 307 Fred W. Coffer, rents $3 month, negro, 60, married first at age 23, born
KS, both parents b. MO no occupation
Ida A. Coffer, wife, negro, 71, married first at age 33, b. MO, both parents b.
MO, no occcupation

On the 1940 US Census, Fred W. Coffer was living Jackson Co., Missouri, Kansas City, Ward 9 in the household of William R. Bass. He is shown as a lodger, negro, age 70, widowed, born Kansas and the same place had been his residence on 1 April 1935. 15

According to Evan Corneal's obituary, Ida was his step-daughter. She is always shown as a

Corneal. However, her mother's obituary indicates that she (Hardenia) had been previously married.

Fred W. Coffer died at home in St. Joseph, Buchanan Co., Missouri, at 1420 N. 7th Street, on 17 September 1944. He was born 12 June 1869 at LaCygne, Linn Co., Kansas. He was widowed and his usual occupation was a hod carrier. 16 He is shown as a negro. His father, Jack Coffer, was born at LaCygne, Kansas. His mother's name and birthplace was unknown. The informant was Mrs. Minnie Turner of 1420 No. 7th Street, St. Joseph, Missouri. Coffer was buried in the St. Joseph Cemetery in St. Joseph, Buchanan Co., Missouri on 26 September 1944. 17

Sally Corneal, daughter of Evan Corneal and Hardina Hutchinson, was born about 1862 in Missouri. She is not found on federal census after her birth. She is shown on the 1865 Kansas State Census, Brown Co., Kansas, Claytonville, in the household of her parents.

Abraham L. Corneal, son of Evan Corneal and Hardenia Hutchinson, was born about 1867 in Kansas. He married first to Lucy Edding on 8 February 1887 in Hiawatha, Brown Co., Kansas. He was 21 and she was 20. They were married by Rev. M. Collins. 18 On 7 August 1895 Abraham Corneal married Ellen Taylor in Hiawatha, Brown Co., Kansas. She was 28 years old and he is shown as age 30. They were married by Rev. J.S. Payne. 19

1900 US Census, Brown Co., Kansas, Hiawatha, ED 23 Page B4   20
58 Kickapoo
98-101 Abraham L. Corneal, black, b. Juy 1866, 33, married 5 years, b. KY,
        father b. KY, mother b. MO, day laborer
Ellen H., wife, black, b. Dec 1866, 33, 0 children, 0 living, b. KY, father b. KY,
        mother b. VA

1910 US Census, Lancaster Co., Nebraska, Lincoln, Ward 1, ED 52, page 5B   21
821 S Street
Abe Corniel, black, second marriage, married 14 years, b. KS, father b. KY,
        mother b. MO, janitor station
Hellen, wife, black, 42, second marriage, married 15 years, 0 children, 0 living, b.
        KY, both parents b. KY post office
Fanny Allen, lodger, black, 59, widow, b. KY, both parents b. KY
Pearl Ervin, male, black, 22, single, b. KS, both parents b. US, porter railroad

Sometime between 1910 and 1921, Abraham and Ellen moved to Portland, Oregon. They are shown in the respective Portland City Directories. 22

1921 Portland City Directory
Abr. L. Corneal (Ellen) r. 839 Tibbetts

1923 Portland City Directory
Abr. L. Corneal (Ellen), r. 839 Tibbetts

1923 Portland City Directory
A.L. Corneal (Ellen), laborer 4. 839 Tibbetts

1930 US Census Multnomah Co, Oregon, Portland, ED 26-151, Sheet 1B   23
839 E. Tibbetts
23-23 Julia Fuller, owns, $6,000, negro, 69, widow, b. KY, both parents b. KY, no
        occupation

Kate Lewis, daughter, negro, 48, widow , b. KY, both parents b. KY, matron city
A.L. Corneal, brother-in-law, negro, 65, married , b. KS, both parents b. US,
        attendant for comfort station, city
Annie Corneal, sister-in-law, negro, 61, married, b. KS, both parents b. US, no
        occupation
Jeanne Jones, daughter, negro, 45, married, b. KY, both parents b. KY , maid,
        railroad
W.M. Jones, son-in-law, negro, 50, married, b. IN, both parents b. US, no
        occupation

1940 US Census Multomah Co., Oregon, Portland, ED 37-164, Sheet 1B   24
2703 S.E. Tibbetts Street
owns $2,000 all living in same house on 1 April 1935
Julia Fuller, negro, 79, widow, 1 year school, b. KY, no occupation
Jeane Jones, informant, negro, daughter, 54, widow, 4 years high school, b. KY,
        no occupation
Abraham Corneal, brother-in-law, negro, 73, widowed, 4 years school, b. KS,
        comfort station, city

Abraham L. Corneal died in 1947 and was buried in the Lincoln Memorial Park, Portland, Multnomah Co., Oregon. His wife, Ellen, died 2 March 1925 at Portland, Multnomah Co., Oregon and was buried in the same cemetery. Between 1925 and 1930, Abraham married a lady named Annie. 25

Benjamin F. "Ben" Corneal, son of Evan Corneal and Hardenia Hutchinson, was born about 1869 in Kansas. In 1893 he was living in Lincoln, Nebraska, working as a barber for A. Ivison. In 1909 he was in Council Bluffs, Iowa where he was employed in a saloon and lived at 1029 W. Broadway. By 1910 he was in Lincoln, Nebraska.

1910 US Census, Lancaster Co., Nebraska, Lincoln, Ward 3, ED 60, page 12B   26
1233 University Avenue
Benj. Corneal, lodger, black, "can't get further information"

On 23 September 1914 in Council Bluffs, Pottawattamie Co., Iowa, Ben F. Corneal, age 45, born Kansas, married Lottie Burles Carter. This was his first marriage and he was living in Lincoln, Nebraska, working as a porter. His parents are shown as Evan Corneal and Ardenia Hutchinson. Lottie was age 38, born in Missouri. She was a resident of Kansas City, Missouri and the daughter Israel Burles and Anna Smith. 27

Cyrus H. Corneal, son of Evan Corneal and Hardenia Hutchinson, was born about 1871 in Kansas. He was living with his brother, William N. "Ephraim" Corneal in 1900 when the federal census was taken in Alliance, Box Butte Co., Nebraska. The enumerator spelled his name as "Sy." He married Miss Sarah A. Harrison on 16 August 1905 in Alliance, Box Butte Co., Nebraska at the home of N.B. Harrison with Rev. C.W. Ray of the M.E. Church officiating. Witnesses were N.B. Harrison and Oleary Crews, who was the daughter of Phannie Corneal, wife of William Nelson Corneal, by a previous marriage. Cyrus had arrived recently in Alliance from San Antonio, Texas. The married couple left after their marriage for Sheridan, Wyoming. While in Alliance in 1900 he was a porter in a saloon. On the marriage license, the parents of Cyrus were listed as Evans Corneal and Ardine Tulay. The parents of Sarah A. Harrison were listed as James Harrison and Josephine Wyatt. She was born in San Antonio, Texas. The parents of N.B. Harrison shown on his marriage license were Thomas Harrison and Josephine Wyatt. 28

1910 US Census Sheridan Co., Wyoming, Sheridan, First Ward, ED 103, page 2B   29

163 N. Gould
45-50 Cye H. Corneal, black, 37, married 5 years, b. KS, both parents b. KY,
         porter club room
Alex Williams, servant, black, 29, single, b. IL, father b. AL, mother b. WA,
         porter saloon
Charlie Williams, roomer, black, 26, married 5 years, b. IL, father b. AL, mother
         b. WA, porter saloon
Charles Lewis, roomer, black, 23, single, b. OH, both parents b. OH, laborer
         barber shop
Sarah Corneal, wife, black, 25, married 5 years, b. TX, both parents b. OH, no
         occupation

Cyrus died on 9 December 1918 in Lincoln, Nebraska. He was buried in the Mount Hope
Cemetery in Hiawatha, Brown Co., Kansas. There is no marker on his grave. 30

Hiawatha Daily World, Wednesday, December 12, 1918:
"Cyrus Corneal, colored, died at his home in Lincoln, Nebr., Monday morning at 9:30. He had been ill a
year with Bright's disease. He is survived by his father, Evans Corneal, two brothers, Ben F. and Abe, of
Lincoln, and four sisters, Mrs. Fannie Young, Lincoln, Nebr., Mrs. O. Howard, Detroit, Mich., Miss
Comora Corneal, Chicago, and Mrs. Libbie Tibbett, of St. Joseph. The two brothers and Mrs. Young
accompanied the body to Hiawatha and there were short funeral services in the Hiawatha Cemetery
Wednesday Afternoon. Cy Corneal went to Lincoln from Hiawatha in 1892."

Fannie Corneal, daughter of Evan Corneal and Hardenia Hutchinson, was born 5 December 1872
in Kansas. She married William Washington on 6 January 1894 in Lancaster Co., Nebraska. At the time
of their marriage, she was shown as age 23 and he was age 32.

1910 US Census, Multnomah Co., Oregon, Portland, ED 212, page 4B   31
268 Wheeler Street
88-114 William M. Washington, black, 48, married 15 years, b. MO, both parents
         b. MO janitor, office
Fannie, black, 37, 1 child, 1 living, b. KS, both parents b. KY, no occupation
Roland, son, black, 9, b. KS
William Lomax, lodger, black, 35, single, b. PA, both parents b. PA, laborer, street
         repairing

William Washington died on 6 March 1934 in Portland, Oregon. His spouse is listed as Fanny
Washington on his death certificate. 32

By 1919 Fannie Corneal Washington was married to Richard H. Young. Her son, Roland
Washington, is shown on the 1920 US Census as Roland Young.

1920 US Census, Lancaster Co., Nebraska, Lincoln, Ward 5, ED 71, page 112   33
1315 Washington Street
345-398 Richard H. Young, owns/mortgaged, black, 57, b. MO, both parents b.
         MO, drapery man, department store
Fannie Young, wife, black, 47, b. KS, father b. KY, mother b. MO, no occupation
Roland Young, son, black, 18, b. KS, father b. MO, mother b. KS, porter work,
         barber shop
Evans Cornell, father-in-law, black, 82, widowed, b. KY, both parents b. KY, no
         occupation

On the 1930 US Census, Richard H. Young was still living in Lincoln, Lancaster County, Nebraska, at 2430 Holdrege Street. He is shown as owning the house, valued at $4,500, and he was widowed. He was a caretaker for city buildings. 34

Fannie Corneal Young died on 6 August 1927 and was buried in Wyuka Cemetery in Lincoln, Lancaster Co., Nebraska. Also buried there was Richard H. Young, born 21 January 1865, died 14 March 1931. The son that Fannie had by William Washington was also buried in Wyuka Cemetery, as Roland Young. He was born 4 July 1901 and died 1 June 1992. 35

The petition for appointmenet of an administrator for the estate of Richard H. Young, filed in Lancaster Co., Nebraska, names a half-sister, Melva White and a half-brother Ed Young, as sole heirs. 36

Lydia Corneal, daughter of Evan Corneal and Hardenia Hutchinson, was born in 1874 in Kansas. Her name is also shown as Libbie. She married Thomas G. "Tom" Tivis.

1920 US Census, Buchanan Co., Missouri, St. Joseph, Ward 3, ED 68, page 190   37
805 Prospect Avenue
60-64 Thomas G. Tivis, rents, black, 49, b. KY, both parents b. KY, janitor
        wholesale house
Lizzie, wife, black, 45, b. KS, father b. KY, mother b. MO
Thomas H., son, black, 12, b. MO
Naomi, daughter, black, 10, b. KS
Georgie, daughter, black, 5, b. MO
Russel, son, black, 2 5/12, b. MO

1930 US Census - Buchanan Co., Missouri, St. Joseph, Ward 6, ED 37, page 6B   38
2015 Charles Street
160-166 Thomas G. Tivis, rents $15 month, negro, 55, married at age 31, b. KY,
        both parents b. US, laborer street work
Elizabeth, wife, negro, 50, married at age 26, b. KS, father b. KY, mother b. MO,
        cleaning private family
Thomas H., son, negro, 22, single, b. MO, porter, hospital
Naomi A., daughter, 20, single, b. KS, cook, private family
Georgie E., daughter, negro, 15, b. MO
Russel C., son, negro, 12, b. MO

Lydia died on 14 July 1934 in St. Joseph, Buchanan Co., Missouri and was buried in the Ashland Cemetery in St. Joseph.

Com(m)ora Corneal, daughter of Evan Corneal and Hardenia Hutchinson, was born about 1877 in Kansas. The obituaries for both parents (1910 and 1923) list her as a "Miss" living in Chicago, Illinois. No further information has been found on her.

Ellen B. Corneal, daughter of Evan Corneal and Hardenia Hutchinson, was born in March of 1880 in Kansas, a twin to Martha F. Corneal. No further information has been found on her.

Martha F. Corneal, daughter of Evan Corneal and Hardenia Hutchson, was born in March of 1880 in Kansas, a twin to Ellen B. Corneal. No further information has been found on her.

Olive M. "Ollie" Corneal, daughter of Evan Corneal and Hardenia Hutchinson, was born October 1881 in Kansas. As a female she is shown in her parents household on the 1900 US Census, Brown Co., Kansas, Hiawatha, Ollie M. Corneal, born October 1881, age 18, born Kansas. According to her mother's obituary of 2 December 1910, she was Mrs. Allie Wallace of Kansas City. When her brother, Cyrus Corneal died in 1918 she was shown as Mrs. O. Howard of Detroit, Michigan. Her sisters were all listed by their given names. Her father's obituary of 1923 indicates that he died at the home of his daughter, Mrs. Olive L. Howard, 2153 U, Lincoln, Nebraska. The 1922 and 1923 city directories for Lincoln, Nebraska indicate Ollie L. Howard (male) with a wife Lola was residing there.

> 1922 Lincoln, Nebraska City Directory
> Ollie L. Howard (c) (Lola), waiter, residence 2153 U
>
> 1923 Lincoln, Nebraska City Directory
> Ollie L. Howard (c) (Lola), barber 219 N. 9th, residence 2153 U

Lincoln Star, Lincoln, Nebraska, 24 April 1923
"Evan Corneal, 92 years old, and resident of Lincoln since 1911, died at the home of his daughter, Mrs. Olive L. Howard, 2153 U street, Tuesday at 4:50 a.m. He is survived by two sons, Benjamin F. Corneal, of Lincoln and Abraham Corneal of Portland, Ore., and four daughters, Mrs. Richard Young of Lincoln; Mrs. Liddie Tides, Mrs. Howard and Miss Comore Corneal of Chicago, and a step daughter Mrs. Ida Coffer, of Kansas City, Kas, … several grandchildren. The body will be taken to Hiawatha, Kas., for funeral services and interment."

Hardenia Corneal was born 16 August 1840 in Howard Co., Missouri and died 23 November 1910 in Brown Co., Kansas. She was buried in the Mount Hope Cemetery at Hiawatha, Brown Co., Kansas. There is a marker on her grave.

Brown County World, Hiawatha, Kansas, 2 Dec 1910
"Hardena, wife of Evan Corneal, of 105 Kickapoo Street, died at 3:10 pm Nov 23, of pneumonia. She was born in Howard County, Missouri August 16, 1840, and moved here in 1864, having previously married and joined a church, and has lived a consistent Christian life since. She was the mother of nine children, four boys and five girls, as follows: Mrs. Ida Coffer, Kansas City; Nelson, St. Paul; Abe and Ben, Lincoln, Nebr.; Cyrus, Sheridan, Wyo.; Mrs. Fannie Washington, Lincoln, Nebr.; Mrs Libbie Tevis, Kansas City; Miss Commora, Chicago; Mrs Allie Wallace, Kansas City. She had 9 grandchildren and one great grand child. Mrs Corneal was a good, kind woman, worked hard and uncomplainingly in raising the large family, is spoken well of by all her neighbors of all classes, as a good woman, loyal to her family, friends, and church. The funeral was held at the Second Baptist church at -- o'clock Friday, Rev. J. R. Richards officiating. Burial was made in Mt. Hope Cemetery. All the children were present except Commora and Nelson."

Hardenia is shown with the maiden name of Hutchinson on the marriage record of her son, Benjamin Corneal. If this was indeed her maiden name, the only Hutchinson in Missouri in 1870 (post Emancipation) was Anna Hutchinson, age 50, black, keeping house, born Virginia, living in Ralls Co., Missouri with her daughter Anna, 20 black, born Missouri. 39

Phannie Lee Stepney Corneal

Phannie Corneal was born Phannie Lee Stepney on 5 December 1865 in Savannah, Andrew Co., Missouri. She married first to Henry Bolts who was born in Kansas and by him had at least two daughters. In about 1887 in Lincoln, Nebraska she married William Nelson "Ephraim" Corneal. Phannie married Harry Tyner on 22 March 1912 in St. Paul, Ramsey Co., Minnesota. 40 Because William Nelson Corneal did not pass away until 1917 in St. Paul, she most likely had divorced him. She is enumerated in the household of her daughter Grazia Corneal in 1920 in Sand Springs Tulsa Co., Oklahoma, where she is shown as Phannie Corneal. On the 1922 Minneapolis, Minnesota City Directory she is shown as Phannie

L. Corneal, widow of Wm., boarding at 516 12th Ave. S. By 1930 she was living in Richmond Heights, St. Louis Co., Missouri, shown as Phannie Corneal. The 1936 Lincoln, Nebraska City Directory shows her as Phannie Corneal, widow of Wm., house at 3918 Madison Ave. She was still living in Lincoln in 1938 at Phannie L. Corneal, widow of Wm., 2239 T Street. On the 1940 US Census, she is Phannie Corneal living in the household of her daughter Grazia Barnes in Richmond Heights, St. Louis Co., Missouri.

Her Missouri Death Certificate #39814 identifies her as Phannie Lee Tyner. Another surname had been typed in and then partially removed and replaced with "Tyner." She was a resident of 1708 Lincoln Ave., Richmond Heights, St. Louis Co., Missouri and died there. She was shown as a widow, husband William Nelson Corneal which was covered over with Tyner. Informant was her daughter Grazia Barnes of 1708 Lincoln, Richmond Heights. She died on 3 November 1940 of lobar pneumonia and was buried in Nelson, Saline Co., Missouri on 9 November 1940.

The Stepney family was prominent in Lincoln, Nebraska. Perry Jefferson Stephen died 20 September 1934, buried in Wyuka Cemetery, Lincoln, Lancaster Co., Nebraska. The obituary of Perry Jefferson Stepheney [sic] from *The Lincoln Star*, Lincoln, Nebraska, 20 September 1934 indicates that he was survived by two sisters, Rev. Sarah McWilliams and Mrs. Phannie Corneal of Lincoln, along with two brothers, Jerry and Mose of Lincoln. The correct surname is Stepney. Perry Stepney was also survived by his wife Grace, daughter Phannie of Omaha and son Morris of Sioux City, Iowa. He died at the home of his sister, Rev. Sarah McWilliams, 2009 U Street, Lincoln, Nebraska. He was buried in Wyuka Cemetery in Lincoln, Nebraska. Perry Stepney was the proprietor of a barber shop in Lincoln.

Grace, wife of Perry Stepney, was born in 1890 in South Dakota. She married first to a Mr. Howard and had a son Marvin Howard, born 5 November 1912 in Nebraska. Grace died in 1952 in California. Marvin died in Los Angeles, California on 8 April 1971. On various census enumerations this Stepney family is shown as being mulatto.

Phannie Stepney Glenn, daughter of Perry and Grace Stepney, was born 31 January 1922 in Nebraska and died 18 April 1987 in Riverside, Riverside Co., California. Morris J. Stepney, son of Perry and Grace Stepney, was born about 1902 in Nebraska.

According to his obituary, Perry Stepney had brothers Jerry and Mose of Lincoln, Nebraska. In 1895 Mose(s) Stepney was living in White Cloud, Doniphan Co., Kansas. There were a number of Stepneys living in Doniphan Co., Kansas in 1865 and 1895. In 1865 John and Poley Stepney were residing in Allen Co., Kansas in Geneva. They were both born in Florida. He was age 65 and she was age 50.

1895 Kansas State Census, Doniphan Co., Kansas, White Cloud, page 3   41
20-24 Moses Stepney, 30, colored, b. MO
Eva Stepney, 27, b. MO
Franklin Stepney, 9, b. KS
Lulu Stepney, 7, b. KS

1900 US Census, Doniphan Co., Kansas, White Cloud, ED 41, Sheet B-1   42
14-16 Moses Stepney, black, b. Feb. 1858, 22, married 14 years, b. VA, both
         parents b. VA, barber
Eva, black, b. March 1876, 24 2 children, 2 living, b. MO, father b. NC, mother
         b. VA
Frank, son, black, b. March 1897, 13, b. KS, at school
Lulu, daughter, black, b. July 1888, 11, b. KS, at school

1910 US Census, Lancaster Co., Nebraska, Lincoln, Ward 3, ED 65, page 191   43
1913 19th Street
208-249 Moses Stepney, black, 50, 1st marriage, married 25 years, b. unknown,
        both parents b. MO, laborer, street
Eva, wife, black, 41, 1st marriage, married 25 years, 3 children, 2 living, b. MO,
        father b. unknown, mother b. MO
Frank, son, black, 24, single, b. KS, porter, car
Lulu Talbot, daughter, black, 21, 1st marriage, 3 children, 3 living, b. KS
Harold Talbot, grandson, black, 6, b. NE
Donald Talbot, grandson, black, 3, b. NE
Delores Talboth, grandson, black, 2, b. NE [should be granddaughter]
Charles Turner, lodger, black, 33, single, b. MO, both parents b. MO, musician
Cliff Gardner, lodger, black, 24, single, b. MO, both parents b. MO, porter,
        barber shop
Claud Wilson, lodger, black, 24, single, b. MO, both parents b. MO, musician
        orchestra

1920 US Census, Lancaster Co., Nebraska, Lincoln, Ward 1, ED 54, page 48   44
856 University Avenue
51-51 Eva Stepney, rents, black, 50, widow, b. MO, father b. SC, mother b.
        MO, no occupation
Lula Talbert, daughter, black, 31, widow, b. KS, both parents b. MO, servant
        private house
Harold Talbert, grandson, black, 15, b. NE, father b. NE, mother b. KS
Donald Talbert, grandson, black, 13, b. NE, father b. NE, mother b. KS
Delorse Talbert, granddaughter, black, 11, b. NE, father b. NE, mother b. KS
Cliff Gardner, boarder, black, 33, widowed, b. MO, both parents b. US, laborer,
        street work
Julius Robertson, boarder, black, 50, single, b. US, both parents b. US, laborer,
        street work
John Kelly, boarder, black, 48, single, b. KS, both parents b. US, laborer, city

Moses Stepney is not shown on the 1920 US Census. While his wife, Eva, indicates that she was a
widow, he was still alive when the 1930 US Census was taken.

1930 US Census, Lancaster Co., Nebraska, Lincoln, Ward 3, ED 19, page 256   45
1906 Vine Street
169-535 Lula Talbot, rents $20 month, negro, 42, married, age 16 at marriage,
        b. KS, father b. VA, mother b. MO, housekeeper, hotel
Harold Talbot, son, negro, 25, married, married at age 21, b. NE, father b. US,
        mother b. KS, porter, railroad
Dolores Holmes, daughter, negro, 20, married, married at age 17, b. NE, father
        b. US, mother b. KS, chambermaid, hotel
Moses Stepney, father, negro, 67, widowed, married at age 22, b. VA, both
        parents b. US, no occupation
Clif Gardner, roomer, black, 43, widowed, married at age 20, b. MO, both parents
        b. MO, asphault tender, paving
Marcela Talbot, granddaughter, negro, 3 9/12, b. NE, father b. NE, mother b. US

1940 US Census, Lancaster Co., Nebraska, Lincoln, Ward 3, ED 55-27, Sheet 6B   46
1970 U Street
rents $16 month

Lula Talbot, informant, negro, 51, widow, 5th grade, b. KS, same house 1 April
    1935, maid hotel
Mose Setpeney [sic], father, negro, 75, widowed, 2nd grade, b. VA, same
    house 1 April 1935
Marcella Talbert, granddaughter, negro, 14, 7th grade, b. NE, same house 1 April
    1935
Clifford Gardner, lodger, negro, 58, widowed, 5th grade, b. MO, same house
    1 April 1935, porter, barber shop

Mose Lee Stepney was born 18 February 1867 and died 18 December 1954. He was buried in Wyuka Cemetery, Lincoln, Lancaster Co., Nebraska. Eva Stepney was born 1 March 1867 and died 19 August 1923. She was also buried in Wyuka Cemetery. Their son Frank A. Stepney was born 1 March 1886 and died 14 April 1943, buried in Wyuka Cemetery. His daughter, Lula May Stepney Talbert was born 22 July 1886 and died 25 July 1962, buried in Wyuka Cemetery. Frank A. Stepney, son of Mose and Eva, was born 1 March 1886 and died 14 April 1943, buried in Wyuka Cemetery.

The Lincoln Star, Lincoln, Nebraska, 29 December 1954
"The family of Moses Lee Stepney wishes to thank the many friends for
the flowers, cards & all other deeds of thoughtfulness during the illness
& death of our beloved. Mrs. Lula Talbert, daughter. Mrs. Delores Kitchen,
granddaughter."

Jerry J. Stepney was born about 1861 in Missouri. Little is known about Jerry, other than what can be gleaned through census.

1920 US Census, Lancaster Co., Nebraska, Lincoln, Ward 3, ED 64, page 16B   47
2014 O Street
295-360 Jerry Stepney, rents, mulatto, 59, widowed, b. MO, father b. US,
    mother b. MO, barber, barber shop
Robert Adams, lodger, black, 45, single, b. KY, both parents b. KY, no
    occupation

1930 US Census, Lancaster Co., Nebraska, Lincoln, Ward 3, ED 19, page 4B   48
 2040 O Street
78-87 Jerre Stepney, rents, negro, 69, widowed, b. MO, both parents b. US,
    barber, barber shop

1940 US Census, Lancaster Co., Nebraska, Lincoln, Ward 3, ED 55-27, page 5-A   49
2014 O Street
Jerry J. Stepney, lodger, negro, 81, widowed, 3rd grade, b. MO, same place on
    1 April 1935, no occupation

Jerry J. Stepney died 9 June 1940 and is buried in Wyuka Cemetery in Lincoln, Lancaster Co., Nebraska.

Besides Perry Jefferson Stepney, Mose(s) Lee Stepney, Phannie Stepney Corneal and Jerry J. Stepney, another sibling was Sarah J. Stepney McWilliams. She was born 30 May 1854 in Kansas. She married John Jefferson McWilliams on 25 December 1868. John was born 17 October 1843 in Kentucky and died 20 March 1917 in Lincoln, Lancaster Co., Nebraska. He is buried in Wyuka Cemetery in Lincoln. Sarah died 22 December 1940 and is buried in Wyuka Cemetery.

Sarah J. Stepney McWilliams was an honorary assistant pastor at the Third Christian Church in

Lincoln, Nebraska. Her brother, P.J. Stepney, was a deacon and treasurer at the church.

1880 US Census, Doniphan Co., Kansas, White Cloud, ED 74 page 45 50
391-404 John McWilliams, black, 33, peddler and preacher, b. KY, both
        parents b. KY
Sarah, wife, mulatto, 24, keeping house, b. KS, father b. MO, mother b. KY
Lily, mulatto, 6, b. KS, father b. KY, mother b. KS
Luella, mulatto, 4, b. KS, father b. KY, mother b. KS
Jeremey A., male, mulatto, 2, b. KS, father b. KY, mother b. KS
Jefferson, mulatto, 7/12, b. October, b. KS, father b. KY, mother b. KS

1900 US Census, Lancaster Co., Nebraska, Lincoln, Ward 3, ED 48, page 219 51
913 N. 18th Street
138-144 J. McWilliams, black, b. 1848, 52, married 27 years, b. KY, both
        parents b. KY, hall janitor
S.J., wife, black, b. May 1857, 43, 12 children, 6 living, b. KS, father b. unknown,
        mother b. KY
J.J., son, black, b. Oct 1879, 20, single, b. KS, father b. KY, mother b. KS, porter,
        barber shop
T.T., son, black, b. Aug 1885, 14, b. NE, father b. KY, mother b. KS, at school
R., son, black, b. Feb 1888, 12, b. NE, father b. KY, mother b. KS, at school
E., son, black, b. June 1892, 7, b. NE, father b. KY, mother b. KS
R.M. Gates, cousin, black, female, b. Dec 1852, 47, married, b. MO, both
        parents b. VA
L.T. Carter, inmate, black, b. Feb 1890, 10, b. NE, father b. KY, mother b.
        unknown, at school

1910 US Census, Lancaster Co., Nebraska, Lincoln, ED 60, page 139 52
851 No. 13th Street
176-195 John McWilliams, black, 65, married 39 years, b. KY, father b. VA,
        mother b. KY, janitor, bank and offices
Sarah, wife, mulatto, 54, 7 children, 7 living, b. KS, father b. unknown, mother
        b. KY
John J., son, mulatto, 26, single, b. KS, father b. KY, mother b. KS, porter,
        pullman car
Ralph, son, mulatto, 21, single, b. NE, father b. KY, mother b. KS, cook, dining
        car
Earl, son, mulatto, 17, b. NE, father b. KY, mother b. KS, porter, barber shop
Paul, son, mulatto, 9, b. NE, father b. KY, mother b. KS
Lloyd Carter, lodger, black, 20, single, b. NE, both parents b. unknown, porter,
        barber shop

1930 US Census, Lancaster Co., Nebraska, Lincoln, Ward 3, ED 19, page 21B 53
2009 U Street
445-510 Sarah J. McWilliams, owns $2,500, negro, 75, widow, b. KS, father
        b. US, mother b. KY, no occupation
Lillian Richards, daughter, negro 56, widow, b. KS, father b. KY, mother b. KS,
        no occupation

Nebraska State Journal, Lincoln, Nebraska, 23 December 1940
   "Rev. Mrs. Sarah J. McWilliams, 86, of 2090 U, died Sunday. Surviving are: five sons, John
Jefferson, Rev. Trago T. and Paul L. of Lincoln, Ralph W. of Pasadena, CA and Earl E of Denver; two

daughters Mrs. Lillian Richards of Lincoln and Mrs. Luella Coleman of Omaha; a sister, Phannie Corneal of St. Louis; a step-brother Mose Stepney of Lincoln and 27 grand children and 13 great grandchildren. Funeral at 2 pm Tuesday at Umbergers, Rev. O.J. Burckhardt officiating, assisted by C.C. Reynolds, C.H. Nicks, Riley Bell and R.M. Dilworth. Wyuka."

The son, John Jefferson McWilliams, was born 8 October 1879 and died 11 January 1953, buried in Wyuka Cemetery, Lincoln, Nebraska.

Sarah Stepney and John McWilliams were parents of Earl McWilliams who was born in June of 1892 in Lincoln, Nebraska. Earl wrote *Negro History of Lincoln 1888 to 1938*. 54   He also was an assistant to John Johnson, taking photographs of blacks in Lincoln, Nebraska.

Paul McWilliams and family was living at 922 S Street in Lincoln, Nebraska in 1940. His wife was Anna and the children were Pauline, Loraine (who provided the information), Rosemary, Richard and Ronald. Paul was doing kitchen work in a fraternity house and Anna was a hotel maid. 55

Rev. Trago T. McWilliams, son of John McWilliams and Sarah Stepney, was born 4 August 1885 and died 14 April 1951. He was buried in Fairview Cemetery in Lincoln, Nebraska. His wife, Idabelle, was born 31 December 1886 and died 12 June 1958, also buried in Fairview Cemetery. The Trago T. McWilliams's house at 1723 N. 29th Street in Lincoln, Nebraska is on the National Register of Historic Places. It is a small, single-story, wood frame cottage, built in about 1890. The house is in what is known as the Clinton neighborhood. Trago and Idabelle lived in the house at 1723 N. 29th Street from 1928 through 1941. Rev. Trago was a leading member of Lincoln's African American community. He worked for the betterment of Lincoln's African American commuity as a pastor and commuity leader.

Trago was born in Falls City, Richardson Co., Nebraska. His parents had been former slaves and moved to Lincoln, Nebraska in about 1887. Both Sarah and John J. McWilliams were ordained pastors in the African Methodist Episcopal Church. In 1896 they left Quinn Chapel AME Church to found the first integrated and nondenominational church in Lincoln.

He graduated from Lincoln High School in 1904 and attended the University of Nebraska in Lincoln. Trago worked at numerous jobs and owned the Quality Lunch diners in downtown Lincoln. He was the owner and editor of the newspaper *The Weekly Review*. In 1922 he was ordained at the Third Christian Church.

Trago helped to organize the Lincoln Chapter of the National Association for the Advancement of Colored People and helped to establish the Prince Hall Mason's Grand Lodge of Nebraska in 1919. In 1933 he actively supported the formation of the Lincoln Urban League through his newspaper. The same year Lincoln Mayor, Frank Zehrung, and Nebraska Governor McMullen recognized him as an outstanding Nebraskan to represent the state at the Educational Council in Kansas City, Missouri. He was a foreman at the Martin Bomber Plant at Fort Crook, Omaha during World War II. When he died in 1951 he was still an active minister of Christ Temple (Holiness) Church. His son, Rev. Trago O. McWilliams (born 1909, died 30 December 1986) continued the ministery at the church. Trago O. McWilliams married Winifred Conrad on 29 March 1928 in Council Bluffs, Pottawattamie Co., Iowa. Winifred was born 4 December 1910 in Broken Bow, Custer Co., Nebraska to William Conrad and Amelia Williams. She died on 20 June 1929 and is buried in Wyuka Cemetery, Lincoln, Lancaster Co., Nebraska. Trago married second to Margaret Emily Stephens. He is buried in Fairview Cemetery in Lincoln, Lancaster Co., Nebraska. Trago and Winifred had one child, Richard McWilliams. 56

A park at 25th and T Streets in Lincoln was named in his honor as McWilliams Park. The Trago Park near 21st and S Streets in Lincoln is also named in his honor. The Urban League is now the Clyde Malone Community Center in Lincoln.

Corneal Newspaper Articles and Legal Records

The Omaha World-Herald, Omaha, Neraska, 14 May 1889
"Eph Corneal, a citizen of color living at O and Twentieth sts., is in the habit of remaining from his domestic hearth until a very late hour in the morning, and Mrs. Eph, who loves her lord and master, has entertained the opinion that he spends his evenings with some other female companion. A fierce jealousy took possession of her mind and on Sunday night she played 'possum on Mr. Eph for the purpose of frightening him back into the virtuous path. When he returned home he found Mrs. Corneal lying in a corpse like state and nothing he could do would rouse her. A copper was called in and he could not make a diagnosis of the case. A physician was called and he assured the mourning husband that there was nothing serious in the case. The next day Mrs. Corneal was about as lively as a cricket on the hearth and Ephraim now spends his nights in the bosom of his family."

The Omaha World-Herald, Omaha, Nebraska, 19 November 1889
"The hearing of Marshal Carder's charges against Officer Ireland began before Mayor Graham this morning. The forenoon was taken up in examining William Corneal, a colored man, who testified that he had been employed by the marshal to watch Officer Ireland. The evidence so far is not of a damaging nature. Eph Corneal is the man who was put into the cell with John Taylor last spring, to extort a confession from him. Officer Ireland denies all the charges made against him."

Lincoln Semi Weekly Nebraska State Journal, Lincoln, Nebraska, 3 June 1892
This is a news article about Charley Thomas being murdered by Green S. Gravely. Among the blacks examined regarding the shooting were W.N. Corneal and Ben Corneal. The account by Ben Corneal differed radically from that of the others.

The Omaha World-Herald, Omaha, Nebraska, 26 July 1892
"Shot In A Saloon
A Drunken Switchman Gets a Bullet in the Neck
A shooting scrape in which James Burke, a white switchman, and William Corneal, better known as "Big Eph," participated, took place at Andy Ivison's saloon at 817 P Street this afternoon. Corneal is employed in the saloon and he, as is the proprietor, is colored. Burke with several switchmen had been putting in the day around town, and just before 2 o'clock got full enough to feel like having a row. He raised a disturbance out on the sidewalk in front of the saloon, and Corneal went out and ordered him away. It is claimed that the order to move was enforced with a kick. Burke left, going up the street towards the Lincoln hotel.

Something like a half hour afterward Burke came in the back door of the saloon walking up to the bar and covered Corneal, who was behind the bar, with his pistol, exclaiming: 'Now, damn you, I've got you!' Corneal squatted behind the bar, and as he went down grabbed a pistol which he kept lying on a shelf in easy reach for such occasions. Burke advanced and fired over the counter, his shot just grazing Corneal's right side. The latter then got in two wild shots, and Burke fired one more and concluded to quit. As he sprang out of the door Corneal shot through the glass door and sent in the only effective bullet of the battle. After cutting a jagged hole through the glass the ball struck Burke in the back part of the neck just to the left of the spinal colunn, ranging upwards and forward. Burke contiued his flight after being shot, but was soon arrested, as was the other participants in the battle. Dr. Hatch endeavored to locate the bullet with a probe, but was unsuccessful. Burke was very drunk and talkative while in the surgeon's hands. It is probable that the bullet is lodged in the muscles of the neck and the wound will not prove serious. Both the principals and serveral of those who were present were locked up, the latter to be held as witnesses."

The Omaha Daily Bee, Omaha, Nebraska, 5 October 1892

Lancaster District Court

"The court is occupied today with the case of the state against James Burk [sic], who is charged with shooting with intent to kill or wound. Burk is the railroad grader who got into a difficulty with W.N. Corneal, the colored bartender of Iveson's saloon, some time last summer. Later in the day Burk returned to the saloon and commenced firing at Corneal at close range. Corneal dropped to the floor and then crawled around the end of the counter and returned the fire. Burk was wounded in the neck and for several days it was believed that he would die. He recovered, however, and is now standing trial."

Lincoln Semi Weekly State Journal, Lincoln, Nebraska, 23 February 1894
"The warrant mentioned in yesterday's *Journal* has been served on J.H. Edson, the real estate man. He was arrested yesterday on the complaint of W.C. Corneal. Corneal operates a saloon west of the Lincoln hotel and claims that Edson obtained some property under false pretenses. He says that Ivison engaged the defendant to draw up a deed transferring to Corneal an eighty-acre farm near Minden, with the understanding that he was to trade it for another farm already selected, but that Edson induced Ivison to sign a blank deed and then he transferred the property to another party in exchange for a farm, which he now holds. Justice McCandless took Edson's personal recognizance in $200 for his appearance on February 26. Referring to the article in yesterday morning's *Journal* Mr. J.H. Edson says he is ready to account to the lawful conservator of Andy Ivison's estate for all business done by him for the estate, but he has no accounting or report to make to Eph Corneal or any other bartender in the city."

The Omaha Daily Bee, Omaha, Nebraska, 14 September 1894
Lincoln, Sept. 13
"There was a shooting scrape early this morning in the vicinity of Twenty-ninth and Fair streets, which resulted from a domestic quarrel between Eph Corneal and his wife. Eph was the sufferer, as he received two bullet wounds in his anatomy, which, it is thought, will not prove fatal. The police were called to the house at 2 o'clock this morning, and Corneal taken into custody on complaint of his wife, who claimed that he assaulted her. He was released on his own recognizance and allowed to depart in search of a physician to look after his injuries. It seems that Corneal is in the habit of abusing his wife, and last night, when she returned late from a party in South Lincoln, he began to pick a quarrel with her, in which she got the better of him. Corneal, who is colored, is a bartender."

Box Butte County, Nebraska
Criminal Case
District Court
State of Nebraska vs W.N. Corneal
Case #1438 Docket G Page 1438

19 May 1902 W.N. Corneal had in his possession and control a certain gambling device known as a roulette wheel used and employed in gaming and did then and there unlawfully exhibit the same to one Ed. Henderson and other persons to affiant unknown to win and gain money. Warrant was issued on 21 May 1902 for Corneal's arrest (first name unknown). Corneal pled not guilty as charged and the hearing continued to 26 May 1902. His surety was set at $500 which was produced by W.N. Corneal and R.C.

Noleman, his attorney. W.G. Simonson appeared for plaintiff on 26 May 1902 and defendant objected to introduction of evidence for reason the complainant does not state a crime. Overruled. Ruled that the defendant (Corneal) committed the offense as charged and be fined $500 as approved by the court and if defaults is to serve time in jail. Sum was paid.

Nebraska State Journal, Lincoln, Nebraska, 28 May 1902
"Rules Against Alliance Saloons.
Alliance, Neb., May 27 — (Special)
A decision rendered last night from the district bench by Judge W.H. Westover may mean that Alliance

will have three less saloons heretofore. H.C. Armstrong, W.H. Brockett and W.H. Corneal had secured saloon licences and paid the license fee of $1,000 each, but upon their failure to comply with the directions of the mayor and council that body rescinded its action and refused to deliver the licenses and ordered the saloons closed. The proprietors secured a temporary restraining order from Judge Westover until last night. At that time he dissolved the injunction, stating that it was not the proper remedy. Mandamus proceedings have been instituted to comply the city council to abide by its first order."

Box Butte County, Nebraska
Criminal Case
District Court
State of Nebraska vs William N. Corneal
Unlawfully selling intoxicating liquor
February 1903
Complaint for Violation of Ordinance No. 9

22 December 1902 S.W. Reese filed a complaint in writing under oath charging William N. Corneal with violation of said ordinance. Warrant was issued for his arrest. [S.W. Reese was the Alliance City Marshall.] Corneal requested continuance of 30 days; denied. 2 January 1903 supoena issued for Thos. Burke, Bacon, W.J. Owens and William Davis.
Trial on 2 January 1903, Corneal pled not guilty. Defendant asked for cause to be dismissed for reason that the evidence failed to sustain the complaint and especially as to selling or giving away liquors. Overruled. Exception. On consideration of evidence the defendant was found guilty of having kept open a building situated on Lot 9 Box 27 in the City of Alliance in which building malt spiritous and vinous liquors were sold as a beverage on Sunday, 21 December 1902, contrary to the ordinances. Charge of selling or giving away liquors on said day dismissed on motion of attorney for the State of Nebraska. Defendant fined $25 and costs taxed at $13.40. He failed to pay so was committed to jail with a bond of $100.00. On the same day the defendant, Corneal, filed a bond in appeal. The bondsman was Simon Spry.

The Alliance Herald of 27 February 1903 announced that four indictments were rendered and arrests were made at Alliance. This involved fraudulent land entries. Those indicted were Eph Corneal, F.E. Reddish, John Leith and Henry H. Miller. They were accused of subornation of perjury, but the accusation is that they procured the making of false entries by negroes. The four accompanied the marshal to Omaha and furnished bond for their appearance at federal court. They were accused of securing fraudulent land entries through the instrumentality of about 25 illerate blacks.

Omaha World Herald, Omaha, Nebraska 28 February 1903
"Fraud in Land Entries
Four Alliance Men Accused of It, Get Bail and Go Home
Eph Corneal, Henry Miller, E.F. Reddish and John Leith, brought in from Alliance Friday night, gave bond in the United States court. They are charged with subornation of perjury. They returned to Alliance this morning. The accusation is that they secured fraudulent land entries, through the instrumentality of about twenty-five illiterate negroes. This is not the first case of the kind in United States court, but no one has ever been convicted on the charge of subornation of perjury in the cases that have been tried. "
More can be learned about the fraudulent land entries from the following newspaper account:

Omaha World Herald, Omaha, Nebraska, Thursday 6 July 1905 page 10
"Stealing Public Lands, A Bit of Nebraska History
Boston Transcript Reviews the Mosby-Summers Prosecution in This State
Charles the Cattle Barons were the Real Decapitors of the Former District Attorney

(Charles R. Lighton, in the *Boston Transcript*)

"During the month of April 1901, and for some time before and after, one F.M. Dorrington was register and one W.R. Akers receiver of the federal land office at Alliance, Neb. This it will be remembered is the office through which the homestead and other frauds were committed which led to the recent indictment, trial and conviction of the Krause brothers.

On April 1 there appeared before these officials a man named Henry Miller, the wealthy owner of one of the large ranches in that district. He was accompanied by his partner, John Leith; by F.E. Reddish, his legal counsellor, and by Eph Corneal of Lincoln ... the latter a well known political thimble rigger and general utility man.

The quartet had in tow on that day several persons, picked up by Corneal at Lincoln, who had suddenly conceived a passon to acquire homesteads in the public domain. The first of these to file was Jesse Cobbs, whose application bears the office number 4109, and whose affidavit of entry recited, among other things, the following:

That my said application is honestly and in good faith made for the purpose of actual settlement and cultivation, and not for the benefit of any other person, persons or corporation, and that I will faithfully and honestly endeavor to comply with the requirements of law as to settlement, residence and cultivation necessary to acquire title to the land applied for: I am not acting as agent of any person, corporation or syndicate in making such entry, nor in collusion with any person, corporation or syndicate to give them the benefit of the land entered or any part thereof; that I do not apply to enter the same for the purpose of speculation, but in good faith to get a home for myself, and that I have not directly or indirectly made, and will not make, any agreement or contract in any way or manner, with any person or persons, corporation or syndicate whatsoever by which the title which I may acquire from the government of the United States shall inure, in whole or in part, to the benefit of any person except myself.

Real Brotherly Love
It appears from the records that the quarter-section of land assigned to this Cobbs, upon strength of his application and affidfavit, lay within the range inclosure of Miller and Leith. It is evident that these gentlemen were preter-naturally large-hearted; for, notwithstanding the fact that Cobbs swore he meant to settle upon and improve a quarter-mile of their pasture, they not only made no protest, but they generously paid his land office fees out of their own pockets. Those western cattlemen are proverbiallly recklessly impulsive in such matters. A beautiful and touching picture of real brotherly love, isn't it? And it did not stop with that; for when a few minutes later, Cobbs was stricken with an acute attack of homesickness and longed to return to the familiar scenes of Lincoln, those two noble-minded ranchmen took a relinquishment of his newly-acquired homestead right, paid him a sum in spot cash, and relieved him of all further care and responsibility in the matter. Just think how happy they have made poor Cobbs, and how thrice-blessed he must have called them! Such instances are by no means rare in cowland. Indeed, the records of the Alliance office for that one day are enough to establish forever the philanthropic reputation of Miller and Leith. Before Cobbs had quite caught his breath, James Woodward stepped up to the desk, made homestead application number 4107, subscribed his name to an affidavit identical in form with that of his predecessor, and was assigned his quarter-section, which happened also to lie inside the wire fence of Cobbs' benefactors. Was it coninicidence, think you, or were these claimants conspiring against the generosity of the ranchmen and endeavoring to ride a free horse to death? On the face of things, the latter seems most likely to be the correct view; for before the ink was dry on Woodard's signature, he, too, was taken with a bad case of homsesickness, got his land office fees paid and a lump sum down for his relinquishment.

And then came Henry Payne, with application No. 4108 and then Edward Baker, with application No. 4106.
A Joyous Procession
One would suppose that even the most reckless profligate would tire of being thus imposed upon. But not

Miller and Leith, for on April 6, five days later, they dropped into the land office again together with Reddish and Corneal, to look on while other lands in their pasture inclosure were shamelessly taken from them by Stephen Jackson (application No. 4123), William Shore (application 4121), Thomas Jackson (application 4120), Peter Martin (application 4126), Annie Groves (application 4125), Lizzie Duncan (application 4124), Ida Taylor (application 4120), Fred Stuart (application 4122), Ben Williams (application 4118) and John Adams (application 4132). In each and every one of these cases, the former procedure was repeated, without a hair's breadth of difference save that when Register Dorrington would get tired of making out papers and raking in the fee money, Receiver Akers would "spell" him for a while.

On April 8 they came again — really as if they enjoyed it! This time the claimants were Abram J. Bell (application 4135), Charles F. Pepper (application 4137), Janie Trefren (application 4134), Lutecin Green (application 4139) and Hattie Housley (application 4138). And again on April 11, with John Corneal (application 4148) and Mattie Parkers (application 4149). And yet again on April 15, the claimants, this time being Addie Taylor (application 4131), Ben Carter (application 4156) and Louis Carter (application 4157). Around twenty-five in all, within just two weeks' time.

They they rested at their labors. Besides the consciousness of so many good deeds, Miller and Leith had aqcquired six and one-quarter square miles of land; Reddish had seen to it that all was in due and legal form; Corneal had stood by chuckling over the crumbs of "rake-off" that were to fall to him as commissions; the claimants had departed, never to return, bearing away $50 each and their traveling and incidental expenses, and Dorrington and Akers were about $500 to the good in lawful fees."

A fencing law was passed by the United States Congress in 1885. This declared that the inclosure or fencing public lands in any State or Territory by any person, association, or coporation not having title to the same was unlawful and thereby prohibited. Because of this the United States district attorney could bring charges in either a United States district or cicuit court against anyone illegally inclosing the public lands. If found to be illegal, the owner was to remove the fence within five days. The same law declared that the use of force, threats, or intimidation to prevent or obstruct any person from making homestead settlement on public lands was illegal. They would be charged with a misdemeanor and subject to a fine not exceeding $1,000, along with imprisonment for not over one year, each offense.

By 1901 a large portion of public domain in western Nebraska was being illegally fenced by cattle barons and ranch operations. Cattlemen fenced the largest portion of grazing domain without legal title or claim. This practice was so common that the Commissioner of the General Land Office sent a special agent to Nebraska in late 1901. He found an increase in hobo filings over the past two years. These were filed by tramps or other irresponsible persons to secure title for cattlemen. By using these fraudulent filings, ranchers could secure title to land around their grazing areas. This was to discourage bonafide homesteaders from filing on what they considered "their land." The agent found that they were not complying with the Homestead Act law, with a claimant maybe building a small shack on the land and spending one night there every six months.

If the cattlemen who could not secure final proof on the fraudulent claims would appeal to the Commissioner of the General Land Office and then the Secretary of the Interior. These appeals would take time so they continued to hold on to land for several years. By the end of 1907, fraudulent entries were almost eliminated in Nebraska. 57

Miller and Leith were ranchmen in Box Butte Co., Nebraska. Henry H. Miller purchased 160 acres of land on 26 September 1890, located in Box Butte County southwest of Alliance near the Morrill County line. He patented 160 acres of land under the Homestead Act on 29 November 1890. It was located southwest of Alliance near the Morrill Co. line. On 22 March 1897 he made a Timber Culture Entry for 160 acres in the same location.

Henry H. and Mary J. Miller's daughter, Annie, was married (second husband) to John Leith. Census enumerations reflect their households and locations.

1900 US Census, Box Butte Co., Nebraska, Snake Creek Prect., ED 10, page A-3 58
37-38 Henry H. Miller, b. March 1842, 58, married 34 years, b. PA, both parents
        b. PA stock farmer
Mary J., wife, b. Nov. 1845, 54, married 34 years, 1 child, 1 living, b. PA, both
        parents b. PA
Blanch L. Chapman, granddaughter, b. June 1889, 10, b. PA, father b. OH,
        mother b. PA

1900 US Census, Box Butte Co., Nebraska, Wright Prect., ED 11, page 2B 59
33-33 John Leith, b. Nov 1895, 54, married 1 year, b. Scotland, both parents b.
        Scotland; came to US in 1847 (no naturalization indicated), farmer
Annie E., wife, b. June 1866, 33, married 1 year, 2 children, 2 living, b. PA, both
        parents b. PA
Blanch L. Chapman, daughter, b. June 1889, 10, b. PA, father b. OH, mother b.
        PA, at school
Mary M. Chapman, daughter, b. May 1891, 9, b. OH, father b. OH, mother b.
        PA, at school
Frank D. Parrish, lodger, b. July 1877, 23, single, b. IA, father b. OH, mother b.
        IA farm laborer

On 26 December 1890 John Leith purchased three parcels of land in Box Butte County at the Chadron Land Office. They consisted of 160 acres in the same sections that Henry H. Miller owned land. John Leith began obtaining land in Box Butte County under the Timber Culture Act twice on 9 September 1895. One was for 151.19 acres and another for 160 acres.   This was west of Alliance and approximately four to five miles north of the Morrill County line. At the Alliance Land Office he patented 160 acres under the Homestead Act on 16 July 1896, located directly south of the Timber Culture land. On 23 May 1898 he purchased 40 acres at the Alliance Land Office, located in the same area. He purchased 160 acres of land on 1 September 1908, located further west of his earlier land and about three miles north of the Morrill County line. On 28 January 1910 he purchased 40 acres of land in the same general area. 60

Henry H. Miller, born 30 September 1842, died 15 March 1904 and was buried in the Alliance Cemetery. He was murdered by James Connelly. His wife Mary J. Miller was born 11 November 1846 and died 7 May 1905, also buried in the Alliance Cemetery.

The Alliance Herald, Alliance, Nebraska, 15 July 1904
"The Connelly Murder Trial On

The trial of James Connelly for the murder of Henry H. Miller of this city is in progress at Harrison and a number of witnesses from here went to that place last Monday and Tuesday. The crime for which Connelly is being tried is well known and needs little if any reviewing. The trouble arose over a steer worth perhaps $30, which was on the defendant's ranch in Sioux county. The animal was claimed by Miller who went out to take possession of the same. While at the ranch of Connelly and walking toward the knoll a short distance from the stable he was shot through the heart and instantly killed. It is said that Connelly was behind the hill and when he got sight of Miller shot and killed him. This is a story of the crime and as far as the details and evidence is concerned it will require the testimony in the trial to determine. Attorney Noleman of this city assisted by Fred Wright of Gering have charge of the defense and Wm. Mitchell and the attorney of Sioux county represents the state. The trial is before Judge Westover. Among those who were subpoenaed from this city were the following: C. Anderson, Ethel

New, J.D. Barry, Valentine King, R.M. Hampton, John Burns, Albert Underwood, Westley Hubbell, Mary Jane Miller, John Leith, Anna E. Leith, Edward Sweezey, Artie L. Kennedy, Zed Goodwin, Jules Zbinden, Jerry Rowan, Robert J. Hill, Dr. J.E. Moore, Guy Lockwood, Wm. Butler, E.A. Hall, Jerry Wells, Andy Cusick Chas. Bangs, Arthur Wicks, R.H. Watkins, Wm. Sherlock, Steve Dolan, Chas. Tiernan."

James Connolly/Connelly was sentenced from Sioux County for manslaughter for eight years. 61

The Alliance Herald, 11 May 1905
"Mrs. H.H. Miller Dead
Mrs. H.H. Miller died suddenly at her home Sunday noon, while her only daughter, Mrs. John Leith was at church. Her husband it will be remembered was murdered in Sioux county about a year ago. Mrs. Miller has not been well of late, being a sufferer of renal calculi, but her condition was not thought critical. She was one of the pioneers of this county and was joint owners of the Zbinen-Miller block in this city. The funeral was conducted by Rev. Ray at the M.E. Church yesterday afternoon."

The Alliance Herald, 21 May 1908   District Court News
"The case of C.L. Hashman vs James, John and Thomas Leith for damages sustained by a prairie fire is now on trial."

The Alliance Herald, 28 May 1908   District Court news
"The case of Hashman vs Leith in which $1500 was asked for damages from a fire set out by Leith, the jury found for plaintiff to the amount of $957.50 and costs. Suits of other parties against Leith were settled out of court."

On the 1910 US Census, Box Butte Co., Nebraska, Annie E. Leith was living at 315 Cheyenne Avenue, shown as age 41, married twice, 3 children, 3 children living. Her husband is not in the household. She apparently had a daughter, Goldie Leith, born in about 1902 in Nebraska. Also in her household were the two daughters, Blanche and Mary Chapman. By 1920 she had moved to Vancouver, Clark Co., Washington where she was living with her husband George Duncan and her nineteen year old daughter, Goldie Leith. 62, 63

John Leith died in 1913. Annie E. Leith filed a petition in the county court of Box Butte County on 30 June 1913 for appointment of administratrix of his estate. 64 In March of 1913, Leith's employee, W.H. Showers and his wife moved to the ranch, eighteen miles west of Alliance. 65

Frank Earl (F.E.) Reddish was born 13 July 1860 in White Co., Indiana and died in Alliance on 31 January 1922, buried in the Alliance Cemetery. On 26 April 1886 he married Mary Eliza "Mollie" Fisher in Nemaha Co., Nebraska. They came to Box Butte County in 1887, homesteading at Barrell Springs on Snake Creek, approximately fourteen miles west-southwest of Alliance. James Leith settled a half mile southwest of the Reddish homestead. In 1894 the Reddishes moved to Alliance where he opened a real estate office. He also was a homestead locator or land attorney in Box Butte County and to areas in Sheridan County and east to Ellsworth. Reddish was a surveyor and conducted an insurance and loan business in addition to being a realtor and land locater. His wife was born on 1 January 1862 in Nemaha Co., Nebraska and died 8 September 1951 in Seirra Madre, Los Angeles Co., California, buried in the Alliance Cemetery. 66

The Omaha Daily Bee, 29 July 1908
Council Bluffs (Iowa)
"William Corneal, colored, filed a voluntary petition in bankruptcy in the federal court yesterday. He schedules his liabilities at $11,761, and his assets at $5,840.15. The secured claims aggregate $4,500. The assets consist of real estate, household goods, etc. Corneal is said to be the first colored person to file a bankruptcy petition in this district."

1. Year: 1900; Census Place: Alliance, Box Butte, Nebraska; Roll: 917; Page: 21A; Enumeration District: 0006; FHL microfilm: 1240917

2. Henry C. Armstrong, owner of the saloon later owned by Corneal, died in March of 1908 at Sheridan, Wyoming.

3. Year: 1910; Census Place: Minneapolis Ward 5, Hennepin, Minnesota; Roll: T624_702; Page: 12A; Enumeration District: 0089; FHL microfilm: 1374715

4. Year: 1920; Census Place: Sand Springs, Tulsa, Oklahoma; Roll: T625_1486; Page: 23A; Enumeration District: 189; Image: 192.

5. Year: 1930; Census Place: Richmond Heights, St Louis, Missouri; Roll: 1224; Page: 10A; Enumeration District: 0053; Image: 443.0; FHL microfilm: 2340959.

6. Year: 1940; Census Place: Richmond Heights, St Louis, Missouri; Roll: T627_2150; Page: 9B; Enumeration District: 95-170.

7. FHL Film 1499059.

8. *Lincoln Star*, Lincoln, Nebraska, 24 April 1923.

9. *Brown County World*, Hiawatha, Kansas, 2 December 1910.

10. Brown County, Kansas Marriage Book, page 68.

11. Kansas State Historical Society; Topeka, Kansas; 1885 Kansas Territory Census; Roll: KS1885_76; Line: 1.

12. Year: 1910; Census Place: Kansas City Ward 3, Wyandotte, Kansas; Roll: T624_460; Page: 2A; Enumeration District: 0167; FHL microfilm: 1374473

13. Year: 1920; Census Place: Kansas City Ward 4, Wyandotte, Kansas; Roll: T625_555; Page: 7A; Enumeration District: 173; Image: 391

14. Year: 1930; Census Place: Pleasanton, Linn, Kansas; Roll: 708; Page: 10B; Enumeration District: 0011; Image: 1006.0; FHL microfilm: 2340443

15. Year: 1940; Census Place: Kansas City, Jackson, Missouri; Roll: T627_2173; Page: 11B; Enumeration District: 116-191.

16. A hod carrier is a laborer employed in carrying supplies to bricklayers, stonesmasons, cement finishers or plasterers.

17. Missouri Death Certificate #30494.

18. Brown County, Kansas Marriages page 216.

19. Brown County, Kansas Marriages page 101.

20. Year: 1900; Census Place: Hiawatha, Brown, Kansas; Roll: 472; Page: 4B; Enumeration District: 0023; FHL microfilm: 1240472

21. Year: 1910; Census Place: Lincoln Ward 1, Lancaster, Nebraska; Roll: T624_850; Page: 5B; Enumeration District: 0052; FHL microfilm: 1374863

22. Ancestry.com. U.S. City Directories, 1822-1995 [database on-line]. Provo, UT, USA: Ancestry.com Operations, Inc., 2011.

23. Year: 1930; Census Place: Portland, Multnomah, Oregon; Roll: 1950; Page: 1B; Enumeration District: 0151; Image: 888.0; FHL microfilm: 2341684

24. Year: 1940; Census Place: Portland, Multnomah, Oregon; Roll: T627_3387; Page: 1B; Enumeration District: 37-164

25. FindAGrave http://www.findagrave.com.

26. Year: 1910; Census Place: Lincoln Ward 3, Lancaster, Nebraska; Roll: T624_850; Page: 12B; Enumeration District: 0060; FHL microfilm: 1374863

27. Return of Marriages in County of Pottawattamie to the Secretary of Iowa State Board of Health.

28. Box Butte Co., Nebraska Marriage Book C, page 74 #955.

29. Year: 1910; Census Place: Sheridan Ward 1, Sheridan, Wyoming; Roll: T624_1747; Page: 2B; Enumeration District: 0103; FHL microfilm: 1375760.

30. FindAGrave.

31. Year: 1910; Census Place: Portland Ward 9, Multnomah, Oregon; Roll: T624_1289; Page: 4B; Enumeration District: 0212; FHL microfilm: 1375302

32. "Oregon Death Index, 1903-1998," database, FamilySearch (https://familysearch.org/ark:/

61903/1:1:VZ4K-WBG), William Washington, 06 Mar 1934; from "Oregon, Death Index, 1898-2008," database and images, Ancestry (http://www.ancestry.com : 2000); citing Portland, Oregon, certificate number 685, Oregon State Archives and Records Center, Salem.

33. Year: 1920; Census Place: Lincoln Ward 5, Lancaster, Nebraska; Roll: T625_996; Page: 14A; Enumeration District: 71; Image: 799

34. Year: 1930; Census Place: Lincoln, Lancaster, Nebraska; Roll: 1285; Page: 18B; Enumeration District: 0031; Image: 1046.0; FHL microfilm: 2341020

35. FindAGrave.

36. "The Lincoln Star", Lincoln, Nebraska 22 March 1931, A-6.

37. Year: 1920; Census Place: St Joseph Ward 3, Buchanan, Missouri; Roll: T625_907; Page: 3A; Enumeration District: 68; Image: 385.

38. Year: 1930; Census Place: St Joseph, Buchanan, Missouri; Roll: 1178; Page: 6B; Enumeration District: 0037; Image: 530.0; FHL microfilm: 2340913

39. Year: 1870; Census Place: Spencer, Ralls, Missouri; Roll: M593_802; Page: 119B; Image: 242; Family History Library Film: 552301.

40. FHL Film#1313418.

41. Kansas State Historical Society; Topeka, Kansas; *1895 Kansas Territory Census;* Roll: *v115_40;* Line: *1.*

42. Year: 1900; Census Place: Iowa, Doniphan, Kansas; Roll: 478; Page: 1B; Enumeration District: 0041; FHL microfilm: 1240478.

43. Year: 1910; Census Place: Lincoln Ward 3, Lancaster, Nebraska; Roll: T624_850; Page: 10B; Enumeration District: 0065; FHL microfilm: 1374863

44. Year: 1920; Census Place: Lincoln Ward 1, Lancaster, Nebraska; Roll: T625_996; Page: 3A; Enumeration District: 54; Image: 99

45. Year: 1930; Census Place: Lincoln, Lancaster, Nebraska; Roll: 1285; Page: 22A; Enumeration District: 0019; Image: 513.0; FHL microfilm: 2341020.

46. Year: 1940; Census Place: Lincoln, Lancaster, Nebraska; Roll: T627_2253; Page: 6B; Enumeration District: 55-27.

47. Year: 1920; Census Place: Lincoln Ward 3, Lancaster, Nebraska; Roll: T625_996; Page: 16B; Enumeration District: 64; Image: 413.

48. Year: 1930; Census Place: Lincoln, Lancaster, Nebraska; Roll: 1285; Page: 4B; Enumeration District: 0019; Image: 478.0; FHL microfilm: 2341020

49. Year: 1940; Census Place: Lincoln, Lancaster, Nebraska; Roll: T627_2253; Page: 5A; Enumeration District: 55-27

50. Year: 1880; Census Place: White Cloud, Doniphan, Kansas; Roll: 379; Family History Film: 1254379; Page: 499A; Enumeration District: 074; Image: 0562.

51. Year: 1900; Census Place: Lincoln Ward 3, Lancaster, Nebraska; Roll: 933; Page: 7A; Enumeration District: 0048; FHL microfilm: 1240933.

52. Year: 1910; Census Place: Lincoln Ward 3, Lancaster, Nebraska; Roll: T624_850; Page: 8A; Enumeration District: 0060; FHL microfilm: 1374863

53. Year: 1930; Census Place: Lincoln, Lancaster, Nebraska; Roll: 1285; Page: 21B; Enumeration District: 0019; Image: 512.0; FHL microfilm: 2341020.

54. *Lincoln in Black and White: 1910-1925* by Douglas Keister, Edward F. Zimmer; Charleston, SC: Arcadia Pub., 2008, p 75.

55. Year: 1940; Census Place: Lincoln, Lancaster, Nebraska; Roll: T627_2253; Page: 23A; Enumeration District: 55-17.

56. National Register of Historic Places, Registration Form, http://www.nebraskahistory.org/histpres/ nebraska/lancaster/LC13-E11-090%20Trago-T-McW.pdf.

57. *Land Frauds and Illegal Fencing in Western Nebraska* by Arthur R. Reynolds, Agricultural History, Vol. 23, No. 3 (Jul, 1949, pp 173-179.

58. Year: 1900; Census Place: Snake Creek, Box Butte, Nebraska; Roll: 917; Page: 3A; Enumeration District: 0010; FHL microfilm: 1240917

59. Year: 1900; Census Place: Wright, Box Butte, Nebraska, Roll: 917; Page: 2B; Enumeration District: 0011; FHL microfilm: 1240917

60. US Department of Interior, Bureau of Land Management, *http://www.glorecords.blm.gov*

61. Prisoner number 4483, RG034#1, Nebraska State Historical Society.

62. Year: 1910; Census Place: Alliance Ward 1, Box Butte, Nebraska; Roll: T624_838; Page: 6A; Enumeration District: 0006; FHL microfilm: 1374851

63. Year: 1920; Census Place: Vancouver, Clark, Washington; Roll: T625_1922; Page: 5A; Enumeration District: 26; Image: 192

64. *The Alliance Herald*, Alliance, Nebraska, 17 July 1913.

65. *The Alliance Herald*, Alliance, Nebraska, 20 March 1913.

66. *History of the City of Alliance and Box Butte Co., Nebraska* Vol. 1, pp 380, 381.

William Crawford

William Crawford and his wife, Sarah, came to Dawson Co., Nebraska with other black settlers from Canada. They are first found on the 1885 Nebraska State Census living next door to Leroy Gields and his sister, Mathilda Robinson. This is the only census that shows William Crawford's birth place as Canada.

> 1885 Nebraska State Census, Dawson Co., Nebraska, Logan Prect., ED 192, 1
> Page 5A
> 60-60 Wm. Crawford, black, 35, farmer, b. Canada, both parents b. Canada
> Sarah, black, 24, wife, keeping house, b. Canada, both parents b. Canada
> Florence, black, 3, daughter, b. Canada, both parents b. Canada
> Charlotte, black, 2, daughter, b. Canada, both parents b. Canada

Along with the Meehans and Emanuels and other black settlers living near Overton, Nebraska, the Crawford remained there until they learned of the availability of land in Cherry Co., Nebraska. While he is shown as married on the 1900 US Census, it does appear that William's wife, Sarah had died between 1895 and 1900.

> 1900 US Census, Dawson Co., Nebraska, Overton, ED 93, Page 3A 2
> 59-59 William Crawford, black, b. Aug 1849, 50, married 21 years, b. TN,
>   both parents b. VA, day laborer
> Florence, daughter, black, b. Nov 1881, 18, single, b. Canada, father b. TN,
>   mother b. NY, at school
> William C., son, black, b. Jan 1886, 14, b. NE, father b. TN, mother b. NY,
>   at school
> Ella, daughter, black, b. June 1888, 11, b. NE, father b. TN, mother b. NY,
>   at school
> Lily, daughter, black, b. Oct. 1890, 9, b. NE, father b. TN, mother b. NY,
>   at school
> Hazel, daughter, black, b. Feb 1893, 7, b. NE, father b. TN, mother b. NY,
>   at school
> Viola, daughter, black, b. May 1895, 5, b. NE, father b. TN, mother b. NY

> 1910 US Census, Cherry Co., Nebraska, Loup Prect., ED 57, Page 6B 3
> 79-79 William Crawford, black, 61, married, married 31 years, b. TN, both
>   parents b. VA, farmer
> Hazel, daughter, black, 17, b. NE, father b. TN, mother b. NY
> Viola, daughter, black, 14, b. NE, father b. TN, mother b. NY

William Crawford purchased 80 acres in Dawson Co., Nebraksa from the federal government on 23 December 1889. It was located in Township 10N, Range 19 W, Section 32, E 1/2 NE 1/4. The land was located about 3 1/2 miles north of Overton. 4

Under the Homestead Act, he secured 635.01 acres of land in Cherry Co., Nebraska, patent issued 5 January 1914 from the Valentine Land Office. The land was located as follows. The land was located near the Dewitty settlement. 5

    Twp 27 N Range 30W, Section 2, NW 1/4
        W 1/2 NE 1/4
    Twp 28 N Range 30W, Section 35, S 1/2
        S 1/2 NE 1/4

William does not appear on the 1920 US Census and most likely died between 1915 and 1920 in Cherry Co., Nebraska. He was buried in the Brownlee Cemetery, Brownlee, Cherry Co., Nebraska. His daughter Hazel was buried in the DeWitty Cemetery near Brownlee. His daughter Lillian "Lily" married a James Allen and also to a Mr. Appleby.

1. Nebraska State Census, 1885," database with images, FamilySearch (https://familysearch.org/ark:/61903/1:1:X3X2-WMX) Wm Crawford, 1885; citing NARA microfilm publication M352 (Washington, D.C.: National Archives and Records Administration, n.d.); FHL microfilm 499,540.
2. Year: 1900; Census Place: Overton, Dawson, Nebraska; Roll: 922; Page: 3A; Enumeration District: 0093; FHL microfilm: 1240922
3. Year: 1910; Census Place: Loup, Cherry, Nebraska; Roll: T624_840; Page: 6B; Enumeration District: 0057; FHL microfilm: 1374853
4. U.S. Department of the Interior, Bureau of Land Management, General Land Office Records, http://www.glorecords.blm.gov/details/patent/default.aspx?accession=NE0820___.298&docClass=STA&sid=1hqrrvyj.jib
5. U.S. Department of the Interior, Bureau of Land Management, General Land Office Records http://www.glorecords.blm.gov/details/patent/default.aspx?accession=NE0820___.298&docClass=STA&sid=1hqrrvyj.jib

Joseph and Cora Crittenden

Joseph W. and Cora Crittenden were well known in Alliance, Nebraska. He was born 15 April 1866 in Texas and died 29 September 1935 in Alliance, Nebraska. For many years he was a farmer and truck gardener in South Alliance. He was a very strong man and died from internal hemorraghing sustained when he lifted a wagon. His wife, Cora, was born 25 September 1882 in Taylor Co., Kentucky and died on 10 November 1961 in Alliance, Nebraska. Both were buried in the Alliance Cemetery. Information in the obituary for Joe Crittenden indicates he was survived by several children. The only child shown to survive Cora was the adopted son, Richard Crittenden.

After being hospitalized for one day, Cora died in St. Joseph's Hospital in Alliance. She was the daughter of James Motley and his wife Sarah Elizabeth "Betty" Anderson. Cora was fondly called "Aunt Billie." She married first to a Mr. Tate. Refer to the Chandler & Motley and Anderson, Volume 1.

Joe and Cora adopted a boy who was named Richard Dean. Joe and Cora went to an orphange in Omaha to possibly adopt a child. They were told that they were too old, but on the sly they took Richard from the home. Nobody came to look for him. 1 It is unknown if the adoption was legalized, but by 1940 he was going by the surname of Crittenden. He was born in Omaha, Douglas Co., Nebraska on 17 August

1924 and died 12 December 1993 in Alliance, Nebraska. He was buried in the Alliance Cemetery. The following census enumerations indicate this family in Box Butte County.

1920 US Census, Box Butte Co., Nebraska, Lawn Prect., ED 15, Page 3A 2
60-61 James Motley, rents, black, 58, b. KY, both parents b. KY, farmer
Sara E., wife, black, 56, b. KY, both parents b. KY
Virgil J., son, black, 19, b. KY, both parents b. KY
Joseph W. Crittenden, son-in-law, mulatto, 49, b. TX, father b. TN, mother b.
      VA, farm laborer
Cora B. Crittenden, daughter, black, 37, b. KY, both parents b. KY
Robert Anderson, uncle, black, 80, single, b. KY, both parents b. KY

1930 US Census, Box Butte Co., Nebraska, Alliance, ED 3, Page 5B 3
South Platte Avenue
93-116 Joseph Crittenden, owns, $3,000, negro, 59, married at age 22, b.
      TX, both parents b. TN, farmer
Cora, wife, negro, 40, married at age 20, b. KY, both parents b. KY,
      laundress, at home
Richard Dean, foster son, negro, 5, b. NE, both parents b. US

1940 US Census, Box Butte Co., Nebraska, Alliance, ED 7-3B, Page 10B 4
214 Platte Avenue, owns #200
Core [sic] Crittenden, female, negro, 56, widow, 4th grade, b. KY, laundress,
      own home
Richard, son, negro, 15, 5th grade, b. NE

Joseph W. Crittenden and Cora B. Tate were married at Checotah, McIntosh Co., Oklahoma on 18 April 1918. He was age 48 and a resident of Checotah. Cora was age 36 and a resident of Hemingford, Box Butte Co., Nebraska. It is thought that her marriage to a Mr. Tate occurred in Omaha, Nebraska. 5

Joseph W. Crittenden married first to Mrs. Sabra Austin on 30 November 1899 in Muskogee Co., Oklahoma. He was age 35 and she was age 36. Joseph was of Eufaula, Indian Territory as was Sabra. 6 She was born to Andy and Nancy Sells in about 1860. Her father registered as a Choctaw Indian in Indian Territory. Even though registered as a Coctaw, he is shown on the Dunn Roll of Creeks in 1896. 7

Index to the Final Rolls of Citizens and Freedmen of the Creek and Seminole
      Tribes enrollment date 1890?
No. 3661 Sabra Austin, 30, female, Census Card #940
(also on the card Arthur Jackson, 16; Jimmie Austin, 9; Rena Austin, 6; Ruben
Austin, 2) 8

Joseph and Sabra Crittenden lived in Checotah Twp., McIntosh Co., Oklahoma in 1910. This is where the Chandlers, Motleys and others lived before coming to Box Butte Co., Nebraska.

1910 US Census, McIntosh Co., Oklahoma, Checotah Twp., ED 70, Page 2A 9
24-24 Joseph W. Crittenden, mulatto, 46, second marriage, married 10 years, b.
      TX, father b. TX, mother b. MS, farmer
Sabra J., wife, black, 48, second marriage, 9 children, 5 living, b. OK, both
      parents b. AL, farm laborer
James G., step son, black, 21, single, b. OK, father b. TX, mother b. OK, farm
      laborer
Lusena, step daughter, black, 16, b. OK, father b. TX, mother b. OK, farm laborer

Ruby C., step son, black, 14, b. OK, father b. TX, mother b. OK, farm laborer
Allie V., daughter, mulatto, 8, b. OK, father b. TX, mother b. OK
Tennessee, niece, black, 15, b. OK, father b. TX, mother b. OK, farm laborer

It is possible that Sabra was married first to a Mr. Jackson and had at least one child by him, then married a Mr. Austin and had more children before her marriage to Joseph Crittenden. Arthur Jackson is shown as being age 16 on her census card #940 in 1896.

According to the 1910 US Census, Joseph Crittenden had only one child by Sabra, that being Allie Viola Crittenden. She was born in 1901 and is shown on the Creek Freedmen Roll #5277. She married Allen B. Bruner, who was born 15 October 1893 in Indian Territory and died September 1873 in Muskogee, Muskogee Co., Oklahoma. He is buried in the Booker T. Washington Cemetery, Muskogee, Muskogee Co., Oklahoma. Allie died between 1926 and 1930 probably in Muskogee Co., Oklahoma. Their marriage license shows his name as Allie Bruner and hers as Viola Crittenden. They were married on 30 January 1917 in Muskogee Co., Oklahoma. Viola was living in Cheotah, McIntosh Co., Oklahoma. 10

The parents of Joseph W. Crittenden were Simon and Jane Crittenden. They were of Victoria Co., Texas. Simon Crittenden registered to vote in Victoria Co., Texas in 1867-1869. 11

1870 US Census, Victoria Co., Texas, Prect. 4, Page 19, PO Kempus Bluff 12
140-135 Simon Crittenden, 30, black, farmer, b. VA
Jane, 27, black, keeps house, b. TN
Ella, 11, mulatto, b. TN
Emeline, 10, mulatto, b. TX
Adam, 8, black, b. TX
Joseph, 6, black, b. TX
Phillip, 5, black, b. TX
Paul, 4, black, b. TX
Samuel, 2, black, b. TX

1880 US Census, Victoria Co., Texas, Prect. 3, ED140, Page 197C   13
43-44 Simon Crittendon, black, 47, laborer, b. VA, father b. VA, mother's
        place of birth unknown
Jane, black, 42, wife, keeping house, b. TN, parents place of birth unknown
Adam, black, 18, son, laborer, b. TX, father b. VA, mother b. TN
Joseph, black, 16, son, laborer, b. TX, father b. VA, mother b. TN
Eliza, black, 15, daughter, b. TX, father b. VA, mother b. TN
Samuel, black, 10, son, b. TX, father b. VA, mother b. TN
Biddie Bland, black, 83, mother-in-law, widow, b. VA, both parents b. VA

By 1900 all of the children born to Simon Crittenden and Jane Bland were no longer living in their household, but they were still in Victoria Co., Texas.

1900 US Census, Victoria Co., Texas, Justice Prect. 3, ED 89, Page 8A   14
128-128 Simon B. Crittenden, black, b. 1837, 62, married 6 years, b. VA, both
        parents b. VA, farmer
Jane, wife, black, no age shown, married 6 years, b. TX, parents place of birth
        not shown
Simeon House, boarder, black, b. Dec 1879, 20, single, b. TX, father b. unknown,
        mother b. MS, farm laborer

FindAGrave on Internet shows that Simon Crittenden was born 1833 and died 1875, buried in Pleasant Green Cemetery, Victoria, Victoria Co., Texas. However, he was still alive in 1900. His wife, Jane Bland, was born about 1837. She died 7 November 1932 in Dacosta, Victoria Co., Texas and was also buried in the Pleasant Green Cemetery.

Samuel Crittenden, son of Simon Crittenden and Jane Bland, was born in September of 1867 in Victoria, Victoria Co., Texas. He married Carrie M. —- in about 1890. Samuel died 9 August 1931 in Victoria, Victoria Co., Texas.

1. Interview, Alliance, Nebraska with Florence Nickens, 3 March 2016
2. Year: 1920; Census Place: Lawn, Box Butte, Nebraska; Roll: T625_979; Page: 3A; Enumeration District: 15; Image: 1120
3. Year: 1930; Census Place: Alliance, Box Butte, Nebraska; Roll: 1266; Page: 5B; Enumeration District: 0003; Image: 863.0; FHL microfilm: 2341001
4. Year: 1940; Census Place: Alliance, Box Butte, Nebraska; Roll: T627_2237; Page: 10B; Enumeration District: 7-3B
5. McIntosh Co., Oklahoma Marriage Book 6, Page 639.
6. "Oklahoma, County Marriages, 1890-1995", database with images, FamilySearch https:// familysearch.org/ark:/61903/1:1:QVP6-SZ9G , Joseph W Crittendon and Sarah Austin, 1899.
7. Ancestry.com. *Oklahoma and Indian Territory, Indian Censuses and Rolls, 1851-1959* [database on-line]. Provo, UT, USA: Ancestry.com Operations, Inc., 2014.
Original data: *Selected Tribal Records*. The National Archives at Fort Worth, Fort Worth, Texas.
8. Ancestry.com. U.S., Native American Enrollment Cards for the Five Civilized Tribes, 1898-1914 [database on-line]. Provo, UT, USA: Ancestry.com Operations Inc, 2008.
Original data: Enrollment Cards for the Five Civilized Tribes, 1898-1914; (National Archives Microfilm Publication M1186, 93 rolls); Records of the Bureau of Indian Affairs, Record Group 75; National Archives, Washington, D.C.
9. Place: Checotah, McIntosh, Oklahoma; Roll: T624_1260; Page: 2A; Enumeration District: 0070; FHL microfilm: 1375273
10. "Oklahoma, County Marriages, 1890-1995", database with images, FamilySearch (https:// familysearch.org/ark:/61903/1:1:QVP6-HJM3 : accessed 30 May 2016), Allie Bruner and Viola Crittenden, 1917.
11. Ancestry.com. *Texas, Voter Registration Lists, 1867-1869* [database on-line]. Provo, UT, USA: Ancestry.com Operations, Inc., 2011.
Original data: 1867 Voter Registration Lists. Microfilm, 12 rolls. Texas State Library and Archives Commission, Austin, Texas.
12. Ancestry.com. *1870 United States Federal Census* [database on-line]. Provo, UT, USA: Ancestry.com Operations, Inc., 2009. Images reproduced by FamilySearch.
13. Year: 1880; Census Place: Precinct 3, Victoria, Texas; Roll: 1330; Family History Film: 1255330; Page: 197C; Enumeration District: 140
14. Year: 1900; Census Place: Justice Precinct 3, Victoria, Texas; Roll: 1676; Page: 8A; Enumeration District: 0089; FHL microfilm: 1241676

Henry Curl

Henry William Curl, a resident of Alliance married Ida Stanton on 5 July 1911 in Alliance, Box Butte Co., Nebraska. He is shown as 26, colored, born Missouri, resident of Alliance, son of Willliam Curl and Marie Reed. Ida was 24, colored, born Delaware, daughter of James Stanton and Lizzie Thomas. The witnesses to their marriage were James Washington and Lilly Hamilton. [1]

He was born 5 August 1880 in Kansas to William Curl and Marie Reed. His wife, Ida Virginia Stanton, was born 15 May 1885 in Wilmington, New Castle Co., Delaware to James Stanton and Lizzie Thomas.

Their daughter, Dorothy Curl was born 2 March 1918 in Alliance and died there on 17 June 1918. She died at their home in South Alliance and was buried in the Alliance Cemetery. Their next child, Evelyn, was born in 1922. The whereabouts of the Curls between 1918 and 1922 are unknown as they are not enumerated on the 1920 US Census. They appear again as a divorced couple in 1930. Henry and Ida divorced in Alliance, Box Butte Co., Nebraska, but the divorce file is missing.

The Alliance Herald, 31 December 1912
"Henry Curl, the colored man, who is charged with attempted rape on the person of six year old Ollie Slaughter was bound over to district court Monday afternoon by Judge Zurn, acting as a justice of the peace. The evidence against Curl is very conflicting. The exact date of the alleged offense has not been proven and while the little girl swore the crime was actually committed, the evidence doesn't seem to substantiate it. But of conditions which are of the very lowest, the little girl and her sister scarecely two years older told a most revolting story. With these facts Curl was not concerned, the man implicated being a boarder and roomer at the home of the mother. A number of white and colored people were in attendance at the preliminary. The principal witness, the little girl, held to her story pretty well. Her mother, however, said she had lied in a number of instances. Curl believes he can prove an alibi, claiming he was not at home on the day this alleged offense was committed."

Box Butte Co., Nebraska Criminal Court Records District Court
Case #2207 Docket J page 147
State of Nebraska vs. Henry Curl
assault with intent to rape
22 January 1913

On about 23 Nov. 1912 Ollie Slaughter accused Henry Curl of an assault on her making bruises, wound and ill-threat with intent against her will feloniously to ravish and carnallly know and abuse her.
Witnesses:

Ollie Slaughter, Ethel Slaughter, Ella Lane, Gertrude Jackson for plaintiff
Henry Curl, Mrs. Curl and Walter Smith for the defendant
Warrant for arrest of Henry Curl was made 30 Dec 1912
He pled not guilty as charged.
Curl was to pay $250 surety which he did not do so; was placed in jail

Box Butte County, Nebraska Criminal Court Case
District Court
Case 3908 Docket O page 271
State of Nebraska vs Henry Curl
Burglary
filed 7 Jan. 1927

Henry Curl did on 22 Nov 1926 commit burglary in Box Butte County by breaking into and entering a building known as the St. James African M.E. Church, situated in the city of Alliance with intent to steal property of value. Warrant was issued for his arrest and he was brought into court on 20 Dec 1926. He pled not guilty to the crime and he declined to accept defense, asking for a premliminary hearing. Witnesses: Charles E. Meehan and Mrs. Gertrude Johnson. Curl declined to cross exam them and offered no defense.

Court found him guilty of the crimes and to be held with a bond fixed at $500 and if he could not post he was to be held in the county jail. Costs of suit $9.70. 20 Dec 1926.

Complaint for Burglary — on 22 Nov 1926 Henry Curl willfully, maliciously and forcibly broke and entered into the St. James African M.E. Church, the property of William Neeham and others as trustees with the intent then and there, and thereby the personal goods, chattles and valuable property of the said William Neeham and others as trustees, then and there being with intent to steal property of value.

The Alliance Herald, 5 April 1928

"Tobe Curl, colored, who was released by the officers a short time ago on a promise to leave the city, failed to leave, and Monday was brought before Police Judge Highland charged with using obscene language in the presence of women. Judge Highland fined Curl $100, but as he could not furnish the money, was given a chance to serve his fine at hard labor for $2.00 per day. He is now working on the city street gang." [Tobe was another name used by Henry Curl.] The following census shows where he and his family were living in Alliance.

> 1930 US Census, Box Butte Co., Nebraska, Alliance, Second Ward, ED 2, Page 2
> 12B
> 101 Sweetwater Ave.
> Henry Curl, lodger, negro, 42, divorced, married at age 19, b. KS, both parents
>   b. Missouri, mortar mixer, plasterer
>
> 1930 US Census, Box Butte Co., Nebraska, Alliance, Second Ward, ED 2, Page 3
> 6B
> 412 East 4th St.
> 126-139 Harvey A. Burks, rents $15 month, negro, 35, married at age 25, b. TX,
>   both parents b. TX, laborer, city
> Charlotte, wife, negro, 29, married at age 15, b. TX, both parents b. TX
> Ida Curl, lodger, negro, 25, divorced, b. DL, father b. US, mother b. MD,
>   chambermaid, hotel
> Evelyn Curl, lodger, negro, 8, b. NE, father b. MO, mother b. DL

On the 1940 US Census, Ida Curl and her daughter Evelyn were living in the household of Ella M. Lane in Lake Precinct, Box Butte Co., Nebraska. Ida is shown as a roomer, 59, divorced, 2 years school, b. Maryland, living in the same house on 1 April 1935, laborer, private home. Her daughter Evelyn Curl is shown as roomer's daughter, 18, 10th grade, b. Nebraska, living in the same house on 1 April 1935. The whereabouts of Henry Curl in 1940 are unknown. 4

Ida Curl died at her home at 101 Sweetwater in Alliance, Nebraska on 9 November 1943. She was buried in the Alliance Cemetery, the owner of the lot being Henry Curl. Her obituary indicates that her family moved to Alliance in 1910. They are not on the 1910 US Census. She had five children, four of whom preceded her in death. The only known children are Dorothy and Evelyn. The obituary indicates she was survived by her husband and one daughter, Evelyn, of Alliance.

Henry Curl died on 15 June 1955 in Alliance at St. Joseph's Hospital following an extended illness. He had lived in Alliance for 40 years according to his obituary. Curl was a retired custodian. He was born 5 August 1880 in Emporia, Lyon Co., Kansas and a member of the Methodist Church. He was survived by his daughter, Mrs. Evelyn Napue of Lincoln, Nebraska, two grandchildren, two brothers William and Clarence, both of Emporia, Kansas and one sister Mrs. Perneutra Thompson of Kansas City, Missouri. He was buried in the Alliance Cemetery.

Evelyn Curl, daughter of Henry Curl and Ida Stanton, married Crosby Napue probably between about 1945 and 1947. They lived in Lincoln, Nebraska and are shown in city directories beginning in about 1947. Crosby was a cook in 1947 and they were living at 1958 S Street. They are shown in 1951 at 2210 U Street and he was employed by the railroad. Evelyn was a maid at the Milner Hotel. Also in the household was an Odell C. Napue. 5

By 1955 Cosby and Evelyn were not living together. He was shown as a painter and living at 704 S. 19th with Odell, also a painter. Mrs. Evelyn Napue was living at 2014 S Street. In 1958 Cosby was shown with a wife Ruby living at 1985 S Street.

Crosby Doil Napue II was born in 1917 and died in 1979. He was buried in the College View Cemetery in Lincoln, Lancaster Co., Nebraska. He was shown having a wife, Ruth Ann Brooks, who was apparently not the mother of his children. She was born 8 April 1933 in Ringgold, Bienville Parish, Louisiana and died 3 February 2008 in Crete, Saline Co., Nebraska. She was also buried in the College View Cemetery. 6

Crosby Napue is shown with a daughter, Avette Marie "Trixie" Napue, born 15 February 1947 in Lincoln, Lancaster Co., Nebraska and died 4 August 2011 in Kansas City, Jackson Co., Missouri. She married Ronald E. Garnett, Airman 2nd Class, US Air Force and was buried in the Leavenworth National Cemetery, Leavenworth Co., Kansas, Section 52, Row 18, Site 4.

Crosby Doil Napue III was born 5 October 1948 in Lincoln, Lancaster Co., Nebraska to Crosby and Evelyn Curl Napue. He died 23 August 2009 in Lincoln, Lancaster Co., Nebraska. He was cremated.

William Curl and Marie Reed

The parents of Henry William Curl do not appear on census enumerations in 1880 and 1900. According to records of Henry Curl, they should have been in Kansas, most likely Lyon County. William Curl was buried in the Maplewood Memorial Lawn Cemetery in Emporia, Lyon Co., Kansas. There is no date of birth shown for him, but he died on 17 January 1905. His wife is shown as Mrs. William Curl, died 8 December 1892, date of birth unknown. They were both buried in Potter's Field. Information on the Curls can be pieced together from newspaper articles in *The Emporia Gazette* of Emporia, Kansas.

Henry Curl is mentioned twice in the newspaper. In the 26 June 1899 issue is an article stating, "Henry Curl, the colored boy who broke into Martin & Martin's store, was sentenced to the Reform School." Other newspaper articles indicate he was sentenced to the reform school for one year. *The Emporia Gazette*, 4 March 1901, page 1 indicates that the sheriff took Henry Curl to the prison at Leavenworth. There is no information as to why he was sentenced to the prison or for how long. He had served his sentence by 1911 when he married Ida Stanton in Alliance.

Piecing together the children of William Curl and Marie Reed is possible from census enumerations and newspaper articles. They appear to be as follows.

1. Henry William Curl, born 5 August 1880 in Kansas (see above)
2. Bessie B. Curl, born October 1882 in Missouri
3. Samuel Curl, born 1884 in Missouri
4. Fred Curl, born about 1889 Kansas
5. William Curl, date of birth unknown
6. Clarence Curl, born 28 December 1893 in Emporia, Kansas

The dates and places of birth lead to confusion. Marie Reed Curl, wife of William Curl, died 8 December 1892 according to the records of Maplewood Memorial Lawn Cemetery in Emporia, Lyon Co., Kansas. Therefore, either her date of death is wrong or the date of birth for Clarence Curl is in error.

The obituary for Henry Curl of Alliance, Nebraska indicates he was survived by two brothers, William and Clarence of Emporia, Kansas and a sister, Mrs. Permeutra Thompson of Kansas City, Missouri.

On 18 April 1905 *The Emporia Gazette* reported the knifing of Permetra Reed, a colored girl returning home from the Church of God meeting. The article reports that she was the step-daughter of the late William Curl. [He died 1 January 1905.] She was slashed across her back with a knife by "Kiss" Wilson a negro. The newspaper reported that Permetra Reed was well respected and worked for a Union street family. She was about 26 years of age, which would place her birth at about 1879. According to census she was born later than 1879. This was the year before the birth of Henry Curl who lived in Alliance. It is possible that Marie had married to a Mr. Reed prior to her marriage to William Curl. However, because the father's place of birth is not shown for Permetra on census enumerations, it is also possible that Permetra was born out of wedlock. The Maggie shown as the wife of Thomas Thompson in 1910 is probably Permetra, perhaps a nickname.

> 1910 US Census, Wyandotte Co., Kansas, Kansas City, Ward 3, ED 163, Page 9A   7
> 1112 Everett Avenue
> 208-210 Thomas Thompson, black, 39, married 12 years, b. AL, both parens b.
>   AL, laborer, railroad shop
> Maggie, wife, mulatto, 30, married 12 years, 6 childfren, 6 living, b. OH, both
>   parents b. OH
> Troussaint, son, mulatto, 11, b. KS, father b. AL, mother b. OH
> Stanley, son, mulatto, 8, b. KS, father b. AL, mother b. OH
> Helen, daughter, mulatto, 7, b. KS, father b. AL, mother b. OH
> Willene, daughter, mulatto, 5, b. KS, father b. AL, mother b. OH
> Odessa, daughter, mulatto, 2, b. KS, father b. AL, mother b. OH
> Thomas, son, mulatto, 7/12, b. KS, father b. AL, mother b. OH
>
> 1915 Kansas State Census, Wyanotte Co., Kansas, Kansas City, Ward 3   8
> 140-142 Thomas Thompson, 41, black
> Permetia, 33, black
> Tossinat, 17, male, black Stanley, 14, black
> Helen, 12, black
> Evelyn, 7, black
>
> 1920 US Census, Wyandotte Co., Kansas, Kansas City, Ward 3, ED 164 9
> 1112 Everett Avenue
> 413-424 Thomas Thompson, owns, free, blak, 54, b. AL, father b. US, mother b.
>   Va, laborer, steel work
> Permetra F., wife, mulatto, 38, b. MO, father b. US, mother b. VA
> Stanley D., son, black, 19, b. KS, father b. AL, mother b. MO
> Helen J., daughter, black, 17, b. KS, father b. AL, mother b. MO
> Evelyn O., daughter, black, 11, b. KS, father b. AL, mother b. MO

Thomas Thompson died between 1925 when the Kansas State Census was taken and 1927 where Permetra is shown as his widow living in Kansas City, Wyandotte Co., Kansas when the City Directory was prepared. She was living at 1112 Everett Ave. with her children Stanley and wife Lois and her daughter Evelyn. Permetra died after 1940.

> 1940 US Census, Wyandotte Co., Kansas, Kansas City, ED 106-21   10
> 1112 Everett Ave.
> owns $1,100

Samuel Grey, negro, 41, 9th grade, b. MO, same house 1 April 1935, service man,
    lounge
Evelyn Grey, wife, informant, negro, 31, 8th grade, b. TX, same house 1 April
    1935, maid, private family
Permetia Thompson, mother-in-law, negro, 58, widow, 9th grade, b. MO, same
    house 1 April 1935, seamstress

Bessie B. Curl, daughter of William Curl and Marie Reed, was born in October 1882 in Missouri.
She is mentioned in a newspaper article as being a sister to Sam Curl.

Emporia Gazette, Emporia, Kansas 22 February 1905, page 4
"Friends of Sam Curl have asked the Gazette to make the statement that Sam Curl
didn't borrow money from Blaine Clay to pay his fine, but that the fine was paid
by Curl's sisters, Mrs. Reed and Bessie Curl."

1900 US Census, Lyon Co., Kansas, Emporia, Ward 1, ED 69, Page 10B   11
Neosho Street
Household of Martha Lyle, black
Bessie B. Curl, housekeeper, black, b. October 1882, 17, single, b. MO, both
    parents b. MO

The only possibility for the Mrs. Reed, sister of Sam Curl, is Uthera? Reed, shown on the 1900
US Census.

1900 US Census, Lyon Co., Kansas, Emporia, ED 73, Page 6A   12
120-120 Harrett Powell, black, b. Dec 1852, 47, married, married 30 years, b.
    VA, father born unknown, mother b. VA
Mary Crutchfield, mother, black, b. Jan 1830, 70, widow, married 15 years, 4
    children, 4 living, b. VA, parents place of birth unknown
Uthera? Reed, niece, black, b. June 1880, 19, married, married 1 year, 1 child, 1
    living, b. MO, father b. unknown, mother b. VA, housekeeper
Rosia Harris, niece, black, b. Dec 1880, 19, single, b. KS, father birth place
    unknown, mother b. Missouri, at school
Alerta Reed, niece, black, b. May 1899, 1, b. KS, parents place of birth unknown

However, if the birth date of June 1880 is correct, this would not be the daughter of William Curl and
Marie Reed.

Samuel "Sam" Curl, son of William Curl and Marie Reed, was born in Missouri in 1884.
According to several years of newspaper articles from the *Emporia Gazette* of Emporia, Lyon Co.,
Kansas, Sam was in and out of court and jail many times. He and his siblings were young children when
their mother died and probably did not have a structured home life. He and his brother, Clarence, were
many times arrested for theft, drunkenness, assault and battery, shooting craps, burglary and bootlegging.
In one newspaper article he is called the Grand High Dealer of the Bones in the Stringtown Ivory Club,
meaning he dealt craps. 13

On 22 May 1905 Sam Curl, age 22 and Lutie Maddux, age 19, were issued a marriage license in
the Lyon County, Kansas courthouse. 14 Their marriage was stormy. Lutie was arrested for distrubing the
peace, slander, bone-dry violation [selling liquor] and keeping a disorderly house. The two of them filed
several times for divorce which apparently was revoked or not fully petitioned in court. The final divorce
proceedings appear to have been in September of 1913. 15

In 1905 when Sam's father, William Curl, was near death, Sam was in jail in Emporia. According to *The Emporia Gazette*, Emporia, Kansas, 13 January 1905, page 8, Bill Curl was sick at his home, 105 Constitution. Because of the sickness Sam Curl, his son, was taken that afternoon from the county jail to his father's home to see him. The first enumeration that shows Sam Curl and his wife Lutie is the 1905 Kansas State Census.

> 1905 Kansas State Census, Lyon Co., Kansas, Emporia   16
> rents
> 122-127 Saml. Curl, 22, black
> Lutie Curl, 21, black
> Jane Johnson, 60, black
> Hattie Wilson, 40, black

> 1920 US Census, Lyon Co., Kansas, Emporia Ward 3, ED 53, page 9B   17
> 28 State Street
> Sam Curl, owns, mortgaged, 36, black, b. MO, both parents b. MO, black
>   hod carrier, day work
> Elizabeth, black, 29, b. KS, both parents b. KS
> William, 13, black, b. KS, father b. MO, mother b. KS
> Ernestine, 12, black, b. KS, father b. MO, mother b. KS

> 1925 Kansas State Census, Lyon Co., Kansas, Emporia   18
> 28 State Street
> 240-245 Samuel Curl, rents, colored, 45, b. MO, came to KS from MO
> Luttie Curl, colored, wife, 45, b. KS
> William Curl, colored, son, 18, b. KS
> Earnestine Holt, colored, daughter, 17, widowed, b. KS
> Elisibeth Holt, colored, granddaughter, b. MO

Sam Curl died 4 July 1929. He was buried in the Maplewood Memorial Lawn Cemetery in Emporia, Lyon Co., Kansas where William Curl and his wife, Marie Reed are buried. His wife is shown as Elizabeth on the 1920 US Census, but this appears to be in error as her actual name was Lutie.

> 1930 US Census, Lyon Co., Kansas, Emporia, ED 16, Page 9B   19
> 28 State Street
> 204-221 Lutie Curl, owns, $700, negro, 42, widow, b. KS, both parents b. TX,
>   house maid, private family
> William A., son, negro, 20, single, b. KS, father b. MO, mother b. KS, laborer
>   steam railway
> Ernestine Holt, daughter, negro, 18, married at age 16, b. KS, father b. MO,
>   mother b. KS, servant, private family
> Elizabeth E. Holt, granddaughter, negro, 6, b. KS, both parents b. KS
> Sarah Maddux, mother, negro, 75, widow, b. TX

According to the City Directory of Emporia, Kansas, 1940 Lute [sic] Curl (widow of Saml) was living at 28 State. Also in the household were Ernestine Curl and Wm. A. Curl.

> 1940 US Census, Lyon Co., Kansas, Emporia, ED 56-20, Page 9B   20
> 28 State Street
> owns, $280
> Ludy E. Curl, female, informant, negro, 53, widow, 5th grade, same house on
>   1 April 1935, b. KS

William A. Curl, 31, son, negro, single, 9th grae, same house on 1 April 1935, b.
    KS, houseboy, private home
Ernestine Holt, 29, negro, daughter, widow, 9th grade, same house on 1 April
    1935, b. KS, maid, hotel
Elizabeth Holt, 15, negro, granddaughter, 3 years high school, b. KS, same house
    1 April 1935

Lutie Edith Maddux Curl was also buried in the Maplewood Memorial Lawn Cemetery in
Emporia, Lyon Co., Kansas. She was born 11 September 1887 in Kansas and died 17 April 1962. Her
parents were Allen J. Maddux and Sarah Osborn. Buried in the same cemetery are the children of Samuel
Curl and Lutie Maddux. William A. Curl was born 1 May 1906 in Kansas and died 19 September 1947.
Ernestine C. Curl Holt was born 3 January 1908 and died 15 March 1993. She married Landa "Landy"
Holt in the Chase County Courthouse in Cottonwood Falls, Kansas.

    Ernestine C. Curl, daughter of Samuel Curl and Lutie Maddux, and husband Landa "Landy" Holt
were separated. He was born 30 April 1906 in Crocus, Adair Co., Kentucky and died 11 May 1935 in
Emporia, Lyon Co., Kansas, son of Jeremiah Samuel Holt and Laura Bell Harrison. Landy was also
buried in the Maplewood Memorial Lawn Cemetery in Emporia. His given name is also shown as
Orlando which is probably his formal given name.

    Their daughter, Elizabeth Holt, was born 13 November 1924 in Emporia, Lyon Co., Kansas. She
married Rex Aaron Williams at Emporia on 5 March 1949. He died at their home on 17 August 2000.
Elizabeth died 20 Marh 2013 in Cottonwood Falls, Chase Co., Kansas and was buried in the Maplewood
Memorial Lawn Cemetery in Emporia, Kansas.

    Frederick H. "Fred" Curl, son of William Curl and Marie Reed, was born 16 March 1886 in
Kansas. It is possible that he never married. There is an article in the *Emporia Gazette*, Emporia, Kansas
2 April 1918, page 4 about the death of Peter Tucker, former slave, of Emporia. He and his wife brought
up fourteen adopted children, one being Fred Curl who lives in Emporia. The newspaper of 18 April
1918 published an interview with Mrs. Peter Tucker. While most of their foster or adopted children took
the name of Tucker, Fred Curl did not. They had him for nineteen years in their house. On the 1940
City Directory of Emporia, Kansas Fred H. Curl is shown as a hlpr AT&SF RR [Atchison, Topeka and
Santa Fe Railroad], living at 102 S. Lawrence. He died on 7 January 1970 and was buried in the
Maplewood Memorial Lawn Cemetery. He is not shown in Henry Curl's obituary as being a surviving
brother.

    1940 US Census, Lyon Co., Kansas, Emporia, ED 56-20, Page 63B 21
    owns $500
    Fred H. Curl, informant, 51, negro, 7th grade, b. KS, same place 1 April 1935,
        boiler washer, steam railroad

    Clarence Curl, son of William Curl and Marie Reed, was born in about 1892 according to census
enumerations. According to his World War I Draft Registration he was born 28 December 1893 in
Emporia, Lyon Co., Kansas. This was filed on 5 June 1917 and he was living at South Pine, Emporia,
Lyon Co., Kansas, laborer for L.R. Bailey Transfer Co. of Emporia, single and colored.

    Like his brother, Sam, he was continually charged with various crimes in Lyon Co., Kansas and
also spent time in the reformatory. Clarence served in World War I and on 17 February 1927 was
admitted to the US National Home for Disabled Volunteer Soldiers at Leavenworth, Leavenworth Co.,
Kansas. Their records indicate that he enlisted in the Army as a private on 16 July 1918 and was
discharged on 15 July 1919 at Camp Funston, Kansas, cause hemorrhoid, external. Clarence was born in
Kansas, age 34, 5 feet 8 inches, dark complexion, dark eyes, black hair, can read and write and has no

religion. He was a laborer in Emporia, Kansas and single. The nearest relative listed was his brother Fred Curl, 27 South Pine Street, Emporia, Kansas. 22

> 1930 US Census, Leavenworth Co., Kansas, Delaware Twp., ED 4, page 20B 23
> National Military Home
> Clarence Curl, negro, 38, b. US, both parents b. US

On the 1940 City Directory of Emporia, Kansas, Clarence and wife Velma E. are shown at 1013 Grand.

> 1940 US Census, Lyon Co., Kansas, Emporia, ED 56-26, Page 10A 24
> owns $2,500
> Clarence Curl, colored, 47, 8th grade, b. KS, same place 1 April 1935, laborer,
>   road work
> Velma, informant, wife, colored, 41, 2 years college, b. KS, same place 1 April
>   1935

Another date of birth appears for Clarence Curl on his Social Security Death Index record. He is shown with a date of birth of 10 January 1892 and death October 1979, number issued in Kansas, last benefit at Emporia, Lyon Co., Kansas. The date of 10 January 1892 would be almost eleven months before his mother's death, and most likely the exact date of his birth. 25

Nothing further is known about William Curl, son of William Curl and Marie Reed. He was alive in 1955, living in Emporia, Kansas, when his brother, Henry Curl, died in Alliance, Nebraska.

After the death of his wife, Marie Reed, on 8 December 1892, the elder William Curl, married a woman named Nannie. She apparently had been married before and had children, one being Pearl Baker who is shown in her household on the 1910 US Census in Lyon Co., Kansas. On 14 November 1904 the Curls both asked for a divorce in the Lyon Co., Kansas court. 26 William Curl passed away on 16 January 1905 at age 48 year, making his birth, if correct, in about 1857.

The Emporia Gazette, Emporia, Kansas, 17 January 1905 page 5
    "William Curl died last night at 2 o'clock. Curl was one of the well known colored men of the town. Several days ago he contracted pneumonia, and was staying at the home of a relative, Mrs. Anderson, who lives at 105 Constitution street. He was about 48 years old, and leaves a wife and several children. The funeral services will probably be held tomorrow."

> 1910 US Census, Lyon Co., Kansas, Emporia, Ward 3, ED 49, Page 6A 27
> 111 State Street
> 116-117 Nannie Curl, black, 42, widow, 8 children, 4 living, b. KY, both parents
>   b. KY, washerwoman, private family
> Pearl Baker, daughter, black, 16, b. KS, father b. PA, mother b. KY
> Clifford Baker, grandson, black, 7/12, b. KS, father b. US, mother b. KS

Nannie Curl died August 1911 at her home at 111 State Street, Emporia, Kansas. Her body was taken on 20 August 1911 for burial in Junction City, Geary Co., Kansas.

In *The Emporia Gazette,* 15 January 1918, page 6 there is a death notice for Mrs. Margaret Carr, colored, who died at the home of her daughter Mrs. Hallie Anderson, 1010 Sylvan Street. Her maiden name was Margaret Curl, and she was born in Saline Co., Missouri in 1845. She came to Emporia, Kansas thirty years before her death, living there most of the time. In 1868 she was married to Dennis Carr at Waco, McLennan Co., Texas. She also had a son, James Carr of Moberly, Missouri. She was buried in the Maplewood Memorial Lawn Cemetery in Emporia, Lyon Co., Kansas.   Margaret would have been a contemporary to William Curl and may have been a sister or cousin.

1880 US Census, Randolph Co., Missouri, Moberly, ED 108, Page 96A   28
188-179 Maggie B. Carr, black, 30, widow, wash and iron, b. MO, both
      parents b. MO
Dennis, black, 13, son, at school, b. TX, both parents b. MO
Halmetta, black, 8, daughter, b. TX, both parents b. MO
Jimmie, black, 7, son, b. TX, both parents b. MO

World War I Draft Registration   29
James Bennett Carr
116 N. Ault, Moberly, Randolph Co., Missouri
Age 44, born 16 February 1874
negro
Janitor Wabash Division Offices, Wabash RR Co., Decatur, Macon Co., Illinois
nearest relative - Edna Grace Carr, 909 Pendleton, St. Joseph, Missouri
9 September 1918

1. Box Butte Co., Nebraska Marriage Book D, page 210 #1570
2. Year: 1930; Census Place: Alliance, Box Butte, Nebraska; Roll: 1266; Page: 12B; Enumeration District: 0002; Image: 829.0; FHL microfilm: 2341001
3. Year: 1930; Census Place: Alliance, Box Butte, Nebraska; Roll: 1266; Page: 6B; Enumeration District: 0002; Image: 817.0; FHL microfilm: 2341001
4. Year: 1940; Census Place: Lake, Box Butte, Nebraska; Roll: T627_2237; Page: 5B; Enumeration District: 7-11
5. Ancestry.com. *U.S. City Directories, 1822-1995* [database on-line]. Provo, UT, USA: Ancestry.com Operations, Inc., 2011.
6. FindAGrave http://www.findagrave.com
7. Year: 1910; Census Place: Kansas City Ward 3, Wyandotte, Kansas; Roll: T624_460; Page: 9A; Enumeration District: 0163; FHL microfilm: 1374473
8. Kansas State Historical Society; Topeka, Kansas; Roll: ks1915_262; Line: 1
9. Year: 1920; Census Place: Kansas City Ward 3, Wyandotte, Kansas; Roll: T625_555; Page: 16A; Enumeration District: 164; Image: 911
10. Year: 1940; Census Place: Kansas City, Wyandotte, Kansas; Roll: T627_1268; Page: 2A; Enumeration District: 106-21
11. Year: 1900; Census Place: Emporia Ward 1, Lyon, Kansas; Roll: 487; Page: 10B; Enumeration District: 0069; FHL microfilm: 1240487
12. Year: 1900; Census Place: Emporia, Lyon, Kansas; Roll: 487; Page: 6A; Enumeration District: 0073; FHL microfilm: 1240487
13. *Emporia Gazette,* 27 October 1914, page 3.
14. *Emporia Gazette*, 23 May 1905.
15. *Emporia Gazette*, 19 September 1913, page 1.
16. Kansas State Historical Society; Topeka, Kansas; 1905 Kansas Territory Census; Roll: ks1905_86; Line: 1.
17. Year: 1920; Census Place: Emporia Ward 3, Lyon, Kansas; Roll: T625_538; Page: 9B; Enumeration District: 53; Image: 888.
18. Kansas State Historical Society; Topeka, Kansas; 1925 Kansas Territory Census; Roll: KS1925_84; Line: 1.
19. Year: 1920; Census Place: Emporia Ward 3, Lyon, Kansas; Roll: T625_538; Page: 9B; Enumeration District: 53; Image: 888.

20. Year: 1920; Census Place: Emporia Ward 3, Lyon, Kansas; Roll: T625_538; Page: 9B; Enumeration District: 53; Image: 888.

21. Year: 1940; Census Place: Emporia, Lyon, Kansas; Roll: T627_1242; Page: 63B; Enumeration District: 56-20

22. Ancestry.com. U.S. National Homes for Disabled Volunteer Soldiers, 1866-1938 [database on-line]. Provo, UT, USA: Ancestry.com Operations Inc, 2007.

23. Year: 1930; Census Place: Delaware, Leavenworth, Kansas; Roll: 707; Page: 20B; Enumeration District: 0004; Image: 904.0; FHL microfilm: 2340442

24. Year: 1940; Census Place: Emporia, Lyon, Kansas; Roll: T627_1242; Page: 10A; Enumeration District: 56-26

25. Ancestry.com. *U.S., Social Security Death Index, 1935-2014* [database on-line]. Provo, UT, USA: Ancestry.com Operations Inc, 2011.

26. *Emporia Gazette,* 14 April 1904, page 4.

27. Year: 1910; Census Place: Emporia Ward 3, Lyon, Kansas; Roll: T624_445; Page: 6A; Enumeration District: 0049; FHL microfilm: 1374458.

28. Year: 1880; Census Place: Moberly, Randolph, Missouri; Roll: 712; Family History Film: 1254712; Page: 96A; Enumeration District: 108; Image: 0194

29. Registration State: Missouri; Registration County: Randolph; Roll: 168350.

Austin Curtis

Austin Curtis and family settled in Cherry Co., Nebraska before 1910. Prior to that they were living in Lincoln, Nebraska. From Cherry Co., Nebraska the family went to Alliance, Box Butte Co., Nebraska to live. The following census enumerations show their family. On the 1910 US Census they were living next door to Dennis and Ida Meehan, another black family.

1900 US Census, Lancaster Co., Nebraska, Lincoln, Ward 4, ED 58, Page 7B   1
715 So. 19th St.
109-111 Austin Curtis, black, b. May 1868, 32, married 11 years, b. MO, both
        parents b. MO, RR porter
Ada M., wife, black, b. Feb 1871, 29, married 11 years, 1 child, 1 living, b. IL,
        both parents b. MO
Wendel, son, black, b. May 1897, 3, b. NE, father b. MO, mother b. IL

—-112 George J. Brown, partner, black, b. Jan 1878, 22, b. KS, both parents b.
        MO, porter, store
Dora Brown, wife, black, b. Dec 1879, 20, 0 children, 0 living, b. MO, father b.
        MO, mother b. GA

1910 US Census, Cherry Co., Nebraska, Kennedy, ED 51, Page 8B   2
18-18 Austin P. Curtis, 42, married 20 years, b. MO, both parents b. MO, farmer
Ida, wife, black, 39, married 22 years, 2 children, 2 living, b. IL, father b. KY,
        mother b. MO
Frank, son, black, 20, single, b. NE, father b. MO, mother b. IL
Vella, daughter, black, 9, b. NE, father b. MO, mother b. IL

Under the Homestead Act, Austin P. Curtis acquired 640 acres in Cherry Co., Nebraska. The patent was issued on 24 November 1916, for Section 35, 6th PM, T 28N, Range 31West, located in the general area of DeWitty in Cherry Co., Nebraska. 3

In 1920, Austin P. Curtis was living in the household of Cleveland R. Lewis and his wife, Luella, in Alliance, Box Butte Co., Nebraska. He is shown as a roomer, married, working as a porter on the train.

1930 US Census, Box Butte Co., Nebraska, Alliance, ED 3, Page 7A 4
115 Dakota Avenue
125-151 Austin Curtis, owns $1300, negro, 63, married at age 22, b. MO, both
       parents b. MO, porter train service
Ida, wife, negro, 59, married at age 17, b. IL, father b. KY, mother b. MO
Novella, daughter, negro, 8, b. NE, father b. MO, father b. IL
Vella Ellis, daughter, negro, 29, divorced, married at age 26, b. NE, father b. MO,
       father b. IL
Shirley Ellis, grandson, negro, 1, b. NE, father b. AZ, mother b. NE

Within a couple of years, Austin and Ida Curtis had moved to Lincoln, Nebraska where they are shown on the 1933 through 1937 Lincoln City Directories. They were living at 2235 S Street.

Austin P. Curtis was born 18 May 1867 and died 15 November 1937. He was buried in the Wyuka Cemetery, Lincoln, Lancaster Co., Nebraska. His son, Wendell Oliver Curtis died 20 April 1949 and was also buried in Wyuka Cemetery. 5

Frank Henry Curtis, son of Austin P. and Ida Curtis, registered for the World War I Draft in Cherry Co., Nebraska. He is shown as living at Audacious, Cherry Co., Nebraska, born 2 May 1889 in Lincoln, Nebraska. He was a farmer with a wife and three children. It was filed at Wells, Cherry Co., Nebraska on 5 June 1917. 6

Vella Wanda Louise Curtis, daughter of Austin P. and Ida Curtis, was born in about 1901 in Nebraska. She married James Perry Ellis in Alliance, Box Butte Co., Nebraska on 7 August 1927 by Neal Johnson, Minister of the Gospel. They were both residents of Alliance and single. James was born in Nelson, Arizona to Adam Ellis, born Texas and Belle Tinsler, born Arkansas. He was a mechanic. Vella was born in Lincoln, Nebraska to Austin P. Curtis, born Lexington, Missouri and Ida M. Curtis, born Galesburg, Illinois. Witnesses at their wedding were Mrs. E.J. Walls and Mrs. M. English. 7 They eventually divorced. She was born 7 January 1901 and died in Alameda Co., California on 13 January 1984. 8

James P. Ellis, the ex-husband of Vella Wanda Louise Curtis, remarried after their divorce, in Alliance, Box Butte Co., Nebraska. According to the marriage application he was 38 years old, divorced, born in Oklahoma, a painter by trade. His parents are shown as Adam Ellis born Texas and Isabelle Timley, born Oklahoma. He married Goldie Boganey of Alliance, colored, widow, age 27, born Missouri. Her parents were shown as W.E. Pleasant and Emma Young, who was born in Missouri. They were married on 8 July 1935 in Alliance by Rev. Herbert W. Bletson of the AME Church. Witnesses were Mrs. James Tatum and John Glass. 9 After the death of Austin, his widow, Ida, moved to California where she is shown in 1940 on the census.

1940 US Census, Alameda Co., California, Okland, ED 61-94 Page 1B 10
1211 Adeline St.
rents $12 month
Ida Curtis, informant, negro, 69, widow, 0 education, b. IL, living at San
      Francisco, CA 1 April 1935
Nella, daughter, negro, divorced, 29, 8th grade, b. NE, living at San
      Francisco, CA 1 April 1935, sewing WPA
Lovella, daughter, negro, 18, 2 years high school, b. NE, living at San Francisco,
      CA 1 April 1935
Shirley, son, 11, 5th grade, b. NE, living at San Francisco, CA 1 April 1935

According to California death records, Ida Mae Curtis was born 28 February 1871 in Illinois and died in Alameda Co., California on 10 December 1948. 11

1. Year: 1900; Census Place: Lincoln Ward 4, Lancaster, Nebraska; Roll: 933; Page: 7B; Enumeration District: 0058; FHL microfilm: 1240933
2. Year: 1910; Census Place: Kennedy, Cherry, Nebraska; Roll: T624_840; Page: 8B; Enumeration District: 0051; FHL microfilm: 1374853
3. U.S. Department of the Interior, Bureau of Land Management, General Land Office Records http://www.glorecords.blm.gov/details/patent/default.aspx?accession=555858&docClass=SER&sid=yn0c1lhf.sjw
4. Year: 1930; Census Place: Alliance, Box Butte, Nebraska; Roll: 1266; Page: 7A; Enumeration District: 0003; Image: 866.0; FHL microfilm: 2341001
5. Wyuka Cemetery http://wyuka.com/cemetery/
6. United States, Selective Service System. *World War I Selective Service System Draft Registration Cards, 1917-1918*. Washington, D.C.: National Archives and Records Administration. M1509, 4,582 rolls.
7. Box Butte Co., Nebraska Marriage Book H, page 391 #3703
8. California Death Records http://vitals.rootsweb.ancestry.com/ca/death/search.cgi
9. Box Butte Co., Nebraska Marriage #4639
10. Year: 1940; Census Place: Oakland, Alameda, California; Roll: T627_443; Page: 1B; Enumeration District: 61-94
11. California Death Records http://vitals.rootsweb.ancestry.com/ca/death/search.cgi

Ward and Alfred Dandridge

Ward and Alfred Dandridge were brothers who came to Chadron, Dawes Co., Nebraska before 1920. They never married and worked at various jobs, but were best known for working in a hotel as a cook and porter. The two men are fondly remembered by Susan Kelley Fry of North Platte, Nebraska who grew up in Chadron and by Art Thomsen of Alliance, Nebraska who worked in Chadron.

Their parents were Kinsey and Lucy Dandridge who lived at Mooresville, Livingston Co., Missouri. The Dandridge family can be found on the 1900 and 1910 US censuses in Missouri. Living next door to Kinsey and Lucy Dandridge in 1900 are Frank and Jane Odell, the parents of Lucy Odell Dandridge. On the 1910 enumeration, the son Alfred is no longer in the household. He had moved to Dawes Co., Nebraska and his brother Ward went to Dawes County after the 1910 US Census.

1900 US Census, Livingston Co., Missouri, Mooresville, ED 104, Page 11B 1
235-237 Kinsey Danridge, black, b. June 1859, 40, married 18 years, b. MO,
 both parents b. MO, railroad laborer
Lucy, wife, black, b. Nov. 1859, 40, married 18 years, 9 children, 9 living, b. MO,
 father b. MD, mother b. MO
Herbert, son, black, b. Aug 1883, 16, b. MO, both parents b. MO
Prudie, son, black, b. Feb 1885, 15, b. MO, both parents b. MO
Alfred, son, black, b. Nov 1886, 13, b. MO, both parents b. MO
Roscoe, son, black, b. Nov 1887, 12, b. MO, both parents b. MO
Leora B., daughter, black, b. March 1891, 9, b. MO, both parents b. MO
Levy W., son, black, b. June 1892, 8, b. MO, both parents b. MO
Chris, son, black, b. Dec 1892, 7, b. MO, both parents b. MO
George C., son, black, b. Feb 1895, 5, b. MO, both parents b. MO
Dora E., daughter, black, b. July 1898, 1, b. MO, both parents b. MO

236-238 Frank Odell, black, b. Sept 1824, 75, married 41 years, b. MD, both
        parents b. MD
Jane, wife, b. Jan. 1843, 57, married 41 years, 15 children, 12 living, b. MO,
        both parents b. VA
Frank, son, black, b. Sept 1868, 31, single, b. MO, father b. MD, mother b. MO
        railroad laborer
Luvene P., daughter, black, b. July 1881, 18, single, b. MO, father b. MD, mother
        b. MO
Birdie M., daughter, black, b. Oct 1883, 16, b. MO, father b. MD, mother b. MO
Joseph, son, black, b. Dec 1886, 13, b. MO, father b. MD, mother b. MO
Effie M., granddaughter, black, b. April 1891, 9, b. MO, father b. MD, mother b.
        MO
Lula, granddaughter, black, b. Mar 1884, 16, b. MO, both parents b. MO

1910 US Census, Livingston Co., Missouri, Mooresville Village, ED 110, Page 2
1B
Martin Street
15-15 Kingy [sic] Dandridge, black, 51, married 27 years, b. MO, both parents b. VA,
        laborer, railroad
Lucy, wife, black, 52, married 27 years, 10 children, 10 living, b. MO, father b.
        MD, mother b. MO, laundress, at home
Ward, son, black, 19, single, b. MO, both parents b. MO, laundress, at home
Leora, daughter, black, 20, single, b. MO, both parents b. MO, servant, private
        family
Christ, son, black, 17, b. MO, both parents b. MO
George, son, black, 14, b. MO, both parents b. MO
Emogene, daughter, black, 11, b. MO, both parents b. MO
Gladys, daughter, black, 7, b. MO, both parents b. MO

1910 US Census, Dawes Co., Nebraska, Chadron, Ward 2, ED 92, Page 4B   3
Second Street
81-84 Eva Haill HH, white
Alfred Dandridge, servant, black, 24, single, b. MO, both parents b. MO, porter,
        Blaine Hotel

1920 US Census, Livingston Co., Missouri, Mooresville Twp., ED 111, Page 7A 4
1-1 Kinzie Dandridge, owns/free, negro, 58, widowed, b. MO, both parents
        b. MO, labor
Christopher, son, negro, 25, single, b. MO, both parents b. MO, labor
George, son, negro, 22, single, b. MO, both parents b. MO, labor
Emogene, daughter, negro, 21, single, b. MO, both parents b. MO
Gladys, daughter, negro, 16, b. MO, both parents b. MO
Orville, son, negro, 2, b. MO, both parents b. MO

1930 US Census, Livingston Co., Missouri, Mooresville, ED 19, Page 1A 5
17-17 Kinsey Dandridge, owns $200, negro, 62, widowed, b. MO, both
        parents b. MO, laborer, farm

On 12 September 1918 Alfred Dandridge filed his World War I Draft Registration in Chadon,
Dawes Co., Nebraska where he was living. He was age 32, born 29 November 1885. Alfred was
employed as a laborer for W.H. Donahue at Chadron. His nearest relative was Kinzie Dandridge of
Mooresville, Missouri. 6

He filed his World War II Draft Registration at Chadron, Dawes Co., Nebraska on 27 April 1942. His address was 172 King St., Chadron, Nebraska. Alfred was 57, born 29 November 1885 at Mooresville, Missouri. The person who would always know his address was Mrs. W.H. Donahue of the Blaine Hotel in Chadron. He was employed at the Blaine Hotel. 7

On 5 June 1917 Ward Dandridge filed his World War I Draft Registration in Chadron, Dawes Co., Nebraska where he was living. He was born born 29 January 1891 at Mooresville, Missouri, employed as a cook at Marralls Restaurant in Chadron. He was single and had one sister. There is a note on the form "#9 - am not acquainted with circumstances." This would reference his sister. 8

Ward Levi Dandridge filed his World War II Draft Registration at Chadron, Dawes Co., Nebraska on 27 April 1942. He was living at 174 King Street in Chadron, born 29 January 1891 in Mooresville, Missouri. The person who would always know his address was George Dandrige of Mooresville, Missouri. Ward was employed at the Blaine Hotel in Chadron. 9

On the 1920 US Census, Alfred and Ward were working at the Blaine Hotel on Second Street in Chadron. On the 1930 US Census they were still employed by the hotel, but living at 174 King.

> 1920 US Census, Dawes Co., Nebraska, Chadron, ED 98, Page 20B   10
> Blaine Hotel, 401 Second Street
> Ward Dandridge, cook, black, 26, single, b. MO, both parents b. MO, cook in
>   hotel
> Alfred Dandridge, porter, black, 32, single, b. MO, both parents b. MO, porter in
>   hotel

> 1930 US Census, Dawes Co., Nebraska, Chadron, ED 2, Page 13A 11
> 174 King
> 303-341 Ward Dandridge, owns, $3,800, negro, 37, single, b. MO, both parents b.
>   MO, cook hotel
> Alfred Dandridge, brother, negro, 44, single, b. MO, both parents b. MO, porter,
>   hotel

The Dandridge brothers were still employed by the hotel in Chadron in 1940, but owned their own house in Chadron

> 1940 US Census, Dawes Co., Nebraska, Chadron, ED 23-2, Page 1A   12
> 216 East 2nd, owns, $2,500
> Ward Dandridge, informant, negro, 49, single, 4 years high school, b. MO, same
>   house 1 April 1935, chef, hotel
> Alfred Dandridge, brother, negro, 54, single, 4 years high school, b. MO, same
>   house 1 April 1935, porter, hotel

Both brothers were buried in the Greenwood Cemetery at Chadron, Dawes Co., Nebraska. Alfred was born in 1888 in Missouri and died in 1956. Ward was born on 29 January 1891 in Mooresville, Livingston Co., Missouri and died on 9 January 1956.

Kinsey Dandridge was born about 1860 in Saline Co., Missouri, the son of Kinsey and Maria Dandridge. He married Lucy Odell on 2 November 1881 in Mooresville, Livingston Co., Missouri. Kinsey was of Chillicothe, Livingston Co., Missouri and Lucy was of Mooresville, Livingston Co., Missouri. They were married by Rev. Hardin Smith. 13   Kinsey died at Mooresville, Livingston Co., Missouri on 15 January 1934 of bronchial pneumonia.   14

Lucy Odell was born 18 November 1856 at Mooresville, Livingston Co., Missouri and died there on 25 April 1912. She was the daughter of Frank Odell and Jane Fife. According to her death certificate she died suddenly of apoplexy and was buried in the Mooresville Cemetery, Mooresville, Livingston Co., Missouri. 15 The following are the known children born to Kinsey Dandridge and Jane Odell.

1. Herbert Dandridge, born 31 August 1883 in Missouri
2. Stilllborn Male Child Dandridge, born 22 February 1884 at Mooresville,
    Livingston Co., Missouri 16
3. Prudie Dandridge (male), born February 1885 in Missouri
4. Alfred Dandridge, born November 1886 in Missouri (see above)
6. Roscoe Dandridge, born 18 November 1888 in Mooresville, Livingston
    Co., Missouri
7. Leora B. Dandridge, born March 1891 in Missouri
8. Ward Levi Dandridge, born 29 January 1891 in Mooresville, Livingston Co.,
    Missouri (see above)
9. Christopher Columbus Dandridge, born 25 December 1892 in Missouri
10. George Carlisle Dandridge, born 23 February 1895 in Mooresville,
    Livingston Co., Missouri
11. Dora Emogene Dandridge, born 1898-1900 in Missouri
12. Gladys Dandridge, born about 1903 in Missouri

Herbert Dandridge, son of Kinsey Dandridge and Lucy Odell, was born 31 August 1883 in Missouri. According to his death certificate he was born 31 August 1870 in Missouri to Kinsey Dandridge and Lucy Odell and was married. He was employed as a chauffeur. The informant was Allene Dandridge of 3506 Clark St. in St. Louis, Missouri. He died there of chronic myocarditis on 25 September 1930. Herbert was buried in the Greenwood Cemetery in St. Louis, Missouri on 27 September 1930. 17

Roscoe Dandridge, son of Kinsey Dandridge and Lucy Odell, was born on 18 November 1888 in Mooresville, Livingston Co., Missouri. On the 1920 US Census he was living in Chariton Co., Missouri. In 1930 he was still in the same household and shown as Maria Blanton's foster son.

1920 US Census, Chariton Co., Missouri, Brunswick, ED 30, Page 4B 18
85-89 Maria Blanton, owns/free, mulatto, 55, widow, b. MO, father b. MO,
    mother b. KY, laborer, laundress
Gertrude Blanton, daughter, mulatto, 27, single, b. MO, both parents b. MO,
    servant, private family
Roscoe Dandridge, boarder, black, 30, single, b. MO, both parents b. MO,
    laborer, section

1930 US Census, Chariton Co., Missouri, Brunswick, ED 4, Page 13A 19
Van Buren St.
314-352 Maria Blanton, owns $700, negro, 55, widow, b. MO, father b. MO,
    mother b. VA, servant, private family
Gertrude Blanton, daughter, negro, 38, single, b. MO, both parents b. MO,
    servant, private family
Rosco Dandridge, foster son, negro, 32, single, b. MO, both parents b. MO,
    laborer, odd jobs

1940 US Census, Chariton Co., Missouri, Brunswick, ED 21-4, Page 61A 20
Roscoe Dandridge, lodger, negro, 51, single, 4th grade, rural Chariton Co.,
    Missouri 1 April 1935, servant, private family

Roscoe filed his World War II Draft Registration Card in Chariton Co., Missouri on 27 April 1942. He was living at Brunswick in Chariton Co., farming for Theo. Manson. His brother, George Dandridge, is listed as the person who would always know his address. 21

He died on 28 May 1945 and was buried in the Mooresville Cemetery, Mooresville, Livingston Co., Missouri, with a military marker on his grave. Roscoe served in World War I from 15 July 1918 to 22 July 1919 as a private in Co. C, 804th Pioneer Infantry. 22

Christopher Columbus "Christ" Danridge, son of Kinsey Dandridge and Lucy Odell, was born 25 December 1892 in Missouri. He never married and died at his home, 59 3rd St., Chillicothe, Livingston Co., Missouri on 10 September 1953 of lobar pneumonia. The informant on his death certificate was his brother George Dandridge. 23 Christopher served in World War I as a private, Co. K, 806 Pioneer Infantry. He was buried in the Mooresville Cemetery, Mooresville, Livingston Co., Missouri and has a military stone on his grave. 24

Christopher filed his World War I Draft Registration in Livingston Co., Missouri on 5 June 1917. He was single, living at Mooresville, Livingston Co., Missouri and working for J.J. Hoffman of Mooresville. 25 He filed his World War II Draft Registration in Livingston Co., Missouri on 25 April 1942. He was living at 130 W. Brunswick in Chillicothe, Livingston Co., Missouri, working for Montgomery Wards in Chillicothe. He listed the person who would always know his address as Mrs. Beatrice Boone, 24 S. Brunswick, Chillicothe, Missouri. Extra comments were that he had a scar on his right leg between the knee and hip about two inches in length. 26

George Carlisle Dandridge, son of Kinsey Dandridge and Lucy Odell, was born 23 February 1895 in Mooresville, Livingston Co., Missouri. He filed his World War I Draft Registration in Livingston Co., Missouri on 5 June 1917. He was single and farming for James Bingham, Jr. of Mooresville, Missouri. 27 George filed his World War II Draft Registration in Livingston Co., Missouri on 25 April 1942. He was living at Mooresville in the county and working for Mrs. Mary Bingham of Mooresville. He listed Elston Stout of Mooresville as a person who would always know his address. 28 He served in World War I, enlisting on 2 August 1918 an was discharged on 5 July 1919. George never married and died on 2 December 1974.

Dora Emogene Dandridge, daughter of Kinsey Dandridge and Lucy Odell, was born about 1898-1900 in Missouri. She married Mathew Kiles on 1 October 1925 in Chillicothe, Livingston Co., Missouri. 29 On the 1930 US Census, she was shown as a widow, living at Chillicothe. Between 1930 and 1940 she married Horace Bruce. Her sons were shown as Kiles on the 1930 enumeration and shown as Bruce on the 1940 enumeration.

1930 US Census, Livingston Co., Missouri, Chillicothe, ED 5, Page 18B 30
Emogene Kiles, rents $6 month, negro, 30, widow, married at age 17, b. MO,
    both parents b. MO, cook, restaurant
Orval, son, negro, 12, b. MO, both parents b. MO
Henry, son, negro, 10, single, b. MO, both parents b. MO

1940 US Census, Livingston Co., Missouri, Chillicothe, Ward 3, ED 59-6, 31
Page 9A
59 3rd St.   rents $5 month
Horace Bruce, negro, 31, 11th grade, b. MO, same place 1 April 1935
Emogene, wife, negro, 40, 6th grade, b. MO, same place 1 April 1935, cook,
    restaurant
Orville W. Bruce, son, negro, 21, single, 6th grade, b. MO, Chillicothe, Livingston
    Co., MO 1 April 1935

Henry K. Bruce, son, negro, 19, single, 1 year high school, b. MO, Chillicothe,
   Livingston Co., MO 1 April 1935
James H. Bruce, son, 6, 1st grade, b. MO, Chillicothe, Livingston Co., MO 1
   April 1935
Rosilie Bruce, daughter, 4, b. MO
Joeani Bruce, daughter, 3, b. MO

Dandridge and Odell

Kinsey Dandridge was born about 1810 in Virginia and his wife Maria was born about March 1814 in Virginia. His given name is also shown as McKinsey. They were parents of the following known children.

1. Elvira Dandridge, born September 1845 in Missouri
2. Minerva Dandridge, born about 1848-1850 in Saline Co., Missouri
3. Stephen Dandridge, born 15 July 1853 in Brunswick, Chariton Co., Missouri
4. Thomas Dandridge, born about 1854 in Missouri
5. Kinsey Dandridge, born about 1860 in Missouri (see above)
6. Jesse Dandridge, born about 1861 in Missouri
7. Bertha Dandridge, born about 1864 in Missouri

1880 US Census, Chariton Co., Missouri, Brunswick, ED 172, Page 574D 32
75-75 Kinsey Dandridge, black, 70, farmer, b. VA, both parents b. VA
Minerva, black, 30, single, at home, b. MO, both parents b. VA (no relationship
   shown)
Maria, black, 55, wife, keeping house, b. VA, both parents b. VA
Thomas, black, 26, son, single, laborer, b. MO, both parents b. VA
Kinsey, black, 20, son, single, works factory, b. MO, both parents b. VA
Jesse, black, 19, son, single, laborer, b. MO, both parents b. VA
Bertha, black, 16, daughter, b. MO, both parents b. VA
Isiah Bradberry, black, 13, nephew, b. MO, both parents b. VA

1900 US Census, Chariton Co., Missouri, Brunswick, ED 31, Page 2A 33
19-19 Maria Dandridge, black, b. March 1814, 86, widow, 11 children, 8 living,
   b. VA, both parents b. VA, housekeeper
Elvira Gayther, daughter, black, b. Sept 1845, 54, widow, 2 children, 1 living,
   b. MO, both parents b. VA, unemployed
Minerva Dandridge, daughter, black, b. May 1853, 47, single, b. MO, both
   parents b. VA, servant
Maria Gayther, granddaughter, black, b. March 1882, 18, single, b. MO, father
   b. KY, mother b. MO, at school

Minerva Dandridge, daughter of Kinsey and Maria Dandridge, was born about 1848-1850 in Saline Co., Missouri. She never married and died 19 May 1910 at home, 2423 Michigan, in Jackson Co., Missouri, buried in the Brunswick City Cemetery, Brunswick Twp., Chariton Co., Missouri. 34

1910 US Census, Jackson Co., Missouri, Kansas City, Ward 11, ED 137, 35
Page 9B
2423 Michigan Avenue
159-175 Jessie Moore, male, black, 35, married 6 years, b. US, both
   parents b. US, teamster, cemetery company

Bertha, wife, black, 35, married 6 years, 3 children, 2 living, b. MO, both
      parents b. VA, general housework, private families
Minerva E., daughter, black, 5, b. MO, father b. US, mother b. MO
Jessie C., son, black, 3, b. MO, father b. US, mother b. MO
Minerva Dandridge, sister-in-law, black, 56, single, b. MO, both parents
      b. US

Stephen Dandridge, son of Kinsey and Maria Dandridge, was born 15 July 1853 in Brunswick, Chariton Co., Missouri. He married Alice Arnold in about 1899-1900. Stephen died on 23 January 1943 at General Hospital No. 2 in Kansas City, Jackson Co., Missouri. His residence was 2409 Michigan, Kansas City, Missouri. He was buried on 5 February 1943 in the Lincoln Cemetery, Kansas City, Jackson Co., Missouri. 36

    1900 US Census, Chariton Co., Missouri, Brunswick, ED 31, Page 2A 37
    18-18 Stephen Dandridge, black, b. July 1854, 45, married 0 years, b. MO,
        both parents b. VA, railroad laborer
    Alice, wife, black, no age shown, 0 years married, 0 children, 0 living, no places
        of birth

    1910 US Census, Chariton Co., Missouri, Brunswick, Ward 1, ED 30, Page 15A 38
    315-334 Stephen Dandridge, black, 53, second marriage, married 10 years, b.
        MO, both parents b. VA, farmer
    Alice, wife, black, 40?, first marriage, married 10 years, 3 children, 3 living, b.
        MO, both parents b. US
    Mary E., daughter, black, 9, b. MO, both parents b. MO
    William, son, black, 8, b. MO, both parents b. MO
    Beth, daughter, black, 5, b. MO, both parents b. MO

    1920 US Census, Chariton Co., Missouri, Brunswick, ED 30, Page 1A 39
    13-13 Stephen Dandridge, owns, mortgaged, black, 67, b. MO, both
        parents b. VA, laborer, farm
    Alice, black, wife, 47, b. MO, both parents b. MO
    William, black, son, 17, single, b. MO, both parents b. MO, laborer, section
    Beth, black, daughter, 14, b. MO, both parents b. MO
    Margery Jackson, granddaughter, 2 3/4, b. MO, both parents b. MO

Stephen and Alice had a son, Lee Arnold Dandridge who was born ON 30 August 1911 in Brunswick, Chariton Co., Missouri. He died there of bronchitis and whooping cough on 6 December 1911 and was buried on 7 December 1911 in the Brunswick City Cemetery, Brunswick, Chariton Co., Missouri. 40

The Dandridges moved from Missouri to Iowa where they are shown on the 1924 City Directory for Council Bluffs, Iowa, living at 1104 Ave C. Stephen was a laborer. On the 1934 City Directory of Indianapolis, Indiana, Stephen and Alice Dandridge are shown living at 624 Udell. He was a laborer and she was a cook.

Stephen's wife, Alice Arnold was born about 1870 in Brunswick, Chariton Co., Missouri. According to her death certificate, her parents were unknown, as was her exact age. She was the widow of Stephen Dandridge. The informant was Samuel Hall, 901 Lock St., Indianapolis, Indiana. She died 6 February 1943 at her home, 2409 Michigan, Kansas City, Jackson Co., Missouri and was buried in the Leeds Cemetery, Kansas City, Jackson Co., Missouri. 41

The parents of Lucy Odell, wife of Kinsey Dandridge, were Frank Odell and Jane Fife. They are shown on the 1880 census enumeration in Missouri.

1880 US Census, Livingston Co., Missouri, Mooresville, ED 171, Page 159D 42
178-180 Frank Odell, black, 58, laborer, b. MD, birth place of parents unknown
Jane, black, 46, wife, keeping house, b. KY, birth place of parents unknown
Amanda, black, 16, daughter, washing and housework, b. MO, father b. MD,
     mother b. KY
Minnie, black, 15, daughter, washing and housework, b. MO, father b. MD,
     mother b. KY
Laura, black, 7, daughter, b. MO, father b. MD, mother b. KY
Frank, black, 10, son, b. MO, father b. MD, mother b. KY
Dora, black, 6, daughter, b. MO, father b. MD, mother b. KY
Liza, black, 5, daughter, b. MO, father b. MD, mother b. KY
Edd, black, 1, son, b. MO, father b. MD, mother b. KY

1. Year: 1900; Census Place: Mooresville, Livingston, Missouri; Roll: 872; Page: 11B; Enumeration District: 0104; FHL microfilm: 1240872
2. Year: 1910; Census Place: Mooresville, Livingston, Missouri; Roll: T624_796; Page: 1B; Enumeration District: 0110; FHL microfilm: 1374809
3. Year: 1910; Census Place: Chadron Ward 2, Dawes, Nebraska; Roll: T624_841; Page: 4B; Enumeration District: 0092; FHL microfilm: 1374854
4. Year: 1920; Census Place: Mooresville, Livingston, Missouri; Roll: T625_919; Page: 7A; Enumeration District: 111; Image: 193
5. Year: 1930; Census Place: Mooresville, Livingston, Missouri; Roll: 1210; Page: 1A; Enumeration District: 0019; Image: 366.0; FHL microfilm: 2340945
6. Registration State: *Nebraska;* Registration County: *Dawes;* Roll: *171152*
7. The National Archives at St. Louis; St. Louis, Missouri; Draft Registration Cards for Fourth Registration for Nebraska, 04/27/1942 - 04/27/1942; NAI Number: 598911; Record Group Title: Records of the Selective Service System; Record Group Number: 147
8.   Registration State: *Nebraska;* Registration County: *Dawes;* Roll: *1711524*
9. The National Archives at St. Louis; St. Louis, Missouri; Draft Registration Cards for Fourth Registration for Nebraska, 04/27/1942 - 04/27/1942; NAI Number: 598911; Record Group Title: Records of the Selective Service System; Record Group Number: 147
10. Year: 1920; Census Place: Chadron, Dawes, Nebraska; Roll: T625_981; Page: 20B; Enumeration District: 98; Image: 390
11. Year: 1930; Census Place: Chadron, Dawes, Nebraska; Roll: 1271; Page: 13A; Enumeration District: 0002; Image: 37.0; FHL microfilm: 2341006
12. Year: 1940; Census Place: Chadron, Dawes, Nebraska; Roll: T627_2243; Page: 1A; Enumeration District: 23-2
13. Ancestry.com. *Missouri, Marriage Records, 1805-2002* [database on-line]. Provo, UT, USA: Ancestry.com Operations, Inc., 2007. Original data: *Missouri Marriage Records.* Jefferson City, MO, USA: Missouri State Archives. Microfilm.
14. Missouri Death Certificate #1826
15. Missouri Death Certificate #14153
16. Ancestry.com. *Missouri, Birth Records, 1847-1910* [database on-line]. Provo, UT, USA: Ancestry.com Operations, Inc., 2007.
Original data: *Missouri Birth Records [Microfilm].* Jefferson City, MO, USA: Missouri State Archives.
17. Missouri Death Certificate #31669
18. Year: 1920; Census Place: Brunswick, Chariton, Missouri; Roll: T625_906; Page: 4B; Enumeration District: 30; Image: 761
19. Year: 1930; Census Place: Brunswick, Chariton, Missouri; Roll: 1182; Page: 13A; Enumeration

District: 0004; Image: 332.0; FHL microfilm: 2340917

20. Year: 1940; Census Place: Brunswick, Chariton, Missouri; Roll: T627_2096; Page: 61A; Enumeration District: 21-4

21. The National Archives at St. Louis; St. Louis, Missouri; Draft Registration Cards for Fourth Registration for Missouri, 04/27/1942 - 04/27/1942; NAI Number: 598884; Record Group Title: Records of the Selective Service System; Record Group Number: 147

22. Ancestry.com. *U.S., Headstone Applications for Military Veterans, 1925-1963* [database on-line]. Provo, UT, USA: Ancestry.com Operations, Inc., 2012.

23. Missouri Death Certificate #32358

24. Ancestry.com. *U.S., Headstone Applications for Military Veterans, 1925-1963* [database on-line]. Provo, UT, USA: Ancestry.com Operations, Inc., 2012.

25. Registration State: *Missouri;* Registration County: *Livingston;* Roll: *1683401*

26. The National Archives at St. Louis; St. Louis, Missouri; Draft Registration Cards for Fourth Registration for Missouri, 04/27/1942 - 04/27/1942; NAI Number: 598884; Record Group Title: Records of the Selective Service System; Record Group Number: 147

27. Registration State: *Missouri;* Registration County: *Livingston;* Roll: *1683401*

28. The National Archives at St. Louis; St. Louis, Missouri; Draft Registration Cards for Fourth Registration for Missouri, 04/27/1942 - 04/27/1942; NAI Number: 598884; Record Group Title: Records of the Selective Service System; Record Group Number: 147

29. Ancestry.com. *Missouri, Marriage Records, 1805-2002* [database on-line]. Provo, UT, USA: Ancestry.com Operations, Inc., 2007. Original data: *Missouri Marriage Records*. Jefferson City, MO, USA: Missouri State Archives. Microfilm.

30. Year: 1930; Census Place: Chillicothe, Livingston, Missouri; Roll: 1210; Page: 18B; Enumeration District: 0005; Image: 155.0; FHL microfilm: 2340945

31. Year: 1940; Census Place: Chillicothe, Livingston, Missouri; Roll: T627_2125; Page: 9A; Enumeration District: 59-6

32. Year: 1880; Census Place: Brunswick, Chariton, Missouri; Roll: 680; Family History Film: 1254680; Page: 574D; Enumeration District: 172; Image: 0812

33. Year: 1900; Census Place: Brunswick, Chariton, Missouri; Roll: 847; Page: 2A; Enumeration District: 0031; FHL microfilm: 1240847

34. Missouri Death Certificate #13244

35. Year: 1910; Census Place: Kansas Ward 11, Jackson, Missouri; Roll: T624_787; Page: 9B; Enumeration District: 0137; FHL microfilm: 1374800

36. Missouri Death Certificate #1038

37. Year: 1900; Census Place: Brunswick, Chariton, Missouri; Roll: 847; Page: 2A; Enumeration District: 0031; FHL microfilm: 1240847

38. Year: 1910; Census Place: Brunswick Ward 1, Chariton, Missouri; Roll: T624_776; Page: 15A; Enumeration District: 0030; FHL microfilm: 1374789

39. Year: 1920; Census Place: Brunswick, Chariton, Missouri; Roll: T625_906; Page: 1A; Enumeration District: 30; Image: 754

40. Missouri Death Certificate #40817

41. Missouri Death Certificate #970

42. Year: 1880; Census Place: Mooresville, Livingston, Missouri; Roll: 700; Family History Film: 1254700; Page: 159D; Enumeration District: 171; Image: 0691

Darnell

The surname of Darnell is found in marriages within the Slaughter and Shelton families of Alliance, Box Butte Co., Nebraska. By 1900 the widow Anna Belle "Annie" Wilson Darnell was living in Ward 2 of Alliance. She had two children in her household, Julia age 15 and William age 7. Julia married Samuel Shelton and William married Ollie Slaughter. The 1900 enumeration indicates that Annie and her husband were living in Nebraska between 1885 and 1892. With eight years difference in age, it is possible that Julia and William had different fathers. According to the marriage license of William to Ollie Slaughter, he was the son of Granville Darnell, mother unknown. Julia's marriage license to Samuel Shelton indicates that her father was Thomas Darnell and her mother was Annie, maiden name unknown.

> 1900 US Census, Box Butte Co., Nebraska, Alliance, Ward 2, ED 6, Page 16B   1
> 39-43 Annie Darnell, black, unknown age, widow, 2 children, 2 living,
>   b. KY, both parents b. KY, wash woman
> Julia, black, daughter, b. Feb 1885, 15, b. KY, both parents b. KY, at school
> William, black, son, b. Nov 1892, 7, b. NE, both parents b. KY, at school

Annie and her children were still living in Alliance when the 1910 US Census was taken. It is interesting to note that she and Julia are shown as mulatto and William as black. 2

> 1910 US Census, Box Butte Co., Nebraska, Alliance, Ward 2, ED 7, Page 6B
> 127 Sweetwater Avenue
> 122-129 Anna Darnell, mulatto, 45, widow, 2 children, 2 living, b. KY, both
>   parents b. KY, laborer, odd jobs
> Julia, daughter, mulatto, 25, single, b. KY, both parents b. KY
> William, son, black, 16, b. NE, both parents b. KY

According to her obituary, Anna Belle Darnell died 22 October 1910 in Alliance and was buried in the Alliance Cemetery. She was preceded in death by her husband, fourteen years prior to her death [about 1896]. Annie and her husband came to Alliance in about 1893. Annie was survived by two children, Mrs. Julia Shelton and Bud Darnell. Her tomsbtone is carved with Shelton on the bottom of it. Nothing can be located on the 1880 US Census for a Thomas or Granville Darnell.

The Alliance Herald of 5 March 1897 contained a card of thanks, "In behalf of myself and two children, I desire to return my most sincere thanks to the many sympathizing friends who so kindly and generously visited and assisted my late husband during his protracted sickness, as well as those who assisted at his burial. Annie Darnell"

Real Estate Transfers - Lincoln, Nebraska   3
Granville S. and Annie Darnell to C.T. Boggs lot 10 block 216, Lincoln $700
There is no Annie or Granville Darnell living in Lancaster Co., Nebraska in 1900 on the census. It is possible that they had lived in Lincoln before coming to Box Butte County and that she decided to sell the property in 1900, after his death in 1897.

On 6 March 1957 in Alliance, Box Butte Co., Nebraska, William Edward "Bud" Darnell applied for a delayed birth certificate. The form indicates that he was born in Lincoln, Lancaster Co., Nebraska. His father is shown as Granville S. Darnell, born in 1857 in Covington, Kenton Co., Kentucky. His mother is shown as Anna Belle Coahman, no year of birth, born in Mt. Sterling, Montgomery Co., Kentucky. It is possible that Coahman is actually meant to be Coleman. She is also shown in other records as Anna Belle Wilson Darnell.

More information on Julia and William "Bud" Darnell can be found in the Shelton and Slaughter families, Volume 2.

1. Year: 1900; Census Place: Alliance, Box Butte, Nebraska; Roll: 917; Page: 16B; Enumeration District: 0006; FHL microfilm: 1240917
2. Year: 1910; Census Place: Alliance Ward 2, Box Butte, Nebraska; Roll: T624_838; Page: 6B; Enumeration District: 0007; FHL microfilm: 1374851

3. *The Nebraska State Journal,* Lincoln, Nebraska 23 March 1900

Arthur Davis

Arthur James Davis is first found in Nebraska on the World War I Draft Registration. He was living at Sumner, Dawson Co., Nebraska, farming for J.M. Downey of Sumner. Arthur was 34, born 15 November 1883 and married to Alice Davis who was also living at Sumner. The registration was filed on 12 September 1918. Prior to this the Davis family were in Kansas. 1

1910 US Census, Riley Co., Kansas, Wild Cat Twp., ED 123, Page 9B   2
117-117 Arthur J. Davis, black, 27, married 4 years, b. KS, both parents b. TN, farm laborer
Alice, wife, black, 20, married 4 years, 2 children, 2 living, b. KS, father b. unknown, mother b. TN
Marcellas, son, black, 3, b. KS, both parents b. KS
Marie, daughter, black, 9/12, b. KS, both parents b. KS

Sometime between 1914 and 1918, they moved to Nebraska. The daughter Marie V. Davis, died while they were in Kansas. She was born in 1910 and died on 5 July 1914, buried in the Sunset Cemetery, Manhattan, Riley Co., Kansas. There is no stone on her grave. 3

1920 US Census, Custer Co., Nebraska, Loup, ED 90, Page 5A   4
87-89 Arthur J. Davis, rents, black, 36, b. KS, both parents b. TN, farmer
Alice, wife, black, 30, b. KS, both parents b. TN
Marcellas, son, black, 13, b. KS, both parents b. KS

By 1930 they were living with their 23 year old son in Grand Island, Nebraska. Both Arthur and his son were janitors at the college.

1930 US Census, Hall Co., Nebraska, Grand Island, Second Ward, ED 11, Page 14A   5
2423 West Second Street
391-341 Marcellas O. Davis, rents $12.50 month, negro, 23, single, b KS, both parents b. KS, janitor, college
Alice E., mother, negro, 40, married at age 16, b. KS, both parents b. TN
Arthur J., father, negro, 46, married at age 21, b. KS, both parents b. US, janitor, college

The family cannot be located on the 1940 US Census. However, Marcellus Davis left Nebraska between 1930 and 1938. He was buried in the Wamego City Cemetery, Wamego, Pottawatomie Co., Kansas, born 1906, died 1938.

Arthur and Alice remained in Nebraska where he is shown on the World War II Draft Registration, as Arthur James Davis, 1821 West 6 Street, Grand Island, Hall Co., Nebraska. He was 58 years old, born 25 December 1883 at Alma, Kansas. The month and day are different from his World War I Draft Registration. His wife, Mrs. Arthur Davis, is shown at the same address. He was working for the WPA, City of Grand Island and reported there were burns on his right hand. It was filed on 27 April 1942 in Grand Island, Hall Co., Nebraska. 6

Alma is in Wabaunsee Co., Kansas. The counties of Riley, Wabaunsee and Pottawatomie all neighbor each other.

Alice Elizabeth Davis, born 11 September 1890, died 12 July 1963. She was buried in the Grand Island Cemetery, Grand Island, Hall Co., Nebraska, Section E, Lot 71A. Arthur is not buried there. 7

From the 1880 US Census of Wabaunsee Co., Kansas, it appears that David Davis and wife Anna were probably the parents who brought their family from Tennessee to Kansas. Arthur James Davis could have been the son of any of them. He was born about 1883 at Alma, Wabaunsee Co., Kansas.

1880 US Census, Wabaunsee Co., Kansas, Alma, ED 117, Page 344A   8
67-70 Archie Davis, black, 32, laborer, b. TN, both parents b. TN
Lena, black, 24, wife, keeping house, b. SC, both parents b. SC
Squire, black, 9, son, b. KS, father b. TN, mother b. SC
Anderson, black, 7, son, b. KS, father b. TN, mother b. SC
Lina, black, 5, daughter, b. KS, father b. TN, mother b. SC
Major, black, 3, son, b. KS, father b. TN, mother b. SC
Mary A., black, 2, daughter, b. KS, father b. TN, mother b. SC
Thomas, black, 3/12, son, b. March, b. KS, father b. TN, mother b. SC

1880 US Census, Wabaunsee Co., Kansas, Alma, ED 117, Page 344B   9
72-75 Gilbert Davis, black, 27, farmer, b. TN, both parents b. VA
Margaret, black, 17, wife, keeping house, b. TN, both parents b. TN

1880 US Census, Wabaunsee Co., Kansas, Alma, ED 117, Page 344B   10
73-76 David Davis, black, 58, farmer, b. VA, both parents b. VA
Anna, black, 58, wife, keeping house, b. VA, both parents b. VA
Kate, black, 23, daughter, b. TN, both parents b. VA
Henry, black, 21, son, b. TN, both parents b. VA
Louisa, black, 15, daughter, b. TN, both parents b. VA
Jesse, black, 13, son, b. TN, both parents b. VA
Nancy, black, 11, daughter, b. TN, both parents b. VA
Lemuel, black, 6, grandson, b. KS, both parents b. TN
Jane, black, 5/12, b. Dec, granddaughter, b. KS, both parents b. TN
John, black, 1/12, b. May, grandson, b. KS, both parents b. TN

1880 US Census, Wabaunsee Co., Kansas, Alma, ED 117, Page 344B   11
74-77 Wiley Davis, black, 30, farmer, b. TN, both parents b. VA
Lina, black, 25, wife, keeping house, b. TN, both parents b. TN
Spencer, black, 8, son, b. TN, both parents b. TN
Jane, black, 7, daughter, b. KS, both parents b. TN
Amanda, black, 4, daughter, b. KS, both parents b. TN
Arlene, black, 4, daughter, b. KS, both parents b. TN
Joseph, 2, son, b. KS, both parents b. TN
Burt, 1, son, b. KS, both parents b. TN
Spencer Simpson, black, 78, father-in-law, stone mason, b. KY, both parents b. KY
Betsey Simpson, black, 70, mother-in-law, b. VA, both parents b. VA
James Allen, black, 15, nephew , b. TN, both parents b. TN
Joseph L. Allen, black, 14, nephew, b. TN, both parents b. TN
Solomon Holford, black, 30, boarder, single, laborer, b. TN, both parents b. TN

1880 US Census, Wabaunsee Co., Kansas, Newbury, ED 120, Page 372A 12
11-11 Dennison household (white)
Henry Davis, black, 21, single, farm laborer, b. TN, both parents b. VA
Catherine Davis, black, 23, single, servant, b. TN, both parents b. VA
Mary J. Davis, black, 5/12, b. January, b. TN, both parents b. VA

According to a tree on Ancestry, David Davis was born about 1822 in Virginia and died 15

August 1877 in Wabaunsee Co., Kansas. However, he was still alive when the 1880 census was taken. He married Anna or Nancy Anne on 25 February 1866 in Carthage, Smith Co., Tennessee. On their marriage license she is also shown as a Davis. However, this was a marriage to legalize their marriage prior to emancipation. 13 According to cemetery records, he died in 1901 and was buried in the Maple Hill Cemetery at Kansas City, Wyanotte Co., Kansas. His wife is shown as Hannah Davis, not Anna Davis. They were parents of the following children.

1. Archibald "Archie" Davis, born Jan 1846 in Tennessee
2. George Davis, born about 1852 in Tennessee
3. Gilbert Davis, born about 1853 in Tennessee
4. Wyley/Wiley Davis, born about 1853 in Tennessee
5. Elizabeth Davis, born about 1854 in Tennessee
6. Laura Davis, born about 1855 in Tennessee
7. Frances David, born about 1856 in Tennessee
8. Catharine "Kate" Davis, born about 1858 in Tennessee
9. Henry Clay Davis, born about 1859 in Tennessee
10. Elira Davis, born about 1864 in Tennessee
11. Louisa Davis, born about 1865 in Tennessee
12. Jesse Davis, born about 1867 in Tennessee
13. Nancy Davis, born about 1870 in Tennessee; died 25 October 1896 in Alma, Wabaunsee Co., Kansas
14. Frank Buckley Davis, born about 1872 in Tennessee
15. Lina Davis, born about 1873 in Tennessee
16. Drucy Davis, born March 1888 in Alma, Wabaunsee Co., Kansas

Archibald "Archie" Davis, son of David and Anna Davis, was born in January of 1846 in Tennessee. He married Tena Saddler on 19 October 1870 in Smith Co., Tennessee. She was born about 1856 in South Carolina. Archie died on 23 July 1909 in Leavenworth, Leavenworth Co., Kansas. His children were Major, Mary, Dewey and Quila.

Gilbert Davis, son of David and Anna Davis, was born in about 1853 in Tennessee. His wife Margaret was born in about 1863 in Tennessee. Wyley/Wiley Davis, son of David and Anna Davis, was born in about 1853 in Tennessee. His wife Lina was born in about 1855 in Tennessee. Catherine "Kate" Davis, daughter of David and Anna Davis, was born in about 1858 in Tennessee. She married Noah McKinney on 11 June 1888 in Alma, Wabaunsee Co., Kansas. He was born about 1850 in Tennessee and died in 1893 in Alma, Wabaunsee Co., Kansas. Henry Clay Davis, son of Davis and Anna Davis, was born in about 1859 in Tennessee. He married Lina Davis on 12 March 1884 in Alma, Wabaunsee Co., Kansas. She was born May 1848 in Tennessee. They had children, Jesse Davis, Dora Davis and Charles Smith Davis.

1. Registration State: *Nebraska;* Registration County: *Custer;* Roll: *1711523;* Draft Board: *9*
2. Year: 1910; Census Place: Wild Cat, Riley, Kansas; Roll: T624_454; Page: 9B; Enumeration District: 0123; FHL microfilm: 1374467
3. FindAGrave http://www.findagrave.com.
4. Year: 1920; Census Place: Loup, Custer, Nebraska; Roll: T625_985; Page: 5A; Enumeration District: 90; Image: 426
5. Year: 1930; Census Place: Grand Island, Hall, Nebraska; Roll: 1282; Page: 14A; Enumeration District: 0011; Image: 240.0; FHL microfilm: 2341017
6. The National Archives at St. Louis; St. Louis, Missouri; Draft Registration Cards for Fourth Registration for Nebraska, 04/27/1942 - 04/27/1942; NAI Number: 598911; Record Group Title: Records of the Selective Service System; Record Group Number: 147
7. Grand Island Cemetery Burial Index, Grand Island, Nebraska.

8. Year: 1880; Census Place: Alma, Wabaunsee, Kansas; Roll: 398; Family History Film: 1254398; Page: 344A; Enumeration District: 117; Image: 0703

9. ibid,

10. Year: 1880; Census Place: Alma, Wabaunsee, Kansas; Roll: 398; Family History Film: 1254398; Page: 344B; Enumeration District: 117; Image: 0704

11. ibid.

12. Year: 1880; Census Place: Newbury, Wabaunsee, Kansas; Roll: 399; Family History Film: 1254399; Page: 372A; Enumeration District: 120; Image: 0004

13. Ancestry.com. *Tennessee, State Marriages, 1780-2002* [database on-line]. Lehi, UT, USA: Ancestry.com Operations Inc, 2008.Original data: *Tennessee State Marriages, 1780-2002*. Nashville, TN, USA: Tennessee State Library and Archives. Microfilm.

George Leonard Dean

George Leonard Dean filed his World War I Draft Registration in Scotts Bluff Co., Nebraska on 12 September 1918. He was living in Scottsbluff, working for A.T. Crawford as a laborer. His nearest relative was his wife, Maggie Dean. George was age 32, born 12 April 1886. Extra notes indicate that he was paralyzed on the right side. [1]

On the 1910 US Census, George Dean was living in Alliance, Box Butte Co., Nebraska and on the 1920 US Census he was in Scotts Bluff Co., Nebraska

1910 US Census, Box Butte Co., Nebraska, Alliance, Ward 2, ED 7, Page 9B [2]
122 Sweetwater Ave.
190-197 Maggie Hardin, black, 28, widow, 2 children, 1 living, b. MO,
        father b. unknown, mother b. M, laborer, odd jobs
George Dean, lodger, black, 26, single, b. KY, both parents b. KY, porter,
        hotel

1920 US Census, Scotts Bluff Co., Nebraska, Scottsbluff, Ward 2, ED 226, Page 21A [3]
605 9th Street
378-481 George Dean, rents, black, 35, b. KY, both parents b. KY, laborer, auto
        garage
Maggie, wife, black, 38, b. MO, both parents b. MO
Jeff? H. Mitchell, boarder, black, 25, single, b. AL, both parents b. AL, laborer,
        auto garage

George Dean married Maggie Patrick on 1 March 1916 in Alliance, Box Butte Co., Nebraska. On the license, he is shown as 31, colored, single, born Kentucky, laborer. His parents were James Dean and Lottie Smith, places of birth unknown. Maggie is shown as 34, colored, widow, second marriage, born Missouri. Her parents are shown as John Hinch and Mary Stapleton, both born in Missouri. [4]

1940 US Census, Scotts Bluff Co., Nebraska, Scottsbluff, ED 79-26A, Page 8B [5]
143 E. 8 Ave.
rents, $9 month
George Leonard Dean, informant, negro, 64, single, 6th grade, b. KY, same
        place 1 April 1935, porter, private home

He filed his World War II Draft Registration on 22 April 1942 in Gering, Scotts Bluff Co., Nebraska. His address is shown as 903 East 8th St., Scottsbluff. He was a janitor for Dr. Malott and Dr.

Hodnett, Scottsbluff. The person who would know where he was is shown as Mary Right, 612 East 9th, Scottsbluff. 6 According to the Social Security Claims, his parents were James Dean and Lottie Smith. 7

George Leonard Dean was born 18 April 1886 in Worthville, Carroll Co., Kentucky and died 13 March 1948. He was buried in the Fairview Cemetery in Scottsbluff, Scottsbluff Co., Nebraska. 8

George Dean is first shown on the 1900 US Census at Louisville, Kentucky. This indicates that his mother was a widow. They cannot be located prior to 1900.

> 1900 US Census, Jefferson Co., Kentucky, Louisville, Ward 11, Ed 105, 22A 9
> 1504 B Kentucky Street
> 392-459 Lottie Dean, black, b. Dec 1863, 36, widow, 6 children, 4 living, b. KY,
> both parents b. KY
> Susie, daughter, black, b. Aug 1883, 16, b. KY, both parents b. KY
> Hale, daughter, black, b. Dec 1885, 15, b. KY, both parents b. KY, at school
> George, son, black, b. April 1886, 14, b. KY, both parents b. KY, at school
> Santorious, son, black, b. Dec 1894, 5, b. KY, both parents b. KY

Hallie C. Dean, daughter of James Dean and Lottie Smith, was born December 1885 in Kentucky. On 2 October 1906 she married Edward W. Barker in Marion Co., Indiana. Her parents are shown on the marriage record. Edward W. Barker was born in about 1884 in Tennessee. 10

James Santorius Dean, son of James Dean and Lottie Smith, was born in December of 1894 in Kentucky. He died 25 January 1945 in Louisville, Jefferson Co., Kentucky. His death record indicates he was 49, born about 1896, son of James Dean and Lottie Smith. 11

The widow, Maggie Hardin, on the 1910 US Census in Box Butte Co., Nebraska is the same age as Maggie Patrick shown on the marriage license in the same county to George Dean in 1916. In 1900 there is a Maggie Patrick shown in Howard Co., Missouri, who might be her.

> 1900 US Census, Howard Co., Missouri, Richmond, ED 70, Page 8A 12
> 129-148 Maggie Patrick, black, b. May 1881, 19, widow, 2 children, 2 living,
>   b. MO, both parents b. MO, no occupation
> Willie, son, black, b. July 1897, 2, b. MO, both parents b. MO

On the same enumeration in Howard Co., Missouri, there is a John Hinch, black, with wife Mary, also black. John was born in August of 1860 and Mary was born in March of 1865. Mary indicates she had 10 children, 7 were living. The oldest in the household was a daughter Pearl, born 1886. 13

1. Registration State: *Nebraska;* Registration County: *Scotts Bluff;* Roll: *1711770*
2. Year: 1910; Census Place: Alliance Ward 2, Box Butte, Nebraska; Roll: T624_838; Page: 9B; Enumeration District: 0007; FHL microfilm: 1374851
3. Year: 1920; Census Place: Scottsbluff Ward 2, Scotts Bluff, Nebraska; Roll: T625_1001; Page: 21A; Enumeration District: 226; Image: 844
4. Box Butte Co., Nebraska Marriage Book E 459
5. Year: 1940; Census Place: Scottsbluff, Scotts Bluff, Nebraska; Roll: T627_2264; Page: 8B; Enumeration District: 79-26A
6. The National Archives at St. Louis; St. Louis, Missouri; Draft Registration Cards for Fourth Registration for Nebraska, 04/27/1942 - 04/27/1942; NAI Number: 598911; Record Group Title: Records of the Selective Service System; Record Group Number: 147
7. Ancestry.com. *U.S., Social Security Applications and Claims Index, 1936-2007* [database on-line]. Provo, UT, USA: Ancestry.com Operations, Inc., 2015.

8. FindAGrave http://www.findagrave.com
9. Year: 1900; Census Place: Louisville Ward 11, Jefferson, Kentucky; Roll: 532; Page: 22A; Enumeration District: 0105; FHL microfilm: 1240532
10. "Indiana Marriages, 1780-1992," database, FamilySearch (https://familysearch.org/pal:/MM9.1.1/ XFJQ-7YF : 3 December 2014), Edw. W. Barker and Hallie C. Dean, 02 Oct 1906; citing reference ; FHL microfilm 413,542.
11. "Kentucky Death Records, 1911-1962," database, *FamilySearch* (https://familysearch.org/ark:/ 61903/1:1:N9CV-8F5 : 20 October 2016), James Dean in entry for James Santonius Dean, 25 Jan 1945; citing Louisville, Jefferson, Kentucky, United States, Office of Vital Statistics, Frankfort; FHL microfilm 1,913,396.
12. Year: 1900; Census Place: Richmond, Howard, Missouri; Roll: 859; Page: 8A; Enumeration District: 0070; FHL microfilm: 1240859
13. Year: 1900; Census Place: Richmond, Howard, Missouri; Roll: 859; Page: 22B; Enumeration District: 0070; FHL microfilm: 1240859

Miles H. DeWitty

Written accounts of the DeWitty settlement in Cherry Co., Nebraska indicate that it was named for a man named DeWitty. One account suggests his name was Jim DeWitty. Searching the land records, the two DeWitty men who obtained land under the Homestead Act in Cherry County, were John H. DeWitty and Miles H. DeWitty. The surname is shown also as Dewitty.

Miles H. DeWitty obtained a patent under the Homestead Act for 637.20 acres in various sections of Cherry County on 23 April 1915 at the Valentine Land Office. This was located exactly where the DeWitty settlement was located in Cherry County. John H. DeWitty obtained patent to 348.45 acres under the Homestead Act in 1919. This was located several miles west of the DeWitty settlement and south of the North Loup River. [1]

The following news announcement appeared in the *Omaha World Herald,* and reveals that the settlement was named after Miles H. DeWitty who became the first postmaster there.

Omaha Daily Bee, 7 April 1915, page 2
Department Orders
Washington, April 6. Special Telegram
Postmasters Appointed: Nebraska
Postoffice established at Dewitty, Cherry County, Nebraska with Miles H.
Dewitty, postmaster

In 1910 Miles H. DeWitty was living in Bourbon Co., Kansas and is seen in the following census enumeration. Since it normally took about five years to prove up and achieve patent, he and his wife probably moved to Cherry County shortly after that enumeration was taken.

1910 US Census Bourbon Co., Kansas Fort Scott Ward 3 ED 41 [2]
1629 E. Oak
484-449 Miles Dewitty, black, 26, married 0 years, b. Mexico, both parents b.
        Mexico, photographer, office
Myrtle, wife, black, 22, married 0 years, 0 children, 0 living, b. MO, father b. KY,
        mother b. MO
Emma M. Batzell, black, 59, mother in law, widow, 10 chilren, 4 living, b. MO,
        both parents b. MD

Miles H. DeWitty and Miss Myrtle Batsell were married on 25 August 1909 in St. Joseph, Buchanan Co., Missouri. They were both residents of St. Joseph and were married by Rev. John A. Gregg of the Ebenezer A.M.E. Church. 3

Miles Henry DeWitty filed his World War I draft registration in Valentine, Cherry Co., Nebraska on 12 September 1918. He was age 45, born 27 August 1873 and a farmer. His nearest relative is shown as his wife, Myrtle Louise DeWitty of Valentine, Cherry Co., Nebraska. 4

From further research in census enumerations, it appears that between 1919 and 1923, Miles H. DeWitty, wife Louise M. (Myrtle) and children moved to California. Miles died on 11 March 1929 in San Diego, San Diego Co., California. 5

> 1930 US Census, San Diego Co., California, San Diego, ED 200 Page 2A 6
> 3660 Filbert Street
> 56-57 Louise M. Dewitty, owns $1,000 negro, 43, widow, b. MO, father b. TX,
>   mother b. KS, washerwoman, at home
> Kersurce R., son, 19, negro, b. NE, father b. TX, mother b. MO, chauffeur, private
>   family
> John H., son, 14, b. NE, father b. TX, mother b. MO
> Miles H., son, negro, 11, b. NE, father b. TX, mother b. MO
> Frank N., son, negro, 7, b. CA, father b. TX, mother b. MO
> Edna L., daughter, negro, 3, b. CA, father b. TX, mother b. MO

> 1940 US Census, San Diego Co., California, San Diego, Ed 62-111, Page 27A 7
> 3532 Filbert Street
> owns, $1,000
> Myrtle De Witty, negro, 53, widow, 1 year high school, b. MO, same house 1 April 1935,
>   seamstress WPA Survey Project
> Miles, son, negro, 21, single, b. NE, 4 years high school, same house 1 April
>   1935, picks and shovel, NYA project
> Frank, son, negro, 17, b. CA, 3 years high school, same house 1 April 1935
> Edna, daughter, negro, 14, b. CA, 1 year high school, same house 1 April 1935

Some information is known about two of their sons, Miles Henry Dewitty and Frank N. Dewitty. According to the claim on the Social Security Deaths for Miles, he was born 23 September 1918 in Valentine, Cherry Co., Nebraska to Miles H. Dewitty and Myrtle Batsell. He died on 15 August 1998 in San Diego, San Diego Co., California. 8

Miles, Jr. served in the U.S. Navy, enlisting on 19 June 1941. On 16 June 1946 in Norfolk, Virginia he married Rosa Brown. Their marriage certificate was filed at Portsmouth, Virginia, showing him as Std 3c in U.S. Navy. His place of birth is shown as Sandhills, Nebraska. His residence was USS Chemung, AO 30, % Fleet, PO, New York, New York. Rosa was 32, divorced, married one other time. She was a packer for Virginia Ice Cream Co. at Southill, Virginia. Her parents were James Brown and Sarah Cuffee, her residence was 726 Queen St., Portsmouth, VA. They were married by Rev. J. H. Harrell, Baptist minister in Norfolk Co., Virginia. 9

Frank N. DeWitty, son of Miles H. DeWitty and Myrtle Batsell, was born 1 April 1923 in California and died 28 April 2009. He served in the U.S. Navy in World War II, the Korean War and Vietnam. He was buried in Fort Rosencrans National Cemetery, San Diego, San Diego Co., California. 10

Miles Henry DeWitty, Sr. was the son of Mo Dewitty, who is shown as a widower on the 1900 US Census.

1900 US Census, Travis Co., Texas, Justice prect. 6, ED 117, Page 26A 11

435-446 Mo Dewitty, black, b. Aug 1841, 58, widowed, b. AL, both parents b.
      VA, farmer

Oliver, son, black, b. Oct 1866, 35, single, b. TX, both parents b. AL, farm laborer

Jessie, grandson, black, b. Feb 1895, 5, b. TX, both parents b. TX

Ransom, son, black, b. Aug. 1868, 31, divorced, b. TX, both parents b. AL, farm
      laborer

Jim, son, black, b. Feb 1872, 28, divorced, b. TX, both parents b. AL, farm laborer

Miles, son, black, b. Aug 1874, 25, single, b. TX, both parents b. AL, student

Lydia, daughter, black, b. March 1877, 23, divorced, 1 child, 1 living, b. TX, both
      parents b. AL

Eliza, daughter, black, b. Sept 1879, 20, divorced, 0 children, b. TX, both parents
      b. AL

Alex, son, black, b. Feb 1882, 18, single, b. TX, both parents b. AL, farm laborer

John, son, black, b. April 1885, 15, b. TX, both parents b. AL, farm laborer

Lucille, daughter, black, b. April 1889, 11, b. TX, both parents b. AL

Louanna Piper, granddaughter, black, b. May 1896, 4, b. TX, both parents b. TX

1. U.S. Department of the Interior, Bureau of Land Management, http://www.glorecords.blm.gov/results/default.aspx?searchCriteria=type=patent|st=NE|cty=031|ln=Dewitty|sp=true|sw=true|sadv=false

2. Year: 1910; Census Place: Fort Scott Ward 3, Bourbon, Kansas; Roll: T624_432; Page: 21B; Enumeration District: 0041; FHL microfilm: 1374445

3. Ancestry.com. *Missouri, Marriage Records, 1805-2002* [database on-line]. Provo, UT, USA: Ancestry.com Operations, Inc., 2007.Original data: *Missouri Marriage Records*. Jefferson City, MO, USA: Missouri State Archives. Microfilm.

4. Registration State: *Nebraska;* Registration County: *Cherry;* Roll: *1711452*

5. Ancestry.com. *California, Death Index, 1905-1939* [database on-line]. Provo, UT, USA: Ancestry.com Operations, Inc., 2013.

6. Year: 1930; Census Place: San Diego, San Diego, California; Roll: 193; Page: 2A; Enumeration District: 0200; Image: 789.0; FHL microfilm: 2339928

7. Year: 1940; Census Place: San Diego, San Diego, California; Roll: T627_453; Page: 27A; Enumeration District: 62-111

8. Ancestry.com. *U.S., Social Security Applications and Claims Index, 1936-2007* [database on-line]. Provo, UT, USA: Ancestry.com Operations, Inc., 2015.

9. Ancestry.com. *Virginia, Marriage Records, 1936-2014* [database on-line]. Provo, UT, USA: Ancestry.com Operations, Inc., 2015. Original data: Virginia, Marriages, 1936-2014. Virginia Department of Health, Richmond, Virginia.

10. FindAGrave http://www.findagrave.com

11. Year: 1900; Census Place: Justice Precinct 6, Travis, Texas; Roll: 1673; Page: 26A; Enumeration District: 0117; FHL microfilm: 1241673

Cherry Co., Nebraska Settlers
Stewart and Boyd

There were several black settlers in Cherry County around Brownlee and particularly in the DeWitty settlement. The information below is about those who only remained in the area a short time.

James H. Stewart was born in about 1859 in Canada to David Stewart and Ann M. Ryan. On 23 December 1902 in Cuyahoga Co., Ohio, he married Ethel Lucas, daughter of William Lucas and Lacy Jackson. 1 They are shown on the 1910 US Census in Cherry Co., Nebraska. On the 1930 US Census, James is shown as only age 49.

1910 US Census, Cherry Co., Nebraska, Loup Prect., ED 57, Page 6B   2
83-83 James H. Stewart, mulatto, 51, second marriage, married 8 years, b.
   Canada (American Citizen, both parents b. VA, came to US in 1892,
   naturalized, plasterer, house
  Ethel M., wife, mulatto, 25, first marriage, married 8 years, b. OH, both parents
   b. OH

1930 US Census, Muskegon Co., Michigan, Muskegon Heights, ED 36, Page   3
16A 1437 Park Avenue
321-325 James H. Stewart, rents $7 month, negro, 49, married at age 28, b.
   Canada, father b. MD, mother b. VA, laborer, foundry
  Ethel M., wife, negro, 45, married at age 18, b. OH, both parents b. OH

1940 US Census, Washtenaw Co., Michigan, Ypsilanti, ED 81-59, Page 5B   4
Frederica Street
rents $15 month
James H. Stewart, negro, 81, 4th grade, b. Canada, same place 1 April 1935
Ethel M., informant, wife, negro, 53, 8th grade, b. OH, same place 1 April
   1935, general housework private family

Under the Homestead Act, James H. Stewart obtained 360 acres of land in Cherry Co., Nebraska. The patent was issued on 6 February 1917. The land was located in the vicinity of DeWitty in Cherry County and is described as follows. 5
  6th PM T 27N R30W Section 15
  North 1/2 North 1/2
  Southwest 1/4 Northwest 1/4

There were several black families and individuals who came to Cherry Co., Nebraska from Merrick County, particularly Central City, Nebraska. Creed F. Boyd was living with his family in 1910 in Central City and is known to have come to the DeWitty area, but went back to eastern Nebraska. He was born in Roane Co., Tennessee in about 1845. His second wife was Rachel C. Finley. She was born 31 March 1865 in Tennessee and died 8 August 1941 in Los Angeles, Los Angeles Co., California. In 1900 Creed and his family were living in Roane Co., Tennessee and by 1910 had moved to Merrick Co., Nebraska. By 1920 Creed had been admitted to the Hospital for the Insane in Norfolk, Nebraska, but is also shown with his family in Merrick County.

1910 US Census, Merrick Co., Nebraska, Central City, Ward 3, ED 148, Page 15A 6
376-328 C.F. Boyd, mulatto, 65, second marriage, b. TN, both parents b. VA
   painter, houses
  Rachel C., wife, black, 45, first marriage, married 25 years, 11 children, 8 living,
   b. TN, both parents b. TN
  Joseph H., son, mulatto, 18, b. TN, both parents b. TN painter, houses
  William, son, mulatto, 16, b. TN, both parents b. TN
  Edna, daughter, mulatto, 11, b. TN, both parents b. TN
  Amanda?, daughter, mulatto, 8, b. TN, both parents b. TN
  Lillie, daughter, mulatto, 6, b. TN, both parents b. TN
  Roger, son, mulatto, 4, b. TN, both parents b. TN
  Mildred, daughter mulatto, 1, b. TN, both parents b. TN

Creed Boyd made the 39th land entry in Cherry Co., Nebraska in 1911. It contained 160 acres and three months after he filed, it was canceled. In 1912 another black, Walter S. Brooks filed a claim on the same 160 acres.   7

While Creed Boyd does not appear to have settled very long in Cherry Co., Nebraska, he did obtain 480 acres of land there under the Homestead Act. The patent was issued on 19 February 1917 and the land was located in the vicinity of DeWitty. The following is the description of this property from the U.S. Department of the Interior, Bureau of Land Management, General Land Office Records

> 6th PM   T 28N R31W, Section 29, South 1/2
> 6th PM   T 28N R 31W, Section 32, North 1/2, North 1/2

Shortly after this, the elderly Creed Boyd was in the Hospital for the Insane in Norfolk, Nebraska. He is shown there as well as in his own household in Merrick Co., Nebraska on the 1920 US Census.

> 1920 US Census, Madison Co., Nebraska, Norfolk, ED 146, Page 14A [8]
> Hospital for the Insane
> Creed F. Boyd, black, 75, married, b. TN, parents b. US

> 1920 US Census, Merrick Co., Nebraska, Central City, ED 158, Page 21A [9]
> 21st Avenue
> 160-168 Creed F. Boyd, rents, black, 75, b. TN, both parents b. TN, painter,
>   house
> Rachel, wife, black, 54, b. TN, both parents b. TN, laborer, day work
> Joe, son, 28, single, b. TN, both parents b. TN, painter, house
> Lillie, daughter, black, 15, b. TN, both parents b. TN, laborer, day work
> Roger, son, black, 13, b. TN, both parents b. TN
> Mildred, daughter, black, 11, b. TN, both parents b. TN

Creed F. Boyd died on 8 December 1923 in the Hospital for the Insane in Norfolk, Madison Co., Nebraska and was buried on 17 December 1923 in the cemetery at the hospital. [10]

1. Cuyahoga County Archive; Cleveland, Ohio; Cuyahoga County, Ohio, Marriage Records, 1810-1973; Volume: Vol 54-55; Page: 164
2. Year: 1910; Census Place: Loup, Cherry, Nebraska; Roll: T624_840; Page: 6B; Enumeration District: 0057; FHL microfilm: 1374853
3. Year: 1930; Census Place: Muskegon Heights, Muskegon, Michigan; Roll: 1015; Page: 16A; Enumeration District: 0036; Image: 293.0; FHL microfilm: 2340750
4. Year: 1940; Census Place: Ypsilanti, Washtenaw, Michigan; Roll: T627_1824; Page: 5B; Enumeration District: 81-59
5. http://www.glorecords.blm.gov/details/patent/default.aspx?accession=565703&docClass=SER&sid=ksz4psg4.c3u
6. Year: 1910; Census Place: Central Ward 3, Merrick, Nebraska; Roll: T624_851; Page: 15A; Enumeration District: 0148; FHL microfilm: 1374864
7. *The Nebraska Sand Hills The Human Landscape* by Charles Barron McIntosh, Lincoln, NE: University of Nebraska Press, 1996, page 231.
8. Year: 1920; Census Place: Norfolk, Madison, Nebraska; Roll: T625_993; Page: 14A; Enumeration District: 146; Image: 304
9. Year: 1920; Census Place: Norfolk, Madison, Nebraska; Roll: T625_993; Page: 14A; Enumeration District: 146; Image: 304
10. FindAGrave http://www.findagrave.com

Edward McKenzie

Sgt. Edward McKenzie of Co. B and Co. I, 9th US Cavalry was one of the few black officers who had family living at Fort Robinson. In May of 1891 according to post orders, he was on extra duty as a wagonmaster. Letters to the Adjutant General, Department of the Platte on 1 May 1891 indicate that he denied signing a petition for the removal of Capt. John Guilfoyle as the commander of Co. I. The medical history records of Fort Robinson indicate that McKenzie and his family lived in the old barrack.

On the 1890 Veterans Schedules for Nebraska (Civil War), Edward McKenzie is shown as a Private in Company G, 4th US Colored Infantry; enlisted 22 July 1863 and discharged 28 October 1865, served 2 years, 3 months and 6 days. His address is shown as Fort Robinson, Dawes Co., Nebraska. 1

The 4th US Colored Infantry was organized at Baltimore, Maryland from 15 July to 1 September 1863. The 4th served in the Department of North Carolina until May of 1866. 2

In February of 1895 his wife, Annie, died of paralysis at Fort Robinson. She was a sister of the wife of 1st Sgt. George Mason, Co. C, 9th Cavalry. Annie was buried at the post cemetery on 16 February 1895. In 1947 her remains were removed to the Fort McPherson National Cemetery at Maxwell, Lincoln Co., Nebraska.

The following are from the Returns of the Regular Army Calvary, Buffalo Soldiers that pertain to Edward McKenzie.

Edward McKenzie, private
Co I, 9th Calvary
Col. Edward Hatch
20 March 1875
San Antonio, Texas

Edward McKenzie
Co. I, 9th Calvary
Col. Edward Hatch
private
9 November 1875
Fort Clark, Texas

Edward McKenzie
Co I, 9th Calvary
Col. Edward Hatch
corporal
30 July 1880
Fort Wingate, New Mexico

Edward McKenzie
Co. I, 9th Calvary
Col. Edward Hatch

Sergeant
29 August 1888
Fort Robinson, Nebraska

Edward McKenzie
Co I, 9th US Cavalry
Colonel Joseph G. Tilford
private
8 June 1890
Fort Robinson, Nebraska

Edward McKenzie
Co I, 9th US Cavalry
Sergeant
27 May 1895
Crawford, Nebraska
on furlough

Edward McKenzie
Co B, 9th US Cavalry
Col. David Perry
24 December 1897
Fort Robinson, Nebraska

Most likely Edward McKenzie was discharged at Fort Robinson. He does not appear to have remained in the area and cannot be located conclusively on the 1900 US Census.

1. Year: 1890; Census Place: Fort Robinson, Dawes, Nebraska; Roll: 37; Page: 3; Enumeration District: Fort Robinson
2. https://www.nps.gov/rich/learn/historyculture/4thusct.htm

Emanuel

The Emanuel family came from Ontario, Canada to Nebraska. They came to Dawson Co., Nebraska, near Overton, with other black families from Ontario. Eventually they took land in Cherry Co., Nebraska in the settlement known as DeWitty, renamed Audacious. Some then left Cherry County and settled in Box Butte Co., Nebraska.

Joshua Dawson Emanuel, son of Joshua Emanuel and Lucinda Travis, was born in March of 1863. Some records indicate that he was born in New York. However, the 1861 Canadian census indicates the family arrived in Canada in 1857 and that he was born in Canada West. He married Mary Ann Robinson, daughter of Richard E. Robinson and Mathilda A. Gields. Mary Ann was born in North Brookston, Ontario Canada in about 1872. Joshua Emanuel Jr. and Mary Robinson married 9 December 1884 in Dodge Co., Nebraska. [1] On the 1880 US Census, Joshua's father, Joshua Emanuel, Sr., was living in Dawson Co., Nebraska, Covington Prect., but Joshua, Jr. is not in the county. [2] Mary Ann Robinson was already living with her parents in Dawson Co., Nebraska in 1880. [3]

> 1885 Nebraska State Census, Dawson Co., Nebraska, Logan Prect., ED 192, [4] Page B2
> 23-23 Josh Emanuel, Jr., black, 22, farmer, b. Canada West, both
>   parents b. Canada, farmer
> Mary Emanuel, black, 16, wife, keeping house, b. Canada West,
>   father b. MI, mother b. OH

> 1900 US Census, Dawson Co., Nebraska, Overton Prect., ED 93, Page 11A [5]
> 207-207 Joshua Emanuel, black, b. March 1865, 35, married 15 years, b. NY,
>   both parents b. NY, farmer
> Mary A., wife, black, b. Sept 1871, 28, 9 children, 8 living, b. Canada, father
>   b. IN, mother b. Canada
> Alfred A., black, b. Nov. 1885, 14, b. NE, father b. NY, mother b. Canada,
>   at school
> Jennie L., black, b. March 1888, 12, b. NE, father b. NY, mother b. Canada,
>   at school
> Wilbert J., black, b. July 1890, 9, b. NE, father b. NY, mother b. Canada, at
>   school
> Mary L., black, b. Oct 1891, 8, b. NE, father b. NY, mother b. Canada, at
>   school

Between 1910 and 1920 the Emanuels moved to Cherry Co., Nebraska, along with other blacks who were living in Dawson Co., Nebraska. Joshua Emanuel, Sr. died in 1887 in Dawson County. The Emanuels first appear on the 1910 US Census in Cherry County. [6]

> 1910 US Census, Cherry Co., Nebraska, Kennedy Prect., ED 51, Page 8A
> 16-16 Joshua Emanuel, black, 45, married 25 years, b. NY, father b. US,
>   mother b. IN, farmer
> Mary, wife, mulatto, 40, 12 children, 12 living, b. Canada, both parents b. US
> Bert, son, mulatto, 18, b. NE, father b. NY, mother b. Canada, farm laborer

Mary L., daughter, mulatto, 17, b. NE, father b. NY, mother b. Canada
Grace, daughter, mulatto, 16, b. NE, father b. NY, mother b. Canada
Lawrence, son, mulatto, 14, b. NE, father b. NY, mother b. Canada
John, son, mulatto, 13, b. NE, father b. NY, mother b. Canada
Dewey, son, mulatto, 11, b. NE, father b. NY, mother b. Canada
Frank, son, mulatto, 9, b. NE, father b. NY, mother b. Canada
Lizzie, daughter, mulatto, 7, b. NE, father b. NY, mother b. Canada
Nellie, daughter, mulatto, 3, b. NE, father b. NY, mother b. Canada
Carl David, son, mulatto, 7/12, b. NE, father b. NY, mother b. Canada

Joshua Emanuel, Jr. died in 1919 in Cherry Co., Nebraska and was buried in the DeWitty Cemetery near Brownlee in Cherry County. His grave is no longer marked. His widow, Mary Ann Robinson Emanuel went to Alliance, Box Butte Co., Nebraska with her younger children. They are shown there on the 1920 US Census.

1920 US Census, Box Butte Co., Nebraska, Alliance, ED 11, Page 23A 7
Reddish Addition
307-347 Mary A. Emanuel, rents, black, widow, 48, came to United States
            in 1879 and naturalized in 1890, b. Canada, father b. IN, mother b.
            Canada, farmer
Richard D., son, black, 20, single, b. NE, father b. NY, mother b. Canada,
            cook, hotel
Chasper F., son, black, 17, b. NE, father b. NY, mother b. Canada, dishwasher,
            hotel
Nellie R., daughter, black, 12, b. NE, father b. NY, mother b. Canada
Carl D., son, black, 10, b. NE, father b. NY, mother b. Canada
Elza I., son, black, 6, b. NE, father b. NY, mother b. Canada
Lulu Young, roomer, black, 39, divorced, b. IN, both parents b. NC, waitress,
            cafe
Glenora M., roomer, black, 18, single, b. NE, father b. NE, mother b. IN
Oscar B. Albert, roomer, black, 45, married, b. KY, father b. KY, mother b. TN,
            cafe, hotel

Mary Ann Robinson Emanuel is last shown on the 1920 US Census and probably died somewhere in Nebraska. She is not buried in the Alliance Cemetery. The children of Joshua Dawson Emanuel and Mary Ann Robinson were as follows.

1. Alfred Andrew Emanuel, born 4 November 1885 near Overton, Dawson Co.,
     Nebraska
2. Jennie L. Emanuel, born March 1888 in Nebraska
3. Wilbert James Emanuel, born 19 July 1890 at Overton, Dawson Co., Nebraska
4. Mary Lucinda Emanuel, born 22 October 1891 in Nebraska
5. Grace L. Emanuel, born January 1894 in Nebraska
6. Lawrence Joshua Emanuel, born 19 July 1896 in Nebraska
7. John Vernon Emanuel, born 19 July 1896 in Nebraska
8. Richard D. Emanuel, born January 1900 in Nebraska
9. Frank Emanuel, born about 1901 in Nebraska
10. Hattie Elizabeth Emanuel, born about 1903 in Nebraska; died in about
     1916 in Nebraska
11. Charles Franklin Emanuel, born 21 September 1903 in Nebraska
12. Nellie Ruth Cherry Emanuel, born 9 Aug 1907 Valentine, Cherry Co.,
     Nebraska

359

13. Carl David Emanuel, born 12 September 1909 in Nebraska

Alfred Andrew Emanuel, son of Joshua Emanuel and Mary Ann Robinson, was born 4 November 1885 near Overton, Dawson Co., Nebraska. He worked for the railroad at Boulder, Colorado from 1916 to 1919, then came to Alliance in February of 1919 as an employee with the Burlington Railroad. In August of 1922 he took up farming. On 23 March 1912 he married Cora Mance in Brownlee, Cherry Co., Nebraska. According to their marriage record Alfred was age 26 and Cora was age 21, daughter of Wm. and Georgia Mance. They were married by H.H. Mance. Cora's father was Wade H. Mance and he was the minister who married them. Refer to Mance section below.

    1930 US Census, Denver Co., Colorado, Denver District V, ED 173, Page 1B   8
    2239 Clarkson St.
    24-24 Alfred Emanuel, rents $18 month, negro, 42, married at age 26, b. NE,
            father b. NY, mother b. Canada, laborer, railroad
    Cora, wife, negro, 33, married at age 17, b. KS, both parents b. SC
    Julia, negro, 16, b. NE, father b. NE, mother b. KS
    Janet, negro, 15, b. NE, father b. NE, mother b. KS
    Raymond, negro, 12, b. CO, father b. NE, mother b. KS
    Gladis, negro, 11, b. CO, father b. NE, mother b. KS
    James, negro, 8, b. NE, father b. NE, mother b. KS
    Dorothy, negro, 6, b. NE, father b. NE, mother b. KS
    Aloin, male, negro, 3, b. NE, father b. NE, mother b. KS

Alfred Emanuel and Cora Mance divorced in 1935 in Box Butte Co., Nebraska. He married second to the widow Leona Glass on 6 May 1944 in Alliance, Box Butte Co., Nebraska. 9

Box Butte County, Nebraska
District Court
Civil Court File #5233
Divorce

Cora Emanuel, Plaintiff
vs
Alfred A. Emanual, Defendant
Petition dated 29 Nov 1935

The plaintiff and defendant were married on 23 March 1912, Cherry Co., Nebraska. The plaintiff has been a faithful, chaste and obedient wife. For more than two years past they have been residents of Box Butte County. The following children were born to them. They all live with the plaintiff who has custody of them.

Julia L. Emanuel, 22
Janet L. Emanuel, age 20
Alfred R. Emanuel, 18
Gladys Emanuel, 16
James Emanuel, 14
Dorothy C. Emanuel, 11
Alvin Emanuel, age 8

The plaintiff claims that the defendant has failed, refused and neglected to provide for her and the children. She has supported and maintained them since 1930. Since April 1943, the defendant has entirely failed to contribute money or provisions or clothing to the plaintiff or any of the children. With the exception during said period he did contribute two bushels of vegetables and two small pigs. The defendant is guilty of extreme cruelty toward plaintiff for more than two years past. He has several times told her that he has lost his regard for her and would no longer live with her, suggesting she get a divorce. She has suffered and anguished which impaired her health. She has received some help from her father.

Voluntary Apperance in District Court of Box Butte County 29 Nov 1935
Alfred A. Emanuel entered his voluntary appearance in the case, waiving the issuance and service of summons, reserving his right to demur, answer or otherwise plead in the said case on or before 30 Dec 1935.

Decree   23 Jan 1936 District Court of Box Butte County, Nebraska
The court finds allegations are true as stated in the petition.
The court declares that the marriage be dissolved and annulled, both parties released from it. The plaintiff is to have exclusive custody, care and control of the children. She is to recover her costs from the defendant.

There is an Alfred Emanuel living in Box Butte Co., Nebraska in 1940 on the census. However, his age and place of birth is incorrect. He is too old to be Alfred and Cora's son, Alfred Raymond Emanuel. Note that both he and Cora indicate they are widowed.

> 1940 US Census, Box Butte Co., Nebraska, Box Butte Prect., ED 7-7, Page 5A 10
> rents $2 Alfred Emanal [sic], negro, 49, widowed, 8th grade, b. CO, rural
>   Sheridan Co., NE 1 April 1935, farmer
>
> 1940 US Census, Box Butte Co., Nebraska, Alliance, ED 7-2A, Page 3B   11
> 412 Niobrara St. rents $5 month
> Cora Emanuel, white, 40, widow, 4 years high school, b. GA, same place
>   1 April 1935, no occupation
> Christina Emanuel, informant, white, daughter, 16, b. NE, same place 1 April
>   1935
> Alvin Emanuel, son, white, 13, b. NE, same place 1 April 1935

The following are the children of Alfred Andrew Emanuel and his first wife, Cora Mance. There were no children born to his second marriage.

1. Julia L. Emanuel, born about 1914 in Nebraska
2. Janet L. Emanuel, born about 1915 in Nebraska
3. Alfred Raymond Emanuel, born about 1918 in Colorado
4. Gladys Emanuel, born about 1919 in Colorado
5. James Andrew Emanuel, born 15 June 1921 in Alliance, Box Butte Co.,
    Nebraska
6. Dorothy Christina Emanuel, born about 1924 in Nebraska
7. Alvin Emanuel, born about 1927 in Nebraska

James Andrew Emanuel, son of Alfred Andrew Emanuel and Cora Mance, was born 15 June 1921 in Alliance, Box Butte Co., Nebraska. As a teenager, James worked on ranches and farms in Box Butte County. He attended Howard University in Washington, DC where he received a B.A. degree. At the age of twenty he joined the US Army, serving as a confidential secretary to the Assistant Inspector General of the US Army, Benjamin O. Davis, Sr. He furthered his education by receiving his M.A. at Northwestern University and his Ph.D. at Columbia University. He was an associate professor of English at The

College of the City of New York. His poems were well known and published in "Ebony Rhythm" as well as the "Negro Digest," "The Midwest Quarterly," "The New York Times," and "Freedomways." His work has been anthologized in about 35 collections and textbooks in the United States, England and France.

In 1966, Emanuel became enbroiled in racial polictics when he ran for the Mount Vernon, New York school board. He called for curriculum reforms, including the addition of teaching black literature. In so doing he organized a black boycott of local merchants. In the late 1960s and early 1970s he taught at French universities. He had married Mattie Etha Johnson and at this time their marriage began to deteriorate, eventually ending in divorce after he returned to New York. He was completely cut off from his son. In 1972 he had met Marie-France Bertrand in Toulouse who became his companion and also the focus of his love poems. He lived at her mother's retreat in Le Barry, France. Eventually he returned to the University of Toulouse where he taught courses in his own poetry. He died in Paris on 28 September 2013. His son, James Andrew Emanuel, Jr., was born 1 January 1954. According to his father he committed suicide after an affray with police. He died 16 January 1983 and is buried in the Silverbrook Cemetery in Niles, Berrien Co., Michigan. 12

Jennie L. Emanuel, daughter of Joshua Dawson Emanuel and Mary Ann Robinson, was born in March of 1888 in Nebraska. She died in 1968 and is buried in the Riverside Cemetery, Denver, Denver Co., Colorado. Jennie married Harry Drisdon in about 1919 or 1920. They were not married in Box Butte Co., Nebraska. The following censuses show where they were living and their family.

> 1920 US Census, Box Butte Co., Nebraska, Alliance, ED 11, Page 22B 13
> Reddish Addition
> 300-340 Harry Drisdon, rents, mulatto, 35, born CA, both parents b. CA, laborer,
>   railroad
> Jennie L., wife, black, 31, b. NE, father b. NE, mother b. Canada
>
> 1930 US Census, Denver Co., Colorado, Denver, ED 174, Page 13B 14
> Washington Street
> #305 Harry Drisdon, rents, negro, 45, married at age 34, b. CA, both parents b.
>   CA, janitor, apartment house
> Jennie, wife, negro, 42, married at age 30, b. NE, father b. NY, mother b. Canada
> Thelma, daughter, negro, 10, b. NE, father b. CA, mother b. NE
> Mable, daughter, negro, 8 11/12, b. NE, father b. CA, mother b. NE
> Victor, negro, 5 6/12, b. NE, father b. CA, mother b. NE
>
> 1940 US Census, Denver Co., Colorado, Denver, ED 16-248, Page 10A 15
> 2307 Emerson Street, rents $14 month
> Harry Drisdon, negro 56, 8th grade, b. CA, same place 1 April 1935, laborer, road
>   construction
> Jennie, wife, negro, 54, 9th grade, b. NE, same place 1 April 1935

Harry Drisdon filed his World War II Draft Registration in Denver Co., Colorado on 17 June 1942. He was living at 2215 Cleveland Place, Denver, Colorado. He was born 2 July 1884 in Alameda, California and employed by the U.S. Goverment, WPA. 16 Harry died on 11 October 1949.

The following are the known children born to Jennie L. Emanuel and Harry Drisdon.

1. Ruby Thelma Drisdon, born 30 March 1920 in Nebraska
2. Mable M. Drisdon, born about 1922 in Nebraska
3. Victor W. Drisdon, born 1 September 1924 in Nebraska

Ruby Thelma Drisdon, daughter of Jennie L. Emanuel and Harry Drisdon, was born 30 March 1920 in Nebraska. She married Joe Foster Casey on 1 April 1937 in Denver, Denver Co., Colorado. They were both age seventeen. 17   She died 8 May 2000 and her last residence was at Denver, Colorado. 18

Mable M. Drisdon, daughter of Jennie L. Emanuel and Harry Drisdon, was born in about 1922 in Nebraska. She married John I. Jefferson on 22 March 1939 in Littleton, Arapahoe Co., Colorado. He was born in about 1920. 19

Victor W. Drisdon, son of Jennie L. Emanuel and Harry Drisdon, was born in 1 September 1924 in Nebraska. He enlisted in the US Army at Camp Beale, Marysville, California on 18 February 1946. As a private he enlisted for the Panama Canal Department. Victor was married, a cook and had achieved three years of high school. His residence was Denver, Colorado. 20 Victor died on 5 September 2002. His last residence was at 94577 San Leandro, Alameda, California. 21

Wilbert James Emanuel, son of Joshua Dawson Emanuel and Mary Ann Robinson, was born 19 July 1890 at Overton, Dawson Co., Nebraska. He filed his World War I Draft Registration in Boulder, Boulder Co., Colorado on 5 June 1917. He was living in Boulder, Colorado, married and shown as African. He was employed as a section man for the Union Pacific RR Co. in Boulder, Colorado. 22   On the 1920 US Census, he shown as being in the Wyoming State Penitentiary.

> 1920 US Census, Carbon Co., Wyoming, State Penitentiary, Rawlins, ED 17,   23
> Page 1B
> Wilbert J. Emanuel, prisoner, mulatto, 29, b. NE, both parents b. Canada, collar
> bender, shirt factory

Wilbert filed his World War II Draft Registration in Denver, Colorado. The card indicates that he was living at Stockyards Station, Rt 3, Denver, Colorado. He was 51, born 19 July 1890 at Overton, Nebraska. He was employed at Bates & Son, Denver, Colorado. The person who would know where he is located is shown as Jennie Drisdon, 2321 Tremont, Denver, Colorado. Personal statistics indicate he was 5 feet 9 inches tall and weighed 160 lbs. He had blue eyes. It was filed 27 April 1942.   24

Mary Lucinda Emanuel, daughter of Joshua Dawson Emanuel and Mary Ann Robinson, was born 22 October 1891 in Nebraska. She married Clarence Eugene Masterson. Mary died on 20 December 1930 and is buried in the Corning Cemetery, Corning, Nemaha Co., Kansas. Their baby who died 22 June 1927 is buried in the same cemetery.   For more information refer to the Masterson.

> 1930 US Census, Nemaha Co., Kansas, Red Vermillion Twp., ED 19, Page 2A 25
> 26-26 Clarence Masterson, rents, negro, 41, married at age 27, b. KS, both
> parents b. KS, farmer
> Mary, wife, negro, 38, married at age 21, b. NE, father b. NY, mother b. Canada
> Ralph, son, negro, 10, b. NE, father b. KS, mother b. NE
> Clarence, Jr., son, negro, 8, b. KS, father b. KS, mother b. NE
> Zelma, daughter, negro, 6, b. KS, father b. KS, mother b. NE
> Vera, daughter, negro, 1 7/12, b. KS, father b. KS, mother b. NE

Grace L. Emanuel, daughter of Joshua Dawson Emanuel and Mary Ann Robinson, was born 8 January 1894 in Nebraska. She married Bert Louis Harris on 30 March 1919 in Alliance, Box Butte Co., Nebraska. He was age 31 living in Alliance, born Alabama to Tom Harris and Maria Hampton, both born in Alabama. Bert was a boiler washer. 26 He died on 11 April 1961 and is buried in the Alliance Cemetery, Alliance, Box Butte Co., Nebraska. His wife, Grace Emanuel Harris died 30 September 1970 and is also buried in the Alliance Cemetery. Refer to Harris.

Nellie Ruth Cherry Emanuel, daughter of Joshua Dawson Emanuel and Mary Ann Robinson was born 29 August 1907 in Valentine, Cherry Co., Nebraska. At the time of her death she was the last living of her thirteen siblings. She was named Cherry after the county where she was born, but she went by Nellie Ruth. After leaving Cherry County, the family moved to Kansas and then later to Boulder, Colorado. She married Norman "Walker" Jenkins, Sr. of Boulder, Colorado. Along with their own three children, Harold, Marian and Norman, Jr., they raised Marvin Jenkins and other family members and foster children. Walker, who was born on 10 October 1905, died on 16 May 1981 and Nellie died on 1 April 2012. She and her husband are buried in Olinger Highland Mortuary and Cemetery, Thornton, Adams Co., Colorado, Garden of Devotion. 27

The Emanuels owned a significant amount of land in Cherry Co., Nebraska and prior to their move there, in Dawson Co., Nebraska. Under the Homestead Act, Joshua Emanuel, Sr. filed for 160 acres of land at the Grand Island Land Office. The land was located approximately three miles east and two and one-half miles north of Overton in Dawson County. Final patent was issued on 27 August 1889 on land described as 6th PM T9N R19W, Section 10, Southwest 1/4. 28

Joshua Emanuel, Sr. made entry No. 10043 on 15 April 1880. At the time he had a minor son named Joshua Emanuel who has since become a man thus he asked that his patent be issued to Joshua Emanuel, Sr. Papers in his Homestead File indicate that he also made a Timber Culture entry and then relinquished his right to it. In June of 1880 he broke 5 acres of land and built a sod house. He had last voted in Overton, Nebraska in November and had voted for seven years. His abode is described as a sod house measuring 16'x24', three rooms, board roof, 3 doors, 2 windows. He also had a house 10'x14', shingle roof with 1 door and 2 window, valued at $400. There was a granary, sod stable, well with pump. He had 40 acres broken for $100 valuation and had planted 15 fruit trees valued at $15. Joshua had 1 wagon, 2 plows, 1 cultivator, 1 mower, 1 shovel plow, 4 horses, 7 head of cattle, 22 hogs and 25 chickens. He owned 1 cook stove and complete furniture, 3 beds, 8 chairs, 1 table, 1 cupboard and a full line of dishes. He had planted corn and wheat. 29

Alfred A. Emanuel received 613.14 acres of land in Cherry Co., Nebraska under the Homestead Act. The land was located in the vicinity of DeWitty. Final patent was issued on 25 June 1913 for land described as follows. 30
> 6th PM T28N R29W
>> Section 19; Southwest 1/4
>> Section 30; North 1/2, Northwest 1/4 of Southeast 1/4, North 1/2 of
>>> Southwest 1/4 and Southwest 1/4 of the Southwest 1/4

Joshua Emanuel received 640 acres of land under the Homestead Act. It was located in the vicnity of DeWitty in Cherry Co., Nebraska. Final patent was issued on 22 April 1914 for the following described land. 31
> 6th PM T28N R30W
>> Section 28; South 1/2 of Southwest 1/4
>> Section 32; North 1/2 of Northwest 1/4 and Northeast 1/4
>> Section 33; North 1/2

Wilbert J. Emanuel received 640 acres of land under the Homestead Act. It was located in Cherry Co., Nebraska in the vicnity of DeWitty. The final patent was issued on 22 September 1915 for land described as follows. 32
> 6th PM T28N R31W
>> Section 15; East 1/2
>> Section 22; North 1/2

Jennie Emanuel received 640 acres of land under the Homestead Act. The land was located in

Cherry Co., Nebraska in the vicinity of DeWitty. She received final patent on the land on 13 June 1916. The land was described as 6th PM T28N R30W, Section 29. 33

Laurence Joshua Emanuel purchased 40 acres of land in Cherry Co., Nebraska, issued on 30 April 1921. The land was located in the vicnity of DeWitty, located at 6th PM T28N R30W, Section 13, Northeast 1/4 of Northeast 1/4. 34

Mance

Cora Manse, who married Alfred Andrew Emanuel as his first wife, is found on the 1900 and 1910 US Census in the household of her parents. It appears that in the ten year period of time, they migrated from Jackson Co., Georgia to Topeka, Shawnee Co., Kansas.

1900 US Census, Jackson Co., Georgia, City of Jefferson, ED 84, Page 6A 35
Athens Street
99-110 Wade Mance, black, b. Aug 1860, 39, married 14 years, b. GA, both
parents b. GA, day laborer
Georgia A., wife, black, b. Jan 1863, 37, married 14 years, 5 children, 5 living,
b. GA, both parents b. GA
Robert, son, black, b. Feb 1888, 12, b. GA, both parents b. GA, at school
Cora, daughter, black, b. July 1890, 9, b. GA, both parents b. GA, at school
Turner, son, black, b. Oct 1892, 7, b. GA, both parents b. GA, at school
Wahoscha, son, black, b. Jan 1896, 4, b. GA, both parents b. GA
Timothy, black, b. May 1898, 2, b. GA, both parents b. GA

1910 US Census, Shawnee Co., Kansas, Topeka, Ward 5, ED 182, Page 3A 36
1907 Harrison
57-58 Wade H. Mance, black, 46, married 23 years, b. SC, both parents b. SC,
grocer, grocery store
Georgia, wife, black, 42, married 23 years, 8 children, 7 living, b. SC, both
parents b. SC
Cora A., daughter, black, 17, b. GA, both parents b. SC
Turner, son, black, 16, b. GA, both parents b. SC
James, son, black, 12, b. GA, both parents b. SC
George, son, black, 10, b. GA, both parents b. SC
Horace, son, black, 8, b. GA, both parents b. SC
Ella, daughter, black, 5, b. GA, both parents b. SC

The Mance family owned land in Cherry Co., Nebraska and lived there for a while before moving to Colorado. Under the Homestead Act, Henry T. Mance acquired 640 acres of land in Cherry County with a final patent issued on 13 June 1916. It was located in the vicinity of DeWitty and described as follows. 37
6th PM T28N R31W, Section 24; West 1/2
6th PM T28N R31W, Section 25; North 1/2

Wade H. Mance acquired 640 acres of land under the Homestead Act, for land located in Cherry Co., Nebraska in the vicinity of DeWitty. The final patent was issued on 4 September 1914 for the following land. 38
6th PM T28N R31W, Section 23; E 1/2 of Northwest 1/4
Section 26; Northeast 1/4

Robert Lee Mance obtained 640 acres of land in Cherry Co., Nebraska under the Homestead Act.

Final patent was issued on 13 June 1916 for land located in the vicinity of DeWitty, 6th PM T28N R31W, all of Section 13. 39

It appears that Wade Mance and his family sold their land in Cherry County just before 1920 and moved to Colorado, as they are shown there on the 1920 US Census.

1920 US Census, Boulder Co., Colorado, Boulder, Ward 4, ED 53, Page 11A 40
2122 Goss St.
241-271 Wade H. Mance, owns, free, black, 53, b. SC, father b. SC, mother b.
        VA, minister
Georgianna, wife, black, 52, b. SC, both parents b. SC
Horace M., son, black, 19, single, b. GA, both parents b. SC, cook, hotel
Ella M., daughter, black, 15, b. GA, both parents b. SC

On the 1930 US Census, Georgianna Mance was living in Denver, Colorado with her son Robert. They were rooming with the Frank C. Pratt family. 41

1930 US Census, Denver Co., Colorado, Denver, ED 173, Page 1A
2232 Washington St.
7-7 Georgiania Mance, room, negro, 61, married, married 18 years, b. SC, father
        b. SC, mother b. FL
Robert Mance, son, negro, lodger, 38, single, b. GA, both parents b. SC, janitor,
        railroad depot

Rev. Wade Hammond (as on tombstone) Mance was born 1869 and died 25 February 1943. He was buried in the Linn Grove Cemetery, Greeley, Weld Co., Colorado. By 1940 he was a widower. 42

1940 US Census, Weld Co., Colorado, Greeley, ED 62-103, Page 10B
104 Twelfth Street   owns, $500
W.H. Mance, informant, negro, 68, widowed, 8th grade, b. SC, same
        house 1 April 1935, no occupation shown

The following children were born to Wade Hamilton/Hammond Mance and Georgia Ann Fisher.

1. Cora A. Mance, born July 1890 in Georgia (see above)
2. Robert Mance, born 24 January 1893 in Georgia
3. Turner Mance, born October 1892 in Georgia
4. Wahoscha Mance, male, b. January 1896 in GA
5. Timothy James Mance, b. May 1898 in GA
6. George Mance, b. about 1900 in GA
7. Horace Mance, b. about 1902 in GA
8. Ella M. Mance, b. about 1905 in GA
9. Eugene Paul Mance, b. about 1913 in CO

Robert Mance, son of Wade Hamilton Mance and Georgia Ann Fisher was born at Washington, Wilkes Co., Georgia on 24 January 1893. His parents are named on his death certificate. He died 28 December 1932 in Detroit, Wayne Co., Michigan from a traumatic cerebral hemorrhage following a bullet wound to his head, suicide, which was committed at his home, 665 Rowena St. in Detroit. He was single and a janitor for the Burlington Railroad. His mother is shown as born in Greenburg, South Carolina. The informant was his brother, James Mance living at 665 Rowena, Detroit, Michigan. 43. Greenburg, South Carolina was probably meant to be Greenville, Greenville Co., South Carolina.

Eugene Paul Mance, son of Wade Hamilton/Hammond Mance and Georgia Ann Fisher, was born about 1913 in Colorado. He married Glenna Dalton, daughter of Luther Oren and Freda C. Dalton. She was born 25 February 1925 in Marietta, Washington Co., Ohio and died 17 May 1998 in Akron, Summit Co., Ohio. Eugene died 6 November 1988 in Canton, Stark Co., Ohio.

Rev. Wade Hampton/Hammond Mance was born about 1860-1862 in South Carolina to William and Phebe Mance. They are shown on the 1870 US Census in Edgefield Co., South Carolina.

1870 US Census, Edgefield Co., South Carolina, Grants Twp., page 6, PO 44
Edgefield
48-50 William Mance, 56, black, farm laborer, b. SC
Phebe, 57, black, keeping house, b. SC
Martha, 26, black, farm laborer, b. SC
Pickens, 12, male, black, farm laborer, b. SC
Wade, 8, black, b. SC
Elbert, 6, black, b. SC
Fannie, 5, black, b. SC
Jane Anderson, 26, black, farm laborer, b. SC

Joshua Emanuel and Lucinda Travis

Joshua Emanuel was born 6 April 1834 in New York. He was the son of Samuel Emanuel and Sallie Peterson. Joshua married Lucinda Travis in 1855 in Grey, Ontario, Canada. Lucinda Travis was born about 1835 in Mercer Co., Pennsylvania to John Travis and Nancy Christina Brunner. She died on 9 March 1872 in Kent, Ontario, Canada. Joshua married second to Ida Delienay on 7 September 1873 in Raleigh, Kent, Ontario, Canada. 45 He came to Dawson Co., Nebraska before 1880 and died on 8 April 1887 in Dawson County, buried in the Evergreen Cemetery, Lexington, Dawson Co., Nebraska. The following US and Canadian censuses reveal more about this family.

1861 Census, Canada West, Grey, ED 2, Personal Census 46
Joshua Manuel, farmer, b. US, came to Canada 1857, age 26
Lucinda Manuel, b. US, age 24
Jane Manuel, b. Canada West, age 2
Sarah Manuel, b. Canada West, age 1
Mary Manuel, b. Canada West, age 3

1871 Census of Canada, Kent, Ontario, Canada, Raleigh Subdivision, page 4 47
12-13 Joshue Manuel, 36, b. US, British Methodist Episcopal, African, farmer
Lucindie Manuel, 35, b. US, British Methodist Episcopal, African
Jane Manuel, 12, b. Canada, British Methodist Episcopal, African
Mary Ann, 9, b. Canada, British Methodist Episcopal, African
Jerushe Ann, 9, b. Canada, British Methodist Episcopal, African
Joshue, 7, b. Canada, British Methodist Episcopal, African
Charles William, 5, b. Canada, British Methodist Episcopal, African
Catherin, 3, b. Canada, British Methodist Episcopal, African
Samuel, 8/12, b. Canada in December, British Methodist Episcopal, African

1880 US Census, Dawson Co., Nebaska, Covington Twp., ED 1, Page 339C 48
33 Joshua Emanuel, black, 44, carpenter, b. NY, both parents b. NY
Ida, black, 29, wife, housework, b. MI, both parents b. MO
Chas. W., black, 14, son, at school, b. Canada, father b. NY, mother b. MI

Catherine L, black, 12, daughter, at school, b. Canada, father b. NY, mother
    b. MI
Saml. R., black, 10, son, at school, b. Canada, father b. NY, mother b. MI

1885 Nebraska State Census, Dawson Co., Nebraska, Overton Prect., ED 191,   49
Page 9C
84-84 Joshua Emanuel, mulatto, 50, farmer, b. NY, both parents b. NY
Ida, wife, mulatto, 34, keeping house, b. MI, both parents b. TN
Catherine, daughter, mulatto, 16, b. Canada, father b. NY, mother b. PA
Samuel, son, mulatto, 14, b. Canada, father b. NY, mother b. PA

The children of Joshua Emanuel and Lucinda Travis were as follows. Not all of them came to Nebraska to live.

1. Emma Jane Emanuel, born about 1855 in New York
2. Sarah Ann Emanuel, born about 1860 in Normanby, Grey, Ontario, Canada
3. Mary Ann Emanuel, born Dec 1860 in Normanby, Grey, Ontario, Canada
4. Jerusha Ann Emanuel, born about 1862 in Canada
5. Joshua Dawson Emanuel, born March 1863 in Canada (see above)
6. Charles William Emanuel, born about 1866 in Canada
7. Catherine Emanuel, born about 1869 in Canada
8. Samuel R. Emanuel, born about 1870 in Canada

According to Ontario, Canada Schedule of Deaths for Raleigh, Kent, Ontario, Canada, Emma Jane Emmanuel [sic], daughter of Joshua Emanuel and Lucinda Travis, died on 29 November 1874 at the age of 16. She had consumption for 15 months. The death record indicates that she was born in County of Grey, Canada and baptized on 16 December 1874, Methodist. [The date of baptism is apparently incorrect as she died on 29 November 1874.] Her father was Joshua Emmanuel, farmer of Raleigh.   50 Emma Jane Emanuel had an illegitimate daughter, Elizabeth Ann Emmanuel, born 29 May 1873 in Kent, Ontario, Canada and died there on 10 June 1873. According to her death record, she died at the age of twelve days from fits and convulsions. Her grandfather, Joshua Emanuel, reported her death.   51

Sarah Ann Emanuel was born about 1860 in Normanby, Grey, Ontario, Canada to Joshua Emanuel and Lucinda Travis. She married William Crawford in Canada. He was born about 1848 in the United States to Jeremiah and Dinah Crawford. They had a daughter Mary Lucinda Crawford who was born 19 February 1880 in North Buxton, Raleigh, Kent, Ontario, Canada.

Mary Ann Emanuel, daughter of Joshua Emanuel and Lucinda Travis, was born in Decmeber of 1860 in Normanby, Grey, Ontario, Canada. On 15 September 1881 in Raleigh, Kent, Ontario, Canada, she married James Henry Kersey. He was born in March of 1859 in Raleigh, Kent, Ontario, Canada to Dennis Kersey and Temperance "Tempy" Acock. They were married by the Methodist minister, Rev. Seth D.W. Smith.   52

The Kersey family came to the United States, settling in Washtenaw Co., Michigan in about 1885. Mary Ann Emanuel Kersey died in 1947. James Henry Kersey died 27 January 1920 in Ypsilanti, Washtenaw Co., Michigan.

1900 US Census, Washtenaw Co., Michigan, Ypsilanti, Ward 1, ED 110,   53
Page 12A
317 First Avenue
270-295 James H. Kersey, black, b. March 1859, 41, married 19 years, b.
    Canada, father b. GA, mother b. SC, American Citizen, carpenter

Mary A., wife, black, b. Dec 1861, 38, married 19 years, 8 children, 7 living,
    b. Canada, both parents b. NY, American Citizen
Herman E., son, black, b. April 1882, 18, b. Canada, both parents b. US,
    15 years in the United States, at school
Ernest L., son, black, b. March 1885, 15, b. MI, both parents b. US, at school
Harrison B., son, black, b. Sept 1887, 12, b. MI, both parents b. US, at school
Bernice V., daughter, black, b. Jan 1893, 7, b. MI, both parents b. US, at school
Arden G., son, black, b. Feb 1895, 5, b. MI, both parents b. US
Nina G., daughter, black, b. May 1897, 3, b. MI, both parents b. US
Leonard D., son, black, b. Feb 1900, 4/12, b. MI, both parents b. US

The following are the children of Mary Ann Emanuel and James Henry Kersey.

1. Hermann Emmanuel Kersey, born 20 April 1882 in Kent, Ontario, Canada
2. Oscar Kersey, born 1883 in Michigan; died 4 May 1888 in Ypsilanti,
    Washtenaw Co., Michigan
3. Ernest L. Kersey, born March 1885 in Michigan; died in 1901
4. Harrison B. Kersey, born 27 September 1887 in Ypsilanti, Washtenaw Co.,
    Michigan
5. Bernice V. Kersey, born January 1893 in Michigan; died in 1969
6. Arden Grant Kersey, born 7 February 1895 in Michigan
7. Nina Gracia Kersey, born May 1897 in Michigan; died in 1969
8. Leonard Darius Kersey, born 16 February 1900 in Ypsilanti, Washtenaw Co.,
    Michigan; died 10 September 1940 in Ypsilanti, Washtenaw Co., Michigan
9. Winand R. Kersey (male), born 1903 in Michigan

Hermann Emmanuel Kersey, son of Mary Ann Emanuel and James Henry Kersey, was born 20 April 1882 in Kent, Ontario, Canada. He came to the United States with his parents about 1885. He married Jessie Reeves on 29 August 1908 in Chatham, Ontario, Canada. She was born 2 August 1886 in Ontario, Canada to George Reeves and Emily Ells and died 30 May 1978 in Camas, Clark Co., Washington. Hermann died in June of 1975 in Michigan.

Arden Grant Kersey, son of Mary Ann Emanuel and James Henry Kersey, was born 7 February 1895 in Michigan and died in 1961. He married Edna Rodrick who was born in Michigan in 1896.

Charles William Emanuel, son of Joshua Emanuel and Lucinda Travis, was born about 1866 in Ontario, Canada. He came to Nebraska with his father and step-mother, settling in Dawson County.

Catherine L. Emanuel, daughter of Joshua Emanuel and Lucinda Travis, was born in about 1869 in Ontario, Canada. She came to Nebraska with her father and step-mother, settling in Dawson County. She married Clinton Jackson and then Frank Johnson.

Samuel R. Emanuel, son of Joshua Emanuel and Lucinda Travis, was born in about 1870 in Ontario, Canada. He came to Nebraska with his father and step mother, settling in Dawson County.

Samuel Emanuel and Sarah A. Peterson

The Emanuels, as free persons of color, were still oppressed by white citizens. In 1840 and 1850 they were living in Allegany Co., New York, and from there migrated to Canada. Living next door was William and Catharine Peterson who may have been Sarah A. "Sally" Peterson Emanuel's relatives. She was born 11 July 1818 in New York.

1840 US Census, Allegany Co., New York, Wirt   54
S. Emanuel
1 free colored male under 10
1 free colored male 24-35
2 free colored females under 10
1 free colored female 10-23

1850 US Census, Allegany Co., New York, Town of Wirt, Page 151B
186-200 Samuel Emanuel, 42, mulatto, $600, farmer, b. NJ
Sally A., 32, mulatto, b. PA
Joshua, 15, mulatto, b. NY
Phebe E., 14, mulatto, b. NY
Mary L., 11, mulatto, b. NY
Caroline, 9, mulatto, b. NY
Sally A., 6, mulatto, b. NY
Cassius M., 3, mulatto, b. NY
Rosena, 9/12, mulatto, b. NY

1850 US Census, Allegany Co., New York, Town of Wirt, Page 151B   55
185-177 Wm. Peterson, 55, mulatto, $1,200, farmer, b. NJ
Catharine, 45, mulatto, b. PA
Wm. B., 23, mullato, farmer, b. NY
Alfred, 16, mulatto, farmer, b. NY
Harriet A., 14, mulatto, b. NY
Ezekial, 10, mulatto, b. NY
Isaih Peterson, 86, mulatto, farmer, b. NJ

Samuel Emanuel, born about 1807 in New Jersey, continued to live in Ontario, Canada and died there before 1875. Sarah Ann "Sally" Peterson, his wife, was born 11 July 1817 in New York and died 3 November 1903 in Essex, Ontario, Canada. She remarried to Walter Toyer on 30 September 1875 in Buxton, Ontario, Canada. He was born in about 1802 and died before 1901.

1901 Census of Canada, Raleigh, Kent, Ontario   56
77-77 John R. Travis, black, married, b. 5 June 1833, 67, b. US, came to Canada
        in 1852, African, Canadian Nationality, Baptist, farmer
Mary Travis, wife, black, married, b. 25 March 1839, 62, b. US, came to Canada
        in 1859, African, Canadian Nationality, Baptist
Samuel Travis, son, black, b. 9 January 1885, 16, b. Canada, African, Canadian
        Nationality, Baptist
Sarah Toyer, mother, black, widow, b. 11 July 1818, 82, b. US, came to Canada in
        1859, African, Canadian Nationality, Methodist

The children of Samuel Emanuel and Sarah Ann "Sally" Peterson were as follows.

1. Joshua Emanuel, born 6 April 1834 in New York (see above)
2. Phoebe Elizabeth Emanuel, born 1835 in New York
3. Mary Louisa Emanuel, born 25 March 1839 in Wirt, Allegeny Co., New York
4. Caroline Emanuel, born about 1841 in New York
5. Sarah Ann Emanuel, born about 1844 in Wirt, Allegeny Co., New York
6. Cassius M. Emanuel, born about 1847 in Wirt, Allegeny Co., New York
7. Rosina Emanuel, born about 1849 in Wirt, Allegeny Co., New York
8. Samuel Emanuel, born September 1852 Gravely Bay, Ontario, Canada

9. William Emanuel, born 1857 in Ontario, Canada
10. Kate Emanuel

Phoebe Elizabeth Emanuel, daughter of Samuel Emanuel and Sarah Ann "Sally" Peterson, was born in 1835 in New York. She married William Doo on 21 May 1866 at North Buxton, Raleigh, Ontario, Canada. He was born in 1837 in Indiana and died 21 February 1879 in Kent, Ontario, Canada. His parents were Green and Abigail Doo. Phoebe died on 3 March 1867 in North Buxton, Raleigh, Ontario, Canada. William Doo married Julia Ann Lawson on 18 March 1869 in North Buxton, Raleigh, Ontario, Canada.

Mary Louisa Emanuel, daughter of Samuel Emanuel and Sarah Ann "Sally" Peterson, was born 25 March 1839 in Wirt, Allegheny Co., New York. She married John Richard Travis, who was a brother to Lucinda Travis, wife of Mary Louisa's brother, Joshua. John Richard Travis was born 5 June 1834 at Coolspring, Mercer Co., Pennsylvania to John Travis and Nancy Christina Brunner. He died on 29 December 1912 in Kent, Ontario, Canada. Mary Louisa Emanuel Travis died 22 July 1910 in Kent, Ontario, Canada.

Caroline Emanuel, daughter of Samuel Emanuel and Sarah Ann "Sally" Peterson, was born about 1841 in New York. She married William L. Dotson in 1861 in Kent, Ontario, Canada. He was born in 1826 in Kentucky to Thomas and Fanny Dotson and died 3 July 1899 at Essex, Ontario, Canada. Caroline married second to Riley Jones.

Sarah Ann Emanuel, daughter of Samuel Emanuel and Sarah Ann "Sally" Peterson was born in about 1844 in Wirt, Allegheny Co., New York. She married William Francis Moore on 22 November 1864 in Kent, Ontario, Canada. He was born 2 May 1847 in Ontario, Canada and died 7 March 1939. Sarah Ann died 23 August 1877 in Kent, Ontario, Canada. They were parents of the following children.

1. Benjamin Franklin Moore, born about 1866 in Ontario, Canada
2. Phoebe Elizabeth Moore, born August 1867 in Ontario, Canada
3. Caroline Marie Moore, born 8 August 1870 in Raleigh, Ontario, Canada; died 17 June 1944 in Canada
4. William Moore, born 9 July 1872 in Kent, Ontario, Canada; married Mary Brooks
5. Charles Wellington Moore, born May 1874 in Ontario, Canada; married Sylvia Shreve
6. Rosana Moore, born 3 February 1877 in Kent, Ontario, Canada; died young

Benjamin Franklin Moore, son of Sarah Ann Emanuel and William Francis Moore, was born in Ontario, Canada in about 1866. He was married to Sarah Ann Baker, born about 1869 in Ontario, Canada and they had William Richard Moore, James Albert Moore and Agatha Viola Moore. He married Rebecca Dungy who was born about 1876 in Ontario, Canada. On 16 September 1918 in Kent, Ontario, Canada, he married Belle Isabella Callender who was born about 1883 in Ontario, Canada.

Phoebe Elizabeth Moore, daughter of Sarah Ann Emanuel and William Francis Moore, was born in Ontario, Canada in August of 1867. She married William Jeremiah Shreve. He was born June 1867 in Ontario, Canada to George Bolivar Shreve and Elizabeth Williams Shadd and died 28 August 1950. They were parents of Edgar Shreve, Ada Elizabeth Shreve, Clarence William Shreve, Oliver Kenneth Shreve, Sarah Eunice Shreve, Charles Harold Shreve, Percy Shreve and Etta Beatrice Shreve.

Caroline Marie Moore, daughter of Sarah Ann Emanuel and William Francis Moore, was born 8 August 1870 in Raleigh, Ontario, Canada. She married Robert Thomas Harding. He was born 14 February 1866 in Peel, Ontario, Canada to Robert Thomas Harding and Elizabeth Travis. Caroline died

17 June 1944 in Canada. They were parents of Robert Harding, Charles Henry Harding, Elsie Harding, Alta Helen Harding, Samuel Wilfred Harding, Albert Sagasta Harding, and Ethel Marie Harding.

Samuel Emanuel, son of Samuel Emanuel and Sarah Ann "Sally" Peterson, was born September 1852 at Gravely Bay, Ontario, Canada. He married Laura L. Kersey on 28 February 1875 in Raleigh, Kent, Ontario, Canada. She was born December 1859 in Raleigh, Kent, Ontario, Canada to John W. and Martha Kersey. He came to Nebraska in 1880, settling in Covington Prect., Dawson County and then went to Illinois to live.

1880 US Census, Dawson Co., Nebraska, Covington Prect., ED 1, Page 339D 57
35 Saml. Emanuel, black, 27, farmer, b. Canada, both parents b. NY
Laura, black, 21, wife, house keeper, b. Canada, father b. IN, mother b. GA
Caroline Moor, black, 9, niece, b. Canada, father's birth place unknown, mother b.
    Canada

1900 US Census, Cook Co., Illinois, Chicago, Ward 3, ED 68, Page 3A 58
2922 State Street
23-51 Samuel Emanuel, black, b. Sept 1852, 47, married 23 years, b. Canada,
    both parents b. NY, came to US in 1880, naturalized, baker
Laura, wife, black, b. Dec 1859, 40, married 23 years, 0 children, 0 living, b.
    Canada, father b. IN, mother b. GA, came to US in 1880
William Blair, boarder, black, b. March 1870, 30, widowed, married 3 years, b.
    TN, both parents b. TN, cook

Travis

Lucinda Travis who married Joshua Emanuel, was born in 1835 in Mercer Co., Pennsylvania to John Travis and Nancy Christina Brunner. She died on 9 March 1872 in Kent, Ontario, Canada. Refer above for her family records.

John Travis was born about 1801 in Virginia to Richard and Lucinda Travis. He married Nancy Christina Brunner before 1826. She was white and born in 1806 in Hempfield, Lancaster Co., Pennsylvania to Henry Brunner and Mary Brown. John died in about 1852 in Coolspring, Mercer Co., Pennsylvania. When the black families began migrating to Ontario, Canada, Nancy Christina Brunner Travis went with them, arriving in about 1852. She died on 10 January 1879 in Raleigh, Kent, Ontario, Canada.

Richard Travis founded a settlement called Liberia in Mercer Co., Pennsylvania. Runaway slaves were secreted on the Underground Railroad to that location. Pandenarium was an experimental colony of manumitted slaves. This was the first stage of future generations going on to Canada in their quest for freedom.

The following census enumerations are helpful for locating John Travis and his family.

1820 US Census, Mercer Co., Pennsylvania, Sandy Lake 7 August 1820 59
Richard Travis
1 free colored male under 14
1 free colored male 14-25
1 free colored male 45 and over
3 free colored females under 14
1 free colored female 14-25

372

1 free colored female 26-44

1830 US Census, Mercer Co., Pennsylvania, Cool Spring 60
Jno. Travice
1 free white female 20-29
1 free colored male 55-99
1 free colored female 55-99

1840 US Census, Mercer Co., Pennsylvania Cool Spring 61
John Travis
1 free white female 30-39
2 free colored males under 10
1 free colored male 10-23
1 free colored male 36-54
4 free colored females under 10
1 free colored female 10-23
2 persons engaged in agriculture

1850 US Census, Mercer Co., Pennsylvania, Cool Spring Twp., Page 338B 62
1247-1269 John Travis, 49, black, farmer $1,800 b. VA
Christena, 41, white, b. PA
John, 15, mulatto, b. PA
Lucinda, 14, mulatto, b. PA
Ruth, 13, mulatto, b. PA
Robert, 11, mulatto, b. PA
Charles, 7, mulatto, b. PA
Elizabeth, 6, mulatto, b. PA
Solomon, 3, mulatto, b. PA
Wm., 1, mulatto, b. PA

1871 Canadian Census, Raleigh, Kent, Ontario, Canada, Page 40 District 2 63
152-153 Cristena Travis, 65, b. United States, Baptist, German, widow
Robert Travis, 28, b. United States, Baptist, African, farmer
William Travis, 21, b. United States, Baptist, African, farmer

According to Christina's death record, she was Christina Scott, died 10 January 1879, age 71 years, born Pennsylvania. She is shown as a farmer's wife, Baptist and died as a paralitic (3 weeks). The informant was her son, John R. Travis, farmer at Raleigh, Kent, Ontario, Canada, where she died. 64

Nancy Christina "Christina" married second to Isaac Scott on 13 March 1865 in Raleigh, Kent, Ontario, Canada. He was born in about 1801 in North Carolina and died in 1871 at Raleigh, Kent, Ontario, Canada. He married first to Jamima —- and had several children by her.

John Travis, son of Richard and Lucinda Travis and Nancy Christina Brunner, daughter of Henry Brunner and Mary Brown, had the following children.

1. James Andrew Travis, born 8 September 1826, Coolspring, Mercer Co., Pennsylvania; died between 1840 and 1850 in Coolspring, Mercer Co., Pennsylvania
2. Catherine Travis, born 14 February 1829 in Coolspring, Mercer Co., Pennsylvania

3. Sarah Ann Travis, born 11 April 1831 in Coolspring, Mercer Co., Pennsylvania
4. John Richard Travis, born 5 June 1834 in Coolspring, Mercer Co., Pennsylvania
5. Lucinda Travis, born about 1835 in Coolspring, Mercer Co., Pennsylvania (see above)
6. Ruth Kinnear Travis, born about 1836 in Coolspring, Mercer Co., Pennsylvania
7. Robert B. Travis, born 29 March 1838 in Coolspring, Mercer Co., Pennsylvania
8. Charles Henry Travis, born 1842 in Coolspring, Mercer Co., Pennsylvania
9. Elizabeth Travis, born 15 September 1843 in Coolspring, Mercer Co., Pennsylvania
10. Solomon Travis, born 1847 in Coolspring, Mercer Co., Pennsylvania
11. William Travis, born about 1848 in Pennsylvania

Catherine Travis, daughter of John Travis and Nancy Christina Brunner, was born 14 February 1829 in Coolspring, Mercer Co., Pennsylvania. She married William Morehead who was born about 1819 in the United States. He died on 1 July 1882 in Kent, Ontario, Canada. Catherine married second to Harrison Webb who was born in about 1819 in the United States. She died on 16 September 1915 in Kent, Ontario, Canada. Catherine Travis Webb is shown on the manifest of Alien Passenger Applying for Admission at the Port of Detroit, Michigan, 151-200- 176, March 1912. She is shown as age 84, widow, seamstress, can read and write, from Canada, English, resident of Raleigh. Her nearest relative in Canada is shown as her sister Elizabeth Harding of Buxton, Ontario, Canada. 65 Catherine and William Morehead had the following children.

1. John Moorehead, born about 1844 in Pennsylvania
2. Sarah May Moorehead, born about 1845 in Pennsylvania; married Jacob Oliver DeLancey 19 March 1863; died 1925
3. Christina Moorehead, born 1848 in Pennsylvania; married Andrew Mordecai Jacobs 4 Nov 1868 in Kent, Ontario, Canada; died 18 March 1877 in Kent, Ontario, Canada
4. Harriet Moorehead, born 1852
5. Lucinda Rebecca Moorehead, born 1856 in Wellington, Ontario, Canada; married Benjamin Edward Harris
6. Elizabeth Moorehead, born 1861 in Ontario, Canada; died 16 August 1879 in Raleigh, Kent, Ontario, Canada
7. William Robert Moorehead, born 1863 in Ontario, Canada
8. Margaret Moorehead, born 1866 in Ontario, Canada

Sarah Ann Travis, daughter of John Travis and Nancy Christina Brunner, was born 11 April 1831 at Coolspring, Mercer Co., Pennsylvania. She married William Scipio in 1854. He was born in about 1824 in Pennsylvania and died in 1900. Sarah died 27 May 1908 in Washtenaw Co., Michigan. They were parents of the following children.

1. John A. Scipio, born in about 1854 in Mercer Co., Pennsylvania; married India Smith in 1875 in Michigan
2. Charles Scipio, born 1855 in Canada West
3. Elizabeth Scipio, born 1856 in Canada West
4. Sarah Jane Scipio, born 1858 in Canada West; married her uncle, William Travis
5. Christina Scipio, born 1861 in Canada West

6. Jennie Scipio, born in 1862 in Canada
7. Mary Scipio, born Sept 1864 in Ontario, Canada
8. James R. Scipio, born 1866 in Canada West; married Rachel Poole 24 May
1893 in Augusta, Washtenaw Co., Michigan; married Jennie Pearl 28
November 1897 in Ypsilanti, Washtenaw Co., Michigan; married Blanche
Lucas 16 November 1903 in Comstock, Kalamazoo Co., Michigan;
married Mattie Hopson Clay 15 January 1920 in Ypsilanti, Washtenaw
Co., Michigan; died 6 June 1941
9. Ruth Scipio, born 1869 in Canada West
10. Samuel Scipio, born January 1873 in Michigan
11. Alice Scipio, born 10 September 1875 in Wayne Co., Michigan

John Richard Travis, son of John Travis and Nancy Christina Brunner, was born 5 June 1834 in
Coolspring, Mercer Co., Pennsylvania. He married Mary Louisa Emanuel. She was born 25 March 1839
in Wirt, Allegheny Co., New York to Samuel Emanuel and Sarah Ann "Sally" Peterson. She died on 22
July 1910 in Kent, Ontario, Canada. John died on 29 December 1912 in Kent, Ontario, Canada. They
had the following children.

1. Elizabeth Caroline Travis, born 18 June 1856 in Normanby, Ontario, Canada;
married James Tyson Robbins 6 May 1875 in Kent, Ontario, Canada; died
August 1944 in Ontario, Canada
2. James Albert Travis, born 22 June 1857 in North Buxton, Ontario, Canada;
married Almira Ennie Elizabeth Robinson 22 April 1885 in North Buxton,
Ontario, Canada; died 28 June 1933 in Kent, Ontario, Canada
3. Mary Lucinda Travis, born 31 October 1860 in Raleigh, Kent, Ontario,
Canada; married Samuel James Henry Zebbs 25 November 1880
Raleigh, Kent, Ontario Canada; died 29 June 1942 in Ontario, Canada
4. Christena Travis, born 22 March 1862, Raleigh, Kent, Ontario, Canada;
married Obadiah Kersey 1 January 1879 Kent, Ontario, Canada; died 1959
5. John Richard Travis, Jr., born 24 August 1865 in Ontario, Canada; married
Sarah A. Maholy; died in Ontario, Canada
6. Sarah Rosina Ann Travis, born 31 July 1869 in North Buxton, Ontario,
Canada; married Allan W. Robinson 15 April 1885 Kent, Ontario,
Canada; married James Albert Scott 23 April 1894 Kent, Ontario,
Canada; died 22 October 1907 in Kent, Ontario, Canada
7. William Charles Lewis Travis, born 21 January 1872 in Raleigh, Kent,
Ontario, Canada; married Sarah Jane Davis 2 October 1893, Ontario,
Canada
8. Clara Alberta Jane Ann Travis, born 7 August 1874 in Raleigh, Kent, Ontario,
Canada; married James Alfred Richardson 28 December 1892 Ontario,
Canada; died 5 November 1911 in Raleigh, Kent, Ontario
9. Rosa Travis, born 19 March 1877 in Buxton, Kent, Ontario, Canada
10. Minnie Amelia Travis, born 9 May 1879 in Kent, Ontario, Canada; married
Joseph Richard Cromwell 28 December 1898 Raleigh, Kent, Ontario,
Canada; died 25 July 1915 in Ontario, Canada
11. Katherine Louisa Travis, born 3 January 1882 in Raleigh, Kent, Ontario,
Canada; married Samuel Sylvester Jones 13 December 1899 North
Buxton, Ontario, Canada
12. Samuel Henry Travis, born 9 January 1885 in Kent, Ontario, Canada; married
Hannah R. Brown 24 December 1904 Kent, Ontario, Canada; married
Melvena Julie Richardson 24 September 1919 Ypsilanti, Washtenaw Co.,
Michigan

13. Angeline Travis

Ruth Kinnear Travis, daughter of John Travis and Nancy Christina Brunner, was born in 1836 in Coolspring, Mercer Co., Pennsylvania. She married first to Thomas Elwood Knox in 1856 in Ontario, Canada. He was born in about 1809 in Philadelphia, Philadelphia Co., Pennsylvania and died 22 November 1874 in Augusta, Washtenaw Co., Michigan. Ruth married second to James W. Jackson on 7 May 1876 in Ypsilanti, Washtenaw Co., Michigan. He was born in January of 1845 in Pennsylvania and died in 1910 in Michigan. Ruth died 21 October 1921 in Augusta, Washtenaw Co., Michigan. The following are children born to Ruth and Thomas Elwood Knox.

1. John Knox, born 1857 in Normanby, Grey, Ontario, Canada; died there in 1870
2. Mary Anne Knox, born 1859 in Ontario, Canada
3. Ruth Kinnear Knox, born 24 May 1863 in Normanby, Grey, Ontario, Canada
4. Jacob Morris Knox, born 12 June 1866 in Ontario, Canada; married Mildred
   Tabitha "Millie" Richardson 7 December 1892 Augusta, Washtenaw Co.,
   Michigan; died 8 May 1939 in Detroit, Wayne Co., Michigan
5. Emeline Knox, born 1872 in Michigan

The following children were born to Ruth and James W. Jackson, her second husband.

1. James William Jackson, born 4 July 1876 in York, Washtenaw Co., Michigan;
   married Grace A. Perkins
2. John Henry Jackson, born 4 July 1876 in York, Washtenaw Co., Michigan;
   married Jane —- about 1896; married Laura B. —-; married Louisa D. —-
3. Alice M. Jackson, born March 1879 in York, Washtenaw Co., Michigan
4. Bert Alvin Jackson, born 30 March 1884 in London, Monroe Co., Michigan;
   married Mary —-.

Robert B. Travis, son of John Travis and Nancy Christina Brunner, was born 29 March 1838 in Coolspring, Mercer Co., Pennsylvania. He married Emma Burnett in Kent, Ontario, Canada. She was born 29 November 1865 in Jackson Co., Michigan and died in Novesta, Tuscola Co., Michigan. Robert died 11 October 1914 in Raleigh, Kent, Ontario, Canada. Robert and Emma had the following children.

1. Robert Travis, born 15 October 1889 in Dawn, Ontario, Canada; died 18
   August 1927 in Kent, Ontario, Canada
2. Minnie Mae Travis, born 15 October 1890 in Ontario, Canada; married Archie
   Reginald Robbins 28 October 1908 in Kent, Ontario, Canada; died
   24 June 1970 in North Buxton, Kent, Ontario, Canada
3. Jane Travis, born 15 March 1892 in Ontario, Canada; married Robert Henry
   Enos 1 June 1910 in Kent, Ontario, Canada
4. Grace Alberta Travis, born about 1894 in Ontario, Canada; married Clarence
   William Shreve
5. Charles Travis , born about 1898 in Ontario, Canada

Before his marriage to Emma Burnett, Robert B. Travis is reported to have had two children by a lady whose surname was Plummer.

1. Christina Travis, born 28 March 1881 in Ontario, Canada; married Enoch
   Wallace
2. Robert A. Travis, born about 1882 in Ontario, Canada; married May Harris

Charles Henry Travis, son of John Travis and Nancy Christina Bruner, was born in about 1842 in

Coolspring, Mercer Co., Pennsylvania. He married Sarah Thomas, who was born about 1859 in Ontario, Canada. They had the following children.

1. Mary Travis, born about 1883 in Ontario, Canada
2. John Travis, born 17 October 1886 in Normanby, Kent, Ontario, Canada; married Florance "Flossis" Hanna; died 15 July 1971 in Fairview, Gloucester Co., New Jersey
3. Charles Henry Travis, born about 1887 in Normanby, Kent, Ontario, Canada; died May 1899 in Grey, Ontario, Canada

Elizabeth Travis, daughter of John Travis and Christina Brunner, was born 15 September 1843 in Coolspring, Mercer Co., Pennsylvania. She married Robert Thomas Harding in 1860 in Peel, Ontario, Canada. He was born 25 December 1830 in Nashville, Davidson Co., Tennessee and died 30 September 1917 in North Buxton, Raleigh, Kent, Ontario, Canada. Elizabeth married second to David M. Lewis on 17 December 1918 in Kent, Ontario, Canada. He was born in 1840 in New York to David Lewis and Sophia Bates. The following children were born to Elizabeth Travis and Robert Thomas Harding.

1. Malvina Rachel Harding, born 21 March 1861 in Ontario, Canada; married Henry Alonzo Enos 21 September 1880 North Buxton, Ontario, Canada
2. William Henry Harding, born 25 December 1865 in Peel, Ontario, Canada; married Rachel Ann Madison; died 23 May 1920 in Raleigh, Kent, Ontario, Canada
3. Robert Thomas Harding, born 14 Feb 1866 in Peel, Ontario, Canada; married Caroline Marie Moore 10 October 1889 Raleigh, Kent, Ontario, Canada; died 1938 in Ontario, Canada (see above)
4. Morris Henry Harding, born January 1867 in Ontario, Canada; married Elsie Elizabeth McCormell
5. Helen Harding, born about 1870 in Ontario, Canada
6. Martha Victoria Mary Ann Harding, born 20 January 1872 in Kent, Ontario, Canada; married James Ervin Steele 29 December 1898 Ontario, Canada; married Benjamin W. Farris; married Charles A. Travis
7. Elizabeth Caroline Harding, born 30 August 1875 in Kent, Ontario, Canada; married Isaac Doros Shadd 23 September 1893 Kent, Ontario, Canada; died 20 July 1900 Kent, Ontario, Canada
8. Emma Harding

Solomon Travis, son of John Travis and Nancy Christina Brunner, was born in about 1847 in Coolspring, Mercer Co., Pennsylvania. He married Margaret McGee. Solomon died on 20 December 1905.

William Travis, son of John Travis and Nancy Christina Brunner, was born in about 1848 in Pennsylvania. He married Sarah Jane Scipio. She was born in 1858 in Canada West to William Scipio and Sarah Ann Travis, who was the daughter of John Travis and Nancy Christina Brunner. William Travis and Sarah Jane Scipio had William N. Travis, born about 1876 in Michigan and died 22 August 1899.

Richard Travis who founded the African American settlement in Mercer Co., Pennslavnia, was born about 1745 in Virginia to John Travis. He married a lady named Lucinda. She was born about 1773 in Virginia and died about 1861 in Sandy Lake, Mercer Co., Pennsylvania. Richard died 23 January 1843 in Mercer Co., Pennsylvania. They had the following children.

1. Rebecca Travis, born about 1798 in Virginia
2. John Travis, born about 1801 in Virginia (see above)
3. Rosannah Travis, born about 1803 in Virginia
4. Eleanor Travis, born about 1810 in Ohio
5. Jane Ann Travis, born about 1814 in Ohio
6. Catherine Travis, born about 1815 in Pennsylvania
7. Richard Travis, born about 1818 in Pennsylvania

Rebecca Travis, daughter of Richard and Lucinda Travis, was born about 1798 in Virginia. She married William Harris, who was born in Virginia and died about 1845 in Coolspring, Mercer Co., Pennsylvania. Rebecca died 16 November 1890 in Kent, Ontario, Canada. They had several children, one being William Harris, born 1821 in Mercer Co., Pennsylvania; married Delilah —; died in 1861.

Rosannah Travis, daughter of Richard and Lucinda Travis, was born about 1803 in Virginia. She married Job Lawson who died before 1850 in Pennsylvania. They had the following children.

1. Female Lawson, born 1820-1830 in Mercer Co., Pennsylvania
2. Male Lawson, born 1820-1830 in Mercer Co., Pennsylvania
3. James Lawson, born about 1829 in Mercer Co., Pennsylvania; married
        Jane —.
4. R.D. Lawson (male), born about 1831 in Mercer Co., Pennsylvania
5. Nathaniel Lawson, born 6 April 1833 in Mercer Co., Pennsylvania;
        married Mariah —- in 1865; died 3 April 1912
6. Rosanna Lawson, born about 1835 in Pennsylvania
7. Lucinda Lawson, born about 1844 in Pennsylvania

Eleanor Travis, daughter of Richard and Lucinda Travis, was born about 1810 in Ohio. She married Charles Lawson in about 1830. He died in 1850 and after his death Eleanor married Josiah Lindsey who was born in Virginia in about 1810. They had no children. Eleanor Travis and Charles Lawson had the following children.

1. Ellen Lawson, born about 1835 in Pennsylvania
2. Lydia Lawson, born about 1836 in Pennsylvania
3. Rebecca Lawson, born about 1838 in Pennsylvania
4. Charles Lawson, born about 1840 in Pennsylvania
5. John Lawson, born about 1843 in Pennsylvania
6. Job Lawson, born about 1845 in Pennsylvania
7. Nancy Mahaly Lawson, born about 1848 in Pennsylvania; married Louis
        Weaver Grandison; married Nelson Humboyd

Jane Ann Travis, daughter of Richard and Lucinda Travis, was born about 1814 in Ohio. She married Solomon Zebbs in 1830 in Mercer Co., Pennsylvania. He was born in about 1800 in Delaware Co., Pennsylvania and died 15 February 1886 in Raleigh, Kent, Ontario, Canada. Jane died 11 June 1885 in Raleigh, Kent, Ontario, Canada. They had the following children.

1. Celia Zebbs, born 1832 in Coolspring, Mercer Co., Pennsylvania; married
        Robert Thomas Harding 4 May 1856, Peel, Ontario, Canada; died 1858
        in Ontario, Canada
2. Mary Ann Zebbs, born about 1837 in Coolspring, Mercer Co., Pennsylvania;
        married Levi Johnson; married — Kemmy
3. Nehemiah Zebbs, born 31 March 1839 in Pennsylvania; married Margaret
        Ann Thomas; died 5 April 1915 in Ontario, Canada

4. Richard J. Zebbs, born 9 April 1841 in Mercer Co., Pennsylvania; married Elizabeth Ann Peterson 1 September 1869, Huron, Huron, Ontario, Canada; died 8 June 1925 in Atlantic City, Atlantic Co., New Jersey
5. Solomon Zebbs, born 26 May 1843 in Coolspring, Mercer Co., Pennsylvania; married Martha Ann Grandison; died April 1918 in Kent, Ontario, Canada
6. Lydia Jane Zebbs, born 25 Jan 1845 in Coolspring, Mercer Co., Pennsylvania; married George Edward Cromwell 13 July 1869, Howick, Ontario, Canada; died 3 April 1911 in Ontario, Canada
7. Charity Rosetta Zebbs, born about 1852 in Pennsylvania; married Samuel Brown; died 4 December 1889 in Kent, Ontario, Canada
8. Samuel James Henry Zebbs, born 2 January 1856 in Peel, Ontario, Canada; married Mary Lucinda Travis 25 Nov 1880, Raleigh, Kent, Ontario, Canada (daughter of John Richard Travis and Mary Louisa Emanuel); died 22 July 1899 in Kent, Ontario, Canada
9. James Colin Zebbs, born about 1857 in Peel, Ontario, Canada; married Martha Priscilla Crosby, 17 January 1878, Peel, Ontario, Canada; died 22 October 1884

Catherine Travis, daughter of Richard and Lucinda Travis, was born about 1815 in Pennsylvania. She married Abraham Ross, who was born about 1807 and died in Mercer Co., Pennsylvania. Catherine died between 1844 and 1850 in Mercer Co., Pennsylvania. They had the following children.

1. Female Ross, born about 1839 in Mercer Co., Pennsylvania; died 1840-1850 in Mercer Co., Pennsylvania
2. John Richard Ross, born about 1841 in Pennsylvania; died 29 June 1916 in Kent, Ontario, Canada
3. Thomas Painter Ross, born 15 April 1843 in Mercer Co., Pennsylvania; married Elizabeth or Caroline Scott; died in 1899
4. Lucy Ross, born 9 August 1844 in Mercer Co., Pennsylvania

Richard Travis, son of Richard and Lucinda Travis, was born about 1818 in Pennsylvania. He married Pollyzena Thomas in 1848 in Pennsylvania. She was born to Henry and Susan Thomas in about 1830 in Pennsylvania. Richard died between 1867 and 1871 in Ontario, Canada. They had the following children.

1. Rosanna Travis, born about 1850 in Pennsylvania; married Joseph Mattison Jackson, in Wellington, Ontario, Canada;
2. Rebecca Travis, born about 1853 in Pennsylvania
3. Mary Travis, born about 1854 in Ontario, Canada
4. John Richard Travis, born about 1856 in Ontario, Canada; married Kate —; died 21 July 1938 in Kent, Ontario, Canada
5. Lucinda Travis, born about 1858 in Ontario, Canada
6. Charles A. Travis, born about 1860 in Ontario, Canada; married Martha Victoria Mary Ann Harding, daughter of Elizabeth Travis and Robert Thomas Harding (see above)
7. James Travis, born 1863 in Ontario, Canada; died 3 May 1908 in Ann Arbor, Washtenaw Co., Michigan
8. Louis Travis, born about 1866 in Ontario, Canada

379

Brunner

Nancy Christina Bruner, wife of John Travis, was the daughter of Henry Brunner by his first wife, Mary Brown. Henry was born 19 August 1785 in Lower Saucon, Northampton Co., Pennsylvania to John Andreas Brunner and Christina Gangewehr. Mary Brown was born about 1787, probably in Pennsylvania. Henry married second on 9 May 1813 in Bucks Co., Pennsylvania to Elizabeth Hess. She was born 26 August 1795 in Bucks Co., Pennsylvania to George Hess and Elizabeth Riegel and died 14 July 1875 in Pleasant Valley, Bucks Co., Pennsylvania. Henry died 31 October 1829 probably in Lower Saucon, Northampton Co., Pennsylvania. The following are children born to Henry Brunner by his second wife, Elizabeth Hess.

1. Ellen Brunner, born 8 October 1814 in Springtown, Bucks Co., Pennsylvania; married Giles Gordon; died 28 December 1900 in Doylestown, Bucks Co., Pennsylvania
2. Samuel Brunner, born 4 November 1817 in Springtown, Bucks Co., Pennsylvania
3. William Conver Brunner, born 12 March 1820 in Pennsylvania; died 12 November 1885 in Bucks Co., Pennsylvania
4. Hannah Brunner, born 17 April 1821 in Springtown, Bucks Co., Pennsylvania; died 13 January 1871 in Springtown, Bucks Co., Pennsylvania
5. Lydia Brunner, born 4 January 1824 in Springtown, Bucks Co., Pennsylvania; died 23 January 1877 in Allentown, Lehigh Co., Pennsylvania

John Andreas Brunner was born 12 February 1758 in Upper Sacon, Northampton Co., Pennsylavnia to Johann Heinrich Brunner/Bruner and Maria Magdalena Sellers. He married Christina Gangewehr in 1779 in Pennsylvania. She was born 24 February 1762 in Pennsylvania to Johann Jacob Gangewehr and Maria Eva Schlosser. Christina died on 14 November 1838 in Springfield, Bucks Co., Pennsylvania. John Andreas "Andrew" died 28 April 1820 in Pennsylvania.

John Andreas Brunner, called Andrew, enlisted on 9 July 1776 in Capt. Henry Haganbucks Company in Northampton Co., Pennstylvania. He was in the 2nd Battalion, which was part of the Flying Camp under Colonel Hart. Andrew was in the Battle of Long Island with General George Washington when he crossed the Delaware. 66

Robinson and Gields

Mary Ann Robinson, who married Joshua Emanuel, was the daughter of Richard E. Robinson and Mathilda A. Gields. Mary Ann was born about 1871 at North Brookston, Ontario, Canada.

Richard Robinson was born about 1852 and according to census enumerations, he was born in Indiana. His parents are unknown. He married Matilda A. Gields who was born about July 1849 in Canada to Leroy Gields and Nancy Ann Wheeler. Richard and Matilda migrated from Ontario, Canada with others to Dawson Co., Nebraska. They divorced in Dawson Co., Nebraska. The petition and decree, dated 4 January 1895 and 13 May 1895 respectively, provides information that they were married on 25 December 1872 in Chatham, Ontario, Canada. Matilda filed for divorce indicating that Richard had deserted her on 4 August 1883 and contributed nothing for her support. They were parents of two children, both over the age of ten and able to take of themselves. Richard had not communicated for over ten years and his whereabouts was unknown. A notice of the petition was posted in the newspaper, but Richard never answered or appeared in court. The divorce was granted to Matilda. 67

On the 1885 Nebraska State Census, Mathilda was living with her brother, Leroy Gields in Dawson County, Nebraska. In 1900 she and Leroy were still living together in Dawson County, but later removed to Cherry Co., Nebraska.

1880 US Census, Dawson Co., Nebraska, Overton, ED 1, Page 341B 68
67 Richard Robinson, black, 28, farmer, b. IN, father b. NC, mother b.
    unknown
Matilda A., black, 30, wife, keeping house, b. Canada, father b. PA, mother
    b. VA
Mary A., black, 8, daughter, b. Canada, father b. IN, mother b. Canada
Lawrence, black, 2, son, b. Canada, father b. IN, mother b. Canada
Nancy Green (crossed through), black, 65, b. PA, father b. SC, mother b. NJ
Leroy Gields, black, 19, son, b. Canada, father b. PA, mother b. VA

1885 Nebraska State Census, Dawson Co., Nebraska, Logan Prect, ED 192,   69
Page 5A
59-59 Leroy Gields, white, 22, single, farmer, b. Canada West, father b. VA,
    mother b. PA
Matilda Robinson, black, 35, sister, divorced, keeping house, b. Canada West,
    father b. VA, mother b. PA
Florence Robinson, black, 7, niece, b. Canada West, father b. IN, mother b.
    Canada
Nancy Green, black, 69, mother, widow, b. PA, both parents b. NJ

1900 US Census, Dawson Co., Nebraska, Logan Prect., ED 93, Page 2B   70
91-91 Matilda Robinson, black, b. July 1849, 50, divorced, married
    15 years, 5 children, 1 living, b. Canada, father b. WV, mother b. PA,
    farmer
Leroy Gields, brother, black, b. August 1849, 40, single, b. Canada, father,
    b. WV, mother b. PA, farm laborer

1910 US Census, Cherry Co., Nebraska, Loup Prect., ED 57, Page 5B   71
50-50 Matilda A. Robinson, mulatto, 60, divorced, 5 children, 1 living, b.
    Canada, father b. VA, mother b. PA, farmer
51-51 Leroy F. Gields, mulatto, 50, single, b. Canada, father b. VA, mother
    b. Pennsylvania

The following are the known children born to Richard Robinson and Matilda A. Gields.

1. Mary A. Robinson, born about 1872 in Canada (see above)
2. Lawrence Robinson, born about 1878 in Canada
3. Florence Robinson, born in Raleigh, Kent, Ontario, Canada

Nothing further is known about Lawrence. Florence married Charles Edward Meehan, son of Charles H. Meehan and Hester C. Freeman. They were married at Lexington, Dawson Co., Nebraska on 16 November 1885. For more information regarding Florence and Charles refer to Meehan information.

Matilda and her brother, Leroy, do not appear on any other census enumerations. Their mother, Nancy Wheeler Gields Green, is buried in the Evergreen Cemetery, Lexington, Dawson Co., Nebraska. Her tombstone is carved only with her name, "Nancy Green."

Leroy Gields and his sister Mathilda Gields Robinson, owned a good of land in Dawson and

Cherry counties in Nebraska. Most of their land was obtained under the Homestead Act and the Kinkaid Act. 72

Matilda A. Robinson
Homestead Act
160 acres in Dawson County
Land Office Grand Island
6th PM; T 10N; R 19W; SE1/4 Section 28
(about 4 miles north of Overton)
Certificate 9886
21 July 1893

Matilda A. Robinson
Homestead Act
two parcels of land in Cherry County
Land Office Valentine
remarks: heirs
6th PM Twp 28 N Range 29 W; west 1/2, Section 15
6th PM Twp. 28 N Range 29 W; NW 1/4 Section 22
slightly west and north of Elsmere
patent issued to heirs through Valentine Land Office
4 April 1912

Leroy F. Gields
Sale-Cash Entry
160 acres
Dawson County
Grand Island Land Office
6th PM Twp 10N Range 19 West; SE 1/4 Section 20
(about 4 miles north of Overton)
2 May 1890

Leroy F. Gields
Homestead Act
3 parcels of land, total 160 acres
Valentine Land Office
land in Cherry County
6th PM Twp 28N Range 29 W Section 20 NE 1/4 NE 1/4
6th PM Twp 28N Range 29 W N1/2 NW 1/4, Section 21
6th PM Twp 28N Range 29W SE 1/4 NW 1/4 Section 21
slightly north and east of Elsmere
13 Jan 1908

Leroy F. Gields
Homestead Act
4 parcels of land totaling 480 acres
located in Cherry County
Valentine Land Office
6th PM Twp 28N Range 29W Section 20 NW 1/4 NE 1/4
6th PM Twp. 28 N Range 29W Section
        SW 1/4 NW 1/4
        NE 1/4

W 1/2 SE 1/4
SW 1/4
26 Dec 1911

The land owned by LeRoy Gields was located about three miles east of the Wamaduze Creek and eight miles northwest of the village of Brownlee in Cherry Co., Nebraska. Less than three weeks after the Kinkaid Act made land available, LeRoy filed on a 480 acre addition, dated 16 July 1904. It is listed as being under the Homestead Act, but the Kinkaid Act made the land available. A month later, his sister Matilda Gields Robinson filed a 480 acre Kinkaid addition next to his claim. Together, they had 1,120 acres.

In 1906 there were other black settlers from Overton in Dawson County who filed Kinkaid claims along the North Loup River, about six miles southwest of LeRoy Gield's claim. It was public domain and had been fenced by the Standard Cattle Company Ranch. The ranch owners removed the fences from the government land. They owned the good land, leaving sandy land and dry valleys that were filed on by the black settlers. By 1911-1912 a good share of the larger areas had already been claimed, however, black settlers continued to file claims from 1912 to about 1923. 73

The following notice was posted in the Valentine, Cherry Co., Nebraska newspaper with regard to the estate of Matilda Robinson.

Valentine Democrat, 25 May 1911
"Order of Hearing and Notice on Petition for Settlement of Account
In the County Court of Cherry county, Nebraska.
STATE OF NEBASKA
        Cherry County.
To the heirs and all persons interested in the estate of Matilda Robinson, deceased: On reading the petition of D.H. White, praying a final settlement and allowance of his account filed in this court, on the 1st day of May, 1910, and for a decree of distribution. It is hereby ordered that you and all persons interested in said matter may, and do, appear at the county court to be held in and for said county, on the 27th day of May, A.D. 1910, at 11 o'clock a.m. to show cause, if any there be, why the prayer of the petitioner should not be granted, and that notice of the pendency of said petition and the hearing thereof be given to all persons interested in said matter by publishing a copy of this order in The Valentine Democrat, a weekly newspaper printed in said county for four successive weeks prior to said day of hearing. James C. Quigley, County Judge."

The newspaper is dated 1911 and the hearing was to be held two days later in 1910, which is undoubtedly an error.

Mathilda/Matilda Gields Robinson was the daughter of Leroy Gields and Nancy Ann Wheeler. She was born in about July 1849 in Canada. Her father Leroy Gields, was born about 1815 in Virginia and most likely died in Canada. Nancy Ann Wheeler was born about 1816 in Pennsylvania and came to Dawson Co., Nebraska with her daughter, son-in-law and son, LeRoy, just prior to 1880 from Canada. Nancy had married ――― Green, probably in Canada before she arrived in Nebraska where she is shown as a widow.

The following are some of known children, born to Leroy Gields and Nancy Ann Wheeler.
1. Mathilda/Matilda Gields, born about July 1849 in Canada (see above)
2. William Henry Gields, born about 1855 in Ontario, Canada

3. Leroy Gields, born about 1859 in Canada; never married

William Henry Gields, son of Leroy Gields and Nancy Ann Wheeler, was born in about 1855 in Ontario, Canada and died there. He married Mary Jane Chase. She was born about 1858 in Ontario, Canada and died 25 September 1896 in Raleigh, Kent, Ontario, Canada. After her death he married Mary Lucinda Travis on 14 April 1902 in North Buxton, Kent, Ontario, Canada. She was born 31 October 1860 in Raleigh, Kent, Ontario, Canada and died in Ontario, Canada on 29 June 1942. The following are children born to William Henry Gields and Mary Jane Chase.

1. Harriet P. Gields, born about 1877 in Ontario, Canada
2. Maggie Lauretta Gields, born about 1879 in Ontario, Canada
3. Mary Gields, born 15 January 1887 in Ontario, Canada
4. Horace Gields, born 23 Aug 1893 in Buxton, Kent, Ontario, Canada;
    married Mary Ann Anderson; died 7 September 1971 in Detroit,
    Wayne Co., Michigan
5. Nellie E. Gields, born 18 June 1894 in Raleigh, Kent, Ontario, Canada

1. Record of this marriage may be found at the Family History Library under microfiche reference number(s) 6110914 through 6110917.
2. Year: 1880; Census Place: Covington, Dawson, Nebraska; Roll: 746; Family History Film: 1254746; Page: 339C; Enumeration District: 001; Image: 0120
3. Year: 1880; Census Place: Covington, Dawson, Nebraska; Roll: 746; Family History Film: 1254746; Page: 341B; Enumeration District: 001; Image: 0124
4. Nebraska State Census, 1885," database with images, FamilySearch (https://familysearch.org/ark:/61903/1:1:X3XK-T1H , Josh Emanuel Jr., 1885; citing NARA microfilm publication M352 (Washington, D.C.: National Archives and Records Administration, n.d.); FHL microfilm 499,540.
5. Year: 1900; Census Place: Overton, Dawson, Nebraska; Roll: 922; Page: 11A; Enumeration District: 0093; FHL microfilm: 1240922
6. Year: 1910 Census Place: Kennedy, Cherry, Nebraska; Roll: T624_840; Page: 8A; Enumeration District: 0051; FHL microfilm: 1374853
7. Year: 1920; Census Place: Alliance, Box Butte, Nebraska; Roll: T625_979; Page: 23A; Enumeration District: 11; Image: 1046
8. Year: 1930; Census Place: Denver, Denver, Colorado; Roll: 239; Page: 1B; Enumeration District: 0173; Image: 483.0; FHL microfilm: 2339974
9. Box Butte Co., Nebraska Marriage Book K, page 315 #6092
10. Year: 1940; Census Place: Box Butte, Box Butte, Nebraska; Roll: T627_2237; Page: 5A; Enumeration District: 7-7
11. Year: 1940; Census Place: Alliance, Box Butte, Nebraska; Roll: T627_2237; Page: 3B; Enumeration District: 7-2A
12. James Emanuel http://www.encyclopedia.com/doc/1G2-3431200023.html
13. Year: 1920; Census Place: Alliance, Box Butte, Nebraska; Roll: T625_979; Page: 22B; Enumeration District: 11; Image: 1045
14. Year: 1930; Census Place: Denver, Denver, Colorado; Roll: 239; Page: 13B; Enumeration District: 0174; Image: 539.0; FHL microfilm: 2339974
15. Year: 1940; Census Place: Denver, Denver, Colorado; Roll: T627_491; Page: 10A; Enumeration District: 16-248
16. The National Archives at St. Louis; St. Louis, Missouri; Draft Registration Cards for Fourth Registration for Colorado, 04/27/1942 - 04/27/1942; NAI Number: 923647; Record Group Title: Records of the Selective Service System; Record Group Number: 147
17. "Colorado Statewide Marriage Index, 1853-2006," database with images, FamilySearch (https://familysearch.org/ark:/61903/1:1:KN31-Z82 : 3 December 2014), Joe Foster Casey and Ruby Thelma

Drisdon, 01 Apr 1937, Denver, Denver, Colorado, United States; citing no. 9366, State Archives, Denver; FHL microfilm 1,690,061.

18. Ancestry.com. U.S., Social Security Death Index, 1935-2014 [database on-line]. Provo, UT, USA: Ancestry.com Operations Inc, 2011.

19. "Colorado Statewide Marriage Index, 1853-2006," database with images, FamilySearch (https://familysearch.org/ark:/61903/1:1:KNQC-HHB : 3 December 2014), John I Jefferson and Mabel M Drisdon, 22 Mar 1939, Littleton, Arapahoe, Colorado, United States; citing no. 22427, State Archives, Denver; FHL microfilm 1,690,092.

20. "Colorado Statewide Marriage Index, 1853-2006," database with images, FamilySearch (https://familysearch.org/ark:/61903/1:1:KNQC-HHB : 3 December 2014), John I Jefferson and Mabel M Drisdon, 22 Mar 1939, Littleton, Arapahoe, Colorado, United States; citing no. 22427, State Archives, Denver; FHL microfilm 1,690,092.

21. Ancestry.com. U.S., Social Security Death Index, 1935-2014 [database on-line]. Provo, UT, USA: Ancestry.com Operations Inc, 2011.

22. United States, Selective Service System. World War I Selective Service System Draft Registration Cards, 1917-1918. Washington, D.C.: National Archives and Records Administration. M1509, 4,582 rolls

23. Year: 1920; Census Place: State Penitentiary, Carbon, Wyoming; Roll: T625_2025; Page: 1B; Enumeration District: 17; Image: 792

24. The National Archives at St. Louis; St. Louis, Missouri; Draft Registration Cards for Fourth Registration for Colorado, 04/27/1942 - 04/27/1942; NAI Number: 923647; Record Group Title: Records of the Selective Service System; Record Group Number: 147

25. Year: 1930; Census Place: Red Vermillion, Nemaha, Kansas; Roll: 713; Page: 2A; Enumeration District: 0019; Image: 817.0; FHL microfilm: 2340448

26. Box Butte Co., Nebraska Marriage Book F, page 83 #2609

27. FindA Grave) Forever Missed Nellie Ruth Cherry Emanuel Jenkins, http://www.forevermissed.com/nellie-ruth-emanuel-jenkins/lifestory#lifestory, used 8 June 2016

28. U.S. Department of the Interior, Bureau of Land Management, General Land Office Records http://www.glorecords.blm.gov/details/patent/default.aspx?accession=NE1030__.126&docClass=STA&sid=bdbr1th1.g0y

29. Fold3 http://www.fold3.com

30. U.S. Department of the Interior, Bureau of Land Management, General Land Office Records http://www.glorecords.blm.gov/details/patent/default.aspx?accession=343406&docClass=SER&sid=bdbr1th1.g0y

31. U.S. Department of the Interior, Bureau of Land Management, General Land Office http://www.glorecords.blm.gov/details/patent/default.aspx?accession=399806&docClass=SER&sid=bdbr1th1.g0y

32. U.S. Department of Interior, Bureau of Land Management, General Land Office Records, http://www.glorecords.blm.gov/details/patent/default.aspx?accession=491101&docClass=SER&sid=bdbr1th1.g0y

33. U.S. Department of the Interior, Bureau of Land Management, General Land Office Records, http://www.glorecords.blm.gov/details/patent/default.aspx?accession=533387&docClass=SER&sid=bdbr1th1.g0y

34. U.S. Department of the Interior, Bureau of Land Management, General Land Office Records, http://www.glorecords.blm.gov/details/patent/default.aspx?accession=804997&docClass=SER&sid=bdbr1th1.g0y

35. Year: 1900; Census Place: Jefferson, Jackson, Georgia; Roll: 206; Page: 6A; Enumeration District: 0084; FHL microfilm: 1240206

36. Year: 1910; Census Place: Topeka Ward 5, Shawnee, Kansas; Roll: T624_457; Page: 3A; Enumeration District: 0182; FHL microfilm: 1374470

37. U.S. Department of the Interior, Bureau of Land Management, General Land Office Records http://www.glorecords.blm.gov/details/patent/default.aspx?accession=533390&docClass=SER&sid=51c230hr.zcx

38. U.S. Department of the Interior, Bureau of Land Management, General Land Office Records, http://www.glorecords.blm.gov/details/patent/default.aspx?accession=429223&docClass=SER&sid=51c230hr.zcx

39. U.S. Department of the Interior, Bureau of Land Management, General Land Office Records, http://www.glorecords.blm.gov/details/patent/default.aspx?accession=533391&docClass=SER&sid=51c230hr.zcx

40. Year: 1920; Census Place: Boulder Ward 4, Boulder, Colorado; Roll: T625_156; Page: 11A; Enumeration District: 53; Image: 541

41. Year: 1930; Census Place: Denver, Denver, Colorado; Roll: 239; Page: 1A; Enumeration District: 0173; Image: 482.0; FHL microfilm: 2339974

42. Year: 1940; Census Place: Greeley, Weld, Colorado; Roll: T627_482; Page: 10B; Enumeration District: 62-103

43. Michigan Death Certificate #165579.

44. Year: 1940; Census Place: Alliance, Box Butte, Nebraska; Roll: T627_2237; Page: 3B; Enumeration District: 7-2A

45. Archives of Ontario; Toronto, Ontario, Canada; *Registrations of Marriages, 1869-1928*; Series: *MS932*; Reel: *30*

46. Ancestry.com and The Church of Jesus Christ of Latter-day Saints. 1861 Census of Canada [database on-line]. Provo, UT, USA: Ancestry.com Operations Inc, 2009.

47. Year: 1871; Census Place: Raleigh, Kent, Ontario; Roll: C-9891; Page: 4; Family No: 10

48. Year: 1880; Census Place: Covington, Dawson, Nebraska; Roll: 746; Family History Film: 1254746; Page: 339C; Enumeration District: 001; Image: 0120

49. Nebraska State Census, 1885," database with images, FamilySearch (https://familysearch.org/ark:/61903/1:1:X3X2-X4J, Ida Emanuel in entry for Joshua Emanuel, 1885; citing NARA microfilm publication M352 (Washington, D.C.: National Archives and Records Administration, n.d.); FHL microfilm 499,540.

50. Archives of Ontario. Registrations of Deaths, 1869-1938. MS 935, reels 1-615. Archives of Ontario, Toronto, Ontario, Canada.Archives of Ontario.

51. Archives of Ontario. Registrations of Deaths, 1869-1938. MS 935, reels 1-615. Archives of Ontario, Toronto, Ontario, Canada.Archives of Ontario.

52. Archives of Ontario; Toronto, Ontario, Canada; Registrations of Marriages, 1869-1928; Series: MS932; Reel: 36

53. Year: 1900; Census Place: Ypsilanti Ward 1, Washtenaw, Michigan; Roll: 747; Page: 12A; Enumeration District: 0110; FHL microfilm: 1240747

54. Online publication - Provo, UT, USA: Ancestry.com Operations, Inc., 2010. Images reproduced by FamilySearch.Original data - Sixth Census of the United States, 1840. (NARA microfilm publication M704, 580 rolls). Records of the Bureau of the Census, Record G

55. Year: 1850; Census Place: Wirt, Allegany, New York; Roll: M432_475; Page: 151B; Image: 307

56. Library and Archives Canada. Census of Canada, 1901. Ottawa, Ontario, Canada: Library and Archives Canada, 2004. http://www.bac-lac.gc.ca/eng/census/1901/Pages/about-census.aspxl. Series RG31-C-1. Statistics Canada Fonds. Microfilm reels: T-6428 to T-6556.

57. Year: 1880; Census Place: Covington, Dawson, Nebraska; Roll: 746; Family History Film: 1254746; Page: 339D; Enumeration District: 001; Image: 0121

58. Year: 1900; Census Place: Chicago Ward 3, Cook, Illinois; Roll: 247; Page: 3A; Enumeration District: 0068; FHL microfilm: 1240247

59. Online publication - Provo, UT, USA: Ancestry.com Operations, Inc., 2010. Images reproduced by FamilySearch.Original data - Fourth Census of the United States, 1820. (NARA microfilm publication M33, 142 rolls). Records of the Bureau of the Census, Record G

60. Online publication - Provo, UT, USA: Ancestry.com Operations, Inc., 2010. Images reproduced by FamilySearch.Original data - Fourth Census of the United States, 1830. (NARA microfilm publication M33, 142 rolls). Records of the Bureau of the Census, Record G

61. Online publication - Provo, UT, USA: Ancestry.com Operations, Inc., 2010. Images reproduced by FamilySearch.Original data - Fourth Census of the United States, 1840. (NARA microfilm publication M33, 142 rolls). Records of the Bureau of the Census, Record G

62. Year: 1850; Census Place: Coolspring, Mercer, Pennsylvania; Roll: M432_796; Page: 338B; Image: 555

63. Ancestry.com and The Church of Jesus Christ of Latter-day Saints. 1871 Census of Canada [database on-line]. Provo, UT, USA: Ancestry.com Operations Inc, 2009.

64. Archives of Ontario; Toronto, Ontario, Canada; Series: MS935; Reel: 21

65. The National Archives at Washington, D.C.; Washington, D.C.; Manifests of Passengers Arriving at St. Albans, VT, District through Canadian Pacific and Atlantic Ports, 1895-1954; National Archives Microfilm Publication: M1464; Roll: 176; Record Group Title: Records of the Immigration and Naturalization Service; Record Group Number: 85

66. Volume: 318; SAR Membership Number: 63431

67. Dawson Co., Nebraska Complete Record Book 6 page 225

68. Year: 1880; Census Place: Covington, Dawson, Nebraska; Roll: 746; Family History Film: 1254746; Page: 341B; Enumeration District: 001; Image: 0124

69. Nebraska State Census, 1885," database with images, FamilySearch (https://familysearch.org/ark:/61903/1:1:X3X2-WMZ, Leroy Gields, 1885; citing NARA microfilm publication M352 (Washington, D.C.: National Archives and Records Administration, n.d.); FHL microfilm 499,540.

70. Year: 1900; Census Place: Logan, Dawson, Nebraska; Roll: 922; Page: 2B; Enumeration District: 0093; FHL microfilm: 1240922

71. Year: 1910; Census Place: Loup, Cherry, Nebraska; Roll: T624_840; Page: 5B; Enumeration District: 0057; FHL microfilm: 1374853

72. Bureau of Land Management http://www.glorecords.blm.gov/default.aspx

73. *The Nebraska Sandhills*, McIntosh, pp 230-231

Mose and Essie English

While Mose(s) and Essie English did not reside very long in Alliance, they should be mentioned as early residents. Between 1910 and 1920 they came to Alliance from Alabama. The following two census enumerations show their household during that time period. Mose English registered for the World War I Draft in Alliance, Nebraska on 11 September 1918. He was living at 111 Sweetwater, age 39, born 1 February 1879, negro. His occupation was a porter on the CB&Q Railroad in Alliance, Nebraska. The nearest relative was Mrs. Mose English of the same address. 1

1910 US Census, Jefferson Co., Alabama, Jonesboro, ED 31, Page 9B   2
262 Raimon
378-385 Mose English, black, 26, 1st marriage, married 2 years, b. GA, both
      parents b. AL, miner, ore mines
Estella, wife, black, 24, second marriage, married 2 years, 3 children, 3 living, b.
      GA, both parents b. GA
Molley Bowen, step-son, black, 7, b. GA, both parents b. GA
Robert Bowen, step-son, black, 6, b. GA, both parents b. GA
Ida L. Bowen, step-daughter, black, 3, b. GA, both parents b. GA

1920 US Census, Box Butte Co., Nebraska, Alliance, ED 272, Page 3A   3
111 Sweetwater Ave.
68-5 O.M. English, rents, black, 38, b. Al, both parents b. AL, labor, railroad
Essie, wife, black, 33, b. AL, both parents b. AL
Robert, son, black, 17, b. AL, both parents b. AL

Mancy, daughter, black, 15, b. AL, both parents b. AL
Jeliene, daughter, black, 13, b. AL, both parents b. AL

1930 US Census, Box Butte Co., Nebraska, Alliance, ED 2, Page 13A 4
111 Sweetwater Ave.
256-276 Mose English, owns $2,000 negro, 50, married at age 24, b. AL, both
     parents b. AL, porter, railroad
Essie, wife, negro, 42, married at age 14, b. AL, both parents b. AL
Richard L., son, negro, 9, b. NE, both parents b. AL
Franklin Riley, boarder, negro, 56, single, b. KS, both parents b. OK, laborer, odd
     jobs
Corine Lewis, lodger, negro, 24, married, at age 18, b. AL, both parents b. AL

The children listed on the 1910 enumeration indicate that the children went by the surname of Bowen. Essie's maiden name was Bowen. They were probably born out of wedlock or took her name. By 1920 they had taken the name of English. The eldest, Robert, was married and living in Alliance by 1930. He and his wife were not married in Box Butte Co., Nebraska.

1930 US Census, Box Butte Co., Nebraska, Alliance, ED 3, Page 2A 5
73 Burlington Railroad Yards
26-26 Robert English, rents $1.50 month, negro, 26, married at age 21, b. AL,
     both parents b. AL, fire knocker, round house
Grace, wife, negro, 21, married at age 16, b. IA, father b. LA, mother b. TX
Bobbie Jean, daughter, negro, 3, 7/12, b. NE, father b. AL, mother b. IA
William, son, negro, 8/12, b. NE, father b. AL, mother b. IA

The daughter shown on census as Mancy was actually Massie C. English. She married Roy Wesley Shores on 29 March 1923 in Box Butte Co., Nebraska. 6 Her parents are shown as Mazelle English, b. Alabama and Essie Bowen, b. Alabama. Roy W. Shores was the son of John W. Shores and Mildred Keyser, both born in North Carolina. Refer to Shores in Volume 2. Their marriage ended in divorce.

Box Butte Co., Nebraska
District Court
Divorce
3 March 1925
Case #3660, Docket O, Page 23
Massie C. Shores
vs
Roy W. Shores

The plaintiff and defendant had lived in Alliance since 1924. She filed for the divorce indicating that he had not supported her, forcing her to live with relatives of his at Halsey, Nebraska on a ranch. She went into the fields doing a man's work. Massie indicated that Roy did not work steadily and moved from one job to another. They lived in Lincoln, Nebraska shortly after their marriage and also near Halsey and with her parents in Alliance. Often he would tell her to go home to her parents. They had a child born in November 1923 who lived only three days. Their son William O. Shores, was born 15 February 1925. Roy wrote to Massie in August of 1924 to come to Alliance from Halsey and that he didn't want her. She moved in with her parents. In November of 1924 she became sick and went to the hospital in Alliance for an operation. She was there five days and when she filed for divorce in March of 1925, she was still under the care of a doctor. Roy refused to pay a medical bill of $46.00, so her mother paid it. Massie indicated that Roy called her vile names, slapped her and threatened to slap her. She stated that he liked other women and spent money on them. Roy owned land in Thomas Co., Nebraska and personal property of 4 horses, 11 hogs and 1 Ford car. Massie asked the court for child support of $50 a month, plus alimony. A summons was dated 12 March 1925 to Roy W. Shores at Thedford, Thomas Co., Nebraska. There is no final decree in the court file.

The child who was born and died in 1923 was Roy Wesley Shores, Jr., born 12 November 1923 and died 14 November 1923. He was buried in the Alliance Cemetery.

Mose and Essie's daughter, Ida Lee English, married Harold Talbert in Box Butte Co., Nebraska in 1924. He was the son of Fred Talbert, born Nebraska and Lulu/Lula Stepney, born Kansas. Lulu/Lula Stepney was the daughter of Moses and Eva Stepney. On Ida and Harold's marriage license, her parents are shown as Moses English and Essie Bowen. Refer to the Corneal family for more information on the Stepney families, Volume 1. 7

Mrs. English (Essie) came to the rescue of Willie Foster, aka Willie Brown, as shown in the newspaper. For more information refer to the section, Rogues, Rascals and Rooming Houses, Volume 1.

The Alliance Herald, 5 March 1920
"Willie Foster testified that on 1 March 1920 she was walking by Sam Shelton's restaurant on upper Box Butte. She saw through the window the outline of Charles Brown. Realizing that 'he had it in for her' she hurried on. She testified that he had threatened to beat her up. She went to the American Hotel where she called Mrs. English for protection who agreed to accompany Willie home. The two started for Willie's home on Sweetwater and got as far as the old Brennan corner, when they saw Brown, standing in front of King's corner. He was apparently waiting for them and crossed over the street walking ahead of them. When they reached Sweetwater, Brown crossed over and approached both Mrs. English and Willie Foster. With his left hand open he hit Willie in the face. He had a knife with blade open in his right hand threatening to use it. Mrs. English seized two bottles and swung them over her head, at which Brown fled. Judge Tash ruled that the motive for Brown's assault was jealousy. He objected to the fact that Willie Foster was attractive to other men, wishing to slash her face and injure her personal beauty. Brown was held for trial at the May term of district court. He could not pay bond of $500 so was placed in jail."

Sometime between 1930 and 1940, Mose and Essie moved to Los Angeles. Their son Richard went with them. They are shown on the 1940 US Census as follows.

1940 US Census, Los Angeles Co., California, Los Angeles, ED 60-551, Page 2B 8
763 East 48th Street, rents $25 month
Mose English, negro, 50, 5 years education, b. AL, same place 1 April 1935,
        janitor, office building
Essie, informant, wife, negro, 47, 3 years education, b. GA, same place 1 April
        1935, maid, private home
Richard, son, negro, 18, 4 years high school, b. NE, same place 1 April 1935

According to family information on Internet, Mose English was born 1 February 1879 in Alabama, the son of Elick and Lusten English. His wife, Estella "Essie" Bowen was born 23 June 1887 in Alabama to a Mr. Bowen and Lucindy Cofield. Mose was buried with his wife in the Evergreen Cemetery, Los Angeles, Los Angeles Co., California. His tombstone indicates he was born 2 February 1883 an died 9 May 1958. Essie's tombstone indicates she was born 23 June 1888 and died 31 October 1959. The date of 1 February 1879 for the birth of Mose also comes from his World War I Draft Registration. It was filed 11 September 1918. 9

There is a marriage of Elleck English, black, to Luster Ball, black, in Russell Co., Alabama in 1879. 10 One year later the couple is shown in Russell Co, Alabama, with two children Rachel, 7 and

Jim, 2. The 60 year old woman, Amey, may be Elick's mother, placing her birth at about 1820. In 1870 there is an Annie or Ammie English living in Russell Co., Alabama. However, Elick is not in her household. There are also other blacks with the surname of English in the same county in 1870. Elick is often used as a nickname for Alexander. There is an Alexander English shown on the Russell Co., Alabama enumeration in 1870, living close to Annie or Ammie English.

> 1870 US Census, Russell Co., Alabama, Silver Run, Page 37
> 281-296 Spencer Doby, 70, black, farm work, b. SC
> Annie or Ammie English, 50, black, farm hand, b. GA

> 1870 US Census, Russell Co., Alabama, Silver Run, page 36
> 275-290 Alexr. English, 24, black, farm hand, b. AL
> Carrie, 34, black, farm hand, b. GA

> 277-292 Ransom English, 60, black, farm hand, b. NC
> Tom, 17, black, farm hand, b. AL
> Wiley?, 16, black, male, farm hand, b. AL
> Dennis, 14, black, farm hand, b. AL
> Shepherd, 10, black, b. AL
> Vick, 9, female, black, b. AL

All of the other English families designated as black living in Russell Co., Alabama, in 1870, were living in Beat No. 4, PO Silver Run.

> 1020-1105 Mary English, 50, black, cook, b. AL
> Frank, 16, black, farm hand, b. AL

> 1033-1120 Mary English, 60, black, cook, b. GA
> Frank, 14, black, farm hand, b. AL
> Rachel, 13, black, b. AL

> 1054-1144 General English, 22, black, farm hand, b. AL; married in May
> Sophia, 20, black, farm hand, b. AL

More information can be found about Shepherd "Shep" English. He was born about 1860 in Georgia to Rawson (Ransom?) English, b. GA and Lucy Smith, b. AL. On 17 August 1922 he died at Pittsview, Russell Co., Alabama. He was a farmer, black, married to a lady named Barbara. 11

There was also a female child, Cillia, born to Ransom English by a wife named Amie. Cilla was born about 1876 in Alabama, black, age 50, died on 7 December 1926 at Pittsview, Russell Co., Alabama. She was the widow of Henry Johnson. 12

If the Alexander English shown with a wife Carrie on the 1870 US Census is the same person as Elick shown with wife Luter on the 1880 US Census, that would explain the two children, Rachel and Jim. They were probably by his marriage to Carrie. Furthermore there is no Alexander English shown in the county in 1880.

> 1880 US Census, Russell Co., Alabama, Glennville, ED 160, Page 636D 13
> Elick English, black, 30, laborer, b. AL, both parents b. AL
> Luter, black, 23, wife, b. AL, both parents b. AL
> Amey, black, female, 60, laborer, b. AL, both parents b. AL
> Rachel, black, 7, b. AL, both parents b. AL

390

Jim, black, 2, b. AL, both parents b. AL

1900 US Census, Russell Co., Alabama, Seale Prect., ED 150, Page 25A   14
399-399 Ellick English, black, b. Jan 1846, 54, married 20 years, b. GA, both
        parents b. GA, farmer
Lusten, wife, black, b. Aug 1862, 37, married 20 years, 11 children, 9 living, b.
        AL, both parents b. AL
Mose, son, black, b. March 1883, 17, b. AL, father b. GA, mother b. AL, farm
        laborer
Rosetta, daughter, b. July 1884, 15, b. AL, father b. GA, mother b. AL
Lugene, son, black, b. June 1885, 14, b. AL, father b. GA, mother b. AL
Willie B., son, black, b. Jan 1889, 11, b. AL, father b. GA, mother b. AL
Julia, daughter, black, b. Feb 1891, 9, b. AL, father b. GA, mother b. AL
Estell, daughter, black, b. Nov 1894, 5, b. AL, father b. GA, mother b. AL
Adella, daughter, black, b. Aug 1876, 3, b. AL, father b. GA, mother b. AL

1910 US Census, Russell Co., Alabam, Seale Prect., Beat 7, ED 194, Page 7B   15
145-145 Elic English, black, 56, married 28 years, b. GA, both parents b. VA,
        farmer
Luster, wife, black, 45, married 28 years, 10 children, 10 living, b. AL, both
        parents b. AL
Julia, daughter, black, 19, single, b. AL, both parents b. AL, laborer on farm
Estella, daughter, black, 14, b. AL, both parents b. AL, laborer on farm
Bessie, daughter, black, 12, b. AL, both parents b. AL
Adell, daughter, black, 10, b. AL, both parents b. AL
Cola, daughter, black, 9, b. AL, both parents b. AL

Alex English, born about 1846, died 21 November 1916 at Hatchechubbie, Russell Co., Alabama. He was 70, black, a farmer and married.   16

1920 US Census, Russell Co., Alabama, Township 15, Hatchechubbee, ED 194,   17
Page 8A
Rutherford Road
146-147 Lester English, rents, female, black, 56, widow, b. AL, both parents b.
        AL
Ceola, daughter, black, 18, b. AL, both parents b. AL, farm laborer
Irene Simmons, granddaughter, black, 14, b. AL, both parents b. AL
Annie Simmons, granddaughter, black, 12, b. AL, both parents b. AL
James Simmons, grandson, black, 8, b. AL, both parents b. AL
John Simmons, grandson, black, 5, b. AL, both parents b. AL

Luster English apparently died between 1920 and 1930 or moved away from Russell Co., Alabama. She is not found on the 1930 US Census for that county.

1. Registration State: *Nebraska;* Registration County: *Box Butte;* Roll: *1711448*
2. Year: 1910; Census Place: Jonesboro, Jefferson, Alabama; Roll: T624_17; Page: 9B; Enumeration District: 0031; FHL microfilm: 1374030
3. Year: 1920; Census Place: Alliance, Box Butte, Nebraska; Roll: T625_979; Page: 3A; Enumeration District: 272; Image: 972
4. Year: 1930; Census Place: Alliance, Box Butte, Nebraska; Roll: 1266; Page: 13A; Enumeration District: 0002; Image: 830.0; FHL microfilm: 234100
5. Year: 1930; Census Place: Alliance, Box Butte, Nebraska; Roll: 1266; Page: 2A; Enumeration District:

0003; Image: 856.0; FHL microfilm: 2341001
6. Box Butte Co., Nebraska Marriage Book G, page 86 #3256
7. Box Butte County, Nebraska Marriage Book H page 120 #3433
8. Year: 1940; Census Place: Los Angeles, Los Angeles, California; Roll: T627_414; Page: 2B; Enumeration District: 60-551
9. Registration State: *Nebraska;* Registration County: *Box Butte;* Roll: *1711448*
10. FHL film #033484, page 6
11. FHL Film #1908243
12. FHL Film #1908439
13. Year: 1880; Census Place: Glennville, Russell, Alabama; Roll: 30; Family History Film: 1254030; Page: 636D; Enumeration District: 160; Image: 0676
14. Year: 1900; Census Place: Seale, Russell, Alabama; Roll: 38; Page: 25A; Enumeration District: 0150; FHL microfilm: 1240038
15. Year: 1910; Census Place: Seale, Russell, Alabama; Roll: T624_32; Page: 7B; Enumeration District: 0194; FHL microfilm: 1374045
16. FHL Film #1894135
17. Year: 1920; Census Place: Hatchechubbee, Russell, Alabama; Roll: T625_40; Page: 8A; Enumeration District: 194; Image: 375

George Evans

On the 1900 US Census, teenager, George Evans, was living in the household of Henry Nehne (white), as his adopted son. On the 1910 US Census, Henry and Martha Nehne are living in Field Prect., Scotts Bluff Co., Nebraska. They indicated that they both came to the United States in 1885 and that the son Ernest, born in Africa, white, came in 1895. [1] Between 1910 and 1920 the Nehne family had moved to Oswego Co., New York. [2] On the 1930 US Census, Henry and Martha were elderly and living with their son Ernest Nehne in Oswego Co., New York. Henry is shown as a Methodist Church missionary. [3]

> 1900 US Census, Scotts Bluff Co., Nebraska, Tabor Prect., ED 168, Page 9A [4]
> 165-165 Henry Nehne, white, b. March 1861, 39, married 8 years, b. Germany,
> both parents b. Germany, came to US in 1885, naturalized, farmer
> Martha, wife, white, b. January 1860, 40, married 8 years, 2 children, 2 living,
> b. Germany, both parents b. Germany, came to US in 1877
> Ernest, son, white, b. July 1893, 6, b. French Congo, both parents b. Germany,
> came to US in 1895
> Dorothea, daughter, white, b. Oct 1897, 2, b. NE, both parents b. Germany
> David Kah, father-in-law, white, b. Sept 1824, 75, widowed, b. Germany, came to
> US in 1876, naturalized, farmer
> George Evans, adopted son, black, b. May 1884, 16, b. French Congo, father b.
> England, mother b. French Congo, came 1896, at school

Henry Nehne is shown on the Hamburg Passenger Lists as sailing from Hamburg, Germany to the United States on 21 May 1896. He was a missionary destined for Minotare [sic]. This would have been Minatare, Nebraska. He came on the ship "Vogelgesang" which was of the Hamburg-Amerika Line. Also with him was Georg Nehne, age 12, shown as his son, born about 1884. This was the George Evans shown in his household in 1900. None of the information on the passenger list indicates place of birth or nationality. Henry Nehne had been in the French Congo as a missionary and brought George back to Germany and thence to the United States. [5]

Martha Kah, wife of Henry Nehne, came to America in 1876. She and her father and siblings departed from Hamburg, Germany on 23 February 1876. Their residence was Quedlinburg, Provinz

Sachsen (Saxony). They came on the "Klopstock" to the port of New York. Her father, David Kah, was shown as a landsman or farmer. The Hamburg Passenger list indicates that Martha was 16 years of age, born about 1860. Thre is no destination shown on the passenger list. 6

She became a missionary of the Methodist Episcopal Church by 1889 and was stationed in the French Congo. The missionary society report of 1889 indicates, "From the West Coast we proceed by steamer two thousand five hundred miles to Congo country. Two days above Congo mouth we land at Mayumba and proceed in boats seventeen miles up an inland lake to Mamby where Miss Martha Kah is stationed." Apparently the station was proposed for abandonment, but Martha was unwilling to leave, so it was decided to keep the station as it was the only one in French territory. 7

In 1889 a new recruit, Henry Nehne, arrived at Mamby to assist Martha Kah. They completed a new mission house, she adopted children to convert to God and they also acted as interpreters and witnesses among the Mamby villages. As late as 1891 the couple is still referred to as Martha Kah and her assistant, Henry Nehne. On 10 September 1880, a treaty with king Makoto established French control over the Congo. By then Henry and Martha had established a small boarding school. Because Mamby was under a French protectorate, they were required to teach French in the school. 8

By 1894 the missionary reports indicate that Henry and Martha were still at Mamby and had married. They had a good mission house and garden and some children. However they were having problems securing a French teacher. Along with the establishment of Roman Catholic schools, they were considering moving the station. 9

Also in the year 1894, Eugene R. Smith edited a book about the Methodist Episcopal Church missionaries. He indicated that Bishop Taylor's Missionaries in Africa, particularly in the Congo Free State included Henry Nehne and Mrs. Kah-Nehne and baby living at Mamby. 10

On the 1920 US Census, George Evans reported that his father was born in France. Previous years, the father is shown as born in England or born in Wales. It is possible that his father was a missionary. The surname Evans is normally considered a Welsh surname. It is doubtful that Henry and Martha Nehne ever legally adopted him, but for some reason Henry brought the 12 year old child to America with him in 1896. His parents may have died or could not care for him. As reflected on the 1900 US Census, Henry and Martha had a son, Ernest who was born in July of 1893 in the French Congo. Henry and Martha were both in the French Congo, but Henry came back later than his wife Martha. She and her son are shown on the New York Passenger lists as arriving on 31 October 1895. She is shown as age 35, an American, destination Minatare [Nebraska]. They sailed on the "Dania" out of Hamburg, Germany. Her son Ernest is shown as age two. They were both considered citizens of the United States. 11 The outbound passenger lists from Hamburg, Germany indicate the same type of information. The ship sailed on 20 October 1895. Their destination is shown as "Minetere." 12

Henry Nehne obtained land in Scotts Bluff Co., Nebraska under the Homestead Act and the Homestead Reclamation Act. A patent was issued to him on 2 May 1905 for 30 acres located in the 6th PM T 21N, Range 53W, Lot/Tract 2, Section 20. This land was located about two miles south of Minatare. Under the Homestead Reclamation Act he obtained a total of 100 acres with the patent issued on 2 September 1913. The land is described as Farm Unit C, 6th PM, T 23N R 53W, Section 23 with the following alliquots: West 1/2 of Southwest 1/4 and West 1/2 of Southwest 1/4 of Northwest 1/4. This land was located several miles northeast of Minatare. 13

George R. Evans obtained 80 acres of land in Scotts Bluff County through the Homestead Reclamation Act. The land office in Alliance, Nebraska issued the patent on 22 June 1918. It was located in 6th PM, T23N R53W, Section 26, West 1/2 of Northwest 1/4. 14 The land was located next to the land Henry Nehne obtained under the Homestead Reclamation Act.

The Homestead file is available for Henry Nehne, but the file for George R. Evans cannot be located. Within the file for Nehne is a deposition about his declaration of intention to become a citizen of the United States. He filed the deposition in the County of Galveston, Texas on 15 October 1888. The deposition states that he was born 14 March 1861 in Germany and emigrated to the United States on 28 March 1885. He filed for the land under the Homestead Act on 26 May 1889 in the Alliance land office and stated he was a married man. On 25 November 1903 he received his naturalization papers in Scotts Bluff Co., Nebraska. Apparently he did not live continuously, as required, on the land as in 1889 he is also shown as being in the French Congo as a missionary. He did not build upon the land until September 1899 when he built a small shed, then a small house 8x8 feet and began residing there. He stated that he had a wife and two children. Nehne found the land having too much alkali in it to be cultivated, so he had to rent adjacent land to make a living. 15

George Evans married Pearl E. Beck, daughter of Elexander and Lucinda Beck. George R. Evans is married and with his wife and two wards, as shown on the 1910 US Census in Field Prect. of Scotts Bluff Co., Nebraska. On the 1900 US Census, the Becks are found living in Diller, Jefferson Co., Nebraska.

> 1900 US Census, Jefferson Co., Nebraska, Village of Diller, ED 92, Page 10B 16
> 208-208 Elexander Beck, black, b. March 1856, 44, married 22 years, b. TN,
> both parents b. TN, ME Minister
> Lucind[a], wife, black, b. May 1863, 37, married 22 years, 5 children, 1 living,
> b. TN, both parents b. TN
> Pearl E., daughter, black, b. February 1881, 19, single, b. TN, both parents b.
> TN, sing. evangelist
> Lillian Elliott, niece, black, b. Nov 1882, 18, single, b. TN, both parents b. TN,
> sing. evangelist

> 1910 US Census, Scotts Bluff Co., Nebraska, Field Prect., ED 204, Page 13A 17
> 35-35 George R. Evans, mulatto, 24, first marriage, married 2 years, b. Africa,
> father b. Wales, mother b. Africa, came to US in 1895, naturalized
> Pearl E., wife, black, 28, first marriage, married 2 years, 0 children, 0 living, b.
> TN, both parents b. TN
> Elmer Wiles, ward, black, 15, b. IL, both parents b. US
> Charlie Smith, ward, black, 13, b. IN, both parents b. US

George Richard Evans, filed his World War I Draft Registration on 12 September 1918 in Scotts Bluff Co., Nebraska. He living at 2123 Broadway in Scottsbluff and born 16 May 1885. His occupation was a fireman for IM Light & P Co., South Broadway in Scottsbluff. His nearest relative was his wife Pearl E. Evans. 18

When the 1920 US Census was taken George Evans was still in Scotts Bluff Co., Nebraska and widowed. On the 1920 Scottsbluff, Nebraska City Directory, George R. Evans and wife Pearl E. were living at 2123 Broadway. He was a fireman for Intermountain Railway Light & P[ower] Co. The city directory information was taken in 1919 for the 1920 publication. Pearl most likely died in late 1919 and before January 1920.

> 1920 US Census, Scotts Bluff, Scottsbluff, Ward 1, ED 225, Page 1B 19
> 2123 Broadway
> 20-20 George Evans, informant, owns/free, mulatto, 34, widowed, came to
> U.S. in about 1892, naturalized, b. Africa (German tongue), father b.
> France, mother b. Africa (German tongue), electrician, light company

Florence Speese, servant, mulatto, 23, single, b. NE, father b. SC, mother b.
    KS
Theodocia Taylor, boarder, mulatto,19, single, b. OK, father b. MO, mother b. KY

The Florence Speese shown in George's household as a servant in 1920, was Florence P. Speese, daughter of John Wesley Speese and Mary J. Wilson. She was in her parents' household on the 1910 US Census, living in Laramie Co., Wyoming, Torrington, Prect. at the Empire Settlement. She was living in the same area in her mother's household, then Goshen Co., Wyoming on the 1920 US Census and was probably also working for George Evans in Scottsbluff which was very close to Empire. Refer to Shores and Speese, Volume 2, for more information.

George Evans remarried and with his family is shown on the 1930 and 1940 US censuses. If the information is accurate on the 1930 US Census, George's wife Jannie or Jane was only married to him for two years. The children shown are children born to him by his first wife, Pearl. They are shown on the 1920 US Census, living in Los Angeles Co., California.

1920 US Census, Los Angeles Co., California, Los Angeles Assembly Dist. 74,   [20]
ED 416, Page 3B
715 Kohler Street
65-70 Benjamin Tibbett, rents, black, 67, b. TN, both parents b. US, porter on
        railroad
Edith R., wife, 60, b. TN, father b. US, mother b. TN
Lucinda J. Evan, step grand niece, black, 5, b. NE, father b. Africa, mother b. TN
Phillip Evan, step grand nephew, black, 3 8/12, b. NE, father b. Africa, mother b.
        TN
Georgetta P. Evan, step grand niece, black, 1 9/12, b. NE, father b. Africa, mother
        b. TN
Edith Warner, step granddaughter, black, 19, single, came to US in 1912,
        naturalized, b. Africa, father b. West Indies, mother b. TN
Minnie E. Reed, lodger, black, 34, married, b. US, father b. TN, mother b. MO,
        laundry
Anthony Adams, lodger, black, 75, single, b. TN, both parents b. US, laborer,
        building wrecking

1930 US Census, Riverside Co., California, Palo Verde, ED 26, Page 1A   [21]
7-7 George R. Evans, rents, negro, 42, married first at age 21, b. Africa, both
        parents b. Africa, laborer on farm
Jannie, wife, negro, 29, married at age 27, b. MS, both parents b. MS
Lucinda, daughter, negro, 16, b. NE, father b. Africa, mother b. MS
Philip, son, negro, b. NE, father b. Africa, mother b. MS
Georgetta, daughter, negro, 12, b. NE, father b. Africa, mother b. MS

1940 US Census Riverside Co., California, Palo Verde, ED 33-25, Page 14A [22]
157 Riverside Drive rents $15 month
George Evans, negro, 53, 6th grade, born French Congo, Africa, same house
        1 April 1935, laborer, agriculture
Jane, informant, wife, negro, 38, 2nd grade, b. MS, same house 1 April 1935,
        housework, private home
Jimmie, son, negro, 3, b. California

According to the California Death Index, George Richard Evans was born 16 May 1885 and died 18 January 1956 in Riverside Co., California. His mother's maiden name was Evans and his father's surname was Bellia. 23

According to the California Death Index, Lucinda J. Evans Smith was born about 1914 in Nebraska. She died in Los Angeles Co., California on 25 October 1986. Her father's surname was Evans and her mother's maiden name was Beck. 24 . Lucinda was born 1 April 1914 and she died 25 Oct 1986, buried in the Riverside National Cemetery, Riverside, Riverside Co., California. Her husband was Allen D. Smith. 25

1940 US Census, Los Angeles Co., California, Los Angeles ED 60-482, Page 12B 26
349 East 42nd Place   owns $2,000
Allen David Smith, negro, 27, 1 year high school, b. AR, same place 1 April 1935,
        truck driver, transportation company
Lucinda, wife, informant, negro, 26, 3 years high school, b. NE, same place
        1 April 1935
Marion Reed, lodger, male, negro, 24, married, 2 years high school, b. LA, same
        place 1 April 1935, porter, retail drug store
Frank White, lodger, negro, 26, single, 8th grade, b. CA, same place 1 April 1935,
        truck washer, transport co.

1940 US Census, Riverside Co., California, Palo Verde, ED 33-26, Page 8A 27
4 — Phillip Evans, negro, 24, 4 years high school, b. NE, living at Blythe,
        Riverside Co., CA 1 April 1935, labor, farm
Helen, informant, wife, negro, 20, 3 years high school, b. OK, living at Wellston,
        Lincoln Co., OK 1 April 1935

California Death Records indicate that Phillip Oliver Evans was born 24 April 1916 in Nebraska. He died 19 June 1985 in Los Angeles Co., California. His mother's maiden name was shown as Beck. 28 According to the California Death Records Georgetta Pearl White, was born 6 Sept 1917 in Nebraska; died 21 Aug 1979 in San Bernardino Co., California. 29

1. Year: 1910; Census Place: Field, Scotts Bluff, Nebraska; Roll: T624_854; Page: 12B; Enumeration District: 0204; FHL microfilm: 1374867
2. Year: 1920; Census Place: Schroeppel, Oswego, New York; Roll: T625_1254; Page: 5B; Enumeration District: 189; Image: 435
3. Year: 1930; Census Place: Schroeppel, Oswego, New York; Roll: 1636; Page: 4A; Enumeration District: 0059; Image: 279.0; FHL microfilm: 2341370
4. Year: 1900; Census Place: Tabor, Scotts Bluff, Nebraska; Roll: 940; Page: 9A; Enumeration District: 0168; FHL microfilm: 1240940
5. Staatsarchiv Hamburg; Hamburg, Deutschland; *Hamburger Passagierlisten; Microfilm No.: K_1754*
6. Staatsarchiv Hamburg; Hamburg, Deutschland; *Hamburger Passagierlisten*; Microfilm No.: *K_1721*
7. *Seventy-Sixth Annual Report of the Missionary Society of the Methodist Episcopal Church for the Year 1889*, p. 32
8. ibid, p. 28
9. ibid, p. 34
10. *The Gospel in All Lands, Methodist Episcopal Church Missionary Society*, ed by Eugene R. Smith, New York, 1894.
11. Year: 1895; Arrival: New York, New York; Microfilm Serial: M237, 1820-1897; Microfilm Roll: Roll 650; Line: 1
12. Staatsarchiv Hamburg; Hamburg, Deutschland; *Hamburger Passagierlisten*; Microfilm No.: *K_1753*

13. US Department of Interior, Bureau of Land Management, General Land Office http://www.glorecords.blm.gov/details/patent/default.aspx?accession=353420&docClass=SER&sid=lucsruaa.oy4

14. US Department of Interior, Bureau of Land Management, General Land Office http://www.glorecords.blm.gov/details/patent/default.aspx?accession=637980&docClass=SER&sid=zh153x30.5pz

15. Fold3 http://www.fold3.com

16. Year: 1900; Census Place: Pleasant, Jefferson, Nebraska; Roll: 931; Page: 10B; Enumeration District: 0092; FHL microfilm: 1240931

17. Year: 1910; Census Place: Field, Scotts Bluff, Nebraska; Roll: T624_854; Page: 13A; Enumeration District: 0204; FHL microfilm: 1374867

18. Registration State: *Nebraska;* Registration County: *Scotts Bluff;* Roll: *1711770*

19. Year: 1920; Census Place: Scottsbluff Ward 1, Scotts Bluff, Nebraska; Roll: T625_1001; Page: 1B; Enumeration District: 225; Image: 757

20. Year: 1920; Census Place: Los Angeles Assembly District 74, Los Angeles, California; Roll: T625_114; Page: 3B; Enumeration District: 416; Image: 749

21. Year: 1930; Census Place: Palo Verde, Riverside, California; Roll: 183; Page: 1A; Enumeration District: 0026; Image: 665.0; FHL microfilm: 2339918

22. Year: 1940; Census Place: Palo Verde, Riverside, California; Roll: T627_277; Page: 14A; Enumeration District: 33-25

23. Ancestry.com. *California, Death Index, 1940-1997* [database on-line]. Provo, UT, USA: Ancestry.com Operations Inc, 2000.

24. ibid.

25. FindAGrave http://www.findagrave.com

26. Year: 1940; Census Place: Los Angeles, Los Angeles, California; Roll: T627_413; Page: 12B; Enumeration District: 60-482

27. Year: 1940; Census Place: Palo Verde, Riverside, California; Roll: T627_277; Page: 8A; Enumeration District: 33-26

28. California Death Records http://vitals.rootsweb.ancestry.com/ca/death/search.cgi

29. ibid.

Charles "Charlie" and Orlando "Orley" Horn

The Horn brothers came to Nebraska in the early 1930s from Kansas. From eastern Nebraska they moved west into the Mitchell, Scotts Bluff Co., Nebraska area. Charles "Charlie" Horn changed the spelling of his last name to Horne, while his brother, Orlando "Orley," retained the original spelling of Horn.

They were sons of Fred D. Horn and Maggie Gordon who lived in Kansas. The birth place of Charlie is shown in a variety of places, all different. On his WWII Draft Registration it is shown as Jackson Co., Kansas 1 and on FindAGrave, it is shown as Pottawatomie Co., Kansas. 2 His obituary indicates he was born at Holy Cross, Kansas. 3 The obituary for Orley Horn indicates he was born in St. Mary, Kansas. 4 FindAGrave indicates he was born in Cedar Rapids, Linn Co., Iowa. 5 All of the children of Fred and Maggie Horn were born in Kansas.

Charles filed his World War II Draft Registration at Gering, Scotts Bluff Co., Nebraska on 25 April 1942. He was living at Michell in Scotts Bluff County, age 45, born 24 July 1896 in Jackson Co., Kansas. His father was shown as Fred Horne of Horton, Kansas. Charlie was shown as a self-employed trucker, negro, with gray eyes, brown hair and dark complexion. He had lost the end of his left thumb.

He served in World War I from 24 September 1918 to 13 March 1919 as a Quartermaster in Corp Remount Co. A No. 415. In 1935 he moved to the Mitchell, Nebraska area where he worked in the potato fields, later establishing his trucking business. Charles was the last surviving veteran of World War I of the Mitchell American Legion Post No. 124. 6

On the 1940 US Census 7 Charles Horn was single and living in Mitchell, Scotts Bluff Co., Nebraska. He was age 48, negro and a drayman. On 1 April 1935 he was living in rural Scotts Bluff County. Charles died on 15 January 1990 in Mitchell and was buried in the Mitchell Cemetery. He was a member of the Berean Fundamental Church where his services were held. 8

Holy Cross, Kansas is a post office in Pottawatomie Co., Kansas. It is on the St. Mary Township line and St. Marys, Kansas is a town five miles south of Holy Cross. Therefore, Charles was definitely born in Pottawatomie Co., Kansas. *The St. Mary's Star*, St. Marys, Kansas of 30 July 1896 announced the birth of a son [Charles] to Mr. and Mrs. Fred Horn. The baby weighed 10 pounds.

Orlando "Orley" Horn was born on 24 January 1900 in St. George, Pottawatomie Co., Kansas and died at Mitchell, Scotts Bluff Co., Nebraska on 7 May 1988. His obituary 9 indicates that he attended Riley and Pottawatomie Co., Kansas schools. Orley's first job was driving a tractor that pulled a road grader for Pottawatomie County. Later he worked on the Miller Ranch in Wabaunsee Co., Kansas. During the early 1930s Orley worked in a meat packing plant in Omaha. His move west was to work at the ammunition depot in Sidney. He came to Mitchell in 1943 where he trucked grain, then later worked for the Missouri Valley Construction Co. Orley never married and was a member of the Berean Fundamental Church. He was buried in the Mitchell Cemetery, Mitchell, Scotts Bluff Co., Nebraska.

On the 1940 US Census, Orley Horn was living in the household of Louise Jackson at 3119 R Street in Omaha. Louise was shown as a negro, age 32, widow, born in Arkansas. She was a seamstress for the WPA Sewing Department. Orley was age 39, single, negro, born in Kansas and living in Omaha on 1 April 1935. He was working in the meat packing plant. Also in the household was Lincoln Bradley, age 47, single, negro, born in Kansas and working in the meat packing plant. 10

The Mitchell Index, Mitchell, Nebraska, 13 February 1965, page 5 published an advertisement for Orley Horn who was sharpening scissors. His address was 1027 14th Ave. in Mitchell. The same newspaper of 25 July 1957, page 3 reported that Charles Horn, a local trucker was the director of the Nebraska Motor Carriers Association.

Fred Horn was born on 1 April 1867 in Sparta, Randolph Co., Illinois to John Horn and his wife Mary. He married Maggie Gordon on 23 October 1895 in Wabaunsee Co., Kansas. Maggie was born about 1876 in Ohio to Jerry Gordon and Louisa White. The following children were born to them.
1. Charles Fredrich Horn, born 24 July 1896 in Holy Cross, Pottawatomie Co., Kansas; see above.
2. Elsie Marie Horn, born in 1898 at St. Marys, Pottawatomie Co., Kansas
3. Orlando Horn, born 24 July 1900 in St. George, Pottawatomie Co., Kansas; see above.
4. Raymond Horn, born in 1903; died 1910 at St. George, Pottawatomie Co., Kansas.
5. Neva Maggie Horn, born 2 May 1907 in Kansas.

Elsie Marie Horn, daughter of Fred and Maggie Gordon Horn, married Max Anthol Walls on 11 April 1918 at Manhattan, Riley Co., Kansas. He born on 23 September 1896 in Kansas and died 26 September 1990. Elsie died on 11 January 1995 in St. Marys, Pottawatomie Co., Kansas. They were both buried in Mount Calvary Cemetery, St. Marys, Pottawatomie Co., Kansas. Max was a carpenter and farmer. In 1925 he helped built Loyola Hall on the St. Marys College Campus. He was in charge of the orchard and vinyard until the college closed in 1933. His parents were James Walls and Milinda Stewart. 11

Neva Maggie Horne, daughter of Fred and Maggie Gordon Horn, married Wilber McKinley Douglas in 1925. Wilber was born 25 August 1901 to Frederk K. Douglas and Henrietta Bradley. He died on 29 July 1967 and was buried in the Newbury Cemetery, Newbury, Wabaunsee Co., Kansas. After his death, Neva married Frank Tucker in 1969. Neva died at the age of 104, on 20 January 2012. She was buried in the Mount Hope Cemetery, Topeka, Shawnee Co., Kansas. 12

John Horn was born in slavery in May of 1838 in Missouri. In about 1879 he married a lady named Sarah and had children by her. By a lady named Mary, he had Fred Horn (see above). The first enumeration that confirms the location of John Horn and his family is as follows.

1900 US Census, Noble Township, Noble Co., Oklahoma 13
John Horn, black, born May 1838, 62, married 21 years, b. MO, both parents b. MO
        farmer
Sarah, wife, black, born March 1861, 39, 11 children, 8 living, born MO, both parents
        born MO
George, black, born December 1879, 20, single, b. MO
Addie, black, born August 1884, 15, b. MO
Annie, black, born December 1886, 13, b. MO
Simon, black, born April 1890, 10, b. MO
Edward, black, born February 1892, 8, b. OK
Mary, black, born May 1896, 4, b. OK

While the parents of John Horn are unknown, it is possible that he is identified with a mother on the 1880 US Census as follows.

1880 US Census, Perry Township, St. Francois Co., Missouri 14
25-25 Disy Taylor, mulatto, 65, mother, widow, b. NC, both parents b. NC
John Horn, black, 40, boarder, laborer, b. MO, both parents b. MO

The *Daily Enterprise Times*, Perry, Oklahoma 11 May 1899 reported "Uncle John Horn is a colored farmer of this county and a staunch supporter of Delegate Flynn, and yesterday morning he wagered a barrel of molasses with Col. R. Cannivan that Flynn would secure free homes for Oklahoma settlers during his present term, and he'll win."

John Horn died at Wellington, Sumner Co., Kansas on 22 June 1918. He was residing at 407 East Lincoln and his furneral was held at the Colored Baptist Church. His wife Sarah was born in March of 1861 in Missouri and died in 1943.

Maggie Gordon, wife of Fred Horn, was born in about 1876 in Ohio to Jerry Gordon and Louisa White. She died on 7 Feburary 1910 in Kansas and was buried in the St. George Cemetery in Pottawatomie Co., Kansas. Her father, Jerry Gordon, was born in about 1847 in Louisiana. He married Louisa White on 3 November 1873 in Wabaunsee Co., Kansas. They are shown in 1880 living in Kansas.

1880 US Census, Alma Township, Wabaunsee Co., Kansas 15
33-34 Jerry Gordon, 33, farmer, mulatto, born LA, both parents b. LA
Louisa, 24, keeping house, mulatto, born LA, both parents b. LA
Mary, 5, mulatto, born KS
Maggie, 3, mulatto, born OH
Salina, 1, mulatto, born KS

Louisa White was born on 8 November 1855 in Tennessee. She died on 13 June 1904 at Paxico, Wabaunsee Co., Kansas. The *Alma Enterprise*, Alma, Kansas, 17 June 1904 published her obituary. She died of consumption. The following children were born to Jerry Gordon and Louisa White.

1. Mary Gordon, born about 1875 in KS
2. Maggie Gordon, born about 1876 in OH, see above.
3. Salina Gordon, born about 1879 in KS
4. Charley Gordon, born August 1881 in KS
5. Luella Gordon, born February 1884 in KS
6. Addie Gordon, born June 1886 in KS
7. Malinda Gordon, born September 1888 in KS
8. Lily Gordon, born May 1891 in KS
9. George E. Gordon born May 1900 in KS

1. The National Archives At St. Louis; St. Louis, Missouri; World War II Draft Cards (Fourth Registration) For the State of Nebraska; Record Group Title: Records of the Selective Service System; Record Group Number: 147; Box or Roll Number: 122
2. FindAGrave, http://www.findagrave.org
3. *The Gering Courier*, Gering, Nebraska, 18 January 1990; page 13.
4. *The Gering Courier*, Gering, Nebraska, 12 May 1988; page 13.
5. FindAGrave, http://www.findagrave.org
6. obituary, Charles Horne.
7. Year: 1940; Census Place: Mitchell, Scotts Bluff, Nebraska; Roll: m-t0627-02264; Page: 20A; Enumeration District: 79-20
8. obituary, Charles Horne.
9. *The Gering Courier*, Gering, Nebraska, 12 May 1988: page 13
10. Year: 1940; Census Place: Omaha, Douglas, Nebraska; Roll: m-t0627-02272; Page: 13A; Enumeration District: 94-104.
11. FindAGrave, http://www.findagrave.org.
12. ibid.
13. Year: 1900; Census Place: Noble, Noble, Oklahoma; Page: 1; Enumeration District: 0153; FHL microfilm: 1241340
14. Year: 1880; Census Place: Perry, St Francois, Missouri; Roll: 714; Page: 451C; Enumeration District: 122
15. Year: 1880; Census Place: Alma, Wabaunsee, Kansas; Roll: 398; Page: 342A; Enumeration District: 117

Ruby Coleman   Cheri L. Hopkins

About the Editors

Ruby Coleman is a professional genealogist, lecturer and writer who resides in North Platte, Nebraska. She has lived in Colorado, Wyoming, South Dakota, Iowa and Nebraska and was a former resident of Alliance, Nebraska. Using her knowledge of the plains states genealogy and history, plus genealogical methodology, Coleman writes, lectures and teaches genealogy. The other Nebraska books she has written include *The Wild Years 1868-1951 North Platte and Lincoln County, Nebraska, Pre-Statehood History of Lincoln County, Nebraska,* revised edition and *Homesteading in Lincoln County Nebraska 1874-1899.*

Cheri Hopkins is an avid genealogist and historian who was born and raised in Alliance, Nebraska. She studies and has a particular interest in Early American history, Nebraska Panhandle settlement and Wyoming Frontier history. Mrs. Hopkins is an enthusiastic collector of historical books, both antique and newly published. She is an avid reader and considers herself to still be a student...always learning. She mostly lectures about events in history and how they may be relevant to or applied to genealogy research. She and her husband spend their free time grave witching, helping individuals or cemeteries who request their service to locate 'forgotten' grave sites.

This is the first book that Hopkins has written. As co-editor, she has collaborated with her sister-in-law in what has been a nearly five year journey.

Made in the USA
Middletown, DE
30 March 2023

27185500R00232